*T*OURISM MANAGEMENT

THIRD EDITION

DAVID WEAVER

LAURA LAWTON

WILEY

John Wiley & Sons Australia, Ltd

Third edition published 2006 by
John Wiley & Sons Australia, Ltd
42 McDougall Street, Milton Qld 4064

Offices also in Sydney and Melbourne
First edition published 2000
Second edition published 2002

Typeset in 10.5/12 pt New Baskerville

© Dave Weaver & Laura Lawton 2000, 2002, 2006

National Library of Australia
Cataloguing-in-Publication data

Weaver, David B. (David Bruce).
    Tourism management.

    3rd ed.
    Includes index.
    For tertiary students.

    ISBN-13 9 78047080 9549.
    ISBN-10 0 470 80954 X.

    1. Tourism — Australia — Marketing. 2. Tourism
    — Australia — Management. 3. Ecotourism — Australia.
    I. Lawton, Laura. II. Title.

338.4791

Cover image. © PhotoDisc, Inc.

Edited by David Rule

Printed in Singapore by
CMO Image Printing Enterprise

10 9 8 7 6 5 4 3 2

CONTENTS

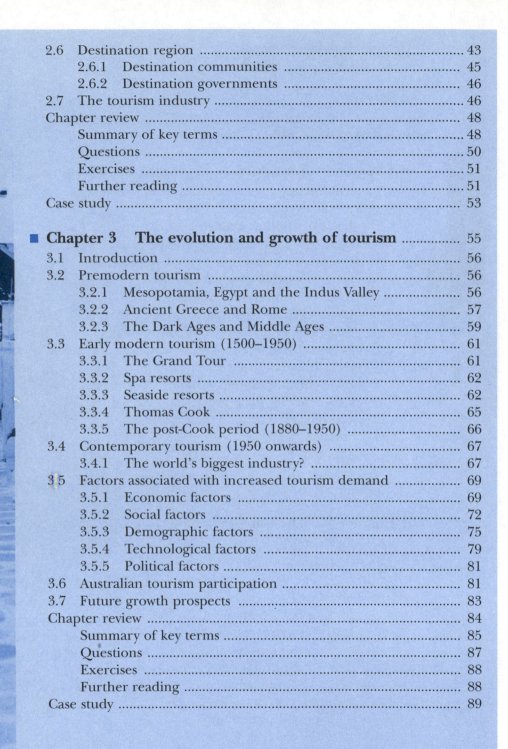

PREFACE

The preface of the second edition of *Tourism management* made two crucial points, which are worth reiterating and expanding for the third edition. First, tourists and the tourism industry are being challenged as never before by acts of violence associated with the phenomenon of 'terrorism'. Just since the submission of the book manuscript to the publisher, we have witnessed the London transit bombings, which killed at least 50 innocent people, and the bombings in the Egyptian Red Sea resort of Sharm-el-Sheik, which are reported to have killed at least another 88. The latter are especially ominous in that, similarly to the Bali bombings of 2003, they deliberately targeted the tourism sector. Such attacks will no doubt increase as the vulnerability of tourists and the growing dependence of countries on tourism revenues become even more apparent to the would-be perpetrators of such despicable acts. In general, there is increased awareness of how much tourism is vulnerable to the external environment, within which terrorism is but one component. In other realms, the natural environment has proven to be a great source of disruption and uncertainty in some destinations in the early 2000s. Nowhere was this better illustrated than in the Indian Ocean basin, where the great tsunami of 26 December 2004 killed at least 180 000 people, including many tourists. Chaos, complexity and uncertainty, without any doubt whatsoever, are core factors that every destination will have to take into consideration in their future management strategies. The content of the third edition of *Tourism management* reflects this contention.

The second point is paradoxical because it emphasises the continuing expansion of tourism despite this increasingly ominous and daunting geopolitical and physical context. Notably, 2004 was particularly surprising given the double-digit percentage growth in international stayover arrivals over the previous year, representing an increase of *70 million* overnight person-trips. Clearly, the impulse to travel is more robust than ever, as is the means of a growing proportion of the world's population to do so. Especially notable in this regard is the emergence of China as a major tourist market as well as an international tourist destination of prime importance. Along with India, Brazil and other rapidly developing countries, China will fuel much of the future growth of international tourism as the traditional mainstays of Europe, Japan, Australia, New Zealand and north America show signs of increasing maturity. All the stake-holders — destination managers and residents, the industry and the new Chinese and Indian tourists themselves — will experience a steep learning curve in terms of behaviour, marketing and the management of impacts. Australia, in particular, is likely to be greatly affected by these new developments, given its geographical proximity to China, India and other leading-edge markets.

As in the previous edition, each chapter of the third edition of *Tourism management* is informed by a 'Technology' feature, which focuses on such topics as the role of biometrics in the tourist entry process, electronic tour guides, Internet marketing, environmentally friendly hotel technologies, and the use of webcams and 3D modelling to facilitate tourism research.

As before, the authors recognise that this edition would not have been possible without the kind cooperation of numerous individuals and agencies. The World Tourism Organization was extremely helpful and generous in providing critical data and permission in a timely fashion. The authors recognise and welcome the organisation's leadership in building a global tourism sector that benefits destinations, the tourism industry and the tourists themselves. We also acknowledge the generous support of the Sustainable Tourism CRC, and Steve Noakes, Leo Jago and Vanessa Atkins in particular, as well as the staff of the leisuretourism.com database operated by CABI Publishing, UK, which has proven to be an indispensable source of published academic research in the tourism field. Our gratitude is extended to all the academics and others who generated with great dedication all the published material listed in the references that made this textbook possible. We particularly thank Dr Justine Digance of Griffith University, Australia, who notified us of new developments within the Australian tourism industry that we otherwise would have missed, and gave us encouragement and cheer throughout the writing process. Dr Neil Leiper of Southern Cross University very kindly provided us with content from his superb tourism management text, which helped us greatly to understand the nuts and bolts of the tourism management process. We also thank the anonymous referees whose helpful comments on the chapters greatly contributed to the quality of this edition. Though the production of this new edition was complicated by our relocation in early 2005 from George Mason University to the University of South Carolina (USC), our efforts were facilitated by the strong support of Dr Pat Moody, dean of the College of Hospitality, Retail and Sport Management at USC and Dr Charles Partlow, interim chair of the School of Hospitality, Restaurant and Tourism Management within the college. Finally, we once again recognise and applaud the superb team at John Wiley & Sons, Australia led by Darren Taylor, executive publisher. We especially thank Nina Crisp, the developmental editor, whose unfailing professionalism, efficiency, good advice and optimism greatly expedited all stages of the writing process. Thank you also to David Rule, the project editor, for all his work on the project.

Dr Dave Weaver
Dr Laura Lawton
University of South Carolina
Columbia, South Carolina, United States

ACKNOWLEDGEMENTS ....

The author and publisher would like to thank the following copyright holders, organisations and individuals for their permission to reproduce copyright material in this book.

Images

P.321 (left): photolibrary.com/Robin Smith; **p. 79:** From Year Book Australia Population Size and Growth 1301.0 2005, ABS included with permission of ABS www.abs.gov.au; **p. 78:** Australian Picture Library/Wolfgang Kaehler; **p. 134:** Australian Picture Library/Buddy Mays; **p. 251:** Australian Picture Library/Anders Ryman; **p. 294:** Australian Picture Library/Corbis/ Martin Harvey; **p. 307:** Reprinted from *The Canadian Geographer*, Vol. 24, Issue 1, 1980, article by RW Butler included with permission; **p. 401:** From 'Tourism in Spain: A Spatial Analysis & Synthesis' by Pearce & Preistly in *Tourism Analysis*, Vol. 2, 1998, p. 195, included with permission of Doug Pearce; **p. 119:** From *Tourism and Development in Tropical Islands — Political Ecology Perspectives*, edited by Stefan Gossling, Edward Elgar, UK included with permission; **p. 40:** Reprinted from 'Methods of analysis and prognosis' in *Crisis Management in the Tourism Industry* Vol. 1, 2003, p. 129 with permission from Elsevier; **pp. 366 & 367:** Reprinted from *Tourism Management Journal*, Vol. 21, Weaver, 'A Broad Context Model of Destination development scenarios', pp. 217–224 © 2000 with permission from Elsevier; **p. 145:** Getty Images/Joe Raedle; **p. 182:** Getty Images/Taxi/Stephanie Rausser; **p. 106:** included with permission of Gold Coast Tourism www.verygc.com; **p. 64:** From: *An Historical Geography of Recreation and Tourism in the Western World 1540-1940* by John Towner © John Wiley & Sons Limited. Reproduced with permission; **p. 187:** From: *Leisure Travel: Making it a Growth Market Again!* by Stanley C Plog © 1991, John Wiley & Sons, Inc reprinted with permission of John Wiley & Sons, Inc; **p. 279:** Kenya Tourist Board © www.magicalkenya.com; **p. 236:** The Kobal Collection/New Line/Saul Zaentz/Wing Nut; **p. 149:** © Linda Ray Wilson; **p. 321 (right):** Lochman Transparencies/ © Marie Lochman, **p. 60:** Mary Evans Picture Library; **pp. 24 & 25:** Adapted from *Tourism Management*, by Neil Leiper, RMIT, 1995, included with permission of Neil Leiper; **p. 31:** Newspix/Colleen Petch; **p. 45:** www.nogravity.com © Jim Campbell; **p. 213:** © Pacific Yurts Inc www.yurts.com; **p. 357:** © Phaphama Initiatives/Anand Madhvani; **p. 376:** © www.penguins.org.au; **p. 352:** © Asia Pacific Economic Corporation/ Pacific Asia Travel Association; **p. 191:** From: Martin Opperman, *Journal of Travel Research* 33 (4) pp. 57–61 fig 1. Reprinted by permission of Sage Publications Inc; **p. 186:** From *Leisure Travel: A Marketing Handbook* by Stanley C Plog, Pearson Prentice Hall, USA 2004, p. 51 included with permission of Stanley C Plog PhD; **p. 258:** © Thredbo.

Text

p. 384: Adapted from: *Social Research Methods: Qualitative and Quantitative Approaches 4e* by W. Lawrence Neuman, 2000, Allyn and Bacon, Boston, MA © Pearson Education; **p. 189:** Reprinted from *Global Tourism 3rd edition*, Theobald (ed), p. 281 © 2005 with permission from Elsevier; **p. 131:** © Hotels Magazine; **p. 246:** From *Tourism: Principles and Practice* by Cooper, Fletcher, Gilbert & Wanhill, 1993, reprinted by permission of Pearson Education Limited; **p. 181:** From: Lawson, *Journal of Travel Research*, 1991, 30 (20) p. 14, reprinted with permission of Sage Publications; **p. 131:** Tourism Research Australia/ Data included with permission of Tourism Research Australia; **p. 344:** From *What Tourism Managers Need to Know: A Practical Guide to the Development and Use of Indicators of Sustainable Tourism*, WTO, 1996, included with permission of WTO.

Every effort has been made to trace the ownership of copyright material. Information that will enable the publisher to rectify any error or omission in subsequent editions will be welcome. In such cases, please contact the Permissions Section of John Wiley & Sons Australia, Ltd, who will arrange for the payment of the usual fee.

1

Introduction to *tourism management*

LEARNING OBJECTIVES

After studying this chapter, you should be able to:

1 define tourism and appreciate its status as one of the world's most important economic sectors

2 describe the factors that have hindered the development of tourism studies as an area of academic investigation

3 explain the importance of theory in the development of an academic discipline

4 identify the four 'platforms' that have characterised the evolution of tourism studies to date, and indicate how this evolution reflects the growing maturity of this field of study

5 discuss the growth of tourism as a university-based field of study

6 describe the importance and growth of refereed tourism journals as a core indicator of development in the field of tourism studies

7 explain the distinctive and mutually reinforcing roles of universities and community colleges in the provision of tourism education and training.

1.1 INTRODUCTION

Tourism is an increasingly widespread and complex activity, which requires sophisticated management to realise its full potential as a positive and sustainable economic, environmental, social and cultural force. Complicating this task is the particular vulnerability of tourism to uncertainty, which was dramatically demonstrated in recent years by three striking events: the terrorist attacks of 11 September 2001, the 2002–03 SARS outbreak and the great Indian Ocean tsunami of 26 December 2004. Informed by the two 'main themes' of complexity and uncertainty, the purpose of this textbook is to give students an introductory exposure to tourism that will provide a foundation for further informed engagement with the sector, first in the remainder of their tertiary studies and then in a management capacity.

This opening chapter provides a general introduction to the text. Section 1.2 defines tourism and gives the reader an initial appreciation of its importance as an economic sector at a global and national level. Section 1.3 traces the development of tourism studies as a field of academic investigation and considers the factors that have hindered (and to some extent continue to hinder) its evolution. Within this context, section 1.4 considers the themes, outline and structure of the book.

1.2 THE PHENOMENON OF TOURISM

Given that this book is concerned with tourism management, it is important to establish what is meant by the term **tourism**. Most people have an intuitive and often simplistic perception of the word, usually focused around an image of people travelling away from their homes for recreational purposes. But how far from home do they have to travel before they are considered to be tourists? And for how long? And what types of travel qualify as tourism? Even without any formal tourism training, most people would acknowledge that a family vacation trip is a form of tourism while the arrival of an invading army or a refugee influx is not. But what about business travellers, Muslims embarking on a pilgrimage to Mecca, a sports team arriving from another country to participate in a tournament or a group of students arriving from another part of the country to continue their education? These examples challenge our sense of who is and who is not a tourist, and indicate the need to establish definitional boundaries. The questions posed here are complex ones that cannot be addressed in this introductory chapter, but it should be apparent that the definition of tourism depends in large part on how we define the **tourist** (see chapter 2).

■ 1.2.1 Definition *of tourism*

There is no single definition of tourism to which everyone adheres. Of the many definitions that have been put forward over the years, some are universal and can be applied to any situation, while others fulfil some specific purpose. Many local tourism boards, for example, establish working definitions that satisfy their own specific requirements and circumstances. The intent here is to offer something more universal that will inform this text. The following definition expands on that of Goeldner and Ritchie (2003), who place tourism in a broad stakeholder context. Additions to the original are indicated by italics:

> ■ Tourism may be defined as the *sum of the* processes, activities, and outcomes arising from the interactions among tourists, tourism suppliers, host governments, host communities, *origin governments, universities, community colleges and nongovernmental organisations, in the process of* attracting, transporting, hosting and *managing tourists and other* visitors. ■

This expanded definition increases the list of stakeholders to include origin governments, tertiary educational institutions and nongovernmental organisations (NGOs), all of which play an increasingly important, if often indirect, role in tourism. Figure 1.1 depicts these stakeholders as members of an interconnected network, in which possibilities exist for interaction among any components within the system. Also notable in the revised definition is the extension of the tourism dynamic to include travel from origin to destination as well as the management process, which is the core theme of this text.

■ **Figure 1.1**
The tourism stakeholders system

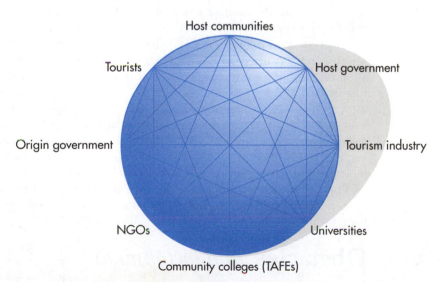

■ 1.2.2 The importance *of tourism*

The importance of tourism as an economic, environmental and socio-cultural phenomenon will be discussed in later chapters. However, it is useful at the outset to convey some sense of tourism's economic significance, if only to assure the reader that this is a field of study very much worthy of their attention. Essentially, tourism evolved during the latter half of the twentieth century from a marginal and locally significant activity to a widely dispersed economic giant, which in 2004 directly and indirectly accounted for more than 10 per cent of the global GDP, or approximately $5.5 trillion. This places tourism roughly on the same global order of magnitude as agriculture or mining. According to the World Tourism and Travel Council (WTTC) (www.wttc.org), the major organisation representing the global tourism industry, 215 million jobs were dependent on the 'tourism economy' in 2004. During that year, more than 750 million tourist trips of at least one night, and involving travel from one country to another, were undertaken. It is further estimated that the cumulative number of overnight domestic tourist trips (i.e. undertaken within the same country) is about ten times greater than this number, or about 7.5 billion trips. Such figures clearly reveal the formidable economic impact of tourism, but also implicate this sector as a primary agent of globalisation which involves billions of host/guest contacts and the incorporation of most places into an integrated global tourism network.

1.3 TOURISM AS AN ACADEMIC FIELD OF STUDY

The previous section suggests that tourism can exercise an enormous impact on host destinations as well as transit and origin regions. How much this impact is positive or negative, however, depends on whether tourism is appropriately managed by the relevant stakeholders, and by host governments, communities and businesses in particular. For a destination, management implies some concerted effort to manipulate the development of tourism to help fulfil the economic, social, cultural and environmental aspirations and strategic goals of the local community. If, in contrast, tourism is allowed to develop without any kind of formal management, experience tells us that the likelihood of negative outcomes is greatly increased, as later chapters will illustrate. The tertiary educational sector has much to contribute to the evolving science of tourism management (see section 1.3.4), and the rapid evolution of tourism studies is an interesting and promising development that has accompanied the expansion of tourism itself.

1.3.1 Obstacles *to development*

The emergence of tourism as a legitimate area of investigation within the university sector is a recent and ongoing development, and one that has encountered many obstacles. It can be argued that this field is still not given the respect and level of support that are provided to the more traditional disciplines. Several factors that help to account for this situation are outlined in the following.

Tourism perceived as a trivial activity

Though attitudes now seem to be changing, many academics and others in positions of authority have regarded tourism over the years as a non-essential and even frivolous activity involving pleasure-based motivations and activities. Hence it was and still often is seldom accorded the same attention, in terms of institutional commitment or financial support, as agriculture, manufacturing, mining or other more 'serious' and 'essential' pursuits (Davidson 2005). Most tourism researchers, and especially those who have been specialising in this area since the 1980s, can relate to tales of repeated grant application rejections, isolation within 'mainstream' discipline departments and ribbing by colleagues who imply that a research trip to the Caribbean or some other tourist destination is little more than a publicly subsidised holiday. These problems still occur, but there is now a much greater awareness of the significant and complex role played by tourism in contemporary society, its magnitude and the profound impacts that it can have on host communities. This growing awareness is contributing to a 'legitimisation' of tourism that is gradually giving tourism studies more credibility within the university system in Australia and elsewhere (see section 1.3.2).

Large-scale tourism as a recent activity

The tendency to downplay the importance of tourism is understandable given that large-scale tourism is a relatively recent development. In the 1950s tourism could legitimately be described at the global level as a marginal economic activity that did not merit focused attention from the university community. By the 1970s its significance was much more difficult to deny. However, aside from the above-noted prejudices about the inherent nature of tourism, the failure of universities to recognise tourism in any serious way until the 1980s can be seen as an example of the 'echo' effect. This effect describes the delay between the appearance of a phenomenon like mass tourism, and the concrete reaction of institutions to that phenomenon.

Such a delay, it must be emphasised, is not necessarily only the result of biases, slow reactions or a failure to appreciate the growth of the tourism sector. Universities, like other bureaucratic institutions, are characterised by a high degree of inertia and are reluctant to change their structures in response to any trend unless forced by government pressure (as in the case of affirmative action, for example). In essence, the university of the early 2000s is therefore a fair reflection of the tourism growth that occurred ten years previously, rather than what is actually occurring at the beginning of the twenty-first century. Given that tourism has continued to grow dramatically through the early 2000s, albeit with some notable interruptions, there is every reason to hope that the universities in Australia and elsewhere will further strengthen their growing commitment to tourism studies.

Tourism perceived as a vocational field of study

To the degree that tourism in the past was accepted as a legitimate area of tertiary study, it was widely assumed to belong within the community college or TAFE system. This reflected the simplistic view that tourism-related education was concerned only with applied vocational and technical skills training, and that relevant employment opportunities were restricted to customer service-oriented sectors such as hotels, travel agencies and restaurants. Accordingly, the appropriate training opportunities were perceived as being best provided by the TAFEs. Even as the complexities of tourism became more apparent, there was often a tendency to introduce new elements of education (such as managerial training in the tourism sector) into the existing TAFE structure, rather than to establish new structures within a resistant or sceptical university sector.

As we will discuss later, the situation changed dramatically during the 1980s and 1990s, and TAFEs and universities are now both recognised as important tertiary stakeholders in the tourism sector. Nevertheless, the TAFE connection continues to be cited in a derogatory and gratuitous way. In 1997, for example, the chair of a committee established by the Australian federal government to review higher education singled out tourism and hospitality programs as 'glorified TAFE courses' unsuited to the university environment (Leiper 1997a). This is a myopic and regressive view that discredits the distinctive but complementary contributions made by the university and TAFE systems.

Lack of clear definitions and reliable data

The development of tourism studies has been impeded by the lack of clear terms of reference. There is no consensus on the definition of tourism, and the term is often used in conjunction or interchangeably with related concepts such as travel, leisure, recreation and hospitality. For many academics and students the focus of tourism and its place within a broader system of academic inquiry is therefore not very clear. A similar lack of precision is evident within tourism itself. It is only since the 1980s that the World Tourism Organization (WTO) (www.world-tourism.org) (see appendix 1) has succeeded in aligning most countries to a standard set of international tourist definitions. Yet, serious inconsistencies persist in the international tourism data that are being reported by member states. This situation, however, is much more positive than the domestic tourism situation, where attempts to achieve standardisation and reliability among WTO member states are still embryonic. Every country has its own definition of domestic tourism, making comparison extremely difficult.

The absence of clear terms of reference extends into the realm of industrial classification. Any attempt to find data on the tourism industry in Australia and New Zealand, for example, is impeded by the lack of a single 'tourism' category within the **Standard Industrial Classification (SIC)** code used by these two countries. Instead, tourism-related activities are subsumed under at least 15 industrial classes, many of which also include a significant amount of nontourism activity (see figure 1.2). This system, in turn, bears no resemblance to the North American Industry Classification System (NAICS) used by the United States, Canada and Mexico, which subsumes tourism under more than 30 individual codes. The tourism 'industry', then, loses respect and influence because of official classification protocols that disguise the sector and divide its massive overall economic contribution into a variety of relatively small affiliated industries such as 'accommodation', 'travel agency services' and 'recreational parks and gardens'.

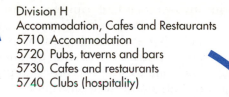

■ Figure 1.2
Australian and
New Zealand
SIC classes
related to
tourism

Division H
Accommodation, Cafes and Restaurants
5710 Accommodation
5720 Pubs, taverns and bars
5730 Cafes and restaurants
5740 Clubs (hospitality)

Division I
Transport and Storage
6121 Long distance bus transport
6401 Scheduled international air transport
6402 Scheduled domestic air transport
6403 Nonscheduled air and space transport
6641 Travel agency services

Division P
Cultural and Recreational Services
9220 Museums
9231 Zoological and botanical gardens
9239 Recreational park and gardens
9241 Music and theatre productions
9322 Casinos
9330 Other recreation services

Lack of indigenous theory or a strong academic tradition

Tourism-related data that are unreliable, inconsistent or dispersed do not facilitate the generation and testing of relevant **theory**. This discourages those who hope to develop the field into a fully fledged **academic discipline**, which has its own **indigenous theories** and methodologies. Theory is essential to the development of an academic field because it provides coherent and unifying explanations for diverse phenomena and processes that may otherwise appear disconnected or unrelated. In other words, theory provides a basis for understanding and organising certain aspects of the real world and is therefore central to the revelation and advancement of knowledge in any field. Students often find theory to be boring, abstract or too difficult to understand, but a grasp of theory is essential for those who intend to pursue tourism, or any other field of study, at the university level.

The lack of indigenous tourism theory can also be associated with the absence of a strong academic tradition in the field of tourism studies. Before the creation of specialised schools and departments (see section 1.3.2), tourism researchers were dispersed among a variety of traditional disciplines, and most notably in social sciences such as geography, anthropology, economics and sociology. Isolated from their tourism colleagues in other departments, tourism researchers could not easily collaborate and generate the synergies and critical mass necessary to stimulate academic progress. Even where tourism researchers have been brought together in tourism studies schools or departments, they still often pursue their research from the perspective of the mainstream disciplines in which they received their education, rather than from a 'tourism studies' perspective. Tourism geographers, for example, emphasise spatial theories involving core/periphery, regional or gravitational models, while tourism economists utilise input/output models, income multiplier effects and other econometric theories. This **multidisciplinary approach** undoubtedly contributes to the advancement of knowledge as tourism researchers come together in tourism departments, but inhibits the development of indigenous tourism theory.

Figure 1.3 suggests that the multidisciplinary approach is gradually giving way to an **interdisciplinary approach** in which the perspectives of various disciplines are combined and synthesised into distinctive new 'tourism' perspectives. This dynamic is more likely to generate the indigenous theories and methodologies that will eventually warrant the description of tourism studies as an academic discipline in its own right. The following subsections support the contention in figure 1.3 that the area of tourism studies is currently moving from a multidisciplinary to an interdisciplinary perspective.

■ **Figure 1.3**

The evolution of tourism studies towards discipline status

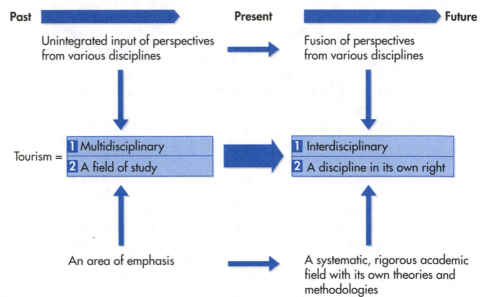

■ *1.3.2* Indications *of development*

The maturation of tourism studies is indicated by its increased visibility within university-level education and research in Australia and beyond. This is apparent in the expanding number of specialised departments and programs as well as the increase in the number of tourism-related refereed journals and other academic publications.

Expansion within the university sector

Many tourism academics are still based in traditional disciplines such as geography and economics, but an increasing proportion are located within more recently established tourism-related units. This is an extremely significant development, given its impact on the field's visibility and its effect of transforming tourism into a formally recognised and structured area of investigation. As noted earlier, this process has also played an important role in creating the critical mass of tourism specialists necessary to progress towards discipline status. Notably, it has been the newer universities (e.g. Griffith University, La Trobe University), the satellite campuses of older universities (e.g. Gatton Agricultural College of the University of Queensland) and institutions with a polytechnic origin (e.g. RMIT University, Curtin University of Technology), that have played a leadership role in the development of such units, less constrained as they are by the elitist pretensions of some of the more established institutions (see table 1.1).

Table 1.1 lists the 28 Australian universities that offered tourism-related programs in 2005. Most were based within business faculties (reflecting the widespread perception of tourism as a primarily economic phenomenon), and frequently in units that combine tourism with related fields, such as hospitality. Note that just two programs were established before 1980, while eight were introduced in 1995 or later. Tourism programs had also been available at Bond University and the Queensland University of Technology during the 1990s but were no longer offered in the early 2000s. In 2005, just ten Australian universities did *not* offer any tourism-related programs. A similar pattern of proliferation is evident in the United Kingdom, where the number of undergraduate tourism programs increased from two in 1986 to 66 in 1997 (Airey & Johnson 1999), and in the United States, where new programs continue to be established by tier one research universities.

■ **Table 1.1**
Australian universities offering tourism programs, domestically, 2005

YEAR	INSTITUTION	NAME OF UNIT	NAME OF FACULTY
1974	University of Queensland (Gatton Agricultural College)	Tourism and Leisure Management	Business, Economics and Law
	Victoria University (Footscray Institute of Technology)	Hospitality, Tourism and Marketing	Business and Law
1985	University of Technology, Sydney (Kuring-gai CAE)[1]	Leisure, Sport and Tourism	Business
1988	James Cook University	Business (tourism program)	Law, Business and the Creative Arts
1989	Edith Cowan University (WA CAE)	Marketing, Tourism and Leisure	Business and Public Management
	Griffith University (Gold Coast CAE)	Tourism, Leisure, Hotel and Sport Management	Griffith Business School
	Southern Cross University (Northern Rivers CAE)	Tourism and Hospitality Management	Division of Business

(continued)

YEAR	INSTITUTION	NAME OF UNIT	NAME OF FACULTY
1989 cont'd	University of Newcastle (Newcastle CAE)	Social Sciences (Leisure and Tourism Studies)	Education and Arts
	University of New England	Bachelor of Commerce (Hospitality and Tourism Management) offered in partnership with Blue Mountains International Hotel Management School	Economics, Business and Law
	University of NSW	Marketing (tourism program)	Commerce and Economics
1990	University of Canberra (Canberra CAE)	Information Management and Tourism	Communication and Education
	Charles Darwin University	Tourism and Hospitality	Law, Business and Arts
	Charles Sturt University (Mitchell CAE — Albury Campus)	Business (tourism program)	Commerce
	Monash University	Postgraduate tourism program	Arts
	RMIT University[2]	Hospitality and Tourism	Business
	University of Western Sydney	Tourism	School of Environment and Agriculture
1991	University of Ballarat (Ballarat CAE)	Business (tourism program)	n/a
1992	Central Queensland University (Capricornia University)	Marketing and Tourism	Business and Law
1993	La Trobe University	Sport, Tourism and Hospitality Management	Law and Management
	University of South Australia	Management (Tourism and Hospitality Group)	Business
1995	Flinders University	Integrated (ecotourism)	Science and Engineering
		Humanities (cultural tourism program)	Education, Humanities, Law and Theology

YEAR	INSTITUTION	NAME OF UNIT	NAME OF FACULTY
1996	University of the Sunshine Coast (Sunshine Coast University College)	(Tourism program)	Business
1997	Murdoch University	(Tourism program)	Social Sciences and Humanities
	Swinburne University of Technology	Business (Tourism and Management)	Business and Enterprise
1998	Curtin University of Technology (Western Australian Institute of Technology)	Management (tourism program)	Business
		(Cultural tourism and ecotourism programs)	Social Sciences
	The International College of Tourism and Hotel Management in association with Macquarie University	(Tourism program)	n/a
2000	University of Tasmania	Sociology, Social Work and Tourism	Arts
	University of Southern Queensland	(Tourism program)	Business

Notes:
[1]CAE = College of Advanced Education
[2]RMIT = Royal Melbourne Institute of Technology
(Inaugurating institution listed in parentheses)

Growth in the number of refereed journals

The growing maturity of tourism studies can also be gauged by the increase in the number of tourism-related **refereed academic journals**, which consolidate tourism research into a single location and thereby encourage interdisciplinary discourse. Because the articles they publish are subject to a normally rigorous procedure of **double-blind peer review**, refereed academic journals are widely considered to be the major showcase of a discipline and the best indicator of its intellectual development (Van Doren, Koh & McCahill 1994). A 'double-blind' process means that the author does not know who the editor has approached to assess the submission, while the reviewers (two or three are usually approached) do not know the identity of the author. A major disadvantage of refereed journals is the large amount of time required between the time the research is submitted to the journal and the time of publication. In addition, the experts who are asked to referee a submission can often guess the identity of the author(s), thereby compromising the objectivity of the double-blind review process.

Appendix 2 lists the English-language refereed tourism journals that existed in 2005, and reveals a pattern of exponential increase that resembles the expansion of tourism departments in Australia and elsewhere. Two stages of development are apparent. The first stage, from 1962 to 1990, was characterised by a small number of general topic tourism journals. Three of these (*Annals of Tourism Research, Journal of Travel Research* and *Tourism Management*) are still widely regarded as the most prestigious journals in the field. The second stage, since 1990, has been marked by the proliferation of new journals, most of which are specialised topically (e.g. *Journal of Travel and Tourism Marketing, Tourism Geographies* and *Journal of Sport Tourism*).

Driving this trend towards highly specialised tourism journals is the generation of tourism-related research output sufficient to warrant their establishment. Moreover, once they have been established, a research momentum is fostered as their very existence encourages even more output by providing outlets for those interested in conducting such specialised research. This specialisation, however, may also have a negative effect. Faulkner (1998) has speculated that the topical specialisation of journals may unintentionally inhibit the integration of the field by further encouraging the generation of theory based on particular disciplines — that is, by encouraging a multidisciplinary approach over an interdisciplinary approach. For example, *Tourism Geographies* makes ample use of geographical theory, and a bias towards economic models and methodologies is evident in *Tourism Economics.*

■ *1.3.3*   **A sequence** *of tourism platforms*

While tourism has become increasingly visible within the university sector, the philosophies through which academics in the field of tourism studies view the world have also evolved. Jafari (2001) has identified four **tourism platforms**, or perspectives, that have dominated the field at various stages of its development and continue to influence the field today.

Advocacy platform

The early tourism literature of the 1950s and 1960s was characterised by a positive and uncritical attitude towards the sector, which was almost universally regarded as an economic saviour for a wide variety of communities. Although this **advocacy platform** can be seen in retrospect as strongly biased and naïve, it must be interpreted in the context of the era in which it emerged. Europe and Asia were recovering from the devastation of World War II, and the issue of global economic development was focused on the emergence of an impoverished 'Third World'. As a potential economic stimulant, tourism offered hope to these regions, especially given that there were then few examples of unsustainable, large-scale tourism development to serve as a counterpoint. The prevalent attitude, therefore, was that communities should do all they can to attract and promote tourism activity within a minimally constrained free market environment.

The advocacy platform can be described as an 'anti-management' perspective, which, in its extreme form, assumes that tourism is an inherently positive force best left to evolve on its own — the role of government, if any, is to facilitate the growth of tourism through the passing of pro-tourism legislation and by maintaining law and order. Mings (1969), who advocated a critical supplementary role for tourism in the economic development of the Caribbean, is representative of the advocacy platform in his failure to emphasise the possibility of negative impacts.

Cautionary platform

The **cautionary platform** emerged in the late 1960s through the interplay of two related factors. First, it was in part an ideological challenge to the advocacy platform by the political left. Where the former advocated free markets, the cautionary platform endorsed a high degree of public sector intervention. Second, tourism's rapid expansion into new environments, and the Third World in particular, produced numerous tangible examples of negative impact by the late 1960s and early 1970s. This led many in the academic community to reconsider the logic of supporting unrestrained 'mass tourism' development.

The cautionary platform, in its extreme, is a management perspective that perceives tourism to be an inherently destructive force that has to be strictly controlled or avoided altogether. It is illustrated by Finney and Watson (1975), editors of *A New Kind of Sugar: Tourism in the Pacific*. In this book, they view tourism as an activity that perpetuates the inequalities of the colonial plantation era. Another cautionary platform classic is *The Golden Hordes: International Tourism and the Pleasure Periphery* by Turner and Ash (1975), who compared the spread of tourism with a barbarian invasion.

The destination lifecycle model of Butler (1980), which argues that unrestricted tourism development eventually leads to product degradation as the place's environmental, social and economic carrying capacities are exceeded (see chapter 10), can be regarded as the culmination of this platform.

Adaptancy platform

Although the cautionary platform effectively exposed many of the negative impacts that could accompany the development of tourism, it was not until the early 1980s that serious efforts were made to identify modes of tourism that would in theory be more positive for host communities. In alignment with the cautionary platform, the **adaptancy platform** introduced and articulated concepts that were conceived as more regulated and small-scale alternatives to mass tourism, such as 'alternative tourism' and 'ecotourism' (see chapter 11). A high degree of management was still implicit, though it was considered vital that control be vested in the host community itself, rather than in big government. Holden's examination of alternative tourism options for Asia is a typical example of the adaptancy platform (Holden 1984).

Knowledge-based platform

According to Jafari's model, the academic study of tourism has moved towards a **knowledge-based platform** since the late 1980s. This involves a shift from the emotive and ideologically driven discourse of past platforms to one that is more objective and cognisant that tourism of *any* type results in positive as well as negative impacts. Moreover, whereas the advocacy and cautionary platforms focus on impacts and the adaptancy platform concentrates on development options, the knowledge-based platform adopts a holistic view of tourism as an integrated and interdependent system in which large scale and small scale are both appropriate, depending on the circumstances of each particular destination. Effective management decisions about this complex system are based not on emotion or ideology, but on sound knowledge obtained through the application of the scientific method (see chapter 12) and informed by relevant models and theory. It is through the adherence of tourism academics to the knowledge-based platform that the field of tourism studies is most likely to achieve the status of a discipline. Leiper's (2004) textbook, *Tourism Management*, is an example of the knowledge-based approach.

■ *1.3.4* **Universities** *and community colleges*

The emphasis in this chapter on the evolution of tourism studies within the university sector is in no way intended to imply an inferior role or status for the TAFE system. Rather, both play a necessary and complementary role within the broader tertiary network of educational and training institutions. In this framework, TAFEs and similar institutions have had, and will likely continue to have, a dominant role in the provision of practical, high-quality training opportunities across a growing array of tourism-related occupations. These will increasingly involve not just entry-level training, but also staff development and enhancement. Universities often provide similar training opportunities, but their primary responsibilities are in the areas of education and research. Specific roles coherent with the knowledge-based platform include the following (no order of priority is intended):

* provide relevant and high-quality undergraduate and postgraduate education, directed especially at producing effective managers for both the public and private sectors
* conduct rigorous and objective scientific research into all aspects of tourism
* accumulate and disseminate a tourism-related knowledge base, especially through refereed journals
* apply and formulate theory, both indigenous and borrowed, to explain and predict tourism-related phenomena
* critically analyse all tourism phenomena
* position this analysis within a broad context of other sectors and processes, and within a framework of complexity and uncertainty
* contribute to policy formulation and improved planning and management.

It is becoming increasingly common for students to earn an advanced diploma in tourism at a TAFE or comparable institution, then attend university for an additional year or more to obtain a bachelor's degree in tourism. The university component, in particular, facilitates entry into occupations that emphasise management, advanced marketing, research and planning.

1.4 CHARACTERISTICS, OUTLINE AND STRUCTURE

This third edition, as did its predecessors, provides university students with an accessible but academically rigorous introduction to topics relevant to tourism management in the Australasian region. It is not, strictly speaking, a guidebook on how to manage tourism; those skills will evolve through the course of the undergraduate program, especially if the tourism component is taken in conjunction with one or more generic management courses or as part of a management degree. No prior knowledge of the tourism sector is assumed.

1.4.1 Characteristics

In concert with the knowledge-based platform, this book maintains a strong academic focus and emphasises methodological rigour, objective research outcomes, theory, critical analysis and healthy scepticism. This is evident in the use of scientific notation throughout the text to reference material obtained in large part from refereed journals and other academic sources. The inclusion of a chapter on research (chapter 12) further supports this focus. At the same time, however, this book is meant to have practical application to the management and resolution of real-world problems, which should be the ultimate goal of any academic discourse.

Second, this book provides a 'state-of-the-art' introduction to a coherent field of tourism studies that is gradually moving towards formulation as a discipline. An interdisciplinary approach is required to realise the outcome envisaged in figure 1.3, recognising that an integrative and comprehensive understanding of tourism requires exposure to the theory and perspectives of other disciplines. The emergence of indigenous theory in tourism studies is likely to involve an amalgamation and synthesis of theory from these other areas. Prominent among the disciplines that inform tourism studies are geography, business, economics, sociology, anthropology, law, psychology, ecology, history, political science and marketing. Figure 1.4 demonstrates how some of these more traditional disciplines are affiliated with selected tourism themes.

Third, the book is national in scope in that the primary geographical focus is on Australia, yet it is also international in the sense that the Australian situation is both influenced and informed by developments in other parts of the world, and especially the Asia–Pacific region.

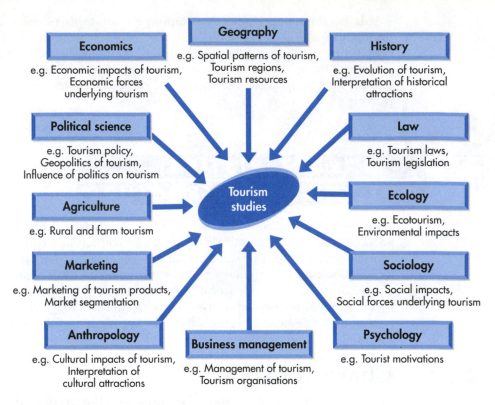

1.4.2 Chapter *outline*

The 12 chapters in this book have been carefully arranged so that together they constitute a logical and sequential introductory tourism management subject that can be delivered over the course of a normal university semester. Chapter 2 builds on the introductory chapter by providing further relevant definitions and presenting tourism within a systems framework. Chapter 3 considers the historical evolution of tourism and the 'push' factors that have contributed to its post–World War II emergence as one of the world's largest industries. Tourist destinations are examined in chapter 4 with regard to the 'pull' factors that attract visitors. Global destination patterns are also described. Chapter 5 concentrates on the tourism product, including attractions and the broader tourism industry. The emphasis shifts from the product (or supply) to the market (or demand) in the next two chapters. Chapter 6 considers the tourist market, examining the tourist's decision-making process as well as the division of this market into distinct segments. Chapter 7 extends this theme by focusing on tourism marketing, which includes the attempt to draw tourists to particular destinations and products. Subsequent chapters represent another major shift in focus, with the emphasis being placed on the impacts of tourism. Chapters 8 and 9, respectively, consider the potential economic and sociocultural/environmental consequences of tourism, while chapter 10 examines the broader context of destination development. The concept of sustainable tourism, which is widely touted as the objective of management efforts, is discussed in chapter 11. Chapter 12 concludes by focusing on the role of research in tourism studies, thereby preparing the reader for further university-level engagement with the topic.

■ 1.4.3   Chapter *structure*

Chapters 2 to 12 are all structured in a similar manner (see figure 1.5). Each begins with a set of learning objectives that students should achieve at the completion of the chapter. This is followed by an introduction and subsequent text that is arranged by topic area into major sections, major subsections, secondary subsections and minor subsections, as per figure 1.5. Dispersed throughout these sections, as appropriate, are four features that support the text.

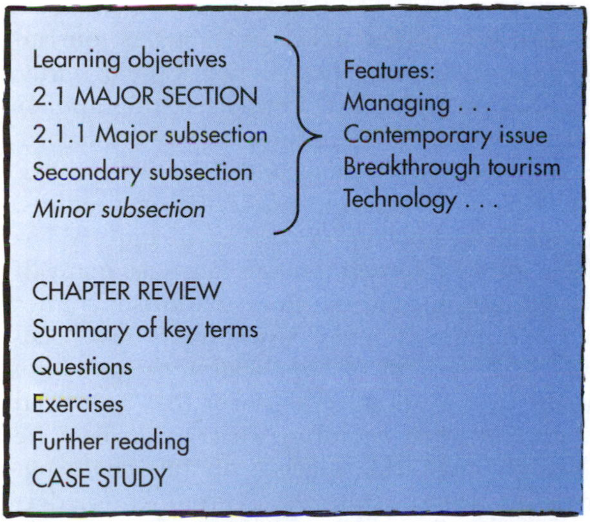

Learning objectives
2.1 MAJOR SECTION
2.1.1 Major subsection
Secondary subsection
Minor subsection

Features:
Managing . . .
Contemporary issue
Breakthrough tourism
Technology . . .

CHAPTER REVIEW
Summary of key terms
Questions
Exercises
Further reading
CASE STUDY

■ **Figure 1.5**
Chapter structure

The 'Managing...' feature focuses on situations related to the chapter theme that have important implications for the management of the tourism sector. The 'Contemporary issue' feature examines a broader theme relevant to the chapter that also has management implications. The 'Breakthrough tourism' feature identifies some very recent developments that could have an important influence on tourism management, while the 'Technology...' feature considers the role of some technological development in shaping the tourism sector and its management.

Following a review of the content, each chapter concludes with a sequence of additional features. The 'Summary of key terms' summarises important concepts and terms in bold type within the chapter. These are listed in the order that they appear and grouped to show the links between the key concepts and their subconcepts. Relevant questions and exercises follow. An annotated 'Further reading' section suggests additional sources that will allow the reader to pursue specific topics in greater depth. Finally, each chapter ends with an expanded case study, which includes several themes relevant to the chapter.

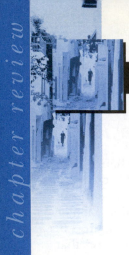

CHAPTER REVIEW

This chapter defines tourism and provides a preliminary indication of its rapid development as a major global economic activity. The evolution of tourism studies as an emerging field of academic inquiry within the university system is also considered. It is seen that this development has long been hindered by the widespread perception of tourism as a trivial subject and the recent nature of large-scale tourism. Also important are its traditional association with vocational training, the lack of clear definitions and a reliable data base, the diffusion of tourism-related activities among numerous categories of the SIC code, the lack of a strong academic tradition and indigenous theory, and the persistence of a multidisciplinary rather than an interdisciplinary approach.

However, these obstacles have been eroded since the 1980s as tourism studies has moved towards an interdisciplinary perspective. Concurrently, there has been a proliferation within Australia and elsewhere in the number of university departments that offer tourism programs. Notably, this proliferation has occurred within the newer universities and those with a CAE background, rather than the more established and traditional institutions. This consolidation of tourism studies as a legitimate area of inquiry has been accompanied by a proliferation of refereed tourism journals, many of which are topically specialised. Philosophically, the field of tourism studies has evolved through a sequence of dominant perspectives. An advocacy platform uncritically supported the development of large-scale tourism in the 1960s, but gave way in the 1970s to a cautionary platform that perceived tourism as an inherently destructive force requiring strict controls. The introduction of purportedly benign small-scale tourism options characterised the adaptancy platform of the 1980s, while the current knowledge-based platform is more scientific and objective than earlier perspectives, regarding tourism as an integrated system incorporating large-scale as well as small-scale tourism activities that requires management based on sound knowledge. This book provides an academically oriented introduction to tourism management that adheres to the philosophy of the knowledge-based platform.

SUMMARY OF KEY TERMS

Tourism

The sum of the processes, activities and outcomes arising from the interactions among tourists, tourism suppliers, host governments, host communities, origin governments, universities, community colleges and nongovernmental organisations, in the process of attracting, transporting, hosting and managing tourists and other visitors

- **Tourist:** a person who travels temporarily outside of his or her usual environment (usually defined by some distance threshold) for certain qualifying purposes

Standard Industrial Classification (SIC)

A system that uses standard alphanumeric codes to classify all types of economic activity. Tourism-related activities are distributed among at least 15 codes.

Theory

A model or statement that explains or represents some phenomenon

Academic discipline

A systematic field of study that is informed by a particular set of theories and methodologies in its attempt to reveal and expand knowledge about some particular theme; e.g. psychology examines individual behaviour, while geography examines spatial patterns and relationships

- **Indigenous theories:** theories that arise out of a particular field of study or discipline
- **Multidisciplinary approach:** involves the input of a variety of disciplines, but without any significant interaction or synthesis of these different perspectives
- **Interdisciplinary approach:** involves the input of a variety of disciplines, with fusion and synthesis occurring among these different perspectives

Refereed academic journals

Publications that are considered to showcase a discipline by merit of the fact that they are subject to a rigorous process of double-blind peer review

- **Double-blind peer review:** a procedure that attempts to maintain objectivity in the manuscript refereeing process by ensuring that the author does not know the identity of the reviewers, while the reviewers do not know the identity of the author

Tourism platforms

Perspectives that have dominated the emerging field of tourism studies at various stages of its evolution

- **Advocacy platform:** the view that tourism is an inherent benefit to communities that should be developed under free market principles
- **Cautionary platform:** a reaction to the advocacy platform that stresses the negative impacts of tourism and the consequent need for strict regulation
- **Adaptancy platform:** a follow-up on the cautionary platform that advocates alternative forms of tourism deemed to be more appropriate than the mass tourism fostered by the advocacy platform
- **Knowledge-based platform:** the most recent dominant perspective in tourism studies, emphasising ideological neutrality and the application of rigorous scientific methodologies to obtain knowledge so that communities can decide whether large- or small-scale tourism is most appropriate

QUESTIONS

1 Many academics and high-profile personalities have argued that there is no place in the university system for tourism programs.
   (a) What is the basis for this view?
   (b) Do you think that it has any validity?

2 Why is tourism usually referred to as a field of study rather than a discipline?

3 Why is theory so important to the development of an academic discipline?

4 How does the evolution of tourism studies through the four 'platforms' indicate the field's increasing maturity?

5 (a) Why are refereed journals considered to be the main source of tourism-related research results?
   (b) What are the weaknesses of refereed journals?

6 (a) What kinds of universities, faculties and units are associated with tourism-related programs in Australia?
   (b) What factors account for these particular patterns?

7 What is the most appropriate 'division of labour' between universities and TAFEs in terms of the provision of tourism education and training?

EXERCISES

1 (a) Obtain a copy of all the articles that were published in *Annals of Tourism Research* during 1973 and 2005.
   (b) Judge how much these articles seem to adhere to the tourism platforms outlined in this chapter.
   (c) Discuss how the difference in the articles reflects the growing maturity of tourism studies as a field of study.

2 (a) From Appendix 2, rank by frequency the countries in which the editors are based.
   (b) Using the appropriate websites or recent copies of each journal, rank by frequency the countries in which the editorial board members of *Annals of Tourism Research*, *Journal of Travel Research* and *Tourism Management* are based.
   (c) Note the geographical patterns that emerge from (a) and (b).
   (d) Discuss the implications that emerge from these patterns, in terms of the production and dissemination of tourism-related knowledge.

Davidson, T. 2005. 'What are Travel and Tourism: Are They Really an Industry?' In Theobald, W. (Ed.) *Global Tourism.* **Third Edition. Sydney: Elsevier, pp. 25–31.** Davidson argues that not only is tourism not a single industry, but it is counterproductive to treat it as such when attempting to gain respect for the field.

Echtner, C. & Jamal, T. 1997. 'The Disciplinary Dilemma of Tourism Studies'. *Annals of Tourism Research* **24: 868–83.** The authors of this article explore the interdisciplinary character of tourism studies and consider whether this area can and should be considered as a discipline.

Jafari, J. 2001. 'The Scientification of Tourism'. In Smith, V. L. & Brent, M. (Eds) *Hosts and Guest Revisited: Tourism Issues of the 21st Century.* **New York: Cognizant, pp. 28–41.** This article updates Jafari's analysis of tourism as having experienced four distinct philosophies or 'platforms'.

Leiper, N. 1997a. 'Those Who Oppose University Courses On Tourism and Hospitality'. In Bushell, R. (Ed.) *Tourism Research: Building a Better Industry. Proceedings from the Australian Tourism and Hospitality Research Conference, 1997.* **Canberra: Bureau of Tourism Research, pp. 75–9.** This article analyses three specific examples where high profile figures in Australia have denigrated the role of tourism within the country's universities.

—— 2000. 'An Emerging Discipline'. *Annals of Tourism Research* **27: 805–09.** Leiper provides a well-written discussion of issues associated with the evolution of tourism as a field of study.

Meyer-Arendt, K. & Justice, C. 2002. 'Tourism as the Subject of North American Dissertations, 1987–2000'. *Annals of Tourism Research* **29: 1171–4.** The exponential increase in the production of tourism dissertations is the focus of this analysis, along with a discussion of the disciplines within which they were produced.

LEARNING OBJECTIVES

After studying this chapter, you should be able to:

1 describe the fundamental structure of the tourism system

2 discuss the external forces that influence tourism and are
influenced by tourism

3 describe the three criteria that are employed to define tourists

4 explain the various purposes for tourism-related travel, and the
relative importance of each

5 identify the four major types of tourist and the definition criteria
that apply to each

6 evaluate the importance of origin and transit regions within the
tourism system

7 explain the role of destination regions and the tourism industry
within the tourism system.

$\mathcal{I}$NTRODUCTION

The introductory chapter defined tourism and described the development of tourism as an expanding area of focus within the university system in Australia and elsewhere, despite lingering prejudices. This is indicated by the growth of tourism-related programs and refereed journals as well as the movement towards a more objective knowledge-based philosophy that recognises tourism as a complex system requiring rigorous scientific investigation.

Chapter 2 discusses the concept of the tourism system and introduces its key components, thereby establishing the basis for further analysis of tourism system dynamics in subsequent chapters. Section 2.2 outlines the systems-based approach and presents tourism within this context. Section 2.3 defines the various types of tourist, considers the travel purposes that qualify as tourism and discusses problems associated with these definitions and the associated data. The origin regions of tourists are considered in section 2.4, while transit and destination regions are discussed in sections 2.5 and 2.6, respectively. The industry component of the tourism system is introduced in section 2.7.

2.2 $\mathcal{A}$ SYSTEMS APPROACH TO TOURISM

A **system** is a group of interrelated, interdependent and interacting elements that together form a single functional structure. Systems theory emerged in the 1930s to clarify and organise complex phenomena that are otherwise too difficult to describe or analyse (Leiper 2004). Systems tend to be hierarchical, in that they consist of subsystems and are themselves part of larger structures. For example, a human body comprises digestive, reproductive and other subsystems, while human beings themselves are members of broader social systems (e.g. families, clans, nations). Systems also involve flows and exchanges of energy which often involve interaction with external systems (e.g. a human fishing or hunting for food). Implicit in the definition of a system is the idea of interdependence, that is, that a change in any component will affect other components of that system. To examine a phenomenon as a system, therefore, is to adopt an integrated or holistic approach to the subject matter that transcends any particular discipline — in essence, an interdisciplinary approach that complements the knowledge-based platform(see chapter 1).

2.2.1 The basic *whole tourism system*

Attempts have been made since the 1960s to analyse tourism from a systems approach, based on the realisation that tourism is a complex phenomenon that involves interdependencies, energy flows and interactions with other systems.

Leiper's **basic whole tourism system** (Leiper 2004) places tourism within a framework that minimally requires five interdependent core elements:
1. at least one tourist
2. at least one tourist-generating region
3. at least one transit route region
4. at least one tourist destination
5. a travel and tourism industry (see figure 2.1).

■ **Figure 2.1**

A basic whole tourism system

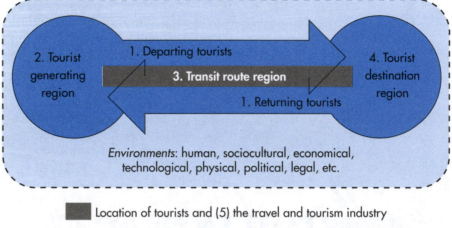

Location of tourists and (5) the travel and tourism industry

Source: *Leiper (1995)*

The movement of tourists between residence and a destination, by way of a transit region, is the primary flow of energy within this system. Other flows of energy involve movement within a destination as well as exchanges of goods and information. Additionally, there are many influential environments and external systems in which the tourism system is embedded. The experience of the tourist, for example, is facilitated (or impeded) by the energy, agricultural and political systems which, respectively, provide or do not provide sufficient fuel, food and accessibility to make the experience possible. Natural and cultural external factors can have a crucial and often unpredictable effect on the configuration of tourism systems. This is illustrated, for example, by the SARS epidemic of 2002 and 2003, which had a major negative impact on prominent destinations such as Toronto and Hong Kong (see Case study: The effect of SARS on tourism in Hong Kong). More recent and far more unpredictable and sudden was the Indian Ocean tsunami of 26 December 2004, which killed an estimated 200 000 local residents and tourists, and had a catastrophic short-term effect on Phuket (Thailand), southern Sri Lanka and other coastal destinations in the region. An as yet unknown repercussion of the tsunami is its long-term effect on the public's perception of coastlines as a highly desirable and low-risk venue for tourism activity.

Tourism systems in turn influence these external environments, for example by stimulating a destination's economy (see section 8.2.3) or helping to improve relations between countries (see section 9.2.1). In the wake of the 2004 tsunami, a high priority was placed by affected destination governments and international relief agencies on restoring the international tourist intake, on the premise that this was the most effective way of bringing about a broader and more rapid economic and psychological recovery. Despite such critical two-way influences, there is a tendency in some tourism system configurations to ignore or gloss over the external environment, as if tourism were somehow a self-contained or closed system (Weaver 1999).

The internal structure of the tourism system is also far more complex than implied by figure 2.1, thereby presenting even more of a challenge to the effective management of tourism. Many tourist flows are actually hierarchical in nature, in that they involve multiple, nested and overlapping destinations and transit regions (see figure 2.2). Cumulatively, the global tourism system encompasses an immense number of individual experiences and bilateral or multilateral flows involving thousands of destinations at the international and domestic level. Regarding the stakeholders depicted in figure 1.1, the tourists and the tourism businesses (or tourism industry) are prominently featured in the shaded portion central to Leiper's model (figure 2.1). Host governments and communities are located in the destination region, and origin governments are situated in the tourist-generating region. NGOs and educational institutions are found in all regions.

■ **Figure 2.2**
Tourism system with multiple transit and destination components

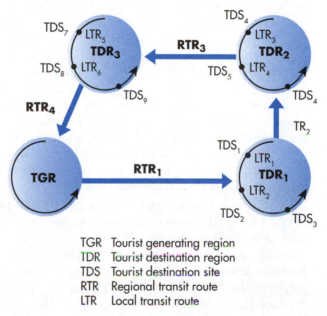

TGR	Tourist generating region
TDR	Tourist destination region
TDS	Tourist destination site
RTR	Regional transit route
LTR	Local transit route

Source: *Adapted from Leiper (1995)*

Finally, the overall tourism system is a hyperdynamic structure that is in a constant state of flux. This is apparent not only in the constant travel of millions of tourists, but also in the continuous opening and closing of accommodation facilities and transportation routes across the globe. This instability represents yet another challenge faced by tourism managers, who must realise that even the most current profile of the sector soon becomes obsolete. In Australia, for example, the strong performance in the Asian inbound traffic during the mid-1990s very quickly gave way to a collapse in many markets as a result of a major economic downturn in that origin region (see chapter 4). Similarly, the robust performance of many destinations in the Muslim world in the late 1990s was largely negated for several years by the terrorist attacks of 11 September 2001.

2.3 *T*HE TOURIST

As suggested in chapter 1, the definition of tourism is dependent on the definition of the **tourist**. It is therefore critical to address this issue in a satisfactory way before any further discussion of management-related issues can take place. Every tourist must simultaneously meet certain spatial, temporal and purposive criteria, as discussed below.

2.3.1 Spatial *component*

To become a tourist, a person must travel away from home. However, not all such travel qualifies as tourism. The WTO and most national and subnational tourism bodies hold that the travel must occur beyond the individual's 'usual environment'. Since this is a highly subjective term that is open to interpretation, these bodies normally stipulate minimum distance thresholds, or other criteria, that distinguish the 'usual environment' from a tourist destination (see section 2.3.5). The designation and use of such thresholds may appear arbitrary, but they serve the useful purpose of differentiating those who bring outside revenue into the local area (and thereby increase the potential for the generation of additional wealth) from those who circulate revenue internally and thereby do not induce such an effect.

Domestic and international tourism

If qualifying travel occurs beyond a person's usual environment but within his or her usual country of residence, then that individual would be classified as a **domestic tourist**. If the experience occurs outside of the usual country of residence, then that person would be classified as an **international tourist**. The concept of 'usual environment' does not normally apply in international tourism. Residents of a border town, for example, become international tourists as soon as they cross the nearby international border (providing that the necessary temporal and purposive criteria are also met), even though this involves a very small amount of travel. Essentially, the border is a geopolitical threshold that separates a person's 'usual environment' from other spaces, no matter what its distance from home. An aspect of international tourism that is seldom recognised is the fact that such travel always involves at least some movement within the international tourist's own country — for example, the trip from home to the airport or international border. Although neglected as a subject of research, this component is nonetheless important, because of the infrastructure and services that are used and the economic activity that is generated.

International tourism differs from domestic tourism in other crucial respects. First, domestic tourists far outnumber international tourists at a global scale and within most countries. In Australia, for example, every night spent by an international tourist in commercial accommodation is matched by three nights accounted for by Australians (Faulkner & Walmsley 1998). This ratio is in line with the World Tourism Organization estimate that domestic tourists account for about 70 per cent of the total world demand for commercial accommodation. In terms of overall global participation and revenue, it is widely accepted that domestic tourism is on the order of ten times larger than international tourism, although the ratio varies dramatically between countries (Goeldner & Ritchie 2003).

Second, relatively little is known about domestic tourists compared with their international counterparts, despite their numbers and economic importance. One reason is that most national governments do not consider domestic tourists to be as worthy of scrutiny, since they do not bring much-valued foreign exchange into the country but 'merely' redistribute wealth from one part of the country to another. It is often only when international tourist numbers are declining, for example in the aftermath of 11 September 2001 or the Indian Ocean tsunami of 2004, that governments are prompted to support tourism businesses by promoting their domestic tourism sector. Another reason for the relative neglect is that domestic tourists are usually more difficult to count than international tourists, since they are not subject, in democratic countries at least, to the border formalities faced by most international tourists. However, where countries are moving towards political and economic integration, and hence more open borders, international tourist flows are becoming just as difficult to monitor as domestic flows. This is well illustrated at present by the 25 countries of the recently enlarged **European Union** (see section 4.3).

Finally, there are some cases where the distinction between domestic and international tourism is not entirely clear. This occurs when the tourism system incorporates geopolitical entities that are not part of a fully fledged country. For example, should a resident of the Israeli-controlled West Bank (Jewish or Arab) be considered an international or domestic tourist when he or she travels to Israel? Travel between the Hong Kong Special Administrative Region and China is another ambiguous situation, as is travel between Taiwan and mainland China.

Outbound and inbound tourists

When referring specifically to international tourism, a distinction is made between **outbound tourists** (those leaving their usual country of residence) and **inbound tourists** (those arriving in a country different from their usual country of residence). Any international tourism trip has both outbound and inbound components, with the distinction being based on whether the classification is being made from the perspective of the country of origin or destination. Take, for example, an Australian who spends two weeks on vacation in Fiji. This person would be considered outbound from an Australian perspective but inbound from the Fijian perspective.

One would assume, intuitively, that the total global number of outbound tourists should equal the total number of inbound tourists over a long period of time. However, this is not the case, as demonstrated by the hypothetical example of an Australian tourist who visits five island–states during a trip to the South Pacific. From Australia's perspective, this trip equates with one outbound tourist experience. However, each of the island–states will record that traveller as one inbound tourist, resulting in five separate instances of inbound tourism. Accordingly, the cumulative number of inbound trips will always exceed the total number of outbound trips at a global scale, since one outbound trip must translate into at least, but possibly more than, one inbound trip.

Long-haul and short-haul travel

A distinction is often made between **long-haul trips** and **short-haul trips**. There are no universal definitions for these terms, which are often defined according to the needs and purposes of different organisations, sectors or destinations (Bowen 2001). The United Nations regards long-haul travel as trips outside the multi-country WTO region in which the traveller lives (Lockwood & Medlik 2001). Thus, a United Kingdom resident travelling to Germany (i.e. within Europe, the same region) is a short-haul tourist, while the same resident travelling to South Africa or Australia is a long-haul tourist. Airines usually base the distinction on distance thresholds, one implication being that long-haul routes require different types of aircraft and passenger management strategies (see the Technology feature in chapter 3). Recent concerns about deep vein thrombosis (or DVT, the formation of blood clots during prolonged periods of inactivity) have focused attention on the effects of long-haul flights. In Australia, the latter are associated with interregional flights six hours or more in duration (Harrison-Hill 2000). From a destination perspective, long-haul tourists are often distinguished from short-haul tourists by expenditure patterns, length of stay and other critical parameters. They may as a result warrant separate marketing and management strategies.

■ 2.3.2 Temporal *component*

The length of time involved in the trip experience is the second basic factor that determines whether someone is a tourist and what type of tourist. Theoretically, there is no minimum time that must be expended, although most trips that meet domestic tourism distance thresholds will require at least a few hours. Again, a crossborder outbound trip involving adjacent origins and destinations could be an exception, as such a trip could possibly be completed in less than an hour and still be considered tourism.

At the other end of the time spectrum, most countries adhere to a WTO threshold of one year as the maximum amount of time that an inbound tourist can remain in the visited country and still be considered a tourist. For domestic tourists this threshold is normally reduced to six months

(Chadwick 1994). Once these upper thresholds are exceeded, the visitor is no longer classified as a tourist, and should be reassigned to another category such as 'temporary resident' or 'migrant'.

Stayovers and excursionists

Within these time limits, the experience of an overnight stay is critical in defining the type of tourist. If the tourist (domestic or international) remains in the destination for at least one night, then that person is commonly classified as a **stayover**. If the trip does not incorporate at least one overnight stay, then the term **excursionist** is often used. The definition of an 'overnight stay' may pose a problem, as in the case of someone arriving in a destination at 2.00 am and departing at 4.00 am. However, the use of overnight stay is a significant improvement over the former criterion of a minimum 24-hour stay, which proved both arbitrary and extremely difficult to apply, given that it would require monitoring of exact times of arrival and departure.

Excursion-based tourism is dominated by two main types of activity. Cruise ship excursionists are among the fastest growing segments of the tourist market, numbering 9.8 million in 2003 (ICCL 2004) but many more if quantified as inbound tourists from the cumulative perspective of each cruise ship destination country. Certain geographically suitable regions, such as the Caribbean and Mediterranean basins, are especially impacted by the cruise ship sector. Crossborder shoppers are the other major type of excursionist. This form of tourism is also spatially constrained, with major flows being associated with adjacent and accessible countries with large concentrations of population along the border. Examples include Canada/United States (Timothy 1999), United States/Mexico, Singapore/Malaysia, Argentina/Uruguay and western Europe.

As with domestic tourists and other domestic travellers, the distinction between stayovers and excursionists is more than a bureaucratic indulgence. Significant differences in the management of tourism systems are likely depending on whether the tourism sector is dominated by one or the other group. An important difference, for example, is the excursionists' lack of need for overnight accommodation in a destination (see the Contemporary issue feature in chapter 4).

▪ 2.3.3 Travel *purpose*

The third basic tourist criterion concerns the **travel purpose**. Not all purposes for travelling qualify as tourism. According to the WTO, major exclusions include travel by active military personnel, daily routine trips, commuter traffic, migrant and guest worker flows, nomadic movements, refugee arrivals and travel by diplomats and consular representatives. The latter exclusion is related to the fact that embassies and consulates are technically considered to be part of the sovereign territory of the country they represent. The purposes that do qualify as tourism are dominated by three major categories:
1. leisure and recreation
2. visiting friends and relatives
3. business.

Leisure and recreation

Leisure and recreation are just two components within a constellation of related purposes that also includes terms such as 'vacation', 'rest and relaxation', 'pleasure' and 'holiday'. This is the category that usually comes to mind when we try to imagine the stereotypical tourism experience. Leisure and recreation account for the largest single share of tourist activity at a global level. As depicted in table 2.1, this also pertains to Australia, where 'holiday' (the Australian version of the category) constitutes the main purpose of visits for both domestic and inbound tourists.

■ **Table 2.1**
Main reason for trip by inbound and domestic visitor nights, Australia, 2003[1]

PURPOSE OF TRIP	DOMESTIC TOURISTS		INBOUND TOURISTS	
	NUMBER[2]	%	NUMBER[2]	%
Holiday	134 900	46	46 265	39
Visiting friends and relatives	97 544	33	21 533	18
Business-related	42 805	15	6 396	5
Other	12 409	4	44 799	38
Total[3]	294 112	100	119 093	100

Notes:
[1] All visitors 15 years of age and older
[2] In thousands
[3] Includes visitor nights where purpose was not stated

Source: *ABS (2003a, 2003b)*

Visiting friends and relatives (VFR)

The intent to visit friends and relatives (i.e. VFR tourism) is the second most important purpose for tourism in Australia (table 2.1). An important management implication is that, unlike pleasure travel, the destination decision is normally predetermined by the place of residence of the person who is to be visited. Thus, while the tourism literature talks about destination choice and the various factors that influence that choice (see chapter 6), the reality is that genuinely 'free' choice really only exists for pleasure-oriented tourists. Another interesting observation is how much VFR-dominated tourism systems are affiliated with migration systems. About one-half of all inbound visitors to Australia from the United Kingdom, for example, list VFR as their primary purpose (as opposed to about one-fifth of inbound tourists in total), and this overrepresentation is due mainly to the continuing importance of the United Kingdom as a source of migrants.

Business

Business is the third most important reason for tourism-related travel at a global level. Even more so than with the VFR category, business tourists are constrained in their travel decisions by the nature of the business that they are required to undertake. Assuming that the appropriate spatial and temporal criteria are met, business travel is a form of tourism only if the traveller is not paid by a source based in the destination. For example, a consultant who travels from Sydney to Perth, and is paid by a company based in Perth, would not be considered a tourist. However, if payment is made by a Sydney-based company, then the consultant is classified as a tourist. This stipulation prevents longer commutes to work from being incorporated into tourism statistics, and once again reflects the principle that tourism involves the input of new money from external sources.

There are numerous subcategories associated with business tourism, including consulting, sales, operations, management and maintenance. However, the largest category involves meetings, incentive travel, conventions and exhibitions, all of which are combined in the acronym **MICE**. Most, but not all, of MICE tourism is related to business. Many meetings and conventions, for example, involve such non-business social activities as school and military reunions. Similarly, exhibitions can be divided into trade and consumer subtypes, with the latter involving participants who attend such events for pleasure/leisure purposes. Incentive tourists are travellers whose trips are paid for all or in part by their employer as a way of rewarding excellent employee performance. In Australia, MICE tourism generates about $7 billion per year in direct expenditure, with about 80 per cent of meetings being oriented to domestic rather than international markets. Weber and Ladkin (2003) note the impetus for the international component of this sector that was created by the 2000 Sydney Olympics but cite competition from ultra-efficient regional competitors such as Singapore and Hong Kong as a major contemporary challenge.

Sport

Several additional purposes that qualify a traveller as a tourist are less numerically important than the three largest categories, though potentially more important in particular destinations or regions. Sport-related tourism involves the travel and activities of athletes, trainers and others associated with competitions and training, as well as the tourist spectators attending sporting events and other sport-related venues. High-profile sporting events such as the Olympic Games and the World Cup of football not only confer a large amount of visibility on the host destination and participating teams (see figure 2.3), but also involve many participants and generate substantial tourism-related and other 'spin-off' effects. For example, the Rugby World

■ **Figure 2.3**
Parade of Australian athletes at the Athens opening ceremony

Cup of 2003, believed to be the world's third-largest sporting event, attracted 65 000 international tourists to Australia and $410 million in direct expenditures within the country from this group. Domestic tourists made about 180 000 interstate trips to attend matches, which were held in ten cities across the country including regional locations such as Gosford (New South Wales), Launceston (Tasmania) and Townsville (Queensland) (DITR 2004). Sporting competitions in some cases have also been used to promote cross-cultural understanding and peaceful relations between countries and cultures (see section 9.2.1).

Spirituality

Spiritual motivation includes travel for religious purposes. Pilgrimage activity constitutes by far the largest form of tourism travel in Saudi Arabia due to the annual pilgrimage or *Hajj* to Mecca by several million Muslims from around the world. Religious travel is also extremely important in India's domestic tourism sector (Singh 2004). One festival alone, the six-week Maha Kumbh Mela, drew an estimated 70 million Hindu pilgrims to the city of Allahabad in 2001.

More ambiguous is the **secular pilgrimage**, which blurs the boundary between the sacred and the profane (Digance 2003). The term has been applied to diverse tourist experiences, including commemorative ANZAC events at the Gallipoli battle site in Turkey (Hall 2002), as well as visits to Graceland (Elvis Presley's mansion in Memphis, Tennessee) (Rigby 2001) and sporting halls of fame (Gammon 2004). Secular pilgrimage is often associated with the New Age movement, which is variably described as a legitimate or pseudoreligious phenomenon. Digance (2003) describes how the central Australian Uluru monolith has become a contested sacred site in part because of conflicts between Aboriginal and New Age pilgrims seeking privileged access to the site.

Health

Tourism for health purposes includes visits to spas, although such travel is often merged with pleasure/leisure motivations. More explicitly health related is travel undertaken in order to receive medical treatment. Cuba, for example, has developed a specialty in providing low-cost surgery for foreign clients. In Australia, the Gold Coast of Queensland is building a reputation as a centre for cosmetic surgery and other elective medical procedures. Many Americans travel to Mexico to gain access to unconventional treatments that are unavailable in the United States.

Study

Study, or formal education more broadly, is a category that most people do not intuitively associate with tourism, even though it is a qualifying WTO criterion. Australia, New Zealand, Canada, the United States and the United Kingdom are especially active in attracting foreign students. Although their numbers may not appear large in relation to the three main categories of purpose, students have a substantial relative impact on the host countries because of the prolonged nature of their stay and the large expenditures, including tuition, that they make during these periods of study. For example, international students accounted for about 8 per cent of all inbound arrivals to Australia in 2002 but more than 27 per cent of all visitor-nights. Educational fees (that is, tuition) were the third-largest inbound expenditure category at more than $1.2 billion, which represented 12 per cent of all expenditures within Australia by inbound tourists (BTR 2003). This compares with just $774 million and 9 per cent, respectively, in 1999 (BTR 2000). Foreign students also often attract visitors from their home country during their period of study, and generate other flow-on effects (see Contemporary issue: Flow-on effects from international students). Yet national tourism organisations have been slow to stimulate this market through the provision of marketing and promotional assistance to universities or other education institutions, as called for by Leiper and Hunt (1998).

Multipurpose tourism

If every tourist had only a single reason for travelling, the classification of tourists by purpose would be a simple task. However, many if not most tourist trips involve **multipurpose travel**, which introduces some confounding elements into the process of data classification and analysis. The current Australian situation illustrates the problem. Departing visitors are asked to state their subsidiary travel purposes as well as their primary purpose for travelling to Australia. It is on the basis of the latter that table 2.1 is derived, and policy and management decisions are subsequently made. These data, however, may not accurately reflect the actual experiences of the tourists.

Take, for example, a hypothetical inbound tourist who, at the conclusion of a two-week visit, states 'business' as the primary trip purpose, and pleasure/holiday and VFR as other purposes. The actual trip of that business tourist may have consisted of conference attendance in Sydney over a three-day period, a three-day visit with friends in the nearby town of Bathurst and the remaining eight days at a resort in Port Douglas. While the primary purpose was business, this is clearly not reflected in the amount of time (and probably expenditure) that the tourist spent on each category of purpose. Yet without the conference, the tourist might not have visited Australia at all. On the other hand, if the delegate had no friends in Australia, the country might not have been as attractive as a destination, and the tourist might have decided not to attend the conference in the first place. Thus, there is an interplay among the various travel purposes, and it is difficult to establish a meaningful 'main' purpose.

A further complication is that people in the same travel group may have different purposes for their trip. The conference delegate, for example, may be accompanied by a spouse who engages solely in pleasure/holiday activities. However, most surveys do not facilitate such multipurpose responses from different members of the same party. Rather, they assume that a single main purpose applies to all members of that group.

Speculation that the contemporary international student generates tourism-related effects far beyond his or her actual educational experience in a destination is supported by Weaver (2004), who in 2001 surveyed 139 international students who had completed a degree at a large public university in the Brisbane–Gold Coast corridor before 2000. One hundred per cent of the sample, which consisted of graduates who had returned to their home countries of Hong Kong, India, Indonesia, Japan and Singapore, stated that they had visited at least three attractions on the Gold Coast during their study. Most of the respondents (82 per cent) additionally indicated that they had travelled elsewhere within Australia for recreational or social purposes during that time, with almost one-half of the sample taking at least two such trips. Each trip entailed an average expenditure of almost $1000 by the student, and consisted on average of 4.4 participants. A similarly high portion, 78 per cent, revealed that they had hosted visitors from their home country while they were studying in Australia. An average of 1.6 visits was hosted, involving on average two visitors and a two-week stay.

Just more than one-half of the students (53 per cent) reported that they had made at least one return visit to Australia since returning to their home country. Vacation or leisure was the main purpose of these trips, followed by VFR involving other students from their home country, other VFR purposes, business, and attending a graduation ceremony. Only nine respondents (7 per cent) indicated that they would probably never visit Australia again. Finally, two-thirds felt that they had influenced other students from their home country to study in Australia, while a similar portion said that they themselves had been influenced in this way. All told, the average respondent generated an estimated $12 000 in direct expenditures as a result of these noneducation-related tourism experiences.

International students in Australia, therefore, seem above and beyond their educational experiences to serve the multiple roles of leisure and VFR tourist, host, return visitor and word-of-mouth recruiter. Additional research using a larger and more representative sample (that is, including European and North American students) is required to gain further insight into the relationship between these various roles, so that destination managers can better devise strategies to maximise these flow-on effects.

2.3.4 Major *tourist categories*

Section 2.3.1 demonstrated that tourists can be either international or domestic, while section 2.3.2 indicated that tourists can also be either stayovers or excursionists. The combination of these spatial and temporal dimensions produces **four major types of tourist**, and these categories account for all tourist possibilities, assuming that the appropriate purposive criteria are also met. **International stayovers** (1) are tourists who remain in a destination outside their usual country of residence for at least one night (e.g. a Brisbane resident who spends a two-week adventure tour in Papua New Guinea). **International excursionists** (2) stay in this destination without experiencing at least one overnight stay (e.g. a Brisbane resident on a cruise who spends three hours in Port Moresby). **Domestic stayovers** (3) stay for at least one night in a destination that is within their own usual country of residence, but outside of a 'usual environment' that is often defined by specific distance thresholds from the home site (e.g. a Brisbane resident who spends one week on holidays in Melbourne). **Domestic excursionists** (4) undertake a similar trip, but without staying overnight (e.g. a Brisbane resident who flies to and from Melbourne on the same day). Figure 2.4 depicts these four categories of tourist within the context of a broad travel typology.

■ **Figure 2.4**
Four types of tourist within a broad travel context

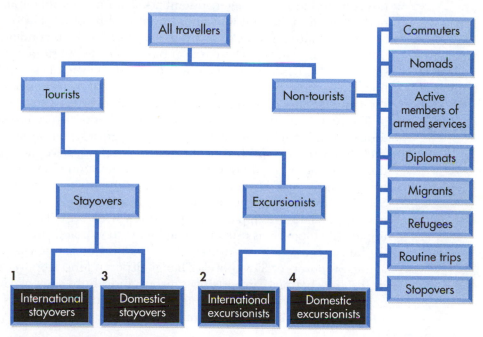

WTO terminology

The above tourist terms, while commonly used in the literature, do not match the terms that are used by the WTO. As indicated in figure 2.5, the WTO refers to tourists as 'visitors' and reserves the word 'tourist' for the specific category of stayovers. In addition, those who are described as excursionists in this text are classified as 'same-day visitors' by the WTO. We reject this terminology as being counterintuitive. If interpreted literally, cruise ship excursionists and cross-border shoppers are excluded in any reference to the 'tourist'. They fall instead under the visitor subcategory of 'same-day visitor'. Nevertheless, students should be aware of the WTO terms, since they will be encountered in the many essential publications released by that organisation, and by governments who adhere to their terminology.

Tourist terms used in this textbook		Tourist terms used by the WTO
■ Tourists	=	Visitors
■ Stayovers	=	Tourists
■ Excursionists	=	Same-day visitors

Stopovers

Stopovers are tourists or other travellers temporarily staying in a location while in transit to or from a destination region. The main criterion that distinguishes a stopover from an inbound stayover or excursionist is that they normally do not clear customs or undergo any other border formalities that signify an official visit to that location. To illustrate the point, a person travelling by air from Sydney to Toronto normally changes flights in Honolulu or Los Angeles. Most passengers disembark from the aeroplane in these transit nodes late at night, and wait in the transit lobby of the airport for three or four hours until it is time to board the aircraft for the second and final leg of this long-haul journey. These transit passengers are all stopovers. If, however, someone chooses to clear customs and spend a few hours shopping in Honolulu, they would be classified as an international excursionist or stayover to the United States, depending on whether an 'overnight stay' was included.

The paradox in this situation is that most stopovers are indeed outbound tourists (unlike the other nontravelling categories), but are not classified as such from the perspective of the transit location. Several factors underlie this exclusion. First, there is the previously mentioned fact that such travellers do not clear border formalities and hence are not official visitors. Second, stopovers are not in the transit location by choice, although many may appreciate the opportunity to stretch their legs. Third, the economic impact of stopovers is usually negligible, with expenditures being restricted to the purchase of a few drinks, some food or a local newspaper (see Managing: Stopovers at Singapore's Changi airport). Most stopover traffic occurs in the international airports of transportation hubs such as Honolulu, Singapore, Bangkok, Dubai and Frankfurt. In contrast, Australia's location and size result in limited stopover traffic.

MANAGING
Stopovers at Singapore's Changi airport

The stopover experience has generally been regarded as little more than a necessary evil by travellers as well as airport authorities. Some major airports, however, appear to be actively exploiting the opportunities provided by the presence of these incidental visitors. Singapore's Changi airport is one example. With the increase in long-haul flights, Singapore has emerged as an ever more important regional transit hub. The Civil Aviation Authority of Singapore (CAAS), the statutory board under the ministry of transport that runs the airport, has the goal of making Changi the best airport in the world and a major global hub. This involves pleasing stopovers and other passengers through a complementary mix of strategies that focus on both utility and pleasure. Ultramodern design that stresses clear visualisation and free movement for easy transfer, for example, is accompanied by strategically located traditional gardens and waterfalls that soften the architecture and provide diversion as well as stress alleviation. A transit hotel in Terminal 1 operates a swimming pool and bar that are open to any stopover for a nominal fee (Jacob 2005). In Terminal 2, the Shower, Fitness and Lifestyle Centre provides napping areas, while other locations provide aromatherapy massage, live music lounges and free access to computer terminals that offer interactive games. Also available are free films at the movie theatre, and an Explorer's Lounge that provides entertainment from the *Discovery* channel and *National Geographic Programme*. The Skyplex Entertainment Lounge is an innovative facility that provides international programming, including live webcam coverage of several cities around the world, on 24 state-of-the-art plasma and LCD screens.

Added to the more conventional shopping and dining opportunities, these facilities generate substantial revenues for the airport and provide the stopover with a pleasurable 'transit as attraction' experience, which may encourage future visits to Singapore as either a stopover or stayover. To bring about this conversion to longer visits, stopovers with sufficient time to pass are given the option of a free Singapore bus tour. One anticipated management challenge, however, is the possibility that all these distractions will cause some stopovers to miss their flights. To minimise this possibility, the Changi website (www.changi airport.com.sg/changi/index.jsp) provides a list of recommended activities suitable for layover periods ranging from half an hour to five hours or more.

■ 2.3.5 Data *problems*

Inbound tourist arrival statistics should be treated with caution, especially if they are being used to identity temporal trends. This is in part because of the high margin of error that characterises older data in particular. For example, the WTO figure of 25 million international stayovers for 1950 (see table 3.1) is nothing more than a rough estimate, given the relatively primitive data-collecting techniques of that era. Yet it is used as a baseline for calculating the relative growth in global tourist arrivals since then. At the scale of any individual country, this margin of error is amplified. More recent statistics have a smaller margin of error as a result of WTO initiatives to standardise definitions and data collection protocols. However, error still results from such things as inconsistencies from country to country in the collection and reporting of arrivals, expenditures and other tourism-related statistics. This is why there is a gap of several years between a given year and the release by the WTO of a relatively reliable profile of the global tourism sector for that year (for example, this book, written during 2005, depends on 2003 WTO data).

Data-related problems are even more pronounced in domestic tourism statistics, owing in part to domestic tourist movements being extremely difficult to monitor in most countries. Such statistics are often derived from the responses to surveys distributed at points of departure or sent to a sample of households, from which broader national or state patterns are extrapolated. However, these surveys do not always employ appropriate survey design or sampling techniques (see chapter 12). At the subnational level, authorities sometimes rely on extremely unreliable information sources such as sign-in books provided at welcome centres, visitor bureaus or attractions. Attempts to compare domestic tourism in different domestic jurisdictions are impeded by the proliferation of idiosyncratic definitions.

For example, most Canadian provinces employ an 80-kilometre radius threshold from a person's residence to distinguish domestic tourists from other travellers. However, tourism authorities in Ontario adhere to a 40-kilometre radius (Chadwick 1994). Australia maintains an idiosyncratic definition of domestic tourism that effectively precludes comparison with any other country. Domestic tourists are defined as Australian residents who take a trip away from home that involves at least one overnight stay, requires a journey of at least 40 kilometres and is undertaken for *any reason* [our emphasis] (BTR 1998). Ironically, any reform of this bizarre definition would complicate any attempt to compare the prereform and postreform data. The experience of both Canada and Australia shows that even highly developed countries continue to face many difficulties in their attempts to understand the magnitude of their domestic tourism systems.

2.4 ORIGIN REGION

The **origin region**, as a component of the tourism system, has been neglected by researchers and managers. No tourism system could evolve but for the generation of demand within the origin region, but little actual tourism activity occurs there. For discussion purposes, it is useful to distinguish between the origin community and the origin government.

2.4.1 Origin *community*

Research into origin regions has concentrated on market segmentation and marketing (see chapters 6 and 7). Almost no attention, in contrast, has been paid to the impacts of tourism on the **origin community**. Yet there are numerous ways in which these impacts can occur. For example, some major origin cities can resemble ghost towns during long weekends or summer vacation periods, when a substantial number of residents travel to nearby beaches for recreational purposes. Local businesses may suffer as a result, while the broader local economy may be adversely affected over a longer period by the associated outflow of revenue. Conversely, local suppliers of travel-related goods and services such as travel agencies may thrive as a result of this tourist activity.

Significant effects can also be felt at the sociocultural level, wherein returning tourists are influenced by the fashions, food and music of various destinations. Such external cultural influences, of course, may be equally or more attributable to immigration and mass media, so the identification of tourism's specific role in disseminating these influences is a useful research directive. Other tangible impacts include the unintended introduction of diseases such as malaria and AIDS, or pathogens that can devastate the local farming sector. The role of the expanding global tourism system as a disseminator of such influences should not be underestimated. For example, of 209 cases of *Plasmodium vivax* malaria infection reported to the Royal Melbourne Hospital between early 1997 and mid-2001, 128 or 61 per cent were associated with Australian travellers who had visited high-risk regions such as the South Pacific, sub-Saharan Africa and Latin America (Elliott et al. 2004). The formation of relationships between tourists and local residents also has potential consequences for origin communities. It is, for example, a common practice for male sex workers (i.e. 'beach boys') in Caribbean destinations such as the Dominican Republic to initiate romantic liaisons with inbound female tourists in the hope of migrating to a prosperous origin country like Canada or Italy (Herold, Garcia & DeMoya 2001).These examples demonstrate that at least some tourism management attention to origin regions is warranted, although another complicating variable is the extent to which the origin region also functions as a destination region, and is thus impacted by both returning and incoming tourists.

■ 2.4.2 Origin *government*

The impacts of the **origin government** on the tourism system have also been largely ignored, in part because it is taken for granted in the more developed countries that citizens are free to travel wherever they wish (within reason). Yet, this freedom is ultimately dependent on the willingness of origin national governments to tolerate a mobile citizenry. Even in democratic countries, some individuals may have their passports seized to prevent them from travelling abroad. At a larger scale, prohibitions on the travel of US citizens to Cuba, imposed by successive US governments hostile to the regime of Fidel Castro, have effectively prevented the development of a major bilateral tourism system incorporating the two countries. In countries, such as North Korea, governed by totalitarian regimes, such restrictions are more normative. An extremely important development in this regard has been the gradual liberalisation of outbound tourist flows by the government of China, which in recent years has dramatically increased the number of countries with approved destination status (ADS) (see section 3.7).

In effect, the role of origin governments can be likened to a safety valve that ultimately determines the amount of energy (i.e. tourist flow) that is allowed into the system (see chapter 3). Outbound flows are also influenced by the various services that origin governments offer to residents travelling or intending to travel abroad. In addition to consular services for citizens who have experienced trouble, these services largely involve advice to potential travellers about risk factors that are present in other countries.

Figure 2.6 depicts the systems of travel advice offered by the governments of five major outbound tourist markets. All include warnings against any travel to particular countries in cases of widespread civil unrest or natural disasters.

■ **Figure 2.6**
The system of travel advice in major source markets

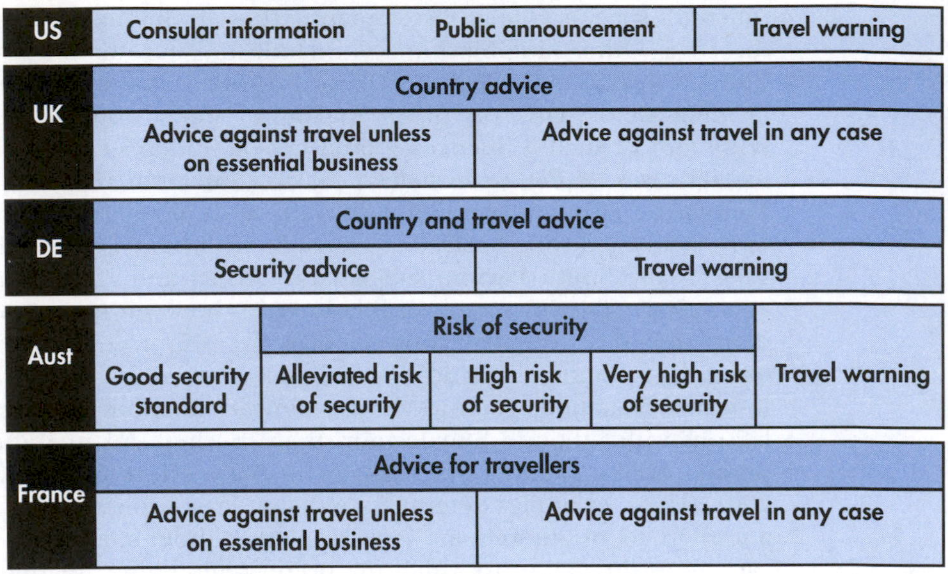

US	Consular information		Public announcement		Travel warning
UK	Country advice				
	Advice against travel unless on essential business		Advice against travel in any case		
DE	Country and travel advice				
	Security advice		Travel warning		
Aust		Risk of security			
	Good security standard	Alleviated risk of security	High risk of security	Very high risk of security	Travel warning
France	Advice for travellers				
	Advice against travel unless on essential business		Advice against travel in any case		

Source: *Glaesser (2003)*

2.5 TRANSIT REGION

As with origin regions, few studies have explicitly recognised the importance of the **transit region** component of the tourism system. This neglect is due in part to its status as a space that the tourist must cross to reach the location that he or she really wants to visit. Reinforcing this negative connotation is the sense, common among tourists, that time spent on the journey to a destination is vacation time that is wasted. Transit passages, moreover, are often uncomfortable, as economy-class passengers on a long- haul flight will attest. Under more positive circumstances, however, the transit region can itself be a destination of sorts as illustrated by the Changi airport example. This may also be the case, for example, if the journey involves a drive through spectacular scenery, or if the trip affords a level of comfort, novelty and/or activity that makes the transit experience comparable to that which is sought in a final destination.

As these examples illustrate, the distinction between transit and destination regions is not always clear, given also that the tourist's itinerary within a destination region will probably include a variety of transit experiences (see figure 2.2). An inbound tourist staying in Sydney, for example, may opt to visit a nearby National Park, which requires a one- or two-hour transit journey. In many instances a location can be important both as a transit and destination region. The Queensland city of Townsville, for instance, is an important transit stop on the road from Brisbane to Cairns, but it is also in itself an important emerging destination. The transit/destination distinction is even more ambiguous in cruise ship tourism, where the actual cruise is a major component of the travel experience and a 'destination' in its own right.

■ 2.5.1 Management *implications of transit regions*

Once the status of a place as a transit node or region is determined, specific management implications become more apparent, such as the need to identify relevant impacts. For airports, this frequently involves increased congestion that impedes the arrival and departure of stayovers. In highway transit situations, a major impact is the development of extensive motel (for *motor* ho*tel*) strips along primary roads on the outskirts of even relatively small urban centres. A related management consideration is the extent to which the transit region can, and wishes to, evolve as a destination in its own right, a scenario that can be assisted by the presence of transit motels or airports.

Managers of destination regions also need to take into consideration the transit component of tourism systems when managing their own tourism sector. Pertinent issues include whether the destination is accessible through multiple or single transit routes and which modes of transportation provide access. Destinations that are accessible by only one route and mode (e.g. an isolated island served by a single airport and a single airline) are disadvantaged by being dependent on a single tourist 'lifeline'. However, this may be offset by the advantage of having all visitor processing consolidated at a single location. A further consideration is the extent to which a transit link is fixed (as with a highway) and can be disrupted if associated infrastructure, such as a bridge, is put out of commission. In contrast to road-based travel, air journeys do not depend on infrastructure during the actual flight, and have greater scope for rerouting if a troublesome situation is encountered (e.g. a war breaking out in a fly-over country or adverse weather conditions).

Destination managers also need to consider the possibility that one or more locations along a transit route could become destinations themselves, and thus serve as **intervening opportunities** that divert visitors from the original destination. Cuba, for example, is currently little more than an incidental transit location in the United States-to-Jamaica tourism system due to the above-mentioned hostility of the US government towards the Castro regime. However, if a change in the political situation led to the re-opening of Cuba to US tourists, then the impact upon the Jamaican tourism sector could be devastating.

■ 2.5.2 Effects *of technology*

Technological change has dramatically affected the character of transit regions. Faster aeroplanes and cars have reduced the amount of time required in the transit phase, thereby increasing the size of transit regions by making long-haul travel more feasible and comfortable. New aircraft models such as the Airbus A380 and Boeing's 777-200 LR Worldliner promise to radically re-shape the transit experience for travellers as well as airports (see Technology: Making room for the monster).

Making room for the monster

The Airbus A380 superjumbo jet, presented to the public in early 2005, is a four-aisle, twin-deck behemoth that can accommodate 555 passengers when fully configured for three seating classes. However, because its 78-metre wingspan is 15 metres wider than the wingspan of its rival Boeing 747 and its weight 30 per cent greater, it cannot be accommodated on the existing runways or gates of even the largest airports. Runway widening and reinforcement were undertaken at Heathrow (London), Charles de Gaulle (Paris), Changi (Singapore), Sydney and a few other airports in anticipation of the aircraft's commercial debut in 2006 but other major hubs were more hesitant. In particular, few US airports indicated an interest in accommodating the superjumbo, on the premise that the anticipated infrequency of use (because of their lack of long-haul routes) did not justify the expensive changes in infrastructure required to host the aircraft.

Airbus defends the A380 as a 'green giant', whose large capacity results in lower per passenger fuel consumption (2.9 litres per passenger per 100 kilometres) and fewer planes in the sky. Critics, however, point out that early adopters such as Emirate Airlines (Dubai) and Singapore Airlines are configuring the aircraft to seat fewer than 500 passengers to accommodate conference rooms, cocktail lounges and other innovative facilities that will differentiate the A380 from its competitor (Lovgren 2005). Assuming additionally that the average A380 flight will not be fully subscribed, the aircraft could then be perceived as an environmental liability, which would further benefit Boeing in its ongoing air wars with Airbus. Ultimately, the two carriers may be banking on different future scenarios for commercial aviation, with Airbus anticipating a pattern of long-haul routes using a relatively small number of 'megahubs' where the congestion and pollution problems allegedly alleviated by the A380 are acute. In contrast, Boeing envisions a preference for more direct flights using smaller aircraft and a larger network of airports, a scenario that its 7E7, scheduled to debut in 2008, is ideally suited for (Lovgren 2005).

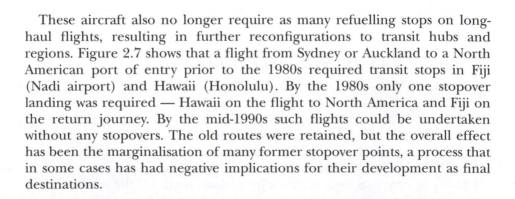

These aircraft also no longer require as many refuelling stops on long-haul flights, resulting in further reconfigurations to transit hubs and regions. Figure 2.7 shows that a flight from Sydney or Auckland to a North American port of entry prior to the 1980s required transit stops in Fiji (Nadi airport) and Hawaii (Honolulu). By the 1980s only one stopover landing was required — Hawaii on the flight to North America and Fiji on the return journey. By the mid-1990s such flights could be undertaken without any stopovers. The old routes were retained, but the overall effect has been the marginalisation of many former stopover points, a process that in some cases has had negative implications for their development as final destinations.

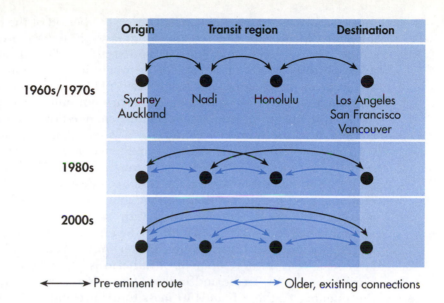

■ **Figure 2.7**
The evolution of the trans-Pacific travel system

A similar marginalisation effect has resulted from the construction of limited access expressways in countries such as the United States, Canada and Australia. By diverting traffic from the old main highways, these expressways have forced the closure of many roadside motels that depended on travellers in transit. In the place of the traditional motel strip, clusters of large motels, usually dominated by major chains (such as Holiday Inn, Motel 6 and Comfort Inn) have emerged at strategic intersections readily accessible to the expressway. These clusters contribute to suburban sprawl by attracting affiliated services such as petrol stations and fast-food outlets. Another implication of technology is the exploitation of otherwise inaccessible areas as transit regions — for example, aeroplanes on the Sydney-to-Buenos Aires route fly over Antarctica (which may itself increase the attractiveness of the journey and thereby increase the volume of traffic). In broad terms, the latter half of the twentieth century was the era in which the car and the aeroplane became pre-eminent, at the expense of the passenger ship and the passenger train (see chapter 3). Places that relied on the ship and the train, accordingly, have declined in importance as transit and destination regions (e.g. train stations and some ports), unless they were able to compensate by developing their road or air access, or by catering to niche nostalgia-motivated markets.

2.6 DESTINATION REGION

The **destination region** is the geographical component of the tourism system that has been subjected to by far the greatest scrutiny. During the era of the advocacy platform (see page 12), this attention focused on the destination-based tourism industry. Researchers were then concerned largely with determining how the industry could effectively attract and satisfy a profit-generating clientele. During the period of the cautionary and adaptancy platforms, the research emphasis shifted towards the identification of host community impacts and strategies for ensuring that these were positive. More of a balance between industry and community is apparent in the present knowledge-based platform, as well as a realisation that the interests of the two components are not mutually exclusive.

The distribution of destination regions changed dramatically during the latter half of the twentieth century, and is constantly being reconfigured, vertically as well as horizontally, through technological change and consumer interest (see Breakthrough tourism: Flipping over zero-gravity flights). Some of this change is the result of internal factors (e.g. active promotional efforts, decision to upgrade an airport), but much is also attributable to external factors associated with the broader tourism system or external environments. An example is the emergence of consumer demand for 3S (i.e. sea, sand, sun) tourism after World War II, which led to the large-scale tourism development of hitherto isolated tropical islands in the Caribbean, South Pacific and Indian Ocean (see chapter 4). Concurrently, the opening of these islands to mass tourism could not have taken place without radical developments in aircraft technology. One implication of this external dependency, and of systems theory in general, is that destinations can effectively manage and control only a very small proportion of the forces and variables that affect their tourism sectors. Even the most effectively managed destinations can be destroyed by the negative intervention of forces over which they have no control.

BREAKTHROUGH TOURISM
Flipping over zero-gravity flights

Extensive publicity was given in the early 2000s to the exploits of Dennis Tito, an American millionaire who became the world's first space tourist (see second edition of Weaver and Lawton's *Tourism Management*). However, because of cost, fitness, technology and liability issues, it is likely to be many decades before space tourism emerges as a significant product niche. Far more promising is the emergence of commercial zero-gravity flights. In 2004, the United States-based Zero Gravity Corp. (www.nogravity.com/index.cfm) became the first company to gain Federal Aviation Administration approval to offer 'parabolic flights' to the public. A parabolic flight entails a rapid 45-degree ascent to 32 000 feet in a specially modified Boeing 727-200 cargo jet, at which point zero-gravity conditions are sustained for 25 seconds before descent. During this period, passengers can fly through the air or do acrobatics in a specially designed padded cabin. The typical commercial parabolic flight lasts for about 90 minutes, involves 25 to 30 passengers and includes 15 sessions of weightlessness (see figure 2.8). The experience, which induces motion sickness in some participants, has been likened to a rollercoaster ride (Boyle 2004).

At approximately US$4000, commercial parabolic flights are affordable for many would-be zero-gravity tourists who want a 'once-in-a-lifetime' opportunity to see what it is like to be an astronaut. Included in the Zero Gravity Corp. product are a preflight training session and a post-flight party that respectively reinforce the anticipation and evaluation phases of the trip. Until the level of demand warrants the full-time use of specially modified aircraft, the company keeps its expenses down through an arrangement whereby conventional 727-200 cargo jets can be rapidly converted to accommodate zero-gravity flights, and then rapidly converted back to regular service until required again. As of early 2005, at least two other companies were offering zero-gravity flights outside the United States. Space Adventures Ltd (www.spaceadventures.com/steps/zerog), based in Russia, includes in its package a tour of the cosmonaut training complex at Star City, meetings with cosmonauts, and a DVD with video coverage that highlights the passenger's zero-gravity experience.

■ **Figure 2.8** *Participants in the parabolic flight experience*

■ 2.6.1 Destination *communities*

Even under the advocacy platform, destination residents were recognised as an important component of the tourism system because of the labour they provided, and in some situations because of their status as cultural tourism attractions. However, only in rare situations when that platform was dominant was the **destination community** recognised as a power in its own right, on par with industry or government. The gradual recognition of host communities as a power and research focus reflected the reality that local residents have the most to lose or gain from tourism of any stakeholder group in the tourism system. As well, government and industry are both more aware that a discontented resident population can negatively affect the tourism industry by fostering a hostile destination image among tourists (see chapter 9). A third factor is that local residents possess knowledge about their area that can assist the planning management and marketing of tourism. For example, residents are best positioned to provide informed interpretation of local historical and cultural attractions to visitors and to indicate whether development at a particular site is likely to cause social or environmental problems. For all these reasons, host communities are now commonly included as equal partners in the management of tourist destinations, and not seen as just a convenient source of labour or local colour, or a group that is already represented by government.

■ 2.6.2 Destination *governments*

If origin governments can be compared with a safety valve that releases energy into the tourism system, then **destination governments** can be likened to safety valves that control the amount of energy absorbed by the destination components of that system. This analogy is especially relevant at the international level, where national governments dictate the conditions under which inbound tourists are allowed entry (see section 4.3.2). To a greater or lesser extent, countries exert control over the number of tourist arrivals by requiring visas or passports from potential visitors, and by restricting the locations through which access to the country can be gained. Most countries, in principle and practice, encourage tourist arrivals because of the foreign exchange that they generate. However, the governments of a few countries (e.g. Bhutan and North Korea) have made conscious decisions to drastically limit entries because of the perception that tourists are a cultural or political threat.

In addition to this entry control function, destination governments also explicitly influence the development and management of their tourism products through the establishment of tourism-related agencies. These include tourism ministries (either tourism by itself or as part of a multi-sectoral portfolio) that are concerned with overall policy and direction, and tourism boards, which focus on destination marketing. Less prevalent are agencies that focus on research, such as Tourism Research Australia (www.tourism. australia.com/Research.asp?sub=0390). Many high-profile tourist destinations, such as the United States and Germany, have no federal-level portfolio emphasising tourism. This reflects to some extent the residual negative perceptions of tourism discussed in chapter 1, but also political systems that devolve responsibilities such as tourism to the state level.

2.7 *T*HE TOURISM INDUSTRY

The **tourism industry** may be defined as the sum of the industrial and commercial activities that produce goods and services wholly or mainly for tourist consumption. Broad categories commonly associated with the tourism industry include accommodation, transportation, food and beverage, tour operations, travel agencies, commercial attractions and merchandising of souvenirs and other goods purchased mainly by tourists. These activities are discussed in chapter 5, but several preliminary observations are in order. First, the tourism industry permeates the tourism system more than any other component other than the tourists themselves. However, as depicted in figure 2.9, segments of the industry vary considerably in their distribution within the tourism system. Not all spatial components of the system, moreover, accommodate an equal share of the industry. Destination regions account for most of the tourism industry, whereas origin regions are represented in significant terms only by travel agencies and some aspects of transportation and merchandising. The inclusion of industry into tourism management considerations is therefore imperative at the destination level, but less so in origin regions.

■ **Figure 2.9**
Status of major tourism industry sectors within the tourism system

Categories	Origin regions	Transit regions	Destination regions
Travel agencies	■	◆	◆
Transportation	●	■	■
Accommodation	◆	■	■
Food and beverages	◆	■	■
Tour operators	●	●	■
Attractions	◆	◆	■
Merchandisers	●	◆	■

■ Major   ● Minor   ◆ Negligible

A confounding element in the above definition of the tourism industry is the extent to which various commercial goods and services are affiliated with tourism. At one extreme almost all activity associated with travel agencies and tour operators is tourism-related. Far more ambiguous is the transportation industry, much of which involves the movement of goods (some related to tourism) or commuters, migrants and other travellers who are not tourists. Great difficulties in particular are encountered when attempting to isolate the tourism component in automobile-related transportation. Similar problems face the accommodation sector despite its clearer link to tourism, since many local residents utilise nearby hotels for wedding receptions, meetings and other functions. It is largely because of these complications that no Standard Industrial Classification (SIC) code has ever been allocated to tourism (see figure 1.2).

CHAPTER REVIEW

The complexities of tourism can be organised for analytical and management purposes by applying a systems perspective to the topic. A basic whole systems approach to tourism incorporates a number of interdependent components, including origin, transit and destination regions, the tourists themselves and the tourism industry. This system, in turn, is influenced by and influences various physical, political, social and other external environments. The challenge of managing a destination is compounded by this complexity. The tourist component of the system is defined by spatial, temporal and purposive parameters, and these lead to the identification of four major tourist types: international and domestic stayovers, and international and domestic excursionists. Recreation and leisure are the single most important purposes for tourism travel, followed by visits to friends and relatives and then business. There are also many qualifying minor purposes including education, sport and pilgrimage. Despite such definitional clarifications, serious problems are still encountered when defining tourists and collecting tourist-related data, especially at the domestic level. In terms of the geography of tourism systems, origin and transit regions are vital but neglected components of the tourism system. Much greater attention has been focused on the higher profile destination region and the tourism industry. Important preliminary observations with regard to the latter include its concentration within the destination region, and the difficulty in isolating the tourism component in many related industries such as transportation.

SUMMARY OF KEY TERMS

System

A group of interrelated, interdependent and interacting elements that together form a single functional structure

- **Basic whole tourism system:** an application of a systems approach to tourism, wherein tourism is seen as consisting of three geographical components (origin, transit and destination regions), tourists and a tourism industry, embedded within a modifying external environment that includes parallel political, social, physical and other systems

Tourist

A person who travels temporarily outside of their usual environment (usually defined by some distance threshold) for certain qualifying purposes

- **Domestic tourist:** a tourist whose itinerary is confined to their usual country of residence
- **International tourist:** a tourist who travels beyond their usual country of residence
- **Outbound tourist:** an international tourist departing from their usual country of residence

- **Inbound tourist:** an international tourist arriving from another country
- **Long-haul trips:** trips variably defined as occurring outside of the world region where the traveller resides, or beyond a given number of flying time hours
- **Short-haul trips:** trips variably defined as occurring within the world region where the traveller resides, or within a given number of flying time hours
- **Stayover:** a tourist who spends at least one night in a destination region
- **Excursionist:** a tourist who spends less than one night in a destination region

Travel purpose

The reason why people travel; in tourism, these involve recreation and leisure, visits to friends and relatives (VFR), business, and less dominant purposes such as study, sport, religion and health

- **MICE:** an acronym combining meetings, incentives, conventions and exhibitions; a form of tourism largely associated with business purposes
- **Secular pilgrimage:** travel for spiritual purposes that are not linked to conventional religions
- **Multipurpose travel:** travel undertaken for more than a single purpose

Four major types of tourist

An inclusive group of tourist categories that combines the spatial and temporal components, and assumes adherence to the qualifying purposes of travel

- **International stayovers:** tourists who stay at least one night in another country
- **International excursionists:** tourists who stay less than one night in another country
- **Domestic stayovers:** tourists who stay within their own country for at least one night
- **Domestic excursionists:** tourists who stay within their own country for less than one night

Stopovers

Travellers who stop in a location in transit to another destination; they normally do not clear customs and are not considered tourists from the transit location's perspective

Origin region

The region (e.g. country, state, city) from which the tourist originates, also referred to as the market or generating region

- **Origin community:** the residents of the origin region
- **Origin government:** the government of the origin region

Transit region

The places and regions that tourists pass through as they travel from origin to destination region

- **Intervening opportunities:** places, often within transit regions, that develop as tourist destinations in their own right and subsequently have the potential to divert tourists from previously patronised destinations

Destination region

The places to which the tourist is travelling

- **Destination community:** the residents of the destination region
- **Destination government:** the government of the destination region

Tourism industry

The sum of the industrial and commercial activities that produce goods and services wholly or mainly for tourist consumption

QUESTIONS

1 (a) Why and how is a systems approach useful in managing the tourism sector?
(b) How does this approach complement the knowledge-based platform?

2 Where do the stakeholders depicted in figure 1.1 fit into the basic whole tourism system (figure 2.1)?

3 (a) What are some of the external natural and cultural environments that interact with the tourism system?
(b) What can destination managers do to minimise the negative impacts of these systems?

4 (a) What three criteria must be considered concurrently when defining the 'tourist'?
(b) What associated problems may be encountered when attempting to determine whether a particular traveller is a tourist or not?

5 (a) Why are domestic tourists relatively neglected by researchers and government in comparison to international tourists?
(b) What can be done to reverse this neglect?

6 (a) To what extent are the various travel purposes discretionary in nature?
(b) What implications does this have for the management of tourism?

7 (a) How do origin regions influence the tourism system?
(b) How are origin regions impacted by outbound tourism, and what can they do to control these impacts?

8 What aspects of the transit region should destination tourism authorities be aware of as they attempt to manage their own tourism sector?

9 Should the local community be recognised as a legitimate tourism stakeholder group in its own right, or is it more appropriate to regard government as the representative of the community?

EXERCISES

1 Write a 1000-word report in which you:
(a) describe the impact of the 26 December 2004 tsunami on the tourism sector of either Thailand, Indonesia, the Maldives, Sri Lanka or India during the following year (2005), and
(b) describe and critically assess the reaction of the applicable national tourism organisation in that time.

2 Write a 1000-word report that:
(a) determines the extent to which the community in which you are currently studying is an origin region, a transit region and also a destination region
(b) identifies the important tourism management issues that emerge from each of these roles.

FURTHER READING

Bennett, M., King, B. & Milner, L. 2004. 'The Health Resort Sector in Australia: A Positioning Study'. *Journal of Vacation Marketing* **10: 122–37.** The authors profile the health resort sector from its mainstream to 'alternative' components, and argue that the lack of traditional spas has resulted in an innovative health tourism sector.

Davidson, T. 2005. 'What Are Travel and Tourism: Are They Really an Industry?' In Theobald, W. (Ed.) *Global Tourism.* **Third Edition. Sydney: Elsevier, pp. 25–31.** In contrast to the perceptions of most tourism stakeholders, Davidson makes the case that it is counterproductive to position tourism as a distinct industry with its own SIC code.

Digance, J. 2003. 'Pilgrimage at Contested Sites'. *Annals of Tourism Research* **30: 143–59.** A useful perspective of this article is the interplay at Uluru between the interests of secular pilgrims and traditional Aboriginal pilgrims, both of whom believe that they should have privileged access. Relevant management considerations are discussed.

Glaesser, D. 2003. *Crisis Management in the Tourism Industry.* **Sydney: Butterworth-Heinemann.** This is one of the first textbooks to focus systematically on the management of crises within the tourism sector. The sphere of 'crisis' is defined, methods of analysis are discussed and crisis management instruments are identified and evaluated.

Leiper, N. 2004. *Tourism Management.* **Third Edition. Sydney: Pearson Education Australia.** This is the third edition of Leiper's textbook, which is the one that most explicitly employs the systems approach as well as a management-oriented framework to the tourism sector.

Ritchie, B. & Adair, D. (Eds) 2004. *Sport Tourism: Interrelationships, Impacts and Issues.* **Clevedon, UK: Channel View.** Fourteen chapters in this edited book cover diverse sport topics related to winter activity, policy, museums, event leverage, secular pilgrimage, host community reactions and urban renewal.

Weaver, D. 2004. 'The Contribution of International Students to Tourism Beyond the Core Educational Experience: Evidence from Australia'. *Tourism Review International* 7: 95–105. This paper, part of a special *Tourism Review International* issue on international tourists, provides details and analysis of a study that was done to measure the flow-on tourism effects resulting from international students at a major Australian university.

The effect of SARS on tourism in Hong Kong

Hong Kong has long been regarded as one of Asia's most successful tourist destinations, and one that successfully withstood the political reincorporation of the colony into mainland China as a special administrative region (SAR) in 1997. One factor underlying this success was the timetable for the reincorporation being known well in advance, which gave politicians and managers ample time to adjust to the looming new geopolitical reality. The same cannot be said for the unexpected SARS epidemic, which devastated Hong Kong's tourism industry during 2003 and therefore better qualifies as a crisis. As chronicled by Pine and McKercher (2004), the first case of pneumonia associated with SARS appeared in China in November 2002. The following February, a doctor who had treated subsequent cases in China infected some guests at the Metropole Hotel in Hong Kong. Mounting reports of the disease prompted the World Health Organization to issue a global alert on 11 March 2003. This was elevated on 2 April to a recommendation that all nonessential travel to Hong Kong be postponed. By late April the outbreak showed signs of peaking and on 23 June Hong Kong was officially declared to be free of SARS. A total of 1755 cases were reported in Hong Kong, of whom 299 died.

The short-term effects of SARS on the Hong Kong tourism system by late April 2003 were profound. These included a cumulative hotel occupancy rate below 20 per cent, the cancellation of 40 per cent of all flights into Hong Kong, 27 000 lost tourism jobs and an 80 per cent decline in both inbound and outbound tourist traffic (McKercher 2003). Unprepared for and lacking any prior knowledge of such a crisis, some accommodation providers such as the Metropole Hotel reacted primarily by initiating unpaid leave and involuntary separation (Leung & Lam 2004). Others closed temporarily, shut down certain floors only, cut employee pay, postponed international promotion involving travel or suspended food and beverage services. Travel agencies and other businesses called for substantial government aid (Chien & Law 2003). Predictions of long-term disaster for the industry, however, were largely unfounded because of the relatively short duration of the crisis. Other factors facilitating the recovery of the tourism sector by mid-2003 were initiatives such as the 'Be my guest' campaign, supported by most Hong Kong hotels (77 per cent), which offered 50 per cent discounts on some rooms and other incentives. High-end hotels also offered a deal in which luxury products available exclusively in Hong Kong were made available at a large discount (Pine & McKercher 2004).

In retrospect, it can be noted that (a) Hong Kong, despite its reputation for efficiency and adaptation, was unprepared for the SARS crisis, (b) the extremely dramatic effects were arguably out of proportion to the actual threat, (c) the response from industry was largely knee jerk and indicative of a panic mentality, and (d) the brevity of the crisis was largely a result of good fortune (i.e. the brevity of the outbreak) and the inherent resilience of tourism rather than good management response. All four observations indicate management failure and the need for destinations such as Hong Kong to have crisis response strategies available should other epidemics eventually appear. McKercher (2003) implicitly attributes much of the crisis to the media, which in his opinion initiated SARS-induced panic (SIP) through the kind of melodramatic coverage that will 'sell newspapers'. He emphasises the discrepancy between the effects on tourism and the actual final infection rate among Hong Kong residents as evidence of SIP (0.02 per cent).

McKercher's perspective is corroborated by Mason, Grabowski and Du (2005), who present a four-stage model of media response to such crises. In the initial preproblem stage (from November 2002 to January 2003 in the case of SARS) the epidemic is a 'nonissue', which receives nominal back-page exposure at best. There is then a quick transition to the 'alarmed discovery' stage (mid-February 2003), which is characterised by dramatic headlines and dire warnings. The third stage entails a gradual marginalisation of coverage as the outbreak recedes (late June 2003), and this is followed by a postproblem stage, in which the issue returns to the back page or disappears altogether. Litvin (2004), however, argues that the market response to SARS in Hong Kong and elsewhere was not evidence of SIP but rather an example of rational consumer behaviour, which suggests different management responses than those implied by the SIP argument. Consumers, he suggests, have at their disposal a huge number of potential destinations. The rational response to uncertainty at any one of them, therefore, is to select an alternative because the original destination can still be visited once the crisis is past. Moreover, the consumer is aware that the risk of contracting an infectious disease such as SARS, however nominal, is a risk that is transferred to family members and other individuals back in the origin region. So managers may have limited scope for preventing collapse during the alarmed discovery stage of media coverage. One possibility raised by Litvin is the mobilisation of the mass media and the Internet to convey positive recovery signals comparable in presentation and impact to those put out by newspapers and television during the alarmed discovery stage.

Questions

1 How could the tourism industry of Hong Kong have been better prepared for the onset of the SARS epidemic?

2 Under what circumstances, if any, would you personally have been prepared to visit Hong Kong as a leisure or vacation tourist during April 2003?

3 Is Litvin justified in suggesting that the collapse of inbound traffic to Hong Kong in April 2003 was an example of rational consumer behaviour rather than SIP?

4 Design a 300-word briefing for the media, intended for lead news coverage, which features the World Health Organization announcement of 23 June 2003 and contributes to efforts to restore confidence in the Hong Kong tourism industry.

3

The evolution and
growth of tourism

LEARNING OBJECTIVES

After studying this chapter, you should be able to:

1 describe the main characteristics and types of premodern tourism in the 'Western' tradition

2 explain the basic distinctions and similarities between premodern and modern tourism

3 identify the role of Thomas Cook and the Industrial Revolution in bringing about the modern era of tourism

4 describe the growth trend of international tourism during the twentieth century

5 discuss the primary factors that have stimulated the demand for tourism during this period of time, and especially since 1950

6 describe global patterns of economic development and associate these patterns with different patterns of tourism demand and behaviour

7 identify the forces that positively and negatively influence the future growth of the tourism industry.

INTRODUCTION

The previous chapter considered tourism from a systems approach and described the spatial, temporal and purposive criteria that distinguish international and domestic tourists from other travellers and from each other. Management-related observations were also made about the origin, transit and destination components of the tourism system. Chapter 3 focuses on the historical development of tourism in the 'Western' or Eurocentric tradition and describes the 'push' factors that have stimulated the demand for tourism especially since the mid-twentieth century.

The first part of chapter 3 (section 3.2) outlines **premodern tourism**, which is defined for the purposes of this textbook as the period prior to about AD 1500 (figure 3.1). Its purpose is to show that while premodern tourism had its own distinctive character, there are also many similarities with modern tourism. Recognition of these timeless impulses and characteristics is valuable to the tourism manager, as they are factors that should be taken into consideration in any contemporary or future situation involving tourism. Moreover, modern tourism would not have been possible without the precedents of Mesopotamia, the Nile and Indus valleys, ancient Greece and Rome, the Dark Ages and the Middle Ages. Section 3.3 considers the early modern era (1500 to 1950), which links the premodern to the contemporary period through the influence of the Renaissance and the Industrial Revolution. Section 3.4 introduces contemporary mass tourism, while section 3.5 describes the major economic, social, demographic, technological and political factors that have stimulated the demand for tourism during this era. Australian tourism participation trends are considered briefly in section 3.6, and section 3.7 considers the future growth prospects of global tourism.

■ **Figure 3.1**
Tourism timelines

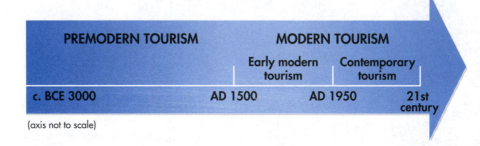

(axis not to scale)

PREMODERN TOURISM

■ 3.2.1 Mesopotamia, *Egypt and the Indus Valley*

Mesopotamia, or the 'land between the rivers' (situated approximately in modern-day Iraq), is known as the 'Cradle of Civilisation' and the first place to experience tourism. The factors that gave rise to civilisation, and hence to emergent tourism systems, include the availability of a permanent water supply (the Tigris and Euphrates rivers), rich alluvial soils (deposited during the annual flooding of these waterways), a warm climate and a central location between Asia, Africa and Europe, all of which contributed to the development of agriculture. For the first time in human history, hunting and gathering societies were replaced by permanent settlements cultivating the same plots of land year after year. Surplus food production was a critical outcome of this process, as it fostered the formation of wealth and the emergence of a small **leisure class** of priests, warriors and others that did not have to worry continually about its day-to-day survival.

The availability of **discretionary time** and **discretionary income** was the most important factor that enabled members of this leisured elite to engage in tourism. Moreover, Mesopotamia was the birthplace of many fundamental inventions and innovations that introduced both the demand and ability to travel for tourism-related purposes. These included the wheel, the wagon, money, the alphabet, domesticated animals such as the horse, and roads. Early cities (another Mesopotamian invention) such as Ur and Nippur were apparently overcrowded and uncomfortable at the best of times, and these inventions allowed the elite to escape them whenever possible. Also critical was the imposition of government structure and civil order over the surrounding countryside, that provided a foundation for the development of destination and transit regions (Casson 1974).

Egypt

Civilisation gradually spread from Mesopotamia westward to the Nile Valley (in modern-day Egypt) and eastward to the Indus Valley (in modern-day Pakistan), where there were similar physical environments. Ancient Egypt provides some of the earliest explicit evidence of pleasure tourism. An inscription, carved into the side of one of the lesser known pyramids and dated 1244 BCE, is among the earliest examples of tourist graffiti (Casson 1974). This and other monuments of the Nile Valley were already ancient at the time of the inscription, and attracted religious and ceremonial tourists as well as the simply curious. Numerous inscriptions from ancient Egypt also describe the acquisition of souvenirs, suggesting that this, along with the urge to leave behind some physical indication of one's presence through graffiti, is an ancient human impulse that is not unique to the modern era.

3.2.2 Ancient *Greece and Rome*

Tourism in ancient Greece is most associated with national festivals such as the **Olympic Games**, where residents of the Greek city–states gathered every four years to hold religious ceremonies and compete in athletic events and artistic performances. The participants and spectators at this festival, estimated to number in the tens of thousands, would have had little difficulty in meeting the modern criteria for international stayovers. Accordingly, the game site at Olympia can be considered as one of the oldest specialised, though periodic, tourist **resorts**. The Games themselves are one of the first recorded examples of sport and event tourism and the precursor to the modern Olympics.

The transit process in ancient Greece was not pleasant or easy. Although a sacred truce was called during the major festivals, tourists were targeted by either highway robbers or pirates, depending on their mode of travel. Roads were primitive and accommodation, if available, was rudimentary, unsanitary and often dangerous. It is useful to point out that the word 'travel' is derived from the French noun *travail*, which translates into English as 'hard work'. As with the Mesopotamians and Egyptians, the proportion of ancient Greeks who could and did travel as tourists was effectively restricted to a small elite. However, the propensity to engage in tourism was socially sanctioned by the prevalent philosophy of the culture (applicable at least to the elite), who valued leisure time for its own sake as an opportunity to engage in artistic, intellectual and athletic pursuits (Lynch & Veal 1996).

Rome

With its impressive technological, economic and political achievements, ancient Rome (which peaked between 200 BCE and AD 200) was able to achieve unprecedented levels of tourism activity that would not be reached again for another 1500 years. An underlying factor was the large population of the Roman Empire. While the elite class was only a fraction of the 200 million-strong population, it constituted a large absolute number of potential tourists. These travellers had a large selection of destination choices, given the size of the Empire, the high level of stability and safety achieved during the *Pax Romana* (Roman Peace) and the remarkably sophisticated network of Roman military roads (many of which are still used today) and associated rest stops. By AD 100 the Roman road network extended over 80 000 kilometres.

The Roman tourism experience is surprisingly modern in its resonance. Fuelled by ample discretionary time and wealth, the propensity of the Roman elite to travel on pleasure holidays (an innovation introduced by Rome) gave rise to an 'industry' of sorts that supplied souvenirs, guidebooks, transport, guides and accommodation. The number of specialised tourism sites and destinations also increased substantially. Famous Roman resorts included the town of Pompeii (destroyed by the eruption of Vesuvius in AD 79), the spas of the appropriately named town of Bath (in Britain), and the beach resort of Tiberius, on the Sea of Galilee. Intriguingly, these sites of ancient tourism are now popular tourist attractions in the contemporary era, and ones that can be authentically presented through modern technology (see Technology and tourism: Pompeii plus with virtual reality). Second homes, or *villas*, were an important mode of retreat in the rural hinterlands of Rome and other major cities. Wealthy Romans often owned villas in a seaside location as well as the interior, to escape the winter cold and summer heat, respectively, of the cities. Villas were clustered so thickly around the Bay of Naples during the first century AD that this area could be described as one of the earliest resort regions.

For Romans wealthy enough to travel a long distance, the historical sites of earlier cultures, especially those of the Greeks, Trojans and Egyptians, held the most interest. This is partly because of cultural connections, but also because sites such as the Pyramids were already ancient during the time of the Roman Empire. In addition, Casson (1974) maintains that the ancient ruins were popular due to the opportunities for acquiring souvenirs, including pieces of the structures themselves.

Virtual reality technologies are usually discussed in the tourism context as phenomena that variably substitute for or inspire travel to real destinations. Often overlooked in this is the potential for such technologies to improve *on-site* visits to tourist attractions. The European Union-funded Lifeplus project is currently investigating the possibility of providing visitors to the ancient Roman resort of Pompeii with mobile augmented reality (MAR) systems that would recreate life there as it was at the time of the Vesuvius eruption of 79, which destroyed the city. In this combination of the real and the virtual, visitors to Pompeii would be fitted with a head-mounted display (HMD) equipped with a miniature camera and backpack computer. The camera feeds the spatial viewpoint of the visitor (e.g. the kitchen in an upper-class house) into software in the computer that superimposes relevant animated virtual elements onto that scene through the HMD (Vlahakis et al. 2003). The visitor standing in the kitchen, for example, will see the actual walls and tables but will additionally observe the preparation of a meal and hear gossip from the cooks. Extremely realistic images of these contemporary scenes are promised by the software company (UK-based 2d3) developing the technology, including scenes where the virtual residents interact directly and personally with the visitor. Odours and stereographic background noise could be added to increase the realism of the encounter further, while future visitors may choose to have their own personal avatar to guide them through the city.

MAR systems, already used to enrich films such as *Troy* and *Lord of the Rings*, could produce a breakthrough in cultural tourism, not only in terms of the realistic on-site encounter provided but also in their potential for generating a level of empathy and understanding that translates into increased visitation levels, growing public interest in history and culture, and higher public support and donations for such sites (Vlahakis et al. 2003). However, while the systems are applicable to any site, not all managers will have access to the resources necessary to implement the technology to its greatest effect. This could in turn have the unfortunate effect of diverting tourists to the cultural and heritage attractions that provide the most impressive MAR interpretation.

3.2.3 The Dark Ages *and Middle Ages*

The decline and collapse of the Roman Empire during the fifth century AD severely eroded the factors that facilitated the development of tourism during the Roman era. Travel infrastructure deteriorated, the size of the elite classes and urban areas declined dramatically, and the relatively safe and open Europe of the Romans was replaced by a proliferation of warring semi-states and lawless frontiers as barbarian tribes occupied what was left of the Roman empire. Justifiably, this period (c. 500–1100) is commonly referred to as the

Dark Ages. The insularity to which Europe descended during this period is evident in contemporary world maps that feature wildly distorted cartographic images dominated by theological themes (e.g. Jerusalem at the centre of the map), grotesque characters and oversized town views. These busy and cluttered maps reveal no useful information to the traveller.

The social, economic and political situation in Europe recovered sufficiently by the end of the eleventh century that historians distinguish the emergence of the **Middle Ages** around this time (c. 1100–1500). Associated tourism phenomena include the Christian **pilgrimage**, stimulated by the construction of the great cathedrals and the consolidation of the Roman Catholic Church as a dominant power base and social influence in Europe. The pilgrimages of the Middle Ages (popularised in the writings of English author Geoffrey Chaucer) are interesting to tourism researchers for several reasons. First, even the poorest people were participants, motivated as they were by the perceived spiritual benefits of the experience. Second, and related to this, was the willingness of many pilgrims to accept and even welcome a high level of risk, since suffering was believed to confer great spiritual rewards. At the same time, the opportunity to go on a pilgrimage was welcomed by many because of the break it provided from the drudgery of daily life (see figure 3.2).

■ **Figure 3.2**
Medieval pilgrims on the way to Canterbury

Another major form of travel, the **Crusades** (1095–1291), also contributed to the development of this travel industry, even though the Crusaders themselves were not tourists, but invaders who attempted to free the Holy Land from Muslim control. Religiously inspired like the pilgrims, the Crusaders unwittingly exposed Europe once again to the outside world, while occasionally engaging in tourist-like behaviour (e.g. souvenir collecting, sightseeing) during their journeys.

3.3 EARLY MODERN TOURISM (1500–1950)

Europe began to emerge from the Middle Ages in the late 1300s, assisted by the experience of the Crusades and later by the impact of the great explorations. By 1500 the **Renaissance** (literally, the 'rebirth') of Europe was well under way, and the world balance of power was beginning to shift to that continent, marking the modern era and the period of **early modern tourism**.

3.3.1 The Grand *Tour*

The **Grand Tour** is a major link between the Middle Ages and contemporary tourism. The term describes the extended travel of young men from the aristocratic classes of the United Kingdom and other parts of northern Europe to continental Europe for educational and cultural purposes (Towner 1996). Because these literate young travellers usually kept diaries of their experiences, it is possible to reconstruct this era in detail. We know, for example, that the classical Grand Tours first became popular during the mid-sixteenth century, and persisted (with modification) until the mid-nineteenth century (Withey 1997). While there was no single circuit or timeframe that defined the Grand Tour, certain destinations feature prominently in the diaries and other written accounts. Paris was usually the first major destination of the *Tourists*, followed by a year or more of visits to the major cities of Italy, and especially Florence, Rome, Naples and Venice (Towner 1996). Though the political and economic power of Italy was in decline by the early 1600s, these centres were still admired for their Renaissance and Roman attractions, which continued to set the cultural standards for Europe. A visit to these cultural centres was vital for anyone aspiring to join the ranks of the elite. The following quote from 1776, attributed to Samuel Johnson, the great English author, captures this status motive:

> ■ A man who has not been in Italy, is always conscious of an inferiority, from his not having seen what it is expected a man should see. The grand object of travelling is to see the shores of the Mediterranean ... All our religion, almost all our law, almost all our arts, almost all that sets us above savages, has come to us from the shores of the Mediterranean (in Burkart & Medlik 1981, p. 4). ■

The journey back to northern Europe usually took the traveller across the Swiss Alps, through Germany and into the Low Countries (Flanders, The Netherlands) where the Renaissance flowered during the mid-1600s (Steinecke 1993).

According to Towner (1996) about 15 000–20 000 members of the British elite were abroad on the Grand Tour at any time during the mid-1700s. Wealthier participants might be accompanied by an entourage of servants, guides, tutors and other retainers. Towards the end of the era, the emphasis in the Grand Tour shifted from the aristocracy to the more affluent middle classes, resulting in a shorter stay within fewer destinations. Other destinations, such as Germany and the Alps, also became more popular (Withey 1997). The classes from which the Grand Tour participants were drawn accounted for between 7 and 9 per cent of the United Kingdom's population in the eighteenth century. Motives also shifted throughout this era. The initial emphasis on education, designed to confer the traveller with full membership into the aristocratic power structure and to make important social connections on the continent, gradually gave way to more stress on simple sightseeing. In either manifestation, however, the Grand Tour had a profound impact on the United Kingdom, as cultural and social trends there were largely shaped by the ideas and goods brought back by the Grand Tourists. These impacts were also felt at least economically in the destination regions through the appearance of the souvenir trade and tour guiding within major destination cities. In addition, the practical travel guide first appeared in the 1820s in response to demand from would-be Grand Tourists (Withey 1997).

■ 3.3.2 Spa *resorts*

The use of hot water springs for therapeutic purposes dates back at least to the ancient Greeks and Romans (e.g. the spas at Bath in the United Kingdom) (Casson 1974). Established in the Middle Ages by the Ottoman Empire within its European possessions, several hundred inland **spas** served the wealthy of continental Europe and the United Kingdom by the middle of the nineteenth century. Many, however, were small and did not survive as tourist destinations. Others, such as Karlsbad (in the modern-day Czech Republic), Vichy (in France) and Baden–Baden (in Germany), were extensive and are still functioning as spas (Towner 1996). The availability of accessible and suitable water resources was, of course, the most important factor in influencing the establishment, character and size of spas, though proximity to transportation, urban areas and related amenities and services were also important.

■ 3.3.3 Seaside *resorts*

By the early 1800s tourism opportunities were becoming accessible to the lower classes of the United Kingdom and parts of western Europe. This was a result of the **Industrial Revolution**, which transformed western Europe (beginning in England during the mid-1700s) from a rural, agricultural society to one that was urban and industrial. Crowded cities and harsh working conditions created a demand for recreational opportunities that would take the workers, at least temporarily, into a more pleasant and relaxing environment. Domestic **seaside resorts** emerged in England to fulfil this demand, facilitated by none of the large population centres being more than 160 kilometres from the English coast. Initially, however, many seaside resorts were small and exclusive communities that, like the inland spas, catered only to the upper classes.

A stimulus for travelling to the coast was the belief, gaining in popularity by the mid-eighteenth century, that sea bathing, combined with the drinking of sea water, was an effective treatment for certain illnesses (Gilbert 1949). Seaside resorts such as Brighton and Scarborough soon rivalled inland spa towns such as Bath as tourist attractions, with the added advantage that the target resource (sea water) was virtually unlimited, and the opportunities for spatial expansion along the coast were numerous.

A primary factor that made the seaside resorts accessible to the working classes was the construction of railways connecting these settlements to nearby large industrial cities. During the 1830s and 1840s, this had the effect of transforming small English coastal towns into sizeable urban areas, illustrating how changes in a transit region can effect fundamental change in a destination region. As the Industrial Revolution spread to the European mainland and overseas to North America and Australia, the same demands were created and the same processes repeated. The well-known American seaside resort of Atlantic City traces its origins as a working-class seaside resort to the construction of a rail link with Philadelphia in 1852 (Stansfield 1978).

In Australia, seaside resorts such as Manly, Glenelg and St Kilda were established in the late nineteenth century to serve, respectively, the growing urban areas of Sydney, Adelaide and Melbourne (Wells 1982). Functionally and structurally, these Australian seaside resorts were similar to their English counterparts. The resort of Port Melbourne was even marketed as 'Brighton-on-the-Sands' in an attempt to emulate its famous English namesake (Hall 1995).

The progression of the Industrial Revolution in England and Wales coincided with the diffusion of seaside resorts to meet the growing demand for a coastal holiday. Figure 3.3 depicts their expansion from seven in 1750 to about 145 by 1911, at which time few sections of the coastline lacked at least one resort (Towner 1996). This pattern of diffusion, like the growth of individual resorts, was largely a haphazard process unassisted by any formal management or planning considerations. Many British seaside resorts today, in large part because of this poorly regulated pattern of expansion, are stagnant or declining destinations that need to innovate in order to revitalise their tourism product (see Contemporary issue: Regenerating the seaside resort).

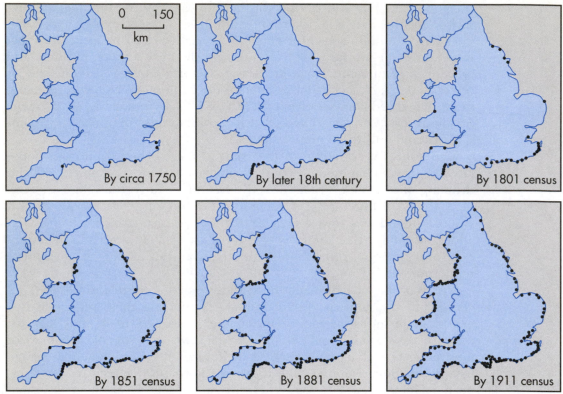

Figure 3.3 *Pattern of seaside resort diffusion in England and Wales, 1750–1911*

Source: *Towner (1996, p. 179)*

CONTEMPORARY ISSUE

REGENERATING THE SEASIDE RESORT

Seaside resorts in the United Kingdom, and to a lesser extent in parts of Australia and the United States, are often perceived collectively as a declining or deteriorating tourism product. This perception is linked to many of these resorts having functioned as such for a century or more but it can also reflect the failure of planners and managers to adapt to external factors such as demographic change, fashion and the emergence of more competitive resorts in other regions. Internal factors such as an unwillingness to invest in new products and facilities have also played a role. It is within this context that the United Kingdom government since the late 1990s has embarked on a program of encouraging the regeneration of seaside resorts. Significantly, the term 'regeneration' is used by the government to describe a strategy of strengthening the local economy through the combination of tourism, culture and leisure services. As such it is substantively different from 'revitalisation' (product enhancement) or 'reinvention' (product innovation), which may however be necessary precedents to regeneration (Smith 2004). The latter may, therefore, be regarded as a more holistic approach to addressing the problem of destination deterioration that basically makes the place more livable and diverse.

Southend-on-Sea was a leading English seaside resort during its heyday from the 1880s to the 1950s. After a period of decline in the 1970s and 1980s, Southend began in the early 2000s to engage in a process of regenerative planning fuelled in large part by European Union funding. The strategy includes the restoration of traditional tourism-related sites such as the pier, foreshore, promenade and main shopping street, although it is felt that resort tourism alone cannot sustain the regeneration effort. Also in the offing is a cultural strategy that aims to make Southend the 'Cultural Capital of the East of England' by 2010 using museums, arts and crafts facilities, sporting events, theatres and heritage attractions to attract visitors as well as local residents (Smith 2004). It is felt that this will engender a stronger sense of place identity for hosts as well as guests, and form the basis for a more resilient local economy. Geographically, one effect would be to encourage spaces where locals and tourists coexist, and to extend these spaces beyond the relatively small core area where traditional attractions are clustered. According to Smith (2004), the foundations have been laid for the regeneration of Southend as a prosperous postmodern seaside resort, although time will tell whether the effort succeeds.

3.3.4 Thomas *Cook*

More than any other individual, **Thomas Cook** is associated with the emergence of tourism as a modern, large-scale industry, even though it would take another 150 years for mass tourism to be realised on a global scale. A Baptist preacher who was concerned with the 'declining morals' of the English working class, Cook conceived the idea of chartering trains at reduced fares to take the workers to temperance (i.e. anti-alcohol) meetings and bible camps in the countryside. The first of these excursions, provided as a day trip from Leicester to Loughborough on 5 July 1841, is sometimes described as the symbolic beginning of the contemporary era of tourism. Gradually, these excursions expanded in the number of participants and the variety of destinations offered. At the same time, the reasons for taking excursions shifted from spiritual purposes to sightseeing and pleasure. By 1845 Cook (who had by then formed the famous travel business Thomas Cook & Son) was offering regular tours between Leicester and London. In 1863 the first international excursion was undertaken (to the Swiss Alps), and in 1872 the first round-the-world excursion was organised with an itinerary that included the British colonies of Australia and New Zealand. The Cook excursions can be considered the beginning of international tourism in the latter two countries, although such trips were, of course, still the prerogative of the wealthy. By the late 1870s, Thomas Cook & Son was operating 60 offices throughout the world (Withey 1997).

Cook's arrangements for the Great Exhibition of 1851, held in London, illustrate the innovations that he introduced into the tourism sector. The

160 000 clients (3 per cent of all visitors) who purchased his company's services were provided with:

- an inclusive, prepaid, one-fee structure that covered transportation, accommodation, guides, food and other goods and services
- organised itineraries based on rigid time schedules
- uniform products of high quality
- affordable prices, made possible by the economies of scale created through large customer volumes.

The genius of Thomas Cook and his imitators, essentially, was to apply the production principles and techniques of the Industrial Revolution to tourism. Standardised, precisely timed, commercialised and high-volume tour packages heralded the 'industrialisation' of the sector. Thus, while the development of the seaside resorts was a mainly unplanned phenomenon, Thomas Cook can be described as an effective managerial pioneer of the industry that fostered and accommodated the *demand* for these and other tourism products. The actual connection between supply and demand, however, was only made possible by communication and transportation innovations of the Industrial Revolution such as the railway, the steamship and the telegraph, which the entrepreneur Cook used to his advantage. As a result of such innovative applications, Thomas Cook exposed an unprecedented pool of potential travellers (i.e. an increased *market*) to an unprecedented number of destinations (i.e. an increased *supply*). Today, the **package tour** is one of the fundamental, taken-for-granted symbols of the contemporary tourism industry.

■ 3.3.5 The post-Cook period *(1880–1950)*

Largely as a result of Cook and his adaptation of Industrial Revolution technologies and principles to the travel industry, tourism expanded significantly from the 1870s onwards. Much of this growth was initially concentrated in the domestic sector of the more industrialised regions such as the United States, western Europe and Australia. The American west, for example, experienced a period of rapid tourism growth associated first with the closing of the frontier in the 1890s and then with the increase in car ownership (Fifer 1988, Gunn 2004). Domestic tourism also flourished in the United Kingdom, and by 1911 it is estimated that 55 per cent of the English population were making day excursions to the seaside, while 20 per cent travelled as stayovers to the coastal resorts (Burton 1995).

International tourism growth in the **post-Cook period** of the early modern era was less robust than in the domestic tourism sector. This was due in part to the feasibility of outbound travel for the middle and working classes only where countries shared an accessible common border, as between Canada and the United States, and between France and Belgium. Switzerland, for example, which shared frontiers with several major countries, received about one million tourists annually by 1880 (Withey 1997). In addition, the period between 1880 and 1950 was characterised by two major wars and two major economic depressions. The first of these major interruptions was caused by the global depression of the 1890s, and this was followed two decades later by World War I (1914–18). Resumed tourism growth in the 1920s was subsequently cancelled out by the Great Depression of the 1930s and World War II (1939–45). No wars or economic downturns of comparable magnitude, however, have interrupted the expansion of the tourism industry since the end of World War II.

Ironically, it can also be argued that World War II, like other major conflicts, while devastating to the tourism industry in the short term, actually stimulated the long-term performance of the sector. This **war dividend** is generated through the creation of conflict-focused attractions (e.g. battlefields, military cemeteries), the provision of millions of people with travel experience and the development of technologies such as the jet aircraft that make cheap mass travel possible (Weaver 2000).

3.4 CONTEMPORARY TOURISM (1950 onwards)

The rapid growth of tourism during the contemporary era of **modern mass tourism** is reflected in the global trend of inbound tourist arrival and associated revenue estimates (table 3.1). The statistics from the 1950s and 1960s are speculative due to the irregular nature of data collection at that time (see chapter 1). But even allowing for a substantial margin of error, an exponential pattern of growth is readily evident, with inbound stayovers increasing more than 30 times between 1950 and 2004, from an estimated 25 million to 750 million. International tourism receipts have grown far more dramatically over the same period, from US$2 billion to well over US$500 billion. An aspect of table 3.1 that is worth noting is the consistent pattern of growth, interrupted only by the economic recession of the early 1980s, the terrorist attacks of 2001, and the combined effects of the Iraq War and SARS in 2003.

3.4.1 The world's *biggest industry?*

Interest groups such as the World Tourism and Travel Council (WTTC) maintain that tourism is the world's single largest industry, accounting directly and indirectly in 2004 for approximately one of every ten jobs and 10 per cent of all economic activity as noted in chapter 1. Whether this does indeed constitute the world's biggest industry, however, depends on how it is quantified and what it is compared against. For example, tourism is larger than the oil or grain industries but probably does not exceed the global mining or agricultural sectors as a whole.

■ **Table 3.1** *International stayover arrivals, 1950–2004*

| YEAR | ARRIVALS OF TOURISTS FROM ABROAD (SAME-DAY VISITORS EXCLUDED) | | RECEIPTS FROM INTERNATIONAL TOURISM (INTERNATIONAL TRANSPORT EXCLUDED) | |
	TOTAL (MILLION)	PER CENT CHANGE OVER PREVIOUS YEAR	TOTAL (US$ BILLION)	PER CENT CHANGE OVER PREVIOUS YEAR
1950	25	–	2	–
1960	69	–	7	–
1961	75	8.7	7	6.1
1962	81	8.0	8	10.2
1963	90	10.7	9	10.7
1964	105	16.1	10	13.4
1965	113	7.9	12	15.2
1966	120	6.3	13	15.0
1967	130	8.2	14	8.4
1968	131	1.1	15	3.7
1969	144	9.4	17	12.1
1970	166	15.5	18	6.6
1971	179	7.9	21	16.5
1972	189	5.8	25	18.1
1973	199	5.2	31	26.1
1974	206	3.4	34	8.9
1975	222	8.1	41	20.3
1976	229	3.0	44	9.2
1977	249	8.9	56	25.2
1978	267	7.2	69	23.7
1979	283	6.0	83	21.1
1980	286	1.0	105	26.4
1981	287	0.4	107	2.0
1982	286	−0.4	101	−6.1
1983	290	1.2	102	1.6
1984	316	9.2	113	10.0
1985	327	3.4	118	4.8
1986	339	3.6	143	21.5
1987	364	7.4	177	23.2
1988	395	8.5	204	15.6
1989	426	8.0	221	8.3
1990	458	7.5	268	21.0
1991	464	1.3	278	3.7
1992	503	8.3	314	13.0
1993	518	3.1	323	23.0
1994	553	6.8	353	9.1
1995	568	2.7	403	14.3
1996	600	5.5	438	8.6
1997	620	3.3	438	0.1
1998	636	2.7	442	0.8
1999	664	4.5	466	5.5
2000	680	3.2	475	1.9
2001	684	−0.3	463	1.7
2002	703	2.8	480	3.7
2003	691	−1.7	523	9.0
2004	760	10.0	n/a	n/a

Source: *WTO (1998a), WTO (1999) and WTO (2004)*

FACTORS ASSOCIATED WITH INCREASED TOURISM DEMAND

Many of the generic factors that influence the growth of tourism have been introduced briefly in the earlier sections on the evolution of tourism. This section focuses specifically on those factors that have stimulated the demand for tourism (or **push factors**) since World War II. However, to maintain historical continuity, the trends are considered in the context of the entire twentieth century. Although outlined under five separate headings, the factors are interdependent and should not be considered in isolation.

■ 3.5.1 Economic *factors*

The most important economic factor associated with increased tourism demand is affluence. In general, the distribution and volume of tourism increases as a society becomes more economically developed and greater discretionary household income subsequently becomes more available. Discretionary household income is the money available to a household after basic needs such as food, clothing, transportation, education and housing have been met. Such funds might be saved, invested or used to purchase luxury goods and services (such as a foreign holiday or expensive restaurant meal), at the 'discretion' of the household decision makers. Average economic wealth is commonly measured by per capita gross national product (GNP), or the total value of all goods and services produced by a country in a given year, divided by the total resident population. It is also important, however, to consider how equitably this wealth is distributed. A per capita GNP of $10 000 could indicate that everyone basically makes $10 000 or that a small elite makes much more than this while most remain in the subsistence economy. The latter scenario greatly constrains the number of potential tourists, and is essentially the structure that prevailed before the modern era.

In the early stages of the development process, regular tourism participation (and pleasure tourism in particular) is feasible only for the elite, as demonstrated by the history of tourism in Europe prior to Thomas Cook. Today, there are still a few societies that demonstrate a level of economic development comparable to Europe before the Industrial Revolution. In her **tourism participation sequence**, Burton (1995) refers to these pre-industrial, mainly agricultural and subsistence-based situations as *Phase One* (table 3.2). In *Phase Two*, the generation of wealth increases and spreads to a wider segment of the population as a consequence of industrialisation and related processes such as urbanisation. This happened first in the United Kingdom, and then elsewhere, during the Industrial Revolution. At present, India and China are roughly at the same stage of development as that which England passed through early last century. Similarly, they are experiencing an explosion in demand for domestic tourism that is fuelling the development of seaside resorts and other tourism facilities. From being almost non-existent in the early 1970s, domestic tourism in China expanded to an estimated 695 million domestic tourist arrivals in 1998 and 878 million in 2002 (CNAT 2003). Concurrently, an ever-increasing number of the *nouveau riche*, or newly rich individuals, are visiting an expanding the array of foreign destinations (see the case study at the end of this chapter).

■ Table 3.2
Burton's four phases of tourism participation

PHASE	ECONOMIC DEVELOPMENTS	TOURISM PARTICIPATION
One	• Mainly subsistence-based and pre-industrial • Rural, agrarian • Large gap between poor masses and small elite	• No mass participation in tourism • Elite travel to domestic and international destinations
Two	• Industrialising • Rapid growth of urban areas • Growing middle class	• Widespread participation in domestic tourism • Increased scope of international tourism by elite
Three	• Almost industrialised • Population mostly urban • Middle class becoming dominant	• Mass participation in domestic tourism, and increase in short-haul international tourism • Elite turn towards long-haul international tourism
Four	• Fully industrialised, 'high tech' orientation • Mostly urban • High levels of affluence throughout the population	• Mass participation in domestic and international (long-haul and short-haul) tourism

By *Phase Three*, the bulk of the population is relatively affluent, leading to further increases in mass domestic travel as well as mass international tourism to nearby countries. The elite, meanwhile, engage in greater long-haul travel. This began to occur in the United Kingdom not long after World War II, and is currently characteristic of newer wealthy countries such as South Korea, Taiwan and Singapore.

Finally, *Phase Four* represents a fully developed country with widespread affluence, and a subsequent pattern of mass international tourism to a diverse array of short- and long-haul destinations. Almost all residents, in addition, engage in a comprehensive variety of domestic tourism experiences that differ greatly from those in the earlier phase societies (see Managing: Domestic tourists in China and the United States). The major regions and countries included in this category are western Europe (including the United Kingdom), the United States and Canada, Japan, Australia and New Zealand. These origin regions have a combined population of approximately 800 million, or 13 per cent of the world's population, but account for roughly 80 per cent of all outbound tourist traffic. With India and China expected to attain Phase Four dynamics within the next two or three decades, the environmental impacts of several billion outbound travellers will probably emerge as a major focus of management in the global tourism system, depending on the extent to which measures are taken to minimise these impacts (see chapter 11).

Given the great economic, social and technological differences between Phase Two and Phase Four countries, it is no surprise that the domestic tourism experiences in each are also dramatically different. This is illustrated in a comparative study of China and the United States (Wang & Qu 2004), which showed that most Chinese domestic tourists travel to their destinations by public buses, trains and, to a lesser extent, air. In contrast, three-quarters of American domestic tourists use private road vehicles. While both groups favour relatively short trips of two nights or less, Americans (43 per cent) are more likely than their Chinese counterparts (18 per cent) to obtain lodging in a hotel or motel. The latter are far more likely to stay in the homes of friends and relatives (48 per cent) or in traditional guesthouses called *luguan* (28 per cent). Favoured domestic tourism activities are more likely to involve interaction with outdoor and natural scenery (73 per cent) and relics or historical sites (32 per cent) than in the United States, where shopping (33 per cent) and outdoor activities (17 per cent) are the main preferences. Because many Chinese are first-time tourists, they tend to visit well-known attractions, whereas Americans are more experienced and more diverse in their destination visitation patterns.

Wang and Qu (2004) note that the scope and quality of the facilities and services provided for domestic tourists in China is inadequate, and that government (especially at the provincial level) and the private sector need to improve the domestic tourist experience through upgrades and partnerships with foreign companies. The lack of information or welcome centres is cited in particular as a major shortcoming. A particular problem for developers wishing to participate in the domestic sector is the tendency of many Chinese to spend frugally within the country to save sufficient funds to travel internationally in the future. Domestic tourism revenues, as a result, may not be seen to compensate for the environmental and social costs generated by increased visitation levels and the concentration of visitors at major attractions. These, along with very rapid rates of growth, are among the issues that need to be considered by tourism managers in Phase Two and Three countries such as China.

Increasing income and expenditure in Australia

The emergence of a prosperous Australian population during the past century mirrors Australia's transition from Phase Two to Phase Four status. Consumption expenditures are a good if partial indicator of living standards, as they show to what extent households are able to meet their material needs through the purchase of goods and services (Saunders 2001). As depicted in figure 3.4, per capita household consumption expenditures in Australia were stable until the early 1940s, due in part to the effects of World War I and the Great Depression (Boehm 1993). Large increases occurred after World War II, and by 2000–01, these expenditures were almost four times higher than the 1941 levels in 'real' terms — that is, after controlling for inflation by calibrating the figure 3.4 data in 1997–98 dollars.

■ **Figure 3.4**
Household final consumption expenditure per capita in 1997–98 dollars, Australia 1900–01 to 2000–01

Source: *Data for 1900 to 1980 from Appendix tables 1 and 4 of Maddock and McLean (1988) supplemented by ABS population and national accounts data from 1981.*

■ *3.5.2* **Social** *factors*

The major social trends that have influenced participation in tourism are the increase in discretionary time, its changing distribution and shifts in the way that society perceives this use of time. During Phase One, the rhythm of life is largely dictated by necessity, the seasons and the weather. Formal clock time or 'periods of life' have little or no meaning as nature imposes its own discipline on human activity. According to Thompson (1967), people in this phase are 'task oriented' rather than 'time oriented', and no fine lines are drawn between notions of 'work', 'rest' or 'play'.

The effect of industrialisation is to introduce a formalised rigour into this equation. Phase Two societies are characterised by a deliberately orchestrated system wherein discrete notions of work, leisure and rest are structured into rigorous segments of clock time, and the life rhythm is regulated by the factory whistle and the alarm clock rather than the rising or setting of the sun. Young (usually male at first) adults are expected to enter the labour force after a short period of rote education, and then to retire after a specified period of workplace participation. The structure that most symbolises this industrial regime is the division of the day into roughly equal portions of work, rest and leisure activity, with the latter constituting the discretionary time component (Veal & Lynch 2001). Time away from work is residual in the sense that it comprises what is left after the individual has fulfilled the work quota. Leisure and rest time are not generally seen as important in their own right, but as a necessary interruption to the work schedule to maintain the labourer's efficiency. The Phase Two industrial era can therefore be said to be dominated by a **play in order to work philosophy**.

Ironically, the early stages of industrialisation are often accompanied by a substantial increase in the amount of time spent at work. For example, the average European industrial labourer by the mid-1800s worked a 70-hour week (or 4000 hours a year), with the weekly work routine interrupted only by the Sunday day of rest. Since then, the situation has improved dramatically in conjunction with the transition to Phases Three and Four. The average working week for the European labour force declined to 46 hours by 1965 and 39 hours by the 1980s. Australia, however, was the first country to institute a standard eight-hour working day (Veal & Lynch 2001). The difference in available discretionary time in Australia between the beginning and end of the twentieth century is illustrated by 44 per cent of time spent by an average Australian male born in 1988 being discretionary, compared with 33 per cent for one born in 1888. Concurrently, the percentage of time devoted to paid work decreased from 20 to 11, according to the Australian Bureau of Statistics.

While the reduction in the amount of working time has clear positive implications for the pursuit of leisure activities in general, the changing distribution of this time is also important to tourism. One of the first major changes was the introduction of the two-day weekend, which was instrumental in making stayover tourism possible to nearby (usually domestic) locations. Before this, tourism for most workers was limited to daytime Sunday excursions. A second major change in the arrangement of working time was the introduction of the annual holiday entitlement. Again, Australia was a pioneer, being one of the first countries to enact legislation to create a four-week holiday standard. Intriguingly, the pressure for such reform came not only from the labour movement, but also from corporations, which realised that the labour force required more discretionary time to purchase and consume the goods and services that they were producing (Veal & Lynch 2001). It can be said therefore that the transition to the more mature phases of economic development is accompanied by the increasing importance of consumption over production. In any event, the holiday portion of the reduced working year makes longer domestic and international holidays accessible to most of the population.

Flexitime and earned time

More recently, the movement of the highly developed Phase Four countries into an information-oriented **postindustrial era** has resulted in innovative work options that are eroding the rigid nine-to-five type work schedules and uniform itineraries of the industrial society. The best known of these options is **flexitime**, which allows workers, within reason, to distribute their working hours in a manner that best suits their individual lifestyles. Common flexitime possibilities include three 12-hour days per week followed by a four-day weekend, or a series of 40-hour working weeks followed by a two-month vacation.

Earned time options are production rather than time-based. They usually involve the right to go on vacation leave once a given production quota is met. If, for example, a worker meets an annual personal production target of 1000 units by 10 August, then the remainder of the year is vacation time, unless the individual decides (and is given the option) to work overtime to earn additional income. Such time management innovations have important implications for tourism, in that lengthy vacation time blocks are conducive to extended long-haul trips and increased tourism participation in general. Only a small minority of workers currently participates in flexitime and earned time, but these arrangements are expected to become more conventional as flexible postindustrial modes of production replace rigid industrial-era schedules in an ever increasing number of sectors.

Changing attitudes

Social attitudes towards leisure time are also changing in the late industrial, early postindustrial period. As in ancient Greece, leisure is generally seen not just as a time to rest between work shifts, but as an end in itself and a time to undertake activities such as foreign travel, which are highly meaningful to some individuals. This change in perception is consistent with the increasing emphasis on consumption over production. In contrast to the industrial era, a **work in order to play philosophy** (i.e. working to obtain the necessary funds to undertake worthwhile leisure pursuits) is emerging to provide a powerful social sanctioning of most types of tourism activity (see Breakthrough tourism: A right to travel?). A related issue, however, is the tendency of many individuals to spend a growing portion of their discretionary time in additional work activity to maintain a particular lifestyle or pay debts, thereby constraining their opportunities for engaging in tourism or other leisure activities. In 2001, over one-half of the Australian labour force worked more than 40 hours per week while one-third exceeded 50 hours. About 60 per cent of all overtime work, moreover, was unpaid (Phillips 2001).

BREAKTHROUGH TOURISM
A right to travel?

Changing social attitudes in Phase Four countries suggest that tourism is increasingly regarded not as a luxury activity or privilege but rather a basic human need in its own right. This is consistent with Maslow (1954), who argued that people try to fulfil higher-level needs such as self-actualisation and self-esteem, which can be met through travel, once lower-level needs such as food, shelter and safety are satisfied. Regarded as such, it is then logical to argue that people should have the *right* to travel. Such a provision is actually contained in Article 13 of the UN 1948 Universal Declaration of Human Rights, which states that 'everyone has the right to leave any country, including his own, and to return to his country'. It is the 1999 WTO Global Code of Ethics for Tourism, however, that ties such rights directly to tourism. Article 7 of the code affirms the right to tourism and emphasises that 'obstacles should not be placed in its way', since 'the prospect of direct and personal access to the discovery and enjoyment of the planet's resources constitutes a right equally open to all the world's inhabitants'. Article 8 goes on to state that 'tourists . . . should benefit, in compliance with international law and national legislation, from the liberty to move within their countries and from one State to another'.

The articulation of tourists' rights under international law has major implications for both origin and destination regions. The former will increasingly be expected to facilitate travel for their residents, while the responsibilities of the latter in receiving and hosting tourists will increase, as will the number of visitors received. The code states, for example, that tourists should have 'access to tourism and cultural sites without being subject to excessive formalities or discrimination' as well as 'prompt and easy access to local administration, legal and health services'. As these rights become more widely recognised, they could have the added effect of increasing the credibility of tourism as a sector worthy of research funding and inclusion in the curricula of major universities.

■ 3.5.3 Demographic *factors*

The later stages of the development process (i.e. Phases Three and Four) are associated with distinctive demographic transformations, at least four of which appear to increase the propensity of the population to engage in tourism-related activities.

Reduced family size

Because of the costs of raising children, small family size is equated with increased discretionary time and household income. If the per capita GNP and fertility rates of the world's countries are examined, a strong inverse relationship between the two can be readily identified. That is, total fertility rates (TFR = the average number of children that a woman can expect to bear in her lifetime) tend to decline as the affluence of societies increases. This was the case for Australia during most of the twentieth century (table 3.3), the post–World War II period of increased fertility (i.e. the 'baby boom') being the primary exception. The overall trend of declining fertility is reflected in the size of the average Australian household, which declined from 4.5 persons in 1911 to 2.6 persons in 2001.

One factor that accounts for this trend is the decline in infant mortality rates. As the vast majority of children in a Phase Four society will survive into adulthood, there is no practical need for couples to produce a large number of children so that at least one or two will survive into adulthood. Also critical is the entry of women into the workforce, the elimination of children as a significant source of labour and the desire of households to attain a high level of material wellbeing (which is more difficult when resources have to be allocated to the raising of children).

However, rather than culminating in a stable situation where couples basically replace themselves with two children, these and other factors have combined in many Phase Four countries to yield a total fertility rate barely above 1.0. While the resulting 'baby bust' may in the short term further enable adults to travel, the long-term effects on tourism if this pattern of low fertility persists are more uncertain. One consideration is the reduction in the tourist market as the population ages and eventually declines (see the following pages). Another is the shrinkage of the labour force, which could reduce the amount of pension income that can be used for discretionary purposes such as travel, while forcing longer working hours and a higher retirement age to fund future pension disbursements.

■ **Table 3.3**   *Australian demographic trends, 1901–2002*

YEAR	POPU-LATION (000s)	PER CENT URBAN	CRUDE BIRTH RATE	TOTAL FERTILITY RATE	LIFE EXPEC-TANCY (M/F)	PER CENT POPU-LATION OVER 64
1901	3 826	n/a	26	n/a	55/59	4.0
1911	4 574	57.8	28	n/a	n/a	4.3
1921	5 511	62.1	24	3.0	58/62	4.4
1931	6 553	63.5	17	2.2	63/67	6.5
1941	7 144	65.0	20	2.5	n/a	7.2
1947	7 579	68.7	23	3.0	66/71	8.0
1954	8 987	78.7	23	3.2	67/73	8.3
1961	10 508	81.7	23	3.3	68/74	8.5
1966	11 551	82.9	21	2.9	68/74	8.5
1971	12 937	85.6	19	2.7	68/75	8.4
1976	14 033	86.0	16	2.0	70/76	8.9
1981	14 923	85.7	16	1.9	71/78	9.8
1986	16 018	85.4	15	1.9	73/79	10.5
1991	17 336	85.3	15	1.9	74/80	11.3
1996	18 311	n/a	14	1.8	75/81	12.0
2002	19 641	n/a	13	1.7	77/82	12.8

Source: *ABS (1998a, 2001 and 2003a)*

Population increase

All things being equal, a larger population base equates with a larger overall incidence of tourism activity. Because of a process described by the **demographic transition model** (**DTM**) (see figure 3.5), Burton's Phase Four societies tend to have relatively large and stable populations. During Stage One (which more or less corresponds to Burton's Phase One), populations are maintained at a stable but low level over the long term due to the balance between high crude birth and death rates. In Stage Two (corresponding to Burton's Phase Two), dramatic declines in mortality are brought about by the introduction of basic health care. However, couples continue to have large families for cultural reasons and for the contributions that offspring make to the household labour force. Rapid population growth is the usual consequence of the resulting gap between the birth and death rates.

As the population becomes more educated and urbanised, the labour advantage from large families is gradually lost. Subsequently, the economic and social factors described in the previous subsections begin to take effect, resulting in a rapidly declining birth rate and a slowing in the rate of net population growth during Stage Three (corresponding to Burton's Phase Three). This is happening currently in heavily populated countries such as India, Brazil, Indonesia and China and is accompanied by the stabilisation of mortality rates. The conventional demographic transition is completed by Stage Four (Burton's Phase Four), wherein a balance between low birth rates and death rates is attained.

The confounding factor not taken into account in the traditional demographic transition model, however, is the pattern of collapsing fertility and eventual population decline described above. If this persists and becomes more prevalent, it may indicate a new, fifth stage of the model (see figure 3.5).

■ **Figure 3.5**
The demographic transition model

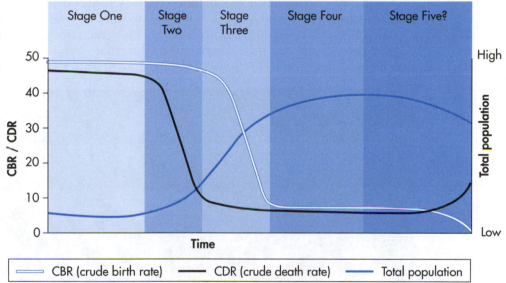

The demographic transition model basically describes the natural growth of the Australian population during the past 150 years, although the overall pattern of population increase was also critically influenced by high immigration levels as in the United States, Canada, New Zealand and western Europe. From a population of less than four million at the time of Federation, Australia's population increased almost fivefold by 2002 (see table 3.3). Similar patterns have been experienced in all of the other Phase Four countries, culminating in the 800 million Phase Four consumers mentioned earlier.

Urbanisation

As happened in Ur and Rome, the concentration of population within large urban areas increases the desire and tendency to engage in certain types of escapist tourism. In part, this is because of urban congestion and crowding, but cities are also associated with higher levels of discretionary income and education, and lower family size. Australia differs from most other Phase Four countries in its exceptionally high level of urban population, and in its concentration within a small number of major metropolitan areas. By 2003, 61 per cent of Australians lived in the five largest metropolitan areas (Sydney, Melbourne, Brisbane, Perth and Adelaide). The 'urban' population in total has peaked at about 85 per cent since the early 1970s.

Increased life expectancy

Increased life expectancies have resulted from the technological advances of the industrial and postindustrial eras. In 1901, Australian men and women could expect a lifespan of just 55 and 59 years, respectively (see table 3.3). This meant that the average male worker survived for only about five years after retirement. By 2002 the respective life expectancies had increased to 77 and 82 years, indicating 15 to 20 years of survival after leaving the workforce. This higher life expectancy, combined with reduced working time means that the Phase Four Australian male born in 1988 can look forward to 298 000 hours of discretionary time during his life, compared with 153 000 hours for his Phase Two counterpart born in 1888 (ABS). However, favouring tourism even more is the provision of pension-based income, and improvements in health that allow older adults to pursue an unprecedented variety of leisure-time activities (see figure 3.6).

■ **Figure 3.6**
German tourists in Montagne d'Ambre National Park, Madagascar

Source: *Weaver (2001)*

Because of increased life expectancies and falling total fertility rates, Australia's population is rapidly ageing, as revealed in the country's 2003 population pyramid (see figure 3.7). From just 4 per cent of the population in 1901, the 65 and older cohort accounted for almost 13 per cent of the nation's population in 2002 (see table 3.3). It is conceivable that within the next two decades Australia's population profile will resemble that of present-day Germany or Scandinavia, where 18–20 per cent of the population is 65 or older.

Contributing to this process is the ageing of the so-called **baby boomers**, those born during the aforementioned (page 75) era of relatively high fertility that prevailed from about 1946 to 1964. The baby boom can be identified in the population pyramid by the bulge in the 35- to 55-year-old age groups. The retirement of this influential cohort, expected to begin around 2010, will have significant implications for Australia's economy and social structure. From a tourism perspective, one critical issue is how much the retiring baby boomers will continue to influence the development and marketing of tourism products, as well as tourism policy.

■ **Figure 3.7**
Australia's population pyramid, 1901 and 2003, by five-year age cohorts

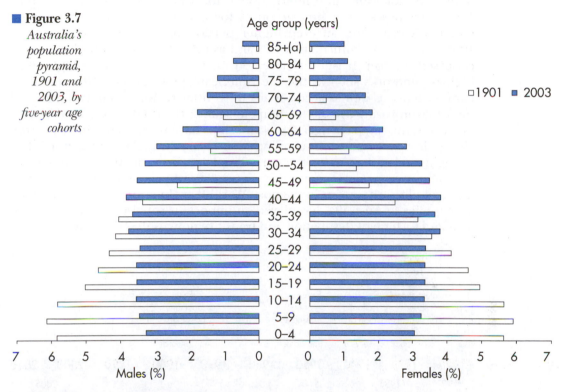

(a) The 85+ age group includes all ages 85 years and over and therefore is not strictly comparable with the five-year age groups in the rest of this graph.

Source: *ABS 2004a and 2004b*

■ *3.5.4* **Technological** *factors*

The crucial role of transportation in the diffusion of tourism is demonstrated by the influence of the railway on the development of seaside resorts and by the steamship on incipient long-haul tourism during the late 1800s. However, these pale in comparison to the impact of aircraft and the automobile. Figure 3.8 illustrates the twentieth-century evolution of the aviation industry. An interesting characteristic of this evolution is the absence of milestone developments in aircraft technology between the 1976 debut of the Concorde (which has now been decommissioned) and the introduction of new long-haul aircraft such as the A380 in the early 2000s. Nevertheless, the world's airline industry now accounts for more than 1.4 billion passengers per year (Goeldner & Ritchie 2003), and is a primary factor underlying the spatial diffusion of tourist destinations.

The development of the automotive industry during the twentieth century paralleled aviation in its rapid technical evolution and growth. The United Kingdom is typical of the Phase Four countries, with private car ownership increasing from 132 000 in 1914 to two million in 1938 and eleven million in 1969 (Burkart & Medlik 1981). The effect has been profound in both the domestic and international tourism sectors. Road transport (including buses, etc.) now accounts for about 77 per cent of all international arrivals and an even higher portion of domestic travel (Burton 1995). War, or the anticipation of war, has played a role in the diffusion of car-based tourism. It is a major reason for the development of high-speed highway networks such as the the American interstate and German autobahn systems, as well as access roads in frontier regions such as Alaska and the Amazon basin. Unable to compete against the dual impact of the aeroplane and the car, passenger trains and ships have been increasingly marginalised, in some cases functioning more as a nostalgic attraction. The changing relative roles of the car, aeroplane, bus and train as modes of tourist conveyance are depicted in figure 3.9, which shows the situation of German pleasure tourists in the post–World War II period. This trend, which also applies to Australia, has played an important role in the changing pattern and fortune of destination and transit regions as described in chapter 1.

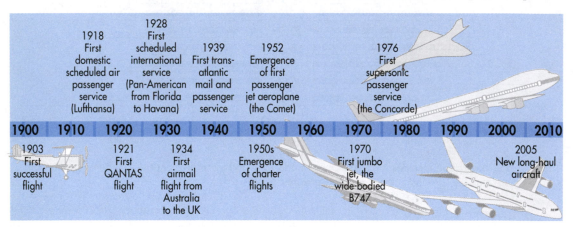

■ **Figure 3.8**   *Milestones in air travel*

Information technologies have also played a vital role in the diffusion of tourism. Computerised reservation systems (CRS), for example, expedite travel by providing travel agencies and carriers with greater flexibility (and thus even further departure from the standardisation and rigidity of industrial era modes of service), integration with other components of the industry and improved cost-effectiveness (Kurtzman & Zauhar 2003). In addition, **virtual reality** (**VR**) technologies have an enormous potential to redefine the tourism industry, and the demand for tourism products. A relevant consideration is whether VR will provide a surrogate or stimulant for actual travel.

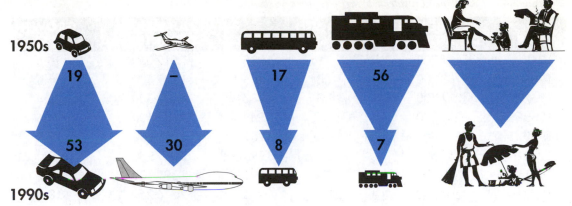

1950s

19   –   17   56

53   30   8   7

1990s

■ **Figure 3.9**   *Transportation modes for German pleasure tourists, 1950s and 1990s (in percentages)*

■ *3.5.5* Political *factors*

Tourism is dependent on the freedom of people to travel both internationally and domestically (see section 2.4.2). Often restricted for political and economic reasons in the earlier development stages, freedom of mobility is seldom an issue in Phase Four countries, where restrictions are usually limited to sensitive domestic military sites and certain prohibited countries (e.g. Cuba relative to the United States). The collapse of the Soviet Union and its socialist orbit in the early 1990s has meant that an additional 400 million people now have greater freedom, if not the money, to travel. More deliberate has been the Chinese government's incremental moves to allow its 1.3 billion people increased access to foreign travel (see the case study at the end of this chapter). A critical factor influencing whether this high level of global mobility is maintained will be concerns over the movement of terrorists and illegal migrants.

3.6 AUSTRALIAN TOURISM PARTICIPATION

The economic, social, demographic, technological and political factors described above have all contributed to increased tourism activity by residents of Phase Four countries. Australia is no exception. Table 3.4 depicts the increasing number of outbound resident departures since 1965, while table 3.5 reveals the growth of domestic tourism. The 73.6 million overnight domestic tourist trips taken within Australia in 2003 equated to 294 million nights away from home, or four nights per trip on average. An additional 139 million day-trip excursions were undertaken that year by Australians, which represents a dramatic decline from the figure of 171 million in 1999. Combined with the steady growth of outbound travel and the stagnation of overnight domestic trips, this indicates that a growing share of the Australian tourism dollar is leaving the country. Government initiatives to retain such expenditures are described in chapter 7.

■ Table 3.4 *Outbound resident departures from Australia, 1965–2003*

YEAR	NUMBER OF DEPARTURES	GROWTH (%)	YEAR	NUMBER OF DEPARTURES	GROWTH (%)
1965	161 700	–	1985	1 512 000	6.6
1966	183 200	13.3	1986	1 539 600	1.8
1967	217 700	18.8	1987	1 622 300	5.4
1968	251 900	13.6	1988	1 697 600	4.6
1969	288 800	14.6	1989	1 989 800	17.2
1970	352 500	22.0	1990	2 169 900	9.0
1971	413 900	17.4	1991	2 099 400	–3.2
1972	504 500	21.9	1992	2 276 260	8.4
1973	638 100	26.5	1993	2 267 080	–0.4
1974	769 700	20.6	1994	2 354 310	3.8
1975	911 800	18.5	1995	2 518 620	7.0
1976	973 800	6.8	1996	2 731 970	8.5
1977	971 300	–0.3	1997	2 932 760	7.3
1978	1 061 200	9.2	1998	3 161 060	7.8
1979	1 175 800	10.8	1999	3 209 990	1.5
1980	1 203 600	2.4	2000	3 498 200	9.0
1981	1 217 300	1.1	2001	3 442 600	–1.6
1982	1 286 900	5.7	2002	3 461 000	0.5
1983	1 253 000	–2.6	2003	3 388 000	–2.1
1984	1 418 500	13.2			

Source: *ABS (1996, 2001 and 2004)*

■ Table 3.5
Domestic tourism trips in Australia, 1984–85 to 2001

YEAR	NUMBER (000s)	YEAR	NUMBER (000s)
1984–85	45 358	1994–95[1]	57 898
1985–86	45 144	1995–96	63 028
1986–87	44 963	1996–97	62 781
1987–88	46 725	1998[2]	73 811
1988–89	46 017	1999	72 981
1989–90	49 962	2000	73 771
1990–91	48 997	2001	74 585
1991–92	48 235	2002	75 339
1992–93	47 878	2003	73 621
1993–94	48 113		

Notes:
[1] Results from this and the 1995–97 reporting periods are not comparable to previous periods due to a change in sampling procedure.
[2] Results from this and subsequent reporting periods are not comparable to earlier periods due to changes in sampling procedure.

Source: *Data derived from BTR (1987–2004)*

Given the incredibly rapid pace of change that is affecting all facets of contemporary life, any attempt to make medium- or long-term predictions about the tourism sector is very risky. It can be confidently predicted that technology will continue to revolutionise the tourism industry, pose new challenges to tourism managers and restructure tourism systems at all levels. However, the specific nature and timing of radical future innovations, or their exact implications, cannot be identified with any precision. In terms of demand, the number of persons living in Phase Four (and Phase Five?) countries is likely to increase dramatically over the next two or three decades as a consequence of the **condensed development sequence** and the nature of the countries currently in Phases Two and Three. The former term refers to the fact that societies today are undergoing the transition towards full economic development (i.e. a Phase Four state) in a reduced amount of time compared to their counterparts in the past. The timeframe for the United Kingdom, for example, was about 200 years (roughly 1750–1950). Japan, however, was able to make the transition within about 80 years (1860–1940) while the timeframe for South Korea was only about 40 years (1950–90).

One reason for this acceleration is the ability of the transitional societies to use technologies introduced during earlier stages of the industrialisation process. Therefore, although England had the great advantage of access to the resources and markets of its colonies, it also had to invent the technology of industrialisation. Today, less developed countries such as India can facilitate their economic and social development through available technologies. It is possible that China, in particular, with its extremely rapid pace of economic growth, will emerge as a Phase Four society by the year 2020. If this is achieved, then tourism managers will have to allow for 1.3 billion additions to the global market for international tourism. However, there are also the countervailing risks of a major economic depression, further spectacular acts of terrorism, health epidemics, or regional or global war involving nuclear, chemical or biological weapons.

CHAPTER REVIEW

Tourism is an ancient phenomenon that was evident in classical Egypt, Greece and Rome, as well as in the Middle Ages. Distinctive characteristics of tourism in the premodern stage include its accessibility to the elite, the importance of religious as well as educational and health motivations, and the lack of a well-defined tourism 'industry'. Other features include the risky, uncomfortable and time-consuming nature of travel, its restriction to relatively few well-defined land and sea routes, and the limited, localised and unplanned spatial impact of tourism upon the landscape. Premodern tourism is similar to modern tourism in the essential role of discretionary time and income in facilitating travel, and the desire to escape congested urban conditions. Other commonalities include curiosity about the past and other cultures, the desire to avoid risk and the proclivity to purchase souvenirs and to leave behind graffiti as a reminder of one's presence in a destination region.

The emergence of Europe from the Middle Ages marked the transition towards the early modern era of tourism, of which spas, seaside resorts and the Grand Tour were important elements. The transition towards modern mass tourism was closely associated with the Industrial Revolution, and especially with Thomas Cook's application of its principles and innovations to the travel sector by way of the package tour. Mass tourism emerged as a result of a convergence between the reduced costs of such travel and the rising wages of the middle and working classes.

The post-Cook era was characterised by the rapid expansion of domestic tourism within the newly industrialised countries. However, large-scale international tourism was delayed by primitive long-haul transportation technology, and by the appearance of two major economic recessions and two world wars between 1880 and 1950. It was not until the 1950s that international tourism began to display an exponential pattern of growth, stimulated by five interrelated 'push' factors that increased the demand for tourism in the economically developed Phase Three and Four countries. Economic growth provided more discretionary income and time for the masses. Concurrently, society perceived leisure time in a more positive way, moving towards a 'work in order to play' philosophy. Demographic changes such as population growth, urbanisation, smaller family size and rising life expectancies increased the propensity of the population to engage in tourism-related activities. Technological developments such as the aeroplane and car provided relatively cheap means of transport, while overall political stability facilitated travel between countries. The experience of Australia is typical, with large-scale increases in outbound and domestic tourism being recorded in the past two decades. The pattern of growth is likely to continue largely on the strength of a condensed development sequence that is rapidly propelling countries such as China and India into the ranks of the Phase Three and Four societies.

SUMMARY OF KEY TERMS ····································

Premodern tourism

Describes the era of tourism activity from the beginning of civilisation to the end of the Middle Ages

- **Mesopotamia:** the region approximately occupied by present-day Iraq, where the earliest impulses of civilisation first emerged, presumably along with the first tourism activity
- **Leisure class:** in premodern tourism, that small portion of the population that had sufficient discretionary time and income to engage in leisure pursuits such as tourism
- **Discretionary time:** normally defined as time not spent at work, or in normal rest and bodily maintenance
- **Discretionary income:** the amount of income that remains after household necessities such as food, housing, clothing, education and transportation have been purchased
- **Olympic Games:** the most important of the ancient Greek art and athletics festivals, held every four years at Olympia. The ancient Olympic Games are one of the most important examples of premodern tourism
- **Resorts:** facilities or urban areas that are specialised in the provision of recreational tourism opportunities
- **Dark Ages:** the period from about AD 500 to 1100, characterised by a serious deterioration in social, economic and political conditions within Europe
- **Middle Ages:** the period from about AD 1100 to the Renaissance (about AD 1500), characterised by an improvement in the social, economic and political situation, in comparison with the Dark Ages
- **Pilgrimage:** generic term for travel undertaken for some religious purpose. Pilgrimages have declined in importance during the modern era compared with recreational, business and social tourism
- **Crusades:** a series of campaigns to 'liberate' Jerusalem and the Holy Land from Muslim control. While not a form of tourism as such, the Crusades helped to reopen Europe to the outside world and spawn an incipient travel industry

Early modern tourism

The transitional era between premodern tourism (about AD 1500) and modern mass tourism (since 1950)

- **Renaissance:** the 'rebirth' of Europe following the Dark Ages, commenced in Italy during the mid-1400s and spread to Germany and the 'low countries' by the early 1600s
- **Grand Tour:** a form of early modern tourism that involved a lengthy trip to the major cities of France and Italy by young adults of the leisure class, for purposes of education and culture
- **Spas:** a type of resort centred on the use of geothermal waters for health purposes
- **Industrial Revolution:** a process that occurred in England from the mid-1700s to the mid-1900s (and spread outwards to other countries), in which society was transformed from an agrarian to an industrial basis, thereby spawning conditions that were conducive to the growth of tourism-related activity

■ **Seaside resort:** a type of resort located on coastlines to take advantage of sea bathing for health and, later, recreational purposes; many of these were established during the Industrial Revolution for both the leisure and working classes

■ **Thomas Cook:** the entrepreneur who applied the principles of the Industrial Revolution to the tourism sector through such innovations as the package tour

■ **Package tour:** a pre-paid travel package that usually includes transportation, accommodation, food and other services

■ **Post-Cook period:** the time from about 1880 to 1950, characterised by the rapid growth of domestic tourism within the wealthier countries, but less rapid expansion in international tourism

■ **War dividend:** the long-term benefits for tourism that derive from large conflicts, including war-related attractions, image creation, and the emergence of new travel markets

Modern mass tourism (Contemporary tourism)

The period from 1950 to the present day, characterised by the rapid expansion of international and domestic tourism

■ **Push factors:** economic, social, demographic, technological and political forces that stimulate a demand for tourism activity by 'pushing' consumers away from their usual place of residence

■ **Tourism participation sequence:** according to Burton, the tendency for a society to participate in tourism increases through a set of four phases that relate to the concurrent process of increased economic development
Phase One: pre-industrial, mainly agricultural and subsistence-based economies where tourism participation is restricted to a small leisure class
Phase Two: the generation of wealth increases and tends to spread to a wider segment of the population as a consequence of industrialisation and related processes such as urbanisation. This leads to increases in the demand for domestic tourism among the middle classes
Phase Three: the bulk of the population becomes increasingly affluent, leading to the emergence of mass domestic travel, as well as extensive international tourism to nearby countries. The elite, meanwhile, engage in greater long-haul travel
Phase Four: represents a fully developed country with almost universal affluence, and a subsequent pattern of mass international tourism to an increasingly diverse array of short- and long-haul destinations. Almost all residents engage in a comprehensive variety of domestic tourism experiences

■ **Play in order to work philosophy:** an industrial-era ethic, which holds that leisure time and activities are necessary in order to make workers more productive, thereby reinforcing the work-focused nature of society

■ **Postindustrial era:** a later Phase Four stage in which hi-tech services and information replace manufacturing and lower-order services as the mainstay of an economy

■ **Flexitime:** a time management option in which workers have some flexibility in distributing a required number of working hours (usually weekly) in a manner that suits the lifestyle and productivity of the individual worker

■ **Earned time:** a time management option in which an individual is no longer obligated to work once a particular quota is attained over a defined period of time (often monthly or annual)

■ **Work in order to play philosophy:** a postindustrial ethic derived from ancient Greek philosophy that holds that leisure and leisure-time activities such as tourism are important in their own right and that we work to be able to afford to engage in leisure pursuits

■ **Demographic transition model (DTM):** an idealised depiction of the process whereby societies evolve from a high fertility/high mortality structure to a low fertility/low mortality structure. This evolution usually parallels the development of a society from a Phase One to a Phase Four profile, as occurred during the Industrial Revolution. A fifth stage may now be emerging, characterised by extremely low birth rates and resultant net population loss

■ **Baby boomers:** people born during the post–World War II period of high TFRs (roughly 1946 to 1964), who constitute a noticeable bulge within the population pyramid of Australia and other Phase Four countries

■ **Virtual reality (VR):** the wide-field presentation of computer-generated, multi-sensory information that allows the user to experience a virtual world

■ **Condensed development sequence:** the process whereby societies undergo the transition to a Phase Four state within an increasingly reduced period of time

QUESTIONS

1 (a) Outline the major forms and types of tourism that occurred in the premodern era.
(b) For each, identify a modern parallel.
(c) What are the similarities and differences between the premodern and modern examples?

2 Does the modern travel of young backpackers offer any parallels to the historical Grand Tour?

3 How do major wars both hinder and stimulate tourism systems?

4 Why is Thomas Cook referred to as the father of modern mass tourism?

5 (a) Do you believe that people have the right to travel?
(b) If so, how far should these rights extend?
(c) What are the implications for destinations?

6 What are the positive and negative implications of an ageing population for the tourism sector of a Phase Four society?

7 How much are VR technologies likely to help or hinder participation in tourism?

8 What factors might account for the higher rates of growth in outbound tourism participation by Australians in the period from 1965 to 1975, as opposed to subsequent years (table 3.4)?

EXERCISES

1 (a) For each country listed in appendix 3 (where such data are provided) calculate the number of outbound trips undertaken for every 100 people in the population, using the following formula:

$$\frac{\text{No. of outbound trips}}{\text{Population}} = 100$$

(b) On graph paper, plot the outcomes for each country (*y* axis) against their per capita GNP (*x* axis).

(c) What trend emerges?

(d) Identify any major anomalies, and discuss possible reasons for these exceptions.

2 Write a 1000-word report in which you describe

(a) how a typical Australian household in 2001 (i.e. Phase Four) differs from its 1901 counterpart (i.e. Phase Two)

(b) the patterns of tourism activity that might be expected from each household over a one-year period

(c) what a future Phase Five Australian household and its tourism-related patterns might look like.

FURTHER READING

Gunn, C. 2004. *Western Tourism: Can Paradise be Reclaimed?* **Elmsford, USA: Cognizant.** Gunn's analysis of tourism in the western United States focuses around a trip that the author made to the region in the late 1920s.

Smith, M. 2004. 'Seeing a New Side to Seasides: Culturally Regenerating the English Seaside Town'. *International Journal of Tourism Research* 6: **17–28.** Smith discusses strategies for the revitalisation of English seaside resorts that focus on a broad perception of cultural resources.

Towner, J. 1996. *An Historical Geography of Recreation and Tourism in the Western World 1540–1940.* **Chichester, UK: Wiley.** Major topic areas within this well-researched, academically oriented text include the Grand Tour and spas and seaside resorts, within both Europe and North America.

Veal, A. & Lynch, R. 2001. *Australian Leisure.* **Second Edition. Sydney: Pearson.** This book provides an Australia-specific account of historical and modern leisure trends, and effectively places these in the broad global context.

Withey, L. 1997. *Grand Tours and Cook's Tours.* **New York: William Morrow & Company, Inc.** Two critical eras in the historical development of tourism are covered in a thorough and well-written manner by Withey.

China's outbound tourism surge

Prior to the 1990s, outbound travel by nationals of China was a rare privilege restricted to a select group of businessmen, bureaucrats, politicians, students and athletes. The World Tourism Organization now predicts that China will become the fourth-largest source of outbound tourists by 2020, when it is expected to send 100 million visitors to other countries. China's transformation into an outbound powerhouse became possible in the late 1970s when the government introduced its Open Door Policy of economic reform and increased international trade. By the late 1980s, the country's GNP tripled and many of China's one billion people soon had enough money to visit other countries. The Chinese government responded to this latent demand by gradually and methodically easing restrictions on outbound travel. Initially, opportunities for leisure travel were 'experimentally' made available only in adjacent Chinese-dominated destinations such as Hong Kong and Macau. In 1991, the range of approved foreign destinations was expanded to include Singapore, Malaysia and Thailand — close-by countries with large ethnic Chinese populations, and with whom China had been establishing close trade relations. In 1999, Australia and New Zealand became the first non-Asian countries to be granted ATD status by the Chinese government. This allows Chinese nationals to enter for leisure purposes rather than just for business (Stolz 1999).

As a result of gradually easing restrictions, the number of Chinese outbound tourists increased from 620 000 in 1990 to 2.1 million in 1991, 3.7 million in 1994, 5.3 million in 1997, and 9.2 million in 1999. This exponential pattern continued during 2002 and 2004, when 16.6 million and 28.9 million outbound tourists were respectively recorded. China has now exceeded Japan as Asia's main source of outbound tourists. This last statistic, while impressive compared with 1990, still represents less than 3 per cent of China's population. By comparison, the 3.4 million Australians who travelled abroad in 2003 represented more than 15 per cent of Australia's population.

There are many factors that continue to hinder Chinese nationals who wish to travel overseas, and especially to destinations beyond Hong Kong and Macau, which account for more than one-half of Chinese outboard tourism. They must first obtain approved leave from his or her employer. The Public Security Bureau must then provide clearance and issue an exit visa. Finally, the would-be tourist needs to obtain a visa from the desired destination. Overseas travel, furthermore, is arranged only by a relatively small number of state-owned travel agencies operating in large cities or provincial capitals. Officially, overseas travellers must be part of organised tour groups, although 40 per cent of exit visas by 1997 were being granted to independent travellers, indicating tacit government approval for further easing travel restrictions (Brady 1998). In

1997, China also abandoned a longstanding policy that required sponsors in the visited country to pay for the travel of their Chinese relations. This was seldom done in practice, and travel agents found many creative ways for getting around the restriction (Lew 2000). Chinese government concerns in this respect were largely based on the desire to minimise the leakage of foreign exchange by discouraging travel for leisure/vacation purposes. But a countervailing factor was that the costs of leisure travel, unlike business or government travel, are not borne by the state. The government has therefore tacitly encouraged the growth of leisure-based travel, even if overseas relatives do not pay for this activity. To avoid a negative balance of tourism payments, the Chinese government concurrently pursues reciprocity in its relations with other countries — that is, every tourist sent by China to country X should ideally be matched to a tourist sent by country X to China (Bailey 1998).

As of late 2004, ATD status had been extended to 73 destinations beyond the mainland. Chinese visitors to Australia increased rapidly from 42 600 in 1995 to 92 600 in 1999 and 190 000 in 2002 but declined in 2003 to 176 100 because of the SARS epidemic and other dissuasive factors (see table 4.5). As a share of the total Australian inbound intake, this represents an increase in the Chinese market from 1.1 to 3.7 per cent, which situated China as the seventh-largest inbound market. Ironically, the United States had not yet attained ATD status as of early 2005, even though it is by far the most preferred overseas destination of Chinese travellers. This is largely because of restrictive US government policy on the issuance of visas to Chinese nationals, an issue that is also regarded as an impediment to the growth of this market in Australia, where overstaying has been a chronic problem. Nevertheless, robust long-term growth is still predicted, and it is therefore important for managers to understand the distinctive characteristics of Chinese outbound travellers. Pending further empirical study, these are likely to include Confucianism-influenced traits such a strong group orientation, a tendency to be influenced by opinion leaders, and a strong emphasis on shopping owing to expectations that returning tourists should give gifts to parents and other elders (Jang, Yu & Pearson 2003).

Questions

1 What factors might underlie the decision of the government of China to ease restrictions on the international leisure travel of its population?

2 How has the government of China influenced the size and destination of the Chinese outbound tourist market?

3 Consult the latest edition of the International Visitor Survey for Australia in order to construct a profile of the Chinese inbound market. Identify, from the perspective of the Australian tourism industry and destination residents, the positive and negative characteristics of this market.

4
Destinations

LEARNING OBJECTIVES

After studying this chapter, you should be able to:

1 describe and explain the relative status of the more developed and less developed world as tourist destination regions

2 identify the major generic factors that attract or 'pull' visitors to tourist destinations

3 discuss how much destinations and various tourism stakeholders can influence these pull factors

4 describe and account for the status of tourism in each of the world's major regions, and assess the pull factors that have contributed to these patterns

5 account for the tendency of tourism at all scales to develop in a spatially uneven pattern

6 assess the basic pattern of inbound and domestic tourism within Australia.

$\mathcal{I}$NTRODUCTION

Chapter 3 described the remarkable growth of contemporary international and domestic tourism from a demand perspective, without reference to the destinations that are the focus of this growth. Chapter 4 addresses the supply issue by considering the spatial variations in the growth and distribution of tourism among and within the world's major regions, and the factors that underlie these patterns. Section 4.2 examines these variations at the most basic level by describing the **global inequality in tourism** that exists between the economically 'more developed' and 'less developed' worlds. The major factors that have stimulated or hindered the development of tourism in each of these two 'macro-regions' are also discussed in this section, but section 4.3 considers the generic 'pull' factors that draw tourists to destinations in general. Section 4.4 describes the tourism situation in each of the world's major geographical regions and examines the pull factors (or lack thereof) that apply in each case. The spatial characteristics of tourism within an individual country are outlined in section 4.5.

$\mathcal{G}$LOBAL DESTINATION PATTERNS: MDCs AND LDCs

4.2

The world can be divided into two 'macro-regions' based on relative levels of economic development and associated sociodemographic characteristics such as social structure and fertility rates. The **more developed countries** (**MDCs**) (collectively constituting the 'more developed world') correspond with Burton's Phase Three and Phase Four countries (see chapter 3). They include Australia, New Zealand, the United States, Canada, Europe, Japan, South Korea, Hong Kong, Taiwan and Singapore. Relatively poor European countries such as Russia, Ukraine, Yugoslavia, Albania and Bulgaria are included because of their cultural affinities with that otherwise prosperous continent.

The **less developed countries** (**LDCs**) (or cumulatively the 'less developed world') are synonymous with those still situated in Burton's Phase Two. The major less developed regions are Latin America and the Caribbean, most of Asia, Africa and the islands of the Pacific and Indian oceans. Wealthy Middle Eastern oil-producing states, including Libya, Kuwait and Saudi Arabia, are included in this category despite their high per capita incomes. This is because of cultural affiliations with other regional countries and social indicators (such as higher fertility and infant mortality rates) that indicate Phase Two dynamics. The designation of countries into either the MDC or LDC category, by convention and perception, remained remarkably stable during the latter half of the twentieth century, though it must not be assumed that all MDCs are more economically developed than all LDCs. Moreover, many countries have MDC-like and LDC-like spaces within their own boundaries (e.g. large cities and Aboriginal reserves).

4.2.1 Tourism *market share and growth*

Table 4.1 depicts the status of the more developed and less developed worlds as recipients of inbound tourism for selected years in the period between 1950 and 2002. While the continuing dominance of the more developed world is evident, so too is the gradual erosion of this status. MDC destinations accounted for about 72 per cent of all international stayovers by the early 2000s, compared with a 90 per cent plus share before 1970. This reduction, moreover, occurred despite the acquisition of MDC status by Singapore, Hong Kong, South Korea and Taiwan, which together accounted for 4.5 per cent of all inbound tourism in 2002. The LDCs cumulatively have experienced about a 100-fold increase in their stayover arrivals (i.e. from 2 million to 200 million) between 1950 and 2002, while the MDCs have experienced a 'mere' 22-fold increase (i.e. from 23 million to 500 million).

■ **Table 4.1**
International stayover arrivals by LDCs and MDCs, 1950–2002

YEAR	MDCs[1] (MILLIONS)	SHARE (%)	LDCs (MILLIONS)	SHARE (%)	GLOBAL TOTAL (MILLIONS)
1950	23.2	91.7	2.1	8.3	25.2
1960	64.8	93.5	4.5	6.5	69.3
1970	142.0	88.9	17.7	11.1	159.7
1980	226.0	79.0	60.1	21.0	286.1
1990	352.7	77.4	103.2	22.6	455.9
1994	419.3	76.8	126.6	23.2	545.9
1998	467.4	73.5	168.6	26.5	636.0
2002	504.5	71.8	198.2	28.2	702.7

Note:
[1] *Includes South Korea, Singapore, Hong Kong and Taiwan since 1990*

Source: *WTO (1998a, 2005)*

4.2.2 Reasons *for the emergence of the LDCs as destinations*

Many factors have combined to elevate the less developed world into the position of an increasingly prominent destination region. However, particularly important are changing consumer preferences in the major international tourist markets, and economic growth within the less developed world itself.

Demand for 3S tourism: the emergence of the pleasure periphery

Seaside resorts were already established as tourist destinations in the era of the Roman Empire (see chapter 3), but became especially important within Europe, North America and Australia in conjunction with the Industrial Revolution. Nineteenth-century limitations in technology as well as discretionary income and time restricted the development of these resorts to domestic coastal locations close to expanding urban markets. However, dramatic twentieth-century advances in air transportation technology combined with the overall development process and changing social perceptions to greatly extend the distribution, scale, and market range of seaside and beach resorts. This modern phase of expansion in **3S tourism** (i.e. sea, sand and sun) initially affected the warmer coastal regions of the more developed countries. Among the destination regions spawned by this trend were the French, Italian and Spanish Rivieras, the east coast of Florida (and the American **sunbelt** in general), Australia's Gold Coast and Japan's Okinawa Island. Tourism development subsequently spread into adjacent parts of the Mediterranean, Caribbean, South Pacific and Indian Ocean basins, most situated within the less developed world.

The expansion of 3S tourism occurred at such a rate and extent that it was possible to discern the emergence of a pan-global **pleasure periphery** by the mid-1970s (Turner & Ash 1975). 'Pleasure' refers to the hedonistic nature of the 3S product, while 'periphery' alludes to the marginal geographic and economic status of its constituent subregions, which straddle both the more developed and less developed world (figure 4.1). The Mediterranean basin is the oldest and largest (in terms of visitation) subcomponent, followed by the Caribbean basin. Less geographically coherent is a band of more recent 3S destinations extending from the South Pacific through South-East Asia, coastal Australia and the Indian Ocean basin.

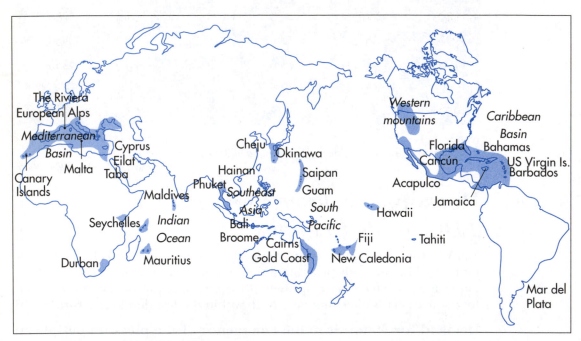

■ **Figure 4.1**   *The pleasure periphery*

The growth of tourism in most pleasure periphery destinations has been dramatic, as illustrated by a selection of relevant countries (see figure 4.2). This growth has been especially apparent in small island states or dependencies (**SISODs**), such as Fiji and the Seychelles, which are concentrated in the pleasure periphery and are for the most part endowed with suitable 3S resources. As a result, they are greatly overrepresented as inbound tourist destinations in proportion to their resident populations. Specifically, the world's 63 SISODs account for only 0.3 per cent of the global population, but around 5 per cent of total international stayover arrivals (see appendix 3).

■ **Figure 4.2**
Performance of selected pleasure periphery destinations: international stayover arrivals

Source:
Weaver (1998)

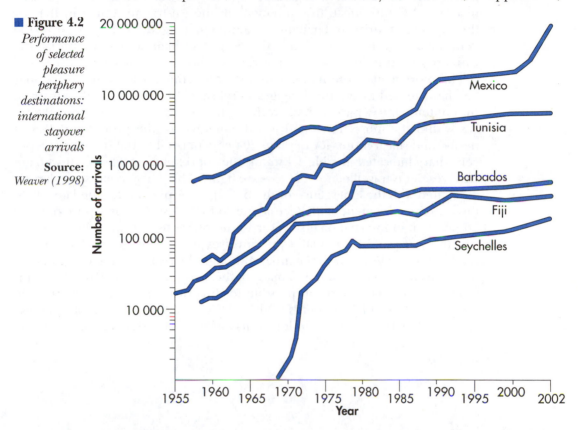

Although best known for its 3S opportunities, the pleasure periphery has expanded to incorporate other types of tourism product. Skiing and other alpine-based winter sporting activities are now widespread in the North American Rockies and the European Alps, while wildlife-based activities are becoming increasingly important in destinations such as Kenya, Australia, New Zealand, Thailand and Costa Rica (see chapter 11).

Economic growth of LDCs

Inbound tourist traffic into the less developed world, and into the pleasure periphery in particular, has traditionally occurred as a **north–south flow** involving North American, European and Japanese travellers (English 1986; Lea 1988). For Australians and New Zealanders the direction of flow is reversed, although the labels are still valid to the extent that developed countries are sometimes referred to collectively as the 'North'. This pattern, however, is now eroding due to accelerated economic growth within the less developed world, which is generating a significant outbound tourist market among its emergent middle and upper classes, and creating greater complexity in the global tourism system. As noted in section 3.5.1, the middle classes in Phase Three societies tend to visit nearby countries, while the rich extend their visits to more prestigious long-haul destinations, often within the more developed world. The net result is that much of the growth in LDC inbound tourism is accounted for by arrivals from other (usually nearby) LDCs. In effect, the stereotype of the Australian tourist in Bali, or the Japanese tourist in Thailand is being challenged by the image of the Venezuelan tourist in Trinidad, the Saudi Arabian tourist in India, the Chinese tourist in Malaysia and the Kenyan tourist in Tanzania.

This movement of international tourists within the less developed world may be characterised as the third geographical stage of international tourism in the contemporary era. The first, involving the movement of international tourists within the more developed world, emerged in the post–World War II period and still accounts for perhaps 70 per cent of all traffic (i.e. the 71.8 per cent share indicated in table 4.1 minus the approximately 2 per cent who are LDC residents travelling to MDCs — see figure 4.3). The second stage, largely associated with the emergence of the pleasure periphery after the late 1960s, involves the movement of MDC residents to LDC destinations. Approximately 20 per cent of international stayover traffic presently falls into this category. The third stage of LDC-to-LDC traffic involves just 5 to 8 per cent of all tourism but has the greatest growth potential, although the realisation of this potential will indicate a transformation of many of these countries into MDCs. With this same proviso, it may also be possible to discern a fourth stage in the still incipient flow of LDC residents to the MDCs, entailing for example Chinese visitors to the United States, Indonesians to Australia and Algerians to France.

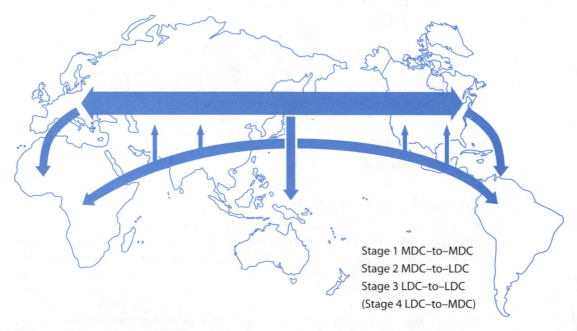

Stage 1 MDC–to–MDC
Stage 2 MDC–to–LDC
Stage 3 LDC–to–LDC
(Stage 4 LDC–to–MDC)

■ **Figure 4.3**   *Three stages of international tourism in the contemporary era*

ᴾULL FACTORS INFLUENCING A DESTINATION

Two of the major forces (i.e. the fashionability of 3S tourism, and internal economic development) that have stimulated growth in the less developed world's share of the inbound tourist market have been examined above. Consideration will now be given to the general factors that can potentially encourage or discourage tourist traffic to any particular destination. These **pull factors** are distinct from the push factors outlined in chapter 3 in being focused on the supply side of tourism (i.e. product or destination-based forces) rather than on tourist demand (i.e. market or origin-based forces). As with the push factors, the use of the term 'pull' is metaphorical.

One important implication of this geographical differentiation between supply and demand is that destinations are better positioned to exert influence over the pull factors than they are over the push factors. For example, a destination does not normally influence whether another country evolves into a tourist-generating MDC, but it can take tangible measures to develop its supply of attractions and create a welcoming environment to attract potential visitors from that MDC. This issue of control will be considered in the discussion of each individual factor. No priority is intended in the order that these factors are presented, since the combination and relative importance of individual factors will vary from one destination to another.

■ 4.3.1 Geographical *proximity to markets*

Controlling for all other factors, an inverse relationship is likely to exist between the volume of traffic flowing from an origin region to a destination region and the distance separating the two. That is, the number of visitors from origin X to destination Y will decrease as distance increases between X and Y, owing to higher transportation costs and longer travel times. This is known as a **distance–decay** effect (McKercher & Lew 2003). The volume of traffic will also be proportional to the size and prosperity of the origin region market, with large and wealthy markets generating larger flows.

These basic relationships are discernible throughout the world. The Caribbean, Mediterranean and South-East Asian subregions of the pleasure periphery, for example, are dominated respectively by American, European and Japanese outbound tourists. A distance–decay relationship is evident as well in the pattern of Australian outbound travel, with eight of the top ten destinations being located in Oceania or South-East Asia (figure 4.4). Although not apparent in figure 4.4, the effect also influences Australian outbound travel to the United States, where most visits are concentrated in the Pacific and western states of Hawaii, California and Nevada (the state where Las Vegas is located). While destination managers cannot alter the location of their city or country relative to the market, distance can serve as an incentive (or disincentive if the distance is short) to pursue strategies such as more aggressive marketing that will help to compensate for this effect. These strategies may include attempts to reduce the psychological distance between the destination and target origin regions.

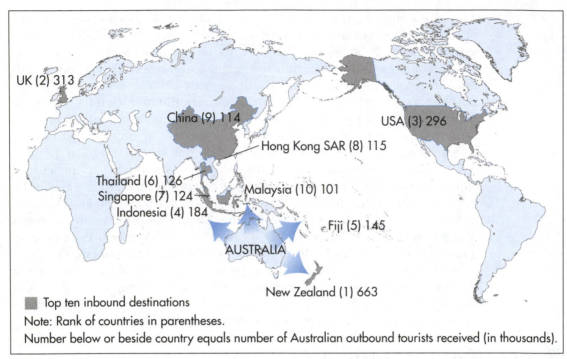

Figure 4.4 *Main destinations for Australian outbound tourists, 2003*

Source: *Data derived from Tourism Australia 2005*

■ *4.3.2* Accessibility *to markets*

The effects of distance can also be reduced by developments that make destinations more accessible to origin regions. **Infrastructural accessibility** refers to the availability and quality of transportation linkages such as air routes, highways and ferry links within transit regions, and of gateway facilities such as seaports and airports within the destination and origin regions. The level of infrastructural accessibility in a destination depends on many factors, including the availability of funds, physical barriers (including distance itself) and cooperation with other destinations as well as intervening jurisdictions in the transit region to establish effective air, land and/or water linkages.

Political accessibility refers to the conditions under which visitors are allowed entry into a destination. Except in authoritarian states such as North Korea, where restrictions on internal travel are imposed, political access is not a significant issue in domestic tourism. However, it is critical in international tourism. The right to allow or deny entry to potential arrivals from other countries is a basic sovereign prerogative of all states, as discussed in chapter 2. In some cases this right has been eroded or conceded altogether through bilateral or multilateral treaties. Citizens and permanent residents of Australia and New Zealand, for example, share a reciprocal right to reside in each other's country for an indefinite period of time. On a larger scale, the 1993 opening of boundaries between the countries of the European Union has meant that travel between Germany and Denmark or the United Kingdom and France is no longer mediated by any border formalities, and is therefore equivalent in effect to domestic tourism. Such initiatives in border liberalisation, however, became subject to new scrutiny and criticism following the events of 11 September 2001, given their effect of expediting the movements of individuals involved with terrorism. There is now a greater possibility, for example, that a 'Fortress Europe' will emerge wherein internal border liberalisation will be accompanied by the tightening of borders with adjacent countries in Eastern Europe and North Africa. Political access is one of the pull factors over which destination countries (though not subnational destinations) can exercise a high level of control.

Government and the tourism industry often differ in their perceptions of the degree to which borders should be opened to inbound tourism. The immigration and security arms of national governments tend to favour less open borders (especially since September 2001), on the assumption that some international visitors may attempt to gain illegal entry or constitute a potential threat to the state in terrorism-related or other ways. In contrast, the business sector views tourists as potential customers, and is therefore supportive of more open borders and an internationally recognised right to travel. This view is usually shared by government departments responsible for the development and promotion of the tourism sector, if such bodies exist within that state. Most destination countries compromise between completely closed and completely open borders by requiring visitors to produce passports or visas and, in some cases, evidence of a local address and return fare (see Technology and tourism: Biometrics as facilitator or impediment to travel?).

TECHNOLOGY AND TOURISM
Biometrics as facilitator or impediment to travel?

A major initiative in the use of biometric data to process inbound tourists was launched in early 2004 by the US government. The US-VISIT program (United States Visitor and Immigrant Status Indicator Technology), involving 115 international airports, 14 major seaports and 50 land border crossings across the country, requires that inbound visitors from countries not participating in the visa exemption program (i.e. all but 28 other countries) have digital photos taken and their two index fingers scanned when they arrive in the United States. This information is compared against databases of criminals and suspected terrorists, and stored for future identification purposes. Touted as a means of ensuring a safer and more secure United States, the program is also presented as a facilitator of open borders, with trials showing it added just 15 seconds to the average security check (IDABC 2004).

(continued)

The program has been widely criticised within the United States, however, for its expense (an estimated $22 billion is required for full implementation over ten years), problems with the technology, lack of a clear governance and account-ability structure and its implications for violating the privacy rights of US citizens and permanent residents. Internationally, several affected countries have for-mally complained that it discriminates against their citizens, prompting a tit-for-tat move by Brazil to photograph and fingerprint arriving US citizens. Many of the 28 countries participating in the visa exemption program were also con-cerned that they could not comply with a related provision requiring passports from all countries to contain machine-readable biometric information by late 2004. Nevertheless, it is likely that the use of biometrics will become more rather than less pervasive. During 2005, the French government carried out a six-month airport trial to determine the relative merits of fingerprints, facial imprints and iris scans as sources of biometric visitor data towards the implementation of a similar program. If the travelling public has any influence over the adoption of such technologies, high levels of support are likely if authorities can demonstrate that they expedite security checks for innocent travellers while effectively intercepting criminals and terrorists.

4.3.3 Availability *of attractions*

A detailed discussion of tourist attractions is provided in chapter 5, but sev-eral introductory comments are appropriate here in relation to their pull effect and the question of control. There is widespread agreement among tourism researchers that attractions, because of their crucial role in drawing tourists, are the most important component of the tourism system, and a major factor around which the development of a destination will depend (Gee, Makens & Choy 1989; Gunn 1994b; Inskeep 1991; Goeldner & Ritchie 2003; Smith, R. 1994). Attractions include specific features such as theme parks and battlefields, and generic or nonspecific features such as scenery and climate. The concept can also be extended to include the pres-ence of friends and relatives as well as business opportunities, which foster VFR (visits to friends and relatives) and business-related tourist flows, respectively. The ability of attractions to draw visitors depends among other factors on their quality, quantity, diversity, uniqueness, carrying capacity, market image and accessibility (see chapter 5).

Pre-existing and created attractions

With regard to the issue of the control that a destination has over its tourism assets, attractions range from those that are 'pre-existing' to those that are entirely 'created'. Examples of the former include climate and spectacular topographical or hydrological features (e.g. the Himalaya or Niagara Falls), or significant historical sites (e.g. the Hastings or Waterloo battlefields). Such features already exist independent of any tourism con-text, and it is really only a question of the extent to which tourism managers and planners exploit the available opportunities that they present. On the other hand, destinations usually possess a great deal of latitude for creating attractions to induce a tourist flow or augment the pre-existing attractions. Examples of augmentation can be found on the Gold Coast, where outstanding inherent natural attractions are supplemented by theme parks, shopping opportunities and other 'built' attractions that contribute to product diversity. In some cases a locality with no significant inherent attractions may emerge as a major destination through the effective introduction of such 'built' opportunities. High profile examples from the United States include Disney World, established in the midst of a scrub pine and orchard landscape outside Orlando, and Las Vegas, the well-known gambling venue. On a much smaller scale, certain Australian towns and cities have become known among tourists for their larger-than-life models of local symbols, including the Big Banana at Coffs Harbour, Nambour's Big Pineapple and Ballina's Big Prawn (Leiper 1997b). Communities also have considerable scope for establishing events and festivals, usually on an annual basis, that may or may not focus on the local culture, economy or climate.

A final point to be made here about attractions is their susceptibility to fashion and social change, suggesting again that the ability of a destination to attract tourists is always subject to demand-side factors beyond its control. For instance, the emergence of the pleasure periphery was in large part a consequence of the high value assigned to sun exposure by Western societies during the latter half of the twentieth century, which converted beaches and warm climates into tourism resources. Throughout most of human history, the idea of lying on a beach to gain a suntan would have been considered ludicrous. Should sun exposure once again become unpopular due to concerns over its relationship to skin cancer and accelerated skin ageing, then the implications for 3S destinations such as the Gold Coast, and Australia in general, could be ominous as tourism managers are forced to reinvent or abandon their product base. This might, for example, require S3 destinations to place more emphasis on cultural attractions or wildlife-based tourism (see chapter 11).

■ 4.3.4 Cultural *links*

A desire to seek out exotic and unfamiliar venues has been an important motivating force for tourism throughout history. However, similarities in culture, language and religion are also a powerful 'pull' factor in some types of tourism (Burton 1995). This is partly because of the increased likelihood that people will migrate to culturally familiar countries (e.g. Finnish people to Sweden, British people to Australia) and subsequently foster VFR tourist flows between their old and new countries. Close cultural links are the main factor underlying the status of the United Kingdom as the second most important destination for outbound Australian tourists (figure 4.4).

Immigration aside, religious links have generated significant spiritually motivated tourist flows, as with American Jews to Israel, Muslim pilgrims to Saudi Arabia, and Roman Catholics to Italy and Vatican City. In addition, the tendency of destinations to attract culturally similar markets attests to the importance of the convenience and risk-minimisation factors in tourism. Simply put, many tourists feel insecure or inconvenienced by having to cope with unfamiliar languages and social norms, and therefore prefer destinations similar to their own origin areas (see chapter 6).

4.3.5 Availability *of services*

Tourists will usually avoid attractions if affiliated services are unavailable or of poor quality. The importance of transportation access has already been discussed in section 4.3.2, and to this must be added the presence of adequate accommodation, toilets and dining facilities. Visitor bureaus are also an important facilitating service. At a broader destination level, the presence of basic services nonspecific to tourism, such as policing and medical facilities, is also critical. The private sector usually provides the tourism-related elements (except for visitor bureaus), while local governments tend to provide the general services. In general, the MDCs are able to offer a superior level of general service provision because of their greater wealth and higher level of physical development.

4.3.6 Affordability

All other factors being equal, reductions in cost generate increased tourist traffic to a destination, as demonstrated by the effect of distance on transportation costs (section 4.3.2). The cost of living in a destination region relative to an origin area is one important component, since a high proportion of total trip costs are normally incurred within the destination through food and accommodation expenditures. Many travellers from the more affluent countries are attracted to LDCs such as Indonesia or Costa Rica because of the low relative costs of locally denominated goods and services. However, this advantage may be lost in situations where accommodation and other tourist-related goods and services are priced in American dollars or other nonlocal currencies. Tourist flows, nevertheless, are usually sensitive to significant exchange rate fluctuations.

A longitudinal study by Webber (2001) for the period between 1983 and 1997 found that in 40 per cent of all cases, Australians abandoned the idea of travelling to a particular country if it was experiencing exchange rate volatility. Moreover, Australians thinking about visiting the United States were found to consider relative prices in Asia and Europe (which are largely affected by exchange rate differentials) before making their decision.

Destination managers can do little to influence cost of living differentials, given that these result from macrolevel forces such as the development process and global or regional economic dynamics such as the so-called Asian economic crisis of the late 1990s. The situation is somewhat different with respect to exchange rates, as national governments can and do intervene in the money markets, or announce radical currency revaluations, when such actions are deemed to be in the national interest. Destinations within a currency bloc (such as most of the European Union), or within a country, however, have no such power. When a high national or bloc currency places the industry at a disadvantage, managers at the provincial or local level can attempt to offset its potentially negative effects through the implementation of price reductions and other incentives. Alternatively, they may restructure their marketing campaigns to attract higher-end markets that are less sensitive to monetary cost.

■ 4.3.7 Peace, *stability and safety*

The tourist market is also sensitive to any suggestion of social or political instability within a destination, given the in situ or 'on site' nature of consumption inherent to tourism — that is, consumers must travel to the product in order to engage in its 'consumption'. Accordingly, and not surprisingly, significant declines in tourist arrivals occur during periods of warfare in the Middle East (Mansfeld 1994) and the Balkans. Overnight visits to Croatia, for example, declined from five million in 1990 (before the Yugoslavian civil war) to 1.3 million in 1995 (immediately after the war), and rebounded to 2.6 million the following year (Needham 1997). In Israel, inbound arrivals during the first six months of 2001 were 53 per cent lower than during the comparable period one year earlier, due to the escalation in violence between the Israelis and Palestinians. One consequence was that the proportion of domestic guests in Israeli hotels increased from 53 per cent in September 2000 to 86 per cent in March 2002 (Israeli & Reichel 2003).

The negative effect of war on tourism, moreover, is not necessarily confined to the actual war zone or period of actual conflict. Richter and Waugh (1986) have demonstrated the destabilising impacts of the Sri Lankan civil war on tourism in India and the Maldives, and of the anti-Soviet war in Afghanistan on tourism in Pakistan. In Zambia, the development of tourism in the 1970s and 1980s was severely curtailed by the liberation wars prevailing in adjacent states during that period (Teye 1986).

More recently, the 2003 decline in cumulative international stayover arrivals (see table 3.1) was due in large part to the uncertainty associated with both the prelude and aftermath of the invasion of Iraq by the United States.

Tourism-directed terrorism

The deliberate targeting of tourists and tourism facilities by terrorists is an increasingly disturbing trend that has resulted from several factors (Nielsen 2001; Smith, V. 2004). Among these is the knowledge that the disruption of tourist flows can have severe economic and sociopolitical repercussions in countries where this sector makes a significant contribution to GNP. This was the main intent of the radical Islamic groups that launched a series of attacks on foreign tourists in Egypt during the 1990s (Weaver & Opperman 2000). Attacks on foreigners (and wealthy, white foreigners in particular) are also guaranteed to generate the publicity and media coverage sought by terrorist groups, while tourists and tourism facilities make easy and 'cost-effective' targets compared with military and political sites that are now better secured against terrorist attacks (see the case study on Bali at the end of this chapter). An extremely important factor is the expansion of tourism into remote areas of the pleasure periphery (e.g. rainforests and isolated beaches) where insurgent and terrorist groups are already established and where it is difficult to ensure the security of visitors. In some destinations, tourists have become attractive targets for kidnappers because of the ransom payments they generate (Aglionby 2001).

Personal safety issues

Beyond the macrolevel forces of war and terrorism, destination viability is affected by the extent to which tourists perceive a place to offer a high level of personal safety in terms of everyday health and wellbeing. Dissuasive factors include high crime levels (see section 9.3.3), susceptibility to natural disasters such as earthquakes and hurricanes, unsafe drinking water and food, and the presence of diseases such as SARS (see the case study at the end of chapter 1), malaria and AIDS. Tourist deaths and injuries associated with traffic-related and other accidents can also generate negative market perceptions, prompting some destinations to pursue strategies that attempt to minimise their occurrence (see Managing: For the minimisation of accidental tourist deaths).

MANAGING

For the minimisation of accidental tourist deaths

The threat of death is the ultimate risk faced by tourists, and one that, when it occurs, can seriously harm the image of a company or destination and result in costly litigation. It is therefore sensible, aside from the obvious humanitarian reasons, for managers to identify and control as much as possible the relevant risk factors so as to minimise the number of tourist deaths. While Australia is generally regarded as a low-risk destination, at least 307 accidental inbound tourist deaths were reported from 1997 to 2000, which represents about 20 per cent of all tourist deaths during that period (the remainder were attributed to natural causes). Ironically, only a few deaths were associated with the dramatic and high-profile deliberate events such as the Childers Backpackers Hostel fire of 2000 that generate widespread publicity. As reported by Wilks, Pendergast and Wood (2003), far more deaths are attributable to more mundane and arguably more preventable factors. The main cause of tourist death and injury, as in most other destinations, was land transport accidents (157), followed by drowning (62). Other causes, such as accidental falls (25), accidental poisoning (18) and plane crashes (10), were deemed too infrequent to yield any meaningful patterns.

Most of the land transport fatalities involved vehicle crashes where one or more occupants were killed, suggesting the importance of factors such as driving on the opposite side of the road to what is familiar, fatigue, signage provided in unfamiliar languages and failure to wear a seatbelt. Drownings were most often associated with exposure to unfamiliar marine environments while surfing, diving or snorkelling, and disproportionately involved males. All these factors, Wilks, Pendergast and Wood emphasise, could be effectively mitigated through prevention-oriented education and awareness initiatives from government as well as industry that target at-risk groups such as drivers from countries where one drives on the right and non-English-speakers. They regard such risk reduction strategies as being preferable to the standard practices of risk avoidance (e.g. cancelling or prohibiting certain events and activities in certain areas or by certain segments) or costly risk transfer (e.g. taking out insurance). The launch of a *Safety Tips for Visitors* video in 2002 as part of the National Visitor Safety Program (www.queenslandholidays.com.au/about_queensland/national_visitor _safety_ program.cfm) is cited as a promising example of a preventative strategy that will ultimately reduce the number of accidental inbound tourist deaths.

■ 4.3.8 Positive *market image*

Image is the sum of beliefs, attitudes and impressions held by a person or group of people towards some phenomenon (Baloglu & Brinberg 1997; Crompton 1979; Murphy 1985). Generally speaking, images can be either descriptive (e.g. the perception that the Gold Coast is a seaside resort) or evaluative (the perception that the Gold Coast is tacky and overdeveloped) (Walmsley & Jenkins 1993). Destination images are often an amalgam of assessments related to previously described pull factors such as accessibility, attractions, cultural links, affordability, stability and safety. Such images are immensely important in discretionary forms of tourism such as recreational vacations, where the destination is not predetermined by business or social considerations. This is because the product, at least for first-time visitors, is an intangible one that cannot be directly experienced prior to its consumption (i.e. prior to the actual visit) — see section 7.3.1. In such cases, potential visitors rely on their images in deciding to patronise one destination over another. Accordingly, image research within tourism studies has traditionally focused on the market awareness and evaluation of destinations and their products as a means of informing the marketing effort. The outcomes of this research often lead destination managers to manipulate their public symbols and promotion in order to improve their market image. This is illustrated by the VeryGC campaign of Australia's Gold Coast, which reinforces the destination's identity as 'active, dynamic and vibrant', according to Gold Coast Tourism (see figure 4.5).

To eventuate in an actual visit, the potential tourist must first be aware that a destination exists. This is seldom a problem for high-profile destination countries such as the United States, France, China or Australia, but a major problem for more obscure countries such as Namibia, Suriname or Qatar, or for less known places within individual countries. Next, it is vital that the awareness of the potential destination is positive. The continuing unrest in Iraq, for example, has made this formerly obscure country familiar to potential tourists in Australia and other MDCs. However, the negative nature of this awareness ensures that most travellers will avoid it. As described earlier, it is often a question of 'guilt by association', as the tourist market extends what is happening in Iraq to the entire Middle East. Similarly, the unsophisticated would-be tourist may apply a national stereotype to all destinations within a particular country, perceiving for example all Swiss localities in alpine/lederhosen terms, or all Californian cities as 'free-fire' zones dominated by street gangs. These stereotypes complicate the ability of tourist destination managers and marketers to disseminate a positive image to the tourism market. A discussion of tourism marketing, which includes the attempt to manipulate destination image within particular tourist markets, is provided in chapter 7.

■ **Figure 4.5**
Gold Coast promotional imagery reinforcing the core product

■ *4.3.9* **Pro-tourism** *policies*

The pull effect of a destination can be positively influenced by the introduction and reinforcement of pro-tourism policies that make a destination more accessible. Governments, for example, can and often do employ awareness campaigns among the resident population to promote a welcoming attitude towards visitors, in order to foster a positive market image. However, because such campaigns depend on widespread social engineering, and because their effects can be counteracted by random acts of violence, positive outcomes cannot be guaranteed. Furthermore, it is the behaviour of some tourists, and the structure and development of tourism itself, that often generate negative attitudes within the host community (see chapter 9). This implies that major structural changes to tourism itself, rather than awareness campaigns, may be required to effect a welcoming attitude.

In contrast, more control is possible at the microlevel, as when employers encourage and reward the pro-tourist behaviour of individual hotel employees, travel guides and customs officials. Other pro-tourism measures available to governments (especially at the national level) include the easing of entry requirements (as within the European Union), the reduction or elimination of tourism-related taxes, duties and other costs incurred by tourists or the tourism industry and the introduction of technologies that expedite security checks (see Technology and tourism: Biometrics as facilitator or impediment to travel?). The willingness of government to initiate financial incentives, however, is usually limited by its concurrent desire to maximise the revenues obtained from the tourism sector (see chapter 8). A special example of pro-tourism advocacy after the September 2001 attacks was when the US travel industry and government collaborated on a $40 million advertising campaign that encouraged Americans to resume their normal domestic travel patterns.

4.4 REGIONAL DESTINATION PATTERNS

The uneven distribution and growth of the global tourism sector is evident in the changing balance of tourism between the more developed and less developed worlds (section 4.2). International tourist destination patterns will now be examined from a regional perspective, along with the combinations of factors that have given rise to these patterns. The regions are outlined below in their order of importance as recipients of tourist arrivals. Table 4.2 provides stayover and population data (actual numbers and percentage shares) by major global regions and subregions, as defined by the World Tourism Organization (WTO). Data for the individual countries that comprise each region and subregion are provided in appendix 3. It is important to emphasise that these and all other stayover statistics in this book are impeded (as a basis for comparing the level of tourist activity between destinations) by their failure to take into account average length of stay. For example, a destination receiving 100 000 stayovers per year with an average stay of ten nights (one million visitor nights) has a greater level of tourism intensity than a destination that receives 200 000 stayovers per year with an average stay of three nights (600 000 visitor nights).

4.4.1 Europe

Europe is by far the most overrepresented destination region relative to its population, accommodating 14 per cent of the world's population but 57 per cent of its stayovers in 2002. This dominant position is further indicated by the fact that six of the top ten destination countries, and 16 of the top 25 (including Turkey), were located within Europe as of 2002 (see table 4.3). In accounting for this status, an examination of Europe reads as a showcase of the push and pull factors discussed in sections 3.5 and 4.3, respectively.

Densely populated and prosperous states border each other, making international travel convenient and affordable. Excellent land and air infrastructure facilitates traffic through increasingly open borders (see section 4.3.2), while the widespread adoption of the euro as a common regional currency eliminates the need to obtain foreign notes or allow for exchange rate differentials in trip budgeting. Tourist and nontourist services are generally excellent, and attractions range from outstanding and diverse historical and cultural opportunities to the natural attributes of the Mediterranean coast,

■ Table 4.2   *International stayover arrivals by region and subregion, 2002*

REGION SUBREGION	ARRIVALS (000s)	% OF ALL ARRIVALS	POPULATION[1] (000s)	% OF WORLD POPULATION
Europe	**399 759**	**56.9**	**853 938**	**13.8**
Northern Europe	46 385	6.6	87 895	1.4
Western Europe	141 099	20.1	185 347	3.0
Central/Eastern Europe	65 241	9.3	361 010	5.9
Southern Europe	130 971	18.6	145 580	2.4
East Mediterranean	16 062	2.3	74 106	1.2
The Americas	**114 853**	**16.3**	**846 134**	**13.7**
North America	81 616	11.6	415 864	6.7
Caribbean	16 058	2.3	37 153	0.6
Central America	4 701	0.7	38 233	0.6
South America	12 479	1.8	354 884	5.8
Asia and the Pacific	**131 294**	**18.7**	**3 563 116**	**57.8**
North-East Asia	73 634	10.5	1 514 834	24.6
South-East Asia	42 228	6.0	547 562	8.9
Australia/South Pacific	9 564	1.4	31 591	0.5
South Asia	5 869	0.8	1 469 129	23.8
Africa	**24 134**	**4.1**	**729 319**	**11.8**
North Africa	10 307	1.5	110 352	1.8
West Africa	2 945	0.4	239 486	3.9
Middle Africa	739	0.1	99 004	1.6
East Africa	6 291	0.9	230 085	3.7
Southern Africa	8 852	1.3	50 392	0.8
Middle East	**27 594**	**3.9**	**177 158**	**2.9**
World	**702 634**	**100.0**	**6 169 665**	**100.0**

Note:
[1]*Includes only those countries reporting data to the WTO*   **Source:** *Data derived from WTO (2003)*

the boreal forests of Scandinavia and the Alps. Since World War II the western half of Europe has experienced a high level of political and economic stability, while the disintegration of the former Soviet Union has eliminated most of the political uncertainty fostered by the Cold War. All these factors have contributed to a market image of 'Europe' as a safe and rewarding tourism experience. Chronic unrest in hotspots such as the Balkans, the Caucasus and Northern Ireland have not negatively affected the market image of 'Europe' as a whole.

Geographically, the above qualities, and hence intensity of tourism activity, are most evident in western Europe. Moving towards the northern and eastern peripheries of Europe (including all the former Soviet Union), the level of activity diminishes significantly. In northern Europe, and Scandinavia in particular, this is due to the reduced density of population. In eastern and southeastern Europe, however, the situation is more complex.

RANK	COUNTRY	INBOUND STAYOVERS (MILLIONS)
1	France	77.0
2	Spain	51.7
3	USA	41.9
4	Italy	39.8
5	China	36.8
6	United Kingdom	24.2
7	Canada	20.1
8	Mexico	19.7
9	Austria	18.6
10	Germany	18.0
11	Hong Kong SAR	16.6
12	Hungary	15.9
13	Greece	14.2
14	Poland	14.0
15	Malaysia	13.3
16	Turkey	12.8
17	Portugal	11.7
18	Thailand	10.9
19	Switzerland	10.0
20	The Netherlands	9.6
21	Russia	7.9
22	Saudi Arabia	7.5
23	Sweden	7.5
24	Singapore	7.0
25	Croatia	6.9

Source: *Data derived from WTO (2003)*

Former Soviet bloc states such as Poland, the Czech Republic and Hungary are already tourism-intensive because of their proximity to western Europe and the dissolution of their restrictive Soviet-era authoritarian systems. Future growth in tourism is likely to be fuelled by the continuing expansion of the European Union and a low cost of living relative to western Europe.

However, these could be somewhat offset by the erosion of the novelty factor that stimulated visitation after the collapse of the Soviet-era political regime. Poland, for example, moved from the number ten position among inbound destinations in 1999 to number 14 in 2004 largely for this reason.

The more easterly countries such as Ukraine, Russia and the former central Asian republics continue to experience problems with accessibility and services, and a high level of economic and political uncertainty, thus contributing to low relative tourist intakes. The Balkan region poses a particular danger for Europe because of the potential for its conflicts to reignite and spread into other parts of Europe, and because of the presence of radical Islamic elements in Bosnia and Macedonia.

■ 4.4.2 The *Americas*

The Americas are overrepresented as a regional tourist destination relative to their population, although not to the same extent as Europe. However, this status disguises significant variations in the relative importance of tourism at the subregional level.

North America

North America accounts for about 7 per cent of the global population, but 12 per cent of all stayovers. Consisting of only three countries (the United States, Mexico and Canada), North America accommodates two of the world's largest bilateral tourist flows: United States/Canada and United States/Mexico. Some 80 per cent of all inbound tourists to Canada are from the United States, while Canadians account for at least one-third of all arrivals to the United States. Proximity is the primary factor accounting for these flows, given that more than 90 per cent of Canadians reside within a one-day drive to the United States. Other factors include strong cultural affinities, the complementarity of attractions (i.e. Americans seeking the open spaces of Canada, and Canadians travelling to the American sunbelt during winter), good two-way infrastructural and political accessibility (i.e. through NAFTA), and a highly stable political and social situation in both countries.

While most crossborder travellers between the two countries apparently do not perceive the international boundary as a significant obstacle (Timothy & Tosun 2003), a somewhat changed climate has been evident as a result of the September 11 terrorist attacks and the invasion of Iraq by the United States. In the first case, elevated security concerns in the United States, often voiced as criticism of the relatively porous Canadian border, have made the crossing a slower and more stressful process for many travellers. In the second case, Canada's decision not to join the so-called 'coalition of the willing' or the continental 'Star Wars' missile defence program has strained bilateral relations, contributing to a growing sense of psychological separation as well as other impediments to crossborder traffic. Similar issues are impeding the travel of Mexicans to the United States, as are concerns about the influx of illegal migrants from that country and Central America.

The Caribbean

Owing to its endowment of 3S resources and its accessibility and proximity to the United States, the Caribbean has emerged as one of the world's most tourism-intensive subregions, with 0.6 per cent of the world's population but 2.3 per cent of its stayovers. The Caribbean is also the single most important region for the cruise ship industry and the region in which the cruise ship industry has the greatest presence relative to tourism as a whole (Wood 2004). This general level of overrepresentation, however, disguises major internal variations. Haiti and Trinidad & Tobago both have relatively weak tourism sectors, which belie the region's image as the personification of the pleasure periphery. In the former case this is due to decades of instability and extreme poverty, and in the latter case due to an economy sustained by oil wealth and industralisation. Cuba's potential, as described in chapter 2, has been hindered by the imposition of restrictions by the US government. In contrast, Caribbean SISODs such as the Bahamas, Antigua and Saint Lucia are among the world's most tourism-dependent countries (Weaver 2001a).

South and Central America

South and Central America, unlike North America, are underrepresented as tourist destinations. Spatially, the highest levels of international tourist traffic occur in the southern destinations of Argentina, Uruguay, Brazil and Chile, which each had between one and four million tourist arrivals during 2002. Most of this traffic is from other subregional countries, given isolation from major international markets (Santana 2001). Factors that account for the overall underrepresentation of South America include isolation from the major origin regions of North America and Europe in particular, poor accessibility and a general lack of international standard tourism services. Other considerations include prolonged periods of political instability throughout the region, resultant negative market images and an atmosphere of hyperinflation and economic uncertainty that prevailed throughout much of the late twentieth century (Santana 2001).

■ 4.4.3 Asia–Pacific

The Asia–Pacific region represents the reverse situation to Europe with respect to relative share of population and stayover totals. However, as with the Americas, its size and complexity warrant analysis at the subregional level.

North-East Asia

North-East Asia has the largest subregional tourism sector in absolute numbers, but this pales in comparison with its one-quarter share of the global population. With almost three-quarters of the intake, China and Hong Kong together dominate the market. To place China's current status as the world's number five destination in perspective, it is interesting to note that only 303 foreign visitors were allowed to enter the country in 1968 (Zhang, Pine & Zhang 2000). Since the 1970s, the Chinese government has expanded inbound tourism through a policy of **incremental access** that has seen the number of cities open to inbound tourists increase from 60 in 1979 to 1068 by 1994 (Bailey 1995). Most of China is now accessible to foreign tourists, except for some areas near international borders and military sites, as well as certain remote regions. Nevertheless, inbound tourism remains concentrated in eastern cities such as Shanghai, Beijing and Shenzen (CNTA, nd). China is unique in that a high proportion of inbound tourists are 'compatriots', that is ethnic Chinese residents of Taiwan, Hong Kong SAR and Macau SAR.

South-East Asia

Next in relative importance on a subregional basis is South-East Asia, where the proportional share of population does not as dramatically exceed its share of stayovers as in Northeast Asia. The internal subregional pattern is diverse, with Malaysia, Singapore and Thailand displaying the most developed tourism sectors, while Cambodia and Laos remain in an incipient phase. The former three countries have benefited from the presence of major transit hubs, good infrastructure, prolonged political and social stability, a diverse array of high-quality attractions, favourable exchange rates relative to major tourist markets, a mostly positive market image and the pursuit of pro-tourism policies by government. Large and prosperous ethnic Chinese populations also engage in extensive travel between these countries (Hall & Page 2000). The emergence of Indonesia as an important destination country was curtailed in the late 1990s by political and social instability, which culminated in the Bali bombings of 2002 (see the case study at the end of this chapter).

Australia/South Pacific (Oceania)

International tourism in Oceania is impeded by the relative remoteness of this region from major market sources. However, it is facilitated by high-profile natural attractions and a favourable exchange rate against the world's major currencies. The regional image, however, has been harmed by recent instability in Fiji (Rao 2002) and the Solomon Islands. As is the Caribbean, the South Pacific islands are overrepresented as a tourist destination, accounting for about 0.5 per cent of the global population, but 1.4 per cent of stayovers. To an even higher degree than in the Caribbean, tourism in the region is unevenly distributed, with just two of 22 destination states or dependencies (Guam and the Northern Mariana Islands) accounting for almost two-thirds of all stayovers (see appendix 3). Also similarly to the Caribbean, Oceania is a subregion of the pleasure periphery where historic and contemporary political and economic linkages largely dictate the nature of local tourism systems. Guam, for example, is dominated by Japanese and American tourists, New Caledonia by French visitors, and the Cook Islands by New Zealanders. Australia is influential in the tourism systems of several Oceanic destinations, including Papua New Guinea, Fiji and Vanuatu. Australia, as a specific destination country, is considered under a separate subsection (section 4.4.6).

South Asia

South Asia is the most underrepresented inbound tourism region relative to population, with almost one-quarter of the world's people but less than one per cent of its inbound tourists. A negative regional destination image, a rudimentary network of services and facilities, widespread poverty and distance from major markets are all factors that have contributed to this deficit. Recent events and issues that have exacerbated the negative image of the region include the United States-led invasion of Afghanistan in 2001 and its aftermath, the acquisition of nuclear technology by Pakistan and ongoing sectarian violence, the Maoist insurgency in Nepal and the massacre of its royal family in 2001, the rogue status of Iran and rising tensions with the United States, and the Indian Ocean tsunami of 2004. Nevertheless, pleasure periphery enclaves flourish in the Maldives as well as in the Indian states of Goa and Kerala.

■ 4.4.4 Africa

Africa as a region displays a high discrepancy between population share and stayover share. This underrepresentation can be accounted for by the persistently negative image of Africa in the tourist market, foreign exchange constraints, chronic political instability, a lack of skilled labour to develop the industry, and weak institutional frameworks that inhibit effective tourism planning and management. Other factors include widespread corruption, distance from the major markets, competition from more stable intervening opportunities, poor infrastructural developments and concerns over personal safety due to high crime rates and widespread infectious diseases such as AIDS (Dieke 2000).

Africa, similarly to South and Central America, is characterised by a skewed pattern of spatial distribution that favours the extreme north (e.g. Tunisia and Morocco) and the extreme south (e.g. South Africa and Botswana). Tourism in the north is fuelled by 3S-motivated tourists from Europe, while intra-regional sources dominate the south. In contrast, Middle and West Africa are minor destinations for international tourist arrivals that embody the dissuasive factors outlined earlier. The largest African state in terms of inbound stayovers, South Africa, managed a global ranking of only twenty-eighth place in 2002, based on 6.55 million recorded arrivals.

■ 4.4.5 The *Middle East*

Resident population and inbound intakes are roughly equal in percentages terms in the Middle East. However, as we have seen with all the other regions, this fact obscures a pattern of internal variability. For example, Egypt, the United Arab Emirates and Jordan have relatively strong tourism industries, while Saudi Arabia's robust tourism sector consists almost entirely of Muslim pilgrims visiting Mecca and other holy sites associated with Islam (Ahmed 1992). In contrast, tourism is embryonic in Yemen and Libya (see Breakthrough tourism: Opening Libya to the world), and almost absent in Iraq. The Middle East, as a Muslim-dominated region, has been disproportionately harmed by the terrorism of September 2001 and the subsequent 'war on terrorism'.

BREAKTHROUGH TOURISM
Opening Libya to the world

Although not included in the infamous 'axis of evil' by US president George W. Bush, Libya has long had the reputation of a rogue state that supported terrorist organisations and pursued weapons of mass destruction under the leadership of the eccentric Colonel Moammar Ghaddafi. Resultant international sanctions, including a ban by many countries on travel and trade with Libya, have forced the regime since the early 2000s to engage in sweeping political and economic reforms. As part of this 'normalisation' strategy, the government is aggressively trying to develop and promote Libya as a major tourist destination. From having an inconsequential tourism industry in the mid-1990s, there are plans for one million inbound visitors and 100 000 hotel beds by 2010 (there were 100 000 inbound visitors in 2003), when it is anticipated that tourism will account for 10 per cent of the economy (MSNBC 2004). Among the resources that are expected to attract these tourists are 2000 km of mainly pristine coastline, extensive ruins from the Roman, Carthaginian and Greek civilisations, and dramatic desert landscapes. Initially, the novelty factor will also be a major draw as tourists vie to be among the first to visit the land of the mercurial colonel.

While converting the country into a major international destination, the Libyans are also adamant that this will not undermine the country's environmental and cultural integrity or sully its strongly Islamic character. Reconciling these two directives will be a major challenge, but one that the Libyans are hoping to achieve by promoting a 'controlled' model of tourism that focuses on education, adventure and the controlled movement of tourists (TravelVideo.TV 2004). Visitors will have to travel in groups connected with approved tour operators, and 'undesirable' (i.e. harder to monitor) markets such as backpackers will be discouraged. Alcohol will be allowed but only within the confines of certain international-standard hotels. Other challenges include moving away from a cash-only orientation, building up basic infrastructure and services, and attracting sufficient foreign investment within the context of a strongly socialised economy. Should Libya succeed in its efforts, this could be a critical step in the transformation of the Middle East from a region of perceived danger and instability to one of openness and opportunity that may eventually embrace other pariahs such as Iran and Syria.

4.4.6 Australia

Australia's share of the global inbound market steadily increased from 0.15 per cent in 1965 to 0.70 in 1997 before stabilising around that level (see table 4.4). It ranked in the thirty-fourth position among country destinations in 2002. The pattern of increase, however, has been uneven. Low or negative growth in the mid-1970s is associated with the rise of oil prices in the wake of the Yom Kippur War between Israel and its Arab neighbours, which negatively affected the affordability of most long-haul destinations. Similar downturns in the early 1980s and 1990s were outcomes of economic recessions in the major markets. The high growth from 1986 to 1988 represented not only good conditions in major

■ **Table 4.4**   *International stayover arrivals in Australia, 1965–2003*

YEAR	NUMBER OF ARRIVALS	GROWTH (%)	% OF GLOBAL STAY OVER ARRIVALS	YEAR	NUMBER OF ARRIVALS	GROWTH (%)	% OF GLOBAL STAY OVER ARRIVALS
1965	173 300	–	0.15	1985	1 142 600	12.6	0.35
1966	187 300	8.1	0.16	1986	1 429 400	25.1	0.42
1967	215 100	14.8	0.17	1987	1 784 900	24.9	0.49
1968	236 700	10.0	0.18	1988	2 249 300	26.0	0.57
1969	275 800	16.5	0.19	1989	2 080 300	–7.5	0.49
1970	338 400	22.7	0.20	1990	2 214 900	6.5	0.48
1971	388 700	14.9	0.22	1991	2 370 400	7.0	0.51
1972	426 400	9.7	0.23	1992	2 603 300	9.8	0.52
1973	472 100	10.7	0.24	1993	2 996 200	15.1	0.58
1974	532 700	12.8	0.26	1994	3 361 700	12.2	0.61
1975	516 000	–3.1	0.23	1995	3 725 800	10.8	0.66
1976	531 900	3.1	0.23	1996	4 164 800	11.8	0.69
1977	563 300	5.9	0.23	1997	4 317 900	3.7	0.70
1978	630 600	11.9	0.24	1998	4 167 200	–3.5	0.65
1979	793 300	25.8	0.28	1999	4 459 500	7.0	0.67
1980	904 600	14.0	0.32	2000	4 931 400	10.6	0.72
1981	936 700	3.5	0.33	2001	4 855 700	–1.5	0.71
1982	954 700	1.9	0.33	2002	4 841 200	–0.3	0.69
1983	943 900	–1.1	0.33	2003	4 745 900	–2.0	0.69
1984	1 015 100	7.5	0.32				

Source: ABS (1996, 2001 and 2005); ONT (1998); WTO (1998a)

market economies, but also the staging of high-profile events such as the 1988 bicentennial of European settlement and the international exposition in Brisbane that same year. The 1989 decline, accordingly, should be interpreted at least in part as a correction or normalisation of visitor intakes following these major events. The same effect occurred in the wake of the 2000 Sydney Olympics, while subsequent declines reflected the sensitivity of Australia to incidents of financial and political instability within the broader region, and its vulnerability as a long-haul destination.

■ Table 4.5   *Australian inbound market regions and major countries, 1991–2003*

MARKET REGION SELECTED COUNTRY	1991 (000s)	SHARE (%)	1995 (000s)	SHARE (%)	1999–2000 (000s)	SHARE (%)	2003 (000s)	SHARE (%)
Asia	**902**	**38.0**	**1872**	**50.2**	**1932**	**41.4**	**1917**	**40.4**
Japan	529	22.3	783	21.0	706	15.2	628	13.2
Singapore	88	3.7	202	5.4	277	6.0	253	5.3
South Korea	24	1.0	168	4.5	139	3.0	207	4.4
China	—	—	43	1.1	120	2.6	176	3.7
Malaysia	48	2.0	108	2.9	147	3.2	156	3.3
Hong Kong	—	—	—	—	—	—	129	2.7
Indonesia	37	1.6	135	3.6	85	1.8	90	1.9
Taiwan	35	1.5	152	4.1	141	3.0	87	1.8
Europe	**531**	**22.4**	**752**	**20.2**	**1132**	**24.4**	**1212**	**25.5**
United Kingdom	273	11.5	365	9.8	598	12.9	673	14.2
Germany	78	3.3	124	3.3	147	3.2	138	2.9
Oceania	**566**	**23.8**	**647**	**17.4**	**909**	**19.5**	**957**	**20.2**
New Zealand	481	20.3	538	14.5	773	16.6	839	17.7
Americas	**336**	**14.2**	**382**	**10.5**	**551**	**11.8**	**538**	**11.3**
United States	272	11.5	305	8.2	437	9.4	422	8.9
Sub-Saharan Africa	**17**	**0.7**	**42**	**1.0**	**72**	**1.5**	**69**	**1.5**
Middle East and North Africa	**15**	**0.6**	**29**	**0.8**	**53**	**1.1**	**53**	**1.1**
Total[1]	**2370**	**100.0**	**3726**	**100.0**	**4652**	**100.0**	**4746**	**100.0**

Notes:
[1] Includes 'not stated'

Source: *Data derived from ABS (1996, 1998b, 2001, 2003)*

Australia's inbound traffic is diverse, and this is a characteristic deliberately cultivated by the federal and state governments in order to avoid dependency on one or two primary markets. As shown in table 4.5, East

Asian sources are dominant, but have displayed an inconsistent pattern of growth through the 1990s and early 2000s. Strong growth in the first half of the decade, attributable to robust domestic economic growth, was followed by decline, especially in South Korea and Indonesia, as a consequence of the Asian economic crisis. More recently, South Korea has recovered well, while the Chinese inbound market has demonstrated consistent and dramatic growth. In contrast to East Asia, traditional markets in the United Kingdom, western Europe, New Zealand and the United States grew slowly in the early 1990s and more rapidly in the late 1990s. The intake from the United States and mainland Europe has since stabilised.

4.5 *I*NTERNAL DESTINATION PATTERNS

The consideration of destinations has thus far been directed towards the global and regional levels, with individual countries, for the sake of simplicity, being treated as uniform entities. In reality, the spatial distribution of tourism within countries also tends to be uneven. This **subnational inequality** is evident even in small pleasure periphery destinations such as Zanzibar (Tanzania), where tourism accommodations are concentrated at seaside locations or in the capital city (figure 4.6). In general, water-focused resources such as coastlines, lakes, rivers and waterfalls are considered potentially attractive as tourist venues in most destinations, and therefore help to promote a spatially uneven pattern of tourism development.

Large urban concentrations also tend to harbour a significant portion of a country's tourism sector. This is because of their status as international gateways, the high level of accommodation and other tourism-related services that they provide, the availability of important urban tourist attractions, and their status as prominent venues for business and VFR tourism (Hinch 1996).

Within these cities the pattern of tourism distribution is also uneven, being highly concentrated in downtown districts where accommodation and attractions are usually clustered (Hall, Jenkins & Kearsley 1997). Increasingly, however, tourism activity is also occurring in the transitional urban–rural fringe that separates the city from the countryside (see Contemporary issue: Distinctive tourism dynamics in the urban–rural fringe). The management implications of spatial concentration are compounded in many destinations by the concurrent presence of temporal concentrations, or the tendency of tourism activity to be focused on particular times of the year. The issue of seasonality is addressed more thoroughly in chapter 8.

Planners, academics and others are accustomed to thinking of the landscape as being divided into clear urban and rural categories. Yet a growing proportion of the population in countries such as Australia, New Zealand, the United States and Canada resides in the **urban–rural fringe** (or **'exurbs'**), a transitional zone that combines urban and rural characteristics and benefits from proximity to each. The urban–rural fringe is created because lower taxes, cheaper land costs, reduced crime and lessened congestion pull residents and businesses deeper into the countryside, while the countervailing attractions of urban employment, markets and services pull them towards the city. The urban–rural mode of thinking prevails among tourism stakeholders as well, even though there is increasing evidence that tourism in the urban–rural fringe is a major sector with distinctive characteristics that require special management considerations (Weaver 2005).

First, it has a distinct combination of products that may include theme and amusement parks (e.g. Dream World on the Gold Coast), **tourist shopping villages** (small towns such as Tamborine Mountain and Maleny (Queensland) where the downtown is dominated by tourist-oriented businesses), factory outlet malls and golf courses. Second, distinct market characteristics are evident in the preponderance of excursionists who maintain overnight accommodation in nearby urban areas, and in the presence of **hyperdestinations** where tourist arrivals dramatically outnumber local residents. In the case of Tamborine Mountain, 7000 residents play host each year to approximately 500 000 visitors. A high proportion of these visitors, moreover, are residents of the nearby urban area who may or may not meet the travel distance thresholds associated with domestic tourism. This all suggests that revenues derived largely from the use of overnight accommodation are minimal and do not compensate for the congestion and utility use generated by large numbers of visitors. Third, management of exurban tourism is complicated by the fact this zone is inherently unstable, in transition and characterised by conflict among the diverse users of this exceptionally complex space.

Given these distinctive traits, Weaver (2005) argues that exurban tourism should be regarded as a distinct subfield alongside urban and rural tourism. Relevant areas of inquiry include analysis of how exurban tourism is linked to adjacent urban and rural tourism products, what strategies are adopted by the residents of hyperdestinations to cope with extreme visitor numbers and how chronic flux in external environments such as residential development and agriculture affects and is affected by the tourism sector.

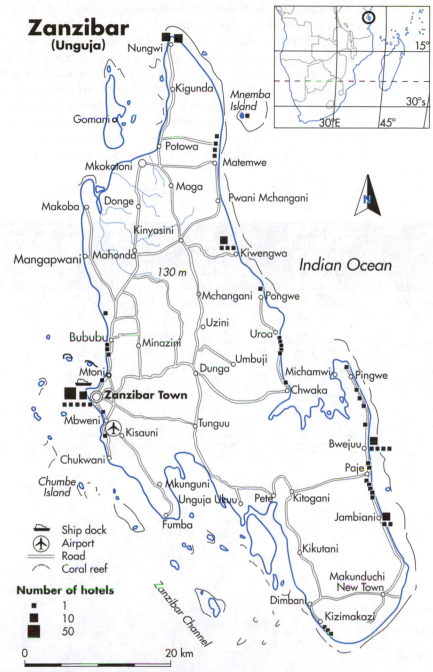

Zanzibar
(Unguja)

Nungwi

Kigunda

Gomani

Potowa

Mkokotoni

Matemwe

Moga

Makoba

Donge

Pwani Mchangani

Kinyasini

Mangapwani Mahonda

130 m

Mchangani Pongwe

Uzini

Uroa

Bububu

Minazini

Umbuji

Mtoni

Dunga

Michamwi Pingwe

Zanzibar Town

Chwaka

Mbweni

Kisauni

Tunguu

Bwejuu

Chukwani

Paje

Chumbe Island

Mkunguni

Kitogani

Unguja Ukuu Pete

Jambiani

Fumba

Kikutani

Makunduchi New Town

Zanzibar Channel

Dimbani

Kizimakazi

Mnemba Island

Indian Ocean

N

Ship dock
Airport
Road
Coral reef

Number of hotels

■ 1
■ 10
■ 50

0   20 km

15°
30°s
30°E   45°

■ 4.5.1 The *Australian pattern*

The basic pattern shown in figure 4.7 pertains to Australia, where New South Wales and Queensland together account for almost 60 per cent of visitor nights in both the inbound and domestic tourism sectors (table 4.6). However, it should also be noted that this figure is similar to the proportion of Australia's total population that resides in these two states. Further analysis at the substate level shows that inbound tourism, as in Zanzibar, is highly concentrated along the coastline, and especially in the portion of coast extending from Cairns to Sydney, and in large urban areas (figure 4.7). The first pattern is consistent with the extension of the pleasure periphery into northeastern Australia. In the remainder of the country inbound tourism is largely a phenomenon of the state or territorial capitals, with the interior represented only by Canberra and three areas within the Northern Territory. Domestic tourism, in contrast to inbound tourism, is more evenly distributed in comparison with state populations, due largely to the high incidence of geographically non-discretionary VFR travel within that sector.

■ **Table 4.6** *Distribution of domestic and inbound visitor-nights in Australia by destination state or territory, 2003*

STATE/ TERRITORY	NO. OF INBOUND VISITOR NIGHTS (000s)	% OF ALL INBOUND VISITOR NIGHTS	NO. OF DOMESTIC VISITOR NIGHTS[1] (000s)	% OF ALL DOMESTIC VISITOR NIGHTS	% OF NATIONAL POPU-LATION
NSW	42 272	36	88 188	30	32
Qld	26 757	23	78 839	27	22
Vic	25 998	22	54 892	19	20
WA	12 790	11	29 997	10	11
SA	4 512	4	21 146	7	1
NT	2 593	2	6 141	2	8
ACT	2 369	2	5 235	2	2
Tas	1 330	1	9 647	3	4
Total	119 093	100	294 112	100	100

Notes:
[1] *Refers to Australians 15 years of age and older.*

Source: *Data derived from ABS (2004)*

■ **Figure 4.7**
Top 16 destination regions in Australia for inbound visitors, 2002

Source: *Data derived from BTR (2002)*

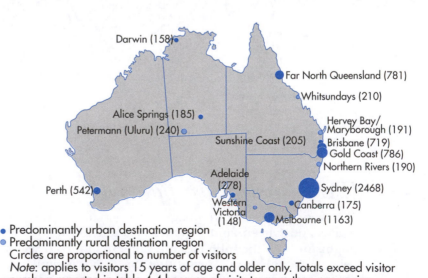

- Predominantly urban destination region
- Predominantly rural destination region
Circles are proportional to number of visitors
Note: applies to visitors 15 years of age and older only. Totals exceed visitor numbers reported in table 4.4 because of visits to more than one region.

CHAPTER REVIEW

Most inbound tourism occurs in the more developed world. However, the less developed world's share is gradually increasing due to the emergence of 3S tourism as a major form of activity after World War II. Furthermore, economic growth and the appearance of a substantial middle class within the LDCs is promoting increased inbound travel between the LDCs as well as from LDCs to MDCs. The formation of a pleasure periphery at the interface of the more and less developed worlds is indicative of tourism's increasing status as a global economic activity and agent of landscape change. Europe, North America, Oceania and the Caribbean are all over-represented as destination regions relative to their resident populations. In contrast, South America, Africa and Asia are all underrepresented. The pattern of uneven distribution is also apparent within each of these regions and within individual countries such as Australia, where coastal areas and metropolitan area cores and exurbs account for most inbound and domestic tourism activity.

Tourism's uneven pattern of distribution reflects differences in the influence of the 'pull' factors that encourage tourism in particular locations, and hence help to determine the global pattern of tourism systems. These pull factors include the geographical proximity of destinations to markets, infrastructural and political accessibility, the availability of sufficient attractions and services, cultural links between origin and destination regions, affordability, political and social stability at the local, national and regional levels, perceived personal safety, market image, and the existence of pro-tourism policies. Central to the management of tourism destinations is how much managers and planners are able to influence these forces. Nothing can be done, for example, to change the actual geographical distance of a destination from a market, or to modify the destination's primary physical features. Similarly, little can be done, especially at the subnational scale, to influence exchange rates or the level of sociopolitical stability. However, the negative effects of these factors, if they exist, can be counteracted at least to some extent through effective image manipulation, the implementation of pro-tourism policies, the establishment of 'created' attractions, and the provision of political and infrastructural access to target markets.

SUMMARY OF KEY TERMS

Global inequality in tourism

A fundamental distinction pertaining to the relative spatial distribution of tourism at a global level

- **More developed countries (MDCs):** countries characterised by a relatively high level of economic development. Collectively, the more developed world remains dominant as a recipient and generator of global tourist flows
- **Less developed countries (LDCs):** countries characterised by a relatively low level of economic development. Until recently, the less developed world has not been very important as a recipient or generator of global tourist flows

3S tourism

A tourism product based on the provision of sea, sand and sun; that is, focusing on beach resorts

- **Sunbelt:** the name frequently applied to the 3S-oriented American portion of the pleasure periphery. Well-known destinations within the sunbelt include Hawaii, southern California, Las Vegas (Nevada), Arizona, Texas and Florida
- **Pleasure periphery:** those less economically developed regions of the globe that are being increasingly mobilised to provide 3S and alpine tourism products
- **SISODs** (small island states or dependencies): geopolitical entities with a population of less than three million permanent residents and a land mass of less than $28\,000$ km^2. SISODs are overrepresented as tourist destinations because of their ample 3S tourism resources
- **North–south flow:** a common term used to describe the dominant pattern of international tourist traffic from the MDCs (located mainly in the northern latitudes, except for Australia and New Zealand) to the LDCs (located mainly to the south of the MDCs)

Pull factors

Forces that help to stimulate a tourism product by 'pulling' consumers towards particular destinations

- **Distance–decay:** in tourism, the tendency of inbound flows to decline as origin regions become more distant from the destination
- **Infrastructural accessibility:** the extent to which a destination is physically accessible to markets by air routes, highways, ferry links, etc., and through entry/exit facilities such as seaports and airports
- **Political accessibility:** the extent to which visitors are allowed entry into a destination by a governing authority
- **Image:** in tourism, the sum of the beliefs, attitudes and impressions that individuals or groups hold towards tourist destinations or aspects of destinations. Destination image is a critical factor in attracting or repelling visitors
- **Incremental access:** a policy, practised most notably in China, whereby new destinations within a country are gradually opened up to international (and possibly domestic) tourists

Subnational inequality

The tendency of tourism within countries, states and individual cities to be spatially concentrated

- **Urban–rural fringe** (or **exurbs**): a transitional zone surrounding larger urban areas that combines urban and rural characteristics and benefits from proximity to each
- **Tourist shopping villages:** small towns where the downtown is dominated by tourism-related businesses such as boutiques, antique shops and cafés
- **Hyperdestinations:** destinations where the annual intake of visitors dramatically outnumbers the permanent resident population; often characteristic of tourist shopping villages

QUESTIONS

1. (a) How much is spatial inequality evident in tourism at the international, national, subnational and local level?
   (b) Why does this inequality occur?
   (c) What are the managerial implications of this inequality at all four levels cited in (a)?

2. (a) Describe the forces that are likely to 'pull' tourists towards particular destinations.
   (b) How much are destinations, and Australia in particular, able to influence or manage each of these forces?

3. (a) What are the arguments for and against the use of biometric technology in clearing inbound tourists for entry into a destination country?
   (b) How else should this technology be applied within the tourism system?

4. (a) Why are tourists being increasingly targeted by terrorist groups?
   (b) What can destination managers do to combat this trend?

5. (a) Why is Europe, in general, far more developed as a tourist destination region than Africa?
   (b) What strategies could African countries implement to improve their status as destinations?

6. What strategies could be implemented in order to increase Australia's share of global stayover tourism to 1 per cent of the total? Take into account the data provided in table 4.5.

7. (a) Why is tourism in the urban–rural fringe described as distinct and especially complex?
   (b) What challenges does this pose to managers of destinations in the urban–rural fringe?

chapter review

EXERCISES

1 (a) Rank the following five destination countries beginning with the one that you would most like to visit for a one-month vacation, and ending with the one that you would be least interested in visiting for a one-month vacation.

Togo   Libya
United States   Switzerland
Indonesia

(b) Indicate the reasons for your rankings.
(c) Assigning a value of '5' for each first choice, '4' for each second choice, and so on, add up the class responses for each of the five destinations.
(d) Identify the overall class rankings.
(e) Do any consistent patterns emerge as to the reasons given for these rankings?

2 (a) Using appendix 3, identify the top 25 destination countries for 1990 in terms of the number of international stayover arrivals.
(b) How does this list of countries compare with table 4.3, which provides the 2002 rankings?
(c) What factors help to account for these patterns?

FURTHER READING

Aramberri, J. & Butler, R. (Eds) 2004 *Tourism Development: Issues for a Vulnerable Industry.* **Clevedon, UK: Channel View.** Several chapters in this edited book discuss the links between tourism and terrorism as well as sociopolitical instability more generally.

Dieke, P. (Ed.) 2000. *The Political Economy of Tourism Development in Africa.* **Elmsford, US: Cognizant Communication.** This compendium of 22 chapters is the first academic book to focus on contemporary tourism in sub-Saharan Africa.

Duval, T. (Ed.) 2004. *Tourism in the Caribbean: Trends, Development, Prospects.* **London: Routledge.** The Caribbean is arguably the most tourism-intensive of the world's regions, and this edited volume considers relevant issues such as the role of hedonism in developing the product, cruise ships, ecotourism, postcolonialism, and community and small business perspectives.

Gössling, S. (Ed.) 2003. *Tourism and Development in Tropical Islands: Political Ecology Perspectives.* **Cheltenham, UK: Edward Elgar.** Ten case studies of SISODs and other tropical island destinations are provided in this book, which focuses on the political and ecological factors that have influenced the growth of this sector.

McKercher, B. & Lew, A. 2003. 'Distance Decay and the Impact of Effective Tourism Exclusion Zones on International Travel Flows'. *Journal of Travel Research* 42: 159–65. The authors analyse the distance–decay effect in Hong Kong outbound tourism and identify the skewing effect of what they term 'effective tourism exclusion zones'.

Crisis and resilience in Bali's tourism sector

During the latter half of the twentieth century, the 2095-square-kilometre Indonesian island of Bali developed into one of the icons of the South-East Asian pleasure periphery. In 2001, it hosted 2.5 million visitors and generated US$1.4 billion of Indonesia's total international tourism intake of US$5.4 billion. This represented 80 per cent of the island's income and 40 per cent of all employment in the formal sector (Henderson 2003). An essential factor in Bali's success as a tourist destination has been its diverse array of tourism products, which range from remote national parks to unique cultural landscapes, prototypical tropical beaches and resort concentrations ranging from the tacky and crowded (Kuta) to the exclusive (Nusa Dua) (Minca 2000). Access to these attractions and products, moreover, is made easy by the compactness of the island and a good road network, so that a trip to the rainforest in the early morning can be followed by a late afternoon session at a beach resort. Accessing Bali itself is simplified by the presence of a major international airport that accommodates direct flights from major origin regions. Dominant among the latter are the regional markets of Japan and Australia, which respectively provided 350 000 and 250 000 visitors to Bali in 2001. Other factors include a low cost of living relative to major market countries, a generally favourable exchange rate on the Indonesian currency (the rupiah), and protourism policies of its government.

For most of its history as a pleasure periphery resort destination, Bali has also enjoyed an entrenched reputation for sociopolitical stability and personal safety that belies the reputation of Indonesia as a whole. Racked by separatist insurgencies in West Papua, Aceh and East Timor, and more recently plagued by sectarian conflicts between Christians and Muslims and a resurgence of Islamic radicalism, Indonesia is a 'chronic crisis' destination that has been unable (outside of Bali) to achieve its potential as a major tourism country. Therefore, for the Balinese tourism authorities, the contrast with Indonesia (i.e. *not* Indonesia, an *enclave* of peace, *Hindu* not Muslim) and its identity as a separate destination have been as much an essential element of its international branding as its presentation as an exotic tropical paradise. This does not mean that Bali has been completely unaffected by its association with and proximity to the rest of Indonesia, as demonstrated by occasional flare-ups between Balinese natives and migrants from other Indonesian islands, and by a 'Boycott Bali' campaign that was organised in the late 1990s by Australian and New Zealander supporters of East Timor's independence movement (Hitchcock 1999). It does mean, however, that such episodes have not seriously damaged its positive image or posed any long-term threat to its tourism industry.

These strategies and assumptions about Balinese tourism were severely tested by the bombings of two nightclubs in Kuta by radical Muslims on 12 October 2002, which killed more than 200 people and injured another 300, many of them Australian. At least 2000 foreign tourists almost immediately left the island, and hotel occupancy rates fell from 75 per cent on 11 October to 33 per cent on 19 October and 10 per cent soon after that in some areas (Henderson 2003). Australians were warned by their government to stay away from 'high-risk' regional destinations that included not only all of Indonesia but also Brunei, Cambodia, Laos, Malaysia, Myanmar, the Philippines, Singapore and Thailand.

The Balinese and Indonesian government authorities responded to this crisis with what Henderson (2003) describes as a four-stage strategy of rescue, rehabilitation, normalisation and expansion. The short-term timeframe of the first two stages included the commitment of funds by the national government to clean and rebuild Kuta, the establishment of crisis media centres in Jakarta and Bali, the formation of a recovery taskforce, the holding of high-level government meetings in Bali to demonstrate confidence in the island's security and lobbying efforts aimed at compelling foreign governments to lift their travel warnings. These were not intended to achieve the unrealistic goal of immediately restoring normal international visitor flows but rather to send a positive message of reassurance and condolence that would prepare the way for that outcome. Concurrently, major efforts were made through aggressive promotion, appeals to patriotism and price discounts to attract domestic tourists, who could keep the tourism economy afloat until the inbound flow was normalised. In preparation for the last two stages, US$3 million was allocated to improve security, develop new products, and devise new marketing campaigns. Some of the themes integrated into these campaigns included the message that Bali was still Bali, that foreigners should show solidarity with the Balinese people and help rebuild the island's economy through their visits, and that Bali is actually safer than ever because of the new security measures.

By the latter part of November 2002, earlier than expected, normal international visitor flows to Bali were effectively restored. Interviews with 200 household heads in heavily affected areas, moreover, indicated the perception of residents that the tourism economy had sufficiently recovered (Toh, Khan & Erawan 2004). While the bombings clearly had had a major negative impact on Bali's tourism industry, the effect was surprisingly temporary. The rapid recovery was first of all an attestation of effective protourism crisis management by the regional and national tourism authorities, which devised and implemented short- and long-term responses that took into consideration, among other things, the need to treat domestic and international markets differently. However, it is unlikely that these strategies would have been as effective had it not been for the fundamental strength and resilience of the pull factors that contributed in the first instance to Bali's emergence as a major destination.

Questions

1 (a) Why is Indonesia referred to as a 'chronic crisis' destination?

  (b) How does Bali being part of Indonesia affect its development as a tourist destination negatively and positively?

  (c) What strategies can the Balinese tourism authorities employ to cope with their location within Indonesia?

2 What are the negative consequences for Bali potentially associated with focusing on the domestic Indonesian tourist market to expedite recovery following the bombings?

3 (a) How much should the experience and memory of the bombings be incorporated into Bali's tourism product development and international marketing?

  (b) Should there be any difference in the bombings-related marketing directed towards Australia (i.e. a country seriously affected by the bombings) and the United States (i.e. a country not seriously affected)?

5

The tourism
product

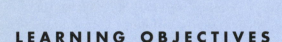

LEARNING OBJECTIVES

After studying this chapter, you should be able to:

1 list the major types of natural and cultural tourist attractions

2 describe the diverse array of these attractions

3 discuss the management implications of the different attraction types

4 identify the various attraction attributes that can be assessed in order to make informed management and planning decisions

5 explain the basic characteristics of the tourism industry's main sectors

6 describe the growing diversification and specialisation of products provided by the tourism industry

7 discuss the concepts of integration and globalisation as they apply to the tourism industry.

5.1 INTRODUCTION

The previous chapter outlined the 'pull' factors that stimulate the development of particular places as tourist destinations, and described the tourism status of the world's major regions in the context of these forces. Chapter 5 continues to examine the supply side of the tourism system by focusing on the **tourism product**, which can be defined as the combination of **tourist attractions** and the tourism industry (figure 2.8). While commercial attractions such as theme parks, casinos and museums are elements of the tourist industry, others, such as generic noncommercial scenery and climate, are not. For this reason, and because they are an essential and diverse component of tourism systems, attractions are examined separately from the industry in this chapter (section 5.2). Section 5.3 follows with a discussion of the other major components of the tourism industry, including travel agents, transportation, accommodation, tour operators and merchandise. The chapter concludes by considering structural changes within the contemporary tourism industry.

5.2 TOURIST ATTRACTIONS

Tourist attractions are an essential 'pull' factor (see chapter 4), and destinations should therefore benefit from having a diversity of such resources. The compilation of an **attraction inventory** is a fundamental step towards ensuring that a destination realises its full tourism potential in this regard. There is at the present time no classification system of attractions that is universally followed among tourism stakeholders. However, a distinction between mainly 'natural' and mainly 'cultural' is commonly made. The classification scheme proposed in figure 5.1 adheres to the natural/cultural distinction for discussion purposes, and makes a further distinction between sites and events. Four categories of attraction are thereby generated: natural sites, natural events, cultural sites and cultural events. The use of dotted lines in figure 5.1 to separate these categories recognises that distinctions between 'natural' and 'cultural', and between 'site' and 'event', are often blurred. The use of these categories therefore should not obscure the fact that many if not most attractions are category hybrids. A national park, for example, may combine topographical, cultural, floral and faunal elements of the site (see the case study at the end of this chapter). With this qualification, tourist attractions and associated activities within each of the four categories are discussed below.

The following material is not an exhaustive treatment of this immense and complex topic, but rather it is meant to illustrate management issues associated with various types of attractions. One underlying theme is the great diversity of tourist attractions, and the possibility that most places are not adequately utilising their potential range of attractions. A related theme is the role of imagination and creativity in transforming apparent destination liabilities into **tourism resources,** reflecting the subjective nature of the latter concept.

■ **Figure 5.1**
Generic inventory of tourist attractions

Category	Site		Event
Natural	TOPOGRAPHY e.g. mountains, canyons, beaches, volcanoes, caves, fossil sites	protected areas, hiking trails	volcanic eruptions
	CLIMATE e.g. temperature, sunshine, precipitation		
	HYDROLOGY e.g. lakes, rivers, waterfalls, hot springs	scenic highways scenic lookouts, cairns	tides
	WILDLIFE e.g. mammals, birds, insects, fish	wildlife parks	animal migrations (e.g. caribou, geese)
	VEGETATION e.g. forests, wildflowers	botanical gardens, spas	
	LOCATION e.g. centrality, extremity		
Cultural	PREHISTORICAL e.g. Aboriginal sites		
	HISTORICAL e.g. battlefields, old buildings, museums, ancient monuments, graveyards, statues		battle re-enactments, commemorations
	CONTEMPORARY CULTURE e.g. architecture, ethnic neighbourhoods, modern technology		festivals, world fairs
	ECONOMIC e.g. farms, mines, factories		
	RECREATIONAL e.g. integrated resorts, golf courses, ski hills, theme parks, casinos		sporting events, Olympics
	RETAIL e.g. mega-malls, shopping districts		markets

■ *5.2.1* Natural *sites*

Natural attractions, as the name implies, are associated more closely with the natural environment rather than the cultural environment. **Natural site** attractions can be subdivided into topography, climate, water, wildlife, vegetation and location. Inbound tourists are strongly influenced to visit Australia by natural sites such as beaches, botanical gardens, zoos and national parks (figure 5.2). Destinations have little scope for changing their natural assets — that is, they either possess high mountains and a tropical climate, or they do not. The challenge, therefore, is to manipulate market image so that 'unattractive' natural phenomena are converted into tourism resources.

Topography

Topography refers to geological features in the physical landscape such as mountains, valleys, plateaus, islands, canyons, deltas, dunes, cliffs, beaches, volcanoes and caves. Gemstones and fossils are a special type of topographical feature, locally important in Australian locations such as Coober Pedy in South Australia (opals), O'Briens Creek in Queensland (topaz) and the New England region of New South Wales (Jenkins 1992). The potential for dinosaur fossils to foster a tourism industry in remote parts of Queensland is considered by Laws and Scott (2003).

Leisure activities undertaken by top five inbound markets to Australia, 2004[1]

Go shopping for pleasure	76 per cent
Go to the beach	59
Go to markets	46
Pubs, clubs, discos	44
Visit national parks/state parks	39
Visit wildlife parks/zoos/aquariums	36
Visit botanical or other public gardens	34
Charter boat/cruise/ferry	28
Visit history/heritage buildings, sites or monuments	26
Visit museums or art galleries	24
Go on guided tours or excursions	21
Bushwalking/rainforest walks	21
Visit casinos	20
Snorkelling	13
Visit wineries	12
Visit amusement/theme parks	12
Attend theatre, concerts or other performing arts	11
Tourist trains	11
Experience aboriginal art/craft and cultural displays	10
Attend an organised sporting event	9
Visit art/craft workshops/studios	8
Go whale/dolphin watching (in the ocean)	7
Visit farms	7
Attend festivals/fairs or cultural events	6
Visit the outback	6
Scuba diving	6
Sailing, windsurfing, kayaking, etc.	6
Go fishing	5
Visit an aboriginal site/community	4
Play golf	4
Surfing	4
Attend aboriginal performance	4
Visit a health spa	1

[1] New Zealand, United Kingdom, Japan, United States, China

Source: *Tourism Research Australia (2005).*

Mountains

Mountains illustrate the subjective and changing nature of tourism resources. Long feared and despised as hazardous wastelands harbouring bandits and dangerous animals, the image of alpine environments was rehabilitated during the European Romanticist period of the early 1800s (Nicholson 1959). As a result, scenically dramatic alpine regions such as the European Alps and the North American Rockies emerged as highly desirable venues for tourist activity, and were gradually incorporated into the global pleasure periphery. A similar process is currently underway in the Himalayan mountains of Asia, the South American Andes, the Southern Alps of New Zealand and the Atlas Mountains of Africa — all previously undeveloped as tourist destinations because of their relative inaccessibility. Beedie and Hudson (2003) describe how this remoteness fostered an elitist 'mountaineer' form of tourism until the latter half of the twentieth century, when improved access (a pull factor) and increased discretionary time and money (push factors) led to the 'democratisation' of alpine landscapes through mass adventure tourism. Lower and less dramatic mountain ranges, such as the American Appalachian Mountains, the Russian Urals and the coastal ranges of Australia, are also highly valued for tourism purposes although arguably they did not undergo the elite-to-mass transition to the same extent (Godde, Price & Zimmermann 2000).

Certain individual mountains, by merit of exceptional height, aesthetics or religious significance, possess a symbolic value as an **iconic attraction** that tourists readily associate with particular destinations. Uluru (formerly Ayers Rock) is the best Australian example, while other well-known examples include Mt Everest (Sagarmatha), the Matterhorn, Kilimanjaro (Tanzania) and Japan's Mt Fuji, which is notable as an almost perfect composite volcano.

Beaches

Similarly to mountains, beaches were not always perceived positively as tourist attractions. Their popularity is associated with the Industrial Revolution and particularly with the emergence of the pleasure periphery after World War II (see chapters 3 and 4). Currently, beaches are perhaps the most stereotypical symbol of mass tourism. Not all types of beaches, however, are equally favoured by tourists. Dark-hued beaches derived from the erosion of volcanic rock are not as popular as the fine white sandy beaches created from limestone or coral, as the former generate very hot sand and the illusion of murky water while the latter produce the turquoise water effect highly valued by tourists and destination marketers. This in large part accounts for the higher level of 3S resort development in 'coral' Caribbean destinations such as Antigua and the Bahamas, as opposed to 'volcanic' islands such as Dominica and Montserrat. The centrality of the beach to the Australian inbound tourism experience is reflected in figure 5.2, which shows that 59 per cent of visitors spent at least some time at the beach during 2003. Going to the beach is also by far the most popular outdoor holiday activity among Australians, with one-quarter of domestic stayovers reporting participation in 1999 (BTR 2000).

Climate

Tourists have been attracted to particular types of climates since ancient times (Boniface & Cooper 2005). Before the era of modern mass tourism, the prevalent attraction of climate was the search for cooler and drier weather relative to the uncomfortable summer heat and humidity of urban areas. Thus, escape to coastal resorts in the United Kingdom and the United States during the summer was and still is a quest for cooler rather than warmer temperatures. The British and Dutch established highland resorts in their Asian colonies for similar purposes, and many of these are still used for tourism purposes by the postcolonial indigenous elite and middle class. Examples include Simla and Darjeeling in India (Jutla 2000), and the Cameron Highlands of Malaysia. This impulse is also evident among the increasing number of Middle Eastern visitors to Australia.

With the emergence of the pleasure periphery, the dominant hot-to-cool movement was reversed as great numbers of 'snowbirds' travelled to Florida, the Caribbean, the Mediterranean, Hawaii and other warm weather destinations to escape cold winter conditions in their home regions. A snowbird-type migration is also apparent on a smaller scale from Australian states such as Victoria to the coast of Queensland (Mings 1997). Thus, hot and sunny conditions complement the white-sand beach and the turquoise water effect to define the dominant stereotypical 3S destination image of the early twenty-first century.

Yet some areas can be too hot for most tourists, as reflected in the low demand for equatorial and hot desert tourism. Essentially, a subtropical range of approximately 20–30°C is considered optimal for 3S tourism, and this is a good climatic indicator of the potential for large-scale tourism development in a particular beach-based destination, provided that other basic 'pull' criteria are also present (Boniface & Cooper 2005). The one major exception to the cool-to-hot trend is the growing popularity of winter sports such as downhill skiing, snowboarding and snowmobiling, which involve a cool-to-cool migration or, more rarely, a warm-to-cool migration. Whatever the specific dynamic, cyclic changes in weather within both the origin and destination regions lead to significant seasonal fluctuations in tourist flows, presenting tourism managers with an additional management challenge (see chapter 8).

Water

Water is a significant tourism resource only under certain conditions. For swimming, prerequisites include high water quality, a comfortable water temperature and calm water conditions. For surfing, however, calm waters are a liability — which accounts for the emergence of only certain parts of the Australian east coast, Hawaii and California as surfing 'hotspots'. Oceans and seas, where they interface subtropical beaches, are probably the most desirable and lucrative venue for nature-based tourism development. Freshwater lakes are also significant for outdoor recreational activities such as boating, and for the establishment of second homes and cottages. Extensive recreational hinterlands, dominated by lake-based cottage or second home developments, are common in parts of Europe and North America. The Muskoka region of Canada is an excellent example, its development having been facilitated by the presence of several thousand highly indented glacial lakes (i.e. the destination region), its proximity to Toronto (i.e. the origin region) and the existence of connecting railways and roads (i.e. the transit region) (Svenson 2004).

Other significant tourist attractions are rivers and waterfalls. Waterfalls in particular hold a strong inherent aesthetic appeal for many people, and often constitute a core iconic attraction around which secondary attractions, and sometimes entire resort communities, are established. Niagara Falls (on the United States/Canada border) is a prime example of a waterfall-based tourism agglomeration. Other examples include Victoria

Falls (on the Zimbabwe/Zambia border) and Iguaçú Falls (on the Brazil/Paraguay border). Small waterfalls, in contrast, are an integral part of the tourism product in the hinterland of Australia's Gold Coast (Hudson 2004)

An important management dimension of water-based tourism is water's status as a resource for other sectors such as agriculture (irrigation), manufacturing (as a water source and an outlet for effluent) and transportation (bulk transport). Accordingly, tourism managers and tourists must often compete for water access with other powerful and frequently incompatible stakeholders.

Geothermal waters

As discussed in chapter 3, spas were an historically important form of tourism that receded in significance during the ascendancy of seaside tourism. The greatest present-day concentration of spas is associated with geologically active areas of the Earth's surface such as Iceland and New Zealand, where geothermal waters with purported therapeutic qualities are readily accessible. Spas are also found along the Czech–German border and in the Appalachian Mountains of the eastern United States. European spas alone are estimated to attract 20 million visitors per year (Smith & Jenner 2000). Australia, however, is characterised by an underdeveloped spa industry (Bennett, King & Milner 2004).

Wildlife

As a tourism resource, wildlife can be classified in several ways for managerial purposes. First, a distinction can be made between captive and non-captive wildlife. The clearest example of the former is a zoo, which is a hybrid natural/cultural attraction (Tribe 2004). At the opposite end of the continuum are wilderness areas where the movement of animals is unrestricted. Trade-offs are implicit in the tourist experience associated with each scenario. For example, a visitor is virtually guaranteed of seeing the animal in a zoo, but there is minimal habitat context and no thrill of discovery. In a wilderness or semi-wilderness situation, the opposite holds true (see figure 5.3). Many zoos are now being reconstructed and reinvented as 'wildlife parks' or 'zoological parks' that provide a viewing experience within a quasi-natural and more humane environment, thereby compromising between these two extremes (Mazur 2001). As indicated in figure 5.2, 37 per cent of main-market inbound tourists in Australia in 2003 visited a wildlife park or zoo.

■ **Figure 5.3**
A human–animal encounter in a semi-wilderness setting

Wildlife is also commonly classified along a consumptive/nonconsumptive spectrum. The former usually refers to hunting and fishing, which are long established as a mainly domestic form of tourism in North America, Australia, New Zealand and Europe. Component activities that have more of an international dimension include big-game hunting (important in parts of Africa and Canada) and deep-sea fishing, which is significant in many coastal destinations of Australia (Bauer & Herr 2004). Because of the consumptive nature of these activities, managers must always be alert to their effect on wildlife population levels. In some destinations, hunting is used as a management tool for keeping wildlife populations in balance with environmental carrying capacities. In many areas 'nonconsumptive' wildlife-based pursuits such as ecotourism are overtaking hunting and fishing in importance (Valentine & Birtles 2004) (see section 11.5.3). This is creating a dilemma for some hunting-oriented businesses and destinations, which must decide whether to remain focused on hunting, switch to ecotourism or attempt to accommodate both of these potentially incompatible activities. One criticism of the 'consumptive/nonconsumptive' mode of classification is both dimensions being inherent in all forms of wildlife-based tourism. The 'nonconsumptive' experience of being outdoors for its own sake, for example, is usually an intrinsic part of hunting and fishing, while ecotourists consume many different products (e.g. petrol, food, souvenirs) as part of the wildlife-viewing experience. Maintaining an inventory of observed wildlife can also be regarded as a symbolic form of 'consumption' (Tremblay 2001).

Vegetation

Vegetation exists interdependently with wildlife and, therefore, cannot be divorced from the ecotourism equation. However, there are also situations where trees, flowers or shrubs are a primary rather than a supportive attraction. Examples include the giant redwood trees of northern California, the wild-flower meadows of Western Australia and the endemic Mediterranean plants of southern Cape Province, South Africa (Turpie & Joubert 2004). The captive/noncaptive continuum is only partially useful in classifying flora resources, since vegetation is essentially immobile. For managers this means that inventories are relatively stable, and tourists can be virtually guaranteed of seeing the attraction (although this may not pertain to weather-dependent attractions such as autumn colour and spring flower displays). However, these same qualities may imply a greater vulnerability to damage and overexploitation. The carving of initials into tree trunks and the removal of limbs for firewood are common examples of vegetation abuse associated with tourism. The 'captive' flora equivalent of a zoo is a botanical garden. These are usually located in larger urban areas, and as a result often attract a very large visitor base (see figure 5.2).

Protected natural areas

Protected natural areas such as national parks are an amalgam of topographical, hydrological, zoological, vegetation and cultural resources that constitute a composite attraction. As natural attractions, high-order protected areas stand out for at least four reasons:
- Their protected status ensures, at least theoretically, that the integrity and attractiveness of their constituent natural resources is safeguarded.

- The amount of land available in a relatively undisturbed state is rapidly declining due to habitat destruction, thereby ensuring that high-order protected areas are a scarce and desirable tourism resource.
- Such areas were usually protected because of exceptional natural qualities that are attractive to some tourists, such as scenic mountain ranges or rare species of animals and plants.
- An area having been designated as a national park or World Heritage Site confers status on that space as an attraction, since most people assume that it must be special to warrant such designation.

For all these reasons, protected natural areas are now among the most popular international and domestic tourism attractions (Butler & Boyd 2000). Some national parks, such as Yellowstone, Grand Canyon and Yosemite (all in the United States), Banff (Canada) and Kakadu and Uluru (Australia) are major attractions in their respective countries. This is ironic given that many protected areas were originally established for preservation purposes, without any consideration being given to the possibility that they might be attractive to large numbers of tourists and other visitors. However, as funding cutbacks and external systems such as agriculture and logging pose an increased threat to these areas, their managers are now more open to tourism as a potentially compatible revenue-generating activity that may serve to pre-empt the intrusion of more destructive activities (see chapter 11).

Location

Extreme or centralised locations fascinate many people and thus have the potential to be exploited as tourist attractions. For example, the town of Rugby (in the US state of North Dakota) has erected a large cairn on its outskirts to publicise its status as 'the geographical centre of North America'. Many tourists stop at this site each year to have their photograph taken and to purchase basic services in transit to other destinations. Other cases where geographical extremity has evolved into a tourism product include Land's End (the most westerly spot on the mainland of England) and the Byron Bay lighthouse in New South Wales, which is close to the most easterly point of land in Australia.

■ 5.2.2 Natural *events*

Natural events are often independent of particular locations and unpredictable in their occurrence and magnitude. Bird migrations are a good illustration. The Canadian province of Saskatchewan is becoming popular for the spring and autumn migrations of massive numbers of waterfowl, but the probability of arriving at the right place at the right time to see the spectacular flocks is dictated by various factors, including local weather and larger-scale climate shifts.

Solar eclipses and comets are rarer but more predictable events that attract large numbers of tourists to locations where good viewing conditions are anticipated. Volcanic eruptions (which appeal to many tourists because of their beauty and danger) are generally associated with known locations (thus they are sites as well as events), but are often less certain with respect to occurrence. However, lodgings have been established in the vicinity of

Costa Rica's Arenal volcano specifically to accommodate the viewing of its nightly eruptions, while the predictable volcanic activity of Mt Yasur is the primary attraction on the island of Tanna in the Pacific archipelagic state of Vanuatu. The eruption of Italy's Mount Etna in 2001 had the interesting effect of attracting curious tourists while at the same time destroying ski facilities, a local tourist attraction.

A natural event associated with oceans and seas is tidal action. To become a tourism resource, tidal activity must have a dramatic or superlative component. One area that has taken advantage of its exceptional tidal action is Canada's Bay of Fundy (between the provinces of Nova Scotia and New Brunswick), where ideal geographical conditions produce tidal fluctuations of 12 to 15 metres, the highest in the world. Extreme weather conditions can produce natural events, as for example when rainfall replenishes the usually dry Lake Eyre basin in South Australia, creating a brief oceanic effect in the desert. This is a good example of an **ephemeral attraction**.

■ 5.2.3   Cultural *sites*

Cultural sites, also known as 'built', 'constructed' or 'human-made' sites, are as or more diverse than their natural counterparts. Categories of convenience include prehistorical, historical, contemporary, economic activity, specialised recreational and retail. As with natural sites, these distinctions are often blurred when considering specific attractions.

Prehistorical

Prehistorical attractions, including rock paintings, rock etchings, middens, mounds and other sites associated with indigenous people, occur in many parts of Australia, New Zealand, Canada and the United States. Many of these attractions are affiliated with existing indigenous groups, and issues of control, appropriation, proper interpretation and effective management against excessive visitation therefore all have contemporary relevance. A distinct category of prehistorical sites is the megalithic sites associated with 'lost' cultures, which are attractive because of their mysterious origins as well as their impressive appearance. The New Age pilgrimage site of Stonehenge (United Kingdom) is a primary example. Others include the giant carved heads of Easter Island and the Nazca lines of Peru.

Historical

Historical sites are distinguished from prehistorical sites by their more definite associations with specific civilisations that fall under the scope of 'recorded history'. There is no single or universal criterion that determines when a contemporary artefact becomes 'historical'. Usually this is a matter of consensus within a local community or among scholars, or simply a promotional tactic. Historical sites can be divided into many subcategories, and only a few of the more prominent of these are outlined below.

Monuments and structures

Ancient monuments and structures that have attained prominence as attractions within their respective countries include the pyramids of Egypt, the Colosseum in Rome and the Parthenon in Athens. More recent examples include Angkor Wat (Cambodia), the Eiffel Tower, the Statue of Liberty, the Taj Mahal, the Kremlin, Mount Rushmore and the Tower of London. The Sydney Harbour Bridge and Opera House also fall in this category. Beyond these marquee attractions, generic structures that have evolved into attractions include the numerous castles of Europe, the Hindu temples of India and the colonial-era sugar mills of the Caribbean.

Battlefields

Battlefields are among the most popular of all tourist attractions, which again demonstrates that the long-term impacts of war on tourism are often positive. Battle sites such as Thermopylae (fought in 480 BC between the Spartans and Persians), Hastings (fought in 1066 between the Anglo-Saxons and Normans) and Waterloo (1815) are still extremely popular centuries after their occurrence. The emergence of more recent battlefields (such as Gallipoli and the American Civil War site at Gettysburg) as even higher profile attractions is due to several factors, including:

- the accurate identification and marking of specific sites and events throughout the battlefields, which is possible because of the degree to which modern battles are documented
- sophisticated levels of interpretation made available to visitors
- park-like settings that are attractive in their own right
- the stature of certain battlefields as 'sacred' sites or events that changed history (e.g. Gettysburg as the 'turning point of the American Civil War' and Gallipoli as the making of the Australian nation)
- personal connections — many current visitors have great-grandparents or other ancestors who fought in these battles.

Other war- or military-related sites that frequently evolve into tourist attractions include military cemeteries, fortresses and barracks (e.g. the Hyde Park Barracks in Sydney), and defensive walls (e.g. the Great Wall of China and Hadrian's Wall in England). Battlefields and other military sites are an example of a particularly fascinating phenomenon known as **dark tourism**, which encompasses sites and events that become attractive to some tourists because of their association with death or suffering (Lennon & Foley 2000). Other examples include assassination sites (e.g. for John F. Kennedy and Martin Luther King), locales of mass killings (e.g. Port Arthur (Tasmania), the World Trade Center site, and Holocaust concentration camps) and places associated with the supernatural (e.g. Dracula's castle in Transylvania, and 'haunted houses').

Heritage districts and landscapes

In many cities, historical districts are preserved and managed as tourism-related areas that combine attractions (e.g. restored historical buildings, shopping) and services (e.g. accommodation, restaurants). Preserved walled cities such as Rothenburg (Germany), York (England), the Forbidden City (Beijing) and the Old Town district of Prague (Czech Republic) fall into this category, as does the French Quarter of New Orleans. The Millers Point precinct of downtown Sydney is one of the best Australian examples, with its mixture of maritime-related historical buildings, small hotels, public open space, theatres and residential areas (Waitt &

McGuirk 1996). Rural heritage landscapes are not as well known or protected. An Australian example is the German cultural landscape of the Barossa Valley in South Australia.

Museums

Unlike battlefields, museums are not site specific, and almost any community can augment their tourism resource inventory by assembling and presenting collections of locally significant artefacts. Museums can range in scale from high-profile, internationally known institutions such as the British Museum in London, to lesser known city sites such as the National Wool Museum in Geelong, Victoria, and small community museums in regional towns such as Gympie in Queensland. That museums differ widely in the way that items are selected, displayed and interpreted is an aspect of these attractions that has important implications for their market segmentation and marketing. Recent trends include the movement towards 'hands-on' interactive interpretation as a way of accommodating leisure visitors (Foley & McPherson 2000), and the opening of decontextualised Holocaust museums in major European and North American cities (Lennon & Foley 1999).

Contemporary

Contemporary or 'living' culture sites include urban phenomena such as ethnic neighbourhoods and rural attractions such as cultural villages. The Polynesian Village in Hawaii and the Taos Pueblo in New Mexico (United States) are well-known examples of cultural villages.

Ethnic neighbourhoods

Large cities in Australia, Canada, the United States and western Europe are becoming increasingly diverse as a result of contemporary international migration patterns. This has led to the emergence of neighbourhoods associated with particular ethnic groups. For many years such areas were effectively alienated from the broader urban community, but now the Chinatowns of San Francisco, Sydney, Vancouver, New York and Toronto, for example, have evolved into high-profile tourist attractions. This trend has been assisted by the placement of Chinese language street signs and the approval of Asian-style outdoor markets and other culturally specific features. The effect is to provide the tourist (as well as local residents) with an experience of the exotic, without having to travel too far afield. More surprising than the 'Chinatown' phenomenon has been the transformation of certain New York neighbourhoods (e.g. parts of Harlem) from what were perceived to be dangerous and hostile ghettos into vibrant centres of African–American music, food and theatre that attract many white visitors.

Food and drink

While taken for granted as a necessary consumable in any tourism experience, food is increasingly becoming an attraction in its own right, as illustrated by the experience of all the ethnic urban neighbourhoods mentioned above and numerous other destinations (Hall et al. 2003). In cases such as Singapore, **food tourism** is encouraged to achieve specific sociopolitical and economic objectives (see Contemporary issue: Food as a tourist attraction in Singapore). For any place, food is a means by which the tourist can literally consume the destination, and if the experience is memorable, it can be exceptionally effective at inducing the highly desired outcome of repeat visitation.

A particularly well-articulated form of food tourism in some destinations is wine tourism (Getz 2000). Scenic **winescapes** are the focus of tourism activity in locations such as the Napa Valley of California, the Hunter Valley of New South Wales, and the Clare and Barossa Valleys of South Australia (Macionis & Cambourne 2000). All have benefited from exceptional wines, a strong and positive market image, well-managed cellar door operations, and exurban locations. But while tourism has been described as a 'perfect partner' for the wine industry (Dowling & Carlsen 1998), Beverland (1999) cites tourism inexperience, diversion from the task of wine production, competition and liability considerations as impediments to the successful participation of individual wineries and vineyards.

CONTEMPORARY ISSUE

Food as a tourist attraction in Singapore

Singapore is a prime example of a destination where food has become an integral component of the local tourism product mix. In part this can be attributed to a diverse and alluring cuisine that has arisen from Singapore's multicultural character and includes Chinese, Malay, Indian and many other influences, often in combinations that are unique to the country. However, Henderson (2004) also emphasises that the development of food-related tourism is part of a deliberate strategy to create a distinct tourism product on a 683-square-kilometre island notably lacking in high-profile cultural or natural attractions. The presentation and celebration of a diverse cuisine, moreover, is intended to send a positive political message to visitors about tolerance for multiculturalism that may not entirely reflect the actual state of intercultural relations on the island. Similarly, the promotion of eating in Singapore as a virtually risk-free experience showcases Singapore's extremely high standards for cleanliness and hygiene and, thence, its success as a state.

Singapore's formal food tourism product includes the month-long Singapore Food Festival, the annual two-week World Gourmet Summit, and an ongoing 'Let's Makan!' campaign (*makan* means 'eat' in Malay) that features ten 'must-try' dishes and encourages residents to recommend different foods and eating places to tourists. This complements the Tasty Singapore campaign, which markets locally produced food by making gift baskets with selected items available as food souvenirs at the airport and other outlets frequented by tourists. Traditional (but licensed and regulated) street stalls provide food in a context that contrasts with the island's otherwise ultramodern image. Additional initiatives, such as the Uniquely Singapore Shop and Eat Tours, which brings tourists into 'local' neighbourhoods and homes, and The Ethnic Trail, which brings tourists into Malay, Chinese and Indian enclaves, further attest to what Henderson (2004) describes as Singapore's status as a high-order food destination.

Economic activity

'Living' economic activities such as mining, agriculture and manufacturing are often taken for granted by the local community, and particularly by the labour force engaged in those livelihoods. However, these activities can also provide a fascinating and unusual experience for those who use the associated products but are divorced from their actual production. At a deeper level, the widespread separation of modern society from the processes of primary production in the 'postindustrial' era, and the subsequent desire to participate at least indirectly in such activities, may help to explain the growing popularity of factory, mine and farm tours (Jansen–Verbeke 1999).

Canals and railways

Recreational canals and railways provide excellent examples of **functional adaptation** (the use of a structure for a purpose other than its original intent). As with factory, mine and farm tours, such adaptations are associated with the movement from an industrial to a postindustrial society, in which some canals and railways are now more valuable as sites for recreation and tourism than as a means of facilitating the bulk transport of industrial goods — their original intent. England is an area where pleasure-boating on canals is especially important, as the Industrial Revolution left behind a legacy of thousands of kilometres of now defunct canals, which have proven ideal for accommodating small pleasure craft. A similar phenomenon is apparent in North American locations such as the Trent and Rideau Canals (Ontario, Canada) and the Erie Canal in New York State. The Puffing Billy scenic rail experience in the Dandenong Ranges of Victoria is Australia's best known example of functional adaptation involving a railway (Critchley 1998), while the 'Rails to Trails' movement is well developed in North America.

Specialised recreational attractions (SRAs)

Of all categories of tourist attraction, specialised recreational attractions (SRAs) are unique because they are constructed specifically to meet the demands of the tourism and recreation markets. With the exception of ski lifts and several other products that require specific environments, SRAs are also among the attractions least constrained by context and location. Their establishment, in other words, does not depend on particular circumstances such as the location of certain cultures or physical conditions. SRAs are in addition the attraction type most clearly related to the tourism industry, since they mostly consist of privately owned businesses (the linear SRAs discussed below are one exception).

Golf courses

Golf courses are an important SRA subcategory for several reasons, including:

- the recent proliferation of golf facilities worldwide (more than 30 000 by the early 2000s)
- the relatively large amount of space that they occupy both individually and collectively
- their association with residential housing developments and integrated resorts
- their controversial environmental impacts.

In addition, high concentrations of golf activity, in areas such as Palm Springs, California, and Orlando, Florida, have led to the appearance of **golfscapes**, or landscapes where golf courses and affiliated developments are a dominant land use. The Gold Coast is the best Australian example of a golfscape, with some 40 courses available within council boundaries, and a similar number under construction or approved.

Casinos

For many years, casinos were synonymous with Monte Carlo, Las Vegas and very few other locations. However, casinos have proliferated well beyond these traditional strongholds as governments have become more aware of, and dependent on gaming-based revenues. Casinos are now a common sight on North American Indian Reserves, in central cities (e.g. Melbourne's Crown Casino and Brisbane's Treasury Casino), and as Mississippi River-style gambling boats in the American South and Midwest (Meyer-Arendt & Hartmann 1998). This diffusion has prompted the Las Vegas tourism industry to remain competitive by erecting ever larger and more fantastic themed casino hotels (e.g. Excalibur, Luxor and MGM Grand), which increasingly blur the distinction between accommodation and attraction. Though ideally intended to attract external revenue, casinos such as Jupiters Casino on the Gold Coast are also attractive to local residents, and their presence is often therefore controversial due to the possibility of negative social side-effects (see chapter 9).

Theme parks

Theme parks are large-scale, topical and mostly exurban SRAs that contain numerous subattractions (e.g. rides, shows, exhibits) intended to provide family groups with an all-inclusive, all-day recreational experience. The Disney-related sites (e.g. Disneyland at Anaheim, California; DisneyWorld at Orlando, Florida; and Eurodisney in Paris) are the best known international examples, while the Gold Coast theme parks (Dreamworld, Sea World and Movieworld) are the best known Australian examples. Theme parks provide a good illustration of social engineering in that they purport to offer thrilling and spontaneous experiences, yet in reality are carefully regulated and orchestrated environments that maximise opportunities for retail expenditure by visitors (Rojek 1993).

Scenic highways, bikeways and hiking trails

Linear recreational attractions are sometimes the result of functional adaptation, as for example canals (see above) and bicycle and walking trails that are constructed on the foundations of abandoned railway lines (e.g. 'Rails to Trails'). In other cases linear SRAs are custom built to meet specific recreational and tourism needs. The Blue Ridge Parkway and Natchez Trace are US examples of custom-built scenic roadways, while the Appalachian Trail is a well-known example of a specialised long-distance walking track. A variation of the road theme is the multipurpose highway that is designated as a scenic route. Australian examples include Victoria's Great Ocean Road and the Birdsville Track from Marree (SA) to Birdsville (Qld).

The linear nature of these attractions poses specific challenges to their managers, including the possibility that they may cross a large number of political jurisdictions, each of which will have some influence over the resource. In addition, long-distance walking trails in particular pass through privately owned land for much of their length, which renders them susceptible to relocation if some landowners decide that they no longer want the trail to pass through their property because of security, liability or vandalism concerns. In the United Kingdom, the status of public walking trails on private property has become a highly contentious and politically charged issue.

Linear SRAs are also likely to share extensive borders with adjacent land uses that may not be compatible with tourism or recreation. There is potential for conflict and dissatisfaction from the fact that these trails, roads and bikeways rely to a large extent on the scenic resources of these adjacent landscapes, yet the latter are vulnerable to modification by forces over which the attraction manager has no control (see section 5.2.5).

Ski resorts

More than most SRAs, ski resort viability is dependent on the availability of specific climatic and topographical conditions, although the invention of affordable snow-making technology greatly facilitated the spread of the industry into regions otherwise unsuitable. A process of consolidation, however, is now evident, with the number of ski areas in the United States declining from 745 to 509 between 1975 and 2000 (Clifford 2002). Concurrently, the average size of resorts has increased and corporate ownership has become prevalent. As with golf courses, the profitability of the contemporary ski megaresort is increasingly dependent on revenues from affiliated housing developments, in which case the actual ski facilities serve primarily as a 'hook' to attract real-estate investors.

Retail

Under certain conditions, retail goods and services, similarly to food, are major tourist attractions in their own right, and not only an associated service activity. Singapore and Hong Kong are South-East Asian examples of destinations that offer shopping opportunities as a core component of their tourism product (Heung & Cheng 2000). In cities such as Kuala Lumpur (Malaysia), shopping malls are built into large hotels to create an integrated accommodation–shopping complex (Oppermann, Din & Amri 1996). The attraction of retail shopping is also evident in Australia, where 81 per cent of main-market inbound tourists reported participation in shopping for pleasure during 2003 (figure 5.2).

Mega-malls

The 'mega-mall' phenomenon is mostly associated with North America, where the West Edmonton Mall (Canada), the Mall of the Americas (Minneapolis) and other complexes vie to be recognised as the world's largest shopping centre. As with theme parks and large casinos, mega-malls are composite attractions that contain numerous individual subattractions designed to maximise the amount of time that visitors remain within the facility and the amount of money that they spend. Similarly, they are usually contrived in character, incorporating fake Italian townscapes or exotic South Pacific themes.

Markets and bazaars

'Colourful' Caribbean markets and 'exotic' Asian bazaars are generic tourism icons of their respective destination regions. The ability to compromise between authenticity (which may repel some tourists) and a comfortable and safe environment for the conventional tourist is a major challenge to the manager of market and bazaar attractions. Within Australia, country or 'farmers' markets in communities such as Mount Tamborine and Eumundi (Queensland) are major local attractions, especially for domestic tourists.

■ 5.2.4 Cultural *events*

Cultural events can be categorised in several ways, including the extent to which they are regular or irregular in occurrence (e.g. the Summer Olympics every four years versus one-time-only special commemorations) or location (the British Open tennis tournament held at Wimbledon versus the changing Olympics site). Cultural events can range in size from a small local arts festival to international mega-events such as the football World Cup. In addition, events may be 'single destination' (e.g. Wimbledon) or 'multiple destination' in space or time (e.g. the Olympics sites spread over a region or the circuit-based Tour de France bicycle race). Finally, thematic classification assigns events to topical categories such as history, sport, religion, music and arts (Getz 1997). For tourism sites such as theme parks, periodic events are an important supplementary attraction that add to product diversity and offer a distraction from routine touring. They may also serve as a management device that redistributes visitors both in time and space. As with museums, communities have the ability to initiate cultural events by creatively capitalising on available local resources.

Historical re-enactments and commemorations

The re-creation of historical events can serve many purposes in addition to its superficial value as a tourist attraction. Participants may be primarily motivated by a deep-seated desire to connect with significant events of the past, while governments may encourage and sponsor such performances to perpetuate the propaganda or mythological value of the original event, especially if the re-creations or commemorations occur at the original sites. Re-enactments associated with the landings of Captain Cook featured prominently in the 1988 Bicentenary commemorations in Australia, although their association with the post-1788 Aboriginal dispossession injected an element of controversy. Less contentious are the periodic re-enactments of American Civil War battles such as Gettysburg. The 135th anniversary re-enactment of Pickett's Charge (the climactic event of the battle), held in 1998, attracted more than 25 000 re-enactors and an estimated 100 000 spectators (see figure 5.4) (EventPlan 2003).

■ **Figure 5.4**
*American
Civil War
re-enactment
at Gettysburg,
1998*

Sporting events

The modern Olympic games are the most prestigious of all sporting events, although the football World Cup is emerging as a legitimate contender for the title in the wake of the highly successful 1998 and 2002 events. That the World Cup and the Olympics do not take place in the same year is a deliberate attempt to avoid competing mega-event coverage. Major sporting events are exceptional in the degree to which they attract extensive media attention, and the number of television viewers far outweighs the on-site audience. These events are therefore additionally important for their potential to induce some of the television audience (which may number several billion consumers) to visit the host city, thereby creating a post-event ripple effect. The fierce competition that accompanies the selection of host Olympic cities or World Cup nations is therefore as much about long-term image enhancement and induced visitation as it is about the actual games. The 2000 Sydney Games were especially symbolic because of their occurrence at the turn of the millennium and their role in positioning the host city as a globalised 'world city' (Waitt 2004). Other sporting events of note are associated with golf and tennis tournaments, while the regular season itineraries of professional sports teams (e.g. baseball, basketball, ice hockey, rugby league) are significant generators of mostly domestic tourist activity.

World fairs

While less prestigious than the Olympics, world fairs (designated as such by an official organisation similar to the International Olympic Committee, or IOC) also confer a significant amount of status and visibility to host cities. The 1988 World Fair in Brisbane, for example, is similar to the 2000 Sydney Games in that it is often associated with that city's 'coming-of-age' as a more open and cosmopolitan place.

Festivals and performances

Most countries, including Australia, host an extremely large and diverse number of festivals and performances. Attendance in Australia (not all of which is accounted for by tourists) is for the most part related to the 'arts' (table 5.1). As mentioned above, destinations have considerable ability to establish festival- and performance-type events, since these can capitalise on anything from a particular local culture or industry to themes completely unrelated to the area. For example, the highly popular Woodford folk festival, held annually in the Sunshine Coast hinterland of Queensland, could just as easily be located on any one of a thousand similar sites within an easy drive from Brisbane. In other cases, festivals are more associated with particular destination qualities. The Barossa Vintage Festival in South Australia is a well-known Australian example that capitalises on the local wine industry.

■ **Table 5.1**   *Attendance at selected cultural events in Australia, 2002*

EVENT	TOTAL ATTENDANCE (000s)	PERCENTAGE								
		TOTAL	NSW	VIC	QLD	SA	WA	TAS	NT	ACT
Popular music concerts	3834	27	27	27	23	25	30	25	25	33
Museums	3623	25	25	24	21	27	26	32	43	57
Art galleries	3606	24	25	23	23	24	29	27	31	48
Musicals/ opera	2706	19	19	21	17	16	16	16	18	20
Theatre	2607	18	18	19	16	16	21	17	16	26
Dance	1581	11	11	10	11	10	12	10	15	18
Classical music concerts	1299	9	10	9	7	9	10	9	10	14

Source: *Data derived from DCITA (2003)*

■ 5.2.5   Attraction *attributes*

Destination managers, as stated earlier, should compile an inventory of their tourism attractions as a prerequisite for the effective management of their tourism sector. It is not sufficient, however, just to list and categorise the attractions. Managers must also periodically assess their status across an array of relevant **attraction attributes** to inform appropriate planning and management decisions (figure 5.5). A spectrum is used in each case to reflect the continuous nature of these variables. Each of the attraction attributes will now be considered, with no order of importance implied by the sequence of presentation. Image is not discussed below, as this attribute is addressed elsewhere in the text in some detail (sections 4.3.8 and 7.7.6).

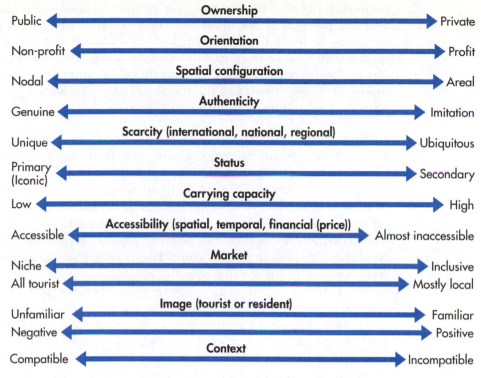

■ **Figure 5.5**
Tourist attraction attributes

Public	Ownership	Private
Non-profit	Orientation	Profit
Nodal	Spatial configuration	Areal
Genuine	Authenticity	Imitation
Unique	Scarcity (international, national, regional)	Ubiquitous
Primary (Iconic)	Status	Secondary
Low	Carrying capacity	High
Accessible	Accessibility (spatial, temporal, financial (price))	Almost inaccessible
Niche	Market	Inclusive
All tourist		Mostly local
Unfamiliar	Image (tourist or resident)	Familiar
Negative		Positive
Compatible	Context	Incompatible

Ownership

The ownership of an attraction significantly affects the planning and management process. For example, the public ownership of Lamington National Park, in the Gold Coast hinterland, implies the injection of public rather than private funding, a high level of government decision-making discretion and the assignment of a higher priority to environmental and social impacts over profit generation. Public ownership also suggests an extensive regulatory environment, and long-term as opposed to shorter-term planning horizons.

Orientation

An emphasis on profitability is affiliated to, but not identical with, private sector ownership. Revenue-starved governments may place more stress on profit generation, which in turn modifies many management assumptions and actions with respect to the attractions that they control. Among the possible implications of a profit reorientation in a national park is the introduction of user fees, an easing of visitor quotas, greater emphasis on visitor satisfaction and increased latitude for the operation of private concessions. The national park, in essence, becomes a 'business' and its visitors 'customers' who must be satisfied.

Spatial configuration

The implications of geographical shape and size were demonstrated earlier by the problems associated with linear attractions. In contrast, a circular or square site (e.g. some national parks) reduces the length of the attraction's boundary and thus the potential for conflict with adjacent land uses. This also has practical implications in matters such as the length of boundary that must be fenced or patrolled. The classification of a site often depends on the scale of investigation. For example, a regional strategy for southeast Queensland would regard Dreamworld as an internally undifferentiated 'node' or 'point', whereas a site-specific master plan would regard the same attraction as an internally differentiated 'area'.

Authenticity

Whereas ownership, orientation and spatial configuration are relatively straightforward, the attribute of 'authenticity' is highly ambiguous and contentious (MacCannell 1976). An exhaustive discussion is beyond the scope of this book, but suffice to say that authenticity can consider how 'genuine' an attraction is as opposed to imitative or contrived. The latter, however, is not necessarily a negative characteristic. For example, the 40 000-year-old Neolithic cave paintings at Lascaux (France) were so threatened by the perspiration and respiration of tourists that an almost exact replica was constructed nearby for viewing purposes. Whether the replica is seen in a positive or negative light depends on how it is presented and interpreted; if the tourist is made aware that it is an imitation, and that it is provided as part of the effort to preserve the original while still providing an educational experience, then the copy may be perceived in a very positive light. Similarly, the mega-casinos of Las Vegas offer a contrived experience, but this is not necessarily problematic as long as patrons recognise this (see chapter 9).

Scarcity

An important management implication of scarcity is that very rare or unique attractions are likely to be both highly vulnerable and highly attractive to tourists because of this scarcity. At the other end of the spectrum are ubiquitous resources; that is, those that are found or can be established almost anywhere. Scarcity or uniqueness is most valuable at the global scale, as the ability of a destination to boast the world's deepest lake, for example, will generate far more tourist interest than claiming the deepest lake in South Australia or Tasmania.

Status

A useful distinction can be made between primary or iconic attractions and secondary attractions, which tourists are likely to visit once they have already been drawn to a destination by the primary attraction. A destination may have more than one primary attraction, as with the Eiffel Tower and Louvre in Paris, or the Opera House and harbour in Sydney. One potential disadvantage of iconic attractions is their power to stereotype entire destinations (e.g. the Royal Canadian Mounted Police or the Pyramids of Egypt). Another potential disadvantage is the negative publicity and loss of visitation that may occur if an iconic attraction is lost due to fire, natural forces or other factors (see Managing the loss of an icon).

On 3 May 2003, the rock formation in the US state of New Hampshire known affectionately as the Old Man of the Mountain finally lost its ancient battle against the freeze/thaw cycle and collapsed into the valley below. The craggy rock profile (see figure 5.6(a)) was an iconic New Hampshire tourist attraction, having been declared the official state emblem in 1945 and subsequently appearing on two US postage stamps and a commemorative state 25-cent coin. Stabilisation repairs on the fragile rock formation had been made periodically since the early twen-

■ **Figure 5.6(a)** *Old Man of the Mountain*

tieth century, but its sudden destruction still provoked shock and disbelief. The first reaction of the governor was to establish a task force to examine how the state should respond. Its recommendations, which were accepted, ruled out any attempt to reconstruct the attraction at its original location due to costs and the instability of the remaining rock (Rayno 2003). Instead, they focused on establishing and enhancing surrounding attractions associated with the rock formation. For example, viewfinders were installed at a major vantage point that juxtaposed a 3D image of the Old Man with the present image. A memorial walking trail was also established at the base of the mountain, and an existing museum dedicated to the attraction was expanded. The governor declared 3 May to be Old Man of the Mountain Day in the state, and a plethora of official and unofficial souvenirs, ranging from the classy to tacky, was made available. The possibility of erecting a replica near the original site is being considered, and the state division of parks has established an online scrapbook to share memories and photos.

Other suggestions proffered over the Internet have included the identification of a new iconic attraction (Mount Washington, the highest point in the northeastern United States and the site of the highest recorded wind speeds, is one poss-ibility), and somewhat wishful attempts to identify a new face in the rock debris (see figure 5.6(b)). The main body of responses, however, indicates an attempt to capitalise on the Old Man as a residual attraction; that is, the lost attraction is being celebrated through a series of peripheral commemorative attractions that

■ **Figure 5.6(b)** *New Man of the Mountain*

perpetuate and enhance its mythological and iconic status. By doing so, it is hoped that many tourists will continue to visit the site to experience the *memory* of the Old Man, prompted perhaps by the extensive publicity generated by its loss.

Carrying capacity

Carrying capacity is difficult to measure since it is not a fixed quality. A national park may have a low carrying capacity in the absence of tourism-related services, but a high carrying capacity once a dirt trail has been covered in cobblestones and biological toilets installed to centralise and treat tourist wastes. In such instances of **site hardening**, managers must be careful to ensure that the remedial actions themselves do not pose a threat to the site or to the carrying capacity of affiliated resources such as wildlife (see chapters 9 and 11). It is crucial that managers have an idea of an attraction's carrying capacity at all times, so that, depending on the circumstances, appropriate measures can be taken to either increase this capacity or reduce the stress so that the existing carrying capacity is not exceeded.

Accessibility

Accessibility can be measured in terms of space, time and affordability. As considered on page 41, spatial access only by a single road will have the positive effect of facilitating entry control, but the negative effects of creating potential bottlenecks and isolating the site in the event of a flood or earthquake. Another dimension of spatial accessibility is how well an attraction is identified on roadmaps and in road signage. Temporal accessibility can be seasonal (e.g. an area closed by winter snowfalls) or assessed on a daily or weekly basis (hours and days of operation). Affordability is important in determining likely markets and visitation levels. All three dimensions should be assessed continually as aspects of an attraction that can be manipulated as part of an effective management strategy.

Market

Destination and attraction markets often vary depending on the season, time of day, cost and other factors. One relevant dimension is whether the attraction appeals to the broad tourism market, as with a theme park, or to a particular segment of the market, as with battle re-enactments or hunting (see chapter 6). A second dimension identifies sites and events that are almost exclusively tourist-oriented, as opposed to those that attract mostly local residents. Because of the tendency of clientele to be mixed to a greater or lesser extent, the all-encompassing term 'visitor attraction' is often used in preference to the term 'tourist attraction'. Positive and negative impacts can be associated with both tourist-dominant and resident-dominant attractions. For instance, an exclusively tourist-oriented site may generate local resentment, but the mixing of tourists and locals in some circumstances can increase the probability of cultural conflict (chapter 9).

Context

Context describes the characteristics of the space and time that surround the relevant site or event and, as such, is an attribute that considers the actual and potential impacts of external systems. An example of a compatible external influence is a designated state forest that serves as a buffer zone surrounding a more environmentally sensitive national park. In contrast, an adjacent strip mine is probably incompatible with that park. The influence of temporal context is demonstrated by a large sporting event that is held shortly after a similar event in another city, which could either stimulate or depress public interest depending on the circumstances.

5.3 *T*HE TOURISM INDUSTRY

The **tourism industry**, as described in chapter 2, includes the businesses that provide goods and services wholly or mainly for tourist consumption. Some but not all attractions belong to the tourism industry. It is worth reiterating that some aspects of the tourism industry are straightforward (e.g. accommodation and travel agencies), but others (e.g. transportation and restaurants) are more difficult to differentiate into their tourism and nontourism components. In addition, commercial activities such as cruise ships and integrated resorts do not readily allow for the isolation of accommodation, transportation, food and beverages, shopping, and so on as distinct components.

5.3.1 Travel *agencies*

More than any other tourism industry sector, **travel agencies** are associated with origin regions (see chapter 2). Their primary function is to provide retail travel services to customers for commission (usually in the 5 to 10 per cent range) on behalf of various tourism industry principals, including carriers, hotels and tour operators. Travel agents also normally offer ancillary services such as traveller's cheques and travel insurance (Medlik 1996). As such, they are an important interface or intermediary between consumers and other tourism businesses. Often overlooked, however, is the critical role of travel agents in shaping tourism systems by providing undecided consumers with information and advice about prospective destinations (Oppermann 1998a). Furthermore, travel agents provide invaluable feedback to destination managers because of their sensitivity to market trends and post-trip tourist attitudes about particular destinations and services.

All the traditional assumptions about the role and importance of travel agents within tourism systems, however, have been challenged by the emerging phenomenon of **disintermediation**, which is the removal of intermediaries such as travel agents from the distribution networks that connect consumers (i.e. the tourist market) with products (e.g. accommodations and destinations). This has been encouraged by the Internet, which allows hotels, carriers and other businesses to offer their products through e-commerce directly to consumers in a more convenient and less expensive package (cheaper because it eliminates the agent's commission). By 2002, an estimated 15 per cent of all leisure travel in the United States was booked online (Tse 2003). To meet this challenge, Tse (2003) recommends that travel agents must 'reintermediate' themselves by offering value-added products, such as face-to-face personal interaction with clients that provides deep and personalised advice and support throughout the travel experience, and possibly within a niche focus such as the gay and lesbian, 'grey' or adventurer markets. Partial or complete adaptation is also possible, with the latter represented by the new wave of online travel agencies such as Travelocity (www.travelocity.com) and Expedia (www.expedia.com) that expedite the mediation process.

■ 5.3.2 Transportation

The overriding trend in **transportation** over the past century (see chapters 2 and 3) is the ascendancy of the car and the aeroplane at the expense of water- and rail-based transport. The technological and historical aspects of these trends have already been outlined in earlier chapters, and the sections that follow focus instead on the business dimension of transportation.

Air

As a commercial activity, air transportation is differentiated between scheduled airlines, charter airlines and private jets. The last category is by far the smallest and most individualised. The major difference between the first two is the flexibility of charter schedules and the ability of charters to accommodate specific requests from organisations or tour operators. Many of the larger airlines have established charter subsidiaries to attain wider market coverage. For example, Air New Zealand controls Freedom Air and controlled Mount Cook Airlines until 1996, while Singapore Airlines owns the charter airline Silk Air.

Recent major developments in the airline industry include the trend towards airline alliances such as the *Star Alliance*, *OneWorld* and *SkyTeam*. Purportedly established on the premise that individual airlines can no longer provide the comprehensive array of services demanded by the contemporary traveller, these alliances offer expanded route networks, ease of transfer between airlines, integrated services and greater reciprocity in frequent flier programs and lounge privileges (Fyall & Garrod 2005). However, more frequent code-sharing (i.e. two airlines sharing the same flight) means fewer flight options, higher prices (because of reduced competition) and more crowded flights for consumers.

A second trend is deregulation (the removal or relaxation of regulations), which is intended to introduce or increase competition within the air transportation sector. Associated with deregulation is the increased application of the so-called seventh and eighth **freedoms of the air**, which respectively allow a carrier based, for example, in Australia to carry passengers between two other countries and to carry passengers on domestic routes within another country (see figure 5.7).

Privatisation, or the transfer of publicly owned airlines to the private sector, is a third significant trend, and one that is closely related to deregulation. This can be undertaken (a) as a wholesale transformation, (b) as a partial measure achieved through the sale of a certain portion of shares, or (c) through the subcontracting of work. The main rationale for privatisation (as also illustrated by national park trends) is the belief that the private sector is more efficient at providing commercial services such as air passenger transportation. One potential concern in such developments is the increased likelihood that privatised airlines will eliminate unprofitable routes vital to regional or rural destinations. In contrast, national carriers are usually mandated in the broader 'national interest' to operate such marginal routes despite their prohibitive costs.

A fourth trend that is affecting the airline industry more than other forms of transportation since September 2001 is the concern over security. Increasingly drastic measures are being adopted to address consumer sensitivities about the vulnerability of aircraft passengers to hijackings and destructive actions. These include the presence of air marshals on some flights and security clearance procedures that require substantially more lead-in time before flight departure.

■ **Figure 5.7**
Freedoms of the air

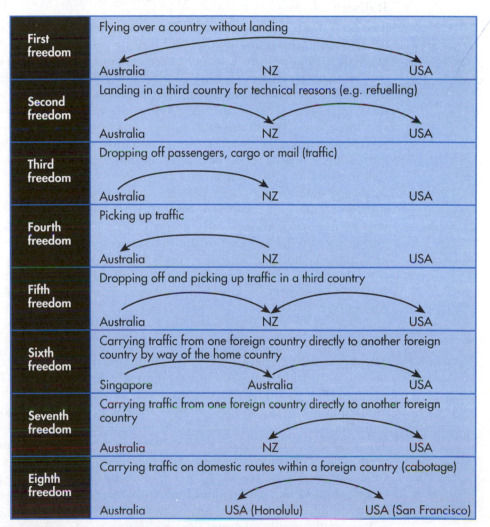

Road

Only certain elements of the road-based transportation industry, including coaches, caravans and rental cars, are directly affiliated with the tourism industry. Coaches remain a potent symbol of the package tour both in their capacity as tour facilitators and as transportation from airport to hotel. Caravans remain popular because of their dual accommodation and transportation function, although the German coach company Rotel (for *ro*lling ho*tel*) has introduced coaches that are provided with berths for overnight accommodation. The car and the aeroplane in many contexts are seen as competing modes of transportation. However, the rental car industry (e.g. Hertz, National, Avis, Budget) has benefited from the expansion of air transportation, as many passengers appreciate the flexibility of having access to their own vehicle once they arrive at a destination.

Railway

The rail industry as a whole now plays a marginal role in tourism, but there are two areas where this involvement is more substantial. The first concerns regions, such as western Europe, where concentrated and well-used rail networks facilitate tourism travel. Rail pass options that allow unlimited access over a given period of time are a popular product among free and independent travellers (FITs). Australia, among many such nationwide and state-specific options, offers the Austrailpass, which provides unlimited economy travel over the entire network over consecutive days, and the Sunshine Rail Pass, which allows 14-, 21- or 30-day unlimited travel over the Queensland Rail network on either a first-class or economy basis.

A very different situation pertains to train tours, the second mode of tourism-related rail travel. As with cruise ships, the trip itself is as much part of the 'destination' as the points of origin and terminus. Train tours also attract the higher end of the market in terms of income. Well-known examples include the Orient Express between London and Istanbul and the Eastern Orient Express between Bangkok and Singapore. An Australian example is the Indian–Pacific route from Perth to eastern Australia.

Water

The great ocean liners that once dominated the trans-Atlantic trade are now in a situation comparable to the great rail journeys — a high-end but residual niche product. Yet the resilience of this sector is indicated by the launching in 2004 of the *Queen Mary II*, which is the first major liner to be launched on the trans-Atlantic route since the *Queen Elizabeth II* in 1969. The regional cruise market in areas such as the Caribbean and Mediterranean has been more robust, expanding continuously since the 1980s. Cruising popularity has also spread to Australia, with P&O permanently basing ships in major ports and lines from other countries basing vessels in Australia for three-to-four-month seasons.

Important trends include the proliferation of mega cruise liners of 140 000 tonnes or more, which are capable of accommodating 3000 passengers or more, and the acquisition of private islands (e.g. Royal Caribbean International's CocoaCay in the Bahamas), which help to sustain passengers' off-ship expenditures within the company.

■ 5.3.3 Accommodation

Notwithstanding the local importance of cruise ships and caravans, the vast majority of stayovers who do not stay in the homes of friends or relatives use commercial tourist accommodation. Once restricted to a narrow range of conventional hotels and motels, the **accommodation** industry is now characterised by a high level of diversity and specialisation, as indicated in the following.

Hotels and apartments

Traditionally, hotels were established in central cities, often near major railway stations, to meet the needs of business travellers. This type of hotel persists today, but is now a specialised facility known as a 'city hotel', and no longer dependent on rail access. Another inner city facility is the 'convention hotel', which emerged during the 1960s to provide specialised meeting, conference and convention services. As such, they are closely affiliated with the MICE tourism phenomenon (chapter 2). 'Airport hotels' are a more recent innovation. Often clustering along distinctive hotel strips, their proximity to major airports attracts aeroplane crews and transit passengers.

In addition, airport hotels increasingly offer meeting facilities to attract business travellers by minimising the time they require to travel from their airport to their hotel. Airport hotels may also become more popular as passengers are forced to allow more lead-in time to clear security for morning flights.

The 'resort hotel' is one of the main 3S tourism symbols. These can range from specialised providers of accommodation to fully integrated resorts that provide comprehensive recreational, retail and other opportunities often in a novel setting (see Breakthrough tourism: Sleeping with the fish at Hydropolis).

Other specialised facilities include the 'apartment hotel', which is distinguished by the provision of cooking facilities and variable levels of service, and **timesharing**, which involves the purchase of 'intervals' (usually measured in weeks) at a resort over a given period of years. In some cases these are consumed during the same week each year, and in others on a more flexible basis. The ability to exchange intervals so that a holiday can be spent at a different resort is a major attraction of timesharing. Finally, 'motels' are a type of hotel with independent access to units for tourists travelling mainly by car (see chapter 2).

As with cruise ships, hotel guest capacities are constantly being increased, with Las Vegas hotel structures such as the MGM Grand and Luxor each offering more than 5000 rooms, or an amount equivalent to all the hotel rooms in Bermuda. From a corporate perspective, the hotel sector is controlled by a relatively small number of large chains (table 5.2). United States-based chains are dominant, reflecting not just the strong global US corporate presence, but also the enormous size of the US domestic tourism sector.

BREAKTHROUGH TOURISM
Sleeping with the fish at Hydropolis

A major milestone in the extension of tourism into the 'fourth dimension' of the hydrosphere was the opening of Hydropolis in late 2006. Located in the United Arab Emirate of Dubai, the world's first underwater hotel is a $700 million complex that extends 20 metres below the surface of the Persian Gulf. The submarine component includes the 220 suites of the hotel itself as well as a spa, ballroom, restaurants and an underwater museum. The jellyfish-shaped facility employs 'biogenic' architecture, which emulates the human body, and all guests in the pressure-resistant bubble-shaped suites have windows that face, as an aquarium does, onto the underwater environment. Control panels allow each guest to create their own personal multimedia environment, which could include dramatic lighting and sound effects. Positioned just above the waterline are floating themed pavilions, which include an e-library, 'silentium', prayer rooms and a Nautilus docking station. Hydropolis also includes a land component, where welcoming, orientation, parking and administrative functions are served. Other features in the land component include a cosmetic surgery clinic, hi-tech cinema, marine biological research laboratory, and business and conference facilities. A fully automated cable-propelled tunnel network connects the land and sea components (Hydropolis 2004).

Hydropolis is clearly intended to be a high-profile attraction rather than just an accommodation facility, given its promotion as a holistic experience that stimulates the wellbeing of mind, body and soul through opportunities for relaxation, education, contemplation, meditation, healing and entertainment. More broadly, Hydropolis is one manifestation of Dubai's strategy, through the auspices of the Dubai Development and Investment Authority, to become a major global tourist destination. Another manifestation is the wave-shaped Burj al Arab structure, which at 321 metres is the world's tallest and arguably most architecturally distinct hotel. One important implication of Hydropolis for the broader tourism system is its role as a prototype for underwater building technology. The groundbreaking research that was required to deal with high water pressure and other aquatic challenges could lead to a proliferation of such structures in other locations. However, with prices at Hydropolis being in the range of $1000 or more per person per night, it is likely that stayover aquatourism, as space tourism is, will be an experience accessible only to wealthy tourists for the foreseeable future (Hydropolis 2004).

■ **Table 5.2**   *The 25 largest hotel chains worldwide, 2003*

RANK	CHAIN	COUNTRY	NUMBER OF ROOMS	NUMBER OF HOTELS
1	InterContinental	United Kingdom	536 318	3 520
2	Cendant	United States	518 747	6 402
3	Marriott	United States	490 564	2 718
4	Accor	France	453 403	3 894
5	Choice Hotels	United States	388 618	4 810
6	Hilton Hotels	United States	348 483	2 173
7	Best Western	United States	310 245	4 110
8	Starwood	United States	229 247	738
9	Carlson	United States	147 624	881
10	Hilton Group	United Kingdom	98 689	392
11	Hyatt	United States	89 602	208
12	Sol Meliá	Spain	80 494	331
13	TUI	Germany	76 000	290
14	Société du Louvre	France	66 356	896
15	Interstate	United States	65 250	295
16	Wyndham	United States	50 980	190
17	Extended Stay America	United States	50 240	472
18	FelCor	United States	45 000	161
19	La Quinta	United States	43 457	363
20	Westmont	United States	40 000	332
21	US Franchise Systems	United States	36 633	470
22	Club Med	France	36 106	103
23	Le Méridien	United Kingdom	35 589	143
24	NH Hotelés	Spain	34 458	239
25	Hospitality Properties	United States	34 284	271

Source: *Hotels 2004, www.hotelsmag.com/archives/2004/07/corporate-300.asp*

■ 5.3.4   Tour *operators*

Tour operators are intermediaries or facilitating businesses within the tourism distribution system that can be differentiated between an outbound (or wholesaler) component and an inbound component. Outbound tour operators are based in origin regions and generally are large companies that organise volume-driven package tours and the travel groups that purchase these. This includes the negotiation of contracts with carriers, travel agencies, hotels and other suppliers of goods and services, including the inbound tour operators that 'take over' the tour groups once they arrive in the destination. Revenue is usually generated on a commission basis. The inbound component, often based in major gateway cities, arranges (also on a commission basis) destination itineraries and local services such as transportation, access to attractions, local tour-guiding services and, in some cases, accommodation (Higgins 1996). By the destinations and services that they choose to assemble, both types of tour operators exercise an important influence over the development of tourism systems.

However, as are travel agencies, contemporary tour operators are challenged by rapidly changing developments in technology and markets and must respond by being innovative. The uniform package tour was suitable for the industrial mode of production that dominated the era of Thomas Cook but is increasingly less suited for postindustrial society. It is necessary now to provide specialised products for a more diverse and discriminating market.

One means of achieving product diversification is to treat each unit of the tourism experience as a separate 'mini-package', thereby allowing consumers to assemble units into a customised package tour that fits their particular needs. One consumer may choose a two-week beach resort holiday with full services, followed by one week in the outback on a coach tour, while another can select from the same operator a two-week stay at an outback lodge, followed by a one-week, limited-service stay at a beach resort.

■ 5.3.5 Merchandise

Tourism-related **merchandise** can be divided into items purchased in the origin region or the destination region. Origin region merchandise includes camping equipment, cameras and film, luggage and travel guidebooks. The last two items are most clearly related to tourism, whereas it is difficult to measure the tourism component of the first two items in terms of total sales. However, unlike items bought in the destination region, even the purchase of a guidebook or luggage does not necessarily eventuate in a tourism experience.

Travel guidebooks are also important because of the influence they have over destination selection and tourist behaviour once in the destination. Established travel guide publishers such as Fodor, Fielding and Frommer have widespread brand recognition within the tourist market and are therefore highly influential in shaping travel patterns and tourism systems. Since the 1980s there has been a proliferation of new travel guides and travel guide publishers, many of which occupy a highly specialised market niche. Perhaps the most bizarre is Fielding's *Guide to the World's Most Dangerous Places* (www.fieldingtravel.com/df/dplaces.htm), which informs the reader how to behave when visiting Iraq, Afghanistan or Angola, among other unlikely destinations. The Lonely Planet series, started in 1973 (www.lonely planet.com/), has evolved from an offbeat, peripheral publication into a mainstream source of information accessed by millions of consumers. All travel guidebooks, however, are handicapped by the transitory nature of tourism systems. Highly recommended hotels and restaurants may no longer exist even before the guide is released. Some publishers cope with such uncertainty by maintaining websites in which updated information is provided, often by tourists who are invited to send in new information to special email addresses provided in the guidebooks. A greater potential challenge to the traditional hard-copy guidebook, perhaps, is the 'mobile tour guide' that capitalises on advances in IT (see Technology and tourism: Getting around with the m-ToGuide).

The traditional hard-copy guidebook may become a relic of the past if the m-ToGuide (Mobile Tourist Guide) is widely adopted by tourists. Sponsored by the European Union's Information Societies Technologies (IST) program and tried in London, Madrid and Siena (Italy), the m-toGuide consists of a portable hand-held terminal that uses cellular telephone networks, global positioning systems (GPS) and the Internet to convey location-specific, immediate, up-to-date and personalised on-site information to the tourist. The tourist can use the voice-activated system to identify his or her location (using maps or photographs or both), relevant attractions and facilities within the vicinity, how to get to these places and the most appropriate mode of transportation for travelling within or out of the area, depending on the time available. The m-ToGuide can also make reservations and purchase tickets, informs the tourist about special deals available in local shops or attractions and provides ratings on restaurants. The tourist can even gain access to information about recent crimes in the area and locations or neighbourhoods that are unsafe (Eyefortravel 2002).

The developers of the m-ToGuide allege that their technology will revolutionise the tourist experience and make it far more satisfying and efficient. However, others argue that such systems undermine the serendipity and uncertainty that makes travel enjoyable for many tourists. They may also not be necessary or effective in remote areas that have few attractions or services. Other potential drawbacks include the cost of the hardware and the information downloads ($15–20 per day in early 2004), possible breakdowns, poor resolution of some images, applicability to only some destinations, inconvenient weight and size, increased risk of theft and the need for training to exploit the system's potential fully. However, if the history of earlier information technologies such as the cell phone is any indication, consumers can expect to access increasingly less expensive, smaller, coverage-comprehensive, lighter and more powerful and efficient mobile tour guides that may indeed relegate the guidebook to the dustbin.

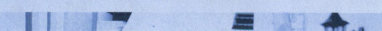

Souvenirs are the dominant form of merchandise purchased by tourists within destinations. These can range from jewellery trinkets and T-shirts to expensive, highly ornate crafts, artworks and clothing. Ironically, many of these items may be imported, calling into question their validity as 'souvenirs' of a particular destination. In contrast, duty-free shopping is based not on the desire to acquire souvenirs, but to obtain luxury items at a discount. Accordingly, whether such items are imported into the destination or not is irrelevant to most tourists. Duty-free shopping is dominated by larger corporations and chains, whereas souvenirs are often more associated with cottage industries. In Australia, the souvenir sector is dominated by Aboriginal-themed artefacts, leading to issues of authenticity, proprietary rights and the formation of 'consumer' images and expectations about the Australian tourism product.

■ 5.3.6 Industry *structure*

Frequent corporate changes and re-alignments are taking place within the tourism industry and illustrate a process known as integration. **Horizontal integration** occurs when firms attain a higher level of consolidation or control within their own sector. This can be achieved through mergers and alliances with competitors, outright takeovers or through the acquisition of shares in other companies within the sector. Horizontal integration also results from the independent establishment of subsidiaries, which diversify the firm's basic product line and thereby cushion the impact of any shifts in consumer demand, for example from first-class to budget accommodation preferences. Figure 5.8 illustrates these options in the context of a hypothetical tour operator.

In contrast, **vertical integration** occurs when a firm obtains greater control over elements of the product chain outside its own sector. If this integration moves further away from the actual consumer (e.g. a large tour operator gains control over a company that manufactures small tour buses), then vertical 'backward' integration is evident. If this integration moves closer to the consumer (e.g. the tour operator acquires a chain of travel agents), then vertical 'forward' integration is occurring. Both forms of integration imply that a firm is gaining control over more components of the tourism system as a way of becoming more competitive and ultimately maximising its profits.

■ **Figure 5.8**
Horizontal and vertical integration

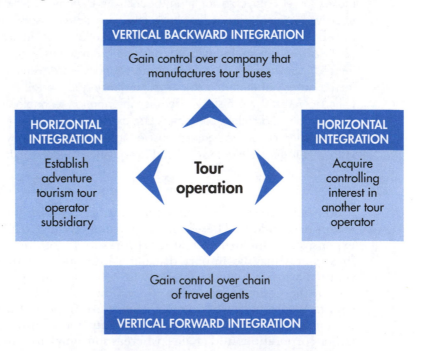

Vertical and horizontal integration are common and longstanding phenomena within the business world, as evidenced by the flurry of acquisitions and mergers that occurred in the car industry during the first half of the twentieth century. What distinguishes integration since the 1980s, however, is its global character. As the world moves towards a single global capitalist system (a process aided by advances in communications technology), firms are less constrained than ever by the presence of national boundaries and regulations in their attempt to maximise profit. This trend is commonly referred to as **globalisation**, although no precise definition actually exists for the term (Harrison 1997). The original five freedoms of the air are an early example of globalisation, while the formation of airline alliances is a more recent example.

Within the context of globalisation, it is likely that the hypothetical tour operation in figure 5.8 will expand from its Sydney base to acquire a rival in Auckland, and then set up its specialised subsidiaries in North America and western Europe, while negotiating to acquire a chain of Japanese travel agencies. The re-aligned tour operator, under the imperatives of globalisation, emerges as a powerful, globally integrated force rather than one that is only nationally influential, and benefits from an increasingly deregulated, privatised global business environment. The private sector tourism manager of the future is a highly mobile individual who expects to reside in several countries during his or her working career.

CHAPTER REVIEW

Tourist attractions are a central element of the tourism product that may or may not be part of the tourism industry, depending on their level of commercialisation and other factors. For organisation and discussion purposes, attractions (excepting VFR and business-related 'attractions') can be categorised into natural sites, natural events, cultural sites and cultural events, recognising that the distinctions between these categories are often blurred. The potential range of attractions is extremely diverse, and destinations benefit from having a broad array, since this increases potential market draw. However, destinations are limited in how much they can influence their attraction inventory — there is considerable flexibility in establishing museums, theme parks and cultural events, for example, but little or no scope for changing a location's history, topography or climate. Whatever a destination's inventory of attractions, it is important to assess and monitor their critical attributes in order to make informed planning and management decisions that will maximise the positive impacts of tourism for operators as well as residents. These attributes include ownership structure, spatial configuration, authenticity, scarcity, carrying capacity, accessibility, market and context. Some variables, such as carrying capacity and image, are difficult to measure and monitor, while others, such as context, are difficult to change or control.

The tourism product also includes the broader tourism industry, which, in addition to some attractions, can be divided into travel agencies, transportation, accommodation, tour operators and merchandise retailers. The available consumer options within all these sectors are becoming more specialised and diverse, but the industry itself, ironically, is growing more consolidated and concentrated within the hands of a few horizontally and vertically integrated corporations. Because of globalisation, this integration is occurring as an increasingly deregulated and transnational phenomenon, suggesting that the large global corporations are gaining more control over international tourism systems.

SUMMARY OF KEY TERMS

Tourism product

Consists of tourist attractions and the tourism industry

Tourist attractions

Specific and generic features of a destination that attract tourists; some, but not all, attractions are part of the tourism industry

Attraction inventory

A systematic list of the tourist attractions found in a particular destination

Tourism resources

Features of a destination that are valued as attractions by tourists at some particular point in time; a feature that was a tourism resource 100 years ago may not be perceived as such now

- **Natural sites:** geographically fixed attractions that are more natural than constructed; these can be subdivided into topography (physical features), climate, hydrology (water resources), wildlife, vegetation and location
- **Iconic attraction:** an attraction that is well-known and closely associated with a particular destination, such as Mt Fuji (Japan) or the Statue of Liberty (United States)
- **Natural events:** attractions that occur over a fixed period of time in one or more locations, and are more natural than constructed
- **Ephemeral attraction:** an attraction, such as a wildflower display or rarely filled lakebed, that occurs over a brief period of time or on rare occasions only
- **Cultural sites:** geographically fixed attractions that are more constructed than natural; these can be classified into prehistorical, historical, contemporary, economic, specialised recreational and retail subcategories
- **Dark tourism:** tourism involving sites or events associated with death or suffering, including battlefields and sites of mass killings or assassinations
- **Food tourism:** tourism that involves the consumption of usually locally produced food and drink
- **Winescapes:** a cultural landscape significantly influenced by the presence of vineyards, wineries and other features associated with viticulture and wine production; an essential element of wine-focused food tourism
- **Functional adaptation:** the use of a structure for a purpose other than its original intent, represented in tourism by canals used by pleasure boaters and old homes converted into bed and breakfasts
- **Golfscapes:** cultural landscapes that are dominated by golf courses and affiliated developments
- **Cultural events:** attractions that occur over a fixed period of time in one or more locations, and are more constructed than natural; these include historical commemorations and re-creations, world fairs, sporting events and festivals

Attraction attributes

Characteristics of an attraction that are relevant to the management of an area as a tourist destination and thus should be periodically measured and monitored; includes ownership, orientation, spatial configuration, authenticity, scarcity, status, carrying capacity, accessibility, market and image

- **Site hardening:** increasing the visitor carrying capacity of a site through structural and other changes that allow more visitors to be accommodated

Tourism industry

The businesses providing goods and services wholly or mainly for tourist consumption

- **Travel agencies:** businesses providing retail travel services to customers for commission on behalf of other tourism industry sectors
- **Disintermediation:** the removal of intermediaries such as travel agents from the product/consumer connection
- **Transportation:** businesses involved with the transportation of tourists by air, road, rail or water
- **Freedoms of the air:** eight privileges, put in place through bilateral agreements, that govern the global airline industry
- **Accommodation:** within the context of the tourism industry, commercial facilities primarily intended to host stayover tourists for overnight stays
  Hotels: the most conventional type of tourist accommodation; can be sub-categorised into city, convention, airport, resort and apartment hotels, and motels
  Timesharing: an accommodation option in which a user purchases one or more intervals (or weeks) per year in a resort, usually over a long period of time
- **Tour operators:** businesses providing a package of tourism-related services for the consumer, including some combination of accommodation, transportation, restaurants and attraction visits
  Outbound tour operators: tour operators based in origin regions that organise and market volume-driven package tours that include transportation, accommodation, attractions and so on
  Inbound tour operators: tour operators that coordinate and manage the component of the package tour within the destination, in cooperation with a partner outbound tour operator
- **Merchandise:** goods purchased as part of the anticipated or actual tourism experience; includes tour guidebooks and luggage in the origin region, and souvenirs and duty-free goods in the destination region

Horizontal integration

Occurs when firms attain a higher level of consolidation or control within their own sector

Vertical integration

Occurs when a corporation obtains greater control over elements of the product chain outside its own sector

Globalisation

The process whereby the operation of businesses and the movement of capital is increasingly less impeded by national boundaries, and is reflected in a general trend towards industry consolidation, deregulation and privatisation

QUESTIONS

1 How and why has the image of mountain areas and ethnic neighbourhoods as tourist attractions changed over the past 200 years?

2 How has climate contributed to the formation of the pleasure periphery?

3 What tourism management problems are posed by linear attractions?

4 (a) What is meant by 'functional adaptation' with respect to tourist attractions?
(b) What are some examples of functional adaptation?

5 How do sites differ from events in terms of their management implications?

6 How can the manager of an attraction deal with the attribute of context (see figure 5.5), which is difficult to control because it involves the external environment?

7 (a) Will the emergence of products such as the m-ToGuide eventually result in the extinction of the hard-copy travel guidebook?
(b) Why?

8 (a) Is the Hydropolis (see page 156) really a breakthrough in accommodation, or is it a novelty that is not likely to be repeated with any frequency outside of Dubai?
(b) Explain your response.

9 (a) What indications of globalisation are evident in the airline industry?
(b) What are the positive and negative implications of these indicators for destinations and consumers?

10 (a) What effect do horizontal and vertical integration have on the structure of tourism systems?
(b) How is this effect influenced by globalisation?

EXERCISES

1 (a) Prepare a 500-word report that discusses how food and drink in your home community can be used to provide a product that is highly attractive to tourists as well as strongly supportive of the local economy and culture.
(b) How would you market this particular food tourism product?

(continued)

2 (a) Contact five travel agencies in your local community to find out
  (i) how much their business is being affected by the phenomenon of disintermediation, and
  (ii) the strategies that they are adopting in response.
(b) Prepare a 500-word report that offers an optimal strategic response, based on a comparative assessment of these responses..

FURTHER READING

Hall, C.M., Sharples, L., Mitchell, R., Macionis, N. & Cambourne, B. (Eds) 2003. *Food Tourism Around the World: Development, Management and Markets.* **Sydney: Butterworth-Heinemann.** Eighteen authored chapters consider a range of related topics, including marketing, product development and inculcating a sense of local place through food and drink. A global case study approach is adopted.

Higginbottom, K. (Ed.) 2004. *Wildlife Tourism: Impacts, Management and Planning.* **Altona, Vic.: Common Ground Publishing.** A comprehensive and up-to-date analysis of wildlife-based tourism, this edited book is divided into three parts: the phenomenon of wildlife tourism, its impacts and appropriate management. The contributors and case studies are mainly Australian.

Higham, J. (Ed.) 2005. *Sport Tourism Destinations: Issues, Opportunities and Analysis.* **Sydney: Elsevier.** Sporting events are featured in this edited book in terms of specialised destinations, policy and planning, marketing and management and economic as well as environmental impacts. International case studies illustrate the analysis.

Hughes, H. 2000. *Arts, Entertainment and Tourism.* **Sydney: Butterworth-Heinemann.** This book uses case studies mainly from the United Kingdom and the United States to analyse the actual and potential synergies between tourism and cultural activities associated with the performing arts and entertainment.

Lennon, J. & Foley, J. 2000. *Dark Tourism: The Attraction of Death and Disaster.* **London: Continuum.** The authors, who coined the term 'dark tourism', explore this phenomenon by examining Holocaust-related tourist attractions and other disaster- and death-related sites.

Wood, R. 2004. 'Global Currents: Cruise Ships in the Caribbean Sea'. In **Duval, T. (Ed.)** *Tourism in the Caribbean: Trends, Development, Prospects.* **London: Routledge, pp. 152–71.** Wood provides a critical analysis of cruise ship tourism in the Caribbean, the world's most cruise-intensive region. The unique circumstances of cruising, including its 'deterritorialisation', are considered primarily in terms of the resulting social and environmental impacts.

Managing Kakadu National Park

Kakadu National Park, a 19 804-square-kilometre protected area established in the late 1970s, is a major attraction of the Northern Territory that has been continuously inhabited for at least 40 000 years and encompasses a unique complex of tidal flats, plateaus, floodplains and lowlands. Evidence of this occupation is provided by abundant cave paintings and rock carvings, while numerous rare or endemic species of plants and animals attest to Kakadu's importance as a stronghold of biodiversity. As with Uluru, the Northern Territory's other iconic tourist attraction, Kakadu is jointly managed by the director of national parks and its traditional Aboriginal owners, who hold title to about one-half of the land in the park and have claimed the remainder. The title lands have been leased back to the director for the purposes of establishing the national park, which is managed by a board consisting of ten Aboriginal and five non-Aboriginal members. This body has been responsible since 1989 for preparing periodic management plans for the park, based on four premises. First, any actions must respect the rights and interests of the traditional owners. Second, they should not negatively affect the ecology of the park, which is regarded as being as much a product of cultural as natural forces. Third, within the constraints of the first two premises, the park should be managed to provide enjoyment and education for the public at large. Finally, the national park should provide economic benefits for the traditional owners (DEH 2005).

Tourism is the vehicle through which most of these economic benefits are obtained. During the early 2000s, Kakadu averaged about 200 000 visitors per year, one-half of whom were international and about 5 per cent of whom were residents of the Northern Territory. A survey of 3410 visitors conducted in 2000–01 indicated that the vast majority could be characterised as ecotourists, given the importance of nature photography (85 per cent) and wildlife viewing (63 per cent) as activities undertaken (DEH 2005). Under the provisions of the current management plan, these tourists share the park with a fluctuating population of Aborigines, who have retained the right under traditional law to hunt and forage within its boundaries and to reside within the park under certain conditions. Unlike the local Aboriginal population, most tourists must engage in a lengthy transit process to reach Kakadu. The major markets and international gateways of Sydney and Brisbane, respectively, are located 4050 and 3500 km from the Northern Territory capital of Darwin, which in turn is a three-hour drive to the park. In addition, many tourists arrive by campervan from the south, after touring Uluru. The park is open to visitors every day of the year but visitation during the summer off-season is about one-half the level of the peak winter season. More specifically, visitor numbers during the January trough month (about 7000) are less than one-quarter of the intake during the July peak month (an average of 33 000), mainly because of uncomfortable levels of heat and humidity and frequent road closures caused by monsoonal flooding. During the off-season, two-thirds of visitors arrive by coach and only one-third as FITs. In the peak season, these proportions are reversed.

Visitors enter Kakadu by way of three major road access points, which used to be open from 7 am to 7 pm, although visitors could enter at other times as long as they obtained their park use ticket as soon as possible once they entered the park. This arrangement was eliminated in December 2004 when entry fees were abolished and entry stations closed to encourage a higher level of visitation after several years of decline and stagnation. To the same end, a new strategic vision was launched in 2005 to position Kakadu as an inter-national iconic attraction by capitalising on its Aboriginal connections and World Heritage status. Kakadu is one of just 22 UNESCO World Heritage sites that are listed for both their cultural and ecological significance. However, it has been overshadowed by the better-known and more recognised Uluru. As part of this new vision, the managers of Kakadu also attempted in the 2000–01 survey to gauge levels of visitor satisfaction so that strengths and weaknesses of the park 'product' could be identified and addressed. Satisfaction levels were found to be very high, yielding on average a value of 6.0 of out 7, where 1 was 'very dissatisfied' and 7 was 'very satisfied'. However, it was also revealed that many tourists were disappointed by their failure to interact or meet with tra-ditional Aboriginal owners or guides, who, it was felt, could better interpret the landscape (DEH 2005).

Other complaints focused on the fact that many of the internal 4WD roads, such as those leading to the major Jim Jim waterfall, were closed because of flooding or bridge repairs. Some respondents were concerned that the small campgrounds were overcrowded or poorly maintained, thereby detracting from the semi-wilderness experience they had expected. Surprisingly, few criticisms of the off-season weather were noted, indicating perhaps that those not dis-posed to such conditions visited at another time or that off-season visitors expected and accepted such conditions as a normal and even positive part of the genuine Kakadu experience. A bigger management challenge for Kakadu's managers is the sheer size of the park, which is almost as big as Tasmania. Related threats include the proliferation of feral animals such as water buffalo over a large area and the arrival of cane toads from northern Queensland. An enormous boundary must be monitored against such negative external influences, though the rectangular shape of the park helps to some degree by minimising the length of these boundaries. However, the latter are also disad-vantageous because they are artificial lines of latitude and longitude that cannot be 'seen' in the landscape and bear no relation to the area's ecological and cultural systems as they cut across rivers and watersheds.

Questions

1 (a) How would you classify Kakadu National Park in terms of the generic inventory of attractions described in figure 5.1?

(b) What are the strengths and weaknesses of this classification with regard to the product management and marketing of this site as a tourist attraction?

2 (a) Describe Kakadu National Park in terms of the attraction attributes outlined on pages 148–51.

(b) Wherever appropriate, indicate characteristics that both help and hinder the management of Kakadu as a site that provides enjoyment and education for visitors within the context of the other three premises described above.

(c) How can the hindrances be dealt with?

6 Tourist
markets

LEARNING OBJECTIVES

After studying this chapter, you should be able to:

1 outline the major tourist market trends since World War II

2 describe the process that culminates in a decision to visit a particular destination

3 explain the need for, and the evaluative criteria involved in, the practice of market segmentation

4 discuss the strengths and limitations of major segmentation criteria, including country of origin and family lifecycle

5 differentiate between allocentric, midcentric and psychocentric forms of psychographic segmentation

6 explain the various dimensions of motivation as a form of psychographic segmentation

7 discuss the types and importance of travel-related behavioural segmentation.

*I*NTRODUCTION

The previous chapter considered the variety and characteristics of attractions within the tourism system and also examined other supply-side components of the tourism industry, including travel agencies, transportation, tour operators and the hospitality sector. Chapter 6 returns to the demand side of the tourism equation by refocusing on the tourist. Section 6.2 reviews the major market trends in the tourism sector since World War II, and this is followed by a discussion of the destination selection process in section 6.3. Section 6.4 considers the importance of tourist market segmentation and examines the geographical, sociodemographical, psychographical and behavioural criteria that are used in segmentation exercises.

6.2 *T*OURIST MARKET TRENDS

The **tourist market** is the overall group of consumers that engages in tourism-related travel. Since World War II there have been several major trends in the evolution of this market and these are discussed below. Essentially, the overall tendency has been towards a gradually increasing level of **market segmentation**, or the division of the tourist market into distinctive **market segments** that are presumed to be relatively consistent in terms of their behaviour.

6.2.1 The democratisation *of travel*

The first trend was considered more thoroughly in chapters 3 and 4 and can be described as the democratisation of travel. This emerged as increased discretionary time and income, among other factors, made domestic and then international travel accessible to the middle and working classes. Involvement in international travel grew rapidly in the 'Western' world during the 1960s and 1970s, while a similar development occurred in certain Asian societies during the 1980s and 1990s. This was the classic era of 'mass tourism', during which the tourism industry perceived tourists as a more or less homogeneous market that demanded and consumed a very similar array of 'cookie-cutter' goods and services (figure 6.1). Such an approach did not differ essentially from that adopted by Thomas Cook during the mid-1800s (see chapter 3).

6.2.2 The emergence *of simple market segmentation and multilevel segmentation*

The second major trend emerged during the mid-1970s, as a large increase in oil prices made marketers and planners come to appreciate that a continuous growth scenario was not practical for every destination, and that some portions of the tourist market were more resistant to crisis conditions than others. This resulted in the practice of **simple market segmentation**, or the division of the tourist market into a minimal number of more or less homogenous subgroups based on certain common characteristics and/or behavioural patterns. Initially, marketers tried to isolate the smallest possible number of market segments in their desire to simplify marketing and product development efforts. Hence, broad market segments were treated as uniform entities (e.g. 'women' versus 'men', 'old' versus 'young', 'Americans' versus 'Europeans' and 'Asians').

By the 1980s the concept of market differentiation was refined through the practice of **multilevel segmentation**, which subdivided the basic market segments into more specific subgroups. For example, 'Americans' were divided into 'East Coast', 'West Coast', 'African–Americans' and other relevant categories that recognised the diverse characteristics and behaviour otherwise disguised by simple market segmentation.

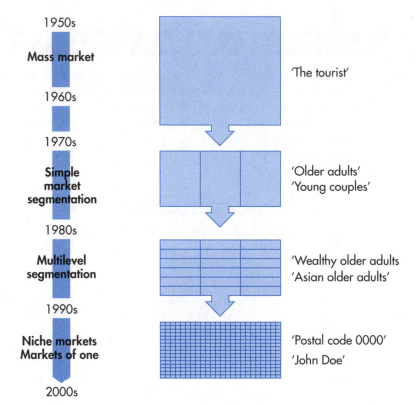

■ **Figure 6.1**
Tourist market trends since World War II

■ 6.2.3 Niche *markets and 'markets of one'*

By the 1990s the tourist market in Phase Four societies was sophisticated and knowledgeable, having had three decades of mass travel experience. Consumers were aware of what the tourism experience could and should be, and thus demanded higher quality and more specialised products that cater to individual needs and tastes. The tourism industry was able to fulfil these demands because of the Internet, flexible production techniques and other technological innovations that made catering to specialised tastes more feasible.

At the same time, the rapid expansion of the tourist market meant that traditionally invisible market segments (e.g. older gay couples, railway enthusiasts, star-gazing ecotourists) were now much larger and thus constituted a potentially lucrative market for the tourism industry. This has led to the identification of **niche markets** encompassing relatively small groups of consumers with specialised characteristics or tastes, and to the targeting of these tourists through an appropriately specialised array of products within the tourism industry (see chapter 5). Extreme segmentation, based on **markets of one**, or segments consisting of just one individual, has also become a normal part of product development and marketing strategies at the beginning of the twenty-first century. This does not mean that mass marketing will disappear, but simply that it will be technologically and financially feasible to tailor a product to just one consumer, in recognition of the fact that each individual is a unique market segment.

6.3 THE DESTINATION SELECTION PROCESS

Further insight is gained into the importance of market segments and the methods that can be used to target these segments for marketing and management purposes by understanding the process whereby tourists arrive at a decision to visit one or more destinations. Destination marketers need to identify and understand the elements of this process that they can influence to achieve their visitation goals. They may, for example, have considerable influence over pull factors such as the design and distribution of brochures and maps, but no influence over push factors (chapter 3) that induce people to travel. This is especially relevant to travel that is undertaken for leisure/recreation purposes, since the destination is usually predetermined in business and VFR tourism (chapter 2). There are many destination selection models in the tourism literature (e.g. Um & Crompton 1990; Goodall 1991), and figure 6.2 represents just one simplified way in which this process can be depicted. This particular model begins with the decision to travel, which is driven by a combination of the 'push' factors discussed in chapter 3 and the potential tourist's personality, motivations, culture, prior life experience, gender, health and education (box A in figure 6.2).

The next stage involves the evaluation of potential destinations from an 'awareness set' of all places known to the decision maker. This awareness set includes places that are known from prior direct or indirect experiences (that is, places known through past visits or through reading, media or word-of-mouth exchanges), as well as new places that emerge from subsequent information search. The latter search, as with the broader process of destination evaluation, is filtered by the characteristics listed in box A as well as push factors such as income, available time and family size. An open-minded, wealthy and well-educated person with no children, for example, is likely to undertake a very different information search and evaluation process than an inhibited person from an insular and proscriptive culture, who also has a large family. The latter individual is likely to begin with a small awareness set and to rule out many destinations straight away because of the limitations just described (i.e. destinations that are too expensive, risky or child-intolerant). This requires assessment of the pull factors described in chapter 4, so that the final selection will likely focus on an affordable, politically stable and accessible destination with many interesting attractions and a culture similar to that of the decision maker. It is widely believed that most consumers reach a final decision after the serious consideration of just three to five options (Crompton 1992), though the original awareness set might contain hundreds of potential destinations. The actual complexity of the evaluation process is also evident in the fact that this often involves 'final' decisions that are subsequently revoked or altered by changing push and pull factors — such as being denied an expected pay increase, or news of a coup d'état. Similarly, a decision could be made as to which specific country to visit (e.g. New Zealand), but uncertainty may continue as to which destinations to visit within that country (North Island or South Island).

■ **Figure 6.2**
The destination selection process

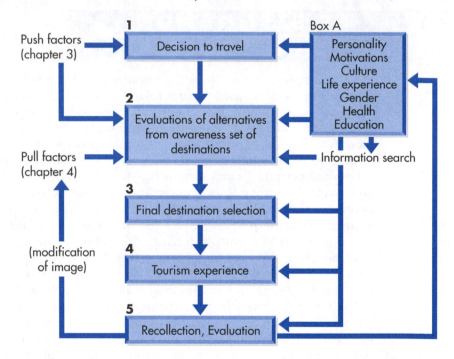

Feedback loops, such as occur when a tentative destination decision is rejected and the evaluation process is revisited, are found elsewhere in the model. Post-trip recollection and evaluation, for example, usually influence subsequent travel decisions. This commonly occurs through the refinement of the destination image 'pull' factor as a result of direct experience (e.g. the traveller had a wonderful vacation and thus carries a strongly positive destination image into the next evaluation process). The influence can also be indirect, as when the travel experience leads to modifications in the individual's personality or culture (e.g. the traveller becomes more open to further travel to exotic destinations).

■ 6.3.1 Multiple *decision makers*

The destination selection process is further complicated by the fact that more than one person is often involved in the decision-making process. In such cases, purchase decisions both before and during the trip therefore tend to require more time, as they often represent a compromise among group members. Wang et al. (2004), with regard to the purchase of group package tours by South Koreans, found that husbands and wives were equally influential in making the decision to travel and selecting a destination, as well as in budgeting, determining length of stay, and selecting airlines and restaurants. However, wives played a dominant role in the information search and in selecting accommodation, travel agents and shopping opportunities. Young children are an interesting factor in the decision-making process, since they do not usually have much of an actual say, but exercise a strong influence over their parents' decisions because of their special needs and wants. In the South Korean study cited, children were found to have a major influence in particular over the activities undertaken during the trip.

6.4 TOURIST MARKET SEGMENTATION

Market segmentation, as stated, divides the total tourist population into smaller, relatively homogeneous subgroups that can be catered to or managed as separate market segments. There are at least eight factors that should be considered concurrently when evaluating the utility of market segmentation in any given situation, including:

- *Measurability*. Can the target characteristics be measured in a meaningful way? Psychological criteria, for example, are more difficult to quantify than age or education level.
- *Size*. Is the market segment large enough to warrant attention? Very small groups, such as female war veterans over 85 years of age, may be insufficiently large to warrant attention by smaller companies or destinations that lack the capacity to engage in niche marketing.
- *Homogeneity*. Is the segmented group sufficiently distinct from other market segments? It may be, for example, that the 45–49 age group of adult males is not significantly different from the 50–54 age group, thereby eliminating any rationale for designating them as separate segments.
- *Compatibility*. Are the values, needs and wants of the segment compatible with the destination or company's own values, corporate strategies, and so on? To use an extreme example, the Muslim holy city of Mecca forbids the presence of non-Muslims, who therefore constitute an incompatible market for that city. Similarly, a company that caters to fundamentalist Christians will alienate its core constituency if it introduces strategies to attract gay and lesbian consumers.
- *Accessibility*. How difficult is it to reach the target market? Sex tourists are relatively inaccessible because they are less likely to admit participation in

a socially unsanctioned activity. A more frequently encountered illustration is a small business in an English-speaking country that lacks the capacity to market its products overseas in languages other than English.

- *Actionability.* Is the company or destination able to serve the needs of the market segment? For example, a wilderness lodge is usually not an appropriate venue for catering to gamblers or those with severe physical disabilities.
- *Durability.* Will the segment exist for a long enough period of time to justify the pursuit of specialised marketing or management strategies? For example, the population of World War II veterans is now experiencing a high rate of attrition, and will be negligible in size by 2020.
- *Relevance.* Is there some underlying logic for targeting a particular segment? Segmentation on the basis of eye colour meets all the previous criteria, but there is no rational basis for thinking that eye colour influences consumer behaviour in any significant way.

The following sections discuss the major market segmentation criteria that are commonly used in the contemporary tourism sector, as well as those that are not widely employed, but could be of potential value to tourism destinations and the tourism industry. These criteria include the box A characteristics in figure 6.2, which also influence the behaviour of individuals during and after the actual tourism experience. Ultimately, the appropriateness of particular segmentation criteria to a destination or business will depend on the conclusions reached in the evaluation of the eight factors outlined above.

■ 6.4.1 Geographic *segmentation*

Geographic segmentation takes into account the country of birth, nationality or current residence of the consumer. Place is the oldest and most popular basis for segmentation. Where budget limitations restrict segmentation to one criterion this is the one usually undertaken. Geographic segmentation declined during the 1980s as other segmentation criteria emerged, but it is now reasserting its former dominance through the emergence of cost-effective **GIS (geographic information systems)** as a tool for facilitating the spatial analysis of tourism-related phenomena. GIS encompasses a variety of sophisticated computer software programs that assemble, store, manipulate, analyse and display spatially referenced information (Feng & Morrison 2002). In a GIS package, the exact location of a person's residence can be specified and related to other criteria relevant to that same location (e.g. income level, age structure, education levels, rainfall, road network, etc.). It is therefore possible to compile detailed combinations of market characteristics at a very high level of geographic resolution (e.g. individual households), making feasible the 'markets of one' described on page 173. Before GIS, the best level of resolution that could be hoped for was the equivalent of the postal code or census subdistrict.

Region and country of residence

The least sophisticated type of geographical analysis, but the simplest to compile, is regional residence, which has often been used as a surrogate for culture. Traditionally, tourism managers were content to differentiate their markets as 'Asian', 'North American' or 'European', because of low numbers and on the assumption that these regional markets exhibited relatively uniform patterns of behaviour. Most destinations and businesses now realise that such generalisations are simplistic and misleading, and prefer to differentiate at least by country of origin. In the case of Australia, for example, useful distinctions can be made between Japanese and American inbound tourist markets (see the case study at the end of this chapter). However, important differences among countries within the same region are also increasingly apparent as arrivals from these individual countries continue to increase. In the East Asian regional market context, it is now imperative for Australians to regard Japan, China, Taiwan, Hong Kong and South Korea as distinctive segments that each warrants its own specialised marketing and management strategies (Chon, Inagaki & Ohashi 2000).

Subnational segmentation

It is appropriate to pursue geographical segmentation at a subnational level under two circumstances. First, larger countries tend to display important differences in behaviour from one internal region to another. Reduced cost and travel time, for example, position the California market as a stronger per capita source of tourists for Australia than New York or Florida.

The second factor is the number of people that travel to a destination from a particular country. A large number justifies the further division of that market into geographical subcomponents. For example, when the number of Chinese inbound tourists to Australia involved only a few thousand visitors, there was no compelling reason to make any further distinction by province of origin. However, as this number approaches 200 000, it makes more sense to consider provincial origins as a basis for market segmentation.

Urban and rural origins

Useful insights may be gained by subdividing the tourist market on the basis of community size. Residents of large metropolitan areas have better access to media and the Internet than other citizens, and more options to choose from at all stages of the destination buying process. Yet within those same communities, the residents of gentrified inner-city neighbourhoods (e.g. North Sydney) are quite distinct from the residents of working-class outer suburbs (e.g. Parramatta) or the exurbs. Rural residents also have distinctive socioeconomic characteristics and behaviour. The urban–rural dichotomy is particularly important in less developed countries, where large metropolitan areas are likely to accommodate Phase Three or Four societies, while the countryside may reflect Phase Two characteristics (see section 3.5.1).

6.4.2 Sociodemographic *segmentation*

Sociodemographic segmentation variables include gender, age, family life cycle, household education, occupation and income. Such variables are popular as segmentation criteria because they are easily collected (except perhaps for income) and often associated with distinct types of behaviour.

Gender and gender orientation

Gender segmentation can be biological or sociocultural. If construed in strictly biological terms, gender is a readily observable and measurable criterion. There are many activities, such as hunting and fishing, which are heavily skewed towards one sex or the other.

Frew and Shaw (1999), for example, found that Australian males living in Melbourne were significantly more likely to have visited or have the interest and intent to attend the Australian Football League Grand Final, the behind the scenes tour of the Melbourne Cricket Council, the Australian Formula One Grand Prix and the Australian Motorcycle Grand Prix. In contrast, their female counterparts were significantly more likely to have visited the Penguin Parade ecotourism site on Phillip Island and had more interest and intent than males to visit the Royal Agricultural Society of Melbourne Show and the National Gallery of Victoria. According to Bond (1997), female travellers tend to be more concerned with issues of physical and psychological security as well as physical comfort, which could have important implications in initiatives to protect tourists against terrorist attacks. Women, according to Westwood, Pritchard and Morgan (2000), also tend to place a higher value on social interaction during travel and appreciate attention to detail in the provision of goods and services. A satisfied female client is more likely to remain loyal to that product and will spread information about her experiences through word-of-mouth contact with other women.

Gender can also be construed in terms of sexual orientation. For many years, gay and lesbian tourism was either ignored by the tourism industry, or existed only as an informal fringe element. With the liberalisation of sexual attitudes in the late twentieth century, this component of tourism became more visible through the emergence of specialised formal businesses and activities, particularly in the areas of accommodation (e.g. Turtle Cove Resort north of Cairns), tour operators (e.g. The Wilson Group in New Zealand), special events and the cruise ship sector. A third phase, which became evident in the 1990s, was the active pursuit of this market by the mainstream tourism industry, in recognition of its formidable purchasing power (Clift, Luongo & Callister 2002). Some estimates suggest that the **pink dollar** accounts for 10–15 per cent of all consumer purchasing power. Destinations that are regarded as gay and lesbian 'friendly' include Sydney, San Francisco, London, Cape Town (Visser 2003) and Amsterdam. Sydney in particular is making a concerted bid to be recognised as a major gay and lesbian tourism destination, with its highly successful annual Gay and Lesbian Mardi Gras, and its hosting of the Gay Games in 2002.

Age and family lifecycle

Age and lifecycle considerations are popular criteria used in socio-demographic segmentation, since these can also have a significant bearing on consumer behaviour. Specific consideration is given in the following subsections to older adults, young adults and the traditional family lifecycle.

Older adults

Along with the emergence and growing acceptance of the gay and lesbian community, the rapid ageing of population is one of the dominant trends in contemporary Phase Four societies (see chapter 3). In the year 2010 the first baby boomers will turn 65, and this will accelerate interest in the 'older adult' market segment. Traditionally, the 65+ market was assumed to require special services and facilities due to deteriorating physical condition. Their travel patterns, moreover, were believed to be influenced by the dual impact of reduced discretionary income and increased discretionary time caused by retirement. Finally, older adults were commonly perceived to constitute a single uniform market. All these assumptions, however, are simplistic. In postindustrial Phase Four societies the 65-year age threshold is no longer a strict indicator of a person's retirement status. Many companies facilitate early retirement options, while there is a concurrent trend to remove artificial age-of-retirement ceilings. As for income, the current cohort of retirees is likely to be better off financially than their predecessors. The assumption of physical deterioration is also false, as the 65-year-old of 2000 is in much better physical condition than their counterpart of 1950, and has a much longer life expectancy. Finally, the assumption of market uniformity is also untenable, as demonstrated by research among Australian older adults (see Contemporary issue: Understanding the complex seniors market). Another relevant trend with implications for tourism participation is the growing number of grandparents who raise their own grandchildren and/or live with them in multi-generational households (ABS 2003).

CONTEMPORARY ISSUE

Understanding the complex seniors market

Recent research by Cleaver Sellick (2004) attests to the heterogeneity of older Australian adults (50 and older) by revealing four travel motivational clusters of roughly equal size. 'Enthusiastic connectors' (20 per cent of 952 respondents to a motivational survey) show the highest levels of motivation in terms of wanting to learn, connect with others, be sociable, be physically active, develop attachment with others, build self-esteem, engage in indulgent relaxation and have nostalgic reminiscences. A second cluster, labelled 'discovery and self-enhancement', (26 per cent), is similarly high on the dimension of learning but somewhat less motivated by the other factors. 'Nostalgic travellers' (29 per cent) rate the desire to have nostalgic reminiscences very highly, while 'reluctant travellers' (25 per cent) register the lowest levels for all the factors. Yet, surprisingly, the latter group were least concerned about perceived risks of travel that are physical (i.e. illness and physical danger), facility-related (i.e. time, amenities, arrangements), psychological (i.e. self-image) and value-related (i.e. personal satisfaction and value for money), while enthusiastic connectors are the most concerned. It may be that those who are not motivated to travel are also therefore not as perceptive of the risks involved. Also, the overall means yielded by enthusiastic connectors were not high in an absolute sense (mostly under 6 on a scale of 1 to 10) suggesting that they did not negatively affect travel decisions. The main demographic distinction among the clusters was the fact that members of the discovery and self-enhancement group tended to have higher levels of education, household income and self-perceived good health.

Some interesting marketing implications of this research are discussed by Cleaver Sellick (2004). One is that older Australians may not be more dissuaded

(continued)

to travel by perceived risks than their younger counterparts, as is commonly assumed. Second, education, income and perceptions of good health all appear useful as discriminating among older adults while gender, marital status and employment status do not, contrary to what some earlier research has found. Third, because most respondents reported that they engaged in activities when travelling that were more likely to be undertaken by persons about ten years younger than themselves, it may be more important in marketing strategies to consider the *cognitive* rather than *chronological* age of older adults.

Young adults

In contrast to the 65+ cohort, young adults, and especially those in their teens and early 20s, are often associated with higher levels of loutish and high-risk behaviour. This is especially evident in ritual events such as the 'spring break' phenomenon in the United States and Australia's 'Schoolies Week' (the celebration of a student's completion of high school), which destination managers on the Gold Coast are attempting to convert into an orderly festival. Involving up to 100 000 young visitors, Schoolies Week is regarded with ambivalence by local residents, who appreciate the positive economic benefits of the influx and its containment largely within the heavily developed Surfers Paradise neighbourhood. However, there is concurrent concern over the event's association with high levels of alcohol and drug abuse, predatory sexual activity, littering and disorderly conduct.

Family lifecycle

The **family lifecycle** (**FLC**) consists of a series of stages through which the majority of people in a Phase Four society are likely to pass during the time from young adulthood to death (figure 6.3). The FLC stages are associated with particular age brackets, although there are many exceptions to this. All stages are also related to significant changes in family status, such as marriage, the appearance and raising of children, and the death of a partner. Retirement (i.e. change in work status) is also identified as an important stage transition.

Lawson (1991) assigned a sample of inbound visitors in New Zealand to appropriate stages in the FLC and found this variable to be important for predicting the tendency to travel, the amount of expenditure made while touring and the types of activities pursued. Regarding tendency to travel, table 6.1 reveals the overrepresentation of young singles, young couples and empty nest Is as tourism participants (i.e. observed cases in the sample) in relation to the overall population structures of major source countries (i.e. expected cases). Young singles in this study were especially enthusiastic as travellers, being overrepresented by a factor (i.e. difference ratio) of almost six.

In contrast, the constraining effect of young children is evident in the underrepresentation of all full nest categories (and especially full nest Is, who are underrepresented by a factor greater than seven). Solitary survivors also demonstrate a pattern of curtailed travel. Only empty nest IIs are represented at a level comparable to their overall population share. Significant differences are also evident in expenditure patterns. Larger groups, such as full

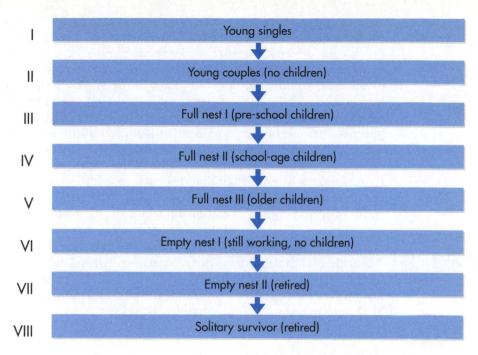

Figure 6.3
The traditional family lifecycle

I — Young singles

II — Young couples (no children)

III — Full nest I (pre-school children)

IV — Full nest II (school-age children)

V — Full nest III (older children)

VI — Empty nest I (still working, no children)

VII — Empty nest II (retired)

VIII — Solitary survivor (retired)

nest IIs and IIIs, not surprisingly, have greater total expenditures, but young singles are the highest spenders on a per capita basis. In terms of activity, young singles and couples are important as markets for rafting, waterskiing, entertainment and spas, while empty nesters place a high priority on museums, tours and Maori-related culture and performances.

Table 6.1
Tourism participation and expenditure in New Zealand by FLC type

| FLC TYPE | OBSERVED CASES | EXPECTED CASES[1] | DIFFERENCE RATIO[2] | EXPENDITURE (NZ$) | |
				PER PERSON	TOTAL
I	312	55	+5.7	913	913
II	392	95	+4.1	851	1702
III	51	375	−7.4	490	1496
IV	192	519	−2.7	468	1831
V	165	227	−1.4	648	2200
VI	587	203	+2.9	832	1666
VII	262	264	1.0	674	1350
VIII	106	329	−3.1	764	764

Note:
[1] Distribution of the observed cases if these were representative of the overall population structure of major source countries
[2] Calculated as a ratio of the higher figure in each row relative to the lower figure, for example 312/55 = +5.7, with the plus sign indicating overrepresentation

Source: *Lawson (1991)*

This evidence from New Zealand suggests that the FLC is a potentially useful sociodemographic basis for tourist market segmentation. However, one major drawback is that an increasing number of people do not conform to the cycle. In Lawson's 1991 study, 1359 individuals, or 40 per cent of the total sample, did not fit into any of the stages. This is likely to be even higher in the early 2000s. Exceptions include permanently childless couples or those who have children relatively late in life, divorced people, single parents, long-term gay and lesbian couples, multi-generational families, 'permanent singles' and those whose spouses die at an early age. In essence, the FLC reflects the traditional nuclear family of the 1950s and 1960s rather than the present era of familial diversity. In addition, even if individuals do conform to the FLC, this is not necessarily reflected in the composition of travel groups. People in relationships may decide to travel by themselves, or with a group of friends, while married couples may be accompanied by one or more parents, nephews or other married couples.

Another confounding factor is pet ownership and the increasing tendency of individuals in all stages of the FLC to regard their animals as household members and desirable travel companions (see figure 6.4 and Technology and tourism: Expediting travel for pets).

■ **Figure 6.4**
Pet-friendly hotels

TECHNOLOGY AND TOURISM
Expediting travel for pets

Pets are an increasingly prevalent and important component of postindustrial societies where people are electing to have fewer and fewer children and have the discretionary income to obtain and maintain companion animals. Two-thirds of Australian households, for example, own at least one pet, and 91 per cent of these owners report that they feel 'very close' to their animals. Moreover, more than one-half of those not owning pets report that they would like to do so sometime in the future (PIAS 2005). It is, therefore, surprising that destination managers have made few efforts to attract animal-owning tourists by being suitably 'pet friendly'. One exception is the United Kingdom, which is a leader in the use of technology to facilitate the entry and re-entry of dogs and cats through its Pet Travel Scheme (PETS) (DEFRA 2005). Pet owners from eligible countries (mostly in the European Union and other developed regions) avoid a costly six-month period of quarantine by following a procedure that begins with the implantation of a microchip that identifies the animal. This is followed by vaccination against rabies and a blood test to ensure that the vaccination provides adequate protection against the latter. With these secured, the owner is then required to obtain a 'pet passport' from their home country that confirms adherence to the above procedure. The only requirements that must still be fulfilled are treatment against tapeworms and ticks, and arrangements to travel by an approved transport company along an authorised route.

The Pet Travel Scheme is a sensible compromise between preventing the spread of rabies and other pet-borne diseases within the United Kingdom and accommodating the needs of a major emerging tourist segment. A similar program should be considered for Australia, where a minimum 30-day quarantine requirement (costing about $700) effectively precludes the entry of tourists travelling with their pets. This would allow inbound tourists to take advantage of pet-friendly tourism initiatives such as the dog passport offered by the company Doggy Holiday (www.doggyholiday.com/passport.htm), which records the good behaviour and medical record of pets at participating businesses and thereby expedites their welcome at other locations.

Education, occupation and income

Education, occupation and income tend to be interrelated in terms of travel behaviour, since education generally influences occupation, which in turn influences income level. University education, for example, often leads to higher-paying professional employment. Income and education are often accessed indirectly by targeting neighbourhoods that display consistent characteristics with regard to these criteria. Not surprisingly, high levels of income and education, as well as professional occupations, are associated with increased tourism activity and in particular with a higher incidence of long-haul travel. One important implication is that high-income earners are less concerned with financial considerations when assessing destination options, and less likely to alter their travel plans in the event of an economic recession. Destinations that cater to high-income earners are therefore themselves less susceptible to recession-induced slumps in visitation. Distinctive forms of educational segmentation include international students (see chapter 2's Contemporary issue feature), schoolies and participants in school excursions.

Race, ethnicity and religion

There is a general reluctance to ascribe distinctive character and behavioural traits on the basis of race, ethnicity or religion, and none of these are, therefore, commonly used for generic segmentation purposes.

However, these are commonly used as segmentation criteria for specialised attractions that cater to particular racial, ethnic or religious groups. Examples include the marketing of heritage slavery sites in western Africa to African–Americans, and religious pilgrimages and festivals to applicable religious groups.

Disability

Persons with disabilities are often neglected or overlooked as a significant tourist segment, even though it is apparent that the number of such individuals is immense and their desire to travel as high as the general population's (Yau, McKercher & Packer 2004; Stumbo & Pegg 2005). According to Australian Bureau of Statistics criteria, 19 per cent of the Australian population (or 3.6 million people) were considered to have a disability in 1998 (ABS 1998). Three factors that indicate the need for tourism managers to pay greater attention to this segment are the ageing of Phase Four populations (given the higher incidence of disabilities among older adults), the availability of technology to expedite travel by persons with disabilities, and increasing recognition of the basic human rights, including the right to travel, of such persons. Some researchers, however, suggest that a fundamental change in the basic perspective of tourism stakeholders is required to accommodate the needs and rights of this segment more appropriately (see Breakthrough tourism: A social perspective on disabilities).

BREAKTHROUGH TOURISM
A social perspective on disabilities

A major problem with segmenting the tourist market on the basis of disability is the contested nature of this concept, which can be situated within a variety of biophysical and sociocultural frameworks. According to Shelton and Tucker (2005), the tourism industry has focused in recent years on providing appropriate physical access (e.g. wheelchair ramps and Braille signage) for persons with disabilities, to the extent that it has become a central supply-side and marketing issue in many destinations. Tourism Australia, for example, provides a 'disabled travelers' link on the front page of its corporate website under 'special travel needs'. Shelton and Tucker regard this kind of accommodation as admirable and an improvement on past approaches but they also argue that the equation of an individual's *impairment* (e.g. missing legs) with associated *disabilities* (e.g. reduced ability to walk) and specialised modes of access (e.g. wheelchair trails and ramps) indicates a narrow person-centred (or personal) model that is itself disabling in so far as it puts the onus on persons with disabilities to identify themselves, focuses unwanted attention on them and confines their activities to specialised structures provided by a benevolent government, charity or business. A social model of disability, they argue, is more appropriate in that it assumes the right of persons with disabilities, like other marginalised groups, to political enfranchisement and an equitable share of a society's available wealth. Accordingly, resources would be allocated to providing individuals currently labelled as 'disabled' with opportunities to participate more fully in tourism beyond the provision of specialised signage or physical access to specific spaces. The effect, in essence, would be to dissociate impairment from the social construct of disability.

Beyond the ethical imperative of such a transformation, Shelton and Tucker maintain that the adoption of an inclusive social approach (which does not mean the removal of wheelchair access and Braille signs but rather their augmentation by more diverse modes of involvement) is a financially sound strategy for destinations and businesses, given the large market of 'disabled' latent tourists who would readily patronise products and places that provide opportunities to join in rather than just to have access. A critical first step in the design and implementation of more suitable facilities and products, according to the authors, is consultation with well-informed travellers with disabilities.

■ 6.4.3 Psychographic *segmentation*

The differentiation of the tourist market on the basis of psychological characteristics is referred to as **psychographic segmentation**. This can include a complex and diverse combination of factors, such as motivation, personality type, attitudes and perceptions, and needs. Psychographic profiles are often difficult to compile due to problems in identifying and measuring such characteristics. Individuals themselves are usually not aware of where they would fit within such a structure. Whereas most people can readily provide their income, age, country of residence and so on for a questionnaire, their psychological dimension often has to be inferred through their responses to complex surveys, and then interpreted by the researcher. Whether they can then be placed into neat categories, as with age or income, is also highly questionable.

Also problematic is how much psychological characteristics can change, depending on circumstances. The factors that motivate a tourist to visit one destination may be entirely absent in the tourist's next trip. Similarly, personality type can change as a result of a person's experiences, but this often occurs imperceptibly and in a way that is difficult to quantify, unlike changes of address or income level. Identification of a person's 'usual' personality can also be misleading to the extent that an 'alternate' personality may be acquired during a tourism experience, since this constitutes a change of routine for the traveller. Because of such complexities, psychographic research usually requires more time and money than other types of segmentation, and often yields conflicting results.

Plog's psychographic typology

The personality typology of Stanley Plog (Plog 1991, 1998) is widely cited within tourism studies. According to Plog, a 'normal' (i.e. representative) population, represented as a bell curve, can be divided into several categories based on personality dimensions with intermediate categories provided to recognise the continual rather than discrete nature of these dimensions (figure 6.5). **Venturers** or 'allocentrics' are intellectually curious travellers who enjoy immersing themselves in other cultures and willingly accept a high level of risk. They tend to make their own travel arrangements, travel by themselves or in pairs and are open to spontaneous changes in itinerary. They tend to avoid places that are heavily developed as tourist destinations, seeking out locales in which tourism is non-existent or incipient. Figure 6.6 provides a more detailed list of characteristics and tourism behaviour attributed to allocentrics.

■ **Figure 6.5**
Plog's psychographic typology

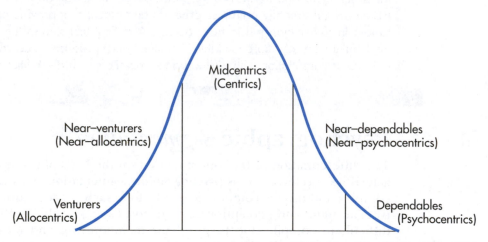

Source: *Adapted from Plog (1991, 1998, 2004)*

In contrast, **dependables** (or 'psychocentrics') are self-absorbed individuals who seek to minimise risk by patronising familiar, extensively developed destinations where a full array of familiar goods and services are available. Plog estimated that only about 4 per cent of the American population were 'pure' venturers and a similar proportion 'pure' dependables, while about 17 per cent were in each of the 'near' categories (Plog 1998). The remaining 60 per cent of the population, as depicted in figure 6.5, are **midcentrics** (or 'centrics') whose personalities compromise between the dependable and venturer dimensions. Typical midcentric behaviour is the visitor to a tropical resort who is eager to attend a local cultural performance and sample the local cuisine, but is equally eager to have access to comfortable accommodation, hygienically prepared meals and a clean bathroom.

Plog's typology has important implications for the evolution and management of tourism systems. Dependables, for example, tend to visit well-established destinations dominated by large corporations and well-articulated tourism distribution systems, while allocentrics display an opposite tendency. A dependable would prefer to eat at McDonald's, stay overnight at the Sheraton and visit a theme park, all mediated by a package tour, while an allocentric would eat at a local market stall, stay overnight in a small guesthouse situated away from the tourist district and explore the local rainforest.

■ **Figure 6.6**

*Personality
and travel-
related
characteristics
of allocentrics
and
psychocentrics*

Venturers	Dependables
Intellectually curious	Intellectually restricted
Moderate risk-taking	Low risk-taking
Use disposable income	Withhold income
Try new products	Use well-known brands
Exploring/searching	Territory bound
Feel in control	Sense of powerlessness
Relatively anxiety free	Free-floating anxiety/nervousness
Interested/involved	Non-active lifestyle
Adventurous	Non-adventurous
Self-confident	Lacking in confidence
Prefer non-touristy areas	Prefer the familiar in travel destinations
Enjoy sense of discovery and delight in new experiences, before others have visited the area	Like commonplace activities at travel destinations
Prefer novel and different destinations	Prefer sun'n'fun spots, including considerable relaxation
High activity level	Low activity level
Prefer flying to destinations	Prefer destinations they can drive to
Tour accommodation should include adequate-to-good hotels and food, not necessarily modern or chain-type hotels, and few 'tourist-type' attractions	Prefer heavy tourist development (lots of hotels, family-type restaurants, tourist shops, etc.)
Enjoy meeting and dealing with people from a strange or foreign culture	Prefer familiar atmosphere (hamburger stands, familiar-type entertainment, absence of foreign atmosphere)
Tour arrangements should include basics (transportation and hotels) and allow considerable freedom and flexibility	Complete tour packaging appropriate, with heavy scheduling of activities
Travel more frequently	Travel less
Spend more of income on travel	Spend more of income on material goods and impulse buys
Inquisitive, curious about the world and its peoples	Little interest in events or activities in other countries
Demanding, sophisticated, active travellers	Naïve, non-demanding, passive travellers
Want much spontaneity in trips	Want structured, routinised travel
Will learn languages or foreign phrases before and during travels	Expect foreigners to speak in English
Seek off-the-beaten-path, little-known local hotels, restaurants	Want standard accommodation and conventional (American) meals
Buy native arts/crafts	Buy souvenirs, trinkets, common items
Want different destination for each trip	Prefer returning to same and familiar places
Prefer small numbers of people	Enjoy crowds

Source: *Plog (1991, 2004)*

The model's conceptual simplicity makes it very popular among tourism students and academics. However, the model should not be accepted without criticism. It is unclear, for example, whether the model can be applied to children, whose personalities may not be fully developed. Also, Plog's methodology for identifying dependable trends has never been publicly revealed due to its commercial sensitivity, and researchers are therefore unable to test the theory using similar methods. The question whether personality is implicit or learned, as discussed, is also relevant: can dependables be converted to midcentrism or venturers by forcing them to face new experiences, or does this just force them further into their shells? In sum, Plog's model is best utilised as a useful indicator of personality dimensions, but not as a definitive predictor of personality distribution or tourist behaviour.

Motivation

Travel **motivation** is different from travel purpose (see section 2.3.3) in that it indicates the intrinsic reasons the individual is embarking on a particular trip. Thus, a person might be travelling for VFR purposes, but the underlying motivation is to resolve a dispute with a parent, or to renew a relationship with a former partner. A pleasure or leisure purpose may indicate a deeper need to escape routine. In all these cases, the apparent motivation may itself have some even more fundamental psychological basis, such as the need for emotional satisfaction. Motivation is implicit in Plog's model, in that allocentrics are more driven by curiosity than psychocentrics, who in turn are more likely to be motivated by hedonism.

There are numerous theories and classification schemes associated with motivation. One of the best known is Maslow's hierarchy of human needs (in Page 2003), which ranges from basic physiological needs (e.g. food, sleep, sex) to the needs for safety and security, love, esteem, self-actualisation, knowledge and understanding, and finally, aesthetics. Maslow has been interpreted within tourism studies to imply that Phase Three and Four societies engage in tourism because their more basic needs have already been met. However, this is misleading. Travel for purposes of health and to access warm weather may be construed as meeting basic physical needs, while 'love needs', the third most basic need according to the hierarchy, are potentially met through the comradeship of group travel or the bonding with like-minded individuals in a battle re-enactment.

It is convenient and pragmatic to group motivations into relatively simple categories such as relaxation, desire to learn, adventure and social contact. This is the approach taken in the American Traveler Survey, which annually surveys a random sample of more than 10 000 households in the United States. Asked why the respondent likes to take a vacation, more than two-thirds indicated the need to get rid of stress, while the desire to spend time with one's spouse, adhere to no schedule, and see or do new things were also cited by at least one-half of the sample (see table 6.3). Context-specific motivations, such as being outdoors, seeking solitude or learning about history and culture, were less prevalent but still important for at least 10 per cent of the sample.

REASON	%	REASON	%
Get rid of stress	70	Have time for friends	23
Time with spouse	60	Learn history/culture	23
Enjoy no schedules	59	Important part of life	21
See/do new things	56	Romantic time	21
I feel alive/energetic	33	Like solitude/isolation	16
Gain perspective	31	Enjoy being outdoors	14
Like being waited on	24	Enjoy physical tests	10

Source: *Plog (2005)*

In contrast to this American research, which simply lists the percentages indicating particular motivations, Lang and O'Leary (1997) identified specific and mutually exclusive clusters within a sample of 1032 Australian outbound 'nature tourists'. The following groups emerged from the study:

- family vacationers (27 per cent)
- culture and entertainment seekers (25 per cent)
- escape and relax vacationers (12 per cent)
- nature tourists (8 per cent)
- physical challenge seekers (8 per cent)
- indifferent travellers (3 per cent).

For the first group, being with family is the major reason for taking the trip, and visits to villages or the countryside, and shopping and sightseeing, are major activity priorities. Cultural performances and other events and entertainment are important driving forces for the second group, along with guided tours and city sightseeing. Escape and relax vacationers seek removal from their daily routines, and prefer water-related activities and nightlife. Nature tourists seek new experiences and participate in nature and heritage-related activities. Physical challenge seekers enjoy sports and water-related pursuits, while indifferent travellers are not specific or articulate about the needs that were being filled by their trip.

6.4.4 Behavioural *segmentation*

The identification of tourist markets on the basis of activities and other actions undertaken during the tourism experience is an exercise in **behavioural segmentation**. In a sense, it employs the *outcomes* of destination buying decisions as a basis for market segmentation, and therefore omits the non-travelling component of the population, unless non-travel behaviour is included as a category. Basic behavioural criteria include:

- travel occasion
- destination coverage (including length of stay)
- activities
- repeat patronage and loyalty.

Travel occasion

Travel occasion is closely related to purpose. Occasion-based segmentation differentiates consumers according to the specific occasion that prompts them to visit a particular tourism product. The honeymoon market is one example that is heavily targeted by various destinations within Australia and South-East Asia. Birthdays, anniversaries, funerals and other rites of passage are other examples of individualised travel occasion, while Schoolies Week and sporting spectacles indicate mass variants.

Destination coverage

Destination coverage can be expressed by length of stay, and also by the number of destinations (as opposed to stopovers and other transit experiences) that are visited during a particular trip. Visitors to Australia, for example, can be segmented by how much their visits are focused on a single state (as in the case of Japanese package tours to Queensland) or a multi-state itinerary (as in the case of backpackers from Europe). Similarly, these visitors can be differentiated by the percentage of total trip time spent in Australia. Inbound tourists from short-haul markets such as New Zealand tend not to visit any other countries during their trips to Australia, while tourists from long-haul markets in the Americas or Europe usually include visits to other countries in their Southern Hemisphere itineraries (Oppermann, Tideswell & Faulkner 1999). In the latter case, it is important to determine whether Australia is a primary, secondary or incidental component of the overall itinerary.

Both single-destination and multi-destination trips usually display a great deal of variety with respect to destination coverage, as modelled by Oppermann (1995) (figure 6.7). Numerous implications follow from this model, including the extent to which tourists are concentrated or dispersed within a country, the length of time (and thus amount of money) spent in different parts of the country and the types of services that are accessed during the tourism experience. Multi-destination itineraries continue to grow in popularity as countries and regions pursue mutually beneficial bilateral and multi-lateral destination marketing and development initiatives. Visitors to East Africa, for example, are taking advantage of tours that combine the accessibility and services of Kenya with the undeveloped natural attractions of neighbouring Tanzania.

Activities

Variables that can be segmented under the generic category of 'activities' include accommodation type, mode of transportation, total and per-day expenditure, attractions visited and types of tourist activities undertaken. The latter, in particular, are extremely diverse. Relevant market segments in Australia include ecotourists (see chapter 11), theme park visitors, honeymooners, beach bathers, bush walkers, visitors to Aboriginal sites and performances, backpackers, heritage tourists and wine tourists (see chapter 5). Whether these activities are of primary or secondary importance to the relevant segment is also a critical factor. The stakeholders who would most obviously be interested in attraction/activity segmentation are the operators of such businesses, or the destinations that specialise in these attractions or

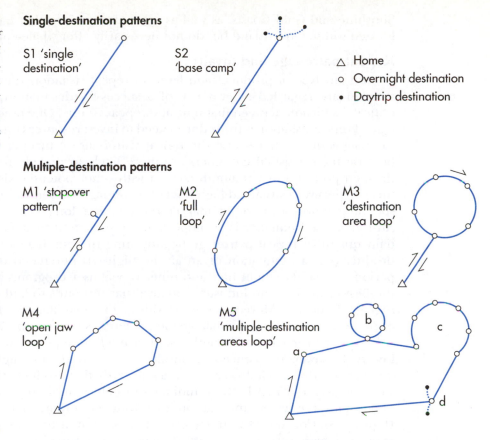

Figure 6.7
Model of single- and multiple-destination itineraries

Source:
Oppermann (1995b)

Single-destination patterns

S1 'single destination'

S2 'base camp'

△ Home
○ Overnight destination
● Daytrip destination

Multiple-destination patterns

M1 'stopover pattern'

M2 'full loop'

M3 'destination area loop'

M4 'open jaw loop'

M5 'multiple-destination areas loop'

a b c d

activities. Backpacking is a particularly interesting type of behavioural segment that represents a composite of activity characteristics (Buchanan & Rosetto 1997; Richards & Wilson 2004).

A relevant issue is whether tourists are mainly interested in specific *activities*, and therefore choose their destination accordingly, or whether they are primarily interested in a particular *destination*, within which available activities are then pursued. The second scenario is less common than the first. This mainly involves tourists who are constrained by financial or time limitations to travel within their own state or country or, more rarely, who are motivated by patriotic considerations or a compelling desire to visit a particular destination that they encountered in a book or the media. The Queensland coastal resort community of Hervey Bay illustrates both scenarios. Some of its whale-watching tourists are there because they are primarily interested in that activity. Others are there because they are primarily interested in visiting Hervey Bay, and whale-watching happens to be one of the available activities. It is important for destinations to determine what proportions of their visitors fall into each category in order to better understand both their markets and their competitors. In attracting tourists mainly interested in whale-watching, Hervey Bay is competing with destinations in other parts of the world (e.g. New Zealand, Canada) and potentially in other parts of Australia. In attracting tourists in the second category, Hervey Bay is competing with the

Sunshine and Gold Coasts, as well as other destinations that happen to be located within Queensland but do not necessarily offer whale-watching.

Repeat patronage and loyalty

As with any type of product, high levels of repeat visitation (i.e. repeat patronage) are regarded as evidence of a successful destination, hence the critical distinction between first-time and repeat visitors. One practical advantage of repeat visitation is the reduced need to invest resources into marketing campaigns, not only because the repeat visitors are returning anyway, but because these satisfied customers are more likely to provide free publicity through positive word-of-mouth contact with other potential visitors. From this perspective, a sustained high level of first-time visitation among the high-spending Japanese inbound market represents a long-term problem for Australia. Use frequency is an important segmentation variable that essentially quantifies repeat patronage by indicating the number of times that a product (e.g. a destination or an airline flight) is purchased over a given period of time. Frequent flier and other repeat-user programs are perhaps the best example of an industry initiative that responds to and encourages high use frequency. Moreover, they provide an excellent database for carrying out relevant marketing and management exercises (see section 7.7.3).

Repeat patronage and lengthy stays are often equated with product **loyalty**. However, the concept of loyalty goes beyond this single factor to incorporate the psychological attitudes towards the products that compel such behaviour. When both attitudinal and behavioural (repeat purchase) dimensions are taken into account, a four-cell loyalty matrix emerges (figure 6.8). Consumers who demonstrate a pattern of repeat visitation and express a high psychological attachment to a destination (or any other tourism-related product) belong in the 'high' loyalty category. Conversely, those who have made only a single visit, and indicate negative attitudes about the destination, are assigned to the 'low' loyalty cell. The other two categories represent contrasting behavioural and attitudinal combinations. 'Spurious' loyalty occurs when a pattern of repeat visitation is exhibited along with a weak psychological attachment. This could result when someone feels compelled to make repeat visits to a destination due to family or peer group pressure, or because of financial limitations that prohibit visits to more desirable destinations. 'Latent' loyalty is the opposite scenario where someone regards a destination very highly, but only makes a single visit. The commonest example of this behaviour is a 'once-in-a-lifetime' visit to an exotic but expensive location.

Though segments such as second-home owners may be controversial (see Managing: Destination loyalty and second-home ownership), high-loyalty visitors are usually highly valued by destinations because of this predictability, and because they are more likely to continue their patronage for longer even if the situation in the destination, or in their personal circumstances, begins to deteriorate (i.e. they are more resistant to the erosion of relevant push and pull factors). These tourists, then, constitute an important indicator group, in that the loss of this group's patronage may show that the product is experiencing a very serious level of deterioration or

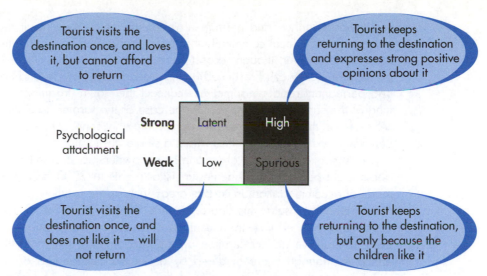

Figure 6.8
The loyalty matrix

change — as, for example, in association with changing destination lifecycle dynamics (see chapter 10). On the other hand, the loss of the spuriously loyal clientele may not indicate any serious problem, since their visits are mainly a matter of habit, convenience or coercion rather than conviction.

MANAGING
Destination loyalty and second-home ownership

The ownership of a periodically occupied second dwelling (or 'holiday home') is a powerful expression of destination loyalty, yet it is a phenomenon that is associated with costs as well as benefits. One major criticism is their contribution to unplanned rural or exurban sprawl, 'overdevelopment' and the fragmentation of farmland and bush (Selwood & Tonts 2004), all of which can undermine the destination's quality of life. Many local businesses and residents clearly benefit from the sale of goods and services to second-home owners over the course of a prolonged visit, but most of the associated economic benefits still accrue to origin regions (e.g. Melbourne or Sydney) where most rentals and other financial exchanges occur, or larger regional towns where supplies and petrol are purchased more cheaply in transit. Property and other taxes constitute a major destination benefit but these revenues may be eroded by increased demands for municipal services such as road maintenance, policing, rubbish collection and utilities. Inflationary effects, which are exacerbated by the speculative motives of many owners, are an ambivalent impact in so far as they benefit property owners wishing to sell but disadvantage those wishing to remain as well as those wanting to move permanently to the community. These motives may also reflect nothing more than an opportunistic loyalty to the destination. From a socio-cultural perspective, second-home owners occupy a half-way position between

(continued)

conventional tourists and permanent residents, which may result in a sense of belonging to the local community that is not recognised as legitimate by permanent residents (even though second-home ownership itself is often a prelude to permanent residency). Frost (2004) cites evidence of how second-home owners and permanent residents sometimes concoct their own 'traditions' (such as visiting at the same time every year in the case of the former) to distinguish themselves from the other group, so reinforcing the sense of two separate and uneasily coexisting communities within a single destination.

For Australia, the issue of second-home ownership is significant given that about eight per cent of all domestic visitor-nights in 2000 occurred within this mode of accommodation. In coastal areas such as the southern part of Victoria's Mornington Peninsula, this figure exceeds 25 per cent. The pull force of the coastline, combined with tax incentives and increased discretionary income, is likely to result in an acceleration of this phenomenon (Frost 2004). However, efforts to manage it are hindered by a poor understanding of second-home development that stems in part from the sector's lack of fit within the formal tourism industry. That municipalities in Australia have jurisdiction over second homes, moreover, has both advantages and disadvantages. For example, it invests planning and management responsibilities with local authorities but they often do not have the expertise or resources to maximise the benefits that are derived locally from this sector.

CHAPTER REVIEW

Since the 1950s there has been a shift in the perception of the tourist market as a homogeneous group of consumers, to the identification of increasingly specific or niche market segments. This has occurred in part because of the growing sophistication and size of the market, which has added complexity to the demand for tourism-related products and made it viable for operators to serve ever more specialised groups of consumers. In addition, technologies have emerged to readily identify these specialised segments and facilitate the development and marketing of appropriate niche tourism products. The culmination of this process has been the ability of marketers and managers to regard each customer as an individual segment, or market of one.

All consumers experience a similar decision-making process when selecting destinations and other tourism products. However, the specifics of the process (and subsequent tourism behaviour) vary according to many push and pull forces as well as personal characteristics such as culture, personality and motivations. Many of these forces and characteristics are therefore potentially useful as segmentation variables, though their relevance in any given situation depends on factors such as measurability, size, homogeneity and compatibility.

Four major categories of market segmentation are widely recognised. Geographic segmentation considers spatial criteria such as region or country of origin, subnational origins and the urban–rural distinction. This type of segmentation is the most commonly employed, and is becoming more sophisticated due to the development of GIS technologies. Sociodemographic segmentation includes gender, age, disability and family lifecycle as well as the highly interrelated criteria of education, occupation and income. Gay and lesbian tourists, along with older adults and women, are three market segments that have attracted industry attention due to their growth and purchasing power. Psychographic segmentation is the most difficult to identify. Plog's distinction between allocentrics, psychocentrics and midcentrics is the best-known example, although motivation is also sometimes used. Finally, behavioural segmentation considers such factors as travel occasion, the number of destinations visited during a trip, activities, and repeat patronage and loyalty.

SUMMARY OF KEY TERMS

Tourist market

The overall group of consumers that engages in some form of tourism-related travel

Market segmentation

The division of the tourist market into more or less homogenous subgroups, or tourist market segments, based on certain common characteristics and/or behavioural patterns

- **Market segments:** portions of the tourist market that are more or less distinct in their characteristics and/or behaviour

- **Simple market segmentation:** the most basic form of market segmentation, involving the identification of a minimal number of market segments
- **Multilevel segmentation:** a refinement of market segmentation that further differentiates basic level segments
- **Niche markets:** highly specialised market segments
- **Markets of one:** an extreme form of market segmentation, in which individual consumers are recognised as distinct market segments

Geographic segmentation

Market segmentation carried out on the basis of the market's origin region; can be carried out at various scales, including region (e.g. Asia), country (Germany), subnational unit (California, Queensland), or urban/rural

- **GIS (geographic information systems):** sophisticated computer software programs that facilitate the assembly, storage, manipulation, analysis and display of spatially referenced information

Sociodemographic segmentation

Market segmentation based on social and demographic variables such as gender, age, family lifecycle, education, occupation and income

- **Gender segmentation:** the grouping of individuals into male and female categories, or according to sexual orientation
- **Pink dollar:** the purchasing power of gay and lesbian consumers, recognised to be much higher than the average purchasing power
- **Family lifecycle (FLC):** a sequence of stages through which the traditional nuclear family passes from early adulthood to the death of a spouse; each stage is associated with distinct patterns of tourism-related behaviour associated with changing family and financial circumstances

Psychographic segmentation

The differentiation of the tourist market on the basis of psychological and motivational characteristics such as personality, motivations and needs

- **Venturers:** according to Plog's typology, 'other-centred' tourists who enjoy exposing themselves to other cultures and new experiences, and are willing to take risks in this process; also known as 'allocentrics'
- **Dependables:** 'self-centred' tourists who prefer familiar and risk-averse experiences; also known as 'psychocentrics'
- **Midcentrics:** 'average' tourists whose personality type is a compromise between venturer and dependable traits; also known as 'centrics'
- **Motivation:** the intrinsic reasons why the individual is embarking on a particular trip

Behavioural segmentation

The identification of tourist markets on the basis of activities and actions undertaken during the actual tourism experience

- **Loyalty:** the extent to which a product, such as a destination, is perceived in a positive way and repeatedly purchased by the consumer

QUESTIONS

1 For managers and marketers, what are the advantages and disadvantages, respectively, of treating the tourist market as a single entity or as a collection of markets of one?

2 What strengths and weaknesses are associated with 'country of residence' and 'region of residence' as criteria for identifying tourist market segments?

3 Describe how the ageing of the population may both encourage and dissuade tourism participation among Australians.

4 (a) Why are certain destinations and businesses showing an increased interest in the pink dollar?
   (b) What risks are inherent in a marketing strategy that focuses on gay and lesbian tourists?

5 What are the strengths and limitations of employing the traditional family lifecycle as a segmentation variable for the tourist market?

6 (a) What fiscally responsible strategies could be implemented by Australian municipalities to make themselves more pet-friendly as destinations?
   (b) How could municipalities who implement these strategies make them known to pet-owning domestic tourists?

7 (a) How much should destinations be required to provide access to tourists with impairments in accordance with a social model of disabilities?
   (b) How should the relevant services and facilities be paid for?

8 What difficulties are associated with the operationalisation of psychographic segmentation in general, and with Plog's typology in particular?

9 (a) What is the difference between trip purpose and trip motivation?
   (b) What are the strengths and weaknesses of each as segmentation criteria?

10 How can the loyalty matrix be operationalised to assist in the management and marketing of destinations?

EXERCISES

1 (a) From the perspective of the destinations of Sydney and Broken Hill, compare and contrast family tourists from the United Arab Emirates and retired couples from the United Kingdom in terms of the eight segmentation criteria outlined in the chapter.
   (b) On the basis of this analysis, what priority should each of these destinations put on marketing to each of these market segments?

(*continued*)

2 Assume that you are the manager of a local wildlife park and that you have obtained funding to identify your market through the use of a questionnaire. Because these funds are very limited, you must keep your questionnaire to only two pages, which allows you to obtain no more than 15 customer characteristics.

  (a) List the 15 characteristics of your market base (e.g. gender, age, eye colour, personality) that you believe to be most important to the successful management of your attraction.
  (b) Indicate why you selected these particular characteristics.
  (c) Design the questionnaire.

FURTHER READING

Clift, S., Luongo, M. & Callister, C. (Eds) 2002. *Gay Tourism: Culture, Identity and Sex.* **London: Continuum.** Theoretical and practical perspectives on the global phenomenon of gay tourism are explored in this multiauthored collection.

Daniels, M. (Ed.) 2005. Special Issue: Travelers with Specialized Needs. *Tourism Review International* **8 (3).** This collection of ten refereed articles is the most thorough compilation of academic research to date on the issue of tourism and disabilities.

Hall, C.M. & Müller, D. (Eds) 2004. *Tourism, Mobility and Second Homes: Between Elite Landscape and Common Ground.* **Clevedon, UK: Channel View.** The 18 chapters in this compilation are divided into sections that look respectively at the meaning of second-home ownership, patterns and issues, and the future.

Jang, S., Yu, L. & Pearson, T. 2003. 'Chinese Travellers to the United States: A Comparison of Business Travel and Visiting Friends and Relatives'. *Tourism Geographies* **5: 87–108.** Internal variations within the rapidly growing Chinese outbound travel market are explored in this empirically based article.

Plog, S. 2005. 'Targeting Segments: More Important than Ever in the Travel Industry'. In Theobald, W. (Ed.) *Global Tourism.* **Third Edition. Sydney: Elsevier, pp. 271–93.** Plog discusses the importance of market segmentation and describes six tourist segments that emerged from a major annual household survey in the United States.

Richards, G. & Wilson, J. (Eds) 2004. *The Global Nomad: Backpacker Travel in Theory and Practice.* **Clevedon, UK: Channel View.** Fifteen chapters, of which at least five focus directly on Australia or New Zealand, examine the phenomenon of backpacking. The editors, through these contributions, attempt to outline a relevant field of study and research agenda.

Differentiating Japanese and American tourists in Australia

Japan and the United States, respectively, were the third and fourth most important overseas markets for the Australian inbound tourism industry in 2003 (see table 4.5), and it is critical in the interests of maintaining and hopefully increasing Australia's international tourism stature that tourism stakeholders fully understand and respond to the characteristics of such major markets. Crucial differences are clearly revealed in table 6.6, which also indicates how much segmentation by country of residence is associated with significant differences in other important segmentation criteria. With regard to trip purpose, for example, Japanese visitors are far more likely than Americans to list 'holiday' as their primary reason for visiting Australia, while Americans are three times more likely to list 'visiting friends or relatives', indicating the relatively small number of Australians of Japanese descent. The differential in the criterion of loyalty is not as pronounced, although there is still concern over 59 per cent of Japanese being first-time visitors, a phenomenon that may be related to the low percentage of VFR-focused motivations. In terms of destination coverage, Queensland, because of its pleasure periphery location, is by far the most popular destination-state for Japanese visitors, while Americans favour New South Wales by a similar margin. The role of Sydney as the main gateway for American arrivals is a major factor behind this pattern. Japanese visitors are somewhat more likely to be female (although it is unclear whether the difference is statistically significant) and much more likely to travel with at least one other person. A distinct segment within the Japanese market that reflects these characteristics is the so-called 'young office lady', who travels internationally in pairs or small groups for leisure purposes (Tourism Australia 2005).

American tourists spend more time in Australia than Japanese tourists, although both figures are skewed by students who remain in the country for a semester or longer. These longer visits are associated in part with the high VFR factor but also with Australia being more of a long-haul destination from the United States. Not surprisingly, the longer American stay results in higher expenditures, although Japanese visitors allocate a higher portion of their expenditures on purchases that are brought home, and less on food, drink and accommodation. This is in part associated with the Japanese custom of presenting gifts purchased during overseas travel to family members and colleagues. The percentage of visitors who go shopping and visit national parks while in Australia is similar for both countries (i.e. 79 per cent in both markets for shopping, and 50 and 45 per cent for Japanese and Americans, respectively, for national parks) (Tourism Australia 2005). The Japanese, however, are much more inclined to visit amusement and theme parks (an important attraction in Queensland's Gold Coast), while Americans are far more likely to visit 'lifestyle' sites, such as pubs, historical sites, museums, sporting venues and festivals.

Of interest to marketers is the importance of travel guidebooks as a source of information on Australia for first-time Japanese visitors. Travel agents are also relatively more important in Japan, while Americans are more likely to rely on friends or relatives who had previously visited Australia (18 per cent against 10 per cent among the Japanese). Japanese visitors are likely to have started planning for their trip within three months of their departure to Australia, while Americans are likely to plan within six months, again reflecting the long-haul nature of the destination. In both cases, domestic holiday periods influence the timing of an Australian visit. Golden Week, in late April and early May, is an important time of domestic travel in Japan, and so is a down period for out-bound travel to Australia and elsewhere. Americans are most likely to visit Australia in July or August (the North American summer), when school is dismissed and annual vacations are usually taken (Tourism Australia 2005).

■ **Table 6.6**   *Characteristics of Japanese and American tourists visiting Australia*

CRITERION	JAPANESE INBOUND	AMERICAN INBOUND
Holiday visitors (%)	78	40
VFR visitors (%)	5	19
Repeat visitors (%)	59	52
Unaccompanied visitors (%)	32	58
Female (%)	52	46
Visiting New South Wales (%)	38	72
Visiting Queensland (%)	71	32
Visiting pubs, clubs, discos (%)	15	56
Visiting history/heritage sites (%)	19	38
Visiting museums/art galleries (%)	14	34
Attending an organised sporting event (%)	4	11
Attending festivals/fairs (%)	3	9
Visiting amusement/theme parks (%)	19	4
Average length of stay (nights)	15	26
First-time visitors consulting travel guides (%)	56	31
First-time visitors consulting travel agents (%)	42	30
First-time visitors consulting the Internet (%)	38	37
First-time visitors consulting friends who have visited Australia previously (%)	10	18
Average total trip expenditure ($)	3760	5631
Percentage of expenditure on shopping for souvenirs and gifts	11	7
Percentage of expenditure on food/drink/ accommodation	15	20

Source: *Data derived from Tourism Australia (2005)*

Other differentiating issues and trends must be taken into account by Australian marketers and managers. The potential for outbound travel, for example, is constrained in the United States by a short average vacation period (often just five to ten vacation days), which is not conducive to long-haul travel, and in Japan by many workers not taking their full allocation of 15 to 20 vacation days. Ageing populations in both societies indicate increasingly 'grey' tourist markets but this factor is exacerbated in the United States by the ageing of the prime baby boomer market 'bulge'. It is ironic in the light of the ageing trend that school excursion groups are one of the fastest-growing subsegments in the Japanese market, with 186 schools booking tours to Australia between April 2004 and March 2005 (Travelbiz.com 2005). A major consideration for all Japanese segments is the Japanese travel industry being one of the most vertically integrated in the world, so that strong relationships with a few influential companies is the key to gaining access to this market. For the US market, key concerns include the declining value of the US dollar, which fell from US$0.52 against the Australian dollar in 2001 to almost US$0.80 in early 2005, persistent fears of terrorism and the precarious financial status of major United States-based carriers. These dissuasive factors, however, are somewhat offset by Australia's high aspirational rating, that is, its status as a destination that a high proportion of Americans would love to visit if they had sufficient time and money (Tourism Australia 2005).

Questions

1 (a) For both the Japanese and American inbound markets, identify three major destination countries that offer Australia the most competition.
  (b) What are the main strengths and weaknesses of each of these competitors?
  (c) How can Australia improve its position relative to each of these competitors?

2 How could Queensland attract a higher proportion of American inbound tourists, and how could New South Wales attract a higher proportion of Japanese inbound tourists?

3 (a) Obtain more information about the Japanese 'young office lady' market segment, and determine how Australia can make itself more attractive to this market.
  (b) What strategies can be employed to attract these individuals back to Australia as they enter subsequent lifecycle stages?

4 How can the factors that dissuade Americans from visiting Australia be overcome, so that their high aspirational attitudes towards this country can be realised?

7

Tourism
marketing

LEARNING OBJECTIVES

After studying this chapter, you should be able to:

1 appreciate the scope of marketing as an essential component of tourism systems

2 list and describe the key characteristics of services marketing and identify how these are different from goods marketing

3 identify the strategies that can be adopted to address imbalances between supply and demand

4 explain why market failure occurs in tourism marketing

5 describe the role of national tourism organisations in tourism marketing

6 outline the rationale for and the stages involved in strategic marketing

7 outline the basic components of the 8P marketing mix model

8 discuss the importance of database marketing in the tourism industry

9 explain the pricing techniques that tourism businesses can use to set prices

10 identify the costs and benefits associated with the various forms of media that are used in tourism promotion.

7.1 INTRODUCTION

Chapter 6 examined market segmentation, or the process whereby consumers are divided into relatively uniform groups with respect to their attitudes and behaviour. This is a critical component of tourism product management in that different market segments, distinguished by one or more geographical, sociodemographic, psychographic or behavioural criteria, are likely to have distinct impacts upon the tourism system. They also require different strategies in the area of tourism marketing, which is the subject of the present chapter. Following a discussion of the nature and definition of marketing in section 7.2, the key characteristics of services marketing, and tourism marketing in particular, are examined in section 7.3. The need to maintain a balance between supply and demand is discussed in section 7.4, while the phenomenon of market failure is addressed in section 7.5. This section also considers the approaches and strategies that can be used to overcome this problem. Strategic marketing, and in particular the components of a SWOT (strengths, weaknesses, opportunities, threats) analysis, forms the core of section 7.6. This is followed in section 7.7 by an overview of the elements involved in the product-focused marketing mix.

7.2 THE NATURE OF MARKETING

Marketing is commonly perceived as involving little more than the promotional advertisements that are displayed through television and other forms of media. However, these advertisements are only one form of promotion, and promotion is only one aspect of marketing. Advertising and promotion, and the people who work in these industries, are important, but marketing involves *everyone* in the tourism and hospitality sector, including tourists and potential tourists. Thus, marketing is pervasive throughout the tourism system.

■ 7.2.1 Definition *of marketing*

There are numerous definitions of marketing (see, for example, Kotler & Keller 2005; Morrison 2002). The following definition, which combines elements of the most commonly cited definitions, is used in this book:

> Marketing involves the interaction and interrelationships among consumers and producers of goods and services, through which ideas, products, services and values are created and exchanged for the mutual benefit of both groups.

In place of the popular perception of marketing as a one-way attempt by producers (e.g. the tourism industry and destinations) to sell their products to the market, this definition emphasises the two-way interactions that occur between these producers and the actual as well as potential tourist market. Successful marketing, for example, depends on feedback (e.g. customer satisfaction, proclivity to purchase new products) flowing from the market to the producer. In addition, it recognises the importance of financial and other benefits to both parties, and includes interactions among the 'internal customers' within a company or organisation and within the tourism market itself.

Services marketing applies to service-sector activities such as tourism and is fundamentally different from the marketing of goods. This holds true even though the tourism sector interfaces with goods such as souvenirs and duty-free merchandise, and notwithstanding the fact that many important marketing principles are equally applicable to both goods and services. In general, the key marketing characteristics that distinguish services from goods are (a) intangibility, (b) inseparability, (c) variability and (d) perishability (Kotler, Bowen & Makens 2003).

7.3.1 Intangibility

In contrast to physical products and goods, services have **intangibility**. This means that they cannot be directly seen, tasted, felt or heard prior to their purchase and consumption. Furthermore, customers usually have only a receipt, a souvenir or other memorabilia such as photographs as evidence that they actually had that experience. Customers purchase tourism and hospitality services with little more than knowledge of the price, some pictures of the destination and its facilities, endorsement by some well-known personality, friends or relatives or the sales intermediary (e.g. travel agent) and, in some instances, their own prior experiences. In the service industry, the concept of compensation for an unsatisfactory purchase is also distinctive. As with goods, money can be refunded or compensating products made available for free, but the product itself cannot be returned once it has been consumed.

Because of the intangible nature of the service sector, word of mouth is especially important as a source of product information, as this involves access to those who have already experienced a particular destination or hotel, or know of someone who has. Accordingly, word of mouth has a high degree of influence among potential customers as an image formation agent (Morrison 2002). However, word of mouth can also be problematic. Circumstances regarding the product may have changed from the time of the informant's experience, or the information may be third- or fourth-hand (e.g. the informant knows someone who knows someone who travelled to Bali and did not like it). In addition, the psychographic profile and tastes of the informant may be different from the person who is receiving the information.

Thus, even with access to word-of-mouth information, the level of perceived risk in purchasing a service, especially for a first-time purchaser, is relatively high compared to goods (although this is not to say that goods purchasing is risk free). To reduce this risk perception, service providers offer tangible clues as to what the customer can expect from the product and the producer, thereby creating confidence in the service. These include articulate and uniformed personnel, a clean and professional office setting, and glossy brochures that convey attractive images to the potential buyer. In the latter regard, virtual reality technologies can be employed to reduce the tangibility gap between goods and services (see chapter 3).

■ 7.3.2 Inseparability

Tourism services are characterised by **inseparability**, meaning that production and consumption occur simultaneously and in the same place. This is demonstrated by the flight of a passenger aboard an aeroplane (i.e. the flight is being 'produced' at the same time the passenger is 'consuming' it), or by a guest's occupation of a hotel room. Because the consumers and producers of these products are in frequent contact, the nature of these interactions has a major impact on customer satisfaction levels. In the tourism industry and other service industries, customer-oriented staff training is thus especially important for 'frontline' employees such as airline attendants and front-desk clerks who work on the product/consumption interface (see Managing: Emotional labour in the tourism sector).

Tourists also need to respect the applicable protocol and regulations, since misbehaviour on their part can also negatively affect the product. For example, patrons who smoke in a smoke-free restaurant detract from the quality of the experience for non-smoking customers. Tourists who walk into a church wearing shorts and talking loudly may offend local residents or other visitors. While it is assumed that frontline service staff should receive training to be made aware of appropriate standards of service behaviour, the same assumption is seldom if ever applied to tourists, even though these two examples clearly demonstrate the negative ramifications of inappropriate tourist behaviour. At the very least, it is incumbent on the service sector to make any relevant rules and regulations evident to tourists in an unambiguous but diplomatic way, so as not to cause offence.

MANAGING
Emotional labour in the tourism sector

High customer satisfaction levels depend on the ability of frontline tourism service providers such as waiters, tour guides, airline attendants and travel agents to display a willingness to be of service and to convey other feelings and attitudes that collectively comprise the performance of **emotional labour**. At least three of the five SERVQUAL scale dimensions of service quality — responsiveness (willingness to provide assistance and prompt service), assurance (courtesy and knowledge that inspire confidence and trust) and empathy (personal and caring attention to the customer) — entail elements of emotional labour (Anderson, Provis & Chappel 2003). Accordingly, managers should try to select employees with personality traits such as sociability and gregariousness that are

(continued)

more likely to translate into an ability to perform this type of work effectively, which tends to be poorly paid and involve long working hours. While appropriate training (e.g. twinning new employees with a more experienced 'buddy' or mentor) should also be provided for all frontline employees to ensure consistency and prevent burnout, evidence from qualitative interviews with managers and service workers in South Australia suggests that emotional labour training is mostly informal and of the on-the-job 'trial and error' variety (ibid.).

The exploratory research of Anderson, Provis and Chappel (2003) indicates the need to educate tourism managers and employees about the concept of emotional labour, which, while grasped intuitively, is not recognised by managers or employees as a formal concept that can be analysed and managed. The importance of personality is also emphasised and the need to apply personality testing to all potential employees and not just management. Finally, the researchers cite the need for formal training programs that focus on the effective performance of emotional labour. A broader issue raised by this research is the role of emotional labour, or something akin to it, in the relations between tourists and destination residents. The latter are under no obligation to perform emotional labour during such contacts and it is reasonable to assume that a high proportion of residents will possess personality traits that are not conducive to doing so. Indeed, increased tourism-related development and associated problems such as congestion could provide a disincentive to friendly behaviour. Yet because the friendliness of locals is an important dimension of satisfying visits, destination managers should investigate strategies through which most residents will readily display the equivalent of emotional labour in their contacts with tourists.

7.3.3 Variability

Tourism services have a high level of **variability**, meaning that each producer–consumer interaction is a unique experience that is influenced by a large number of often unpredictable 'human element' factors. These include the mood and expectations of each participant at the particular time during which the service encounter takes place. A tourist in a restaurant, for example, may be completely relaxed, expecting that their every whim will be satisfied, while the attending waiter may have high levels of stress from overwork and expect the customer to be 'more reasonable' in their demands. Such expectation incongruities are extremely common in the tourism sector, given the tourist's perception of this experience as a 'special', out-of-the-ordinary (and expensive) occasion, and the waiter's view that this is just a routine experience associated with the job. The next encounter, however, even if the same waiter is involved, could involve an entirely different set of circumstances with a more positive outcome.

The problem for managers is that these incongruities can lead to unpleasant and unsatisfying encounters, and a consequent reduction in customer satisfaction levels and deteriorating local attitudes towards tourists. Often, just one such experience can sour a tourist's view about a particular destination, offsetting a very large number of entirely satisfactory experiences during the same tourism experience that, because they were expected, do not make the same impression. This is why a tourist returning to the same hotel may have a completely different experience during the second trip — the combination of moods, expectations, experiences and other factors among all participants is likely to be entirely different from the first trip. This uncertainty element, combined with the simultaneous nature of production and consumption (i.e. it is more difficult to undo any mistakes), makes it very difficult to introduce quality control mechanisms in tourism similar in rigour to those that govern the production of tangible goods such as cars and clothing. For tourism destinations and products, it is again a matter of decreasing the likelihood of negative outcomes by ensuring that employees are exposed to high-quality training opportunities, and that tourists are sensitised to standards of appropriate behaviour and reasonable expectations.

■ 7.3.4 Perishability

Tourism services cannot be produced and stored today for consumption in the future. For example, an airline flight that has 100 empty seats on a 400-seat aeroplane cannot compensate for the shortfall by selling 500 seats on the next flight of that aeroplane. The 100 seats are irrevocably lost, along with the revenue that they would normally generate. Because some of this loss is attributable to airline passengers or hotel guests who do not take up their reservations, most businesses 'overbook' their services on the basis of the average number of seats that have not been claimed in the past. This characteristic of **perishability** also helps to explain why airlines and other businesses such as wotif.com (http://wotif.com) offer last-minute sales or stand-by rates at drastically reduced prices. While they will not obtain as much profit from these clients, at least some revenue can be recouped at minimal extra cost. For a tourism manager, one of the greatest challenges in marketing is to compensate for perishability by effectively matching demand with supply. An optimal match contributes to higher profitability, and therefore the supply and demand balance is discussed more thoroughly in the following section.

7.4 MANAGING SUPPLY AND DEMAND

If possible, the tourism manager will attempt to produce an exact match between the supply and the corresponding demand for a product. This is because, all other things being equal, resources that are not fully used will result in reduced profits. When considering the supply and demand balance, there are two main cost components that must be taken into account. **Fixed costs** are entrenched costs that the operation has little flexibility to change over the short term. Examples include taxes, the interest that has to be paid on borrowed funds and the heating costs that are incurred in a hotel during the winter season. In the latter case, these must be paid whether the rooms are occupied or not, as otherwise building damage could result. **Variable costs** are those costs that can be adjusted in the short term. For example, during the low season hotels can dismiss their casual nonunionised staff and cut back on their advertising, thereby adjusting to low occupancy rates by saving on salaries and promotion. It may also be possible to obtain cheaper and smaller supplies of food if the hotel is not already under an inflexible long-term contract with a specific supplier.

There is no set boundary between these two categories, and it is helpful to think of costs as falling along a fixed-to-variable spectrum that varies from one operation to another. Tourism businesses tend to have a relatively high proportion of costs concentrated in the fixed segment of the spectrum, implying that large amounts of money have to be budgeted whether a flight or hotel is fully booked or almost empty. As a result, even small shortfalls in occupancy can lead to significant declines in profit. Figure 7.1 demonstrates this problem by showing the contrasting profits that result from two different levels of occupancy in a hypothetical hotel with 50 rooms and monthly fixed costs of $64 000. In scenario A, full occupancy results in a $20 000 monthly profit when costs are subtracted from revenues. However, in scenario B, with just a 20 per cent decline in occupancy, the corresponding profit declines to $3200 (i.e. 84 per cent), since the variable costs fall by 20 per cent (the same as the occupancy rate fall), but the $64 000 fixed costs cannot move at all. Being able to maintain a high occupancy rate is therefore absolutely critical for the hotel. Demand for tourism-related services such as accommodation, however, is usually very difficult to predict, given the complexity of the destination or product decision-making process (chapter 6), and the uncertainty factor (see the case study at the end of chapter 2). To help achieve a better understanding and thus a higher level of control over the demand portion of the supply/demand equation, daily, weekly, seasonal and long-term patterns in demand can be identified.

7.4.1 Daily *variations in demand*

The level of demand for most tourism services changes on a daily basis. For example, in a hotel reception area, the peak check-out time is in the morning between approximately 7 am and 10 am, and in large hotels queues commonly form during that period. Similarly, late afternoon and early evening is a busy time, as guests arrive to check in. However, for the housekeeping department, the intervening period is usually the busiest time as rooms are cleaned and prepared for the next guests to arrive. Different types of hotels also have different demand patterns. An airport hotel, for example, often faces unpredicted demand surges at any time of the day or night if aeroplanes are delayed or cancelled. In many types of attractions, such as theme parks, a peak often occurs between midday and late afternoon, while country markets usually experience peak visitation in the early morning. Cruise ship tourism has a particularly unbalanced daily variation from a destination perspective, with periods of intense activity in ports of call being followed by periods of calm. When analysed from the perspective of daily demand, salaries are a fixed cost unless there is provision for sending staff home early without compensation.

Figure 7.1
Effect of a high fixed cost structure on hotel room profits

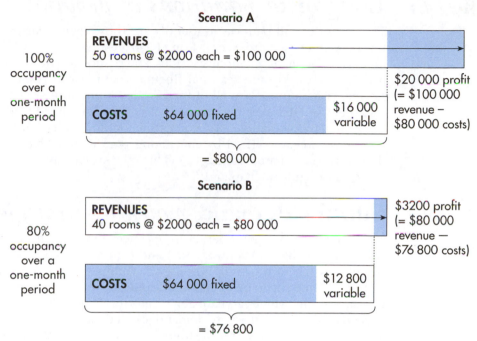

7.4.2 Weekly *variations in demand*

Differential demand patterns on a weekly basis are illustrated in the hotel industry by the distinction between the 'four-day' and 'three-day' market. The four-day market is a largely business-oriented clientele that concentrates in the Monday to Thursday period. Hotels that focus on this market tend to experience a downturn on the weekend. Conversely, the three-day or short holiday market peaks on the weekend and during national or state holidays. Exurban tourist shopping villages that draw much of their tourist traffic from nearby large cities, such as Tamborine Mountain and Maleny, also tend to experience weekend peak use periods.

7.4.3 Seasonal *variations in demand*

Variations can also be identified over the one-year cycle, with a distinction being made between the high season, the low season and shoulder periods in many types of destinations and operations. 3S resort communities and facilities often experience 100 per cent occupancy rates during the high season, which is in the summer for high-latitude resorts and in the winter for tropical or subtropical pleasure periphery resorts. This may then be offset by closures during the low season due to very low occupancy rates, with subsequent negative impacts throughout the local community (see section

8.3.3). In contrast, business-oriented city hotels and urban attractions often experience their seasonal downturn during the summer, when business activity is at a low ebb.

7.4.4 Long-term *variations in demand*

The most difficult patterns to identify are those that occur over a period of several years or even decades. Long-term business cycles, which have been identified by many economists (Ralf 2000), do not necessarily affect the usual daily, weekly and seasonal fluctuations, but can result in lower-than-normal visitation levels at all of these scales. Some tourism researchers have also theorised that destinations and other tourism-related facilities, irrespective of macro-fluctuations in the overall economy, experience a product life-cycle that is characterised by alternating periods of stable and accelerated demand (Toh, Khan & Koh 2001). This very important concept is discussed more thoroughly in chapter 10.

7.4.5 Supply/demand *matching strategies*

Most tourism managers operate in an environment that is largely capacity restrained — that is, supply is fixed and cannot be expanded rapidly. They therefore concentrate on optimising the volume of demand, although there is usually some scope for modifying supply as well. There are two broad circumstances in which a manager needs to take action — when supply exceeds demand and when demand exceeds supply — each of which is accompanied by its own set of strategies (see figure 7.2). The strategies that are adopted (see below) depend in large part on whether the imbalances are daily, weekly, seasonal or long term in nature.

If supply exceeds demand: *increase demand*

The assumptions underlying this strategy are that either the total demand is below capacity or the demand is low only at certain times. Potentially, demand can be increased through a number of strategies.

An example of *product modification or diversification* is the attempts since the mid-1990s to incorporate the rainforests and farms of the Gold Coast's exurban hinterland into that destination's tourism product. To prevent supply from exceeding demand, during the 1990s many casinos in Las Vegas developed 'family-friendly' attractions and ambience to diversify their client base beyond hardcore gamblers (Becker 1994). Another strategy is the *alteration or strengthening of distribution channels*, as when a small bed and breakfast operation is linked with a large tour operator through its membership in a bed and breakfast consortium. Attempts during the early 2000s to attract Middle Eastern tourists to the Gold Coast, and to encourage domestic tourism within Australia, indicate the *identification of new or alternative sources of demand*, without necessarily modifying the existing product. *Pricing discounts*, such as those provided by wotif.com (see preceding), and *redesigned promotional campaigns* that focus more effectively on the existing product and market mix are other options.

Some Caribbean 3S destinations employ all these strategies in response to low summer occupancy levels. For example, casinos and ecotourism are being promoted on some islands to attract summer visitors. VFR tourism from within the region and from the Caribbean diaspora in North America and Europe is also being pursued, as these visitors also tend to take their holidays during the summer period. Furthermore, steep price discounts ('summer rates') are offered to attract traditional hotel-oriented markets.

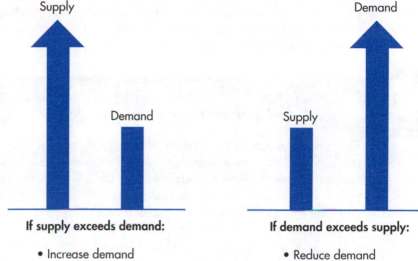

■ **Figure 7.2**
Supply/ demand imbalances and appropriate strategies

If supply exceeds demand:

- Increase demand
- Reduce supply
- Redistribute supply.

If demand exceeds supply:

- Reduce demand
- Increase supply
- Redistribute demand.

Reduce supply

This strategy assumes that it is not possible or desirable to increase demand in any substantial way, and that it is desirable or essential to reduce costs. In hotels supply can be reduced by closing individual rooms or wings, or by closing the entire hotel in the low season as an extreme measure to reduce fixed and variable costs. This strategy is commonly adopted in the Caribbean at the level of individual operations. Airlines react in a similar fashion by putting certain aircraft out of service, renting these out to other companies, or cancelling flights.

Redistribute supply

Redistribution or restructuring of supply is necessary when the existing product is no longer suited to the demand it was originally intended to satisfy. In the case of a hotel, rooms can be modified to better reflect contemporary demand. This could involve the conversion of two rooms into an executive suite, the conversion of some rooms into 'courtesy suites' (used only during the day for showers and resting) and the provision of non-smoking rooms. The conversion of hotel rooms into timeshare units is an illustration of a long-term adaptive strategy in the accommodation sector. Theme parks usually introduce new rides or renovate old rides periodically to sustain demand, while the conversion of scheduled flights to charter flights in the airline industry is another example of adaptive supply redistribution.

If demand exceeds supply: *reduce demand*

Where demand for a product exceeds its capacity, tourism product managers can raise the price of a seat or room, thereby reducing demand while obtaining additional revenue per unit. A similar demand reduction strategy is to increase entrance fees in national parks that are being negatively impacted by excessive visitation levels (see chapter 9). Another option often applied to protected areas and other natural or cultural sites but seldom to countries or municipalities is a formal quota on the number of visitors allowed per day, month, season or year. Some destination managers may also take the controversial move of proactively discouraging visits from some or all tourists on a temporary or permanent basis (see Contemporary issue: Reducing demand through demarketing).

CONTEMPORARY ISSUE
Reducing demand through demarketing

The concept of marketing, which implies creating and fulfilling demand for certain products, is taken for granted in the tourism field. Less known or applied is the idea of tourism **demarketing**, which can be defined as the process of discouraging all or certain tourists from visiting a particular destination temporarily or permanently. Yet this is an option that can be employed by managers effectively to reduce demand in the early stages of the destination decision-making process, either because the supply of product is limited or because certain market segments are perceived as causing carrying capacity problems when present even in small numbers (Beeton & Benfield 2002). The first scenario indicates a strategy of **general demarketing** directed towards all tourists. An example is Venice, Italy, where municipal authorities occasionally sponsor television advertisements depicting unpleasant local scenes of crowding and water pollution to discourage visitation during peak summer periods. These applications, however, are unusual given the proclivity of tourism promotion agencies to support increased visitation and concerns that negative imagery and messages may have a longer-term dissuasive effect on visitation even during times when this is desired.

The second scenario involves a strategy of **selective demarketing**. Examples are more numerous, and include South-East Asian destinations that threaten certain kinds of sex tourist with punishment, and French and Belgian destinations that send unwelcoming messages to English football hooligans. In Australia and the United States respectively, many coastal destinations actively discourage schoolies and spring break visitors because of their alleged disruptive influence. A more subtle form of demarketing occurs when promotional emphasis on a certain aspect of the destination, such as its appeal to the wealthy, conveys an implicit message that mass tourists are unwelcome. In all cases of selective demarketing, accusations of overt or even illegal discrimination are an inherent risk, as is the possibility of generating resentment well beyond the target segment. Liberal heterosexuals, for example, may choose to boycott destinations that actively or implicitly demarket gay or lesbian tourists. General and selective demarketing, therefore, are strategic alternatives within the marketing mix that should be employed only after the utmost consideration of their social and economic consequences.

Increase supply

As an alternative to induced demand reduction, managers can accommodate higher demand levels by expanding current capacity. Many 3S resort communities respond effectively to short-term demand fluctuations by making their patrolled beaches available on the basis of daily or weekly patterns of demand. A hotel can build an additional wing, acquire new facilities or utilise external facilities on a temporary basis. To increase bed capacity in a single room, cots and convertible sofas are often provided. Primitive hut-type accommodation, such as the *bures* provided by some Fijian hotels, have the great advantage of being highly attractive to 3S tourists. However, at the same time, they can be erected and disassembled rapidly depending on seasonal fluctuations. A similar principle applies to the tent-like structures available commercially from the US-based company Pacific Yurts (www.yurts.com), which are patterned after the traditional Mongolian nomad tent, the yurt. These inexpensive and lightweight structures can be erected or disassembled in less than a day (as demand permits) and make minimal environmental impact, yet they provide a roomy and comfortable experience for guests (see figures 7.3 and 7.4). As with bures, they are an effective means of meeting the problem of high fixed costs associated with 'permanent' facilities.

■ **Figure 7.3** *A Pacific Yurt in a natural setting*
Source: *Bair (1995)*

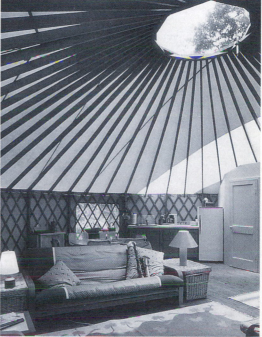

■ **Figure 7.4** *An optional interior for a Pacific Yurt*
Source: *Bair (1995)*

Redistribute demand

This strategy works by transferring demand from times of excess use to times of low demand. The differential seasonal price structure in many Caribbean resorts, for example, is an attempt to redistribute demand from the high-demand winter period to the low-demand summer season. At the weekly scale, many attractions attempt to divert traffic from the busy weekend period to the rest of the week by offering weekday discounts on entrance fees and other prices.

7.5 MARKET FAILURE

Tourism is an industry where **market failure** occurs frequently. Mainstream economic theory suggests that market demand and product supply will attain equilibrium in the long term. Companies that identify a need for promotion to fill their hotel rooms or aeroplane seats, therefore, will spend the necessary funds on that promotion. In return, they will benefit financially from their investment when the anticipated increase in demand materialises. In destination marketing, however, the case is not so straightforward. It is widely recognised that tourists usually decide first on a particular destination, and then select specific tourism products (e.g. accommodation) within that destination. However, specific tourism operators are rarely willing to invest money in destination promotion, since this type of investment will provide benefits to their competitors as well as to themselves. Hence, the situation arises where financial investment is required for destination promotion to achieve demand/supply equilibrium but operators are unwilling to contribute since the returns do not accrue directly to the individual companies. The market therefore does not function as it should in taking action to attain supply and demand equilibrium.

7.5.1 Government *tourism organisations*

Destination promotion, as a result, is normally the responsibility of government-based **national tourism organisations** (**NTOs**) and their regional or municipal counterparts. This is a role that serves to reinforce the importance of destination governments within the overall tourism system. Historically, such bodies have been funded from general tax revenues, and therefore individual tourism operators receive direct benefits from destination promotion that the wider community (including the tourism businesses) has funded. However, this public funding is usually justified by the tax revenues, jobs and other economic benefits that trickle down from prosperous businesses to the broader community (see chapter 8).

Market failure has implications not only for destination promotion and marketing but also applies to the provision of infrastructure (i.e. the roads and airports that benefit businesses but are also funded through general tax revenues), specific tourism facilities (e.g. convention centres) and tourism research. However, in the present context of tourism marketing it is the area of promotion and those related activities that are particularly relevant. The following subsections will therefore discuss some of the marketing functions that are usually performed by NTOs such as Tourism Australia (www.tourism.australia.com). Similar functions are carried out by the states (e.g. Tourism Queensland (www.tq.com.au)) and some municipalities (e.g. Gold Coast Tourism (www.goldcoasttourism.com.au/)), depending on mandate and level of available funding.

Marketing functions of government tourism organisations

Historically, the principal marketing role of NTOs has been promotional. However, despite widespread funding reductions, this is changing as the contemporary international tourism industry becomes more competitive and complex, and tourists become increasingly sophisticated in their destination choice behaviour. Progressive elements within the tourism industry, accordingly, recognise the importance of collaboration between the public and private sector in implementing effective marketing strategies (Formica & Littlefield 2000).

The following sections describe the array of activities that ideally are carried out by a well-funded and collaborative government tourism organisation.

Promotion

Advertising directed at key market segments is a core activity. The extremely successful '100% Pure New Zealand' campaign, for example, employs the common logo and slogan but different activities and images in the key inbound markets of Australia, Japan, the United States, the United Kingdom, Germany and Singapore (Morgan, Pritchard & Piggott 2002) (see the case study at the end of this chapter). To expedite these campaigns, larger NTOs often maintain offices in the major cities of key market countries. Related activities include participation in domestic and international tourism trade shows, the organisation of familiarisation tours for media and industry mediators, handling media inquiries and coordinating press releases. Government tourism organisations also produce and distribute or coordinate the production and distribution of promotional material and work to promote a favourable destination image in key origin regions. Some organisations engage in joint promotion with other jurisdictions.

Research

Research, or the informed acquisition of strategic knowledge and information (see chapter 12), is an increasingly important activity pursued by government tourism organisations. This can focus on visitation trends and forecasting, identification of key market segments and their expenditure and activity patterns, perceptions of visitor satisfaction and effectiveness of prior or current promotional campaigns. If resources are available, these bodies may also try to identify the key threats and opportunities presented by external environments (see section 7.6.1).

Coordination of the tourism industry

Although the tourism industry and its constituent subsectors maintain their own representative bodies, government tourism organisations often provide support to new and existing tourism businesses, advise on their product development and otherwise assist in educating and encouraging the industry.

Information for tourists

This function is distinct from promotion in its emphasis on providing basic information to tourists who are already in the destination through tourist information centres at key destination sites and gateways.

These functions are usually informed by and directed towards the overriding strategic objectives of the NTO. In the case of Tourism Australia, the latter include (a) influencing tourists to travel to Australia to see sites as well as to attend events, (b) influencing visitors to travel throughout Australia, (c) influencing Australians to travel throughout Australia, (d) fostering sustainable tourism within Australia and (e) helping to realise economic benefits for Australia from tourism (Tourism Australia 2005b). Such broad objectives are usually shared with the **national tourism authority (NTA)**, which is the government agency (usually a department or office within a department, and sometimes the same agency as the NTO) that is responsible for broad tourism policy and planning.

NTOs are normally mandated to promote the country as a whole, which can generate conflict with states or provinces that perceive an imbalance in coverage with respect to their own jurisdiction. For example, South Australia and Western Australia might complain that Tourism Australia places too much emphasis on iconic attractions such as the Sydney Opera House, the Great Barrier Reef and Uluru, thereby reinforcing the tendency of inbound tourism to concentrate at these locations. While NTOs are sympathetic with such concerns and do try to integrate less frequented locations into their publicity and strategic planning (see the mandate of Tourism Australia on the previous page), the presentation of icons serves to reinforce distinctive and positive images that are pivotal for inducing potential tourists to favour Australia over its competitors. One way that NTOs can compromise between the more popular and less-known internal destinations is to portray generic lifestyles (e.g. the 'shrimp on the barbie' ads featuring Paul Hogan that were popular in the United States during the 1990s) and landscapes (e.g. beaches and kangaroos) that do not evoke specific locations. Frequently, these images are varied to target particular markets identified by segmentation research.

7.6 STRATEGIC TOURISM MARKETING

Whether undertaken by an NTO or an NTA for a country destination, or by a business just for itself, effective tourism marketing must take into account the basic mission statement of the organisation, and both the internal and external environment of the destination or company (figure 7.5). The mission statement is usually some very basic directive that influences any further statement of objectives or goals. For example, an NTO's mission statement usually espouses a viable and expanding tourism industry as a means of improving the quality of life for the broad local community. A business, in contrast, may have a mission of offering the highest quality products within a particular sector.

■ Figure 7.5
Strategic tourism marketing

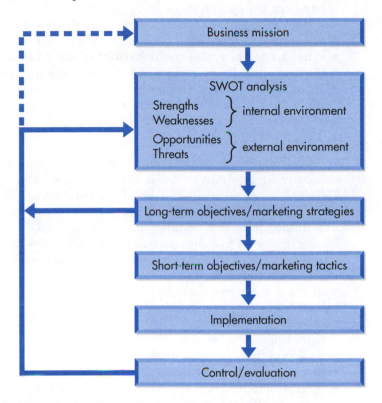

■ 7.6.1 SWOT *analysis and objectives*

SWOT analysis (strengths, weaknesses, opportunities, threats) is a very popular method for facilitating **strategic marketing** and management. The strengths and weaknesses component refers to the internal environment of the destination or business, while opportunities and threats are factors associated with the external environment.

The external environment includes not only elements of the general environment (i.e. the external technological, political, social, cultural and physical environments of tourism systems, as discussed in chapters 2, 3 and 4), but also an analysis of competing destinations or businesses. Key questions when examining the external environment include the following:

• Who are the competitors?
• What strategies are being employed by these competitors?
• What are *their* strengths and weaknesses?
• Who are their customers, and why do they purchase their products?
• What are their resources?
• What nontourism external environments are affecting or are going to affect us? How much can we influence these environments?

Questions that are pertinent to the internal environment of the destination or company include the following:

- What is the current level of visitation or patronage, and how does this compare with past trends?
- What products are actually and potentially available?
- Who are the customers, and how are they segmented?
- What are the activities and behaviour of the customers?
- How satisfied are customers with the available products?
- What are the reasons for these satisfaction levels?
- What are the available financial and human resources?

■ 7.6.2 Objectives

A SWOT analysis assists in the identification of long-term objectives for the company or destination. Such horizons may extend to the next ten or 15 years, but are usually not less than five years. Given the complex and unpredictable nature of the factors that will influence tourism over that timeframe, it is not sensible to stipulate specific long-term objectives. Rather, the objectives should reflect characteristics that are likely to remain desirable in ten or 15 years whatever else transpires. Relevant long-term objectives for a destination might include:

- increase the average length of stay
- increase average visitor expenditures per day
- increase the proportion of inputs (e.g. food, labour) that are obtained from the local region
- achieve a more dispersed distribution of the tourism sector
- diversify the market base to reduce dependence on the primary markets
- increase the number of tourists in a sustainable way.

Given a different set of priorities, the long-term objectives for a company are likely to be very different to those identified by destination managers — for example, to be the most highly capitalised company and to capture the largest share of consumer dollar in the sector.

Based on the broad and deliberately vague objectives and goals that are formulated for this extended timeframe, more specific short-term goals and marketing tactics should be established that have a horizon of six months to three years, depending on feasibility. Short-term goals that parallel the long-term objectives noted above might include:

- increase the average length of stay from 2.6 days to 3.2 days within the next two years
- increase average expenditures from $100 to $150 per day over the next two years
- initiate legislation within the next year that requires hotels to obtain at least one-half of their food inputs from local suppliers
- increase the promotional budget for regional tourism attractions by 10 per cent in the next financial year
- open three new tourist offices in large but nontraditional markets over the next three years
- limit the increase in annual arrivals to 5 per cent a year over the next two years.

■ 7.6.3 Control/*evaluation*

These precise figures and target dates inform the implementation process, and allow for a performance evaluation — have they been achieved or not? The control/evaluation process provides feedback for further SWOT analyses, which reassess the internal and external environmental factors that have helped or hindered the attainment of the objectives. This in turn may lead to a reassessment of the long-term and short-term objectives, as well as associated marketing strategies and tactics.

Strategic marketing recognises that a tourist destination or company does not exist in a vacuum. Such entities are just one component in complex tourism systems that are in turn affected by a myriad of factors generated in environments that are external to those systems. It also recognises that the managers of successful destinations, however success is defined, have a vision for the future, an awareness of the strategies that are required to achieve success and the will and means to carry out those strategies. Only by thinking in the long term will destinations and businesses minimise negative impacts and attain a sustainable tourism sector (as discussed in the next four chapters).

7.7 MARKETING MIX

The critical components that determine the demand for a business or destination product are collectively known as the **marketing mix**. Several different marketing mix structures have been proposed, a popular one being the **8P model** (Morrison 2002), which includes the following:

- place
- people
- packaging
- promotion
- product
- price
- programming
- partnerships.

All these components need to come together in a mutually reinforcing way to achieve maximum effectiveness. In many respects the marketing mix factors discussed below overlap with the pull factors that were considered in chapter 4. One major difference is that the 8P model reconfigures those factors in a way that facilitates marketing and promotional efforts. That is, they are conceptualised as factors that can be marketed and managed to the greatest possible extent. In addition, the marketing mix is applicable to individual companies as well as destinations.

■ 7.7.1 Place

As indicated in chapter 4, place is essential because tourists must travel to the destination in order to consume the tourist product. Relative location (proximity to actual and potential markets and competitors) is a critical element of place, as is coverage (the other places that are identified or not identified as target markets for marketing and promotional efforts). Australia, for example, maintains a highly visible presence in east Asia, western Europe and North America, but places a low priority on emerging markets in Africa, eastern Europe and Latin America. Accessibility represents the extent to which the markets and destinations are connected, and this too must be taken into account in marketing strategies. Essentially, these three elements encompass the three geographical elements of tourism systems, as discussed in chapter 2 — destination regions, origin regions and transit regions.

An increasingly important concept in the marketing mix is **sense of place**, which in a tourism context can be defined as the package of natural and cultural characteristics that distinguishes a particular destination from any other destination. By promoting sense of place, marketers are in essence branding the destination as a unique product that is offered nowhere else, thereby enhancing its competitive advantage by positioning it at the 'unique' pole of the scarcity continuum (see page 148). This strategy, moreover, has important implications for a destination's environmental and sociocultural sustainability, because it counteracts the tendency towards uniformity and community alienation that characterises many destinations as they become more developed (see chapters 9 to 11) (Walsh, Jamrozy & Burr 2001).

■ 7.7.2 Product

The product component encompasses the range of available goods and services, their quality and warranty and aftersales service. Range is a measure of diversification, and can be illustrated by a tour operator that offers a broad array of opportunities, as opposed to a niche operator. Similarly, a destination may provide a large number of diverse attractions, or just one specific attraction. The concepts of quality and warranty must be approached differently when comparing a destination with a specific operator. In the case of a specific operator, the manager of the business exercises considerable control in ensuring that the customer receives certain specific services in a satisfactory way, and that some kind of restitution is available if the customer is unsatisfied. In a destination, however, there is relatively little that the manager can do about litter-strewn streets, unfriendly residents and the persistence of rainy weather during a tourist's entire visit. This is because much of the 'product' consists of generic, public goods over which the tourism manager has minimal control and no scope or direct obligation to provide any warranties for unsatisfactory quality. Similarly, the notion of aftersales service is difficult to apply to tourism services or destinations, and is mainly restricted to determining tourists' post-trip attitudes about their tourism experience.

■ 7.7.3 People

People enter the marketing mix equation in at least three ways:
• service personnel
• the tourists themselves
• local residents.

The service personnel issue was considered earlier under the topics of inseparability and variability, which demonstrated the critical role of highly trained employees at the consumer/product interface. The importance of fostering tourist sensitivity and awareness was also stressed, since inappropriate tourist behaviour can reduce the quality of the product for all participants. For many destinations, the local residents also fall into the category of product, since tourists may be attracted by the culture and hospitality of the resident population. Again, tourism managers can attempt to control public behaviour towards tourists through education programs, but there is very little that can be done in the way of quality control if some local residents maintain a hostile attitude, unless this is expressed in unlawful activities.

It has been argued that the treatment of residents as a mere element of 'product' that can be manipulated for the benefit of the tourism industry and tourists is an approach that breeds hostility and resentment within the local community. As a result, a community-based approach to tourism management and planning, which gives first priority to the needs and wants of residents and acknowledges their lead role as decision makers, has become more popular (Singh, Timothy & Dowling 2003). High-level input from the community is, moreover, more conducive to the development and presentation of a product that effectively conveys the destination's sense of place.

Database marketing

The incorporation of the 'people' component in the marketing mix (and the tourist component in particular) has been greatly assisted by the emergence of **database marketing**, which can be defined as a comprehensive computer-driven marketing approach that is based on a memory of prior business transactions with customers. It involves the continuous collection, accumulation and analysis of data on customer behaviour and characteristics as a means of informing market segmentation and subsequent marketing decisions (Opperman 1999). As such, it exemplifies the holistic, two-way model of marketing advocated in this chapter (section 7.2.1). Database marketing makes feasible the identification and targeting of very small niche markets as well as 'markets of one' (see chapter 6). In addition, it is an effective device for identifying customers who are most likely to continue patronising the tourism business or destination (i.e. high-loyalty customers), and those who are likely to provide the most business. This latter point recognises the marketing adage that 20 per cent of a company's customer base accounts for 80 per cent of its business (Alford 1999). In the tourism industry, database marketing is exemplified in loyalty schemes such as airline frequent flyer and hotel frequent user programs, which involve the compilation of sophisticated databases on a large array of consumer variables. The utility of these variables in dealing with the special challenges of services marketing is illustrated by a situation where a hotel's database shows that a customer requested several packages of macadamia nuts during a previous stay, prompting the hotel to provide extra macadamia nuts in the room of that customer prior to their next visit. This is pleasing and personalised service that fosters continued high loyalty.

■ 7.7.4 Price

Price is a critical marketing mix element, since affordability constitutes an important pull factor in drawing tourists to particular destinations. Airlines, attractions and hotels commonly reduce their prices until a desirable level of occupancy is achieved (i.e. a strategy of increasing the demand), given the profit implications of empty seats or rooms for products that have high fixed costs (see figure 7.1). However, the relationship between reduced price and increased patronage is not entirely straightforward, as many consumers perceive price as an indicator of quality — if the price is too low, this might indicate a poor-quality product. For this reason, reduced price may dissuade wealthier travellers who can afford higher prices, and may convey a lasting image of cheapness. Permanent or temporary discounts, nevertheless, are often used to target specific groups who are sensitive to high prices, including older adults, students and young children.

Given the importance of price in a high fixed cost environment, it is important for tourism managers to be aware of the pricing techniques that can be employed by businesses. The emphasis here is on companies, since the cost of a destination is based on the cumulative pricing decisions of the businesses and operations, public and private, that function within that destination. Destination managers might possibly influence those prices through tax concessions, grants, regulations and other means, but cannot by themselves determine the pricing structure. The pricing techniques can be separated into four main and largely self-explanatory categories as follows.

Profit-oriented pricing

Pricing techniques that are oriented towards profit include typical approaches such as the maximisation of profits and the attainment of satisfactory profits (however these might be defined) and target return on investment. Such strategies do not place the priority on what the competition is doing.

Sales-oriented pricing

There are many varieties of pricing techniques that focus on consumer sales. These include basing the strategy on the prices that the market, or some target segment thereof, is willing to pay for a product, maximising the volume of sales, increasing market share through (for example) aggressive promotion and reduced prices, gaining market penetration through low initial entry prices, and maintaining high prices as a signal of outstanding quality (prestige pricing).

Competition-oriented pricing

The emphasis here is on competitor behaviour as the major criterion for setting prices. This reactive approach can involve the matching of a competitor's prices, or the maintenance of price differentials at a level above or below the competitor's prices, depending on the type of market that is being targeted.

Cost-oriented pricing

These strategies base pricing structures on the actual cost of providing the goods or services. First, costs are established, and then an appropriate profit margin is added. This margin can be either a fixed sum (e.g. $50 per ticket) or a relative amount (e.g. 10 per cent profit per ticket). It is a common practice in cost-oriented pricing to calculate break-even points — that is, combinations of price and occupancy where revenues and costs are equal (e.g. $100 per room at 84 per cent occupancy, or $120 per room at 70 per cent occupancy). Any incremental increase in occupancy above the break-even point represents a profit margin.

■ 7.7.5 Packaging

Packaging refers to the deliberate grouping together of two or more elements of the tourism experience into a single product. This is best illustrated in the private sector by the provision of set-price package tours that integrate transportation, accommodation, visits to attractions and other complementary tourism components (see chapter 5). For destinations, the packaging element can be more ambiguous and informal, involving attempts by NTOs or subnational tourism organisations to market the destination as an integrated 'package' of attractions, activities, relevant services and other tourism-related opportunities.

According to Morrison (2002), packaging is popular because it provides greater convenience and economy for customers, allows them to budget more easily, and eliminates the time required to assemble the constituent items individually. From an operator perspective, packages can stimulate demand in off-season periods (e.g. 'summer special packages'), attract new customers, encourage the establishment of partnerships with operators offering the complementary services and make business planning easier (in part because packages are often paid for well in advance of the experience).

■ 7.7.6 Programming

Programming is closely related to packaging in that it involves the addition of special events, activities or programs to a product to make it more diverse and appealing (Morrison 2002). Examples include the inclusion of scuba diving lessons or academic lectures on a cruise, 'chance' encounters with historical impersonators at a heritage theme park, broadcasting live rugby matches at a sports bar and the periodic announcement of prizewinners at a convention. For the theme park or sports bar (or, potentially, the destination), such program add-ons allow the operator to alter their product package frequently and inexpensively without having to undertake risky and costly actions such as introducing new rides or menus. Moreover, the programs could be altered to draw specific market segments (e.g. broadcasting women's hockey to attract young adult females).

■ 7.7.7 Promotion

As indicated earlier, many people see promotion as being synonymous with marketing. Promotion attempts to increase demand by conveying a positive image of the product to potential customers through appeals to the perceived demands, needs, tastes, values and attitudes of the market or a particular target market segment (see the case study at the end of this chapter).

Promotion consists of:

- presentation
- personal selling
- sales promotion
- publicity
- merchandising
- advertising.

Presentation can include the provision of uniformed and well-groomed staff and an attractive physical environment, which give potential customers a favourable impression of the company. Personal selling entails a direct approach to a particular client, usually a large corporation whose potential patronage justifies the added costs of this individual approach. Sales promotions are short-term strategies that promote a product through temporary discounts (e.g. special discount of 80 per cent off a product for one day only in order to increase exposure to consumers).

Publicity

Publicity can occur through press releases and is one of the least expensive means of promotion, and one that can be readily used by destination managers. Even better is coverage by way of a *National Geographic* magazine article or television special accessed by millions of consumers. However, there is a higher risk in such unsolicited media coverage that the publicity, and resulting product image, will be negative, one example being the media presentation of Thailand following the 2004 tsunami. This forces the destination or company to engage in damage control by releasing its own counterbalancing publicity.

Merchandising

Merchandising can be used very effectively as a promotional tool when it involves the sale of products that are readily associated with a particular company or destination (Doyle 2004). This might involve items of clothing on which a resort or tour operator's logo is prominently displayed. There are several advantages associated with well-formulated merchandising strategies. First, unlike other forms of promotion, merchandising also generates direct income, and all the more so since logo products often sell at a premium. Second, since such products are usually purchased as souvenirs, they tend to be prominently displayed as status symbols back in the origin region, thereby maximising exposure to potential customers. Third, it is commonly the more frequently worn items of clothing, such as baseball caps and T-shirts, that are merchandised, and therefore the purchasers of these products are likely to spend more time acting as walking billboards for the company or destination.

Hard Rock Café illustrates the effective application of merchandising to the tourism sector. More of the company's revenue is generated from the sale of Hard Rock Café-branded merchandise than from food and beverages. The range of available items has expanded from simple but enormously popular T-shirts to lapel pins, teddy bears and beer glasses. Because of their desirability as collectables, many consumers purchase two items — one for display as a status symbol (e.g. a T-shirt or key chain) and one preserved in mint condition for its future resale value. Even more ingeniously, names of individual locations (e.g. Surfers Paradise, Las Vegas) are included on certain items of merchandise, making each a discrete collectable and prompting dedicated collectors to accumulate specimens from all Hard Rock Cafés worldwide.

Advertising

Advertising is the most common form of promotion, and constitutes a major topic of investigation and management in its own right (see for example Morgan & Pritchard 2000). An important distinction in advertising can be made between a 'shotgun approach' and a 'rifle approach'. In **shotgun marketing**, an advertisement is placed in a mainstream media source that is accessed by a broad cross-section of the tourist market. As with a shotgun, much of the delivery will miss the target audience altogether, but the high level of saturation will ensure that the target audience will also be affected. For example, an advertisement for a backpacker hotel in *Time* magazine will be ignored by most readers, but will almost certainly reach a large number of backpackers who read this magazine. Shotgun marketing also attracts new recruits to the product, that is, non-backpackers whose interest is aroused by the advertisement. The high costs associated with the mainstream media, however, are a major drawback to this approach.

In contrast, **rifle marketing** occurs when the advertisement is directed specifically to the target market, like a single bullet fired from a rifle. This would occur if the above-mentioned hotel advertisement were placed in a backpackers' magazine. Its major disadvantages are the lack of product exposure to the broader tourist market and competition with the advertisers of similar products. Beyond the shotgun/rifle dichotomy, a major decision in advertising and public relations dissemination is the selection of a media type that will best convey the desired message to the target market. Major media outlets are discussed below, except for travel guides, which were discussed in chapter 5.

Television

The attraction of television as a media outlet is based in part on its ubiquity, at least within high-spending Phase Four societies. Moreover, television is more effective than any other contemporary mainstream media in conveying an animated, realistic image of a product. To be cost-effective (since television advertising time is relatively expensive), television-oriented advertisements must capture the viewer's attention quickly (else the viewer may leave to visit the kitchen or toilet) and convey the message within a short period of time (e.g. 30 seconds). Also, they should be timed to optimise exposure to the target audience. For example, it is a wasted effort to target young children during the late evening hours. Similarly, it is critical to match the product with the program. Highly educated viewers, for example, are more likely to watch news programs or documentaries.

Radio

As a media outlet, radio has long been overtaken by television, but it is still important in Phase Two and Three societies as a promotional device. In Phase Four societies radio remains important as a source of information during work time. From 9 am to 5 pm radio may reach as many potential customers as television. Although less expensive than television, a major disadvantage of radio is the inability to convey visual information. Effective auditory stimuli, however, can evoke desirable and attractive mental images.

Newspapers and magazines

Newspapers and magazines have the advantage of containing messages that can be accessed at any time, and may persist for many years in the form of accumulated or circulating copies. However, this also means that the advertisement becomes obsolete as prices increase and the product is modified. In addition, the images are static and the quality of reproduction can be quite crude in newspapers, even when colour is used. Print media also assumes a literate market, which is a serious impediment in Phase Two and some Phase Three societies. An added complication in highly literate countries is the abundance of newspaper and magazine options, which requires marketers to conduct extensive research in order to identify the most effective target outlets. An estimated 4500 magazine titles are available in Australia alone, and 90 per cent of all such sales occurring through retail outlets rather than subscription makes it difficult to predict the readership of any particular issue (Magazine Publishers of Australia 2005).

Brochures

Tourism brochures are perhaps the most utilised form of promotion across the tourism industry and within destinations, and are a very important means through which package tours and products within particular destinations are selected. Research, however, suggests that brochures have more influence on those with no prior experience of a destination or product than those who have (Zhou 1998). A characteristic that distinguishes brochures from television or other printed media is their specialised nature — they are not provided as an appendage to a newspaper article or a television program, but concentrate 100 per cent on the promotional effort. Brochures are usually printed in bulk quantities, and made available for distribution through travel agencies, tourism information centres, hotels, attractions and other strategic locations, as well as by mail. Brochures can range in complexity from a simple black-and-white leaflet to a glossy booklet, such as those commonly available from large tour operators.

A way of making brochures more attractive and of minimising their disposal is to include practical information (e.g. safety suggestions, directions) and discount coupons or to treat the brochure itself as a means of gaining discounted entry at qualifying attractions.

Internet

The Internet is emerging as a mainstream media outlet that will eventually rival or even exceed television or newspapers and magazines. Its creative use as a promotional tool and distribution channel is illustrated by the rapid development of **webcasting** technologies, which deliver interactive multimedia (video and audio) in real time. Configured effectively, webcasting can help to overcome the intangibility dilemma discussed in section 7.3.1. Another innovative marketing application of the Internet involves the facilitated provision and delivery of postcards (see Breakthrough tourism:

marketing with the e-postcard). Given the rapid development of such technological innovations, it is not surprising that the Internet is growing in popularity as a means of accessing information about potential destinations and other tourism-related goods and services (see Technology and tourism: Using the Internet to find out about Australia).

An extremely important charateristic of the Internet is that almost anyone can develop and update a website due to their low cost and technical simplicity, which means that even the smallest operator or destination can obtain the same potential exposure as any large corporation. In this sense the Internet is instrumental in levelling the promotional 'playing field'.

BREAKTHROUGH TOURISM

Marketing with the e-postcard

An inevitable consequence of the Internet has been the appearance of postcards that can be selected online and delivered through email. Unlike the traditional postcard, these **e-postcards** can be obtained and sent almost instantaneously from an Internet café or other location and at a much reduced cost since there is no need to purchase the physical item or a postage stamp. It is also possible to deliver the image to a large number of recipients (as, for example, through a mailing list) without having to write a separate message for each. Websites maintained by organisations such as Sunlover Holidays (part of the commercial division of Tourism Queensland) and Tourism Western Australia offer a diverse selection of images and require the tourist simply to pick the desired image, add a message and write in the email address of the recipient or recipients. The organisation never runs out of images, controls and can add to the images that are offered and can maintain the site at minimal cost. It is even possible for the tourist to send e-postcards after the trip has been completed.

While the marketing and image-formation implications of the e-postcard are enormous, this innovation is not without problems. The sender has to know the web address from which to initiate the process, yet the names of the relevant promotional agencies (for example, see above) and their web addresses are often not well known to tourists. Moreover, there is nothing to stop maverick sites from making available irreverent or otherwise uncomplimentary images. The range of potential recipients is restricted to individuals having access to computers, and high-quality printers are also required if the image is to have any longer-term impact as a tangible representation of the destination and not just an ephemeral electronic file. In addition, the receipt of e-postcards will be further disturbed by the likelihood that they will be mistaken for spam, and deleted, or by their use as direct marketing spam. Finally, the psychological impact of e-postcards is diluted by their lack of a handwritten message or cancelled postage stamp: signifiers of authenticity, uniqueness and personalisation that better ensure that a traditional postcard will be retained, valued and revisited periodically by the recipient and potential visitor.

Consumers are increasingly relying on the Internet as a travel-planning and decision-making tool. According to the Tourism Australia (2004), 22 per cent of all inbound visitors in 2003, or just fewer than one million, reported using the Internet to obtain information about Australia in planning that visit, down from 26 per cent in 2002 but up from 13 per cent in 2000. Significantly, only 8 per cent of these users were influenced by the Internet to visit Australia, while 54 per cent used it to find out more about Australia *after* their decision had already been made. In either case, the Internet was accessed by a large proportion of users to find out about accommodation (42 per cent), events or activities (41 per cent) and itinerary planning (40 per cent). Less frequent was the search for airfares to Australia (22 per cent), air travel within Australia (11 per cent) and other internal transportation options (20 per cent). Internet usage was found to vary among major markets, with Germans being the most involved (33 per cent) and Indonesians the least (5 per cent). Marketers should note, moreover, that one-third of Koreans were influenced to visit Australia by the Internet, compared with just 2 per cent of visitors from the United Kingdom. The proportions are reversed in the search for low airfares to Australia, with 10 and 33 per cent, respectively, accessing the Internet for this purpose. Promotional efforts that try to exploit the marketing potential of the Internet should also factor in the strong correlation between usage and age. More than one in four visitors between 15 and 34 accessed the Internet, compared with one in ten in the 65 or older cohort. In addition to revealing differences among major geographic and demographic market segments, the above results indicate considerable room for growth in the use of the Internet as a destination decision-making tool and source of transportation options for travel within Australia. The high proportion of VFR motivations among British visitors is probably a major reason for this market's tendency not to be influenced by the Internet but followup research should be undertaken to determine whether additional factors also play an important role.

7.7.8 Partnerships

As illustrated by the formation of airline alliances (see page 152) and credit cards that feature a particular business or organisation (e.g. the Marriott Rewards VISA card), mutual benefits can result when similar or dissimilar businesses embark in cooperative product development and marketing on a temporary or longer-term basis (Fyall & Garrod 2005). These include exposure to new markets, expanded product packages, greater ability to serve customer needs, more efficient use of resources through sharing, image improvement through association with well-regarded brands and access to partners' databases and expertise (Morrison 2002). Partnerships are especially important for small operations that lack the economies of scale to engage in these efforts efficiently and effectively on their own. For example, vacation farms in countries such as Austria have formed consortiums of ten or more operators, which benefit from the collective pooling of resources. Another illustration is the Silk Road marketing campaign, which employs a well-known overriding historical theme to promote tourism in otherwise obscure central Asian countries such as Kyrgyzstan, Turkmenistan, Uzbekistan and Tajikistan (World Tourism Organization 2001). Partnerships can also be created between suppliers of products and their customers, as demonstrated by repeat-user programs.

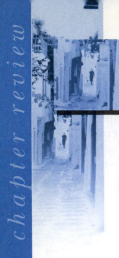

CHAPTER REVIEW

Marketing involves communication and other interactions among the producers and consumers of tourism experiences. The marketing of a service such as tourism differs from goods because of the intangibility, inseparability, variability and perishability of the former. These qualities present challenges to managers and marketers in their attempt to match the supply of tourism products with market demand. For example, intangibility means that the consumer cannot directly experience the product before its consumption, while inseparability implies that production and consumption occur simultaneously, thus limiting the scope for introducing quality control mechanisms. Because profit margins in the tourism sector are narrowed by high fixed costs, and because demand varies considerably over a daily, weekly, seasonal and long-term timeframe, managers must be aware of the strategies that can be implemented to foster an equilibrium between demand and supply. Depending on the circumstances, these involve the reduction, increase or redistribution of supply or demand.

Conventional macro-economic theory suggests that an equilibrium between supply and demand will eventually be achieved, but market failure (i.e. the failure to attain this balance) often occurs in the marketing of 'public goods' such as an entire tourist destination. To compensate for market failure, national and subnational tourism organisations are established to market and promote destinations. Whether undertaken by these public authorities or private companies, strategic marketing procedures should be practised in order to achieve optimum outcomes. This includes the use of a SWOT analysis to inform long- and short-term objectives. In strategic marketing, demand can be gauged and manipulated through the use of marketing mix frameworks such as the product-focused 8P model, which takes into account place, product, people, price, packaging, programming, promotion and partnerships.

SUMMARY OF KEY TERMS

Marketing

The interactions and interrelationships that occur among consumers and producers of goods and services, through which ideas, products, services and values are created and exchanged for the mutual benefit of both groups

Services marketing

The marketing of services such as those associated with the tourism industry, as opposed to the marketing of the goods industry. The following characteristics distinguish service marketing from goods marketing:

- **Intangibility:** the actual tourism service cannot be seen, touched or tried before its purchase and consumption
- **Inseparability:** production and consumption of tourist services both occur at the same time and place and are thus inseparable

- **Emotional labour:** the expression of the willingness to be of service to customers, as through responsiveness and empathy
- **Variability:** service encounters, even if they involve a similar kind of experience, are highly variable due to the differences and rapid changes in mood, expectation and other human element factors that affect the participants
- **Perishability:** because production and consumption are simultaneous, services cannot be produced and stored in advance for future consumption; empty aircraft seats, for example, are a permanent loss that cannot be recouped

Fixed costs

Costs that the operation has little flexibility to change over the short term, such as interest costs on borrowed funds and basic facility maintenance costs

Variable costs

Costs that can be readily reduced in the short term, such as salaries of casual staff

Demarketing

The process of discouraging all or certain tourists from visiting a particular destination temporarily or permanently

- **General demarketing:** demarketing that is directed towards all tourists, usually temporarily
- **Selective demarketing:** demarketing that is directed towards a particular tourist segment, usually intended as a permanent measure against groups deemed to be undesirable

Market failure

The failure of market forces to produce a longer-term equilibrium in supply and demand, such as when individual businesses in the tourism industry are unwilling to provide the funds for destination promotion (to increase demand) because such investment will provide benefits to their competitors as well as to themselves

- **National tourism organisations (NTOs):** publicly funded government agencies that undertake promotion and other forms of marketing at the country-destination scale, usually directed towards inbound tourists; these are distinct from the government departments or bodies, or national tourism authorities, that dictate tourism-related policy
- **National tourism authority (NTA):** the government agency responsible for broad tourism policy and planning within a destination country

Strategic marketing

Marketing that takes into consideration an extensive analysis of external and internal environmental factors in identifying strategies that attain specific goals

- **SWOT analysis:** an analysis of a company or destination's strengths, weaknesses, opportunities and threats that emerges from an examination of its internal and external environment

Marketing mix

The critical components that determine the demand for a business or destination product

- **8P model:** a product-focused marketing mix model that incorporates place, product, people, price, packaging, programming, promotion and partnerships
- **Sense of place:** the combination of natural and cultural characteristics that makes a destination unique in comparison to any other destination, and thus provides it with a competitive advantage
- **Database marketing:** a comprehensive marketing strategy that is based on a memory of prior business transactions with customers; the use of accumulated customer data to inform marketing decisions
- **Shotgun marketing:** a mode of promotional advertising where the message is disseminated to a broad audience on the assumption that this saturation will reach target markets and perhaps attract new recruits
- **Rifle marketing:** a mode of promotional advertising that is aimed just at the target market
- **Webcasting:** the delivery of interactive multimedia to customers through the Internet on either an 'on demand' or 'real-time' basis
- **e-postcards:** virtual postcards that are selected through the Internet and sent to recipients by email

QUESTIONS

1 In what ways does marketing go beyond the simple presentation of advertisements through various forms of media?

2 What marketing strategies can be adopted by NTO and NTA managers to compensate for the intangibility, inseparability, variability and perishability that are implicit in a visit to a destination?

3 Bures and yurts are temporary accommodation types that help to address a hotel's problem of high fixed costs. What are the potential disadvantages associated with their use?

4 (a) What are the risks of using demarketing as a tactic for reducing the demand for a particular destination?
(b) How can these risks be minimised?

5 (a) What is market failure?
(b) Why does it occur frequently within the tourism industry?

6 (a) What dilemma do NTOs face in trying to promote their country overseas, while at the same time giving fair representation to all their country's states or provinces?
(b) How can NTOs try to overcome this dilemma?

7 How could a manager prioritise the strengths, weaknesses, opportunities and threats in a SWOT analysis in terms of devising management and marketing strategies?

8 What are the strengths and weaknesses associated with the various forms of media that can be used to promote tourism destinations and products?

9 (a) How is the Internet revolutionising the process of strategic marketing in the tourism industry?

(b) What future innovations in Internet technology are likely to revolutionise tourism marketing further in the next ten years?

E X E R C I S E S

1 (a) Divide the class into four groups and have each group conduct a SWOT analysis of a particular destination. Each of the four destinations should be located adjacent to one another either at the international scale (e.g. Singapore, Malaysia, Indonesia and Thailand) or at the subnational scale (e.g. Gold Coast, Brisbane, Sunshine Coast and Hervey Bay).

(b) Show how the other three destinations fit into the SWOT analysis of each destination.

(c) Indicate ways in which the competition-related threats of these other destinations can be converted into opportunities.

2 Write a 1000-word essay that conveys the sense of place of your home town in such a way that it would induce the reader to visit that destination.

3 List ten critical questions that a destination manager should ask departing tourists in compiling a visitor database that can effectively aid the marketing of that destination.

F U R T H E R   R E A D I N G

Anderson, B., Provis, C. & Chappel, S. 2003. 'The Selection and Training of Workers in the Tourism and Hospitality Industries for the Performance of Emotional Labour'. *Journal of Hospitality and Tourism Management* **10: 1–12.** The authors present the concept of emotional labour as a way of compensating for the problem of inseparability in the hospitality industry.

Beirman, D. 2003. *Restoring Tourism Destinations in Crisis: A Strategic Marketing Approach.* **Sydney: Allen & Unwin.** This text contains in-depth international case studies from past tourism crises and analyses the strengths and weaknesses of the responses made by tourism operators.

Fyall, A. & Garrod, B. 2005. 'From Competition to Collaboration in the Tourism Industry'. In Theobald, W. (Ed.) *Global Tourism.* **Third Edition. Sydney: Elsevier, pp. 52–73.** The rationale for collaborative partnerships in the tourism industry, and illustrations of them, are covered in this chapter.

Kotler, P., Bowen, J. & Makens, J. 2003. *Marketing for Hospitality & Tourism.* **Third Edition. Upper Saddle River, New Jersey: Prentice Hall.** This is an adaptation of Kotler's classic marketing text for the hospitality and tourism sector. It provides a systematic overview of the issues involved in marketing, although the tourism component is not featured as prominently as the hospitality component.

Morgan, N. & Pritchard, A. 2000. *Advertising in Tourism and Leisure.* **Oxford: Butterworth–Heinemann.** This text focuses on the promotional aspects of marketing and is well illustrated with international case studies.

Morgan, N., Pritchard, A. & Pride, R. (Eds) 2004. *Destination Branding: Creating the Unique Destination Proposition.* **Second Edition. Sydney: Elsevier.** Using a mixture of theoretically and practically oriented chapters, this book provides a global perspective on the issue of destination branding, a vital component in the marketing of public tourist places.

Morrison, A. 2002. *Hospitality and Travel Marketing.* **Third Edition. Albany, New York: Delmar Publishers.** This is a key textbook in the area of tourism marketing, and one of the few that emphasises a tourism rather than a hospitality perspective. It makes extensive use of systems theory.

Pike, S. 2004. *Destination Marketing Organisations.* **Oxford: Elsevier.** Written by a former destination marketer, this text bridges industry and theory by synthesising a wealth of academic literature of practical value to destination-marketing organisations.

Walsh, J., Jamrozy, U. & Burr, S. 2001. 'Sense of Place as a Component of Sustainable Tourism Marketing'. In McCool, S. & Moisey, R. (Eds) *Tourism, Recreation and Sustainability.* **Wallingford, UK: CABI Publishing, pp. 195–216.** The authors discuss the idea of sense of place as a strategically critical marketing concept rooted in the context of sustainable tourism, which assumes the empowerment of the local community.

Marketing 100% Pure New Zealand

In mid-1999, New Zealand launched its first global branding campaign, which it hoped would double the country's international tourism revenues by 2005 by encouraging new visitors, more repeat visitors and longer stays (Morgan, Pritchard & Piggott 2002). The 100% Pure New Zealand campaign has since been recognised as an exemplar of effective destination branding, as demonstrated by its selection for the Pacific Asia Travel Association's 2004 Grand Award for Marketing from a field of 332 contestants. An early assumption of the campaign was the need to engage in niche marketing, given the realisation that New Zealand is a small, isolated destination that cannot broadly compete with Australia in terms of size, attraction diversity and marketing resources. Extensive market research in the United Kingdom, a major inbound market for New Zealand, revealed that the country held the greatest appeal for the special interest and 'real travel' market segments, which includes backpackers, well-travelled professionals, adventure tourists and ecotourists. These segments regard New Zealand as a laid-back, down-to-earth destination with an outstanding natural environment. Because motivations such as relaxation, family entertainment, nightlife and sunbathing were not seen to be satisfied, it was decided to focus the campaign instead on 'energising the traveller' and on positioning New Zealand as 'an adventurous new land and an adventurous new culture on the edge of the Pacific Ocean' (Morgan, Pritchard & Piggott 2002).

The '100% Pure' tagline was consequently created to evoke a strong sense of a 'real', authentic, healthy, wholesome and unadulterated destination in which visitors are free to express themselves within a variety of highly appealing natural landscapes. Typical ads employ four primary features. First, there is a backdrop of spectacular natural scenery against which one or more people are engaging in appealing and satisfying activities, such as walking along the beach, mountain biking or relaxing in a mountain pond. Second, the primary text at the base of this image employs the '100% Pure' tagline within the specific context of that theme, e.g. 100% Pure Adventure, 100% Pure Solitude, 100% Pure Adrenaline, 100% Pure Romance, 100% Pure Spirit. A more specific application in the early 2000s used the slogan 'In Five Days You'll Feel 100%' to attract the short-stay Australian market. Small print detailing the specifics and logistics of a New Zealand vacation are the third element of the ads but one that is clearly subordinate to the first two elements and is not meant to be read until the image and tagline have made their initial impression on the observer. Finally, the statement '100% Pure New Zealand' is included at the bottom of the ad as the unifying slogan that relates all the depicted experiences to Brand New Zealand. In both taglines, the '%' symbol incorporates a map of New Zealand that explicitly ties the destination with the slogan.

The New Zealand campaign is widely regarded as a success because it effectively conveys a concise, consistent, emotionally appealing and durable message to a variety of desired target markets in the key origin countries of the United States, United Kingdom, Australia and Japan (Morgan, Pritchard & Piggott 2002). An additional factor involved efforts to compensate for New Zealand's small marketing 'voice' by linking its campaign to the America's Cup yacht race and, more importantly, to the *Lord of the Rings* trilogy, which was filmed in New Zealand (see figure 7.6). Capitalising on the exposure of New Zealand's Middle Earth landscapes to hundreds of millions of moviegoers over a three-year period, 100% Pure New Zealand ads were released during the time of the 2002–04 Oscars ceremony in newspapers such as the *Los Angeles Times* with the modified slogan 'Best Supporting Country in a Motion Picture' (Piggott, Morgan & Pritchard, 2004). In another example of targeted and leveraged public relations, Tourism New Zealand, the country's NTO, also successfully negotiated with US-based TV channels such as *National Geographic* and *Sci Fi* to incorporate New Zealand tourism footage in three documentaries examining the making of the trilogy (Morgan, Pritchard & Piggott 2002).

Some indication of the campaign's success is provided by the fact that the number of international stayovers to New Zealand increased from 1 607 000 in 1999 to 2 334 000 in 2004 with increases reported in all intervening years (TRCNZ 2005). Market satisfaction research by Tourism New Zealand (2005) also reveals that fully 96 per cent of international visitors intend to recommend New Zealand as a destination to their friends and relatives. However, the campaign can also be criticised because it creates a high visitor expectation that may not always be realised in the actual New Zealand landscape, resulting in dissatisfaction and negative word-of-mouth advertising. It can also result in a paradox in which the many visitors who are attracted by the ads serve to undermine the very environmental qualities that attracted them in the first instance, thereby also giving rise to the first scenario. An additional concern is that the campaign's success will result in an embedded image of New Zealand, which will constrain future efforts to broaden its appeal beyond a basically undeveloped rural landscape. The greater Auckland region, for example, is an urban and exurban destination that does not directly benefit from the campaign beyond the enhancement of its role as the country's gateway.

■ **Figure 7.6** *Tourism New Zealand adopted the slogan 'Best supporting country in a motion picture' after the filming of* Lord of the Rings

Questions

1 (a) How are the 8Ps evident in the 100% Pure New Zealand campaign?

(b) How could the campaign be enhanced through further capitalisation on the 8P model? Consult the Tourism New Zealand website at www.newzealand.com/travel to inform your response.

2 Write a 500-word report in which you:

(a) describe your level of interest in visiting New Zealand prior to being exposed to the 100% Pure New Zealand branding campaign

(b) indicate how much your desire to visit New Zealand has increased, decreased, or stayed the same as a result of this exposure

(c) explain the reasons for your response in (b) and comment on what this says about the effectiveness of the campaign.

3 Write a 1000-word SWOT analysis on New Zealand as an inbound destination. Identify the top three strengths, weaknesses, opportunities and threats, and explain why you consider these to be major considerations.

8 Economic impacts
of tourism

After studying this chapter, you should be able to:

1 name the top destination countries in terms of tourism revenue earnings and compare these with the top stayover-receiving countries

2 outline the main positive and negative economic impacts of tourism

3 explain the concept of the income multiplier effect (IME) and describe the circumstances under which a high or low IME is likely to occur

4 describe how tourism can function as a propulsive activity within a growth pole strategy

5 differentiate between the informal and formal sectors and describe their implications for tourism management

6 identify the circumstances under which a destination is more likely to experience negative rather than positive economic impacts from tourism

7 discuss the negative consequences of revenue leakages for a destination and explain where and why they occur

8 explain the fluctuating patterns of demand that characterise tourism and the implications of this for destinations

9 indicate how tourism can maintain a competitive or complementary relationship with agriculture

10 discuss employment-related problems that are associated with tourism.

ᛎNTRODUCTION

Marketing, as discussed in chapter 7, is a pervasive process, which includes attempts to attract and retain a client base for individual tourism-related businesses or entire destinations. Once the client–product link is established, however, a range of potential positive and negative impacts is possible and these must be taken into account in the strategic marketing and planning undertaken by destination managers. It is common in the tourism literature to distinguish between economic, sociocultural and environmental impacts. This tendency to use discrete categories, however, should not detract from the fact that impacts are often closely interrelated. For example, negative social reactions to tourism could result from its perceived economic and environmental costs. The placement of economic impacts as the first topic of discussion does not imply that these are inherently any more important than the sociocultural or environmental dimension. Rather, this reflects the primary importance that destinations have tended to place on economic benefits as a rationale for pursuing tourism. The structure of this chapter is straightforward, with section 8.2 examining the potential economic benefits of tourism and section 8.3 considering the potential economic costs.

ᛖCONOMIC BENEFITS

When tourism emerged as a significant economic sector in the decades following World War II, most researchers and government administrators assumed its growth to be a positive and desirable process. Conspicuous by its absence through the 1950s and 1960s was any concerted critique of tourism, prompting the description of this period as the era of the advocacy platform (see chapter 1). It is essentially this perspective that is represented below in the discussion of economic benefits.

■ 8.2.1 Direct *revenue*

The prospect of substantial tourism-derived **direct revenue** has long been the most compelling incentive for destinations to attract tourism activity. Fuelling this incentive is the global tourism revenue reported since 1950. **International tourism receipts** are defined by the World Tourism Organization (WTO 1996) as encompassing all consumption expenditure, or payments for goods and services, made by international tourists (stayovers and excursionists) for their own use or to give away. These receipts have increased at a substantially higher rate than the actual global intake of international stayovers, and exceeded US$520 billion per year by 2003 (table 3.1). At the level of the individual destination country, the revenue statistics for international tourism are also impressive, with 28 countries recording US$4 billion or more in tourism receipts for 2002 (table 8.1).

■ Table 8.1   *World's top tourism earners, 1980 and 2002*

RANK 1980	RANK 2002	COUNTRY	TOURISM RECEIPTS (US$ MILLION) 1980	TOURISM RECEIPTS (US$ MILLION) 2002	% SHARE OF RECEIPTS WORLDWIDE 1980	% SHARE OF RECEIPTS WORLDWIDE 2002
1	1	United States	10 058	66 547	9.6	14.0
4	2	Spain	6 968	33 609	6.6	7.1
2	3	France	8 235	32 329	7.8	6.8
3	4	Italy	8 213	26 915	7.8	5.7
34	5	China	617	20 385	0.6	4.3
6	6	Germany	6 566	19 158	6.2	4.0
5	7	United Kingdom	6 932	17 591	6.6	3.7
7	8	Austria	6 442	11 237	6.1	2.4
19	9	China, Hong Kong SAR	1 317	10 117	1.3	2.1
14	10	Greece	1 734	9 741	1.7	3.1
10	11	Canada	2 284	9 700	2.2	2.0
46	12	Turkey	327	9 010	0.3	1.9
8	13	Mexico	5 393	8 858	5.1	1.9
24	14	Australia	967	8 087	0.9	1.7
27	15	Thailand	867	7 902	0.8	1.7
15	16	Netherlands	1 668	7 706	1.6	1.6
9	17	Switzerland	3 149	7 628	3.0	1.6
12	18	Belgium	1 810	6 892	1.7	1.5
52	19	Malaysia	265	6 785	0.3	1.4
21	20	Portugal	1 147	5 919	1.1	1.2
18	21	Denmark	1 337	5 785	1.3	1.2
41	22	Korea, Republic of	369	5 277	0.4	1.1
16	23	Singapore	1 433	4 932	1.4	1.0
51	24	Poland	282	4 500	0.3	0.9
25	25	Sweden	962	4 496	0.9	0.9
—	26	Macau	—	4 415	—	0.9
23	27	Taiwan	988	4 197	0.9	0.8
—	28	Russia	—	4 188	0.9	0.8
—	29	Croatia	—	3 811	0.8	0.8
28	30	Egypt	808	3 764	0.8	0.8

Source: *Weaver & Oppermann (2000) and appendix 3*

These figures do not reflect all expenses that are incurred by tourists, but only those that accrue to the destination itself. The first component of these accruing expenditures are those paid in advance in the origin region, as through a package tour arrangement, while the other component involves money spent at the actual destination. The latter is usually characterised by a highly diverse array of expenditure categories, as illustrated by Australia's International Visitor Survey (see table 8.2). The data from table 8.2 reveal the importance of the accommodation, food and beverage, and merchandise subsectors as beneficiaries of tourist expenditure within Australia, while the transportation categories (rented vehicles, organised tours and airfares) are also significant, representing about one billion dollars in 1999. The status of education fees as the third-largest expenditure category is notable given the neglect of this sector by Australia's NTO (see chapter 2). It is also notable that one-half of total trip expenditures belong to the first component described above — that is, they occur within origin countries.

■ **Table 8.2** *Total international tourist expenditure on trips to Australia, 1995–2002 (AUS$ million)*

EXPENDITURE CATEGORY	1995	1997	1999	2002
Food, drink and accommodation	2 197	2 582	3 436	4 582
Shopping	2 027	1 897	1 814	2 155
Education fees	313	552	774	1 264
Rental, leasing fees and petrol for rented vehicles	235	270	326	361
Entertainment	205	206	232	306
Horse racing and gambling	107	253	193	153
Organised tours	240	336	421	524
Other transport fees	157	270	330	414
International airfares bought in Australia	102	129	153	184
Domestic airfares	80	78	95	140
Other[1]	405	598	639	648
Total expenditure on trips in Australia (a)	**6068**	**7 171**	**8413**	**10 731**
Total expenditure on trips to Australia by package tourists and other visitors (b)	13 872	14 769	16 592	n/a
(a) as a percentage of (b)	43.7	48.6	50.7	n/a

Note:
[1] *Includes purchase of motor vehicles and phone, fax or postage*   **Source:** *Data derived from BTR (2003)*

Taxation revenue

Subsumed under the umbrella of tourism receipts are levies such as the Australian departure tax, a fee paid by all departing inbound visitors. Governments regard taxes as an attractive form of revenue generation, and one that costs very little to collect. Taxes are often hidden as part of a package arrangement or within the overall cost of a good or service, so that the consumer is unaware of their existence. In addition, taxes can be increased substantially without bringing about a significant negative response from the tourist market. This is because taxes usually comprise only a very small portion of the overall trip expenditure. For example, a 100 per cent increase in a $10 departure tax will not add significant costs to a $3000 trip. Governments, on the other hand, stand to gain a substantial increase in revenue from the cumulative intake of such a doubled levy (e.g. 500 000 inbound tourists paying a departure tax of $20 each instead of $10 equates to added revenue of $5 million).

Wason (1998) has identified 40 different taxes applicable to the tourism industry. Common examples include airport departure taxes (like the Australian departure tax), bed (or hotel room) taxes, permits for entry to public attractions such as national parks, entry or transit visas, and gaming licences. Tourists also generate taxation revenue through the purchase of goods and services subject to sales tax (e.g. Australia's GST) and other levies. Bed and sales taxes are examples of *ad valorem* taxes (that is, they are set as a percentage of price), while departure taxes and visas are *specific* (that is, they are set at a given price). More unusual are taxes directed at the outbound tourist flow, which are usually implemented to reduce the loss of foreign exchange.

Influence of other government departments

One potentially frustrating aspect of taxation from the destination manager or tourism department's perspective is the control exercised by destination government departments, which may not always be sympathetic to the interests of the tourism sector. For example, the Department of Immigration and Multicultural and Indigenous Affairs (DIMIA) is the Australian federal body responsible for issuing and pricing visas and for establishing qualification requirements. A possible decision to ease or tighten these requirements, to greatly increase the visa costs or to take more time in processing applications could thus create a major deterrent to travel that the tourism stakeholders have little power to control. This was demonstrated in 1998 by the introduction of a $50 visa fee (increased to $65 by 2005) on all visitors except New Zealanders. Conversely, the introduction of the electronic travel authority (ETA) in 1996 illustrates how agencies such as DIMIA can facilitate tourism by expediting application procedures. The ETA can be obtained by potential visitors from qualifying countries (e.g. major markets such as the United States, Canada, Japan, Singapore, Hong Kong and South Korea) in just a few minutes from the DIMIA website for a fee of $20. It replaces the visa stamp normally affixed to the traveller's passport, and when the tourist arrives at the airport to board their flight to Australia, check-in staff can quickly confirm electronically whether they are ETA approved. In general, however, more concerns have been expressed within the tourism industry over the increasing tendency of governments to regard tourism as a revenue-generating 'cash cow', with little of the revenue typically re-invested within the tourism industry itself (Wason 1998).

Strategies to increase direct revenue

Tourism receipts (taxes aside), can be expanded by increasing:
• the number of visitors
• their average length of stay
• their average daily expenditure (figure 8.1).

Most basic is the visitor intake, and it is the fluctuation in this statistic that usually receives the greatest attention from managers. However, it is the average length of stay and the amount spent per day that actually determine the amount of revenue generated by these tourists. The impact of these factors among different market segments is demonstrated by the contrasting length of stay and spending patterns of Japanese and American inbound tourists to Australia. As depicted in table 6.4, per-day expenditures are similar, but a longer length of stay results in much larger total expenditures from American visitors. Accordingly, many destinations devise strategies that encourage longer vacations and high-spending markets. In some cases, a 'quality' over 'quantity' approach is deliberately implemented to reduce the social and environmental impacts of high visitation levels (chapter 9).

■ **Figure 8.1**
Factors influencing tourism revenue in a destination

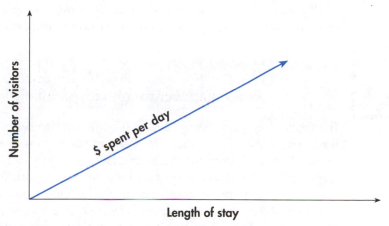

Contribution of tourism to GNP

Tourism receipts, while a crucial indicator of the sector's size, do not on their own allow for a comparison of tourism's relative importance from one destination to another or within the overall economy of a particular destination. To facilitate such comparisons, the value of international tourism receipts is calculated for a one-year period as a percentage of a country's gross national product (GNP; or sometimes gross domestic product, GDP) (see appendix 3). There is no definitive percentage threshold that differentiates the countries where tourism is a critical component of the economy. However, a 5 per cent figure can be taken to indicate a highly significant contribution in lieu of more sophisticated techniques, such as the Tourism Satellite Account (TSA), that more accurately measure tourism's economic contribution but have not yet been widely adopted.

Statistics on the contribution of tourism to GNP are available for 168 countries or dependencies (appendix 3). Of these, 70 (or 42 per cent) meet or exceed the 5 per cent criterion. However, about one-half of these destinations are pleasure periphery SISODs (section 4.2.2), some of which display a pattern of 'hyperdependency' on tourism. Extreme cases include the Maldives (46.4 per cent), Anguilla (74.4 per cent) and St Lucia (41.2 per cent). It is interesting to note that in many destination countries with large absolute tourism receipts, such as the United States and France, tourism's contribution to GNP is relatively small (0.6 per cent and 2.4 per cent, respectively). This apparent anomaly reflects the immense and highly diverse economies of these countries, wherein even a very large tourism industry still represents only a small portion of overall economic output. This also applies to Australia, which was the fourteenth-ranked country in terms of inbound tourism receipts in 2002, but derived only 2.1 per cent of its GNP from this source (or about 4 per cent of GDP). In contrast, New Zealand occupied the thirty-ninth rank in 2002 (indicating less *absolute* importance of tourism compared with other countries), but obtained 5.6 per cent of its GNP from tourism (indicating greater *relative* importance of tourism within the national economy). Such statistics are critical in determining the allocation of government resources to the tourism sector, and therefore any recalibrations that reduce the percentage contribution to GNP constitute a serious threat to destination managers (see Breakthrough tourism: Redefining tourism and its economic impact).

BREAKTHROUGH TOURISM
Redefining tourism and its economic impact

The Productivity Commission (2005), a body that reviews and advises on microeconomic policy and regulation for the Australian government, generated a firestorm of criticism from the Australian tourism industry in April 2005 when it suggested that the contribution of the latter to GDP is much smaller than the 4 per cent figure that is conventionally accepted. The commission's estimate of a 1.6 to 2.2 per cent contribution was obtained by restricting the definition of 'tourism' only to travel focused on leisure or vacation purposes or what it considers to be the 'true nature' of tourism activity as described in the dictionary (Productivity Commission 2005). From this perspective, the economic contributions of international students, business travellers and convention attendees are all excluded as 'visitor oriented' rather than 'tourism oriented'. Industry criticism, led by the Australian Tourism Export Council (ATEC 2005), stressed that the conventional estimate of 4 per cent was derived from adherence to the globally accepted World Tourism Organization definition of tourism, and to a consumption-based model that considers *what* goods and services individuals purchase rather than *which* individuals do the purchasing.

By significantly downgrading the economic contributions of the tourism industry to the Australian economy, ATEC and other industry bodies are concerned that the work of the commission could trigger a concomitant reduction in the amount of tourism funding provided by government, which was estimated to average $900 million to $1.1 billion per year from combined federal and state sources during the three years from 2000–01 to 2002–03 (Productivity Commission 2005). Among other reasons, the commission implies that reductions may be warranted given that a large portion of government funding is marketing and promotion related, and therefore influences the intake of discretionary leisure or vacation travellers but not 'nondiscretionary' education or business travellers. Whether or not its assumptions are warranted, the work of the commission illustrates how much the definitional assumptions of the tourism industry and other stakeholders are not necessarily held by outside groups, including those that influence the allocation of public resources. More ominous is the possibility that it could indicate a general trend towards perceiving tourism in restrictive recreation-oriented terms.

■ 8.2.2 **Indirect** *revenue*

The economic impact of tourist expenditures on a destination does not end once the tourists have given their money directly to the supplier of a commercial tourist product. Rather, **indirect revenues** continue to be generated by the ongoing circulation of these expenditures within the economy of the destination (Cooper et al. 2004). This **multiplier effect** has both an indirect and induced component that come into play once the **direct (or primary) impact**, that is the actual spending of money by the tourist, has taken place (see (a) of figure 8.2). The first-round **indirect impacts**, (b), occurs when the business (e.g. a hotel) uses a portion of these direct expenditures to purchase goods (e.g. food, pool-cleaning equipment) and pay wages to its employees. Second-round indirect impacts, (c), then occur when the suppliers of these goods and services use a portion of revenues received from the hotel to buy goods and services for their own use. This process continues into subsequent rounds, (d), although the revenues involved by this time are substantially diminished and often very difficult to trace.

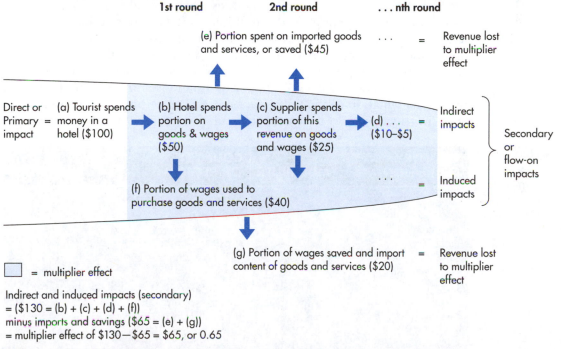

Indirect and induced impacts (secondary)
= ($130 = (b) + (c) + (d) + (f))
minus imports and savings ($65 = (e) + (g))
= multiplier effect of $130−$65 = $65, or 0.65

■ **Figure 8.2**   *The multiplier effect in tourism: a simplified example*

Through each round of indirect impact, revenues are lost to the destination multiplier effect due to the purchase of imported goods and services, and the allocation of money to savings, (e). If the initial hotel purchases in stage (a) are all allocated to imported goods and services, then essentially no multiplier effect takes place (i.e. there is no circulation of any portion of the revenue within the destination). Also in each indirect impact round, the multiplier effect is increased by **induced impacts** that take place when wages paid by the hotels and their suppliers are used by employees to purchase goods and services such as televisions, food, cars and haircuts, (f). However, as in (e), the multiplier effect of these wages is also eroded by savings, and by the import component of the goods and services that they purchase, (g). In simple terms (since its actual calculation is very complicated), the multiplier effect is obtained by adding together the sequential rounds of the indirect and induced impacts (i.e. **secondary (or flow-on) impacts**), and subtracting the revenue that is lost through allocations to imports and savings. The $100 initial expenditure shown in figure 8.2 thereby produces an additional multiplier effect of $65, or 0.65.

Historical multiplier effects from a variety of destinations are depicted in table 8.3. Using the United Kingdom as an example to illustrate the concept, the number 1.73 means that every $1 of direct expenditure has been estimated to generate an additional $1.73 in secondary impacts. In other words, if the 1.73 figure is still applicable, the total international United Kingdom receipts of US$17.6 billion (in 2002) generate more than US$36 billion in additional revenue, making an overall total of $48.1 billion if the primary and secondary effects are combined. In contrast, $1 spent in the Scottish city of Edinburgh generates only an additional $0.35. When added to direct expenditure the multiplier effect better reflects the gross economic benefits of tourism to a destination economy and the broader involvement of external environments such as the agriculture, construction and manufacturing sectors that supply goods and services to tourism. The association in table 8.3 between larger destinations and larger multipliers is not coincidental, since the former are more likely to have the economic size and diversity to sustain the internal circulation of direct tourism revenue.

■ **Table 8.3**
Multiplier effects for selected destinations

COUNTRY OR REGION	MULTIPLIER	COUNTRY OR REGION	MULTIPLIER
United Kingdom	1.73	Walworth County, USA	0.78
Republic of Ireland	1.72	Malta	0.68
Sri Lanka	1.59	Gibraltar	0.66
Jamaica	1.27	Western Samoa	0.66
Egypt	1.23	Cayman Islands	0.65
Dominican Republic	1.20	Iceland	0.64
Cyprus	1.14	Barbados	0.60
Northern Ireland	1.10	Grand County, USA	0.60
Bermuda	1.09	British Virgin Islands	0.58
Fiji	1.07	Door County, USA	0.55
Seychelles	1.03	Solomon Islands	0.52
Malta	1.00	Republic of Palau	0.51
Mauritius	0.97	Victoria Metropolitan Area, Canada	0.50
Antigua	0.88	Sullivan County, USA	0.44
Missouri State, USA	0.88	City of Carlisle, UK	0.40
Hong Kong	0.87	Edinburgh, Scotland, UK	0.35
Philippines	0.82	East Anglia, UK	0.34
The Bahamas	0.79		

Source: *Cooper, Fletcher, Gilbert & Wanhill (1993).*
Reprinted by permission of Pearson Education Limited

8.2.3   **Economic** *integration and diversification*

The multiplier effect is closely linked to the idea of **backward linkages**, which encompass the goods and services that 'feed into' the tourism industry through the indirect impacts described above. The link occurs when these goods and services are obtained from within the destination rather than through imports. The sectors that typically account for most of the backward linkages in tourism include agriculture and commercial fisheries, transportation, entertainment, construction and manufacturing. The full list of backward linkages in tourism is extensive and complex, attesting to tourism's great potential to stimulate local economic integration and diversification, provided that these goods and services can be supplied from within the destination. For example, the manufacturing component in tourism ranges from the furniture and appliances used in resort hotels, to pool-cleaning equipment, kitchen utensils and bathroom sinks. Returning to table 8.3, it is evident that destinations such as the United Kingdom and Sri Lanka are better positioned to supply this array of goods than Sullivan County or Edinburgh.

8.2.4   **Employment** *(direct and indirect)*

From the perspective of the destination community, the creation of jobs is an especially relevant reason for a destination to promote its tourism sector. Just how much employment tourism generates, however, is a subject of controversy. The World Travel and Tourism Council (the WTTC), as described in chapter 1, espouses a figure of 215 million jobs worldwide. Australia's Department of Industry, Tourism and Resources estimates that tourism accounts directly and indirectly for about one million jobs in Australia. Leiper (1999), however, regards the one million figure as being politically motivated, as well as greatly exaggerated because of the failure to distinguish between 'real jobs' within tourism itself and full-time job equivalents spread across the entire economy. To illustrate, Leiper uses the example of tourists using dental services. In any given year, many dentists in Australia obtain some business from tourists. If all of this business is combined, the resulting number of work hours is equivalent to several hundred full-time jobs. The WTTC statistics include such cumulative incidental contributions. However, there are very few individual dentists who actually depend on tourism to sustain their livelihood. Leiper (1999) estimated that the actual number of real tourism-dependent jobs in Australia was about 200 000 in the late 1990s, while another 500 000 were full-time job *equivalents* accounted for by dentists, university employees, workers in backward linkages and a myriad of others. This argument implies that exaggerated statistics (the one million jobs figure is still used by government and tourism industry advocates) are best avoided — first, because they raise questions about the credibility of the tourism industry and tourism statistics in general, second because they confuse attempts to identify the true economic impacts of tourism, and third because the employment effect of tourism is enormous even without the recourse to exaggeration.

■ 8.2.5 Regional *development*

Proponents of the advocacy platform, and other stakeholders, emphasise the effectiveness of tourism in initiating and promoting the development of regions where economic options are otherwise constrained. The classic example of tourism as a vehicle for regional economic development is 3S (sea, sand, sun) tourism, wherein 'unspoiled' natural sites and regions possessing little value for most conventional economic activities have been redefined as valuable resources for the tourism industry. Environmental consequences aside, the rapid physical development of the European Riviera, the small islands of the Caribbean, Australia's Gold and Sunshine coasts and other parts of the pleasure periphery is fundamentally an outcome of the sustained global demand for 3S tourism. A similar effect, though within a different kind of physical environment, is evident in the ecotourism sector, which places a high value on rainforests, national parks and other relatively natural settings as tourism venues (see chapter 11).

Other types of tourism product suited to marginal settings include the vacation farm sector (Weaver & Fennell 1997) and specialised components of agriculture such as wineries (see chapter 5). Skiing and other winter sports have a substantial economic impact on Australia's small alpine region. Casinos, as noted in chapter 5, contribute substantially to the economic development of economically underdeveloped locations such as Native American reservations in the United States. The Mashantucket Pequot tribal land in the American state of Connecticut, for example, now hosts the world's largest single casino, and its presence is responsible for converting the tribe from one of the poorest communities in the United States to one of the richest (Carmichael, Peppard & Boudreau 1996). In the Australian and New Zealand context, nature-based and cultural tourism are providing a stimulus for the economic development of historically marginalised indigenous communities and other peripheral areas (see Managing: Tourism as a vehicle for economic development in regional Australia).

MANAGING
Tourism as a vehicle for economic development in regional Australia

Among the more developed countries, Australia has earned a reputation for actively promoting regional social and economic development through government-sponsored tourism programs. The recent See Australia marketing campaign, for example, was especially relevant to regional Australia because of its emphasis on promoting domestic tourism, which accounts for 80 per cent of all visits to the country's nonmetropolitan destinations. Moreover, niche products such as food and wine tourism, ecotourism, caravanning, backpacking and cultural and heritage tourism are all targeted for development and promotion by the federal government in large part because of their viability in rural and small-town Australia. Other related federal initiatives include the Business Ready

Program for Indigenous Tourism, which promotes business management skills and capacities within Aboriginal communities, and the establishment of a Regional Advisory Service within Tourism Research Australia to focus on the acquisition of knowledge that will increase tourism in nonmetropolitan Australia (DITR 2005a).

An important initiative is the Australian Tourism Development Program (ATDP), which has sought to promote the development of tourism in nonmetropolitan regions by providing funds to boost the capacity of operators to provide attractive tourism products to domestic and international visitors. The program was intended to provide $24 million in competitive grants to incorporated organisations between 2004 and 2007. In the first round, $6 million was allocated to 39 applicants from a pool of 1469, with a requirement that the designated work be completed within two years of funding beginning. Category I grants are valued at $100 000 or less and are focused on specific products, while Category II grants, valued in excess of this amount, are designed to fund large-scale, collaborative projects that focus on regional development and marketing strategies. Among the successful first-round Category I projects in 2004 were the Lismore Café and Culture Trail, which links a series of cultural, gastronomical and historical attractions along the Wilson River in northern New South Wales ($100 000); an International Indigenous Festival of Arts and Culture at the site of the Woodford Folk Festival in southern Queensland ($100 000); the fencing and rehabilitation of 16 square kilometres of native habitat at Banrock, South Australia, to attract ecotourists ($100 000); and the construction of a day spa facility in Marysville, Victoria ($100 000). Successful Category II projects included a corridor implementation plan for the Overlanders Way highway in the Northern Territory and Queensland ($295 000); a proposal to develop the town of Broome as the tourist gateway to northwestern Australia ($250 000); and the Cradle Coast Experience Strategy, which seeks to expand the quality and array of themed tourist experiences in a remote part of Tasmania ($200 000) (AusIndustry 2005).

Growth pole strategy

In most cases the development of tourism in a peripheral area occurs as a spontaneous, mostly unplanned process. However, there are countries where tourism is deliberately mobilised as a **propulsive activity** in a so-called **growth pole strategy**. Examples are found in the Dominican Republic (Freitag 1994), Mexico (e.g. Cancún) and Indonesia (e.g. Bintan). In essence, this involves the establishment of resorts at a strategically selected location (i.e. the growth pole) as a way of stimulating economic development in the region. A growth pole strategy in tourism entails a sequence of stages along the following lines:

1. An appropriate site (growth pole) is identified by government, usually in an economically marginal area that is deemed suitable for sustaining some predetermined form of tourism development such as 3S resorts.

2. Through government initiative and incentives, public and private investment is injected into this area, commonly in the form of subsidised facilities and infrastructure.
3. This investment attracts employees, supportive services and other tourism facilities, often induced by continuing government incentives.
4. Economic growth eventually becomes self-sustaining and independent of tourism in a direct sense when a critical mass of residential population is attained (i.e. new investment and settlement is attracted by the large local market rather than by tourism opportunities *per se*). At this point incentives are normally withdrawn. At the same time, the developmental benefits of tourism 'trickle down' from the growth pole into the surrounding region.

The use of tourism in growth pole strategies is an attractive option for destination countries where certain economically marginal regions are perceived as having some form of tourism potential.

■ *8.2.6* **Formal** *and informal sectors*

Managers and governments within most destinations usually assume that economic benefits are most efficiently achieved through a strong **formal sector** — that is, the component of the economy that is subject to official systems of regulation and remuneration. Because the formal sector includes the largest and most technologically sophisticated businesses, it is seen as the primary generator of wealth and indicator of economic development. Government bias in its favour also owes in no small part to the formal sector generating substantial tax revenue and being subject to a significant degree of government control.

In contrast, the **informal sector** is unregulated and external to the formal institutions of that society. Participating businesses generally operate beyond the legal system, are not subject to formal quality control measures, are not registered or enumerated, do not provide regular working hours for their employees and do not officially pay any regular wages or taxes (Dahles 2001). Because the informal sector cannot be measured or regulated easily, and because it does not generate tax revenue for government, public officials often try to suppress, or at best ignore, this element. A large informal sector, in addition, is psychologically perceived as an indicator of economic underdevelopment, and its incorporation into or replacement by the formal sector is therefore generally seen as a prerequisite for attaining Phase Four status.

Within the tourism industry, the informal sector is often criticised by the formal sector and government for its 'harassing' and 'unprofessional' attitude towards tourists, who are thought to be offended by the often aggressive behaviour of souvenir hawkers and other itinerant businesspeople. This relates directly to the concept of inseparability, and the consequent importance of service quality control, as discussed in chapter 7. However, the formal sector also opposes the informal sector because it captures a significant portion of tourist expenditures and may be perceived by many tourists as a more authentic form of host/guest encounter. This is a valid argument in many LDCs, where a substantial and highly visible informal sector paralleling the mainstream tourism system is evident in tourism subsectors such as guest houses, services and crafts-related activities, souvenir vending, prostitution, guiding, pedicab driving, markets, beach hawking and food stalls (see figure 8.3).

■ **Figure 8.3**
Beach hawkers in Bali: authentic or intimidating experience?

Government authorities often harass and discourage such operations, and only in a few isolated instances, such as the Indonesian city of Yogyakarta (Timothy & Wall 1997; Dahles 2001), are they attempting to work out a mutually beneficial strategy of peaceful coexistence or cooperation. In the case of Yogyakarta, the positive attitude was prompted by the realisation that street vendors were a major tourist attraction in their own right, as well as a major employer that formed backward linkages with local industry and had great resilience in adapting to changing business conditions. The informal tourism sector also exists within many MDCs, but is less visible and less of a 'problem' because of the dominance of formal sector businesses.

8.3 ℰCONOMIC COSTS

As the size and scope of the global tourism industry continued to increase through the late 1960s and 1970s, evidence accumulated that the economic impacts of the sector were not all positive. It was in response to this evidence that the cautionary platform emerged within the field of tourism studies to argue that the economic, social, cultural and environmental costs of unregulated tourism tend to outweigh its benefits. Destination managers, they argued, should therefore be extremely cautious about pursuing tourism in an uncritical way (see chapter 1). This section considers the major economic costs that are potentially incurred by tourist destinations, and is thus essentially a summary of the cautionary platform's economic critique.

▪ 8.3.1 Direct *financial costs*

Proper assessments of revenue intake from tourism should first of all take into account the **direct financial costs** that are necessarily incurred by the public sector to generate and sustain this intake. To point out these costs is not to be critical, but merely to indicate that tourism, as with any other economic activity, requires financial inputs to realise financial benefits. The situation in Australia illustrates the nature and magnitude of these costs. For the four years from 2004 to 2007, the federal Department of Industry, Tourism and Resources (DITR) committed almost $240 million to tourism promotion and development, with most of the funds allocated towards international and domestic marketing (see table 8.4). Tourism Australia alone had a gross budget of about $140 million in 2001–02, about $100 million of which came from the federal government and the remainder from direct contributions from industry (Tourism Australia 2005c).

▪ **Table 8.4**
DITR funding allocations to tourism 2004–07

FUNDING AREA	AMOUNT ($ MILLIONS)
International marketing	120.6
Domestic regional marketing and development	45.5
Australian Tourism Development Program (ATDP)	24.0
Enhanced research and statistics capacity	21.5
Niche segment development	14.7
Tourism and conservation programs	4.6
Business Ready Program for Indigenous Tourism	3.8
National Voluntary Tourism Accreditation System	2.3
Administration, implementation and coordination of Tourism White Paper	1.5
World Tourism Organization membership	1.4
Total	239.9

Source: *Data derived from DITR (2005b)*

To these amounts should be added a similar spectrum of cost allocations incurred at the state and territory level. For example, Tourism Queensland, which is similar to Tourism Australia in its mandate and responsibilities, reported operating expenses for the year ending 30 June 2004 of more than $108 million, of which $36 million was for marketing and promotion, $35 million for operation costs, and $31 million for employee costs (Tourism Queensland 2005).

Direct incentives, usually disbursed by nontourism agencies within government, constitute a distinct set of costs in the development of the tourism sector (Wanhill 2005). Potential entrepreneurs are usually willing to commit their own resources into a project in anticipation of strong profits. However, in more uncertain situations, destination governments may have to entice these entrepreneurs with capital grants, labour and training subsidies or the provision of infrastructure at public expense (as demonstrated in growth pole strategies). Incentives are more likely to be available when several destinations offer a similar product, such as a generic 3S experience, and therefore must compete with each other for investment. In such a situation, the entrepreneur will usually locate within the destination that offers the most lucrative incentive package, all other things being equal. This was demonstrated in early 1999 when the producers of the popular television series *Baywatch* entered negotiations with both Hawaii and the Gold Coast of Australia to obtain the best package of incentives in its attempt to select a long-term filming site (Hawaii was selected). Where a destination, in contrast, is in a monopolistic situation of offering iconic attractions (as with Niagara Falls, Uluru, the Sydney Opera House or the Eiffel Tower), the level of anticipated long-term demand is more likely to attract entrepreneurs even without the offer of incentives.

■ 8.3.2 **Indirect** *financial costs*

A major thrust of the cautionary platform was its emphasis on the substantial **indirect financial costs** that are incurred by tourism in a destination. The best-known are the costs subsumed under the category of **revenue leakages**. Some or all of the following leakages may curtail the circulation of tourist receipts in the destination economy as depicted in segment (e) of figure 8.2, and thereby erode the multiplier effect:

* imported current goods and services that are required by tourists or the tourist industry (e.g. petrol, food)
* imported capital goods and services required by the tourist industry (e.g. furnishings, taxis, architect's fees)
* factor payments abroad, including repatriated profits, wages and hotel management fees
* imports for government expenditure (airport, road and port equipment)
* induced imports for domestic producers who supply the tourist industry (e.g. fertiliser to grow the food consumed by tourists) (English 1986).

Serious revenue leakages, as suggested in section 8.2.3, are more likely to occur in small economies, given their lack of capacity to supply the goods and services required by the local tourism industry. In addition, the residents of these destinations do not normally possess sufficient investment capital to sustain desired levels of tourism development. Severe revenue leakages are associated with *enclave resort* situations, or self-contained facilities where patrons are discouraged from spending their money outside of the operation's confines, and where most of the goods are imported from beyond the local community (Freitag 1994). More broadly, the term *enclave tourism* has been used to describe formal sector tourism industries in regions such as the Okavango Delta of Botswana that are controlled by foreign interests, include enclave resorts, and have only weak linkages with the local space-economy (Mbaiwa 2005). They may also be induced more indirectly by the *demonstration effect* of tourism, where for status or role-model reasons, locals seek to emulate the behaviour of tourists by consuming the imported goods favoured by the tourists (Shaw & Williams 1994).

Problems with revenue leakage

Revenue leakages are regarded as insidious for several reasons, particularly when the leakages accrue to a different country rather than another region within the same country:

1. They siphon away circulation effects (i.e. the multiplier effect) that could benefit the economy of the destination rather than the exporting country or region.
2. The cumulative indirect component is less tangible and harder to measure than direct expenses, and therefore more difficult to quantify as a first step towards addressing the problem.
3. Even if they can be measured, their existence usually reflects basic short-comings in the economic structure of the destination that are extremely difficult to resolve.
4. Imports not only dissuade local entrepreneurs from supplying similar goods, but they may displace existing local (i.e. small-scale) producers who cannot match the quality, price or quantity provided by the exporter (see Contemporary issue: Weak linkages between tourism and local agriculture).
5. The presence of leakages implies, to a greater or lesser extent, an economic dependency of the destination on the exporter, which constrains the ability of destination stakeholders to manage their own affairs. This is especially problematic when businesses are dominated by expatriate managers.

For all these reasons, integrated and long-term tourism management strategies should try to foster linkages between tourism and the destination economy, so as to reduce the potential for revenue leakage and maximise the multiplier effect.

Indirect incentives

Augmenting the direct incentives outlined in section 8.3.1 are various indirect incentives. These include preferential or reduced interest rates, the provision of land for sale or lease on favourable terms, depreciation allowances, tariff and quota exemptions on tourism-related imports, and tax holidays. An example of the latter are the ten-year tax-free periods commonly offered to developers who construct hotels of a certain size in the Caribbean. Other indirect incentives include loan guarantees and special depreciation allowances on tourism-related capital goods. Such provisions are often more popular in governments than direct incentives because they do not involve the direct outlay of money. Rather, governments obtain less revenue than they would if the incentives were not offered (e.g. the interest realised at full market rates rather than reduced interest rates).

A major rationale for encouraging tourism development in peripheral regions is the stimulation of local agriculture, since food typically accounts for one-third of expenditure in the average tourist trip (Torres 2003). However, research in the late 1990s by Torres (2003) revealed that hotels in Cancún, the best-known resort in the Mexican state of Quintana Roo, received just 1 per cent of their meat, 3.4 per cent of their vegetables, 4.5 per cent of their fruit, 9 per cent of their poultry and none of their dairy products from within the state. This research revealed several factors that collectively have inhibited the establishment of local food linkages, including the proximity of Yucatan state with its established agro-industries that supply Cancún hotels with one-fifth of their fruit and meat, almost one-quarter of their vegetables, and 64 per cent of their poultry. A small group of specialised wholesalers from Yucatan and elsewhere in Mexico dominate the hotel supply chain, in part because of kickbacks they provide to chefs and food managers.

Impoverished local farmers cannot break into these entrenched supply chains, in part because of the prejudices held against the mostly indigenous subsistence peasants by the mainly mixed-race food purchasers. This in turn contributes to a deep and pervasive atmosphere of mutual mistrust between local farmers (especially the directors of the communal *ejidos*) on the one hand, and hoteliers and wholesalers on the other. The prejudice and mistrust are fuelled by real inefficiencies in the local farming sector that dissuade linkages with hotels by giving rise to unreliable supplies and low quantities of goods of often inferior quality. Yet these goods are often more expensive than nonlocal food because of the high agricultural labour costs that arise because of labour competition with the tourism industry. Macroeconomic policies of the Mexican government do not help the *ejidos* because they have led to the elimination of most farm subsidies, and the provision of collateral-based loans at market rates only to larger commercial operations. Another problem is the lack of unity among the *ejidos*, so that all crops tend to ripen at once, leading to low prices and intense competition among local farmers.

The weak supply chain between local farmers and hoteliers currently entails the occasional truck sent out by the larger hotels to purchase unusual local produce, or basic fresh fruit and vegetables in the off-season. Local *ejidos* also occasionally send unsolicited truckloads of goods to the hotels in hopes of making a sale. In both cases, however, exchanges are hampered by the inability of local farmers to supply an official revenue receipt required for hotel tax accounting. Ultimately, whether the linkage issue is judged as successful depends in part on the definition of 'destination': what is deemed unsuccessful in the context of 'Quintana Roo' is regarded as a great success for 'Mexico' because almost all the food supplied to the hotels of Cancún is sourced domestically. If the latter perception is held, there is little incentive to reform the system so that local producers receive a greater share of the pie.

■ 8.3.3 Fluctuations *in intake*

A stable and predictable flow of inputs and outputs in many industries contributes to financial stability and facilitates the management process, as enormous investments in time and energy are not required to gauge and prepare for continual changes in the supply/demand equation (see section 7.4). The dairy industry is an example of a sector with low demand uncertainty. Demand in this sector is not significantly influenced by weather or other changeable factors, nor is the market likely to suddenly stop purchasing dairy products. In addition, since consumers consider dairy products to be a basic necessity, consumption patterns will not be seriously affected by a downturn in the economy.

Tourism is an example of an activity that is frequently at the opposite end of the spectrum to the dairy industry, being highly vulnerable in some manifestations to changes in weather, fashion and sociopolitical conditions (see section 7.4). It is worth re-emphasising that the in situ nature of consumption inherent in tourism is one reason for this uncertainty in demand. Tourists must travel to the place of 'production' (i.e. the destination), whereas dairy products travel from the place of production to the homes of consumers. Supply-side disruptions within the destination, such as political uncertainty or a disruption of infrastructure, thus have a major and sometimes overwhelming bearing on visitor intakes (see section 4.3 and also the case study at the end of chapter 1). Factors that are not specific to particular destinations can also be influential, as indicated by the 12–14 per cent decrease in global travel reservations that followed the terrorism actions of September 2001, and the 26 per cent decrease in the number of inbound tourists to Thailand in January 2005 (i.e. the month following the tsunami) over the same month in 2004 (ILO 2005).

Second and also by way of reiteration, demand-side factors such as the availability of discretionary income have a particularly harsh effect on tourism, given its status as an essentially luxury or discretionary product. Most consumers will direct their first cutbacks towards their tourism activities rather than dairy products should disruptions in the economy reduce their discretionary income or generate feelings of financial insecurity (see section 3.5.1). As noted in chapter 7, tourism suffers an additional liability in that the products cannot be stockpiled — an empty hotel room produces no economic value, but is a fixed cost that still requires maintenance, mortgage repayment, etc.

These cautionary comments about the instability of tourism demand and supply do not contradict earlier information in this textbook that claims a positive global outlook for the tourism sector. Rather, problems can arise for managers when the patterns and underlying factors that apply at the global level are assumed to be valid for individual destinations as well. In other words, the steady growth experienced worldwide represents a pattern of cumulative behaviour that does not necessarily indicate the performance of specific destinations. For any individual destination country, a similar analysis of arrival trends since 1950 would likely reveal a great deal of fluctuation. In the wake of the 2001 terrorist attacks, for example, many Muslim-dominated countries experienced a prolonged period of reduced inbound visitation.

Seasonality

The tendency to report destination arrival data for an entire year (as in table 3.1) is misleading, since such statistics usually disguise significant variations in intake that affect the supply/demand equilibrium These temporal variations are caused partially by demand-side factors such as holiday time availability in the origin markets (e.g. summer holidays, winter break). However, as, or more, influential are supply-side factors such as changing opportunities in attractions and activities and how much the destination is dependent on these changeable products. Resorts that are dependent on winter sports or 3S-based activities readily come to mind as tourism products that are subject to significant seasonal variations in demand.

Australia is not plagued by seasonality to the same extent as pleasure periphery destinations such as Spain (Pearce 1989) or the Caribbean, partly because of the diversity of major market sources and variations in their peak periods of outbound travel (Lim & McAleer 2001). Substantial variations in climatic conditions within Australia at any given time mean additionally that there is no particular season in which the country can be uniformly characterised as 'hot' or 'cold'. Yet, as depicted in figure 8.4, a seasonality effect is still evident within the inbound tourist intake, with May and December respectively accounting for 5.5 and 13.8 per cent of the latter in 2003. A further complication is the deviation of specific market segments from this pattern. Holiday travellers, for example, more or less paralleled the overall trend, while business travel peaked in the period from July to November and then dropped sharply in December and January.

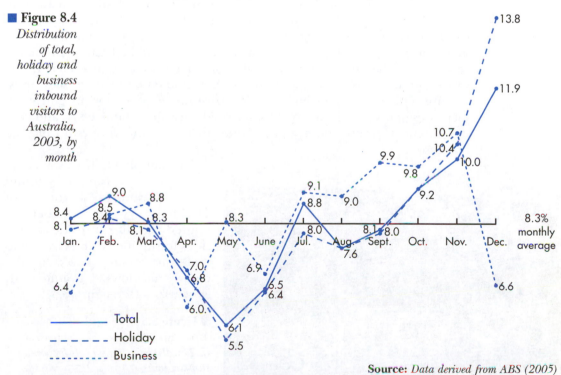

■ **Figure 8.4**
Distribution of total, holiday and business inbound visitors to Australia, 2003, by month

Source: *Data derived from ABS (2005)*

Where strong seasonal variations are part of the normal annual tourism cycle of a destination, a large amount of economic and social disruption can occur if appropriate compensating measures are not taken by tourism managers. The problem can be described as one of undercapacity and overcapacity, or to use an analogy from the farming sector, a 'drought-deluge' cycle. In the context of the supply/demand matching strategies outlined in section 7.4, the off-season is a period when supply exceeds demand, while the high season is characterised by an excess of demand over supply. During the off-season, low occupancy rates result in reduced business, which subsequently reverberates in a negative way throughout the economy and labour force in a sort of reverse multiplier effect. In contrast, the high season is often characterised by overbookings, stress on infrastructure, overcrowding, and shortages of goods and services (which may in turn give rise to inflation).

Strategies that individual companies can adopt to address seasonal and other demand fluctuations have been outlined in chapter 7. Destination managers, however, are more constrained in their options, because they can only influence the strategies and tactics of the businesses that dominate the tourism sector, and themselves only control a portion of the sector. Among the options for destination managers and governments are the stimulation of alternative economic activities such as hi-tech industries and manufacturing, so that the off-season effect in tourism is offset by the continuing output from these other sectors (see Technology and tourism: Diversifying the Gold Coast with hi-tech). Within tourism itself, local governments can withdraw or restrict certain variable cost services, such as beach patrolling and garbage collection. They can also promote their destination to non-traditional markets that have unconventional patterns of seasonal travel. Gold Coast tourism managers, for example, have become more active in marketing to the United Arab Emirates and other Middle Eastern countries, recognising that their residents are more likely to visit Australia in the winter off-season when temperatures in their home region are at their most intense. Other strategies include the provision of off-season incentives to local residents (such as NTO-sponsored discount booklets), and the development of attractions and activities that will draw visitors during the off-season.

An example of off-season adaptation of infrastructure is found at the Australian ski resort of Thredbo, where otherwise unused ski lifts provide scenic rides to summer visitors as well as access to walking tracks in the high meadows around Mt Kosciuszko (see figure 8.5).

■ **Figure 8.5**

Minimising the seasonality of tourism in Thredbo by using ski lifts for scenic summer tours

TECHNOLOGY AND TOURISM
Diversifying the Gold Coast with hi-tech

The managers of pleasure periphery tourism cities such as Las Vegas, Orlando and Nice increasingly recognise the role that hi-tech and innovation industries can play in diversifying the economies of tourism-dependent cities. This is because the factors that encourage the growth of tourism, such as an amenity-rich lifestyle, progrowth planning regimes and encouragement of entrepreneurialism are factors that also cause hi-tech businesses to flourish. Within Australia, the Gold Coast is positioning itself as a centre of technical innovation across a broad range of activities, encouraging the establishment of such businesses since 1995 through the Gold Coast City Council's Economic Development and Major Projects Directorate. Among the local innovation leaders featured in a series of publications available from the Gold Coast City Council (GCCC 2004, 2005) are Eracom, an electronic security technology firm; Bond Wireless, a leader in mobile phone messaging; Eduss, pioneer in developing education software that facilitates flexible learning; Digga, a manufacturer of excavation devices such as rock augers and hydraulic posthole borers; Chocolate Graphics, which embosses intricate designs into chocolate candies; the Institute for Glycomics, which investigates the pharmaceutical potential of carbohydrates; Photon, a producer of sophisticated visual effects used in movies; and Bustech, a builder of environmentally friendly mass transit vehicles.

Especially intriguing are cutting-edge companies more directly focused on the tourism industry. The Sunland Group is the developer of the 80-storey Q1 apartment building in Surfers Paradise, which incorporates innovative technology in its super-fast lifts, 17-storey underground foundation and cyclone-resistant anti-sway design, all of which are equally applicable to the new generation of high-rise hotels. Riviera and Mustang Cruisers, builders of luxury marine cruisers, are two rapidly growing companies located in the Gold Coast's Marine Precinct, where 2500 workers were employed in 2005. The Sanderson Group is a leader among a group of emerging theme park display and setting creators, while AustMarine is a pioneer in the development of holding tanks for marine life destined for hotels and restaurants. Finally, the Gold Coast is a centre of artificial reef technology involving the strategic placement of sand-filled geotextile bags to minimise the erosional effects of storms. All these initiatives increase the quality of the Gold Coast tourism product but also generate local year-round economic benefits through their export to other pleasure periphery destinations, which may, ironically, provide more competition to the Gold Coast as a result.

Fashion

Much less predictable than the seasonal variations are the effects of fashion. As discussed in section 4.3, this is demonstrated by the shifting perceptions in 'Western' societies towards sunbathing, beaches and water sports, which became popular during the Industrial Revolution but may eventually fall out of general favour due to concerns about skin cancer. This would force 3S destinations to develop and promote alternative tourism products.

Another perspective on fashion is the rise and fall of specific destinations. Places often become fashionable due to novelty and curiosity, but are soon superseded by newer destinations offering a similar (i.e. easily substitutable) product. Thus, St Lucia may have the status of being the 'in' Caribbean destination one particular year, only to be replaced in turn by Anguilla, St Martin and Grenada. This effect is experienced in many other industries, but one dilemma for tourism is the tendency in destinations to acquire an accommodation inventory commensurate with the level of the highest demand. When visitor arrivals decline because of the fashion factor (as opposed to the cyclic seasonal effect), the specialised nature of hotels means that they are difficult to convert permanently to other uses when high fixed costs become too much of a burden. The fashion effect is closely associated with the resort cycle concept, which is discussed in chapter 10.

Vulnerability to instability

More uncertain and potentially harmful to destinations than the vagaries of fashion are the effects of social and political instability (both in situ and external), which can lead to drastic declines in visitor intakes (see section 4.3.7). Especially insidious is the potential for just one random and completely unpredictable act of terrorism or sabotage to cripple a destination's tourism industry, as demonstrated by the terrorist attacks on the United States in September 2001 and the Bali bombings of 2002 (see the case study at the end of chapter 4). Even though little can be done to prevent such occurrences, tourism managers need to be aware of this vulnerability, and of the possibility that very positive growth performance can be reversed in an instant. Accordingly, a strategy of broader economic diversification would help to cushion such impacts, as it would with seasonal variations.

■ 8.3.4 Competition *with other sectors*

The attraction of the multiplier effect is the stimulation of a diverse local economy through the generation of significant backward linkages within the destination. In some cases, however, a competitive rather than a complementary relationship evolves between tourism and other sectors in the local economy. It was noted in section 8.3.2 and the Contemporary issue feature, for example, that tourism-induced food imports may displace or dissuade local production if the scale economies of the exporter and the bilateral trade environment are such that a cheaper and better quality product can be offered to the hotels.

Further marginalisation of agriculture occurs because of tourism's status as a more competitive bidder for land. A golf course or resort hotel, for instance, represents a far more lucrative use of prime agricultural land than a sugar cane operation. Where farming is already a marginal activity, as the sugar industry was on the Caribbean island of Antigua in the 1960s, tourism serves to accelerate its decline by offering strategically located land owners a viable alternative land use (Weaver 1988). Finally, the **opportunity cost** of using a resource for tourism over some other activity should be taken into consideration. Money or land allocated to tourism, in effect, is money or land denied to agriculture, which thus represents a forgone opportunity for the destination. This effect has been noted in the wine-producing regions of South Australia, where investment in tourism is seen to divert attention and investment from wine production (Beverland 1999).

■ 8.3.5 Employment *problems*

It cannot be denied that tourism is an efficient generator of direct and indirect employment, but the nature of this employment may not always be conducive to the economic development of the destination. Wages in the tourism sector tend to be low compared with other sectors (although agriculture in many cases is an exception). Bull (1995) contends that the average wage in travel, hospitality and retail (there is no specific category for tourism) in North America, western Europe and Australasia is 5–35 per cent below national average wages. Bull attributes this situation to the following factors:

- the unskilled nature of most tourism jobs, with relatively few opportunities for upward mobility and few training opportunities
- the tendency of employers to treat jobs requiring higher levels of skill (as in customer service) as unskilled
- high labour turnover (i.e. unstable labour force)
- the weakness of unionisation and collective bargaining
- the tendency of many employers to flout minimum wage regulations
- where there are few or no alternatives to tourism, depression of local wages because of the lack of competition.

Because of the seasonal and cyclical nature of tourism, the sector is also characterised by a high incidence of seasonal, part-time and casual employment, thereby further contributing to the discrepancy between the number of people employed and the actual hours and wages achieved. Tourism in Australia and elsewhere has additionally been criticised, like certain other sectors, for fostering a ghetto-like environment that provides women with lower pay, poorer working conditions, less career mobility, less access to training programs and less effective trade union support. Gender/occupation statistics from the 2001 Census corroborate these criticisms in revealing that females accounted for a higher proportion of workers in lower status occupations related to tourism (see table 8.5). It is, therefore, not surprising that male and female workers in the 'accommodation, cafés and restaurants' category earned an average weekly wage of $479.80 and $376.90, respectively (ABS 2003).

Ironically, the advocacy platform has interpreted many of these alleged shortcomings as advantages, in that low wages mean that more workers can be hired, and unskilled workers can find employment opportunities more readily. Furthermore, part-time and seasonal jobs may be more desirable among certain segments in the workforce, such as single mothers.

■ **Table 8.5**
*Selected
tourism-
related
occupations
in Australia
by sex,
2001 Census*

OCCUPATION CATEGORY	TOTAL WORKERS	MALES	FEMALES	MALE (%)	FEMALE (%)
Air transport professionals	10 960	10 324	636	94.2	5.8
Hospitality and accommodation managers, not further defined	1 575	1 007	568	63.9	36.1
Hotel and motel managers	20 534	12 293	8 241	59.9	40.1
Caravan park and camping ground managers	3 705	2 009	1 696	54.2	45.8
Restaurant and catering managers	39 076	17 079	21 997	43.7	56.3
Hotel service supervisors	4 095	1 701	2 394	41.5	58.3
Hospitality workers, not further defined	4 289	1 659	2 630	38.7	61.3
Hospitality trainees	830	300	530	36.1	63.9
Travel attendants	8 242	2 561	5 681	31.1	68.9
Travel and tourism agents	25 172	7 217	17 955	28.7	71.3
Waiters	79 826	18 377	61 449	23.0	77.0

Source: *ABS (2003)*

CHAPTER REVIEW ....

This chapter has considered the potential economic costs and benefits of tourism for a destination. The main argument for tourism, as expounded by supporters of the advocacy platform, is the generation of earnings through direct tourist expenditures and related taxation. Another important economic benefit is the generation of indirect local revenue through the multiplier effect, and the concurrent diversification and integration of the local economy through the stimulation of backward linkages with agriculture and other sectors within the destination. Tourism is also an effective stimulant for direct and indirect employment opportunities and a vehicle for regional development. This can occur as a result of spontaneous processes (such as the development of most vacation farms or nature-based operations), or as the consequence of a deliberate growth pole strategy, as with the Mexican resort of Cancún. When considering the economic benefits of tourism, it is generally assumed that a strong formal sector is the best engine for achieving these benefits, rather than the unregulated informal sector.

The cautionary platform, in contrast to the advocacy platform, holds that the positive economic impacts of tourism may be much lower than alleged. First, the direct financial costs involved in maintaining an effective administrative bureaucracy, marketing activities and providing incentives are substantial. Second, revenue leakages, which result from a high import content, profit repatriation and other processes, can drastically reduce the multiplier effect. Tourism, moreover, engenders economic uncertainty because of its vulnerability to fluctuations in intake arising from seasonal variations, the effects of fashion and social or political unrest, in both the destination and source regions. Tourism also has the capacity to foster a competitive rather than a complementary relationship with agriculture and other local sectors, and a tendency to create part-time, low-wage and low-skill employment dominated by females. How much a destination derives net economic benefits or costs from tourism depends on the circumstances that pertain to each particular place. In general, destinations with large and diverse economies are most likely to benefit from tourism, since these can generate the backward linkages that give rise to a strong multiplier effect. In contrast, small destination economies, such as those found in the SISODs, are most likely to incur the economic costs described in this chapter. Essentially, the destinations that are therefore most desperate to obtain economic benefits from tourism are those that are most likely to experience the negative economic impacts of tourism.

SUMMARY OF KEY TERMS ....

Direct revenue

Money that is obtained directly from tourists through advance or immediate expenditures in the destination and associated taxes

- **International tourism receipts:** all consumption expenditure, or payments for goods and services, made by international tourists (stayovers and excursionists) to use themselves or to give away

Indirect revenues

Revenue obtained through the circulation of direct tourist expenditures within a destination

Multiplier effect

A measure of the subsequent income generated in a destination's economy by direct tourist expenditure

- **Direct (or primary) impact:** expenditure or direct revenue obtained from tourists
- **Indirect impacts:** revenues that are used by tourism businesses and their suppliers to purchase goods and services
- **Induced impacts:** revenue circulation that results from the use of wages in tourism businesses and their suppliers to purchase goods and services
- **Secondary (or 'flow-on') impacts:** the indirect and induced stages of money circulation in the multiplier effect that follows the actual tourist expenditure

Backward linkages

Sectors of an economy that provide goods and services for the tourism sector; includes agriculture, fisheries and construction

Growth pole strategy

A strategy that uses tourism to stimulate economic development in a suitably located area (or growth pole), so that this growth will eventually become self-sustaining

- **Propulsive activity:** an economic activity that is suited to a particular area and thus facilitates the growth pole strategy; in the case of Cancún and other subtropical or tropical coastal regions 3S tourism is an effective propulsive activity

Formal sector

The portion of a society's economy that is subject to official systems of regulation and remuneration; formal sector businesses provide regular wage or salaried employment, and are subject to taxation by various levels of government; the formal sector dominates Phase Four societies

Informal sector

The portion of a society's economy that is external to the official systems of regulation and remuneration; dominant in many parts of the less developed world, informal sector businesses are characterised by small size, the absence of regular working hours or wage payments, family ownership and a lack of any regulating quality control

Direct financial costs

Direct expenses that are necessarily incurred to sustain the tourism sector; within the public sector, typical areas of outlay include administration and bureaucracy, marketing, research and direct incentives

Indirect financial costs

Costs that do not entail a direct outlay of funds, but indicate lost revenue

- **Revenue leakages:** a major category of indirect financial costs, entailing erosion in the multiplier effect due to the importation of goods and services that are required by tourists or the tourist industry, through factor payments abroad such as repatriated profits, and through imports required for government expenditure on tourism-related infrastructure such as airports, road and port equipment

  Enclave resort: a self-contained resort complex; enclave resorts are associated with high revenue leakages because of their propensity to encourage internal spending on imported goods

  Enclave tourism: a mode of tourism characterised by external domination and weak linkages with the local economy

  Demonstration effect: the tendency of a population, or some portion thereof, to imitate the consumption patterns and other behaviour of another group; this can result in increased importation of goods and services to meet these changing consumer demands

Opportunity cost

The idea that the use of a resource for some activity (e.g. tourism) precludes its use for some other activity that may yield a better financial return (e.g. agriculture)

QUESTIONS

1 What factors might account for France and the United States being ranked first and third, respectively, in international stayovers received in 2002 (table 4.3) but third and first, respectively, in the receipts received from this intake (table 8.1)?

(continued)

2 Under what circumstances is a destination likely to have (i) a low income multiplier effect and (ii) a high income multiplier effect?

3 (a) How does a growth pole strategy benefit peripheral areas?
(b) How do the public and private sectors work together in such a strategy?

4 (a) Are governments in less developed countries such as Mexico justified in favouring the formal tourism sector over its informal sector counterpart?
(b) Why?

5 What strategies could be implemented in the Cancún hotel sector to increase the proportion of food products originating in Quintana Roo state?

6 (a) Why is tourism vulnerable to fluctuating levels of visitor intake?
(b) What are the economic implications of these fluctuations?
(c) How do the measures outlined in section 8.3.3 fit into the supply/demand matching strategies described in section 7.4?

7 (a) What kind of employment structure tends to be characteristic of the tourism industry?
(b) What are the positive and negative impacts of this structure?

EXERCISES

1 (a) On a base map of the world, colour in red all countries and dependencies in which tourism accounts for at least 5 per cent of GNP and colour in blue all countries and dependencies where tourism accounts for less than 1 per cent of GNP.
(b) Write a 500-word report in which you describe and account for the spatial patterns that emerge.

2 (a) Assess the economic benefits and costs discussed in this chapter as you would expect them to apply to Australia and the Cook Islands, respectively.
(b) Gather as much economic information as possible about the tourism sectors in both destinations, and determine whether the actual situation meets your expectations.
(c) Account for those instances where your expectations are not met.

FURTHER READING

Bull, A. 1995. *The Economics of Travel and Tourism.* **Second Edition. Melbourne: Longman.** This text discusses microeconomic and macroeconomic factors associated with tourism that are still relevant today.

Cooper, C., Fletcher, J., Wanhill, S., Gilbert, D. & Fyall, A. 2004. *Tourism Principles and Practice.* **Third Edition. London: Prentice Hall.** The economic dimension of tourism is thoroughly covered in this general tourism textbook.

Dahles, H. (Ed.) 2001. *Tourism, Heritage and National Culture in Java: Dilemmas of a Local Community.* **Richmond, UK: Curzon Press.** Dahles provides an insightful discussion of the relationships among the formal and informal tourism sectors, tourists and government in Java, Indonesia.

Lundberg, D., Krishnamoorthy, M. & Stavenga, M. H. 1995. *Tourism Economics.* **New York: Wiley.** A major strength of this book is its ability to convey complex ideas about the economics of tourism in a readily understandable way.

Mbaiwa, J. 2005. 'Enclave Tourism and its Socio-economic Impacts in the Okavango Delta, Botswana'. *Tourism Management* **26: 157–72.** This case study from northern Botswana effectively describes the phenomenon of enclave tourism and its negative consequences for peripheral destinations.

Timothy, D. & Wall, G. 1997. 'Selling to Tourists: Indonesian Street Vendors'. *Annals of Tourism Research* **24: 322–40.** An excellent case study of the informal street vendor sector in the Indonesian city of Yogyakarta, demonstrating how the fostering of these entrepreneurs can result in several positive impacts for an LDC destination.

Torres, R. 2003. 'Linkages Between Tourism and Agriculture in Mexico'. *Annals of Tourism Research* **30: 546–66.** Torres relies on an extensive series of interviews with hoteliers, food wholesalers, tourists and local farmers to investigate the reasons hotels in Cancún do not obtain their food supplies from within the state of Quintana Roo.

Wanhill, S. 2005. 'Role of Government Incentives'. In Theobald, W. (Ed.) *Global Tourism.* **Third Edition. Sydney: Elsevier, pp. 367–90.** A comprehensive outline of government incentives to the tourism industry is provided in this chapter, which includes a short discussion of market failure.

Economic impact of Rugby World Cup 2003 on Australia

Sports-related mega-events are a type of attraction that larger destinations are increasingly pursuing in order to stimulate short-term as well as long-term economic development. The Rugby World Cup (RWC), consisting of 48 matches held at multiple venues (i.e. Adelaide, Brisbane, Canberra, Gosford, Launceston, Melbourne, Perth, Sydney, Townsville, Wollongong) across Australia between 10 October and 22 November 2003, is widely regarded as the largest sporting event of that year (a non-Olympic or FIFA World Cup year). It therefore provides an appropriate case study for estimating the national economic impacts of this type of activity, which in turn indicates the degree to which governments should pursue and support similar mega-events in future. Finally, the study design provides a prototype for estimating the economic impact of those future events (DITR 2004).

Based on regular and special surveys conducted by the Bureau of Tourism Research (the precursor to Tourism Research Australia) and several states, it was estimated that 65 000 additional international stayovers came to Australia specifically because of the RWC, including spectators, accompanying persons, media, VIP and corporate visitors, and team members from the 20 participating countries. Incorporated into this calculation was allowance for an unknown but probably small number of tourists who would have come to Australia anyway but rescheduled their trip to coincide with the rugby event. The estimated intake figure is critical, because it is the basis from which inbound tourist expenditure, arguably the most important short-term economic impact of the RWC, is calculated. Using data from the surveys and existing statistics about the behaviour of specific market segments, an international expenditure estimate of $400 million was obtained. This consisted of:

- 32 000 European visitors @ 36 nights and $230 per day = $8302 each, or $256.1 million cumulative
- 19 000 New Zealand/Asia visitors @15 nights and $210 per day = $3153 each, or $59.2 million cumulative
- 11 000 African visitors @ 24 nights and $260 per day = $6260 each, or $64.5 million cumulative
- 3000 American visitors @ 22 nights and $306 per day = $6741 each, or $20.6 million cumulative.

International airfares, at $103 million, accounted for the largest expenditure category, of which 30 per cent was estimated to have been spent in the origin countries of the visitors. Food, drink and accommodation, at $87.2 million, was the second most important category and one that accrued entirely to the host country, as with shopping, the fourth most important category ($45.2 million). The third most important category was package tours ($78.6 million), of which

28 per cent spent was spent internationally through commissions. In total, 87 per cent of the total $400 million was thought to have been spent within Australia. In addition to these expenditures, international visitors accounted for $63 million of the $200 million in ticket sales realised by the Australian Rugby Union.

The accrual of out-of-state economic benefits to individual states is more difficult to compile, since this involves monitoring not only the interstate travel of inbound tourists once they arrive in Australia, but also the interstate travel of Australians. For the latter group, the location of matches between specific countries was regarded as a critical indicator of how the expenditures were distributed by state, although this did not take into account where the inbound tourists might be in between matches. Rather than assume that every visitor from every country would automatically attend matches where their country was a participant, a weighting was applied to each country that represented the latter likelihood. Teams most likely to attract their compatriots, such as England, New Zealand and South Africa, were assigned a '1', while teams with a lesser proclivity were given reduced weightings, from which a lower allocation of expenditures from their compatriots was assigned (e.g. France 0.85, Romania and Fiji 0.15 and Namibia 0.05). It could subsequently be calculated, for example, that New South Wales received 32 per cent of all expenditures from European visitors, Victoria 20 per cent, and so on. It was then estimated from these cumulative calculations that 75 per cent of all international expenditures occurred in New South Wales (in large part because all semifinal and final matches were held there), 10 per cent in Queensland, 8 per cent in Victoria, and 2 per cent in the ACT.

For interstate visitors, the main expenditure calculations were based on the state of origin of ticket purchases and the state within which the match was being played. So, of 66 916 tickets for matches located in New South Wales, 49 948 (75 per cent) were sold to out-of-state Australians. Adjustments were then made to allow for double-header matches, persons accompanying ticket holders but not attending the games and tickets (an estimated 9 per cent) purchased domestically by international visitors. Independent surveys of interstate visitors were used to derive average expenditures per visit, which ranged from $1446 in Western Australia to $566 in the ACT, and these figures were multiplied by the visitor estimates obtained from the ticket calculations. It was found that interstate expenditures by domestic tourists amounted to $143 million, with New South Wales (34 per cent) and Victoria (29 per cent) receiving the largest share, followed by Queensland (20 per cent), Western Australia (9 per cent), South Australia (5 per cent), the ACT (3 per cent) and Tasmania (0.7 per cent).

The study determined that New South Wales received about three-quarters of combined international and interstate expenditures. However, subsequent modelling adjusted these figures to take into account the displacement effect, that is, the loss of expenditures from state residents travelling to other states. This modelling, employing a complicated array of assumptions, cautiously estimated that the RWC created $494 million in additional industry sales, 4476 full- and part-time jobs, $55 million in Commonwealth government revenue and $289 million in added contribution to the Australian GDP. The study avoided making any long-term estimates of the RWC economic contributions because of the high level of uncertainty involved in specifying the contribution of the mega-event to future visitation and expenditure levels.

Questions

1 (a) How much were the visitation and expenditure benefits of the RWC evenly distributed among the states?

  (b) How could the distribution be made more equitable in a future RWC hosted by Australia?

  (c) What risks are taken when implementation strategies are undertaken to make the distribution more equitable?

2 (a) Using the above case study and the study document (www.industry.gov.au/assets/documents/itrinternet/Final EconomicImpactOfRWC2003_20040604150504.pdf?CFID=8115941&CFTOKEN=88567173), compile a list of assumptions made that could skew the accuracy of the results.

  (b) What does this list say about the reliability of the calculations obtained from such studies of economic impact?

  (c) What are the policy implications of (b)?

9

Sociocultural and *environmental impacts of tourism*

LEARNING OBJECTIVES

After studying this chapter, you should be able to:

1 list the potential benefits of tourism for the society and culture of a destination

2 describe how tourism can promote both traditional culture and the modernisation process in less developed regions

3 explain the concept of commodification and its consequences, and understand how tourism can contribute to this process

4 differentiate between frontstage and backstage and discuss their implications for the management of tourist destinations

5 explain the linkages that can exist between tourism and crime

6 identify the circumstances that increase or decrease the probability that a destination will experience negative sociocultural impacts from tourism

7 assess the concept of the irridex

8 describe the potential positive and negative environmental consequences of tourism for destinations

9 cite examples of the environmental impact sequence using an array of stressor activities.

The basic aim of tourism management at a destination-wide scale is to maximise the sector's economic, sociocultural and environmental benefits, while minimising its associated costs. To meet this objective, destination managers must understand the potential positive and negative impacts of tourism, and the circumstances under which these are most likely to occur. Chapter 8 considered these costs and benefits from an economic perspective, and concluded that small-scale, developing destinations are most likely to incur the costs of continued tourism development. Chapter 9 extends our understanding of tourism impacts by considering their sociocultural and environmental dimensions. Section 9.2 examines the alleged sociocultural benefits of tourism, while section 9.3 considers its potential sociocultural costs as expressed through the phenomenon of commodification, the demonstration effect and the relationship between tourism and crime. The possible environmental benefits of tourism are discussed in section 9.4, and this is followed in section 9.5 by an examination of its environmental costs, as modelled through the environmental impact sequence. The consideration of the sociocultural dimension before the environmental dimension is not intended to suggest the greater importance of the former, but rather that the cautionary platform (see chapter 1) initially placed more emphasis on social and cultural issues in its critique of the tourism sector. The two dimensions, in reality, are often closely interrelated.

9.2 SOCIOCULTURAL BENEFITS

Although supporters of the advocacy platform emphasise the economic benefits that could result from tourism for a destination, they also cite various secondary sociocultural advantages. These include:
- the promotion of cross-cultural understanding
- the incentive value of tourism in preserving local culture and heritage
- the promotion of social stability through positive economic outcomes.

Counter-arguments are made for all of these impacts in section 9.3, but the intention in this section is to present only the advocacy point of view.

9.2.1 Promotion of cross-cultural understanding

When individuals have had only very limited or no contact at all with a particular culture, they commonly hold stereotypical, or broad and usually distorted behavioural generalisations, about that culture and its members. In the absence of direct experience, stereotypes provide a set of guidelines that are used to indicate what can be expected when encountering members of that culture. In times of impending or actual warfare, governments frequently evoke exceptionally crude stereotypes that demonise and depersonalise the enemy, or 'other', making it easier for the public, or 'us', to hate and kill 'them' (D'Amore 1988). Such attitudes, for example, were cultivated by the Australian government towards the Japanese people during World War II, while the 'White Australia' immigration policy, which prevailed until the 1970s, was based in large part on fears of the 'yellow peril'. Similar fears have persisted about Arabs and Muslims in general in the aftermath of the terrorist attacks on the United States in late 2001.

The advocacy platform contends that direct contacts between tourists and residents dispel such stereotypes and allow the members of each group to perceive one another as individuals and, potentially, as friends (Tomljenovic & Faulkner 2000). Tourism is thus seen as a potent force for cross-cultural understanding because huge numbers of people come into contact with members of other cultures both at home and abroad. In Australia, direct contacts with Japanese and other Asian tourists have undoubtedly contributed to the erosion of stereotypes held by some Australians, while the same effect has also occurred in reverse through the exposure of outbound Australians to Asia and other overseas destinations.

A force for world peace

One manifestation of this cross-cultural perspective is D'Amore's contention that tourism is a vital force for world peace. Aside from spontaneous day-to-day contacts, he cites the role of tourism in facilitating deliberate 'track-two diplomacy', or unofficial face-to-face contacts that augment official or 'track-one' avenues of communication (D'Amore 1988; D'Amore & Jafari 1988). This phenomenon is illustrated by the way that cricket Test matches in 2004 helped to build rapprochement between India and Pakistan, which have fought three wars since 1947 (Beech et al. 2005). Preceded by confidence-building measures such as an agreement to resume normal diplomatic and civil aviation links, a decision was made in 2003 to hold a Test series between the countries in Pakistan during the following year. The government of Pakistan issued visas for 10 000 Indians, whose warm and hospitable treatment by their Pakistani counterparts during the match was widely reported in the Indian press. More importantly, a regional television audience of 600 million was treated to a remarkable spectacle of incident-free sporting conduct and camaraderie throughout this 'proxy war', which ended in an Indian victory. Beech et al. (2005) speculate that this massive grassroots exposure to a sustained atmosphere of mutual goodwill has done and will do much to build the impetus for further improvement in the bilateral relationship, a consideration that is of no small import given the nuclear-weapon capabilities of both countries. Within the tourism sector itself, initiatives that explicitly attempt to foster peace and cross-cultural understanding include Oxfam's Community Aid Abroad tours to Guatemala, and Camp Coorong's reconciliation tourism in South Australia (see 'Contemporary issue: Seeking reconciliation at Camp Coorong').

While reconciliation between Aboriginal and non-Aboriginal Australians has been official federal government policy since the early 1990s, major disagreements among participating groups about implementation and other fundamental issues have resulted in a questionable record of progress at the political level. More potentially promising perhaps are the informal outcomes that can be achieved by grassroots initiatives such as Camp Coorong, which attempt to increase cross-cultural understanding by exposing non-Aboriginal Australians to Aboriginal culture and issues. Located two hours from Adelaide, Camp Coorong was established in 1985 as a community-based project of the Ngarrindjeri people. Visitors, accommodated in dormitories and cabins, are exposed to a variety of cultural experiences, including bush tucker and bush medicine walks, basket-weaving workshops and visits to a midden and a community museum. Each experience has an explicit political dimension, which aims to lead to an understanding of the problems that have led to the need for reconciliation. For example, bush walk interpretation emphasises the devastating effect that the European colonisation has had on the local natural environment, while the basket-weaving workshops demonstrate how Aboriginal culture has been held to external standards of authenticity and legitimacy. Guides on the midden tour indicate the damage that might occur to similar traditional sites as a result of increased tourism, and a more extensive tour of the traditional Ngarrindjeri lands emphasises how much of the latter has been lost to European colonists (Higgins-Desbiolles 2003).

It is unclear whether this example of 'reconciliation tourism' (Higgins-Desbiolles 2003) is achieving its objectives. Comments from Aboriginal visitors contained in the museum guestbooks reveal the apparent success of the site in raising political and cultural awareness among indigenous Australians. Strongly positive comments by non-Aboriginal visitors have also been noted (Higgins-Desbiolles 2003), although the apparent preponderance of university students, environmentalists and members of reconciliation groups among the former suggest that Camp Coorong may to a large extent be preaching to the converted. Less clear is how much other non-Aboriginal Australian markets are being affected. Ryan (2002a) notes that non-Maori New Zealanders are ambivalent about the Maori tourism product and it is probable that similar attitudes are held by many non-Aboriginal Australians towards the Aboriginal tourism product. The challenge for reconciliation tourism sites such as Camp Coorong is to offer product interpretation that is not so politicised as to threaten or alienate the average non-Aboriginal Australian but not so diluted that it fails to convey an awareness of and empathy for the cross-cultural events and issues that have led in the first place to the need for reconciliation.

■ 9.2.2 Incentive *to preserve culture and heritage*

Tourism may stimulate the preservation or restoration of historical buildings and sites. This can occur directly, through the collection of entrance fees, souvenir sales and donations that are allocated to the site, or indirectly, through the allocation of general tourism or other revenues to preservation or restoration efforts intended to attract or sustain visitation. This is best illustrated at a destinationwide scale by **tourist–historic cities** such as Quebec City (Canada), Bruges (Belgium) and York (UK) where the restoration and revitalisation of entire inner-city districts has been induced and sustained at least in part by tourism (Ashworth & Tunbridge 1990, 2004). Australia does not have any urban places that would qualify as a tourist–historic city but has examples of tourism-related historical preservation ranging from relatively large sites such as the Port Arthur convict ruins in Tasmania and the Millers Point district of Sydney, to small sites such as the Springvale Homestead in Katherine, Northern Territory. Destination residents benefit from these actions to the extent that restored sites are more attractive to tourists and therefore generate additional revenues, and because they provide residents with opportunities to appreciate and experience their history that might not otherwise exist.

The same principles apply to culture. Ceremonies and traditions that might otherwise die out due to modernisation may be preserved or revitalised because of tourist demand. As with historical sites, the examples are numerous, and include the revival of the *gol* ceremony in Vanuatu, where boys and young men jump from tall wooden towers in a way that superficially resembles bungee jumping (de Burlo 1996), and the revival of traditional textile and glass crafts in Malta. Other examples are the expansion of Native American arts and crafts in the American Southwest (Turco 1999), and the revitalisation of traditional dances and ceremonies on Bali (Hitchcock 2000). Similar processes are evident in Australia, with tourism serving to stimulate the production and presentation of some Aboriginal crafts and dances. For example, the traditional sand painting of certain Aboriginal groups in the Northern Territory has been successfully adapted to other media such as acrylic and canvas because of the interest expressed by tourists, while 'bark paintings' have similarly been revived and marketed as a lucrative commercial product.

■ 9.2.3 Promoting *social wellbeing and stability*

Through the generation of employment and revenue, tourism promotes a level of economic development conducive to increased social wellbeing and stability. This promotion also occurs when a destination attempts to improve its international competitiveness by offering services and health standards at a level acceptable to visitors from the more developed countries. Although implemented because of tourism, local residents derive an obvious and tangible social benefit from, for example, the elimination of a local malaria hazard or the introduction of electricity, anticrime measures or paved roads to the district where an international-class hotel is located.

Tourism can also moderate the actions of repressive governments. The presence of tourists, for example, was credited with softening the Chinese reaction towards antigovernment demonstrations in the Tibetan capital of Lhasa during 1987 and with disseminating news of the event to the outside world (Schwartz 1991). Similarly, the presence of international athletes and media in Kuala Lumpur during the 1998 Commonwealth Games had the effect of moderating the Malaysian government's actions against opposition protesters.

9.3 SOCIOCULTURAL COSTS

Supporters of the cautionary platform have acknowledged that tourism can produce positive sociocultural outcomes under certain conditions, but maintain that the conventional model of mass tourism development is more likely to result in social and cultural costs to destination residents. This is especially true, it is argued, if those destinations are located in less developed countries or peripheral areas within more developed countries. The widespread dissatisfaction of local residents as a result of inappropriate tourism development is an extremely important consideration for destination managers, since this can lead to direct and indirect actions against tourists and tourism that will destabilise a destination and give rise to a negative market image. The maintenance of support among local residents through the prevention and amelioration of negative impacts is, therefore, a prerequisite for the long-term wellbeing of the tourism sector. The following subsections examine the main sociocultural issues that influence the management of tourism destinations.

9.3.1 Commodification

The **commodification** of a destination's culture, or its conversion into a commodity in response to the perceived or actual demands of the tourist market, is commonly perceived as a major negative sociocultural impact associated with tourism (Greenwood 1989; King & Stewart 1996). To the extent that this confers a tangible monetary value on a product (i.e. the culture) that already exists but otherwise generates no economic return, it may be regarded as a positive impact. The problem, however, occurs when the inherent qualities and meanings of cultural artefacts and performances become less important than the goal of earning revenue from their reproduction and sale. Concurrently, the culture may be modified in accordance with the demands of the tourist market, and its original significance eroded or lost altogether. There are several ways that cultural commodification can occur as a result of tourism, and the following scenario gives one extreme possibility:

- *Phase 1.* Tourists are rarely seen in the community, and when they do appear, are invited as 'honoured guests' to observe or participate in authentic local ceremonies without charge. They may be given genuine artefacts as a sign of the high esteem in which they are held by the local community.

- *Phase 2.* Visiting tourists become more frequent and hence less of a novelty. They are allowed to observe local ceremonies for a small fee, and genuine artefacts may be sold to them at a small charge.
- *Phase 3.* The community is regularly visited by a large number of tourists. Ceremonies are altered to provide more appeal to tourists, and performances are made at regular intervals suitable to the tourist market. Authenticity thus gives way to attractions of a more contrived nature. Prices are set at the highest possible levels allowed by the market. Large amounts of cheaply produced souvenirs are made available for sale.
- *Phase 4.* The integrity of the original culture is entirely lost due to the combined effects of commodification and modernisation. Commodification extends into the most sacred and profound aspects of the culture, despite measures taken to safeguard it.

While the residents of a destination may obtain significant financial returns from tourism by the fourth stage, the contention is that serious social problems arise in association with the loss of cultural identity and the concomitant disruption of traditional norms and structures that maintained social stability. According to Greenwood (1989, p. 179), 'commoditisation of culture in effect robs people of the very meanings by which they organise their lives'. In addition, conflicts can erupt in the community over the distribution of revenue, appropriate rates of remuneration for performers and producers (who may have formerly volunteered their services) and other market-related issues with which the society may not be equipped to cope. Compounding the issue is the possibility that the progression will occur over a relatively short time period, reducing the opportunity to devise and implement effective adaptive strategies.

Traditional societies that are exposed to intensive and invasive levels of tourism development are especially susceptible to commodification. Classic case studies include Tana Toraja in Indonesia (Crystal 1989), the Basque community of Fuenterrabia in Spain (Greenwood 1989) and Tonga (Urbanowicz 1989). Maori cultural performances in New Zealand carried out in hotels tend to be more commodified and altered than performances that are given in villages, suggesting that venue can play an important role in the process (Tahana & Oppermann 1998).

Frontstage and backstage

Local residents are not powerless in the face of commodification pressures, and can adopt various measures to minimise their negative impact. One of these strategies, as identified by MacCannell (1976), is the recognition of **frontstage** and **backstage** distinctions within the destination. The frontstage is an area where commercial and possibly modified performances and displays are provided for the bulk of visiting tourists. The backstage, in contrast, is an area set aside for the personal or in-group use of local people and, potentially, selected VFR or business tourists. The backstage accommodates the 'real life' of the community and maintains its 'authentic' culture. As long as the distinctions are maintained and respected by the tourists and local residents, then the community can in theory achieve the dual objectives of income generation from tourism (in the frontstage) and the preservation of the local way of life (in the backstage).

The distinction between frontstage and backstage can be implicit, or some kind of physical barrier may be used to differentiate the two spaces. These range from the crude canvas screens that are erected by Alaskan Inuit to shield their backyards from the gazing eyes of tourists, to walls, ditches and 'do not enter' signs that attempt to confine tourists to the frontstage. It is possible that the very same space can be differentiated as frontstage or backstage depending on the time, so that, for example, a beach is tacitly recognised as tourist space on weekdays during daylight hours, and as local space at other times. Such distinctions can also be made on a seasonal basis. In some countries, the frontstage/backstage principle is applied as part of a comprehensive nationwide strategy for regulating contact between local residents and tourists. For example, all of Bhutan is effectively a backstage, given the government's policy of strictly limiting the number of inbound tourists and ensuring that the effects of westernisation are minimised throughout the country (Brunet et al 2001). The government of the Maldives (an Indian Ocean SISOD) isolates 3S tourism development on selected uninhabited atolls as a means of curtailing the influence of tourists on the country's traditional way of life (Bosselman, Peterson & McCarthy 1999).

The frontstage/backstage distinction, however, can have unexpected consequences and dimensions that raise difficult questions about cultural authenticity. In some native Indian communities in North America, the frontstage is occupied by traditional cultural artefacts and performances that have long been abandoned or modified by the community as items of everyday use, but are of great interest to tourists. The backstage, in contrast, is occupied by a cultural landscape that is similar in many respects to that found in nonindigenous communities of a similar size and location, reflecting the evolving and adaptive nature of the living indigenous culture. It is important to note that the frontstage/backstage distinction is by no means confined to traditional communities. Most local governments in Australia and other Phase Four countries use zoning by-laws to prevent the intrusion of tourism-related activities and businesses into residential areas, thus effectively demarcating the latter as backstage territory.

Servility

The issue of commodification has manifestations and implications that extend beyond the frontstage/backstage distinction. Additional concerns include the presentation and exploitation of residents themselves as a commodity, as demonstrated in advertisements and imagery that degrade and stereotype local people in the interests of successful promotion. The following is a frequently quoted excerpt from a Jamaican Tourist Board advertisement that appeared during the 1970s. Accompanying the advertisement was a photograph of a matronly black servant standing and smiling benignly over a white couple relaxing at a balcony table:

■ You can rent a lovely life in Jamaica by the week. It starts with a country house or a beach cottage hilltop hideaway that comes equipped with gentle people named Ivy or Maude or Malcolm who will cook, tend, mend, diaper and launder for you. Who will 'Mr Peter, please' you all day long, pamper you with homemade coconut pie, admire you when you look 'soft' (handsome), giggle at your jokes and weep when you leave (quoted in Erisman 1983). ■

This kind of imagery has been strongly condemned by supporters of the cautionary platform as evidence of racial exploitation. Especially vocal have been the supporters of **black servility theory**, who see tourism in regions such as the Caribbean and South Pacific as an activity that perpetuates the subjugation of formerly colonised or enslaved peoples through the servant–served relationship (Erisman 1983). The basic argument is that menial workers such as maids and servants, mostly of African or indigenous descent, are 'commodities' expected to meet the whims of the pampered tourists, who are mainly of European background. Local people, in addition, are expected to act as a compliant and picturesque part of the tourism landscape. The comparison with the era of slavery and colonialism extends to the pyramidical structure of tourism employment in such societies, wherein menial workers at the bottom tend to be black, middle managers mixed race, and top managers white. Advertisements as blatantly patronising as the one quoted above are now rarely used, but the same message is still conveyed in more subtle ways, as, for example, in promotional images that display local people in a traditional guise that does not accurately reflect the contemporary society of the destination (see figure 9.1).

■ **Figure 9.1**
Presentation of locals by the Kenya Tourism Authority

Prostitution

Sociocultural stereotypes and sexual imagery (which often belie the conservative nature of the destination society) are still frequently used because they are effective in purveying an attractive destination image to certain tourist market segments. Pleasure periphery destinations seem to be particularly susceptible to sex-oriented advertising, with the use of the coco de mer and other sexually-suggestive symbols in the tourism promotion of the Seychelles being just one particularly well-known example (Wilson 1994).

While successful in attracting some types of tourists, it is less clear whether this form of advertising actually leads tourists to expect sexual promiscuity among local women, or whether such demands, if they exist, are met through increased levels of prostitution. However, there is no doubt that prostitution is well established either formally or informally in many destinations as a result of tourist demand. The male prostitute, or 'beach boy', is a familiar figure on the beaches of the Caribbean and parts of Africa, where competition for female tourists is associated with increased social and economic status for impoverished local males (de Albuquerque 1998). The sex industry is a very large and well-established formal component of tourism in European cities such as Amsterdam and Hamburg, in South-East Asian destinations such as Thailand and the Philippines, and within some areas of Australia and New Zealand, such as the Kings Cross district of Sydney. Yet sex tourism is a complex phenomenon that should not automatically be condemned as unequivocally negative. Coercive and child-focused sex tourism are clearly great evils that cannot be justified. However, under other circumstances, sex tourism may be benign, empowering and financially beneficial to sex workers, according to some researchers (e.g. Oppermann 1998; Bauer & McKercher 2003).

■ 9.3.2 The demonstration *effect revisited*

The concept of the demonstration effect as a potential economic cost for destinations was considered in section 8.3.2. From a sociocultural perspective, problems occur when residents (usually the young) gravitate towards the luxurious goods paraded by the wealthier tourists (Shaw & Williams 1994) or the drugs and liberal sexual mores demonstrated by some 'backpacker'-type tourists. As a result, tensions may result between the older and younger community members, as the latter increasingly reject local culture and tradition as inferior, in favour of modern outside influences (Mathieson & Wall 1982).

Case studies as diverse as the Cook Islands (Cowan 1977) and Singapore (Teo 1994) provide evidence for a tourism-related demonstration effect within local societies. However, as with most phenomena associated with tourism, this process is more complex and ambiguous than it first appears. First, the overall role of tourism in conveying and promoting outside influences is relatively minor compared with the pervasive impact of television and other media, especially since the latter are also effective vehicles for the deliberate promotion of consumer goods. Hence, it is not easy to isolate the specific demonstration effect of tourism. Second, the effect is not always unidimensional (i.e. tourists influencing locals), but may also involve the adoption of destination culture attributes by the tourists (see section 2.4.1). Finally, the demonstration effect can have beneficial outcomes depending on the motivations of the adopter and the elements of the tourist culture that are adopted (see Breakthrough tourism: Shedding light on the demonstration effect).

The demonstration effect is a vague and problematic idea in tourism because it is more taken for granted than based on hard evidence, yet is generally assumed by supporters of the cautionary platform in particular to be a negative process, in which locals with weak and vulnerable cultures blindly attempt to adopt attributes of the dominant cultures of the tourist. Fisher (2004) argues that the demonstration effect is far more complex than this and that an understanding of the relevant processes and variants is necessary for it to evolve as a meaningful concept from which testable hypotheses can be drawn. He distinguishes between *exact imitation* (e.g. acquiring and drinking a bottle of Perrier water), *deliberately inexact imitation* (filling an empty Perrier bottle with tap water), *accidental inexact imitation* (holding the bottle incorrectly) and *social learning* (drinking cola or some other bottled liquid). Which option (if any) a local resident selects after observing a tourist drinking a bottle of Perrier water depends on many factors associated with the decision-making process. Incomplete or out-of-context observation, for example, will increase the likelihood of accidental inexact imitation, as will complete or partial incomprehension at the analysis stage. Here, the observer will also determine whether the action is relevant to their life and should be imitated for status or other reasons. Evaluations are also made as to whether it is feasible to imitate. In this light, it is perfectly rational (and not an indication of a gullible or ignorant local resident) to decide to drink tap water from a Perrier bottle because it confers the desired status without inflicting an unacceptable financial penalty.

Fisher (2004) models the demonstration effect as a complex, multifaceted, active process in which decisions are knowingly taken that benefit the observer. Useful lines of investigation that arise from this model include determining what makes some people or cultures are more susceptible to the effect, whether some types of tourist behaviour are more likely to be imitated, how much the copied behaviour is retained and how positive or negative its impact is. This approach suggests a critical engagement with the demonstration effect, which adheres to the knowledge-based platform and provides a more sophisticated indication of the positive and negative impacts that result from tourism.

9.3.3 The relationship *between tourism and crime*

The growth of tourism often occurs in conjunction with increases in certain types of crime, including illegal prostitution (Brunt, Mawby & Hambly 2000; Clift & Carter 2000; Mathieson & Wall 1982; Pizam & Mansfeld 1996). The tourism-intensive Surfers Paradise neighbourhood of the Gold Coast, for example, reports significantly higher levels of criminal activity than adjacent suburbs (Prideaux 1996). It is tempting to conclude from such evidence that the presence and growth in tourism are *causing* increased illegal behaviour, but the linkage is more complicated. As with the demonstration effect, the growth of tourism may coincide with a broader process of modernisation and development that could be the primary underlying source of social instability and hence criminal behaviour. Yet tourism makes a good scapegoat because of its visibility, ubiquity and emphasis on 'others' as perpetrators. In addition, some tourism-related crimes are highly publicised, resulting in a disproportionate emphasis on tourism as the reason for such activity. Another perspective is that tourism growth is usually accompanied by growth in the resident population, so that the actual number of criminal acts might be increasing without any actual growth in the per capita crime rate.

The link between tourism and crime, with the above qualifications, can be discussed first with respect to tourism in general and then with reference to specific types of tourism that entail or foster a criminal connection. A distinction can also be made between criminal acts directed *towards* tourists (i.e. ultimately a sociocultural impact mainly on the origin region) and those committed *by* tourists (i.e. a sociocultural impact mainly on the destination region). The general connection in the first scenario largely occurs because tourists are often wealthier than local people, and the two groups come into close contact with one another. As a result, tourists offer a tempting and convenient target for the minority of local residents that is determined to acquire some of this wealth for themselves, or who wish to exploit the tourists in some other way. Workers within tourism may be culprits, as evidenced by sexual assaults on tourists by some guides in Nepal (Brown 1999). At one end of the spectrum where the element of illegality is vague or borderline are residents who engage in deliberate overpricing or begging. Progressing towards the other end of the spectrum are unambiguously criminal activities involving theft, assault and murder such as those connected with tourism-targeted terrorism. The attractiveness of tourists as targets of crime is increased by several factors, as depicted in figure 9.2.

■ **Figure 9.2**
Factors that make tourists targets of criminal activity

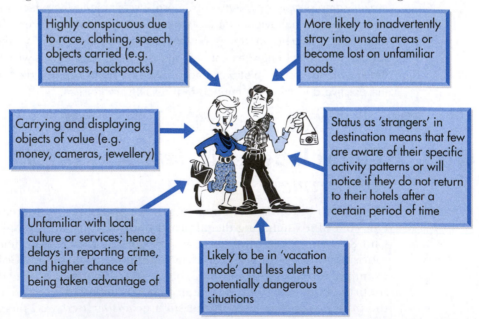

Highly conspicuous due to race, clothing, speech, objects carried (e.g. cameras, backpacks)

More likely to inadvertently stray into unsafe areas or become lost on unfamiliar roads

Carrying and displaying objects of value (e.g. money, cameras, jewellery)

Status as 'strangers' in destination means that few are aware of their specific activity patterns or will notice if they do not return to their hotels after a certain period of time

Unfamiliar with local culture or services; hence delays in reporting crime, and higher chance of being taken advantage of

Likely to be in 'vacation mode' and less alert to potentially dangerous situations

In this general perspective, the tourist is usually the victim. However, criminal acts are also committed by the tourists themselves, either against the locals or other tourists. Where certain forms of tourism either encourage or cause criminal activities, tourists are often the initiator or lead player. Sex-related activity that is defined as illegal by destination authorities is a common example. In other cases, the tourism activity is not inherently illegal, but brings with it a strong criminal association. Gambling is an example of this indirect relationship, given the involvement of organised crime elements, prostitutes and participants who may engage in criminal activity to feed their gaming addictions. Finally, there are tourist activities that have a high probability of degenerating into criminal behaviour because of the presence of alcohol (e.g. Australia's 'Schoolies Week'), rivalry situations (e.g. English soccer hooligans travelling to France during the 1998 World Cup) or other crime stimulants.

■ 9.3.4 Factors *contributing to the increased likelihood of sociocultural costs*

For the managers of destinations, it is vital to know the circumstances under which negative sociocultural impacts are most likely to occur. This allows them to assess whether these circumstances are present in the destination, and if so, to identify demand- or supply- side ameliorative measures that are warranted and feasible. If these actual or potential impacts are ignored, there is a danger that the social or cultural **carrying capacity** of the destination (or the amount of tourism activity that can be accommodated without incurring serious damage) will be exceeded. Each of the factors outlined here should not be looked at in isolation, since it is more probable that negative effects will result from a combination of mutually reinforcing circumstances. Thus, the greater the number of factors present, the greater the probability of negative outcomes. No order of priority is intended in this inventory.

Extensive inequality in wealth between tourists and residents

As mentioned earlier, tourists who are visibly wealthier than the majority of the resident population, as in an LDC destination, are more likely to generate resentment and induce a demonstration effect among some residents that cannot be fulfilled by conventional means (e.g. increased earnings). Hence, there is a greater probability that these individuals will revert to tourist-directed crime to meet these perceived needs. A broader issue of relevance to this factor of wealth disparity is that residents are just as likely to rely on stereotypes as tourists, prompting many to assume that *all* tourists from Australia or the United States are extremely wealthy. A widespread sense of envy and resentment can emerge under such circumstances.

Cultural and behavioural differences between tourists and residents

Large cultural differences can result in the identification of tourists as a group distinct from the 'local' population, hence reinforcing the sense of the 'other' and, as discussed above, making them more vulnerable to crime.

Where the gap between the tourist and resident cultures is wide, the probability of culturally based misunderstandings is also increased, even if tourist actions are motivated by the best of intentions. The problem is exacerbated when tourists make little or no attempt to recognise and respect local sensibilities and persist in adhering to their own cultural norms. The same also applies to the attitudes of local residents, although more of an onus is placed on the visitor since the latter cannot reasonably expect that a destination will transform itself just for their convenience. Inappropriate behaviour is fairly or unfairly associated with psychocentric tourists (section 6.4.3), who become more prevalent as a destination becomes more developed. For such groups, contact with other cultures is likely to reinforce rather than remove existing cultural stereotypes, producing an effect that is opposite to what the advocacy platform assumes will occur.

Overly intrusive or exclusive contact

How much differentials in wealth and culture create social problems is also influenced by the nature of contact between tourists and residents. As discussed in section 7.3, this is an extremely complex factor, given the large number of individual face-to-face contacts that occur over the course of a typical visit and the numerous variables that mediate such interactions, which include personality type, group characteristics (e.g. a bus tour group or a young couple), the moods of the individuals involved and how extroverted or introverted the culture or individuals within the culture are.

Some supporters of the advocacy platform argue that direct contact can dissolve stereotypes, but it has been suggested earlier that this can make the situation even worse under certain circumstances, for example when the contacts are overly intrusive and extend into backstage areas. However, problems can also result when tourists are channelled into exclusively tourism-focused spaces such as retail frontstages or enclave resorts (see section 8.3.2). Accusations may arise in such cases that the tourists are monopolising the most desirable spaces, that they are being deliberately snobbish or that small operators are being denied the opportunity to engage tourists in commercial transactions. Further, the reduction in direct contact that results from these attempts to remove tourists from local areas may indeed reinforce the cultural stereotypes that each group holds about the other. This discussion illustrates the **paradox of resentment** faced by tourism managers, which recognises that tensions can be generated whether destination managers choose to maximise contact between tourists and locals through a strategy of dispersal or to minimise these contacts by pursuing a policy of isolation.

High proportion of tourists relative to the local population

Where the number of tourists is high compared with the resident population, the former may be perceived as a threat that is 'swamping' the destination. Again, the influence of other variables should be considered, as the perceived number of tourists may be inflated by their cultural or racial visibility, or by their concentration within confined boundaries of space or time. An excellent example of this phenomenon occurs in the cruise ship industry when a large number of passengers is discharged into a port of call. These excursionists tend to concentrate within restricted shopping areas in the central business district for a short period of time, and are usually unaware of and unprepared for the actual sociocultural conditions prevailing in the destination.

Hyperdestinations are the extreme expression of the spatial and temporal distortions that emerge in most tourist destinations under free market conditions (see sections 4.5 and 8.3.3). The situation is especially acute in tourist shopping villages, on small islands and in remote villages, where even a small number of tourists can be overwhelming. For this reason, managers should be extremely careful about placing too much reliance on ratios that measure the number of locals per tourist or visitor-night over an entire country or state. For example, for Australia as a whole, there were 4.2 residents for every inbound tourist in 2004. However, this statistic is rendered almost meaningless because the number would be much lower for an area such as the Gold Coast (and would vary considerably between the coastal and inland suburbs and between summer and winter), and much higher in inland farming areas.

Rapid growth of tourism

If tourism is growing at a rapid pace, the local society, along with its economy and culture, may not have time to effectively adjust to the associated changes. For example, sufficient time may not be available to devise and formalise the necessary backstage/frontstage distinctions. The result can be a growing sense of anxiety and powerlessness within the local community. As with the tourist/host ratio factor, this issue is closely related to the size of the destination — even a small absolute increase in visitor numbers, or the construction of just one mid-sized hotel, can represent high relative growth that challenges the capacities and capabilities of the small destination.

Dependency

Problems can occur if a destination becomes too dependent on tourism, or if the sector is controlled (or is perceived to be controlled) by outside interests. In the first scenario, sociocultural problems occur indirectly as seasonal or cyclical fluctuations in demand generate widespread unemployment or, alternatively, an influx of outside workers (see section 8.3.3). High levels of control by outside forces, as per the second scenario, are problematic for several reasons, including resentment over the repatriation of profits and monopolisation of high-status jobs (e.g. hotel managers and owners) by nonlocals. In addition, locals may feel that they are not in control of events that affect their everyday lives. This sense is reinforced by the increased power of large transnational corporations and the uncertainty associated with globalisation (see section 5.3.7).

Different expectations with respect to authenticity

Cultural differences notwithstanding, tourist–resident tensions arise if there is a misunderstanding about the status of a cultural performance or other tourism products in terms of their perceived 'authenticity', which itself is a contentious and highly subjective concept (see sections 5.2.5 and 9.3.1). On one level it can be argued that everything, including fake copies of local art, is 'authentic' or 'genuine' because of the simple fact that it exists and conveys some kind of meaning. However, this view is not helpful, since the concept can then no longer be used to distinguish between different tourism products and experiences. A more conventional view is to consider authentic goods and experiences as those that embody the actual culture (past or present) of the destination community. But even this is problematic. In the example of the Native American village noted earlier, is the non-traditional culture that is being practised in the backstage, which represents the contemporary reality of that group of people, any less authentic than the tepee displayed in the frontstage?

One way of approaching the issue is to consider perceptions of authenticity. Four generalised scenarios are possible, as depicted in figure 9.3. In the first scenario, (a), the attraction is presented as authentic and is perceived as such by the visiting tourist. This is the ideal option that is likely to characterise the first two stages of the commodification model outlined in section 9.3.1. The opposite situation, (b), is also acceptable in terms of its implications for host–guest relationships. In this scenario, a performance is presented as contrived and is perceived as such by the tourists. While a philosophical argument can be made as to the inherent value or legitimacy of a contrived (or 'inauthentic') product, the crucial point is that both parties recognise and accept this contrived status. There is no attempt at deception, and no fundamental misunderstanding among most participants. Disneyworld and Las Vegas are classic examples of venues hosting 'doubly contrived' attractions. In these fantasy worlds, no one believes, or is seriously deceived into believing, that the Magic Kingdom or the Excalibur casino are 'real' — everyone accepts that these are hardcore frontstage fantasy environments designed to attract and entertain tourists.

■ **Figure 9.3**
Resident–tourist cross-perception of attractions

Residents' presentation of attraction	Tourists' perception of attraction	
	Genuine	Contrived
Genuine	(a) Positive impact (both parties recognise authentic nature)	(d) Negative impact (tourists believe that a genuine production is contrived)
Contrived	(c) Negative impact (tourists misled or confused into mistaking the contrived for the genuine)	(b) Positive impact (both parties recognise inauthentic nature)

The remaining two scenarios are more problematic and require special attention from managers. In one case, (c), the performance is contrived, but tourists believe, through inadvertent (e.g. frontstage is confused with or misinterpreted as backstage) or deliberate reasons (e.g. frontstage is deliberately purveyed as backstage or the two are mixed), that they are viewing something that is genuine. The limbo performance in a Caribbean hotel, the sale of 'genuine' religious artefacts at Lourdes and the 'greeting' given to visitors by 'native' Hawaiian women, are all examples of this perceptual discord. Tourists may emerge from such experiences feeling cheated, embarrassed or exploited. MacCannell (1976) describes as 'staged authenticity' the deliberate attempt to convey contrived culture as authentic.

The opposite situation, (d), occurs when the performance is genuine, but tourists see it as contrived, in some cases because of scepticism obtained from previous experience with scenario (c). Residents may be offended when tourists react to a sombre local ceremony, for example, in a disrespectful or flippant manner, as sometimes occurs in the religious events that are held during Carnival time in the Caribbean or Latin America.

■ 9.3.5   The irridex

Doxey (1976) has proposed an index of resident irritation, or **irridex**, to describe the evolution of local attitudes in response to accelerating tourism development (figure 9.4). In the initial stage, residents are 'euphoric' as a growing number of allocentric-type tourists provide good company and good monetary returns for the local community. As the flow becomes larger, tourists are taken for granted and interactions become more formal and commercial (commodified). This 'apathy' stage gives way to 'irritation' or 'annoyance', and then outright 'antagonism', as the social, cultural and environmental carrying capacities of the destination are approached and exceeded. An attitude of 'resignation' then sets in once the residents realise that they must adapt to a drastically altered community setting. For some residents, resignation is manifested in a quiet acceptance of the tourism-intensive destination, while others choose to leave the destination altogether, presumably to live in a place that has substantially less tourism intensity.

Empirical research has revealed only partial support for the irridex. A major criticism involves its treatment of the local community as a homogeneous entity evolving along a single perceptual trajectory. In reality, any community is likely to display an array of reactions to tourism at any given stage of development, depending on such factors as the residents' proximity to the tourist districts, the amount of time that they have resided in the destination, their socioeconomic status and whether or not they are employed within the tourism industry. A major factor is how much any particular individual derives personal or family benefits from the presence of tourists, whatever the overall effect for the community. Also, if it is possible to undertake a psychographical differentiation of the tourist market, then the same can be said of residents — local allocentrics are likely to react to tourists in a very different manner than local psychocentrics, although this proposition has not yet been empirically tested. Finally, many residents will harbour mixed views towards tourism — for example, they despise its social costs to the destination but highly value its economic benefits. This is apparent in the Gold Coast hinterland hyperdestination of Tamborine Mountain,

■ **Figure 9.4**
Stages of the irridex

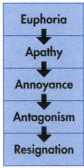

Source:
Doxey (1976)

where 51 per cent of residents in a recent survey displayed this ambivalent tendency, while the remainder was about evenly divided between 'supporters' and 'opponents'. Yet even supporters conceded that tourism created high levels of traffic congestion, while opponents admitted that tourism created local employment and attracted desirable services (Weaver & Lawton 2001). In some situations residents may tolerate a significant level of personal inconvenience if they perceive that the benefits of tourism to the community as a whole are also substantial. This is evident in the attitudes of Gold Coast residents towards the annual Indy car race (Fredline & Faulkner 2000).

The irridex can also be criticised for its assumption of a reactive rather than a proactive community response. As the local situation deteriorates, many communities implement official or unofficial measures (e.g. staying indoors, curtailing development, introducing or changing zoning, introducing quotas, introducing education programs, improving infrastructure) to cope with tourism, pre-empting antagonistic responses.

9.4 ENVIRONMENTAL BENEFITS

Various environmental benefits have been cited by the advocacy platform as a supplement to the dominant economic benefits. First, the argument is made that clean, scenic settings are desirable assets for attracting tourists in most places, whatever their specific attractions. Destinations therefore have an incentive to protect and enhance their environmental assets. Second, in certain kinds of tourism (e.g. ecotourism), an 'unspoiled' environment and its associated wildlife may in itself constitute a tourist attraction, providing an added incentive for its preservation. In each respective case, market demand defines the natural environment as an indirect or direct tourism resource. The resultant use of such resources for tourism may be a more economically rational option than potentially less benign activities such as agriculture or logging, provided that the associated generation of revenue is sufficiently large (this idea is discussed more thoroughly in chapter 11).

Third, just as tourists were credited with exposing government suppression in Tibet (see section 9.2.3), a similar phenomenon can occur with respect to abuses within the natural environment. Tourists, for example, have been instrumental in publicising the practice of clear-cutting in the forests of British Columbia and in exposing pollution problems in Antarctica (Stonehouse & Crosbie 1995). Fourth and more generally, it can be argued that individuals who personally experience endangered natural sites through tourism are more likely to value and support their preservation in the political arena, and to become more sensitive to environmental issues. Eighty-three per cent of a sample of ecolodge guests in Lamington National Park, Queensland, for example, agreed or strongly agreed that participation in ecotourism had made them more environmentally conscious (Weaver & Lawton 2002).

In the latter half of the twentieth century, the tourism industry demonstrated a remarkable capacity to intrude on, and sometimes overwhelm, certain kinds of physical environment, thereby providing contrary evidence to the earlier argument that tourism protects such environments from less benign forms of use. Of particular concern has been the affinity displayed by 3S tourism for coastal areas and inland bodies of water. Because of market demands, the developers of 3S accommodation and other tourism facilities try to locate as close as possible to water-based attractions. However, ironically, these high-demand coastal and shoreline settings are also among the most complex, spatially constrained and vulnerable of the Earth's natural environments (French 1997; Viles & Spencer 1995). In effect, the greatest concentrations of tourism activity have been established, within a very short period of time, in the very settings that are least capable in terms of their inherent carrying capacity of accommodating such levels of development.

The sprawling and ever expanding coastal resort agglomerations of eastern Florida, the Riviera, the insular Caribbean and Southeast Queensland all demonstrate this dilemma. On a smaller scale, a similar problem is being experienced in fragile mountain environments such as the European Alps, the Australian Alps (see the case study at the end of this chapter), the Himalaya and the Rockies. Small islands are also highly vulnerable because of their limited environmental resource base, and the fact that just one or two major resort developments can impact on a significant proportion of the total environment. A great problem for tourism is that environmental deterioration, like cultural commodification, may progress to a state where visitors are no longer attracted to the destination — and the destination is then faced with the double dilemma of a degraded environment and a degraded tourism sector (see chapter 10).

9.5.1 Environmental *impact sequence*

In the late 1970s the Organisation for Economic Cooperation and Development (OECD 1980) formulated a simple and still relevant four-stage **environmental impact sequence**, which models the environmental effects associated with tourism, whether oriented to the coast or elsewhere (figure 9.5):

- **stressor activities** initiate the environmental impact sequence
- **environmental stresses** associated with these activities alter the environment
- **environmental responses** occur as a result of the stresses; these can be immediate or longer term, and direct or indirect
- **human responses** occur as various stakeholders and participants react to the environmental responses; these can also range from immediate to long term, and from direct to indirect.

Four categories of stressor activity ('permanent' environmental restructuring, generation of waste residuals, tourist activities and indirect and induced activities), as described in the subsections below, account for all such impacts.

STAGE A STRESSOR ACTIVITIES
1. Permanent environment restructuring
2. Generation of waste residuals
3. Tourist activities
4. Indirect and induced activities

STAGE B ENVIRONMENTAL STRESSES
What deliberate changes are made?

STAGE C ENVIRONMENTAL RESPONSES
How does the environment respond to those changes?
Short term to long term
Direct to indirect

STAGE D HUMAN RESPONSES TO STAGE C
How do people react to the environmental responses?
Short term to long term
Direct to indirect

■ *9.5.2* 'Permanent' *environmental restructuring*

This category encompasses environmental alterations directly related to tourism that are intended to be permanent. Associated stressor activities include the construction of specialised facilities such as resort hotels and theme parks, as well as tourist-dominated golf courses, marinas and airports. Focusing on the construction of a new resort hotel, the following list indicates just some of the possible associated environmental stresses:

- clearance of existing natural vegetation
- selective introduction of exotic plants
- levelling of terrain
- reclamation of natural wetlands such as mangroves or estuaries
- sand mining on local beaches
- quarrying
- blocking of breezes and sunshine by tall structures (see Technology for visualising the impacts of tourism: GIS and 3D modelling)
- tapping into groundwater.

The potential environmental responses to clearance include the reduced biodiversity of native flora and fauna and increased numbers of undesirable and opportunistic exotic plants and animals. Levelling is commonly associated in the short term with soil erosion and landslides, and in the longer term, particularly in more distant locations, with flooding problems due to increased run-off and the raising of streambeds by the downstream deposition of sediments. Note also that sand mining and quarrying may be carried out at a considerable distance from the actual development site. It is important to stress that environmental responses are also not restricted to the site where restructuring is occurring, but can be realised in far away locations within the ecosystem. This can be problematic for a destination that is itself well managed, but suffers the effects of poor management within, say, an upstream destination that discharges untreated wastes into the river shared by both destinations.

In coastal areas an adverse environmental impact sequence is frequently associated with activities such as the construction of beach piers for the accommodation of small watercraft that interfere with normal geophysical processes. Under normal conditions the stability of the beachfront is maintained as sand particles removed by lateral offshore currents are replaced by new material eroded from nearby headlands or other beaches and are deposited elsewhere by this same current (figure 9.6). The effect of constructing a pier (i.e. the environmental stress) is to interrupt this pattern, causing sand to pile up behind the pier in a spit-like formation. Lacking replenishment by this sand, the beach on the other side of the pier is eroded by the modified current. This eventually eliminates portions of the beach, and threatens adjacent resorts and other structures. Possible human responses in the short term include reduced visitor numbers in the eroded beach environment, which would lead to a loss of income in the adjacent resorts. The resort owners could respond by constructing their own small pier to trap sand in front of the resorts. In the longer term the facilities might have to be abandoned if no countervailing measures are undertaken. Remedial measures relevant to this or other coastal development scenarios include the removal of the pier, the pumping of sand across the pier from the artificial spit to the down-current beach, or the construction of an offshore artificial reef to modify wave action.

■ Figure 9.6
Environmental impact sequence involving construction of a pier

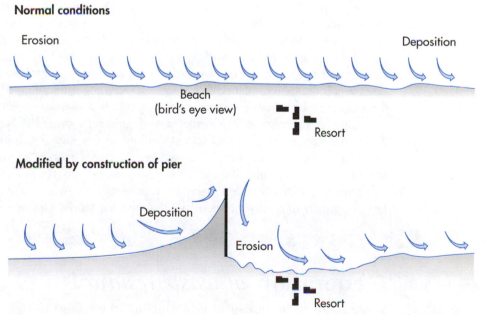

Normal conditions

Erosion

Deposition

Beach
(bird's eye view)

Resort

Modified by construction of pier

Deposition

Erosion

Resort

In April 2002, the city council of Virginia Beach, a major United States coastal resort, approved zoning changes that increase the allowable height of beach-front hotels from 100 feet (30 metres) to a maximum of 200 feet (60 metres) depending on how far the facility is constructed from the beach and retains that intervening land, or land between adjacent hotels, as publicly accessible open space. The changes were intended to increase tourist activity by opening new accommodation units, while at the same time maintaining the attractiveness of the resort by avoiding the creation of a high-rise hotel 'wall' along the beach. The height increases, however, may produce their own environmental stresses, such as increased afternoon shadowing on the beach and disruption of ocean breezes, as well as interrupted viewscapes of the ocean from locations inland from the hotel strip. To assess these potential impacts, Shellito et al. (2004) employed geographic information systems (GIS) to construct three-dimensional virtual models of the Virginia Beach resort strip in which the height of existing and potential new hotels are manipulated and 'viewshed analysis' conducted, that is, a person's view of the ocean from any vantage point can be visualised. Specific objects are assessed by the computer as 'being seen' or 'not being seen' from those positions, while any beach location at any time can be evaluated as to whether it will be shaded.

As expected, the researchers found that a scenario that permits all actual and potential hotels to increase their height to allowable limits would result in severely restricted views of the water, as well as extensive shadowing and breeze interruption, which could have the effect of diminishing visitor satisfaction. However, they were able to construct several other scenarios that retained broad viewscapes while providing for significant increases in the number of additional hotel rooms. Thus, even with increased visitor numbers, a feeling of openness could be maintained that would increase the satisfaction of visitors and the reputation of Virginia Beach as a quality resort destination, without inducing unacceptably negative environmental stresses and responses. The implications of this technology for any type of tourist destination are enormous, as they allow visual and other impacts to be assessed before rather than after any new construction or renovation. As such, they provide destination managers with a powerful tool that can inform efforts to zone or otherwise regulate areas of tourism activity in a way that does not diminish the tourist experience.

9.5.3 Generation *of waste residuals*

Waste residuals in tourism typically include the following:

- blackwater (i.e. sewage) and greywater (e.g. water from showers and kitchens)
- garbage (organic and inorganic)

- atmospheric emissions from aircraft, vehicles, generators and air-conditioners
- noise from aircraft and vehicles
- run-off of fertilisers and pesticides from golf courses and lawns.

Focusing on the first of these stressor activities as an example, blackwater is a significant environmental stress when it is discharged in large quantities directly into a nearby body of water or into a local water table. Environmental responses might include localised water contamination, the harming or killing of marine life and a loss in aesthetic appeal. Initial human responses, which include various health problems, will likely lead to reduced visitation unless steps are taken to deal with the problems (as with the beach erosion scenario).

9.5.4 Tourist *activities*

There is a relatively large literature on the effects of tourist activity on various natural environments (Buckley 2004; French 1997; Marion & Farrell 1998; Newsome, Moore & Dowling 2002). Associated stressor activities in tourism include:

- walking on coral reefs
- disturbing aquatic sediments by divers and boaters
- trampling vegetation
- littering
- approaching and observing wildlife
- pedestrian or vehicular traffic congestion
- the use of trail bikes, jet-skis and off-road vehicles
- elimination of bodily wastes while undertaking outdoor activities.

While some of the environmental stress results from actions of a deliberately destructive nature (e.g. littering, harassment of wildlife or destroying vegetation with an off-road vehicle), apparently benign acts also cause damage when their cumulative impact exceeds local environmental carrying capacities. Examples include trail erosion and disruption of wildlife caused by too much hiking or wildlife-viewing activity (see figure 9.7). Even more insidious is the inadvertent diffusion of potentially harmful pathogens into remote areas by hikers, backpackers and other tourists. Buckley, King and Zubrinich (2004), for example, describe how spores of the jarrah die-back pathogen (*Phytophthora cinnamomi*), which can destroy 50–75 per cent of plant species in some Australian plant communities, are readily dispersed by off-road vehicles, trail bikes, mountain bikes, hiking boots and horses. Solutions to contain this spread, such as the quarantine of unaffected areas or the complete sterilisation of all equipment, vehicles and clothing before entering such areas, are widely regarded as prohibitively expensive, draconian or ineffective.

In a coastal context, the negative effects of tourist activity on coral reefs are well documented. For example, research has shown that 35 per cent of the coral colonies of Watamu in Kenya have been damaged by inadvertent tourist trampling (Viles & Spencer 1995). Similar effects have been identified in the Cayman Islands (Tratalos & Austin 2001). More dramatically and deliberately,

■ **Figure 9.7**
*Wildlife
viewing in
Africa: how
close is too
close?*

the anchor of a cruise ship docked off Grand Cayman Island in the mid-1980s caused the destruction of 3150 square metres of previously intact coral reef in one incident. It was estimated that at least 50 years of natural regeneration would be required to repair the damage (Smith, S. H. 1988). In large part (though not solely) as a consequence of tourism, most coral reefs in the Caribbean became severely degraded by the late 1980s (Wells & Price 1992).

The issue of coral destruction is also relevant to Australia, given the presence of the Great Barrier Reef and other coral formations in the northern and western parts of the country. It has been estimated that more than 100 000 diving certificates are issued annually in Australia, with much of the resulting diving activity occurring in areas where coral reefs can be accessed. Research on the eastern coast of Australia has revealed that diving produces environmental stresses such as coral breakage, due mainly to contact with fins (Harriott, Davis & Banks 1997). This is corroborated by research in Eilat, Israel, which revealed that the average dive yielded ten instances of contact with coral, mostly by sediments raised from fin activity (Zakai & Chadwick-Furman 2002). Even though most serious coral damage in the Australian study could be attributed to a small minority of careless or inexperienced divers, the increase in overall diver numbers suggests that this destructive minority will grow in numbers accordingly.

■ 9.5.5 Indirect *and induced activities*

In earlier discussions on tourism revenue and employment (sections 8.2.2 and 8.2.4), the concept of ongoing indirect and induced impacts was noted. A similar effect applies to the stressor activities associated with the environmental impact sequence. Road improvements or airport expansions that occur because of tourism are examples of indirect permanent environmental restructuring. Induced effects include the construction of houses for people who have moved into an area to work in the tourist industry, and migrants who move to an area after experiencing that area as a tourist (see Managing: The impacts of amenity migration).

The indirect and induced effects of tourism at a global scale are enormous, given the number of facilities that are at least partly affiliated with tourism, and the number of people who are employed in the tourism industry or are dependent on those who are. It is evident, for example, that most of the inland (and non-tourism oriented) suburbs of Australia's Gold Coast would have never been developed had it not been for the presence of tourism as a propulsive industry and generator of regional wealth. However, as with revenue and employment, it is difficult to measure the extent of tourism-related effects on such 'external' environments when the interrelationship is not immediate and direct.

MANAGING

The impacts of amenity migration

A major but poorly understood induced consequence of tourism in some destinations is permanent population growth and associated development that results from **amenity migration**. This can be defined as migration that is motivated by the desire to reside in areas that offer a perceived high quality of life because they have attractive natural amenities such as coastlines, inland water, mountains and forests. The link between amenity migration and tourism is based on the premise that an area attractive enough to visit for outdoor recreation is attractive enough to draw permanent migrants, and that anyone making such a migration decision is unlikely to do so without having first had direct personal experience with that area as a tourist. As the eastern coastline of Australia and the Sunbelt of the southern United States are, the Greater Yellowstone area in the mountains of the western United States is a major region for amenity migration, based on the scenic natural attractions found in Yellowstone National Park and adjacent lower order protected areas. As with the Rocky Mountains region more generally, the rate of population growth in the Greater Yellowstone area between 1980 and 2000 greatly exceeded the rate for the country as a whole, primarily because of the arrival of amenity migrants. Among the groups that account for most of this movement are retirees and the semiretired, younger 'lifestyle' migrants seeking a better place to raise their children, and entrepreneurs seeking to take advantage of the economic opportunities created by tourists and migrants. Approximately four of every ten local business owners themselves first experienced the region through tourism (Johnson, Maxwell & Aspinall 2003).

Amenity migration is supported and encouraged by many local residents because of its role in counterbalancing emigration and stimulating the local economy through increased expenditure and tax base. The employment and expenditure associated with new housing construction is a particularly important outcome but one that has also been criticised because of its role in fragmenting agricultural land and natural habitat. Between 1974 and 1997, the Greater Yellowstone area lost 18 per cent of its farmland, due largely to the subdivision

(continued)

of privately owned land into 'ranchettes' and commercial properties (Johnson, Maxwell & Aspinall 2003). This new construction, if not properly planned, can also have the effect of undermining the scenic natural vistas and sense of openness that are the basis of the region's attractiveness as a destination. It is for this reason that municipal government in western communities such as Boulder, Colorado, allocates money for conservation easements that essentially pay landowners to keep their land permanently in an undeveloped state. Related negative effects of amenity migration include land inflation, overtaxed local infrastructure and inadequate affordable housing. Social conflict may also arise as incoming retirees use their growing political clout to lobby for health care allocations instead of the education and recreation disbursements favoured by young families.

9.5.6 Management *implications of sociocultural and environmental impacts*

The discourse on impact, whether environmental or sociocultural, is informed by the following observations. First, it must be re-emphasised that *all* tourism-related activity causes a certain amount of stress, and this stress is likely to include both positive and negative effects for different stakeholders. The critical issue is not whether stress can be avoided altogether, but whether the net effects are acceptable to the destination community or can be reduced to an acceptable level through proactive management strategies. Acceptability, in turn, is influenced by the perception of benefits received — residents normally try to realise optimum benefits, but a high level of environmental or sociocultural stress may be tolerated in exchange for significant job and revenue opportunities for the local community. It may also be reasoned that the negative environmental or sociocultural impacts of tourism are less than those that would result from alternative economic activities such as logging.

Second, stress is linked to carrying capacity, which varies from site to site, and is a malleable concept that can be manipulated through site hardening, the formal designation of frontstage/backstage distinctions and other adaptive measures. Ecosystems, as do cultures and societies, have different levels of resilience and adaptability. Thus, a concentration of 500 tourists in a closed-canopy temperate forest would probably have no discernible impact on that biome, but could seriously disrupt an Antarctic site. However, even within the same type of environment (e.g. a tropical rainforest or a coral reef), site-specific carrying capacity will be influenced by variables such as slope, biodiversity, soil type and hydrology. Generalisations about carrying capacity should, therefore, be made with great caution.

Finally, carrying capacities are often extremely difficult to identify, since stress and its impact are not always dramatic, but rather incremental and long term. A large resort destination such as the Gold Coast may appear to be functioning within local environmental carrying capacities, until a

100-year cyclone event destroys the community because of alterations to the protective dune and estuarine environments that occurred over previous decades. Similarly, a local community may appear to be coexisting peacefully with an adjacent enclave resort, until one particular incident triggers a violent community-wide reaction against that resort. As discussed in more detail in chapter 11, a strong element of uncertainty and ambiguity must always be taken into account when attempting to identify the long-term costs and benefits of tourism in any destination.

CHAPTER REVIEW

This chapter has considered an array of sociocultural and environmental impacts potentially associated with the development of tourism. The major sociocultural benefits focus on tourism's potential to promote cross-cultural understanding, to function as an incentive to preserve a destination's culture and historical heritage and to foster wellbeing and stability within the local society. These advantages were cited by the advocacy platform as secondary benefits to the all-important economic consequences. Sociocultural costs, as emphasised by the cautionary platform, include the gradual commodification of culture and related perspectives on servility and prostitution. Commodification is the process of the local culture becoming more commercialised, and more modified and cheapened, as local residents respond to the opportunities provided by the increased intake of visitors. Other aspects involve the sociocultural consequences of the tourism demonstration effect, and the direct and indirect connections between tourism and crime, wherein tourists and residents can both be victims or perpetrators.

Negative sociocultural impacts that may eventually breach a destination's carrying capacity are more likely to occur in a destination when there is inequality in material wealth between the residents and tourists, strong cultural differentiation and a tendency on the part of tourists to adhere strongly to their own culture. Other factors include tourist–resident contacts that are overly intrusive or exclusive, the extent to which residents are able to differentiate between 'backstage' and 'frontstage' spaces, a high proportion of tourists to residents, an overly rapid pace of tourism growth, a level of dependency on tourism and external control over the same, and differential expectations as to the meaning and authenticity of cultural and historical products. The irridex shows how resident reactions towards tourism and tourists can deteriorate as a result of increased levels of tourism activity, although it fails to recognise that communities and individuals can harbour contradictory attitudes at any stage of development, and have the capacity to pre-empt inappropriate tourism activity that may precipitate negative responses.

The main environmental benefit associated with tourism is its provision of an incentive for the protection of natural resources that would probably otherwise be subject to less benign forms of exploitation. However, the environmental impact sequence suggests that tourism development itself may produce negative consequences. This sequence is a four-stage process involving the appearance of stressor activities, environmental stresses that result from these activities, environmental responses to those stresses and human reactions to the responses. The four categories of stressor activities are permanent environmental restructuring, the generation of waste residuals, tourist activities and indirect and induced activities associated with tourism. Empirical evidence suggests that these impacts can often be subtle, indirect, delayed and evident in regions far removed from the location of the original stress.

SUMMARY OF KEY TERMS ....

Tourist–historic city

An urban place where the preservation of historical districts helps to sustain and is at least in part sustained by a significant level of tourist activity

Commodification

In tourism, the process whereby a destination's culture is gradually converted into a saleable commodity or product in response to the perceived or actual demands of the tourist market

- **Frontstage:** explicitly or tacitly recognised spaces within the destination that are mobilised for tourism purposes such as commodified cultural performances
- **Backstage:** the opposite of frontstage; areas of the destination where personal or intragroup activities occur, such as noncommercialised cultural performances. A particular space may be designated as either frontstage or backstage depending on the time of day or year
- **Black servility theory:** the belief that tourism, in regions such as the Caribbean or South Pacific, is an activity that perpetuates the subjugation of formerly colonised or enslaved peoples through the maintenance of the servant (black) and served (white) relationship

Carrying capacity

The amount of tourism activity (e.g. number of visitors, amount of development) that can be accommodated without incurring serious harm to a destination; distinctions can be made between social, cultural and environmental carrying capacity

Paradox of resentment

The idea that problems of resentment and tension can result whether tourists are integrated with, or isolated from, the local community

Irridex

A theoretical model proposing that resident attitudes evolve from euphoria to apathy, then irritation (or annoyance), antagonism and finally resignation, as the intensity of tourism development increases within a destination

Environmental impact sequence

A four-stage model formulated by the OECD to account for the impacts of tourism on the natural environment:

- **Stressor activities:** activities that initiate the environmental impact sequence; these can be divided into permanent environmental restructuring, the generation of waste residuals, tourist activities and indirect and induced activities
- **Environmental stresses:** the deliberate changes in the environment that are entailed in the stressor activities

- **Environmental responses:** the way that the environment reacts to the stresses, both in the short and long term, and both directly and indirectly
- **Human responses:** the reactions of individuals, communities, the tourism industry, tourists, NGOs and governments to the various environmental responses
- **Amenity migration:** migration induced by the quality-of-life characteristics of a place, including comfortable weather and beautiful scenery. Amenity migrants are usually first exposed to such places through their own tourist experiences

QUESTIONS

1 (a) Why is tourism sometimes referred to as a vehicle for the promotion of world peace?
(b) How valid is this description of tourism?
(c) How could Camp Coorong attract a larger number of Australian visitors?

2 (a) How much is commodification a positive or negative impact of tourism for destinations?
(b) What strategies can a destination adopt to minimise its negative effects while maximising its benefits?

3 (a) Does black servility theory apply to a highly developed country such as Australia, New Zealand or the United States?
(b) Why?

4 (a) How can the demonstration effect indicate both the weakness and strength of the individual or society in which it is occurring?
(b) How could destination managers mobilise the demonstration effect so that it has positive effects on the society and culture of the destination?

5 (a) In what ways can tourism promote criminal behaviour in a destination?
(b) How can these effects be minimised?
(c) Under what circumstances is sex tourism related to crime?

6 (a) What is meant by the 'paradox of resentment'?
(b) How can tourism managers avoid this problem?

7 What are the opportunities and difficulties of using 'authenticity' as an indicator of tourism's sociocultural impacts within a destination?

8 (a) What is the 'irridex', and what are its strengths and weaknesses?
(b) How could this be made into a useful tool for destination management?

9 (a) Why is it difficult to measure the indirect and induced environmental impacts of tourism?

(b) How much should the developers and managers of a tourism facility be required to take responsibility for these indirect and induced impacts?

10 (a) What kinds of physical environment are (i) more likely and (ii) less likely to have a high environmental carrying capacity for tourism-related activity?

(b) What could be done to increase a site's environmental carrying capacity for tourism?

EXERCISES

1 Try to recall at least three unpleasant social or cultural incidents that you have personally experienced when travelling to a tourist destination where the dominant culture is different to your own.

(a) In each case, to what extent was the problem attributable to your own actions or to the actions of a person or persons in that other culture?

(b) What measures could or should be taken by the managers of that destination to prevent future incidents of that nature?

(c) What sociocultural impacts might these measures have on the destination?

2 (a) For each of the factors outlined in section 9.3.4, suggest a variable that would allow it to be measured and monitored at a reasonable cost by destination managers.

(b) Outline a strategy for collecting the information associated with each of these variables.

(c) Describe some of the problems that might be encountered in using this information to determine how much negative impact tourism is having on the destination.

FURTHER READING

Brunet, S., Bauer, J., de Lacy, T. & Tshering, K. 2001. 'Tourism Development in Bhutan: Tensions between Tradition and Modernity'. *Journal of Sustainable Tourism* 9: 243–63. Challenges associated with designating an entire country as a backstage, while slowly opening the door to international tourism, are discussed in this article.

Buckley, R. (Ed.) 2004. *Environmental Impacts of Tourism.* Wallingford, UK: CABI Publishing. The 25 chapters in this book focus mainly on Australia, and encompass an array of outdoor nature-based activities within a variety of physical environments. Several chapters provide comprehensive literature reviews of impacts associated with specific activities.

Clift, S. & Carter, S. (Eds) 2000. *Tourism and Sex: Culture, Commerce and Coercion.* **London: Pinter.** This compendium of 16 chapters examines various sociocultural impacts associated with sex tourism.

Krippendorf, J. 1989. *The Holiday Makers: Understanding the Impact of Leisure and Travel.* **Oxford: Heinemann.** Described by the *Sunday Times* as a 'revolutionary work', Krippendorf examines the social and cultural impacts of mass tourism in the broad context of social transition.

Smith, V. (Ed.) 2001. *Hosts and Guests: The Anthropology of Tourism.* **Third Edition. New York: Cognizant Communications.** Smith's edited volume of 14 contributions is considered one of the classics in the field of the anthropology of tourism. Most of the case studies are taken from LDCs or peripheral destinations within the MDCs, including Bali.

Tomljenovic, R. & Faulkner, B. 2000. 'Tourism and World Peace: A Conundrum for the Twenty-first Century.' In Faulkner, B., Moscardo, G. & Laws, E. (Eds) *Tourism in the 21st Century: Lessons from Experience.* **London: Continuum, pp. 18–33.** The authors consider both the positive and negative impacts of tourism with regard to its effects on encouraging world peace.

Zakai, D. & Chadwick-Furman, N. 2002. 'Impacts of intensive recreational diving on reef corals at Eilat, northern Red Sea'. *Biological Conservation* **105: 179–87.** Empirical scientific research described in this article illustrates how much diving can negatively affect coral reefs.

Environmental impacts of tourism in alpine Australia

The 100-square-kilometre alpine area surrounding Mt Kosciuszko (Australia's highest peak) is one of Australia's most unique and constricted ecosystems, home to 33 rare animal species and 21 that are endemic (i.e. found nowhere else in their natural state) (Buckley, Pickering & Warnken 2000). Yet it is also one in which tourism demand has dramatically escalated during the past three decades. While most downhill skiing and other winter activity in the area occurs in the lower subalpine environments, summer visits to the alpine area have increased from an estimated 20 000 in 1978 to 36 000 per year in the early 1980s and 70 000 in the 1999/2000 season (Pickering et al. 2003). Summer activities include backcountry camping, bushwalking, sightseeing, wildflower viewing, climbing, mountain biking, fishing, swimming, picnicking and paragliding, while some cross-country skiing, snowshoeing and snow and ice climbing occur in the winter. These activities, rather than permanent facilities such as hotels, have the greatest impact on the alpine environment.

Bushwalking and other walking activities, including hikes to the summit of Mt Kosciuszko account for perhaps 80 per cent of all summer visitor activity, while sightseeing accounts for perhaps another 10 per cent (Pickering et al. 2003). Most walking occurs along designated trails, but Pickering et al. report that the growing volume of such activity has resulted in problems of soil compaction, clearing of vegetation, changes in local soil chemistry, and the introduction of alien plants. Off-track walking, though much less frequent, is disproportionately harmful to the alpine ecosystem, given the finding that most vegetation loss, soil compaction, organic litter loss and vegetation composition change in most ecosystems tends to occur during initial use (Marion & Farrell 1998). For alpine regions, this is especially significant, given the fragility of associated vegetation and soil and the possibility that some areas affected beyond a certain threshold may never recover (Pickering et al. 2003). These off-trail problems also occur because of the role of the Mt Kosciuszko summit as a visitor magnet, which leads to crowding (especially since about one-half of visitors arrive at the peak around noon) and the subsequent tendency to spread out away from the site-hardened core area onto unhardened surrounding natural vegetation. There is also evidence that mountain-biking occurs in non-designated areas, while it can be argued that the introduction of rainbow and brown trout — exotic species that negatively affect stream ecosystems — is related to tourism because it was done to attract recreational fishers. Temporary accommodations such as tents and snow caves are associated with faecal contamination and nutrient enrichment of water and soil; there are no permanent facilities in the area to accommodate human or other wastes. Other impacts are related to the compaction of snow during the winter, although these effects are far more pronounced in adjacent ski areas than in the high alpine zone (Pickering & Hill 2003).

Pickering et al. (2003) conclude that the amount of tourism-related activity in this core alpine zone is probably exceeding the area's environmental carrying capacity, even though most of the area is located within a national park. One management response has been the introduction of educational programs and codes of conduct, which try to prevent potential and actual visitors from engaging in careless activities such as off-trail walking and collecting vegetation. In addition, a rehabilitation program exists to revegetate areas that have already been negatively affected and work has been done to increase the capacity of existing trails to accommodate more walkers without damaging the environment. At a regional scale, the principle of establishing permanent facilities at the edges of the alpine area has been followed to prevent the need for onsite infrastructure and other facilities, although this has the negative consequence of ensuring a low carrying capacity. Of broader concern is the fact that the alpine zone of Australia is readily accessible to 80 per cent of the population, including residents of Sydney and Melbourne (Buckley, Pickering & Warnken 2000), and that national parks are mandated not just to protect relatively undisturbed natural habitats but to make these available, within reason, for public visitation and appreciation.

Strategic planning to ensure sustainable tourism outcomes must also take into account the prospect of climate change, which is expected to drastically diminish this already tiny area over the next 30 years (Whetton, Haylock & Galloway 1996), rendering it even more vulnerable to tourism-related activity. The implication of climate change, however, is that the rare and endemic species of the alpine zone are likely to disappear even if an exemplary model of sustainable tourism is pursued in the area. Another consideration is that existing ski resorts will diversify the range of activities they offer to compensate for the shortened skiing season, which could result in even more visitors being diverted to the alpine zone and more types of recreational activities being introduced. Climate change, finally, may lead to an increased risk of bushfires in the national park (some of which may be caused by careless tourists), which, as can climate change itself, could have a far more devastating effect on the alpine ecosystem than tourism.

Questions

1 (a) Construct an environmental impact sequence that focuses on tourism as it is currently practised in the alpine areas of Australia.

  (b) Show how pre-emptive and reactive human responses by the management of the national park could result in an altered sequence having fewer negative environmental impacts.

2 Using a variety of secondary academic sources, write a 1000-word paper that describes the likely effects of climate change on alpine and subalpine Australia and its tourism industry, and the responses that the tourism industry will need to make to these changes.

10 Destination *development*

LEARNING OBJECTIVES

After studying this chapter, you should be able to:

1 discuss the implications of the destination lifecycle concept for tourism managers

2 describe the destination lifecycle model as presented in the Butler sequence

3 explain how different elements of the tourism experience can be incorporated into the destination lifecycle model

4 indicate the strengths and limitations of the Butler sequence, and of the destination lifecycle concept in general, as a device to assist destination managers

5 categorise the factors that contribute to changes in the destination lifecycle process

6 explain how tourism development at a national scale can be described as a combined process of contagious and hierarchical spatial diffusion

7 describe how the destination lifecycle concept can be accommodated within the pattern of tourism development that occurs at the national scale.

10.1 INTRODUCTION

The previous two chapters considered the economic, sociocultural and environmental costs and benefits that are potentially associated with tourism, primarily from a destination perspective. All tourism activity results in change within a destination, and this usually involves a combination of both costs and benefits. Whether the net impacts are positive or negative depends on a variety of factors, including the destination's level of economic development and diversity, its sociocultural and physical carrying capacity, and, critically, the amount, rate and type of tourism development relative to these internal factors. This chapter examines the process of destination development in more detail, by integrating the content of earlier chapters on impacts, markets, destinations and the tourism product. Section 10.2 considers the concept of destination lifecycles, and focuses specifically on the Butler sequence, which is the most frequently cited and applied destination lifecycle model. This section also provides a critique of the model, and examines the factors that can contribute to changes in the destination lifecycle. The dynamics of tourism development at a national scale, which are not adequately described by the lifecycle concept as represented by the Butler sequence, are considered in section 10.3. The concept of spatial diffusion is presented as an alternative model that more accurately describes the evolution of tourism at a national scale.

10.2 DESTINATION LIFECYCLE

The idea that destinations experience a process analogous to birth, growth, maturation and perhaps decline or even death is embodied in the concept of the **destination lifecycle**. This theory, if demonstrated to have widespread application to the real world, is of great interest to tourism managers, who would then know where a particular destination is positioned within the cycle at a given point in time and what implications this has if no intervention is undertaken. The destination lifecycle, this latter clause suggests, should not be regarded as an unavoidable process, but rather one that can be redirected through appropriate management measures to realise the outcomes that are desired by destination stakeholders (see chapter 11).

Allusions to the destination lifecycle were made in the early tourism literature, as illustrated in the following 1963 quotation by Walter Christaller:

■ The typical course of development has the following pattern. Painters search out untouched unusual places to paint. Step by step the place develops as a so-called artist colony. Soon a cluster of poets follows, kindred to the painters; then cinema people, gourmets, and the jeunesse dorée. The place becomes fashionable and the entrepreneur takes note. The fisherman's cottage, the shelter-huts become converted into boarding houses and hotels come on the scene. Meanwhile the painters have fled and sought out another periphery ... More and more townsmen choose this place, now en vogue and advertised in the newspapers. Subsequently, the gourmets, and all those who seek real recreation, stay away. At last the tourist agencies come with their package rate travelling parties; now, the indulged public avoids such places. At the same time, in other places the same cycle occurs again; more and more places come into fashion, change their type, turn into everybody's tourist haunt (Christaller 1963, p. 103). ■

During the 1970s the work of Plog (psychographic segmentation) and Doxey (the irridex) also implied a destination lifecycle, though their research focused only on specific aspects of that progression rather than the macro-process (see chapter 9). Particularly influential in the tourism evolution literature of that decade was a detailed empirical case study of Atlantic City (New Jersey, United States) by Stansfield (1978). This study described how the famous seaside resort attained prominence, gradually declined through the first half of the twentieth century and then experienced a process of revitalisation following the introduction of casino-based gambling. The title of this article made specific use of the term 'resort cycle', but did not attempt to translate the findings of this specific case into any broader theoretical model.

■ 10.2.1 The Butler *sequence*

Drawing on this earlier research, in 1980 Butler presented his S-shaped resort cycle model, or **Butler sequence**, which proposes that tourist destinations tend to experience five distinct stages of growth (i.e. exploration, involvement, development, consolidation, stagnation) under free market and sustained demand conditions (Butler 1980). Depending on the response of destination managers to the onset of stagnation, various scenarios are then possible, including continued stagnation, decline or rejuvenation (see figure 10.1). Although usually not stated in applications of the model, the Butler sequence assumes a sufficient level of demand to fuel its progression, as per the 'push' factors outlined in chapter 3.

■ **Figure 10.1**
The Butler sequence
Source: *Butler (1980)*

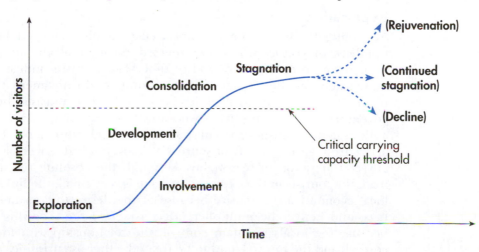

Before describing the stages in more detail, it is important to stress that this model quickly attained, and has maintained, its status as one of the most cited and applied models within the field of tourism studies. Its long-standing appeal is based on several factors, some of which merit mention here, and others that will be elaborated on in the critique that follows the presentation of the stages. First, the model is structurally simple, being based on a concept — the product lifecycle curve — that has long been used by economists and marketers to describe the behaviour of the market in purchasing consumer goods such as televisions and cars. The reader will also note its superficial similarity to the pattern of population growth depicted in the demographic transition model (see figure 3.5). Its simplicity and prior applications to areas such as marketing and demography make Butler's resort cycle curve accessible and attractive, as well as readily applicable using available data such as visitor arrivals or a surrogate such as accommodation units. Second, Butler's model has intuitive appeal, in that anyone who has travelled extensively or who has participated in the field of tourism studies will agree that some kind of lifecycle dynamic is indeed evident across a broad array of destinations. According to Lundgren (1984, p. 22), 'Butler put into the realistic cyclical context a reality that everyone knew about, and clearly recognised, but had never formulated into an overall theory'.

Third, to elaborate on the previous point, the Butler sequence is a comprehensive, integrated model that allows for the simultaneous incorporation of all facets of tourism in a destination beyond the visitor numbers that are used to construct the curve. Table 10.1 summarises the more important of these facets in terms of their relationship to the first five stages of the model and forms the basis for the following discussion of the individual stages. Fourth, the Butler sequence appears to be universally applicable, in that there is nothing inherent in its structure that restricts its relevance to only certain types of destination or environment at least at a localised scale. It is for all of these reasons that the Butler sequence may be described as the culmination of the tourism-critical cautionary platform.

Exploration

According to Butler, the *exploration* stage is characterised by very small numbers of visitors who are dispersed throughout the destination and remain for an extended period of time. The tourism 'industry' as such is nonexistent, as the negligible visitor numbers do not merit the establishment of any specialised facilities or services. The tourists themselves are adventurous, allocentric types who are drawn by what they perceive to be authentic and 'unspoiled' cultural and natural attractions. These visitors arrive from a wide variety of sources and are not influenced significantly by any consideration of seasonality. Although the absolute revenue obtained from the tourists in the exploration stage is very small, the linkages with the local economy are extensive because of the desire to consume local products, and hence the multiplier effect is very large. For this reason, and because the locals maintain control, the relationship with tourists is very cordial, and the tourists tend to be treated either as curiosities or honoured guests. These attitudes may be described as pre-euphoric, in that tourism is not yet making a large enough impact to substantially benefit the economy of the destination.

■ Table 10.1   *Changing characteristics within the Butler sequence*

VARIABLE	EXPLORATION	INVOLVEMENT	DEVELOPMENT	CONSOLIDATION/ STAGNATION
Status of the destination within the tourism system	Peripheral	Gradual incorporation	Full integration	Full integration
Rate of growth in visitation	None (low-level equilibrium)	Low growth	Rapid growth	None (high-level equilibrium)
Spatial pattern of tourism activity	Dispersed	Nodes of concentration appear	Concentrated	Highly concentrated
Attractions	Cultural/natural, unique to destination	Mainly cultural/ natural	Mainly specialised tourist orientation	Specialised and contrived tourist orientation; generic
Ownership of operations	Local	Local, some nonlocal	Mainly nonlocal	Nonlocal
Accommodation	No specialised accommodation	Small-scale, unobtrusive	Mainly large-scale	Large-scale 'international' style
Market origins	Diverse	Less diverse	Dominant markets emerge	Dominant markets
Psychographics of market	Allocentric	Allocentric– midcentric	Midcentric– psychocentric	Psychocentric
Seasonality	None	Emergent	Seasonal	Highly seasonal
Length of stay	Extended	Relatively long	Relatively short	Brief
Economic status of tourism	Insignificant	Minor, supplementary	Dominant	Overwhelming dependency
Tourism-derived revenue	Insignificant and stable	Small and growing	Large and growing	Large and stable
Multiplier effect	Extremely high	High	Declining	Low
Linkages	Local	Mainly local	Mainly nonlocal	Nonlocal
Leakages	None	Minor	Major	Very high
Commodification of attractions	Noncommercial, 'authentic'	Somewhat commercial, mainly authentic	Commercial, increasingly contrived	Highly commercial, contrived
Irridex	Pre-euphoria	Euphoria	Apathy (early), annoyance (later)	Antagonism, then resignation
Environmental stress	Very low	Low but increasing	High	Very high

In essence, exploration can be described as a kind of informal 'pre-tourism' stage where visitors must accommodate themselves to the services and facilities that already exist in the area to serve local residents. For example, tourists would have to shop in the local market and travel by the local bus system. From a systems perspective, the exploration-stage destination is only peripherally and informally connected to any origin or transit regions.

On a worldwide scale, the number of places that can be described as being in the true exploration stage is rapidly diminishing due to the explosive growth of tourism since World War II. The remaining exploration-stage places largely coincide first with wilderness or semiwilderness areas where any kind of formal economic activity is absent, rudimentary or focused on some specialised primary activity such as mining or forestry. Most of the Australian interior and northern coast, aside from urban areas and certain high-profile national parks, is in the exploration stage. A similar logic applies to many locations within northern Canada, the Amazon basin, Siberia and central Asia, Antarctica, Greenland and the Congo River Basin in Africa. Residual exploration-stage locations also include settled areas that lack tourism activity due to conditions of war or civil unrest (e.g. Afghanistan), inaccessibility imposed internally or externally (e.g. North Korea and Iraq before the US invasion, respectively) or a general combined lack of significant pull effects (e.g. large parts of rural China and India).

One aspect of exploration that is generally left unanswered is when or if this stage actually begins. Weaver (1988) argues that the exploration stage in the Caribbean island of Antigua began with the arrival of European settlers in the 1600s, when some kind of connection was first established to accommodate the arrival of tourist visitors. However, this then assumes that the indigenous population did not function in any way as 'tourists' before this time, an issue that has not yet been addressed by tourism researchers.

Involvement

Two major developments characterise the *involvement* stage. First, the visitor intake begins to increase slowly, ending the low-level equilibrium of visitor arrivals that characterised the exploration stage. Second, local entrepreneurs begin to provide a limited amount of specialised services and facilities for these tourists, thereby inaugurating an incipient tourism industry as they both respond to and stimulate this visitor flow. These services and facilities typically consist of small guesthouses and inns, eating places, the provision of guides, small tour operations and a few small semi-commercial attractions. Often, residents simply make one or two rooms within their houses available for a nominal fee. The budding and still largely informal tourism sector begins to show signs of concentration within local settlements, transportation gateways or near tourist attractions. However, the sector is still small-scale, and has little visual or environmental impact on the landscape.

The involvement stage is associated with the 'euphoria' phase of the irridex. This is due to the confluence of two facts: visitor numbers are large enough to generate significant revenues, but tourism is still incipient enough that the destination maintains local control, extensive backward linkages with agriculture and other local sectors, a high multiplier effect and a mainly allocentric-oriented visitor intake. However, the growing intake is already mediated to some extent by the formal tourism system, thereby opening the way for nonlocal participation and for greater numbers of midcentric tourists. For example, while some backpackers and academics might still arrive by walking or by four-wheel drive or relatively primitive local transport, others of a less adventurous persuasion begin to arrive by minivans provided by tour operators in a nearby city or by small aeroplane. These developments indicate that the area is gradually being integrated more formally into the tourism system, with formal businesses becoming more involved because of the increased tourist demand. Concurrently, residents begin to consciously or subconsciously demarcate backstage and frontstage spaces and times to cope with the growing number of visitors.

Factors that trigger the involvement stage

The factors that trigger the transition from exploration to involvement can be either internal or external. Internal forces are those that arise from within the destination community itself, such as the adventurous entrepreneur who builds and advertises a new kind of attraction as a way of inducing increased visitation levels (see Contemporary issue: Chaos, entrepreneurship and the destination lifecycle). External forces originate from outside the destination. These can be small-scale and cumulative, as in word-of-mouth marketing by previous visitors within their origin regions. Each visitor, for example, might relate their adventures in the 'untouched' destination to ten other people, some of whom are subsequently inspired to visit the destination. The result is a gradual increase in tourism numbers. This can also result in the coverage of a remote destination by a weblog, or a travel publication, such as *Lonely Planet*, that is read by thousands of potential visitors.

Conversely, the external factor can be a high-profile event, such as the publication of a *National Geographic Magazine* article, a television documentary, the visit of a celebrity or the release of a popular movie. The construction of a major airport or road are other possible triggers. In these instances, specific events serve as catalysts for dramatic and almost immediate increases in visitation. All of the examples given, of course, can also occur at later stages, though in those instances the tourism sector and the lifecycle dynamics are already well established (see section 10.3).

The importance of understanding the trigger factors is demonstrated by the effect that these can have on the subsequent dynamics of the destination lifecycle. Internal forces imply that the destination is taking a proactive approach towards tourism development, which increases the likelihood that local control will be retained and the community will be better equipped to adjust to increases in visitation, perhaps through a deliberately prolonged involvement stage. In contrast, external forces of the singular, large-scale variety tend to induce rapid change that is directed by outside interests — the community has the immediate disadvantage of being placed on the defensive, having to react to events rather than directing them. Under these circumstances, the involvement stage is likely to be little more than a brief prelude to the development stage.

In Australia the involvement stage characterises many rural Aboriginal communities, which are making tentative attempts to pursue tourism as a means of bringing about effective economic development. In such cases, the employment of a proactive approach to the trigger factors is essential given the cultural and economic circumstances of those communities (Altman & Finlayson 2003). The issue is also imperative in non-Aboriginal rural areas and settlements, which, while faced with different circumstances and issues, are also increasingly entering the involvement stage in their own quest for a viable economy.

CONTEMPORARY ISSUE
Chaos, entrepreneurship and the destination lifecycle

It is increasingly being argued by academics such as Russell and Faulkner (2004) and McKercher (1999) that the deterministic, reductionist linear approach of conventional science is inadequate for understanding and managing complex systems such as tourism. Instead, they contend that a chaos approach is warranted. 'Chaos' describes a situation where often random and unpredictable trigger effects cause a system to be dislodged from a steady state, resulting in disequilibrium and a new ordering of that system as its elements regroup and adjust. Phenomena that are associated with a chaos approach include the 'butterfly effect', which is a small effect that leads to disproportionate change, often through an 'avalanche effect' (e.g. the one additional snowflake that triggers an avalanche). The butterfly effect, in turn, is likely to happen when the system is in an 'edge-of-chaos' state; that is, when the system is in tenuous equilibrium and is vulnerable to large-scale change (e.g. a bubble ready to burst). Whether a system is in an edge-of-chaos state depends in part on the presence of 'lock-in' effects or factors such as strict regulations or a strongly conservative mindset that support the status quo and make the system more resistant to change. Lock-in effects can have an enormous impact on systems despite sometimes being highly irrational or relict (think of the QWERTY keyboard).

Russell and Faulkner (2004) emphasise the role of entrepreneurs as agents of chaos ('chaos-makers') in tourism. They are risktakers who use their intuition and business acumen to identify and exploit edge-of-chaos states, or even introduce the conditions to induce such states. Thomas Cook is cited as a classic example (see section 3.3.4) in so far as he was able to exploit new innovations of the early Industrial Revolution (an edge-of-chaos era) such as the steamship and passenger trains to trigger major change in the contemporary tourism sector. Walt Disney is a well-known modern equivalent. Within Australia, Russell and Faulkner describe the Gold Coast neighbourhood of Surfers Paradise as a destination where the historical lack of lock-in effects has favoured innovative change and constant upheaval as initiated by a sequence of colourful entrepreneurs. Coolangatta (on the southern edge of the Gold Coast), in contrast, experienced stagnation and decline from the 1950s because of the lock-in effects associated with a conservative low-risk culture. However, in keeping with the cyclic nature of the chaos approach, it is now Surfers Paradise that seems to have entered a period of stagnation while Coolangatta shows evidence of being on the verge of a major rejuvenation.

Development

The *development* stage is characterised by rapid tourism growth and dramatic changes in all aspects of the tourism sector over a relatively short period of time. As with all other phases of the model, the change from involvement to development is usually marked by a transition rather than a sharp boundary, although specific events (e.g. construction of the first mega-resort) can act as clear turning points. The rate and character of the growth will depend on the pull factors (see chapter 4) that prevail during the stage, and the attempts made in the destination to manage the process. In the Butler sequence, a rapid erosion in the level of local control occurs as the community is overwhelmed by the scale of tourism development. As the destination is rapidly integrated into the formal tourism system, larger non-local and transnational companies gain control over the process, attracting the midcentric and psychocentric consumers who happily arrange and facilitate their travel experiences (often through package tours) within these highly organised structures.

Spatially, the development stage is a time of rapid landscape change, as small hotels and guest houses give way to large multistorey resorts, agricultural land is replaced by golf courses, second-home developments and theme parks, and mangroves are removed to make way for marinas. Large areas of farmland may be abandoned after being purchased by speculators, or because labour has been diverted towards tourism. The 'sense of place' or uniqueness of the destination that was associated with the exploration and involvement stages gives way to a generic, 'international'-style landscape. Concentrated tourism districts form along coastlines, in alpine valleys or in any other area that is close to associated attractions or gateways. At this point environmental stresses are widespread, and negative environmental responses are apparent. The attitudes of residents towards visitors also experience a rapid transformation. In the early development stage, tourists become a normal part of the local routine, prompting reactions of apathy. However, as tourist numbers continue to mount, and as resultant pressures are placed on local carrying capacities, apathy may give way to annoyance within a growing portion of the population.

Australian destinations that appear to be in the development stage include the Sunshine Coast, Cairns, New South Wales coastal resorts such as Port Macquarie, Coffs Harbour and Byron Bay, and the Western Australian resort of Broome. Noncoastal destinations that also appear to qualify include alpine resorts such as Thredbo, and tourist shopping villages such as Maleny, Mount Tamborine and Hahndorf in the respective hinterlands of the Sunshine Coast, the Gold Coast and Adelaide.

Consolidation

The *consolidation* stage is characterised by a decline in the growth rate of visitor arrivals and other tourism-related activity, although the total amount of activity continues to increase. Visitor numbers over a 12-month period are usually well in excess of the resident population. Of paramount importance in this stage is the fact that the level of tourism development begins to exceed the environmental, social and economic carrying capacities of the destination, thereby indicating increased deterioration of the tourism product and bringing about the aforementioned deceleration of the growth rate.

During consolidation, crowded, high-density tourism districts emerge and are dominated by a psychocentric clientele who rely largely on short-stay package tour arrangements affiliated with large tour operators and hotel chains. The destination is wholly integrated into large-scale, globalised tourism systems, and tourism dominates the economy of the area. Attractions are largely specialised recreational sites of a contrived, generic nature (symbolised by theme parks and casinos), which overwhelm or replace authentic natural or cultural attractions that previously formed the basis for the destination's popularity. Seasonality emerges as a major influence on the destination's economy, along with product deterioration, high turnover in hotel and restaurant ownership, and abandonment of facilities and areas due to a lack of interest in redevelopment. Much of this is due to transnational companies that 'abandon' the destination to seek the greener pastures alluded to by Christaller (see page 308).

It is in the consolidation stage that the local social 'breaking' point is reached, with some residents becoming blatantly antagonistic towards tourists, while others become resigned to the situation and either adjust to the new environment or leave the area altogether. As predicted by Doxey, a large proportion of residents blames tourism for all problems, whether the blame is justified or not. As negative encounters with the local residents and local tourism product increase, word-of-mouth exchange of information contributes to the reduced visitor intakes.

The Surfers Paradise district of the Gold Coast is perhaps the best Australian example of consolidation stage dynamics, while international examples include pleasure periphery resort areas along the French and Spanish Rivieras, in Florida and the Bahamas, and in the Waikiki area of Honolulu.

Stagnation

Peak visitor numbers and levels of associated facilities, such as available accommodation units, are attained during the *stagnation* (or 'saturation') stage. Surplus capacity is a persistent problem, prompting frequent price wars that lead to further product deterioration and bankruptcies, given the high fixed costs involved in the sector. One way that companies respond to this dilemma is to convert hotel-type accommodation into self-catering apartments, timeshare units or even permanent residences for retirees, students or others. The affected destination may have a high profile, but this does not translate into increases in visitation due to the fact that the location is perceived to be 'out of fashion' or otherwise less desirable as a destination. Indicative of stagnation, aside from the stability in the visitor intake curve, is the reliance on repeat visits by psychocentrically oriented visitors — the moribund destination is now virtually incapable of attracting new visitors.

The best examples of the stagnation stage are found in parts of the Riviera, such as Spain's Costa Brava, and in some areas of Florida and the Caribbean (e.g. the Bahamas' New Providence Island). Beyond the global pleasure periphery, it is discernible in the recreational hinterlands that have developed within a one-day drive of large North American cities, including Muskoka (Toronto), the Laurentians (Montreal) and the Catskills (New York City). The rural nature of these regions, however, suggests different structural characteristics than those associated with urban areas.

Decline or rejuvenation

The stagnation stage can theoretically persist for an indefinite period, but it is likely that the destination will eventually experience either an upturn or a downturn in its fortunes.

Decline

The scenario of *decline* will occur as a result of some combination of the following factors:

- Repeat clients are no longer satisfied with the available product, while efforts to recruit new visitors fail.
- No attempts are made by destination stakeholders to revitalise the local tourism product, or these attempts are made but are unsuccessful.
- Resident antagonism progresses to the level of outright and widespread hostility, which contributes to the negative image of the destination.
- New competitors, and particularly intervening opportunities, emerge to divert and capture traditional market sources.

As tourist numbers decline, more hotels and other specialised tourism facilities are abandoned or converted into apartments, health care centres or other uses suitable for retirees. Ironically, this may have the effect of allowing locals to re-enter the tourism industry, since outmoded facilities can be obtained at a relatively low price. Similarly, the decline of tourism often reduces that sector's dominance of the destination as other service industries (e.g. health care, call centres, government) are attracted to the area in response to its changing demographics. The decline stage may be accelerated by a 'snowballing' effect, wherein the abandonment of a major hotel or attraction impacts negatively on the viability of other accommodation or attractions, thereby increasing the possibility of their own demise.

The number of destinations that have experienced significant decline-stage dynamics is not large. The Coolangatta district of the Gold Coast is probably the best Australian example (Faulkner & Russell 1998), while one of the most illustrative international cases is Atlantic City from the post–World War I period to the 1970s (Stansfield 1978). Other historical examples include Cape May (New Jersey) whose pre-eminence as a summer seaside resort for Philadelphia ironically was destroyed in the late 1800s by the emergence of Atlantic City. Additional examples can be found within the older established areas of southern Florida (e.g. Miami Beach in the 1970s), the French and Spanish Rivieras and Hawaii.

Rejuvenation

The other alternative is a *rejuvenation* of the destination's tourism industry. While the Butler sequence shows this occurring after the stagnation stage, it is also possible that rejuvenation will take place following a period of decline, with decreasing numbers serving as a catalyst for action. This was the case with Atlantic City's decision to introduce legalised casino-based gambling, breaking the monopoly held by Las Vegas. According to Butler, rejuvenation is almost always accompanied by the introduction of entirely new tourism products, or at least the radical reimaging of the existing product, as a way of recapturing the destination's competitive advantage and sense of uniqueness. Instances of reliance on new products include Atlantic City with its gambling initiative, and Miami Beach, which restructured the existing 3S product in the 1980s to capitalise on the city's remarkable art deco hotel architecture, which had appeal to the nostalgia market. A similar scenario of nostalgia-based reimaging is feasible for Coolangatta and older summer resorts on the Atlantic coast and Great Lakes shoreline of North America. Miami's rejuvenation was assisted in the mid-1990s by a crackdown on crime, which did much to change the city's image as a dangerous destination.

The implication of these examples is that rejuvenation seldom occurs as a spontaneous process, but arises from deliberate, proactive strategies adopted by destination managers and entrepreneurs. Success in achieving revitalisation is associated with the ability of the public and private sectors to cooperate in focusing on what each does best. The public sector provides destination marketing, suitable services and the management of public attractions, and the private sector assumes a lead role in industry sectors such as accommodation, food and beverages, tour operations, transportation and some categories of attraction (see Managing: Rejuvenation in Las Vegas).

MANAGING

Rejuvenation in Las Vegas

With its stagnant pattern of visitation growth, focus on gambling, sleazy image and abundance of contrived attractions and discount accommodations, Las Vegas during the mid-1980s was a consummate 'mature' destination. Yet rather than accept continued stagnation or imminent decline, managers and entrepreneurs in this desert oasis demonstrated a remarkable capacity for reinvigoration and sustained growth through creative product and image redefinition — what Douglass and Raento (2004) describe as part of a longstanding 'tradition of invention'. One aspect of this contemporary reinvention was the rebranding of Las Vegas as a wholesome family destination in the late 1980s, symbolised by the addition of inclusive-market attractions at major casinos such as Caesar's Palace (the animatronic figures in the Atlantis atrium), the Hilton (Star Trek adventure) and the Sahara (Speedworld) (Weaver & Oppermann 2000), and the opening of themed casinos such as Treasure Island, Excalibur and Circus

Circus. Regarded as only partly successful, the family trend was supplanted in the mid-1990s by new trends concentrating on size and sophistication. Led by innovative entrepreneurs such as Steve Wynn and Kerk Kerkorian, Las Vegas witnessed the erection of increasingly large casinos such as the 5005-room MGM Grand (the world's largest hotel), as well as ultraluxurious facilities such as the Bellagio and Venetian. Belying a reputation for $1.99 buffets and $99 package tours, Las Vegas emerged as a centre of fine art and world-class shopping and gourmet dining (Douglass & Raento 2004).

The latest reinvention, in the early 2000s, borrowed from the past by colouring this sophistication with explicit appeals to the risqué. However, this campaign, manifest in the slogan 'What happens here – stays here', has been criticised by some in the convention and meetings industry (Jones 2003) and others who believe that it panders to the core gambling market and sends an alienating and disturbing message to families. While the long-term impact of this campaign is not yet apparent, its effects may be limited by Las Vegas having always managed to retain elements of previous reinventions and thereby extend its appeal to an ever broader market. Thus, contemporary Las Vegas continues to attract families while simultaneously catering to top- and bottom-end gamer, gourmand, business and convention and inveterate shopper market segments.

10.2.2 Critique *of the Butler sequence*

The examples used in the preceding discussion illustrate the broad potential applicability and intuitive appeal of the Butler sequence as a model to describe the development of tourist destinations, wherein negative economic, sociocultural and environmental impacts increase and accumulate as the destination moves through the development stage. A major implication of the model is the idea that tourism carries within itself the seeds of its own destruction, and that proactive management strategies are essential if this self-destruction is to be avoided.

Lifecycle applications

Since its publication in 1980, the Butler sequence has been empirically tested no fewer than 50 times just within the published English-language literature. Most of these applications have identified a general conformity to the broad contours of the model, supporting its potential as an important theoretical as well as practical device for describing and predicting the evolution of destinations (Prosser 1995). However, most applications have also identified one or more aspects where the sequence does not apply to the targeted case study. For example, Weaver (1990) and Douglas (1997), in the respective cases of Grand Cayman Island and Melanesia, found that the earliest tourism initiatives in these colonial situations were carried out by external interests associated with the colonial power, and that local, nonelite participation increased as tourism became more developed.

Douglas also found evidence of serious resident annoyance and antagonism in the Solomon Islands when this destination was barely into the involvement stage.

In the case of Niagara Falls, there was no evidence for the loss of local control until well into the late development stage, nor was there evidence that the clientele was shifting towards a psychocentric mode. Furthermore, specialised recreational attractions, such as theme parks, have not superseded the iconic waterfall as the destination's primary draw (Getz 1992). Agarwal (1997) found, in the case of the English seaside resort of Torbay, that local control was retained during the development stage and beyond. In addition, visitors did not display any behaviour during these later stages suggestive of psychocentrism. Faulkner and Russell (1997) found that the involvement stage in Coolangatta (on the southern Gold Coast) was effectively bypassed by the very rapid onset of mass tourism, and that the dynamics of the consolidation stage were far more complex and multifaceted than proposed by Butler (see Breakthrough tourism: Reassessing the resort cycle in Lancaster County). (Butler himself recognised that the involvement stage could be pre-empted by the 'instant resort' effect created by Cancún-like growth pole strategies.) Baum (1998) noted that although the Canadian province of Prince Edward Island could be described as experiencing stagnation on the basis of visitation levels, the destination retained a structure of small-scale and local ownership typical of the involvement stage. With regard to seasonality, Digance (1997) points out that Thredbo, the Australian ski resort, evolved from an essentially winter-only resort to a year-round destination.

BREAKTHROUGH TOURISM

Reassessing the resort cycle in Lancaster County

Lancaster County is a largely rural municipality in eastern Pennsylvania that has developed into a major tourism destination because of its proximity to major metropolitan markets such as Philadelphia, New York and Washington. Extensive research by Hovinen (2002) into the application of the resort cycle to Lancaster County has revealed the simultaneous presence of all the later stages of the model. Based on an analysis of 1995–99 gross sales for a sample of almost 100 tourism-related businesses, he found, for example, that family-oriented rural cultural attractions displayed characteristics of stagnation and decline. These attractions (e.g. Amish Village, Amish Farm and House, Dutch Wonderland) were largely focused on or themed around the traditional horse-and-buggy Amish cultural groups that triggered the region's initial entry into the involvement and development stages in the 1950s and 1960s. In contrast, businesses focused on shopping, including suburban factory outlet malls (e.g. Rockvale Square) and urban or semirural antique outlets, indicated extremely robust growth, as did new theatre complexes, such as the Sight and Sound facility that features religious spectacles.

Because a specific stage such as stagnation, decline or development cannot be discerned in present-day Lancaster County, Hovinen argues that such situations are best characterised as being in a multidimensional and highly complex 'maturity' phase, in which stagnating and declining products coexist over the long term with rapidly growing enterprises serving different markets. This echoes Agarwal's (1994) observation that different aspects of tourism in the same destination can exhibit different lifecycles, and indicates that some entrepreneurs find opportunity in circumstances that compel other operators to disengage from a destination. With this mixture of growing and declining products, the maturity stage is characterised by an equilibrium in visitor numbers and revenues that superficially rather than functionally resembles Butler's stagnation phase. This levelling of the curve, for example, does not necessarily indicate that the destination's social and environmental carrying capacities have been breeched but only that some products have fallen out of fashion or otherwise reached the end of their own specific lifecycle.

General criticisms

Clearly, then, many deviations have been identified when the Butler sequence has been subjected to empirical testing. At a general level, the model can be criticised for its determinism, that is, the implication that a destination's progression through a particular sequence of stages is inevitable. In reality, there is no inherent reason to assume that all exploration- or involvement-stage destinations are fated to pass beyond these initial phases. Such a progression may be highly probable in a small fishing village on a scenic coastline, but much less so in an isolated agricultural settlement in New South Wales or northern China. Tourism planners and managers should therefore make the effort to identify and then focus on those early stage destinations that are *likely* to experience further development, rather than worrying that every such destination *will* face this problem.

This issue of determinism extends to the proposed carrying capacity thresholds (figure 10.1). According to the Butler sequence, tourism development escalates until these thresholds are exceeded, but communities can and often do override free market forces and take proactive measures to ensure that tourism does not impact negatively on the destination. As depicted in figure 10.2, there are two basic ways in which this can be achieved. In supply-driven scenario (a), the carrying capacities are left as they are, but the level of development is curtailed so that they remain below the relevant thresholds. Essentially, a long involvement stage of slow growth is induced, followed by consolidation at a desired level, with 'development' being avoided altogether. This could be achieved through a number of strategies, alone or in combination, including the following:

- Place restrictions or quotas on the allowable number of visitors (as in Bhutan).
- Impose development standards.
- Introduce limitations to the size and number of accommodation facilities.

- Zone only certain limited areas for tourism development.
- Prohibit the expansion of infrastructure, such as airports, that would facilitate additional tourism development.
- Increase entry fees to the destination (e.g. visa fee) in order to reduce demand.

Many of these strategies relate to the tactics of obtaining supply/demand equilibrium as outlined in section 7.4.5, although the emphasis there was mainly in the private sector, at a microscale, and related to corporate profitability rather than destination-wide impacts. It should be noted here, however, that such public sector strategies may be resisted by a local tourism industry that sees this as an erosion of its customer base and profitability.

In demand-driven scenario (b), the conventional sequence of involvement and development takes place, but measures are taken to raise carrying capacity thresholds in concert with the increased visitor intake. This can be achieved on the sociocultural front by demarcating and enforcing frontstage/backstage distinctions (see chapter 9) or by introducing tourist and resident education and awareness programs (see chapter 7). On the environmental front, destinations can make pre-emptive human responses to environmental stresses, including site-hardening initiatives such as the installation of improved sewage and water treatment facilities. Economic adjustments might include the expansion of local industries in order to supply the required backward linkages (see chapter 8). In effect, scenario (b) involves the increase of supply to meet demand, while scenario (a) involves the reduction of demand to fit the existing supply. The issue of proactive responses to the 'classic' Butler sequence is pursued further in chapter 11.

■ **Figure 10.2**
Alternative responses to the Butler sequence

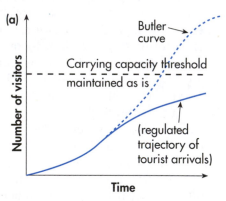

Maintain tourist numbers below existing carrying capacity thresholds = Supply driven

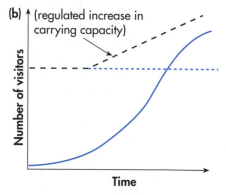

Increase carrying capacity in conjunction with increased tourist numbers = Demand driven

The question of geographic scale

As discussed in earlier chapters, the term 'destination' can be applied at different scales, ranging from a single small attraction to an entire continent (e.g. Asia or Europe) or macroregion (e.g. the pleasure periphery). This raises the question as to whether certain scales are more suited to the application of the Butler sequence than others. Because visitation levels and surrogates such as the number of accommodation units can be graphed at any scale, there has been a tendency in the lifecycle literature to assume that the Butler sequence can be applied across the geographical spectrum.

The resemblance to Butler's curve, however, is often superficial. This is because the dynamics discussed by Butler cannot be meaningfully applied at the country level, unless the country happens to be very small. The problem can be illustrated by considering Spain, where visitation levels indicate the later development or very early consolidation stage. However, it is absurd to imagine that all or most of Spain's 40 million residents are now expressing antagonism towards tourists, or that all of its tourist accommodation is now accounted for by large, 'international'-style hotels. Such circumstances may apply to parts of the Spanish Riviera, but not to most parts of inland rural Spain, which is mostly at the involvement or early development stage. Similarly, the appearance of early 'development' in a graph of inbound arrivals to Australia disguises great disparities between the exploration-stage Outback and poststagnation dynamics occurring in parts of the Gold Coast. In essence, Butler's cycle, in its classic format, does not apply to such large countries because of the tendency of large-scale tourism to concentrate only in certain areas of these countries (see section 4.5) (Toh, Khan & Koh 2001). More productive, as discussed in section 10.4, are attempts to model the diffusion of tourism, and hence the differential progression of the resort cycle, within large areas.

The Butler sequence itself is more appropriately applied at the scale of an individual resort concentration such as the Gold Coast, Byron Bay, Spain's Costa Brava, a small Caribbean island such as Antigua, or an alpine resort such as Thredbo or St Moritz (Switzerland). However, caution must still be exercised since significant internal variations often occur even at this scale. This is illustrated by the Gold Coast, where the apparent stagnation stage of Surfers Paradise contrasts with the appearance of exploration-type dynamics in many parts of the hinterland (see figures 10.3(a) and 10.3(b)).

■ **Figure 10.3(a)** *Surfers Paradise*

■ **Figure 10.3(b)** *Hinterland rainforest*

Cross-sectoral considerations

A related concern is the influence on destination development of sectors other than tourism. Applications of the resort cycle model often give the impression that tourism is the only economic activity carried out in the destination, so that resident reactions and environmental change are influenced only by this one sector. This isolationist approach ignores the external environment that must be taken into consideration in the analysis of tourism systems (see chapter 2). In reality, few destinations are wholly reliant on the tourism industry. In the case of Las Vegas, the city is also extremely important as a wholesale distribution point, centre for military activity and health care, and a magnet for hi-tech industry. The question of tourism growth leading to the breaching of carrying capacity thresholds must therefore take into account the moderating (or exacerbating) influences of these co-existing activities. The problem can also be illustrated by a large nonresort city such as London or Paris. Such centres have a very large tourism industry that appears to be in the consolidation stage, but this sector accounts for only a small portion of the city's total economic output. Hence, it is not rational to assume that the onset of tourism consolidation in Paris or London will result in widespread antagonism, or a complete dependency on tourism.

Tourism dynamics are additionally affected by noneconomic external factors such as political unrest and natural disasters, which also need to be taken into account in the management of destination development. High-profile examples mentioned earlier in the text include the dramatic decline in visitation induced by the 2004 tsunami in Phuket (Thailand), the 2003 bombings in Bali, and the 2003 SARS epidemic in Hong Kong. Within Australia, the 1998 flood in the Northern Territory town of Katherine had a similar devastating short-term impact on visitation. However, community mobilisation and effective managerial responses to sensationalist media coverage and damaged tourism infrastructure allowed the tourism industry in Katherine to recover rapidly, resulting in only a small glitch in the visitation curve (Faulkner & Vikulov 2001).

The Butler sequence as an 'ideal type'

The Butler sequence, in summary, best describes relatively small, highly specialised resort destinations, in free market (or 'laissez-faire') situations, where demand is sustained and few if any measures are taken to manipulate the lifecycle progression and its consequent degradation of the destination's tourism product. Its applicability to real-life situations, therefore, seems to be very limited, and out of all proportion to the considerable attention that it has received in the tourism literature. Yet the attention paid to the Butler sequence is justified because of the model's utility as an **ideal type** against which real-life situations can be measured and compared (Harrison 1995). In other words, the Butler model (as any model) shows what takes places when the distortions of real life are removed — it is, in essence, an idealised situation.

With this 'pure' structure as a frame of reference, the researcher can see how much a real-life case study situation deviates from that structure, and then try to identify why this deviation occurs. For example, it was noted that local control actually increased with accelerated tourism development on

Grand Cayman Island, a situation that can be attributed to the status of this island as a colony where British and Jamaican interests had the capital and freedom to initiate the involvement stage. In the case of Niagara Falls, the presence of an overwhelmingly dominant and iconic natural attraction appears to prevent a situation where contrived, specialised recreational attractions become more important than the original primary cultural or natural attractions. The implication, which can be illustrated with many more examples, is that different types of circumstances result in different types of deviations to the model. These deviations can be placed into categories, which should eventually result in a constellation of modified resort cycle models that take these real-life circumstances into account.

10.3 FACTORS THAT CHANGE THE DESTINATION LIFECYCLE

The trigger factors that induce a transformation from the exploration stage to the involvement stage have been considered. These and other factors also influence change in later stages of the cycle, whether the latter conforms to the Butler sequence or not. Managers benefit from a better understanding of these ongoing influences, in particular because the destination in the post-involvement stages can experience not only further growth, but also decline. This understanding includes an awareness of the degree to which various factors can be controlled and manipulated. Clearly, it is desirable that the managers of a destination should retain control over as many of these as possible, so that they can shape a desirable evolutionary path for the destination.

The factors that influence the evolution of tourism in destinations can be positioned within a simple eight-cell **matrix model of lifecycle trigger factors** (figure 10.4). As with the attraction inventory discussed in chapter 5, the dotted lines indicate that each variable can be measured along a continuum — discrete categories are used as a matter of convenience for discussion purposes, rather than as an indication that all factors neatly fit into four homogeneous cells.

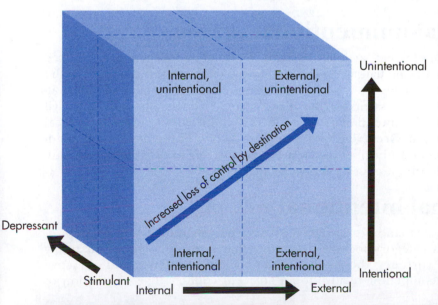

■ **Figure 10.4**
Matrix model for classifying lifecycle trigger factors

■ 10.3.1 **Internal-intentional** *actions*

From a destination perspective, the 'ideal' situation involves actions that originate deliberately from within the destination, or **internal-intentional actions**. Stimulants that trigger further growth include infrastructure upgrading, effective marketing campaigns directed by the local tourism organisation, and the decision by local authorities to pursue a growth pole-type strategy based on tourism. Conversely, internal and intentional depressants, such as entry fees and infrastructure restrictions, can be used to restrict or reverse the growth of tourism. Not all these factors, however, are instigated or desired by destination managers, as illustrated by the actions of home-grown terrorist groups.

■ 10.3.2 **External-unintentional** *actions*

Trigger factors that originate from beyond the destination, and in an unintentional way, can be described as **external-unintentional actions**. Because they are spatially removed in origin from the destination, and because they are not the deliberate result of certain actions, they tend to be highly unpredictable both in character and in outcome, and mostly uncontrollable by destination managers. They are therefore the least desirable outcome from a destination perspective, and furthermore, indicate how much developments within the destination are vulnerable to uncertain, external forces. Examples of external-unintentional depressants include cyclones that periodically disrupt the tourism industry in northern Queensland or Vanuatu, climate change and its harmful impact on the Great Barrier Reef, and political chaos in Indonesia in so far as it hinders tourism in Bali. Ironically, many of these same factors are tourism stimulants for other destinations. For example, political instability in Indonesia has had the effect of diverting many Australian tourists to destinations within Australia itself or to long-haul regions such as Europe.

■ 10.3.3 **Internal-unintentional** *actions*

Internal-unintentional actions, as with external-intentional actions (see below), are intermediate between the first two categories with respect to the control that can be exercised by the destination. Examples of internal-unintentional depressants include a prolonged civil war (though some civil wars can also be intentional) or coral reef destruction caused by a local pollution source. Occurring within the jurisdiction of the destination, managers and other authorities are in a better position to deal with these situations than if they are associated with outside forces.

■ 10.3.4 **External-intentional** *actions*

The opposite situation is described by **external-intentional actions**. Depressants in this category include a country that drastically and dramatically devalues its currency, thereby becoming a more affordable and attractive destination competitor relative to an adjacent country. The legalisation of gambling in Atlantic City was a potential depressant for Las Vegas, but in retrospect could be considered a stimulant because of its role in inducing Las Vegas to redefine its product base. A clearer example of a stimulating effect is the opening of a new transportation corridor such as a railway within a transit region, to expedite the movement of tourists from an origin to a destination region. Movies and television shows are also potential external-intentional stimulants, as demonstrated by the role of the *Lord of the Rings* film trilogy in stimulating interest in New Zealand as a destination (see the case study at the end of chapter 7). In regions where tourism is dissuaded by the presence of infectious diseases, counteracting advances in medical technology can have a trigger effect (see Technology and tourism: Medicine, hygiene and the resort cycle).

TECHNOLOGY AND TOURISM
Medicine, hygiene and the resort cycle

The spread of tourism in many less developed countries has been hindered by the presence of infectious diseases such as malaria, yellow fever, hepatitis and Japanese encephalitis. Malaria is especially problematic because of its widespread distribution (most of sub-Saharan Africa, the Amazon basin, Central America, South Asia and South-East Asia), high public profile, ability to mutate rapidly and the absence of vaccines to prevent infection (Steffen 1997). In areas of transmission where tourism has become established, much credit must be given to the development of antimalarial medications such as chloroquine, proguanil and mefloquine, as well as repellents (e.g. pyrethroids and diethyltoluamides), which decrease the probability of being bitten by *Anopheles* mosquito carriers. Public health authorities have also contributed in many areas by reducing mosquito populations through insecticide spraying and removing debris and habitat that facilitate breeding.

These antimalarial successes, however, should not lead to complacency among destination managers, who might assume that the disease is no longer a barrier to continued tourism development. One reason is the emergence of resistant strains of the dangerous *falciparum* variety since the late 1980s, so that chloroquine and proguanil, once the standard treatments, are now no longer considered appropriate in many areas of transmission. More recently, strains resistant to mefloquine, a more recent and powerful treatment, have appeared. An associated problem is that the more effective treatments are associated with a higher risk of medical side-effects, especially if taken over a longer period of time by backpackers, volunteer tourists and other long-stay segments (Knopfen 2004). With drug-resistant strains of malaria expected to increase, Trampuz et al (2003) estimate that between 10 000 and 30 000 tourists from the more developed countries will contract malaria each year within the next decade, leading to drastically reduced tourism flows in highly infectious regions such as east Africa and west Africa if no effective counteracting medications are developed.

As argued, the Butler sequence, and the destination lifecycle concept in general, are not applicable at the scale of entire countries, except for those that are very small. To gain insight into the process of tourism development at the country scale, it is helpful to revisit the internal spatial patterns described in section 4.5, which involve the concentration of tourism within large urban centres and in built-up areas adjacent to attractions such as beaches and mountains. To understand how these patterns have emerged and are likely to evolve in the future, an understanding of the concept of **spatial diffusion** is essential.

10.4.1 Spatial *diffusion*

Spatial or geographical diffusion is the process whereby an innovation or idea spreads from a point of origin to other locations (Getis, Getis & Fellman 2004). Spatial diffusion can be either contagious or hierarchical. In **hierarchical diffusion**, the idea or innovation originates in the largest urban centre, and gradually spreads through communications and transportation systems to smaller centres within the urban hierarchy. This process is modelled in part (a) of figure 10.5. To illustrate, television stations in the United States first became established in large metropolitan areas such as New York and Chicago in the late 1940s, and within a year or so started to open in second-order cities such as Boston and Denver. Within five years, they were established in small regional cities of about 100 000 population and in many cities of 50 000 or fewer by 1960. Hence, the larger the city, the higher the probability of early adoption.

■ **Figure 10.5**
Hierarchical and contagious spatial diffusion

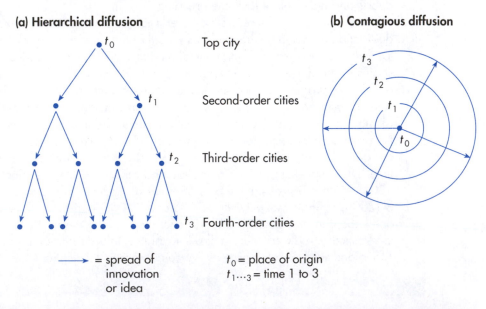

(a) **Hierarchical diffusion**

- t_0 — Top city
- t_1 — Second-order cities
- t_2 — Third-order cities
- t_3 — Fourth-order cities

(b) **Contagious diffusion**

- t_3
- t_2
- t_1
- t_0

→ = spread of innovation or idea

t_0 = place of origin
$t_{1...3}$ = time 1 to 3

In **contagious diffusion**, the spread occurs as a function of spatial proximity, as demonstrated by the likelihood that a contagious disease carried by a student in a classroom will spread first to the students sitting next to the infected student, and lastly to those sitting farthest away. Contagious diffusion is sometimes likened to the ripple effect made when a pebble is thrown into a body of still water. A good example is the expansion of Islam from its origins around the cities of Mecca and Medina to the remainder of the Arabian Peninsula, and then rapidly into the rest of the Middle East and north Africa.

In both modes of diffusion, the ideal depictions in figure 10.5 are distorted by real-life situations, as with the Butler sequence. It is useful in the diffusion discourse, therefore, to identify barriers that delay or accelerate the process, and that channel the process in specific directions. The contagious diffusion of Islam, for example, was halted by effective resistance from Ethiopian Christians and the French. The discussion will now focus on the combined application of these spatial diffusion concepts to national-scale tourism development.

■ 10.4.2 Effects *of hierarchical diffusion*

The concentration of tourism activity in urban areas is a manifestation of hierarchical diffusion. A country's largest city (e.g. Paris, Sydney, Toronto, New York, Nairobi, Auckland) is likely to function as the primary gateway for inbound tourists. Also, because of its prominence, it will contain sites and events of interest to tourists (e.g. opera house, parliament buildings, museums and so on). The dominant city, then, is often the first location in a country to host international tourism activity on a formal basis. For the same reasons, this centre also acts as a magnet for domestic visitors.

As the urban hierarchy of the country evolves, the same effect occurs on a smaller scale as the smaller cities (e.g. state capitals, regional centres) offer more services and provide more attractions in their own right. Thus, tourism spreads over time into lower levels of the urban system, a process that is assisted by improvements in the transportation networks that integrate the urban hierarchy — in essence, the tourism system expands by 'piggybacking' on the expansion of external systems such as transportation. However, tourism itself may contribute in some measure to this expansion of the urban hierarchy, in so far as it acts as a propulsive activity for spontaneous (e.g. Gold Coast) or planned (e.g. Cancún) urban development in coastal areas or other regions where tourist attractions are available.

■ 10.4.3 Effects *of contagious diffusion*

The effects of contagious diffusion follow on from the effects of hierarchical diffusion. As cities grow, they emerge as significant domestic tourism markets in their own right as well as increasingly important destinations for inbound tourists. Both markets stimulate the development of recreational hinterlands around these cities, the size of which is usually proportional to the size of the urban area. As the city grows, the recreational hinterland expands accordingly. The tourist shopping villages in the urban–rural fringe of the Gold and Sunshine coasts are examples of this phenomenon at the excursionist level, while Muskoka (in the Canadian province of Ontario) and the Catskills (in the American state of New York) illustrate stayover-oriented recreational hinterlands.

Once a community becomes tourism oriented (i.e. 'adopts' the 'innovation' of tourism, in diffusion terminology), nearby communities become more likely to also experience a similar process within the next few years because of their proximity to centres of growing tourism activity. This observation is also relevant to Christaller's description of early tourists escaping to less-developed destinations when their old haunts become over-crowded (see page 306), and thus links the process of national tourism development with the destination lifecycle. In other words, the destination lifecycle will first affect communities on the edge of existing tourism regions, and then gradually incorporate adjacent communities as the recreational hinterland spreads further into the countryside. The same effect can occur in a hierarchical way — as a country develops, funds may be made available to upgrade the airport or road connection to third-order regional cities, which then becomes a trigger factor that initiates the involvement stage.

Barriers to diffusion

This process, however, is not likely to continue indefinitely, in part because demand is not unlimited, but also because of barriers that terminate, slow or redirect the tourism diffusion process. These can take numerous forms, the most common being the lack of attractions capable of carrying the destination beyond the exploration stage. Other barriers include community resistance, political boundaries and climate (e.g. 3S tourism can only develop within a certain latitudinal range). Conversely, factors that can accelerate the diffusion process include an extensive area of tourism potential such as a beach-lined coast or an alpine valley, and upgraded transportation networks. It should be noted here that a road network is likely to facilitate contagious diffusion, while an air network will facilitate hierarchical diffusion.

■ 10.4.4 Model *of national tourism development*

Figure 10.6 provides a model of national-scale tourism development that takes into account both hierarchical and contagious diffusion in a hypothetical country. The following sequence is depicted, with each interval representing, for the sake of illustration, a ten-year period:

- *Time 0*: in this earliest phase of evolution, there is some inbound and domestic tourism activity, indicative of the involvement stage, in the capital city and main gateway.
- *Time 1*: ten years later, a small recreational hinterland forms around the capital city, while tourism is introduced to a coastal city because of the presence of beaches in the vicinity; this introduction may be spontaneous, or the result of a deliberate growth pole strategy.

- *Time 2*: the recreational hinterland of the dominant city expands outward (= contagious diffusion), while tourism is introduced as a significant activity in several second-order cities (= hierarchical diffusion); concurrently, tourism development takes hold in other coastal communities because of their 3S resources, while the hinterland of the original resort expands further, both inland and along the coast.
- *Time 3*: the pattern identified at Time 2 continues: recreational hinterlands expand and new places experience 'involvement'; in addition, where physical geography permits, fourth-order settlements in the interior become important as alpine tourist resorts.
- *Time 4*: expansion continues, with the limits of development stretched along transportation corridors, alpine valleys and the coastline.

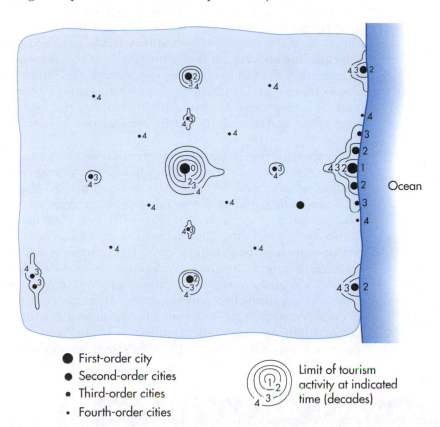

■ **Figure 10.6**
Tourism development in a hypothetical country

- ● First-order city
- ● Second-order cities
- • Third-order cities
- • Fourth-order cities

Limit of tourism activity at indicated time (decades)

Models such as figure 10.6 are potentially useful for predicting when and whether a particular place within a country is likely to enter the lifecycle process beyond the exploration stage. It is also valuable to those who are responsible for the management and planning of destination-countries, and in particular those who are seeking to direct this process. Like the Butler sequence, the ideal type depicted in the figure can probably be augmented by a constellation of subtypes that take into consideration different types of countries. These might include landlocked states, alpine states, very large states (e.g. Australia, Russia, Canada), LDCs and 3S SISODs.

CHAPTER REVIEW

Although allusions to the destination lifecycle were already made in the 1960s, this concept is most closely associated with the Butler sequence or 'S' curve introduced in 1980. This integrative model proposes that destinations tend to pass through a series of stages: involvement, development, consolidation and stagnation. Depending on circumstances, the destination may then undergo continuing stagnation, decline or rejuvenation. One major implication of the model is that tourism appears to contain within itself the seeds of its own destruction, as negative impacts accumulate and finally undermine the local tourism product as the stages progress. Applications of the intuitively appealing and simple Butler sequence to case study situations have revealed a broad adherence to the model, although most of these studies have also uncovered deviations. While criticised as well for being too deterministic and for not taking into account the existence and influence of sectors other than tourism in the destination, the Butler sequence has enormous value as an 'ideal type' against which real-life situations can be measured. It is also clear, however, that the model is applicable only at certain geographic scales, and should in general not be applied at the national scale.

Whether the evolution of a destination is best described by the Butler sequence per se or by some variation, tourism managers should try to gain an understanding of the trigger factors and actions that induce significant change in a destination. These range from internal-intentional factors (the most favourable scenario) to those that are external-unintentional (the factors over which the destination has the least control). These factors, furthermore, can be generally classed as tourism stimulants or depressants. In larger countries tourism development is best described as a combined hierarchical and contagious diffusion process that is distorted both positively and negatively by assorted barriers and opportunities. The destination lifecycle concept can be situated conveniently within this context of national tourism development, in that it is possible to anticipate when and whether a particular place is likely to move beyond the incipient stages of the cycle.

SUMMARY OF KEY TERMS

Destination lifecycle

The theory that tourism-oriented places experience a sequential process of birth, growth, maturation, and then possibly something similar to death, in their evolution as destinations

- **Butler sequence:** the most widely cited and applied destination lifecycle model, which proposes five stages of evolution that are described by an S-shaped curve; these might then be followed by three other possible scenarios
  Exploration: the earliest stage, characterised by very few tourist arrivals and very little impact associated with tourism

Involvement: the second stage, where the local community responds to the opportunities created by tourism by offering specialised services; associated with a gradual increase in visitor numbers

Development: the accelerated growth of tourism within a relatively short period of time, as this sector becomes a dominant feature of the destination economy and landscape

Consolidation: as local carrying capacities are exceeded, the rate of growth declines; the destination is now almost wholly dominated by tourism

Stagnation: the stage wherein visitor numbers and tourism growth stagnate due to the deterioration of the product

Decline: the scenario of declining visitor intake that is likely to ensue if no measures are taken to arrest the process of product deterioration and resident/tourist discontent

Rejuvenation: the scenario of a renewed development-like growth that occurs if steps are taken to revitalise the tourism product offered by the destination

- **Ideal type:** an idealised model of some phenomenon or process against which real-life situations can be measured and compared

Matrix model of lifecycle trigger factors

An eight-cell model that classifies the various actions that induce change in the evolution of tourism in a destination. Each of the following categories can be further divided into tourism stimulants and depressants

- **Internal-intentional actions:** deliberate actions that originate from within the destination itself; the best case scenario for destinations in terms of control and management

- **External-unintentional actions:** actions that affect the destination, but originate from outside that destination, and are not intentional; the worst case scenario from a destination perspective

- **Internal-unintentional actions:** actions that originate from within the destination, but are not deliberate

- **External-intentional actions:** deliberate actions that originate from outside the destination

Spatial diffusion

The process whereby some innovation or idea spreads from a point of origin to other locations; this model is more appropriate than the destination lifecycle to describe the development of tourism at the country level

- **Hierarchical diffusion:** spread occurs through an urban or other hierarchy, usually from the largest to the smallest centres, independent of where these centres are located

- **Contagious diffusion:** spread occurs as a function of spatial proximity; the closer a site is to the place of the innovation's origin, the sooner it is likely to be exposed to that phenomenon

QUESTIONS

1 (a) Is the popularity that the Butler sequence has maintained since the early 1980s justified?
(b) Why?

2 Why is the Butler sequence referred to as the culmination of the cautionary platform?

3 (a) What is meant by the statement that tourism carries within itself the seeds of its own destruction?
(b) If true, what can be done to overcome this dilemma?

4 Why are models such as the Butler sequence extremely useful to managers, even though they seldom if ever describe real-life situations?

5 (a) To what extent can destination managers influence the actions that can induce significant change in the evolution of the destination?
(b) What, if anything, can destinations do to prepare, or react to, changes that are external and unintentional?

6 (a) How can the concept of spatial diffusion help to explain the process of tourism development at the national level?
(b) How do contagious and hierarchical diffusion work together to describe tourism development at the national scale?

7 How does figure 4.7 reveal the effects of hierarchical diffusion on the distribution of inbound tourism in Australia?

8 How does the destination lifecycle concept fit into the pattern of tourism development that is described in figure 10.6?

EXERCISES

1 (a) For any major resort destination (e.g. the Gold Coast, Phuket, Bali, Cairns, the Sunshine Coast), obtain visitor statistics for as many years as possible and plot these on a graph similar to the format of figure 10.1 (i.e. time on the *x*-axis and quantity on the *y*-axis).
(b) According to the resultant curves, where does this destination situate within the Butler sequence?
(c) Gather as much evidence as you can about the tourism industry within the selected destination, and determine the extent to which Butler's model is both corroborated and contradicted by this material.
(d) Where the information does not conform to the model, what factors might account for these deviations?
(e) What factors appear to be influential in triggering the transition from one stage to another?

2 Select any large country (e.g. Australia, New Zealand, Canada, the United States, Germany, France, South Africa) and write a 1000-word report in which you consider the strengths and weaknesses of employing the destination lifecycle model to describe the evolution of tourism in this country.

FURTHER READING

Butler, R. W. 1980. 'The Concept of a Tourist Area Cycle of Evolution: Implications for Management of Resources'. *Canadian Geographer* 24: 5–12. This is the original article that introduced the Butler sequence; it is better for students to read this and other original articles, rather than rely entirely on the interpretations of others.

Butler, R. (Ed.) 2005a. *The Tourism Area Life Cycle: Theoretical and Conceptual Implications.* Clevedon, UK: Channel View.

Butler, R. (Ed.) 2005b. *The Tourism Area Life Cycle: Applications and Modifications.* Clevedon, UK: Channel View. These two volumes comprise a major collection of articles that critically explore the origins, theory, applications and modifications of the destination lifecycle in a wide variety of case studies. Butler, the editor of both volumes and originator of the S-curve lifecycle, provides a valuable personal commentary and synthesis of contributions.

Hovinen, G. 2002. 'Revisiting the Destination Lifecycle Model'. *Annals of Tourism Research* 29: 209–30. Hovinen's third article on Lancaster County, Pennsylvania, focuses on the simultaneous presence of growth, stagnation and decline dynamics, prompting its characterisation as a 'mature' destination.

Russell, R. & Faulkner, B. 2004. 'Entrepreneurship, Chaos and the Tourism Area Lifecycle'. *Annals of Tourism Research* 31: 556–79. The authors make a strong case for the role of individual entrepreneurs as agents of change — i.e. chaos makers — within destinations such as the Gold Coast.

Weaver, D. 2000. 'The War-Distorted Destination Life Cycle.' *International Journal of Tourism Research* 2: 151–61. This unusual application of the destination lifecycle model suggests devastating short-term but positive long-term outcomes for destinations as a result of a major war such as World War II or the American Civil War.

....

Revisiting Byron Bay

In the early years of the twenty-first century, the northern New South Wales resort town of Byron Bay continues to exemplify the complexities, ambiguities and conflicts that characterise the evolution of tourist destinations. Organised tourism in the area was induced by the construction of a jetty and railway link in the late 1800s but this sector maintained a low profile until the 1960s when Byron Bay began to establish its international reputation as an offbeat destination catering to backpackers, surfers, hippies and other counter-culture tourists. Through the 1970s and 1980s, with the decline in primary sector activities such as lumbering and whaling, the town's visual and functional identity as a tourism resort became more evident, as did the emerging tension between pro- and antidevelopment factions within the community. Key events in this contemporary era include the election of a 'green' (i.e. antidevelopment) shire council in 1987, which Bradbury and Mourdant (1996) describe as the beginning of the 'Battle for Byron'. Armed with its power to make local decisions about land use zoning and the provision of infrastructure and other services, since the late 1980s the council has adopted a restrictive approach towards growth (except for the period from 1991 to 1994 when a progrowth slate was elected), assisted by sympathetic activist ad hoc community groups such as BEACON (Byron Environmental and Conservation Organisation) and BRACE (Byron Residents Against Community Erosion) (Essex & Brown 1997; Kinninment 2005a). Perhaps the highest-profile success of the green faction to date was the defeat in 1994 of a proposal by Club Med to convert an existing 800-bed resort into a 1200-bed facility on the edge of town. Essex and Brown (1997) describe this as an excellent illustration of the power of well-mobilised interest groups to use media and other means to defeat (in this case on a technicality) a proposal deemed to symbolise all that they oppose on ideological grounds. Even more substantive in terms of curtailing growth, however, was the council's imposition in 1998 of a moratorium on all major development, on the grounds of infrastructure inadequacy.

Although the dominance of a green council and activist community organisations have been unusually successful in curtailing major tourism-related construction activity in Byron Bay since the late 1980s, this has not prevented the onset of environmental and social stresses that are normally associated with the later stages of the destination lifecycle. Ironically, this is largely attributable to the inability of the town's highly constrained built landscape to accommodate the continued growth of tourist arrivals, which have increased from an estimated 350 000–400 000 per year in the early 1990s to 750 000–1 000 000 in 2000 in a town with just 6000 permanent residents (Templeton 2001). Resultant chronic stresses in this hyperdestination have included continual severe congestion along major arteries and in the commercial core (especially on weekends and holidays) and inadequate parking. Other stresses borne by middle- and working-class residents in particular are escalating housing costs and property tax inflation, present because the supply of available houses does not meet the demand for Byron Bay real estate.

There is additional irony in how much Byron Bay's reputation as an alternative, laidback counter-culture magnet has contributed to the community's problems. On the one hand, this 'alternative' identity sustains the increasing number of conventional visitors, many of them day-only excursionists from the Gold Coast. On the other hand, the backpackers themselves, more than 50 000 of whom are drawn to Byron Bay per year (Gibson & Connell 2003), have a disproportionate impact because of their tendency to stay in the area for several days. Their large numbers, additionally, have given rise to an 'industrial' backpacking sector, which unintentionally undermines the counter-culture identity that they were instrumental in growing in the 1960s and 1970s. The opening in 2005 of 'Backpackers World', a large and highly commercialised facility catering to youthful tourists, is cited by Kinninment (2005b) as a particularly notable example of this industrialisation. Not all of these backpackers, however, can be accommodated in the town's 12 youth hostels, leading to the lucrative business of holiday letting in private homes, about 600 (or 30 per cent) of which are available for this purpose. BRACE and other groups have lobbied against this activity, arguing that renters often disturb the peace of residential areas because of their fondness for partying, and because the community's tolerant attitude towards alcohol and drugs facilitates their use and abuse by such visitors (Kinninment 2005a).

This tolerance, and the party atmosphere it fosters, has given rise to some of Byron Bay's most pressing social and environmental problems. An infamous event was the New Years 'riot' of 1993, in which disruptive behaviour by many of the 25 000 revellers in the central business district culminated in 78 arrests and 61 hospital admissions (Crime Prevention Division 2002). Less controversial and informal events have been an integral part of Byron Bay's distinctive identity and attraction base for several decades. The East Coast International Blues and Roots Festival, Splendour in the Grass, and the Byron Bay Arts and Music Festival all attract tens of thousands of attendees, and while not associated with arrests and hospitalisations, do add enormously to traffic congestion and stress on services (e.g. spillage of raw sewage on residents' lawns) during event periods (Gibson & Connell 2003).

The Byron Bay status quo of continuing visitor increases, inadequate physical development to cope with these increases, rampant property inflation, increasingly alienated local residents and hyper-stressful periods associated with formal and informal events, does not appear to be tenable over the long term, and recent and potential developments associated with the future of the tourism sector should be evaluated with this in mind. Paramount among these developments are the recent completion of a motorway from the Gold Coast (which may well serve to increase excursionist tourism even more and tie Byron Bay into the sprawling conurbation of that tourism city) and the lifting of the development moratorium following improvements to the town's sewage treatment capacity. Another issue is the re-emergence of resort plans for the Club Med site, which was acquired in 2001 by a Melbourne property developer, who is proposing to build a complex of low-density holiday homes under the name North Beach Byron. As of mid-2005, activist community groups such as BEACON were successful in opposing this proposal, despite claims from the developer that it will exemplify best practice in environmental design (North Beach Byron 2005).

Questions

1 Write a 1000-word report in which you
   (a) describe how much Byron Bay has conformed to the destination life-cycle as modelled in the Butler sequence, and
   (b) outline the reasons for these deviations.

2 In a 1000-word report,
   (a) construct a vision of what Byron Bay should ideally look like in 2020 in terms of the variables outlined in table 10.1, and
   (b) describe the factors that are likely to obstruct this vision or make it happen.

11
Sustainable
tourism

LEARNING OBJECTIVES

After studying this chapter, you should be able to:

1 explain the concept of a 'paradigm shift' and its relevance to contemporary society

2 indicate how the problems of contemporary mass tourism discussed in chapters 8 to 10 are related to the dominant Western environmental paradigm

3 define sustainable tourism and show how this is related to the emergence of the green paradigm and the concept of sustainable development

4 identify key indicators that can be used to gauge sustainability, and list their shortcomings

5 list the reasons for the tourism industry's adoption of sustainable tourism, and explain the advantages that larger companies have in its implementation

6 describe the sustainable tourism measures taken by the tourist industry

7 define and list the major types of alternative tourism, and discuss their potential advantages and disadvantages

8 appreciate how ecotourism differs from other nature-based tourism activities such as 3S and adventure tourism, and describe its characteristics

9 discuss the positive and negative arguments for encouraging tourism within protected areas

10 outline and explain the broad context model of destination development scenarios as a framework for describing the range of evolutionary possibilities for tourist destinations.

As manifested in the Butler sequence, the destination lifecycle concept suggests that tourism degrades destinations and ultimately destroys itself if managers implement no remedial or precautionary measures during the development of the sector. The desire to avoid these negative impacts and still derive positive economic, sociocultural and environmental impacts from tourism has given rise to the concept of sustainable tourism, or tourism that occurs within the accepted carrying capacities of a particular destination. This chapter on sustainable tourism begins by examining the nature of paradigms and paradigm shifts, and considers the possibility that the dominant scientific paradigm and its associated environmental perspective are in the process of being modified or replaced by a more environmentally sensitive 'green paradigm' that emphasises the concept of 'sustainable development' (section 11.2). This provides a context for understanding the emergence of 'sustainable tourism', as discussed in section 11.3. After outlining potential key indicators of sustainable tourism and the shortcomings of indicator monitoring, we examine sustainability in the context of mass tourism in section 11.4. The reasons for the tourism industry's interest in sustainability are considered, along with associated practices and measures. A critique of these developments is also provided. Section 11.5 focuses on 'alternative tourism' and its various manifestations, as well as the problems that potentially accompany this small-scale counterpoint to mass tourism. Section 11.6 examines ecotourism, while section 11.7 considers strategies that potentially improve the sustainability of destinations. It concludes with a broad context model of destination development scenarios that integrates these concepts and incorporates the Butler sequence.

11.2 *A* PARADIGM SHIFT? ······································

Defined in its broadest sense, a **paradigm** is the entire constellation of beliefs, assumptions and values that underlie the way in which a society interprets reality at a given point in time. A paradigm can therefore also be described as a 'worldview' or 'cosmology'. According to Kuhn (1962), a **paradigm shift** is likely to occur when the prevailing paradigm is faced with contradictions and anomalies in the real world that it cannot explain or accommodate. In response to this crisis, one or more alternative paradigms appear that seemingly account for these contradictions and anomalies, and one of these gradually emerges as the new dominant paradigm for that society. The period from when the contradictions are first apparent to the replacement of the old paradigm with the competing paradigm can last for many decades, or even centuries. It is also important to note that the replacement of one dominant paradigm by another does not usually involve the complete destruction or disappearence of the formerly dominant paradigm. Rather, the latter can persist as a co-existent worldview retained by some groups or individuals. As well, the new dominant paradigm often incorporates compatible (or at least non-contradictory) aspects of the old paradigm, and may even emerge as a synthesis between the old paradigm and other radically opposing worldviews that initially arise.

■ 11.2.1 Dominant *Western environmental paradigm*

Such a paradigm shift occurred in Europe during the fifteenth and sixteenth centuries. During this time, the Catholic Church was dominant, and its theological worldview held that the world was a flat planet located in the centre of the universe, and that humans were created spontaneously in the image of God. This theological paradigm, however, was challenged by the findings of Christopher Columbus and other explorers, and by the discoveries of scientists such as Copernicus and Galileo. Gradually, the theological paradigm was replaced by a **scientific paradigm** that offered coherent and logical explanations for the radical new evidence uncovered by these pioneers. Fundamentally, the scientific paradigm perceives the universe as a 'giant machine', not unlike an automobile, that can be 'disassembled' in order to see how it operates. Once these subcomponents and their functions are perfectly understood, then future events within the universe can be predicted with certainty. Underlying the scientific paradigm is the 'scientific method', which reveals knowledge through a rigorously objective procedure of hypothesis formulation and empirical testing (see chapter 12).

By the nineteenth century, science was established as the dominant paradigm within Europe, and then within the world as a whole through the colonial expansion of England, France, Spain and other major European powers. Accompanying the scientific paradigm was growth in the anthropocentric belief that humans are the centre of all things and are apart from and superior to the natural environment. The latter in this perspective is seen as having no intrinsic value, but only extrinsic value in relation to its perceived usefulness for people. Thus, some types of woodland such as conifer plantations came to be valued because of their usefulness as a fuel and source of timber, while swamps were assigned little or no value, as they are perceived to be economically unproductive.

Related to this is the belief in 'progress', or the idea that the application of science and technology will result in a continuous improvement in the quality of human life. Ideologically, the parallel view that progress can best be attained through a growth-oriented capitalist economic system became widely accepted in countries such as the United Kingdom and the United States. This perspective emphasises the role of individual incentive and competitive free market forces that determine the value (defined in terms of contribution to GDP) of various elements of the natural environment, such as oil (high) and swampland (low). These natural environment-related aspects of the scientific paradigm are described by Knill (1991) as comprising the **dominant Western environmental paradigm**.

■ 11.2.2 **Contradictions** *in the dominant Western environmental paradigm*

During the twentieth century, and especially since 1950, the dominant Western environmental paradigm (and the scientific paradigm more broadly) experienced a crisis similar to what the Catholic Church underwent in the sixteenth century, with many anomalies and contradictions being identified that challenge its fundamental assumptions about progress and nature. Ironically, many of these inconsistencies were revealed by science itself. For example, the field of physics demonstrated the apparently random and chaotic behaviour of subatomic particles, and revealed that the very act of observation can change the nature of these particles (Faulkner & Russell 1997). Such findings call into doubt the universal applicability of the objective, mechanistic, deterministic worldview proffered by the dominant Western environmental paradigm and science more generally.

At the same time, research in biology, geography and ecology shows that present levels of economic development and growth, deriving from notions of progress and dominance over nature, may be inconsistent with the world's environmental carrying capacity. Processes and events that support this contention include:

- a series of high-profile environmental disasters, including the *Torrey Canyon* oil tanker spill off the coast of the United Kingdom in 1967, the part meltdown of the Three Mile Island nuclear power plant in the United States in 1979, the gas leak from the Union Carbide pesticide plant in Bhopal, India, in 1984, the nuclear power plant meltdown at Chernobyl, Ukraine, in 1986 and the *Exxon Valdez* oil tanker spill off Alaska in 1989, and Hurricane Katrina's impact on New Orleans in 2005
- escalation in anthropogenic (human-induced) climate change
- accelerating ozone depletion, especially in polar regions
- increased incidence of dangerous viral and bacterial mutations
- rampant desertification and deforestation.

Some supporters of the dominant Western environmental paradigm, described as 'technological utopians', argue that technology will solve all these problems. Critics, however, point out that many of the problems are themselves caused by the same modern technologies (such as nuclear power and genetic manipulation) that claim to address other problems, such as depleted fossil fuels and increased population growth. Critics also suggest that the damage to the environment may soon progress to a point of irreversibility, if this is not already the case.

The dominant Western environmental paradigm and tourism

The tourism sector has also been implicated in these developments. The criticisms of contemporary mass tourism raised in chapters 8 and 9, and the cautionary platform that articulated these criticisms, are reactions against a prevalent pattern of large-scale tourism development that is an outcome of the dominant Western environmental paradigm. As encapsulated in the Butler sequence (section 10.2), this critique holds that the emphasis on unlimited free-market growth produces the contradiction of initially desirable tourist destinations that eventually self-destruct as they become overcrowded, polluted and crime-ridden, and hence increasingly less desirable to both tourists and residents.

■ 11.2.3 **Towards** *a green paradigm?*

Criticism of the dominant Western environmental paradigm was made long before the present century — for example, in the writings of the American author Henry David Thoreau and the English author and social critic Charles Dickens. However, these were individual and isolated voices that initially did little to challenge the dominant paradigm and its damaging environmental or social impacts, especially since these problems were offset by demonstrable improvements in the physical wellbeing of societies undergoing the Industrial Revolution (see page 71). Since World War II the critique has gained momentum, and has been popularised through a sequence of high-profile publications that have influenced the post–World War II environmental movement (figure 11.1). Challenges to the dominant Western environmental paradigm are also evident in allied perspectives such as contemporary feminism and the global reassertion of the rights of indigenous people, as well as through interest in the New Age movement.

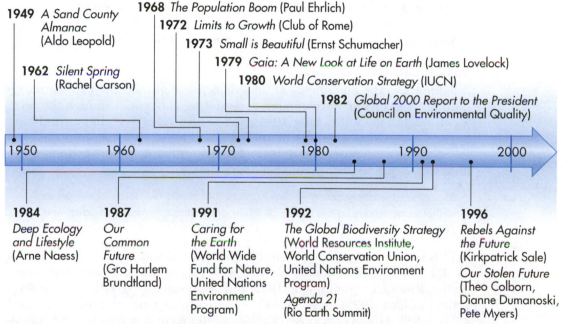

1949 *A Sand County Almanac* (Aldo Leopold)

1962 *Silent Spring* (Rachel Carson)

1968 *The Population Boom* (Paul Ehrlich)

1972 *Limits to Growth* (Club of Rome)

1973 *Small is Beautiful* (Ernst Schumacher)

1979 *Gaia: A New Look at Life on Earth* (James Lovelock)

1980 *World Conservation Strategy* (IUCN)

1982 *Global 2000 Report to the President* (Council on Environmental Quality)

1984 *Deep Ecology and Lifestyle* (Arne Naess)

1987 *Our Common Future* (Gro Harlem Brundtland)

1991 *Caring for the Earth* (World Wide Fund for Nature, United Nations Environment Program)

1992 *The Global Biodiversity Strategy* (World Resources Institute, World Conservation Union, United Nations Environment Program) *Agenda 21* (Rio Earth Summit)

1996 *Rebels Against the Future* (Kirkpatrick Sale) *Our Stolen Future* (Theo Colborn, Dianne Dumanoski, Pete Myers)

■ **Figure 11.1** *Milestone publications in the modern environmental movement*

The growing crisis in the dominant Western environmental paradigm is, therefore, resulting in the articulation of a competing worldview that can be described as the **green paradigm** (Knill 1991). It is premature to claim in any definitive way that our society is now in the midst of a paradigm shift, but evidence of such a transition is mounting across a growing array of sectors, including tourism (see below). Figure 11.2 depicts the contrasting characteristics that are associated with the dominant Western environmental paradigm and the emerging green paradigm. Both are depicted as ideal types (see page 324), and it should be reiterated that any dominant paradigm of the future is likely to emerge as a synthesis of these contrasting characteristics.

■ **Figure 11.2**
The dominant Western environmental paradigm and the green paradigm as ideal types

Dominant Western environmental paradigm	Green paradigm
Humans are **separate from nature**	Humans are **part of nature**
Humans are **superior to nature**	Humans are **equal with the rest of nature**
Reality is **objective**	Reality is **subjective**
Reality can be **compartmentalised**	Reality is **integrated** and **holistic**
The future is **predictable**	The future is **unpredictable**
The universe has **order**	The universe is **chaotic**
The importance of **rationality** and **reason**	The importance of **intuition**
Hierarchical structures	**Consensus-based** structures
Competitive structures	**Cooperative** structures
Emphasis on the **individual**	Emphasis on the **communal**
Facilitation through **capitalism**	Facilitation through **socialism**
Linear **progress** and **growth**	Maintenance of a **steady state**
Use of **hard technology**	Use of **soft technology**
Patriarchal and **male**	**Matriarchal** and **female**

Sustainable development

A hallmark in the emergence of the green paradigm was the explicit recognition of **sustainable development** as a guiding concept. Although the term was introduced in the early 1980s, it was the release of the Brundtland Report (*Our Common Future*) in 1987 that launched this idea into the forefront of the environmental debate. The Brundtland Report proposed the following definition of sustainable development:

> ■ Sustainable development is development that meets the needs of the present without compromising the ability of future generations to meet their own needs (WCED 1987, p. 43). ■

This simple and enticing definition has gained widespread support from all sides of the environmental debate, and was employed as a central theme in the Rio Earth Summit of 1992 and its resultant *Agenda 21* manifesto (Miller & Kaae 1993) as well as in the sequel Johannesburg Summit of 2002 ('Rio + 10'). However, a closer scrutiny of the term reveals a number of difficulties. Some critics suggest that the term is an oxymoron, or an 'essentially contested concept' (Hall 1998, p. 13) with 'sustainability' (with its steady state implications) and 'development' (with its growth implications) being mutually exclusive. The widespread support that the term enjoys, therefore, may simply reflect the ease with which it can be appropriated by the supporters of various ideologies or platforms to perpetuate and legitimise their own perspective (McKercher 1993). A resultant danger, according to Mowforth and Munt (1998) and others, is that the term can be used for **greenwashing** purposes; that is, to convey an impression of environmental responsibility for a product or business that does not deserve the reputation for it.

Others, however, regard the semantic flexibility of sustainable development as an asset that recognises and is responsive to the complexity and diversity of the real world. Hunter (1997), for example, describes sustainable development as an adaptive paradigm that accommodates both weak and strong manifestations. **Weak sustainable development** strategies are relevant to heavily modified environments (e.g. urban cores, intensively farmed areas), where human quality of life is a more realistic and relevant goal than, say, preserving rare species and their undisturbed habitats. In contrast to this anthropocentric approach, **strong sustainable development** strategies that emphasise biocentric goals such as the latter *are* warranted in relatively undisturbed environments such as Antarctica and most of the Amazon basin.

11.3 SUSTAINABLE TOURISM

The term **sustainable tourism** became popular following the release of the Brundtland Report. The term at its most basic represents a direct application of the sustainable development concept. Sustainable tourism, in this context, is tourism that meets the needs of present generations without compromising the ability of future generations to meet their own needs. More commonly, sustainable tourism is regarded as tourism managed in such a way that it does not exceed the environmental, social, cultural or economic carrying capacity of a given destination. Weaver (2006) adds the caveat that even responsible operators may inadvertently operate on occasion in an unsustainable way, in which case the litmus test for a sustainable tourism operator is the willingness to redress the problem as soon as it is made apparent. Weaver also suggests that the definition should incorporate the need for operators to be *financially* sustainable, since tourism that is not financially viable is not likely to survive for long, no matter how viable it is from an environmental or sociocultural perspective. As with sustainable development, the term 'sustainable tourism' is susceptible to appropriation by those pursuing a particular political agenda (see section 11.3.5), but is also amenable to weak and strong interpretations that adapt to different kinds of destinations.

■ 11.3.1 Indicators

Whether perceived from a weak or strong perspective, criteria must be selected and monitored to determine whether sustainable tourism is present in a destination or not. The first step is to identify a set of appropriate **indicators**, or variables that provide information about the status of some phenomenon (in this case, sustainability), so that tourism and affiliated sectors can be managed accordingly (Hamilton & Attwater 1997). Since the early 1990s, the World Tourism Organization (WTO) has played a lead role in identifying and 'road testing' tourism-related indicators, recommending a basic management framework of 11 practical core indicators that is deemed relevant to any destination (see table 11.1). In addition, it has identified a variety of supplementary specialised indicators that can be added to the management frameworks of relevant destinations such as beach resorts (levels of beach erosion and beach use intensity [persons per metre of accessible beach]) and managed wildlife parks (human population in park and surrounding area, amount of poaching activity) (WTO 1996).

■ **Table 11.1**
WTO core indicators of sustainable tourism

INDICATOR	SPECIFIC MEASURES
1. Site protection	Category of site protection according to IUCN index
2. Stress	Tourist numbers visiting site (per annum/peak month)
3. Use intensity	Intensity of use in peak period (persons per hectare)
4. Social impact	Ratio of tourists to locals (peak period and over time)
5. Development control	Existence of environmental review procedure or formal controls over development of site and use densities
6. Waste management	Percentage of sewage from site receiving treatment (also structural limits of other infrastructural capacity on site, such as water supply)
7. Planning process	Existence of organised regional plan for tourist destination region
8. Critical ecosystems	Number of rare or endangered species
9. Consumer satisfaction	Level of satisfaction by visitors (questionnaire based)
10. Local satisfaction	Level of satisfaction by visitors (questionnaire based)
11. Tourism contribution to local economy	Proportion of total economic activity generated by tourism only

Source: *WTO (1996)*

Challenges of indicators

Even if it is assumed that the WTO framework provides an indicator selection that adequately reflects the diversity of variables that need to be considered by destination managers, several operational challenges must still be confronted, including:

• Fuzzy boundaries of complex tourism systems, which makes it difficult to determine how much a change in an indicator is related to tourism directly (e.g. construction of a resort), indirectly (e.g. construction of a road to a resort) or in an induced way (e.g. construction of housing for workers in the resort), if at all (see chapter 9). Complex systems also produce the possibility of discontinuities between cause and effect through both time and space. For example, a negative impact in a destination (e.g. *E. coli* appearing in the water) may be caused by unsustainable tourism activity that occurred one month earlier 50 kilometres upstream.

- Incompatibility between the timeframe of indicator monitoring, which is long term, and the timelines of the political process that supports monitoring, which is short term and unpredictable. Budgetary fluctuations and the election of new political parties, accordingly, can result in changes to monitoring methodologies, the indicators monitored and so on, thereby complicating the long-term tracking of patterns.
- Nonlinear relationships between cause and effect, so that a given input into a system does not necessarily result in a given output that can be reliably extrapolated into the future. This is illustrated by the **avalanche effect**, in which a small input that caused no apparent problems in the past (e.g. a snowflake), acts unpredictably as a catalyst or trigger for massive change in the system (e.g. an avalanche).
- Lack of knowledge about the **benchmark** and **threshold** values that indicate sustainability for a particular destination. A benchmark is a value against which the performance of an indicator can be assessed (e.g. it may be determined in a particular ecosystem that at least 50 per cent of the area should be occupied by relatively undisturbed habitat for that ecosystem to remain viable). The benchmark may be the same as a threshold, which is a critical value or value range beyond which the carrying capacity is being exceeded (e.g. if tourist density exceeds 1.7 persons per metre for more than one hour at a particular beach).
- Potential incompatibility between environmental and social or cultural sustainability. For example, the creation of a new high-order protected area geared towards ecotourism might result in a more sustainable outcome for WTO variable #1 (site protection) but unsustainable outcomes for variable #10 (local satisfaction) as local residents express their anger over being displaced from their traditional tribal lands and hunting grounds to accommodate tourists. This raises the possibility of mixed assessments in indicator performance (e.g. five indicate sustainability and five do not), making it difficult to make an overall assessment of the sustainability of tourism in that destination.

Because of the uncertainties and complexities associated with indicators, it is perhaps impossible to determine with complete certainty whether a destination is sustainable, as Weaver (2006) suggests. More prudent is to assess that an apparently successful destination *appears* to be sustainable in so far as it conforms to best practice knowledge. In any case, the effort of pursuing and assessing sustainability is clearly worthwhile, since to abandon the effort is to virtually guarantee an unsustainable outcome.

11.4 SUSTAINABILITY AND MASS TOURISM

Although much of the early attention to sustainable tourism was focused on small-scale and low-intensity situations (see section 11.5), its relevance to mass tourism is arguably more important, since the latter accounts for most global tourism activity. The following discussion considers why the mass tourism industry should be interested in sustainability, and outlines practices and measures that reflect apparent adherence to sustainable tourism.

■ 11.4.1 Reasons *for adoption*

Several factors justify the adoption of sustainable practices within the mainstream tourism industry in addition to the availability of a compatible weak approach to sustainability (see above). These include:
- ethical considerations
- the growth of the 'new traveller' market
- the profitability of sustainability
- the suitability of larger corporations to adopt sustainable practices.

Ethical considerations

One school of thought is that corporations need to pursue sustainability because ethical behaviour is what society expects from entities that exercise such great power over the environment and culture, even if such expectations are not enshrined in the law (Walle 1995). For some executives and managers, this may be motivated by religious fiat (e.g. the Golden Rule), while for others it may reflect an attitude of enlightened self-interest; that is, a belief that a failure to behave ethically will at some point result in a negative public image or consumer boycotts.

Growth of the green consumer market

As a consequence of the growing environmental movement, consumers are gradually becoming more discerning, sophisticated and responsible when it comes to purchasing decisions and behaviour, including travel (Roberts 1996). In Phase Four societies such as Australia, the United States and the United Kingdom, various surveys suggest that approximately one-quarter of consumers can be described as 'true' green consumers, meaning that environmental considerations continuously influence their purchasing behaviour (Weaver 2006). For example, they are more or less willing to pay extra for 'environmentally friendly' food and cars and believe that government should spend more on social and environmental issues. A larger group, consisting of about one-half of the population, are marginal or 'veneer' green consumers, who are concerned about the issues but tend to purchase appropriate goods and services only if they are competitive with their 'nongreen' counterparts. However, many will temporarily or permanently convert to 'true' green behaviour once convinced that an environmental crisis is at hand. Business ignores this diverse phenomenon of **green consumerism** at its peril, particularly since these attitudes and behaviour within society were virtually indiscernible before the emergence of the environmental movement after World War II, a fact that lends credence to the theory of a contemporary paradigm shift (see section 11.2.3). One financial indication of this shift is the growth in socially responsible investment (SRI) portfolios, whose assets increased in value from about US$40 billion in 1984 to US$2.16 trillion in 2003, or about 12 per cent of all professionally managed funds (Social Investment Forum 2003).

Poon (1993) argues that green consumerism is evident within tourism in the emergence of the **new traveller** segment (see figure 11.3) and there is empirical evidence to back this contention. A survey of 489 air travellers in the United States, for example, showed that 70 per cent were more likely to patronise a hotel with a good environmental record, while more than 90 per cent agreed that hotels should offer energy-efficient lighting (Webster 2000). Sixty-two per cent of Australian consumers, in a survey conducted in the late 1990s, indicated a willingness to pay a 10 per cent premium for environmentally quality-assured tourism products (Horneman, Beeton & Huie 1997). More recently, green consumerism in conventional tourism was evident in the high-profile debate that followed the 2004 tsunami, which considered whether it was appropriate for tourists to visit the devastated Thai resort of Phuket in the months immediately after the disaster (see Contemporary issue: To visit or not in the wake of a disaster).

■ **Figure 11.3**
Characteristics of the new traveller

The new traveller

Green consumer
Sensitive to local cultures
Conscious of social justice concerns
More independent-minded and discerning
Knowledgeable about environmental issues
Prefers flexible and spontaneous itineraries
Carefully assesses tourism products in advance
Searches for authentic and meaningful experiences
Wishes to have a positive impact on the destination
Motivated by a desire for self-fulfilment and learning
Searches for physically and mentally challenging experiences

CONTEMPORARY ISSUE

To visit or not in the wake of a disaster

The Indian Ocean tsunami of 26 December 2004, with its estimated 200 000 fatalities and widespread coastline destruction, will be remembered as one of the great natural catastrophes of our era. With 5000 or more tourists included in that statistic, the tsunami also rates as the greatest natural disaster that has affected the tourism industry. In the wake of the devastation, it is not surprising that most tourists elected to stay away from seriously affected destinations, such as Phuket (Thailand). Yet by doing so, are they contributing to or hindering the re-establishment of a sustainable tourism sector? The argument for staying away is partly practical (i.e. damaged facilities, attractions and infrastructure), partly ethical (i.e. the insensitivity of having pleasure tourists in the area so soon after the disaster and the need to focus resources first on the recovery of villages and agriculture) and partly psychological (i.e fears of another tsunami and guilt). Accordingly, the premature return of tourists could breed resentment among local residents and give the tourism sector a bad reputation.

(continued)

The counterargument, apparently supported by most residents and tourism stakeholders in the region, is that the quick return of the tourists is the most effective way of recovering from the tsunami (Leinwand 2005). They point out that damage to most of the tourism facilities was superficial and that more visitors would mean the creation of much needed local jobs as well as a reduced probability of hotels and other tourist-dependent businesses having to shut permanently because of insufficient clientele. The perception that the situation is returning to normal is also an important psychological consideration for traumatised local residents and hesitant tourist markets. For all these reasons, it is understandable that tourism authorities and operators in the region actively sought to encourage visitors soon after the disaster. Describing the absence of tourists as the 'second wave' of the tsunami, authorities in the region banked on media tours, greatly discounted prices and 'welcome campaigns' to attract visitors, many of whom did return. One aspect that may have been overlooked, however, is the importance of providing potential tourist markets with post-disaster behavioural education, so that returning tourists behave in a sensitive and appropriate manner conducive to the achievement of a socially sustainable tourism sector. To this effect, more efforts could also have been made to encourage tourists and foreign-owned tourism businesses to actively and visibly participate in recovery efforts through donations and volunteering.

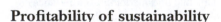

Profitability of sustainability

The inherent profitability of many related activities is a major incentive for conventional businesses to become more involved in sustainability (Rowe 1998). Reduced energy consumption, for example, is a tangible long-term direct cost saving, as is the recycling of certain kinds of materials. Webster (2000) describes a recycling program of Sheraton Hotels that saved US $7000 per month from the sale of plastic and reduced dumping fees. Indirect profits are realised through the introduction of streamlined, non-hierarchical organisational structures, and through the improved employee morale that often accompanies such 'green' reforms. In addition, the fostering of positive community relations may create a friendly tourist–host rapport that enhances the quality of the vacation experience for tourists, and hence encourages repeat visitation and positive word-of-mouth publicity.

Suitability of larger corporations to adopt sustainable practices

Larger corporations are better positioned in many ways than their small-scale counterparts to implement and profit from sustainable tourism measures (McKercher 2001), as demonstrated by the Sheraton example described above. Economies of scale allow big businesses to allocate resources to fund specialised job positions that address sustainability-related issues (e.g. environmental officer, community relations officer), as well as relevant staff training, public education programs and comprehensive environmental audits. Cost-effective recycling and reduction programs are feasible because of the high levels of resource and energy consumption, while vertical and horizontal integration (see section 5.4) allow a company so structured to coordinate its sustainability efforts across a broad array of backward and forward linkages. Because of the volume of business they generate, these companies can also exert pressure on external suppliers to 'go green'. An example is the UK hotel chain Forte, which saved $75 000 in one year just by negotiating a reduction in the packaging of sugar sachets (Webster 2000).

■ 11.4.2 Practices

In a review of sustainability-related practices within the conventional tourism industry, Weaver (2006) finds that:

- Formal institutional mechanisms have been initiated in most sectors to stimulate and facilitate the collective pursuit of sustainable tourism. These include the Cruise Industry Waste Management Practices and Procedures (CIWMPP) program, the International Hotels Environment Initiative (IHEI) and the Tour Operators Initiative (TOI) for Sustainable Tourism Development. Most sectors have also now introduced sustainability-related codes of practice (see section 11.4.3).
- Each sector is led by a small number of high-profile innovative leaders. These include British Airways and American Airlines among air carriers, Marriott, Starwood and Grecotel among accommodation providers, and TUI among outbound tour operators.
- Sustainability measures adopted by these leaders and other companies focus on activities that increase profits and lower costs (e.g. high-volume recycling of glass and aluminium, energy use reduction, cogeneration), encourage brand visibility (sponsor tourism awards such as the British Airways Tourism for Tomorrow Awards) and are not expensive to implement (e.g. provide informational brochures and signage). High-level quality control mechanisms have not yet been widely adopted (see section 11.4.3).
- A high level of unawareness and noninvolvement remains within each sector beyond the high-profile activities of sector leaders.

Weaver (2006) speculates that while significant and demonstrable progress has been achieved in the conventional tourism industry over the late 1980s, this progress is uneven and indicates a 'veneer' pattern of sustainability that responds to and parallels the dominance of veneer green consumerism within society. The lack of a 'deep' commitment, which could for example be expressed in a voluntary decision by industry to declare a moratorium on tourism development in some destinations, is not evident mainly because there is not yet widespread public agitation for such a radically biocentric policy shift. The institutional and leadership foundation for a deeper level of involvement, however, has been established and this could evolve as conventional fossil fuel price increases and technology advances make a wider range of sustainability practices more profitable and practical (see Technology and tourism: State-of-the-art sustainability at the Orchid Hotel, Mumbai).

The ECOTEL-certified Orchid Hotel, a five-star facility in the heart of India's commercial capital of Mumbai, illustrates the soft and hard technological innovations that are available to the contemporary hotel wishing to improve its environmental sustainability (Orchid Hotel 2005). Construction innovations include the use of autoclaved aerated concrete, made with 60 per cent fly ash, as an environmentally friendly substitute for brick in external walling, having superior thermal insulation properties. External paint is a water-based variety with negligible volatile organic compound content of 0.0125 per cent. Internal wall partitions use QED ('Quite Easily Done') panels made from fertiliser waste, which can be easily removed and reused, while other interior works use medium-density fibre wood made from otherwise useless cotton stalks. Triple-glazed windows consisting of a hermetically sealed double-glazed unit and added reflective glass prevent the heat and ultraviolet rays of the sun from entering rooms and improves the longevity of furniture and carpets by preventing fading.

Energy-conserving technologies permeate every guestroom. The master control panel, for example, features a 'green button', which allows the guest to raise the air-conditioning thermostat by two degrees Celsius over a two-hour period. Room lights (using compact fluorescent instead of incandescent bulbs) and air-conditioning are activated only when the guest's key card is inserted, and CFC-free mini bars save up to 40 per cent in energy use by using 'fuzzy logic' software that senses the load inside and adjusts their thermostats accordingly. Unit air-conditioners use eco-friendly R22 refrigerants instead of CFCs, which has reduced the hotel's contribution to stratospheric ozone depletion by 99.55 per cent. Heat generated by these air-conditioners, moreover, is diverted through a cogeneration system to provide hot water to guestrooms, the laundry room and the kitchen. Efforts to achieve 'zero garbage' generation through the hotel include an experimental vermiculture project consisting of nine bins in which organic kitchen wastes are decomposed by worms. Another example of 'low' or 'soft' tech innovation is the use of a herbal paste to eradicate cockroaches. Unlike conventional treatments, this substance includes no poisonous chemicals, requires no followup cleaning and can be applied anywhere (Orchid Hotel 2005).

■ 11.4.3 Quality *control*

A critical issue in the pursuit of sustainable tourism is the conveyance of assurance, through **quality control mechanisms**, that a particular hotel, ski resort, tour operator or carrier is as environmentally or socially sustainable as it claims to be. **Codes of practice** and **ecolabels** are two of the main quality control mechanisms that attempt to provide this assurance in the tourism industry.

Codes of practice

The adoption of 'green' codes of practice is one of the most widespread and visible sustainability initiatives undertaken by the tourism industry. Among examples are the:

- Code of Ethics and Guidelines for Sustainable Tourism (Tourism Industry Association of Canada)
- Environmental Codes of Conduct for Tourism (United Nations Environment Program)
- Sustainable Tourism Principles (Worldwide Fund for Nature and Tourism Concern)
- APEC/PATA Code for Sustainable Tourism.
- Code of Ethics (Belize Ecotourism Association — BETA)
- Environmental Charter for Ski Areas (National Ski Areas Association)

The APEC/PATA code (figure 11.4) is representative in terms of content. Members are urged to adopt measures related to environmental and social sustainability, many of which relate to the sustainability indicators provided in table 11.1. While acceptance of the code is supposed to indicate that the member is committed to achieving sustainable outcomes (Ryan 2002b), the voluntary nature of the commitment has been much criticised. These codes of practice have also been criticised because of the vague and general nature of the clauses (which allegedly makes them hard to put into operation and too open to interpretation), the lack of timelines for attaining compliance and them almost all being based on the principle of self-regulation.

However, there are several arguments in favour of codes. First, the membership of organisations such as PATA (Pacific Asia Travel Association) and APEC (Asia Pacific Economic Cooperation) are too diverse to accommodate detailed objectives and relevant indicators within a single code. The codes provide the generic principles that everyone can agree with, and each type of member can then be referred to relevant best practice parameters as defined by a monitoring or other organisation. In this respect, second, Bendell and Font (2004) regard codes of practice as a low-cost and low-risk gateway for moving towards higher forms of quality control. Third, the codes are a powerful form of moral suasion in that uncomfortable questions and scrutiny may be directed at members who do not consciously pursue sustainability, given that members are assumed to have made such a commitment. Fourth, private corporations in particular (i.e. most of the tourism industry) are more likely to cooperate with sustainability initiatives if they are not threatened or forced to accept obligatory objectives and deadlines. Finally, the self-regulation that is implicit or explicit in these codes is based on the premise that voluntary adherence to good practice within the industry itself will pre-empt governments from imposing their own regulations. Businesses, as a result, will be able to maintain greater control over their own operations if they show themselves to be good 'corporate citizens'.

APEC/PATA CODE FOR SUSTAINABLE TOURISM

This code urges PATA Association and Chapter members and APEC Member Economies to:

Conserve the natural environment, ecosystems and biodiversity

- **CONTRIBUTE** to the conservation of any habitat of flora and fauna, affected by tourism
- **ENCOURAGE** relevant authorities to identify areas worthy of conservation and to determine the level of development, if any, which would be compatible in or adjacent to those areas
- **INCLUDE** enhancement and corrective actions at tourism sites to conserve wildlife and natural ecosystems.

Respect and support local traditions, cultures and communities

- **ENSURE** that community attitudes, local customs and cultural values, and the role of women and children, are understood in the planning and implementation of all our tourism related projects
- **PROVIDE** opportunities for the wider community to take part in discussions on tourism planning issues where these affect the tourism industry and the community
- **ENCOURAGE** relevant authorities to identify cultural heritage worthy of conservation and to determine the level of development if any which would be compatible in or adjacent to those areas
- **CONTRIBUTE** to the identity and pride of local communities through providing quality tourism products and services sensitive to those communities.

Maintain environmental management systems

- **ENSURE** that environmental assessment is an integral step in planning for a tourism project
- **ENCOURAGE** regular environmental audits of practices throughout the tourism industry and to promote desireable changes to those practices
- **ESTABLISH** detailed environmental policies and indicators, and/or guidelines for the various sectors of the tourism industry
- **INCORPORATE** environmentally sensitive design and construction solutions in any building or landscaping for tourism purposes.

Conserve and reduce energy, waste and pollutants

- **FOSTER** environmentally responsible practices for:
  - reducing pollutants and greenhouse gases
  - conserving water and protecting water quality
  - managing efficiently waste and energy
  - controlling the noise levels and
  - promoting the use of recyclable and biodegradable materials.

Encourage a tourism commitment to environment and cultures

- **ENCOURAGE** those involved in tourism to comply with local, regional and national planning policies and to participate in the planning process
- **FOSTER,** in both management and staff of all tourism projects and activities, an awareness of environmental and cultural values
- **ENCOURAGE** all those who provide services to tourism enterprises to participate through environmentally and socially responsible actions
- **SUPPORT** environmental and cultural awareness through tourism marketing.

Educate and inform others about local environments and cultures

- **SUPPORT** the inclusion of environmental and cultural values in tourism education, training and planning
- **ENHANCE** the appreciation and understanding by tourists of natural environments and cultural sensitivities through the provision of accurate information and appropriate interpretation
- **ENCOURAGE** and support research on the environmental and cultural impacts of tourism.

Cooperate with others to sustain environments and cultures

- **COOPERATE** with other individuals and organisations to advance environmental improvements and sustainable development practices, including establishing indicators and monitoring
- **COMPLY** with all international conventions and national, state and local laws which safeguard natural environments and cultural sensitivities.

Source: PATA

Ecolabels

Font (2001, p. 3) defines ecolabels as 'methods [that] standardize the promotion of environmental claims by following compliance to set criteria, generally based on third party, impartial verification, usually by governments or non-profit organizations'. As such, they are considered a stronger quality control mechanism than codes of practice. Ecolabels are focused on the interrelated concepts of **certification** and **accreditation**. The former involves an independent expert third party (i.e. other than the applicant or the governing ecolabel body), which investigates and confirms for an ecolabel body whether an applicant complies with that body's specified sustainability standards or indicators. If so, then the ecolabel will formally certify the applicant. The latter is a process in which an overarching organisation evaluates the ecolabel itself and confers accreditation if it is assessed as being sufficiently rigorous and credible. In essence, the accrediting body certifies the ecolabel (Buckley 2002).

Most of the approximately 100 tourism-related ecolabels are focused on a particular product or region (e.g. the Blue Flag ecolabel certifies European beaches). Green Globe 21 (www.greenglobe21.com) is an exception because it encompasses all tourism products and all regions, and in doing so is attempting to position itself as the world's primary tourism ecolabel. Central to the Green Globe 21 system is a graded membership structure in which members progress from low-risk, low-effort Affiliate to Benchmarked and then Certified status. The latter entails full third-party certification based on performing above the baseline level of an array of relevant indicators. As of mid-2005, only about 500 tourism products worldwide were participating in the scheme and only a small proportion of these had attained Certified status. The problem for Green Globe 21 is that companies are reluctant to join until it achieves greater visibility among consumers but this is unlikely to occur without a higher level of participation from industry in the first place. This may also indicate that the level of green consumerism within the conventional tourist market is not yet as developed as it is in the marketplace more generally.

11.5 SUSTAINABILITY AND SMALL-SCALE TOURISM

As suggested, much attention in the sustainable tourism literature, perhaps inordinately, has been devoted to small-scale tourism projects and destinations, on the assumption that such tourism is more likely to have positive environmental, economic and sociocultural impacts within a destination. As discussed in the following, the theoretical case for this assumption is sound, and there are indeed many examples of small-scale sustainable tourism. However, it should never be automatically assumed that the outcomes of small-scale tourism are always positive.

11.5.1 Alternative *tourism*

The cautionary platform identified the problems associated with mass tourism, but did not articulate more appropriate options in response. Alternative options appeared in the early 1980s in association with the adaptancy platform (see chapter 1). This new perspective held that large-scale tourism was problematic, and that small-scale alternatives were therefore inherently more desirable in most cases. The associated options, combined under the umbrella term of **alternative tourism**, were thus primarily conceived as alternatives to large-scale or mass tourism specifically, rather than other types of tourism.

Figure 11.5 depicts mass tourism and alternative tourism as contrasting ideal types. These came to be widely perceived as models of 'bad' and 'good' tourism, respectively. Where mass tourism attractions are 'contrived', alternative tourism attractions are 'authentic'; where mass tourism fosters externally controlled, high-leakage operations, alternative tourism offers locally controlled, high-linkage opportunities and so on. It may be added that alternative tourism is expected to adhere to a strong interpretation of sustainability, while mass tourism was seen by supporters of the adaptancy platform as following an unacceptably weak version.

CHARACTERISTICS	UNSUSTAINABLE MASS TOURISM	DELIBERATE ALTERNATIVE TOURISM
Markets		
Segment	Psychocentric–midcentric	Allocentric–midcentric
Volume and mode	High; package tours	Low; individual arrangements
Seasonality	Distinct high and low seasons	No distinct seasonality
Origins	A few dominant markets	No dominant markets
Attractions		
Emphasis	Highly commercialised	Moderately commercialised
Character	Generic, 'contrived'	Area specific, 'authentic'
Orientation	Tourists only or mainly	Tourists and locals
Accommodation		
Size	Large scale	Small scale
Spatial pattern	Concentrated in 'tourist areas'	Dispersed throughout area
Density	High density	Low density
Architecture	'International' style; obtrusive, non-sympathetic	Vernacular style, unobtrusive, complementary
Ownership	Nonlocal, large corporations	Local, small businesses
Economic status		
Role of tourism	Dominates local economy	Complements existing activity
Linkages	Mainly external	Mainly internal
Leakages	Extensive	Minimal
Multiplier effect	Low	High
Regulation		
Control	Nonlocal private sector	Local 'community'
Amount	Minimal; to facilitate private sector	Extensive; to minimise local negative impacts
Ideology	Free market forces	Public intervention
Emphasis	Economic growth, profits; sector-specific	Community stability and wellbeing; integrated, holistic
Timeframe	Short term	Long term

■ **Figure 11.5** *Mass tourism and alternative tourism: ideal types*

Source: *Weaver 1998 (adapted from Butler (1992) and Weaver (1993))*

Circumstantial and deliberate alternative tourism

In some cases, a destination's affiliation with alternative tourism is superficial, the presence of the associated characteristics being simply a function of the fact that the destination is in the 'exploration' or 'involvement' stage of the Butler sequence (see section 10.2). This 'unintentional' variation can be referred to as **circumstantial alternative tourism** (**CAT**) meaning that this status is associated with early circumstances of the resort cycle. In contrast, **deliberate alternative tourism** (**DAT**) occurs when a regulatory environment is present that 'deliberately' maintains the destination in that involvement-type state (Weaver 2000). Returning to figure 11.5, the full set of alternative tourism characteristics in a destination is therefore indicative of the deliberate variation. If, however, the characteristics listed under 'regulation' are absent, then this indicates the presence of the circumstantial version. The reader should note the similarities between the latter situation and the exploration/involvement stage characteristics listed in table 10.1. The distinction between circumstantial and deliberate alternative tourism is critical, since a CAT destination has the potential to evolve along an unsustainable path of development(there being no measures in place to prevent this). In contrast, DAT reflects the influence of specific policy directives and controls (e.g. indicator thresholds and benchmark objectives that reflect a strong sustainability interpretation) that better ensure the maintenance of a sustainable, low-intensity tourism option.

■ *11.5.2* Manifestations

The earliest manifestations of DAT were social or cultural in nature, perhaps reflecting the cautionary platform's initial emphasis on the sociocultural impacts of tourism. In addition, most of the attention was focused on the underdeveloped or 'Third World', which was regarded as especially susceptible to the negative effects of tourism. Pioneering examples include the 'Tourism for Discovery' project in Senegal, which was established in 1972 as a way for tourists to experience traditional village life in an authentic west African setting (Gningue 1992). Other early initiatives were introduced in Jamaica, India, Tanzania and Mauritius (Dernoi 1981). While some of these programs received substantial publicity because of their innovative character, they constituted only a minuscule proportion of total tourism activity in those countries. Indian alternative tourism operations, for example, accounted for only 0.1 per cent of all overnight stays by international tourists in that country during the late 1970s (Dernoi 1981).

Since the 1980s sociocultural DAT opportunities have expanded rapidly, but still account for only a very small proportion of all tourism activity. Stimulated by growth in the 'new traveller' market, sociocultural DAT products include the following (with product examples given in italics):

- cultural villages — *Tourism for Discovery* (Senegal)
- homestays — *Meet the People* (Jamaica), *Home Visit System* (Japan), *Friendship Force* (International)
- feminist travel — *Womantrek* (United States)
- indigenous tourism — *Wanuskewin* (Saskatchewan, Canada), *Tiwi Tours, Camp Coorong* (Australia)
- older adult tourism — *Elderhostel* (international)
- vacation farms — *Willing Workers on Organic Farms* (international)

- social awareness travel — *Center for Global Education, Global Exchange, Plowshares Institute* (all in the United States)
- youth hostels
- personal awareness tourism — *ESALEN Institute* (California)
- religious tourism — monastery retreats
- educational tourism — *The Humanities Institute* (United States)
- volunteer activity — *Habitat for Humanity, Global Volunteers* (both in the United States)
- guesthouses.

While the above activities mostly occur in rural areas, urban DAT is also possible. One example is the urban cultural heritage tourism that is being developed in the African-American Shaw neighbourhood of Washington, DC (Peckham 2003) and in the Soweto township of Johannesburg, South Africa (Rogerson 2004) (see figure 11.6). Ecotourism, another primarily rural activity, first emerged in the 1980s as a nature-based form of alternative tourism. However, because it is now widely recognised as having mass as well as alternative manifestations, it is discussed separately in this chapter (see section 11.6).

■ **Figure 11.6**
Getting to know Soweto

■ *11.5.3* **Critique** *of alternative tourism*

Although a small-scale level of activity is implicit in alternative tourism, the absence of negative impacts cannot be assumed. Problems that can occur in association with this apparently benign form of tourism are depicted in figure 11.7. In conjunction with earlier comments made about the suitability of large-scale enterprises to implement sustainable practices (see section 11.4.1), the opposite can be said about small operations. Operators of the latter often lack the resources or expertise to implement measures compatible with sustainable tourism. Alternative tourists themselves may cause sociocultural stress by being overly intrusive in their desire to experience 'backstage' lifestyles over a prolonged period of time (see section 9.3.4). Similarly, they may unintentionally distress wildlife by their presence, or introduce harmful pathogens into sensitive natural locales that have not been site-hardened to accommodate even small numbers of visitors. In both situations, these tourists may function as 'explorers', as per the Butler sequence, who inadvertently open the destination to less benign forms of tourism development. Despite their discomfort with mass tourism, alternative tourists also use related products, such as air transport, which contribute to unsustainability at a global level.

A commonly cited criticism is the association of alternative tourism with elite 'green' value systems that place a high value on principles (such as the nonconsumption of natural resources) that may be incompatible with local hunting traditions or slash-and-burn farming techniques. Great pressure may be placed on locals to adopt the alternative tourism model, even though local residents in some cases might prefer a more intensive and larger-scale form of tourism that generates higher economic returns. Small-scale ecotourism is even seen as a way of keeping an area in an underdeveloped, primitive state for the benefit of a few wealthy ecotourists from the developed countries.

■ **Figure 11.7** *Criticisms of alternative tourism*   **Source:** *Adapted from Weaver (1998)*

Where local residents are actually in control of an alternative tourism enterprise, most of this power may rest in the hands of the local elite, whose economic and social dominance in the community is reinforced. Similarly, clan rivalries may be exacerbated if one group perceives that a rival group is gaining an advantage, as happened during the 1980s with the development of alternative tourism guesthouses in the Tufi region of Papua New Guinea

(Ranck 1987). Other problems include the continued naïvety of many advocates, who may be unwilling or unable to see its potential shortcomings, and the possibility that unscrupulous businesses may use the alternative tourism or ecotourism label to legitimise products that do not meet the appropriate criteria.

11.6 ECOTOURISM

Ecotourism is distinguished in three main ways from other types of tourism:
* It emphasises the natural environment, or some component thereof (e.g. noncaptive wildlife), as the focus of attraction, with associated cultural resources being a secondary attraction.
* Interaction with nature is motivated by a desire to appreciate or learn about the attraction. This contrasts with nature-based 3S or adventure tourism, where the natural environment serves as a convenient setting to fulfil some other motivation (e.g. sunbathing or thrill-seeking, respectively, in the two cases given here).
* Every attempt must be made to operate in an environmentally, socioculturally and economically sustainable manner. Unlike other types of tourism, the sustainability mandate is explicit.

Within these parameters there are many activities that cluster under the ecotourism umbrella. As depicted in figure 11.8, activities such as birdwatching, whale-watching and stargazing tend to position entirely within ecotourism, while safaris, trekking and nature photography usually overlap with the nature-based components of adventure tourism, 3S tourism and/or sociocultural alternative tourism. For example, participants in an African safari excursion may be motivated simultaneously by the thrill and risk of the experience, as well as by a desire to observe large predators in their natural habitat.

11.6.1 Soft *and hard ecotourism*

Ecotourism activities can be further classified as hard or soft, although as with mass and alternative tourism, these labels should be seen as two ends of a spectrum rather than as mutually exclusive categories (Weaver 2001a). **Hard ecotourism**, as an ideal type, emphasises an intense, personal and prolonged encounter with nature. Associated trips are usually specialised (i.e. undertaken solely for ecotourism purposes) and take place within a wilderness setting or some other mainly undisturbed natural venue where access to services and facilities is virtually nonexistent. Participants are environmentalists who are highly committed to the principles of sustainability. This form of ecotourism is most clearly aligned with alternative tourism and with a strong interpretation of sustainability.

In contrast, **soft ecotourism** is characterised by short-term, mediated interactions with nature that are often just one component of a multipurpose tourism experience. Participants have some appreciation for the attraction and are open to learning more about sustainability and related issues, but the level of commitment to environmentalism, as a philosophy, is not as strong, indicating a higher incidence of veneer green consumer participation. Soft ecotourism takes place within less natural settings (e.g. park interpretation centre, scenic lookout, signed hiking trail, wildlife park) that provide a high level of services and facilities. This form of ecotourism can potentially exist as a type of mass tourism informed by a weaker interpretation of sustainability. Nevertheless, with appropriate educational opportunities, there is evidence that soft as well as hard ecotourism can produce positive environmental impacts (see Managing: Environmental impacts through effective interpretation).

■ **Figure 11.8**
Major types of ecotourism activity

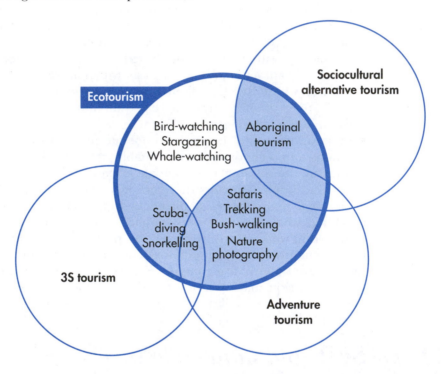

MANAGING
Environmental impacts through effective interpretation

Expensive 'hard' option strategies such as fencing and policing are often employed by protected area managers to avoid negative environmental impacts resulting from tourism. Increasingly, however, less expensive 'soft' option measures such as interpretation are being used to influence the behaviour of tourists so that the heavy-handed options are rendered unnecessary. Evidence that effective interpretation positively influences visitor behaviour is provided by Littlefair (2004), who from 1999 to 2002 observed the reactions of 449 ecotourists in Lamington National Park, Queensland, to 41 guided natural tours that offered varying levels of minimal impact content. Three types of impact-related behaviour — taking shortcuts to avoid trail switchbacks, picking up litter and talking quietly — were measured.

In hikes where the tour guide not only provided comprehensive environmental interpretation but also served as a role model of appropriate behaviour and made strategically timed appeals to the ecotourists to also behave appropriately, the amount of negative impact behaviour was significantly reduced. For example, at the three switchbacks where well-defined shortcuts were available, 100 per cent of participants took those shortcuts when the appeals were absent (even though the guide stayed on the trail). Where the appeals were made, the proportion taking the shortcut was reduced to 6–10 per cent. To test for litter pickup, typical pieces of litter were preplaced at three specified locations just before the groups reached those spots. Again, the role model and appeals hikes were accompanied by a much higher proclivity to behave positively (80 per cent of the litter was picked up by the ecotourists) than the generic hikes (about 15 per cent was removed). In this case, the role modelling appeared to be a less important influence than the appeal. Finally, to measure whether the tourists were talking loudly, the tours were continuously recorded with a concealed microcassette and each five-second segment was categorised into one of 11 noise levels, based on loudness and number of people talking. Less time was spent engaged in noisy talk on the role model and appeals tours, although the differences were not statistically significant.

Littlefair (2004) concludes that minimal impact interpretation can be effective in positively influencing behaviour that is explicitly targeted in that interpretation. In addition, role modelling is seen as essential for demonstrating correct behaviour, especially with shortcutting, since it was unclear to many participants where the correct path was. The research, however, did not reveal whether the participants were likely to continue behaving positively in future tours that lacked the role model or appeals component.

11.6.2 Magnitude

The magnitude that one attributes to ecotourism depends on how much of the hard–soft spectrum and how many overlapping activities are embraced in the accepted definition. If one restricts ecotourism to the hard ideal type, then this sector will account for considerably less than 1 per cent of all tourism activity. A liberal definition that embraces an array of soft ecotourism products and hybrid activities such as scuba diving produces a much higher figure, probably in the 15–20 per cent range. Complicating such calculations is the multipurpose nature of most travel (see page 33). The difficulties that arise in quantifying ecotourism are illustrated by inbound tourism patterns in Kenya. The great majority of inbound visitors are conventional mass tourists who spend most of their time in the capital city (Nairobi) or in Indian Ocean beach resorts. However, surveys have revealed that 70 per cent of these visitors selected Kenya for their 3S holiday because of the opportunity to participate in a wildlife-watching safari excursion (Akama 1996). The resultant soft ecotourism activity often occurs on a large scale within certain accessible protected areas, leading to the observation that ecotourism can and often does also occur as a form of mass tourism (see the case study at the end of this chapter).

■ *11.6.3* **Location**

Ecotourism destinations are usually associated with 'natural' or 'relatively undisturbed' settings. It is therefore not surprising that most ecotourism activity takes place within protected areas such as national parks, which provide both a relatively undisturbed setting and a DAT-like regulatory environment that restricts potentially harmful activities (Butler & Boyd 2000). Hard ecotourism tends to occur in the more remote regions of countries or individual parks, while soft ecotourism, as noted above, concentrates in the more accessible portions of parks that are located within a few hours drive from major cities or 3S resort areas (Weaver 1998). In the latter situations, it is typical for 90–99 per cent of all tourist activity to occur within just 1–5 per cent of the park area. Given that such protected areas are expected to fulfil two potentially conflicting mandates — the preservation of local biodiversity and the accommodation of increasing visitor numbers — it is not surprising that situations arise and management decisions are taken that call into question the sustainability of tourism in such areas.

Protected areas and other relatively undisturbed natural environments clearly do provide a potentially optimal venue for authentic, high-quality encounters with nature, but there is no inherent reason for excluding modified environments such as reservoirs and farmland that may also attract interesting birds or mammals. Weaver (2005) even makes the case for urban ecotourism, arguing that extremely site-hardened locations such as bridges and skyscrapers can provide excellent wildlife-viewing opportunities. The Congress Avenue Bridge in Austin, Texas, for example, hosts a colony of 1.5 million Mexican free-tailed bats that annually attracts 100 000 visitors and $10 million in revenue.

Ecotourism activity occurs in all parts of the world, but some regions and countries have attained a reputation as ecotourism destinations. Prominent among these are Australia (see the following), New Zealand and the Central American corridor extending from the Yucatan Peninsula and Belize to Costa Rica. Other important regions are the Amazon Basin, the 'safari corridor' from Kenya to South Africa, the Himalaya, the Pacific Northwest of Canada and the United States, peripheral Europe, and southeast Asian destinations such as Thailand, Borneo and Sumatra (figure 11.9). Rainforest, savanna, coastal and marine environments are especially well represented as ecotourism venues, while deserts and grasslands have relatively little related activity.

■ Figure 11.9 *Prominent world ecotourism destinations*

Ecotourism in Australia

An indication of the magnitude of ecotourism in Australia is provided by figure 5.2, which shows that 39 per cent of the combined five top inbound markets (i.e. New Zealand, the United Kingdom, Japan, the United States, Singapore) visited a national or state park on their visit to Australia in 2003. The likelihood that many of these visits were related to soft ecotourism is indicated by the fact that just 23 per cent of these visitors reported that they bushwalked or went on a rainforest walk. With just 6 per cent reporting visits to the Outback, it is also apparent that ecotourism activity among international tourists is primarily a coastal or near-coastal phenomenon. High-profile Australian ecotourism destinations include the Great Barrier Reef, the tropical and temperate rainforests that extend intermittently from Cape York to Tasmania, Fraser Island (Queensland), and Rottnest Island, the Kimberleys and Shark Bay (Western Australia). Other venues include Kakadu National Park (Northern Territory), the alpine region extending through New South Wales and Victoria, Phillip Island (Victoria), and Kangaroo Island and the Flinders Ranges (South Australia).

The Gold Coast is particularly interesting given the proximity of rainforest-based ecotourism to a high-density 3S resort agglomeration.

Destinations encompass a diverse array of public and private interests, of which those related to tourism may constitute only a small proportion. Accordingly, they pose distinctive challenges with regard to the implementation of sustainable tourism. In particular, municipal, state and national governments, unlike corporations, are limited in the amount of control that they can exercise over these constituent elements, and are additionally constrained by the powers invested in higher- as well as lower-order jurisdictions. The Commonwealth government, for example, may deem that an environmentally sensitive area is critical for training the armed forces and may expropriate this area for this purpose, even though the local shire regards that land as essential for its municipal pursuit of sustainable tourism. Governments are further constrained by them not being able to show preference to tourism interests over those of other constituents.

Nevertheless, destination governments do have access to mechanisms that facilitate the pursuit of sustainable tourism. Development standards, or legal restrictions that dictate the physical aspects of development (Bosselman, Peterson & McCarthy 1999), are one such option. Included in this category are density and height restrictions, setbacks (distances separating the outer edge of a development from another object, such as a footpath, floodplain or beach high water mark), building standards (e.g. conformance of new construction to traditional architectural styles, minimum insulation requirements), noise regulation and signage control (e.g. prohibitions on motorway billboards). In addition, municipalities can pursue social sustainability by requiring resorts to provide reasonable pedestrian access between a public road and a public beach, as is often done in the Caribbean.

Zoning regulations, which demarcate specific areas for defined uses and development standards, are another important tool for destination planning and management, as are districting strategies that designate special urban or rural landscapes for focused management or planning that seeks to preserve the special historical, natural or cultural properties of these places. In the designated Chinatown district of Toronto, bilingual Chinese and English road signs and relaxed standards for the display of food and other commercial goods are both permitted in order to distinguish this neighbourhood as a Chinese–Canadian culture area and tourist attraction. Destination governments also have considerable scope for offering sustainability-related incentives to their constituent private sector tourism operators. One example is the Barbados *Tourism Development Act* of 2002, which allows a 150 per cent tax deduction on expenses related to the pursuit of Green Globe 21 hotel certification. Finally, destination governments may enhance their power to implement sustainable tourism by working collectively through organisations such as the Australian Local Government Association. Ad hoc municipal interest groups have recently been established in Australia to address problems associated with rapid tourism-related development (see Breakthrough tourism: The National Sea Change Task Force).

The sea change phenomenon, or the temporary and permanent lifestyle-motivated movement of people to places adjacent to or near the coastline, is a major geographic trend in Australia, and one that has major environmental, economic and social implications. Sea change councils, or those affected most directly by this trend, presently account for about 20 per cent of the country's population, and this is expected to increase substantially by 2020 because of the retirement of the baby-boomer cohort and escalating housing costs in major metropolitan areas. Concerned about the effects of this trend on inadequate infrastructure and vulnerable natural environments, 27 CEOs from these councils attended a Sea Change Summit on the Sunshine Coast in early 2004. A major achievement of the summit was the creation of a National Sea Change Task Force empowered to effectively tackle problems associated with this trend through advocacy, coordinated regional planning for sustainability, and community engagement (Shire of Augusta-Margaret River 2004).

As of early 2005, the number of councils participating in the task force had increased to more than 70. Its increased visibility, however, has been mainly the result of several controversial proposals, including a 50 per cent 'sustainability surcharge' to be levied on the rates bills of absentee-owned holiday homes to mitigate their environmental, economic and social impacts (Millar 2005). For similar purposes, councils in the shires where Kangaroo Island and the Great Ocean Road are located have suggested the introduction of bridge and road tolls, while the Shire of Byron Bay (New South Wales) has gone further by proposing that the town be declared a national park accessible only by entry fees. Other revenue-generating ideas include the imposition of an offsetting levy on all inbound tourists, and a 'shadow tolling' program where state governments pay a GST-generated fee to local councils based on how many domestic tourists they accommodate (Dick 2005). While each of the above proposals is likely to be met with enormous resistance from those who will be financially affected, the task force has succeeded in placing the sea change phenomenon on the national agenda while providing a structure to both propose and lobby for innovations that will hopefully lead to a more sustainable tourism sector on the Australian coastline.

11.7.1 Extending *the Butler sequence*

Attempts to model the process of tourist destination development in the field of tourism studies have mostly focused on the Butler sequence and its unfortunate outcomes (see chapter 10). However, recent developments in the field of sustainable tourism suggest that a broader framework is necessary in order to encompass the full range of possible developmental scenarios. Such a framework is provided in figure 11.10. This **broad context**

model of destination development scenarios consists of four basic tourism ideal types, based on the scale of the sector (small to large) and the amount of sustainability-related regulation that is present (Weaver 2000).

■ **Figure 11.10**
Broad context model of destination development scenarios

Source: *Weaver (2000)*

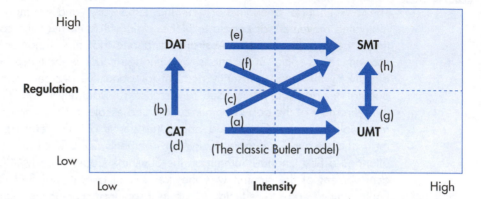

DAT	Deliberate alternative tourism	**SMT**	Sustainable mass tourism
CAT	Circumstantial alternative tourism	**UMT**	Unsustainable mass tourism

In this model, small-scale destinations fall into either the CAT (i.e. little or no regulation) or DAT (extensive regulation) category (see section 11.5.1). Similarly, large-scale destinations in theory are either unsustainable (= unsustainable mass tourism, or UMT) or sustainable, depending on the presence or absence of a suitable regulatory environment (= sustainable mass tourism, or SMT). As with other category-based models cited previously in this book (e.g. the attraction inventory in chapter 5 or Plog's psychographic model in chapter 6), the graphed data fall along a continuum rather than into discrete categories. Thus, many different types of CAT destination will emerge, depending on the extent to which CAT-like criteria of scale and regulation are evident.

Possible paths of evolution

If only CAT destinations are taken into consideration initially, the broad context model offers four distinct possibilities for future development. The Butler sequence is but one possible scenario, involving the movement of a destination from CAT to UMT (a). The progression in this scenario is from an unregulated 'involvement' stage to an unregulated and unsustainable 'consolidation' stage or beyond. Evidence from a large variety of destinations suggests that such a sequence occurs frequently, but consideration must also be given to the possibility that a CAT destination can move to DAT through the implementation of the regulatory environment required to maintain the characteristics of alternative tourism (b). The Caribbean island of Dominica and the South Pacific island–state of Samoa appear to illustrate this possibility (Weaver 1998). Additionally, a CAT-to-SMT sequence can occur when a mass tourism industry is superimposed over an undeveloped region in a highly regulated way (c). The Indonesian growth pole resort of Bintan and the early stages of the development of Cancún possibly adhere to this scenario (chapter 8).

A fourth possibility for CAT destinations is the absence of any evolution at all (d). This scenario assumes that not all CAT destinations will attract sufficient levels of demand to stimulate any further tourism development. For example, most of Outback Australia is not likely within any foreseeable timeframe to move beyond exploration- or involvement-stage dynamics, given the absence of push or pull factors that would draw these areas into a more robust tourism system. One implication is the lack of need in such cases to allocate resources towards the establishment of DAT. Instead, resources should be directed to identifying and managing locations where the potential for intensification to occur is higher, such as coastal and alpine destinations.

Moving beyond CAT, other depicted scenarios include the movement from DAT to either SMT (e) or UMT (f). The former situation occurs when the destination is able and wants to increase its carrying capacity thresholds to accommodate higher visitation levels. A DAT destination, however, can also move towards UMT if the appropriate adjustments to carrying capacity are not made, or cannot be made. This is illustrated by national parks such as Amboseli (Kenya), where visitation levels during the 1970s far outpaced the capacity of park managers to cope with the resultant stresses (Weaver 1998).

Finally, SMT can be transformed into UMT as a result of similar dynamics (g), while the opposite is also possible. Calviá, on the Spanish pleasure periphery island of Mallorca, is an example of a previously unsustainable tourism-intensive destination that is making significant progress towards the attainment of sustainability (Calviá 1998).

Application of the broad context model to the Gold Coast

The broad context model can be used to depict the current status of tourism on the Gold Coast, as well as a more desirable long-term tourism outcome. As shown in figure 11.11, the coastal strip of the Gold Coast is characteristic of UMT, while the hinterland can generally be described as CAT. The preferred outcome is for each area to retain its current scale of development, but in a sustainable way. Thus, the Gold Coast, in terms of policy directives, should seek to implement SMT along the coast and DAT in the hinterland. The double-headed arrow implies that this strategy should be accompanied by the mutually reinforcing integration of the two Gold Coast product components.

■ **Figure 11.11**
Application of the broad context model to the Gold Coast
Source:
Weaver (2000)

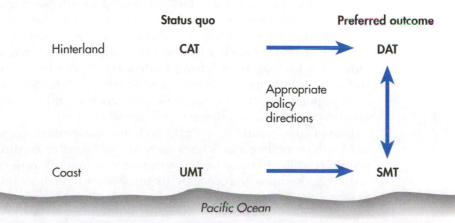

CHAPTER REVIEW

In response to increasing contradictions and anomalies in the dominant Western environmental paradigm, our society appears to be shifting towards an ecocentric green paradigm. This shift has seen the concept of sustainable development become the focus of contemporary tourism sector management, with weak and strong interpretations possible depending on whether a particular destination consists mainly of undeveloped natural habitat or heavily modified landscapes, respectively. The identification and monitoring of indicators at the destination and operations level is essential if sustainable tourism is to be achieved, but associated procedures are marred by our basic lack of understanding about the complexities of tourism systems, and other problems. Nevertheless, the concept is still worth pursuing, since not to do so is to virtually ensure unsustainable outcomes. The mass tourism industry, long notorious for following an unsustainable path of development, is now pursuing sustainable tourism more seriously because of the rapid growth in green consumerism and the potential profitability of sustainability-related measures as well as self-enlightened ethical considerations. It is assisted in this effort by its own economies of scale. Nevertheless, the penetration of sustainability-related practices within the conventional tourism industry does not appear to extend much beyond the establishment of facilitating structures within various sectors and the leadership of a few corporate innovators, suggesting a shallow level of adherence that complements the dominance of 'veneer' environmentalists within society at large. The rudimentary state of specialised quality control mechanisms supports this contention. Codes of practice, for example, are abundant but controversial, while the highest-profile certification-focused global ecolabel, Green Globe 21, has attracted only minimal participation to date.

Many researchers, therefore, remain sceptical about the motives of the conventional mass tourism industry, and a great amount of attention is still being given to the concept of alternative tourism as a presumably more benign alternative to mass tourism. Even so, alternative tourism itself has been criticised on many grounds, including its intrusiveness into backstage spaces, its limitations of scale, and its potential for opening destinations to less benign forms of tourism. Ecotourism was initially conceived in the 1980s as a nature-based form of alternative tourism but has since been widely acknowledged as having both a hard (mainly alternative tourism) and soft (mainly mass tourism) manifestation. Protected areas remain the most popular ecotourism venue, though more attention is being paid to the suitability of urban and other highly modified spaces.

Tourist destinations, as opposed to businesses, present distinctive sustainability-related challenges such as the presence of diverse public and private constituencies as well as a usually dominant nontourism sector. Nevertheless, destination governments possess tools such as the establishment of development standards and zoning regulations that aid the pursuit of sustainable tourism. They are assisted in this pursuit by the broad context model of destination development scenarios, which depicts the range of potential tourism options, of which the Butler scenario (CAT-to-UMT) is just one. Deliberate alternative tourism (DAT) and sustainable mass tourism (SMT) are the desirable scenarios, depending on whether a weak or strong interpretation of sustainability is warranted.

SUMMARY OF KEY TERMS

Paradigm

The entire constellation of beliefs, assumptions and values that underlie the way that a society interprets the nature of reality

- **Paradigm shift:** the replacement of one paradigm with another when the formerly dominant paradigm can no longer adequately account for various contradictions and anomalies

Scientific paradigm

The currently dominant paradigm, which holds that reality is reducible and deterministic and can be understood through the application of the 'scientific method'

- **Dominant Western environmental paradigm:** the scientific paradigm as applied to environmental and related issues, holding the anthropocentric view that humankind is at the centre of all things, and constitutes the primary focus of reference in all relationships with the natural environment; humans are seen as being superior to nature, which exists only for their benefit

Green paradigm

An emerging ecocentric worldview that is challenging the basic assumptions of the dominant Western environmental paradigm and accounting for its related anomalies and contradictions

Sustainable development

In principle, development that meets the needs of present generations while ensuring that future generations are able to meet their own needs

- **Greenwashing:** the process of conveying an impression of environmental responsibility that is not actually deserved; often associated with the misuse of terms such as 'sustainable tourism' and 'ecotourism'
- **Weak sustainable development:** an approach to sustainable development that assumes relatively relaxed environmental expectations in recognition of areas, such as intensively developed beach resorts, that are already extensively modified and have high carrying capacities
- **Strong sustainable development:** an approach to sustainable development that assumes relatively rigorous environmental expectations in recognition of areas, such as wilderness, that are relatively undisturbed and have a low carrying capacity

Sustainable tourism

Tourism that is developed in such a way so as to meet the needs of the present without compromising the ability of future generations to meet their own needs

- **Indicators:** a variable or parameter that provides information about some phenomenon in order to facilitate its management in a desirable way
- **Avalanche effect:** the process whereby a small incremental change in a system triggers a disproportionate and usually unexpected response
- **Benchmark:** an indicator value, often based on some past desirable state, against which subsequent change in that indicator can be gauged
- **Threshold:** a critical value of indicator sustainability; when the threshold is exceeded, this indicates an unsustainable situation

Green consumerism

The proclivity to purchase goods and services that are deemed to be environmentally and socially sustainable; situates along a spectrum from 'true' green to 'veneer' green attitudes and behaviour

- **New traveller:** an emerging market niche that is highly discerning and critical in ensuring that its travel behaviour does not negatively affect destinations; similar to Plog's allocentric tourist

Quality control mechanisms

Mechanisms that provide some degree of assurance to consumers, government or others that a particular operation, product or destination follows standards associated with sustainable tourism

- **Codes of practice:** commonly developed and espoused by tourism corporations and industry associations, these are intended to provide general guidelines for achieving sustainability-related outcomes
- **Ecolabels:** mechanisms that certify products or companies that meet specified standards of practice
- **Certification:** the outcome of a process in which an independent third party verifies that a product or company meets specified standards, allowing it to be certified by the ecolabel
- **Accreditation:** the process by which the ecolabel is determined by an overarching organisation to meet specified standards of quality and credibility

Alternative tourism

The major contribution of the adaptancy platform, alternative tourism as an ideal type is characterised by its contrast with mass tourism

- **Circumstantial alternative tourism (CAT):** alternative tourism that results from the fact that the destination is currently situated within the early, low-intensity stages of the resort cycle
- **Deliberate alternative tourism (DAT):** alternative tourism that is deliberately maintained as such through the implementation of an appropriate regulatory environment

Ecotourism

A form of alternative tourism (and potentially mass tourism) that places primary emphasis on a sustainable, learning-based interaction with the natural environment or some constituent element

- **Hard ecotourism:** a form of ecotourism that stresses an intensive, specialised and prolonged interaction with nature in a relatively undisturbed natural environment with few available amenities; a form of alternative tourism
- **Soft ecotourism:** a form of ecotourism that emphasises a short-term interaction with nature as part of a multipurpose trip with ample provision for services and facilities; can exist as a form of mass tourism

Broad context model of destination development scenarios

A framework for modelling the evolution of tourist destinations, which takes into account scale and sustainability-related regulations; various transformations are possible among four ideal tourism types CAT, DAT, UMT (unsustainable mass tourism) and SMT (sustainable mass tourism)

QUESTIONS

1 (a) What is the evidence both for and against the contention that contemporary society is currently experiencing a paradigm shift?
  (b) Based on this evidence, how much effort should conventional tourism operators put into pursuing a sustainable tourism agenda?
  (c) What other considerations should dictate such a decision?

2 Under what circumstances is a weak or strong interpretation of sustainable development warranted in tourism?

3 What are some of the major challenges associated with the collection and use of sustainable tourism indicators?

4 (a) How much has the conventional mass tourism industry actually embraced the practice of sustainable tourism?
  (b) What accounts for this?

5 (a) What is the difference between certification and accreditation?
  (b) Why are these important to the pursuit of sustainable tourism?

6 What is the difference between deliberate and circumstantial alternative tourism, and why is this distinction important to tourism managers?

7 Why should it not be assumed that all forms of alternative tourism are sustainable?

8 (a) What are the distinguishing characteristics of ecotourism?
  (b) How does it differ fundamentally from other nature-based tourism activities such as 3S and adventure tourism?

9 How is the broad context model of destination development scenarios potentially useful to the managers of tourist destinations?

EXERCISES

1 Assume that budgetary constraints allow you, as a destination manager, to collect only five of the WTO core sustainable tourism indicators listed in table 11.1. List your choice of five indicators, and write a 500-word report in which you justify your selection of each.

2 (a) Identify a region or locale in your country that has the appearance of circumstantial alternative tourism (CAT).
(b) Discuss the likelihood that this destination will experience each of the four scenarios that can affect such a destination, according to the broad context model of destination development.
(c) As a class, compare and contrast the findings from the various destinations.

FURTHER READING

Butler, R. W. 1990. 'Alternative Tourism: Pious Hope or Trojan Horse?' *Journal of Travel Research* **28: 40–5.** Butler offers one of the most insightful and articulate critiques of alternative tourism, pointing out the problems associated with different aspects of this subsector.

Fennell, D. & Dowling, R. (Eds) 2003. *Ecotourism Policy and Planning.* **Wallingford, UK: CABI Publishing.** Leading ecotourism researchers contribute case study chapters that include indigenous territories, World Heritage sites and Australian protected areas.

Font, X. & Buckley, R. (Eds) 2001. *Tourism Ecolabelling: Certification and Promotion of Sustainable Management.* **Wallingford, UK: CABI Publishing**. The 16 chapters in this volume provide a critical analysis on ecolabelling and accreditation initiatives, including those put forward by Green Globe 21.

Hunter, C. J. 1997. 'Sustainable Tourism as an Adaptive Paradigm'. *Annals of Tourism Research* **24: 850–67.** Hunter suggests that the concept of sustainable tourism acquires a different meaning depending on the context of each destination. Sustainability in a large urban resort, for example, means something very different to sustainability in a sensitive natural area.

Stabler, M. J. (Ed.) 1997. *Tourism & Sustainability: Principles to Practice.* **Wallingford, UK: CAB International.** This selection of 24 chapters considers a broad range of issues associated with sustainable tourism, including theory and method, industry responses, alternative tourism and policy issues.

Wearing, S. 2001. *Volunteer Tourism: Experiences that Make a Difference.* **Wallingford, UK: CABI Publishing.** This detailed analysis of a volunteer ecotourism project in Costa Rica, which adopts a sociological perspective, is one of the few examples of a text devoted to a specific type of alternative tourism.

Weaver, D. B. (Ed.) 2001. *The Encyclopedia of Ecotourism.* **Wallingford, UK: CABI Publishing.** This 41-chapter compilation considers all aspects of ecotourism, including impacts, businesses, destinations and management.

Weaver, D. 2006. *Sustainable Tourism: Theory and Practice.* **London: Elsevier.** Weaver provides a comprehensive overview of sustainable tourism practices and theories in the context of alternative tourism, mass tourism and destinations, using global case studies.

Webster, K. 2000. *Environmental Management in the Hospitality Industry: A Guide for Students and Managers.* **London: Cassell.** This book provides detailed and thorough information about the implementation of sustainable practices in the accommodation sector. International case studies are included.

Penguins as spectacle on Phillip Island

There is increasing debate both for and against the idea that mass ecotourism supports the survival of plants and animals that would otherwise be destroyed by farming, urbanisation and other forms of development that provide more revenue than less intensive forms of tourism. Few sites offer a better opportunity to explore this issue than Phillip Island Nature Park, a protected area about 100 kilometres south of Melbourne, where a colony of charismatic but endangered little penguins attracts hundreds of thousands of visitors each year. To contextualise this debate, it is useful to chronicle the history of the Phillip Island penguins before the introduction of mass tourism in the late 1970s. As described by Harris (2002), there were ten little penguin colonies on the island at the time of European settlement in the mid-1800s. Over the next 130 years, this was reduced to a single colony by the combination of wholesale land clearance, the accompanying introduction of nonnative predators (e.g. cats, dogs, foxes) and invasive plants, and the development of housing subdivisions in prime penguin nesting habitat.

Early tourism and recreation activity apparently played a role in this depletion of the penguin population. Island residents began to offer organised penguin tours in the 1920s but these were unregulated until the 1960s, resulting in considerable damage from visitor trampling of burrows and dunes and from the physical handling and flash-photographing of penguins. Further stress to the colony occurred with the introduction of vehicles, many of them used by tourists, when Phillip Island was connected to the mainland by a bridge (Harris 2002). Efforts to protect the remaining penguins commenced in the 1930s when a local family, and then the local shire council, reserved a small amount of land for this purpose. The Victorian state government, concerned over the continuing decline of the penguins, assumed control over the reserve in 1981 and established the Phillip Island Nature Park Board of Management (PINPBM) to protect the penguins and other native wildlife, provide opportunities for visitation and interpretation, and operate the park as an efficient business (ibid.). One of its prime tasks is the creation and implementation of a management plan to carry out its various mandates.

The establishment of the board initiated a period of tourism intensification at the 2000-hectare park, with visits to the penguin area increasing from 250 000 per year in the mid-1980s to more than 500 000 per year in the early 2000s, 60 per cent of it inbound and 50 per cent arranged through package tours (ibid.). During 2004, 627 000 paying visitors were recorded for the park as a whole, with 467 000 specifically visiting the Penguin Parade, which features the return of the penguins from their feeding at sea. About $7.7 million in revenue was obtained from parade visitors, and 52 full-time and

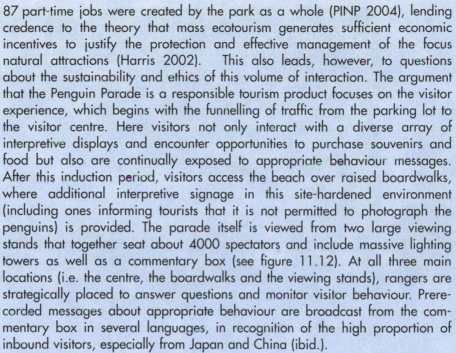

87 part-time jobs were created by the park as a whole (PINP 2004), lending credence to the theory that mass ecotourism generates sufficient economic incentives to justify the protection and effective management of the focus natural attractions (Harris 2002).   This also leads, however, to questions about the sustainability and ethics of this volume of interaction. The argument that the Penguin Parade is a responsible tourism product focuses on the visitor experience, which begins with the funnelling of traffic from the parking lot to the visitor centre. Here visitors not only interact with a diverse array of interpretive displays and encounter opportunities to purchase souvenirs and food but also are continually exposed to appropriate behaviour messages. After this induction period, visitors access the beach over raised boardwalks, where additional interpretive signage in this site-hardened environment (including ones informing tourists that it is not permitted to photograph the penguins) is provided. The parade itself is viewed from two large viewing stands that together seat about 4000 spectators and include massive lighting towers as well as a commentary box (see figure 11.12). At all three main locations (i.e. the centre, the boardwalks and the viewing stands), rangers are strategically placed to answer questions and monitor visitor behaviour. Prerecorded messages about appropriate behaviour are broadcast from the commentary box in several languages, in recognition of the high proportion of inbound visitors, especially from Japan and China (ibid.).

Harris emphasises, in further support of the incentive theory, that the ecological situation in the park has improved significantly despite the concomitant increase in the number of visitors. The penguin population, for example, has returned to its pre-1950 level of 28 000–30 000 and chick production is well above the historical average. Large areas of habitat have been restored through the eradication of nonnative plants and animals. Virtually unprecedented is the Victorian government's policy of gradually buying out all the houses and vacant lots in a nearby subdivision so that this area can be ecologically restored, which Harris argues would not likely have been implemented but for the lucrative economic benefits derived from the penguins. The Penguin Parade itself has attained Ecotourism Australia certification in recognition of its responsible practices. More contentious, perhaps, are the ethical questions related to the way in which the penguins are put on display in such a visible and even voyeuristic way, so that the Penguin Parade assumes the characteristics of a sporting megaevent or circus performance. How much this spectacle provides in meaningful and respectful education or mere entertainment and amusement is unclear, although it is unlikely that it will be tampered with given its status as the culmination of the visitor experience. Another contentious issue is pressure to expand the site-hardened environment to accommodate future growth in tourism demand and to generate even more revenue, which could conflict with the conservation efforts of the park. There is a risk, moreover, that such an escalation could exceed the carrying capacity of the penguin colony and trigger an avalanche effect of population stress and decline.

■ **Figure 11.12** *Waiting for penguins on Phillip Island*

Questions

1 (a) Compile a list of five indicators specific to the Penguin Parade that would help to determine whether this product is sustainable.

(b) For each indicator, describe how you would collect and measure the relevant information.

2 (a) Describe how the history of penguin-viewing on Phillip Island from the 1920s to the present fits into the broad context model of destination development scenarios (figure 11.10).

(b) Speculate on the possible scenarios as to where the penguin-viewing area would situate in the broad context model if the number of annual visitors was allowed to increase from 500 000 to 1 000 000.

12
Tourism
research

LEARNING OBJECTIVES

After studying this chapter, you should be able to:

1 explain the critical role of research within the field of tourism management

2 describe the main types of research that are relevant to the field of tourism studies and outline the circumstances under which each is best applied

3 differentiate between induction and deduction, and describe how these two approaches are complementary

4 classify specific research initiatives as per their adherence to the main types of research

5 list the major types of techniques associated with primary and secondary research

6 discuss the basic stages of the research process

7 describe the four main levels of investigation and explain how they complement each other within a comprehensive research project.

12.1 INTRODUCTION

The previous chapters of this book demonstrate that tourism is an increasingly diverse and complex phenomenon that requires sophisticated management and planning if it is to be pursued in a sustainable as well as competitive manner by destinations and businesses. Whether the primary motivation is to maximise the positive impacts and minimise the negative impacts of tourism (as with most destinations) or to maximise profits (as with most businesses), stakeholder objectives can only be achieved if decisions are informed by a sound knowledge base. This in turn is derived through the pursuit of properly conceived and executed **research**, or the systematic search for knowledge. It is therefore critical for students of tourism management to be familiar with the research process and related issues. The purpose of this chapter is to provide an introduction to research as it relates to the field of tourism studies. The first section (section 12.2) examines the various types of research and illustrates their applicability to tourism. The broader research process, including problem recognition and formulation, identification of appropriate methodologies or methods, data collection, data analysis and interpretation, and data presentation, is described in section 12.3 in the context of the tourism sector.

12.2 TYPES OF RESEARCH

There are several standard ways of classifying research in the field of tourism studies and elsewhere, and four of the most important are discussed in the following:
- basic versus applied
- cross-sectional versus longitudinal
- qualitative versus quantitative
- primary versus secondary.

Allowing for a certain amount of overlap within each pairing (e.g. a particular research design may combine elements of the qualitative and quantitative approach), it should be possible to classify any research initiative as containing an element of each of these four approaches. For example, a research project may be applied, longitudinal, quantitative and primary all at the same time. Each of these research types in turn is associated with a particular **research methodology**, or set of procedures and methods that is used to carry out the research process. Methodological issues, because they are pervasive, are raised in the following section as well as in the discussion of the research process (section 12.3).

12.2.1 Basic *research*

The distinction between **basic research** (sometimes referred to as pure research) and **applied research** is based on the intended end result of the investigation. Basic research reveals knowledge that will increase the understanding of tourism-related phenomena per se, and is not intended to address specific short-term problems or to achieve specific short-term outcomes (Jennings 2001). However, the knowledge gained from basic research may prove relevant in the subsequent context of more specific issues, especially if the knowledge is expressed in the form of general laws, theories or models. This is illustrated by the Butler sequence, which is an outcome of basic research that has proven to be highly relevant to the field of applied tourism. The same can be said for Doxey's irridex (see chapter 9) and the broad context model of destination development scenarios (see chapter 11).

Basic research is commonly associated with universities, given their core mandate to engage in the unfettered search for knowledge. Corporations, and smaller ones in particular, are less inclined to carry out this type of investigation, since the ensuing applications are not usually apparent right away, and therefore cannot be readily justified on financial grounds (see Contemporary issue: What is research and how important is it?). One intriguing type of basic research is sometimes referred to as the 'fishing expedition'. This occurs when the researcher applies many different techniques and experiments to some database or subject matter without knowing what will result, but in the hope that some major 'big catch' revelation will emerge.

CONTEMPORARY ISSUE
What is research and how important is it?

The assumptions made by academics about the definition, structure and objectives of research are not necessarily shared by other tourism stakeholders or by members of the private sector tourism industry in particular. This disconnect has been made apparent during the international WHATT (Worldwide Hospitality and Tourism Trends) roundtables, which seek industry input into the academic research agenda for the tourism and hospitality sectors. As reported by Jones and Phillips (2003), the Australian WHATT forum confirmed the contention that the research cultures of the two groups are fundamentally different. Where the industry (dominated by the hospitality sector) basically wants to use research for short-term problem solving and business decision making that increases competitive advantage, academics (mainly tourism specialists with social science backgrounds) are focused on the long-term objective of extending the body of public knowledge. Accordingly, industry research outcomes are usually presented in short and often confidential executive summaries that highlight key points, while academics concentrate on publishing in publicly accessible (but not always intellectually accessible) refereed journal articles. Academics (in theory) are also allegedly more likely to conduct research that involves carefully framed questions or hypotheses, rigorous scientific methodologies and critical and objective analysis of results. Tellingly, many in industry prefer the term 'intelligence gathering' over 'research'.

(continued)

To a large extent, the vector of interaction between industry and universities (see figure 1.1) is mediated by consultants who collect and distil material from academic publications and then present it in 'user friendly' form to industry. The WHATT roundtables are attempting to forge a more direct and more mutually beneficial relationship. They do this inherently by providing a venue for cross-cultural dialogue but also through suggestions such as the creation of a web portal that would serve as a gateway for ongoing communication and information access. Another proposal calls for academics to write simple synoptic summaries of their articles for inclusion in trade journals and other media used by the industry. It is doubtful that these initiatives will result in any breakthroughs, however, until there is some kind of resolution or compromise between the divergent objectives of the two camps. That is, academics must 'publish or perish', while industry managers must report a healthy 'bottom line' to shareholders. Other obstacles include the entrenched nature of the respective cultures, and the industry being mainly 'hospitality' oriented while academics are mainly 'tourism' focused.

Induction and deduction

Basic research can be carried out through methodologies of **induction** or **deduction**. In induction, the repeated observation and analysis of data lead to the formulation of theories or models that link these observations in a meaningful way. Deduction, in contrast, begins with an existing theory or model, and applies this to a particular situation to see whether it is valid in that case. In other words, induction progresses from the specific (i.e. the evidence) to the general (i.e. the theory), while deduction moves from the general to the specific (Sarantakos 2004). Gilbert (1993) alludes to the close association between the two approaches by pointing out that theories are generated through induction and then applied through deduction.

Figure 12.1 illustrates this relationship with respect to the Butler sequence, wherein many different observations and unconnected studies led to the formulation of the resort cycle concept through a process of inductive generalisation. These observations pointed towards a common process of accelerated growth culminating in the breaching of a destination's carrying capacities (see chapter 10). Subsequently, many other researchers have applied Butler's general model in a deductive way to specific destinations, leading to varying conclusions about its applicability as well as refinements and extensions (e.g. section 11.5) that take into account these new investigations. These notions of refinement and extension are very important to basic research, since they imply an evolution in our knowledge of tourism-related phenomena.

Often, the testing of a model through the inductive or deductive approach is informed by the formulation of one or more **hypotheses**, which are informed tentative statements or conjecture about the nature of certain relationships that can be subsequently proved or disproved through systematic hypothesis testing and other investigation. For example, a researcher testing the Butler sequence (i.e. a deductive approach) may establish the following hypothesis to address one particular aspect of the model:

'The control of the tourism sector tends to pass from the local community to external interests as the level of tourism development increases.'

Such a statement then provides a focal point for research into the applicability of the model. As long as investigations continue to verify the hypothesis, then there is no need to alter the model. However, once the hypothesis is rejected, then the model itself needs to be reconsidered. In some cases, the rejection may be a 'one-off' occurrence resulting from unusual local circumstances. However, as with paradigm shifts, a pattern of repeated rejection warrants a fundamental modification of the original model.

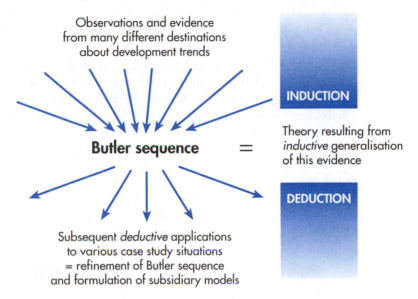

■ **Figure 12.1**
The place of induction and deduction in the Butler sequence

Observations and evidence from many different destinations about development trends

INDUCTION

Butler sequence =

Theory resulting from *inductive* generalisation of this evidence

DEDUCTION

Subsequent *deductive* applications to various case study situations = refinement of Butler sequence and formulation of subsidiary models

■ *12.2.2* **Applied** *research*

As implied in the term, the orientation in applied research is directed towards specific practical problems and outcomes. These may be associated with product development, the identification of target market segments or community reactions towards specific planning scenarios, among a great number of other tourism-related issues. Applied research is commonly associated with private corporations or government agencies charged with the task of addressing specific issues within certain time and resource constraints. If industry-based, the research results may be kept confidential so that competitors cannot use this same information for their own purposes. However, like basic research, applied research can also lead to theoretical breakthroughs and the advancement of knowledge if the results are made available to the public. Plog's psychographic segmentation is one example (see chapter 6). The establishment of the CRC (Cooperative Research Centre) for Sustainable Tourism in the late 1990s (renamed the Sustainable Tourism CRC in 2004) was a major development in the evolution of applied tourism research in Australia given its core mandate of delivering innovative knowledge to Australian tourism stakeholders that will enhance the sector's sustainability and international competitiveness As a not-for-profit company owned by a consortium of partners from industry, government and the university sector, the Sustainable Tourism CRC research program develops and manages relevant intellectual property focused on the three key areas of destinations, enterprises and resources (STCRC 2005).

■ 12.2.3 Cross-sectional *research*

The difference between **cross-sectional research** (sometimes referred to as latitudinal research) and **longitudinal research** is based on the time period that is represented by the resulting data. Cross-sectional research entails a 'snapshot' approach that describes a situation essentially at one point in time (although the data may be collected over several weeks or months) (Ryan 1995). In its simplest form, cross-sectional research is undertaken at a single site (scenario (a) of figure 12.2). A more complex variation involves the collection of information at multiple sites (scenario (b)). Scenario (a) might involve the administration of a one-time survey over a two-week period in 2000 to determine the attitude of Perth residents towards the Americas Cup yachting competition. Scenario (b) might involve a similar one-off survey that is carried out in Perth, Broome, Geraldton, Bunbury and Kalgoorlie. The advantage of the second scenario is the opportunity that is provided to make comparisons and perhaps identify common trends, but it has the disadvantage of being more expensive. In addition, careful planning must be exercised in order to ensure that all the surveys are carried out at about the same time and in a similar manner.

■ **Figure 12.2**
Basic cross-sectional and longitudinal surveying options

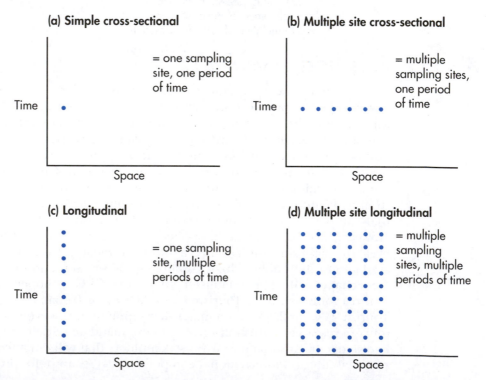

■ 12.2.4 **Longitudinal** *research*

Longitudinal research or 'trend' research is undertaken during several time periods during which a sequence of snapshots is produced. An example of scenario (c) of figure 12.2 (i.e. single-site longitudinal research) is the monitoring of Perth resident attitudes over a ten-year period. The most comprehensive (and most expensive) form of longitudinal research entails the examination of many sites over multiple time periods (scenario (d) of figure 12.2). This scenario would occur if the Perth residential survey was also administered concurrently on an annual basis to the residents of Broome, Geraldton, Bunbury and Kalgoorlie. The International and National Visitor Surveys, conducted by Tourism Research Australia, are good illustrations of this approach. As a result of such ambitious investigations, considerable insight is gained into spatial as well as temporal patterns, and on this basis we are more likely to generate useful models and theories. One continuing problem, however, is the possible necessity of extending the time period of the inquiry if no clear trends emerge within a given timeframe.

A variation in longitudinal research carried out by survey is the continued solicitation of the same respondents from one time period to the next. The advantage of this approach is the ability to monitor the changing behaviour of a given sample. However, such an approach may not be practical due to the attrition of respondents due to death, migration or respondent fatigue. This is a more realistic option where the time period of the research is more limited. For example, consumers who have already booked a trip to a particular location may be asked to express their expectations about that destination. Upon their return several weeks later, they could be asked whether their expectations were met. Note that this form of longitudinal research is also distinguished by the different questions that are asked in each phase of the surveying.

A major challenge for longitudinal research is the maintenance of consistency in the research design over the entire period. If, for instance, the survey questions, definition of 'resident' or sample size is radically altered halfway through the period, or a change is made in the cities where residents are surveyed, the subsequent results will no longer be neatly comparable to data collected prior to the changes. Any apparent trends that emerge from the study will therefore be misleading.

■ 12.2.5 **Qualitative** *research*

The distinction between **qualitative research** and **quantitative research** is concerned mainly with the type of data that is sought. Qualitative research can be initially defined as a mode of research that does not place its emphasis on statistics or statistical analysis; that is, on the objective measurement and analysis of the data collected (Goodson & Phillimore 2004). In terms of subject matter, it usually involves a small number of respondents or observations, but considers these in depth. It is for this reason that qualitative research methods are sometimes referred to as 'data enhancers' that allow crucial elements of a problem or phenomenon to be seen more clearly (Ragin 1994). Qualitative research is suited for situations where little is known about the subject matter, since the associated methodology is intended to gain insight into the phenomenon in question.

An example of qualitative research would be a situation where the researcher non-randomly selects a group of ten Gold Coast residents and conducts an in-depth two-hour interview with each to see what they think about the tourism sector in their community. Many researchers criticise such qualitative research for lacking the objective rigour and validity of a statistical approach, and for not necessarily being representative of any group larger than that which was actually interviewed or observed. This criticism, however, is best directed towards the careless execution of qualitative methods, and not to qualitative methodology itself, which can be extremely rigorous and challenging in its assumptions and applications. Sections 12.2.7 and 12.2.8 provide more information about particular qualitative research methods.

■ 12.2.6 Quantitative *research*

Quantitative research relies on the collection of statistics that are then analysed through a variety of statistical techniques. Numerous quantitative research methods are used in the field of tourism studies, and it is beyond the scope of this introductory tourism management text to describe these methods. It can be said, however, that quantitative research techniques typically are 'data condensers' that yield a relatively small amount of information about a large number of respondents or observations (Ragin 1994). Table 12.1 depicts some of the contrasting characteristics associated with quantitative and qualitative research techniques and in so doing illustrates the very different assumptions and philosophies that inform each approach.

■ **Table 12.1**
Quantitative and qualitative research styles

QUANTITATIVE STYLE	QUALITATIVE STYLE
Measure objective facts	Construct social reality, cultural meaning
Focus on variables	Focus on interactive processes, events
Reliability is the key	Authenticity is the key
Value free	Values are present and explicit
Independent of context	Situationally constrained
Many cases or subjects	Few cases or subjects
Statistical analysis	Thematic analysis
Researcher is detached from subject	Researcher is involved in subject

Source: *Neuman (1997, p. 14)*

Because it often involves a very rigorous process of hypothesis formulation, detached observation, data collection, data analysis and acceptance or rejection of the hypotheses, quantitative research is regarded as the very core of the scientific method. This paradigm has always been at the heart of the natural sciences, but has only recently become more prevalent in tourism studies, in association with the emergence of the knowledge-based platform. It claims to 'reliably' reflect the 'real world' through its rigorous procedures and the ability to extrapolate its results to a wider population. Many of its exponents, accordingly and unfairly, adopt a dismissive attitude towards 'soft' and subjective qualitative research approaches.

This perception is unfortunate, since the two research approaches are not uncomplementary. For example, much inductive research is qualitative and intuitive, but this can generate models and hypotheses that can then be tested using quantitative (or qualitative) techniques. Similarly, we may accept or reject a hypothesis based on some test of statistical significance, but find that we subsequently have to conduct in-depth qualitative interviews to interpret or account for these outcomes. Another link is the possibility of analysing qualitative data, such as newspaper letters to the editor, using quantitative methods such as content analysis (see section 12.2.7).

The student, therefore, should be aware of the circumstances under which a qualitative or quantitative approach is warranted, but should further realise that a particular research agenda can usefully combine both. This potential for synergy is illustrated by questionnaires that provide for quantitative response patterns (e.g. 'How old are you?' or 'On a scale of 1 to 5, how would you rate Uluru as a tourist attraction?') as well as qualitative insights through open-ended questions (e.g. 'Why did you rate Uluru in this way?'). Such a synergy between quantitative and qualitative methodologies is compatible with the emergence of the green paradigm (see chapter 11).

■ 12.2.7 Primary *research*

The distinction between **primary research** and **secondary research** depends on the source of the data that are being used by the researcher. In primary research, the data are collected directly by the researcher, and did not exist prior to their collection. This is usually undertaken when the data required to address some issue or problem that is of concern to the researcher are absent. Hence, a major advantage of primary research is the ability of the investigator to design a tailored research framework relevant to the specific topic and questions of interest. As with longitudinal and multiple site cross-sectional data, a major problem is high cost in time and money. There are numerous techniques associated with primary research methodology, some of the most important of which are described in the following.

Surveys

The survey is undoubtedly the most common method for conducting primary research in tourism studies, as well as in the social sciences more generally. Accordingly, much useful generic information is available for students wishing to undertake this type of investigation (e.g. Alreck & Settle 1995). The design and administration of any specific survey (and whether a survey is even the right way to proceed), however, still ultimately depends on the goals of the researcher and the resources that are available to conduct the survey (see Managing: Research to measure the effectiveness of visitor information centres). Depending on the responses to those concerns, the researcher can select from three basic types of surveys:

- face-to-face interviewing (conducted at households or in the field)
- telephone interviewing
- mail-out surveys (with fax and email variations).

Table 12.2 provides an overview of the key characteristics associated with each of these surveying techniques. If the researcher has a limited budget and no access to trained interviewers, then a mail-out survey is usually the best way to proceed. Similarly, a face-to-face procedure is warranted where the researcher is interested mainly in in-depth, qualitative responses with a small number of respondents.

MANAGING

Research to measure the effectiveness of visitor information centres

Visitor information centres (VICs) attempt to facilitate and increase tourist activity within a defined jurisdiction but it is not always clear whether their performance justifies the costs of their establishment and operation. The Sustainable Tourism CRC has developed the VICkit as a survey-based tool that allows VIC managers to assess their performance cost-effectively through 15 questions that can be administered to VIC visitors on a face-to-face or self-completed basis. The VICkit contains a user handbook (CD-ROM and hard copy), the questionnaire itself, a prototype cover letter and an Excel spreadsheet in which the questionnaire data can be entered and analysed. Aside from standard questions that ask about the respondents' gender, postcode of residence, age and travel group, the questionnaire focuses on:

- whether a prior visit to the VIC influenced the decision to make the current visit
- whether their current visit to the VIC is occurring at the beginning, middle or end of their trip
- how the VIC rated in terms of staff knowledge, touchscreen technology, friendliness, availability of information on local products and brochures
- how much the information obtained at the VIC increased or decreased the time they spent in the region and the number and range of activities pursued
- whether the VIC visit influenced them to seriously consider making a future visit (Sustainable Tourism CRC 2005).

Most of the questions simply require the visitor or interviewer to check the appropriate box (e.g. ☐ Male, ☐ Female) or write a short response (e.g. Postcode/ZIP: _____), which helps both completion and data entry. The VICkit authors recommend that at least 150 surveys be completed to generate valid outcomes, and provide suggestions for ensuring the collection of a representative random sample.

The results generated by the VICkit data analysis tool are primarily descriptive, providing for example the percentage of visitors who engaged in more activities than anticipated as a result of their visit to the target VIC. A cross-tabulation function is also provided that allows any variable to be analysed relative to any other variable. One can see, for example, whether males are more likely than females to engage in more activities as a result of their VIC encounter, or whether those reporting more activities also reported high satisfaction levels with staff knowledge. Detailed statistical analysis using multivariate techniques, however, is not available in the package. The authors encourage managers to employ the VICkit consistently over time to monitor trends but less anticipated perhaps are the possibilities that the package provides for multiple site longitudinal research if it becomes widely adopted.

■ Table 12.2
Characteristics of three ideal survey types

CHARACTERISTIC	FACE-TO-FACE SURVEYS	TELEPHONE SURVEYS	MAIL-OUT SURVEYS
Cost	High	Medium	Low
Response time	Medium	Fast	Slow
Response rate	High	Medium	Low
Interviewer bias	High	Medium	Low
Need for trained interviewers	Very high	High	None
Accommodation of sensitive questions	Difficult	Good	Good
Accommodation of multiple item scales and ranking questions	Reasonable	Difficult	Good
Accommodation of qualitative questions	Very good	Good	Difficult
Survey length	Medium	Short	Long
Sample size	Small	Medium	Large

Focus groups

Focus groups involve face-to-face group discussions conducted with a small number of people usually pre-selected because of their relevance to a particular research problem (Bloor 2001). A researcher who is concerned about resident reactions to a proposed resort hotel, for example, may gather together ten community leaders who are judged to be informed, concerned and representative of a broader cross-section of the local community. Focus groups rely a great deal on the interactions and synergies that take place among the participants, and are an excellent means of obtaining in-depth, qualitative data. They are often used in the initial phases of research to identify problems and issues, and as a prelude to quantitative inquiry. Yau, McKercher and Packer (2004) used focus groups along with in-depth interviews to explore the tourism experiences of people with disabilities in Hong Kong.

Relevant questions that must be asked when considering focus groups as a research method include how large a group to form (optimum group size may be affected by cultural and political factors), who to include and whether to offer some kind of incentive to participants. A more detailed analysis of the advantages and disadvantages of this approach, including the possibilities of virtual focus groups, is provided by Krueger and Casey (2000) and Bloor (2001).

The Delphi technique

The Delphi technique involves a panel of experts, ranging in size from ten or less to several hundred, who are asked to respond to several rounds (usually three or four) of questioning about a particular research issue (Adler & Ziglio 1996). In each subsequent round, all participants (who remain anonymous) are made aware of the results of the previous round of questioning, so that the opinions expressed in that new round are influenced by those earlier outcomes. Knowledge and opinion are thus systemically focused as feedback to arrive at an eventual consensus about the issue. The Delphi technique is often applied as a forecasting tool to obtain a general picture of the future, rather than as a means of achieving highly accurate predictions (which are almost always impossible to attain). Its fundamental principle is that useful speculations will emerge from the repeated and focused questioning of a group of individuals who are highly qualified and informed about a particular issue (Moeller & Shafer 1994). Among the problems associated with this technique are:

- identifying the appropriate pool of experts who represent the desired balance of opinions, philosophies, experience, etc.
- soliciting their participation
- obtaining panel feedback in a timely fashion
- panel attrition (tight time commitments are a common reason for this and the previous two problems)
- misinterpretation of responses
- an inability to obtain consensus or the temptation to 'fit' responses into a pattern of consensus.

From a student perspective, few if any experts are likely to participate in a study that is not being sponsored and coordinated by a well-known professor or university. Despite these pitfalls, the results can still be prophetic. One Delphi study undertaken in 1974 (Shafer & Moeller 1974) predicted that wildlife resources would be used mainly for nonconsumptive recreational uses such as photography by the year 2000, a forecast which has largely been realised through the growth of ecotourism (see chapter 11). More recently, the Delphi technique was used by Garrod (2003) to define 'ecotourism'. This approach revealed consensus as to its core criteria, but exposed divisions as to the importance of local ownership, and the status of ecotourism as a process rather than just a type of tourism. Participating experts also tended to favour medium-length definitions that compromised between simplicity and comprehensiveness.

Observation

The collection of information through observation is relevant to many tourism-related research problems. Applications include:

- noting the changing number and condition of hotels in a particular resort strip over a given period of time
- recording the average length of time that visitors to a theme park have to wait in a queue before gaining entry, and noting their body language during the wait
- counting the number of people who attend a large festival (Raybould et al. 2000)
- observing where a hotel disposes of its garbage over a certain time period
- recording the reaction of tourists towards souvenir hawkers at the entrance to a scenic site
- following a tour group to observe the behaviour and spatial distribution of tourists.

Because there is no direct interference with the subject matter in any of these cases, the researcher is able to observe the 'unselfconscious' behaviour of the subjects — that is, the reactions and responses of the tourists or residents are not influenced by interaction with an interviewer.

To capture this authentic behaviour, researchers undertaking observation will sometimes make a great effort to ensure that their activities and motives remain undetected. Serious ethical questions are raised if this involves the 'stalking' of people in order to avoid detection, or the use of deception so that subjects are unaware that they are the subject of an investigation. The latter can occur in certain types of 'participant observation', as when the researcher temporarily assumes a certain false identity in order to gain access to the unselfconscious views and behaviour of a particular group (Bowen 2002). For example, a researcher might work for several months among a group of lifeguards who assume that the researcher is 'one of them'. In reality, the real intention of the researcher is to gain the confidence of the group so that the authentic behaviour and perceptions of the lifesaving subculture can be observed as part of a research project. New technologies such as webcams enhance the possibilities for observation-based research, but generate additional ethical concerns (see Technology and tourism: Using webcams to aid research).

Most universities maintain special committees that assess the ethical dimensions of such research and define the conditions under which the projects are allowed to proceed. Because of the ethical questions raised and the amount of time involved, observation is not widely practised as a research technique within tourism studies despite its potential to yield knowledge that cannot be obtained through survey or questionnaire-based methods.

The webcam, or stationary camera linked to computer systems that broadcasts still and animated real-time images through the Internet or other media, is an emerging technology that is now being widely employed to market a variety of tourism products. It also has great utility as a device for gathering observational research data, in part because of its unobtrusive and increasingly cost-effective qualities. However, webcams are not yet being widely used for research purposes. To ascertain their potential as a data collection source, Timothy and Groves (2001) during early 2000 tracked and analysed the visual data conveyed by a convenience Internet sample of 300 tourism-related webcams. Most of the imagery focused on the target attraction and it was possible to identify four distinct categories of information. The most visible of these was the *weather*, from which it would be possible for researchers to identify seasonal and long-term patterns and to correlate weather conditions with *crowd density and distribution*, the second type of data that was yielded. Density and distribution data are extremely useful for identifying carrying capacity thresholds, differential use of sites and facilities during different times of the day, traffic patterns and crowd behaviour, all of which are useful in visitor management. Third, the sites provided information about structural *land use*, although meaningful patterns required a much longer time. Finally, some of the sites provided information on *licence plates*, which could be used to identify visitor market origins. While not evident from the sites, the researchers speculate that certain camera angles would allow for the closeup observation of tourist behaviour.

Timothy and Groves then identify four interrelated factors that cumulatively influence the capacity of webcams to provide useful visual data. Update interlude is one critical factor that takes into account whether the data are essentially continuous or static. Most images were 'refreshed' every ten seconds to five minutes, although some provided a near constant flow. Resolution or clarity is a second factor, critical if the researcher wishes to observe details such as licence plate jurisdictions, facial expressions or small animal behaviour (e.g. in ecotourism). Range of coverage, the third factor, includes distance from the observed site and angle (e.g. bird's eye, lateral or oblique). Finally, quality of coverage includes whether the view is fully or only partly visible. The researchers conclude by arguing that webcams are impressive but imperfect sources of data that are best used in conjunction with other more conventional modes of data collection, including field observation and surveys.

Content analysis

Content analysis describes a variety of techniques that are used to systematically examine and measure the meaning of communicated material by classifying and evaluating selected words, themes or images (Wheeler 1994). For example, the researcher might record the number and type of sexual images that appear in tourism advertisements for the Gold Coast in a sample of brochures. Insight into Doxey's irridex, to give a further illustration, might be gained by undertaking a content analysis of letters to the editor in a local newspaper. Within the tourism literature, a content analysis of human images in the tourism advertisements of 33 United States-based popular magazines was undertaken by Peterson (1998) to show that older adults are more likely to be depicted less frequently and more unfavourably than younger adults. Burns and Murphy (1998) content analysed a selection of brochures against actual visitor behaviour to determine that the promotion of the Great Barrier Reef underemphasised the educational motives of visitors and overemphasised participation in scuba diving. A study of 50 airline mission statements by Kemp and Dwyer (2003) found self-concept (88 per cent), philosophy (80 per cent) and customers (72 per cent) to be the most prevalent, and technology (22 per cent), concern for employees (22 per cent) and concern for public image (30 per cent) the least prevalent of nine core components characteristic of effective corporate mission statements.

■ 12.2.8 Secondary *research*

In secondary research, the investigator relies on material and research that has been compiled previously by other researchers. This substantially reduces the time and money required to obtain the desired information, especially given the availability of comprehensive and easily searched databases that contain a large number of secondary sources (see Breakthrough tourism: Leisuretourism.com and the dissemination of knowledge). However, a disadvantage is that users of this information cannot be entirely sure about its validity or reliability, since they were not involved in its original collection or compilation (Neuman 1997). Information sources that are important in secondary research are discussed below.

BREAKTHROUGH TOURISM
Leisuretourism.com and the dissemination of knowledge

The effective use of tourism-related knowledge to aid research and management depends upon how easily it can be accessed. Leisuretourism.com is a website operated by United Kingdom-based CABI Publishing that provides tourism, leisure, sport and hospitality stakeholders with access to a comprehensive database of mostly academic journal articles, books and conference proceedings. As of early 2005, this database included more than 70 000 items, most of them in English. The database can be searched using the 'quick', 'advanced' or 'expert' keyword search options, from which relevant material is displayed chronologically beginning with the most recent. Each item is accompanied by a full bibliographic reference and an abstract that briefly describes the item. Of particular

(continued)

interest are the links that allow the user to search for a full online copy of the item, and send an email to the contact author. In addition, a 'marked list' feature allows up to 500 items to be saved in a personalised database, which can then be printed, emailed, saved or exported.

Whereas the database is accessible only to paid subscribers, leisuretourism.com additionally includes a variety of free features, including relevant daily news headlines and briefs, a calendar of conferences and other meetings, academic job postings and a showcase featuring a current 'hot topic' such as ecotourism or domestic tourism. One intriguing feature is the provision of monthly usage statistics, which track the journals most frequently accessed and the terms used most frequently to search for items. During December 2003, for example, the top ten terms were (in order) 'tourism', 'leisure', 'ecotourism', 'sport', 'tourist behaviour', 'pro poor tourism', 'leisure education', 'product life cycle', 'authenticity' and 'tourism place'. This kind of information, tracked over time, is knowledge in its own right since it indicates the pattern of topics that are popular with researchers over time, and the journals from which information about these topics is obtained.

Academic journals

The proliferation of refereed journals within the field of tourism studies was discussed in chapter 1. Articles in academic journals, as described in that chapter, have the advantage of having undergone a double-blind reviewing process, which in theory increases the quality and objectivity of the published results. However, the time involved in undertaking the review process means that the results are often outdated by the time the journal appears on the library shelf. In addition, refereed journals often tolerate tedious and difficult writing styles that are not readily accessible to students, the tourism industry or even other academics. Proliferation itself is an emerging problem in the tourism field to the extent that there may not be enough quality manuscripts being submitted to sustain the many titles, forcing the editors of many of the newer journals in particular to accept mediocre manuscripts, which would otherwise be rejected. Nevertheless, academic journals are a core source of secondary data for students and other researchers wishing to access research outcomes in all aspects of tourism.

Academic books

Academic books have also proliferated since the early 1990s. Although books usually undergo a less rigorous process of peer review, they are also generally subject to much less stringent page limitations, allowing for more in-depth analyses of particular issues. Increasingly, academic tourism books are edited works covering specific themes, in which individual authors or author teams prepare one or more chapters. The following are just a few of the edited academic books useful to researchers wishing to investigate the indicated themes:

- *Food Tourism Around the World: Development, Management and Markets* (edited by Hall et al. 2003)

- *Gay Tourism: Culture, Identity and Sex* (edited by Clift, Luongo & Callister 2002)
- *Mediterranean Islands and Sustainable Tourism Development* (edited by Ioannides, Apostolopoulous & Sonmez 2001)
- *The Global Nomad: Backpacker Travel in Theory and Practice* (edited by Richards & Wilson 2004)
- *Tourism and National Parks* (edited by Butler & Boyd 2000)
- *Tourism and Recreation in Rural Areas* (edited by Butler, Hall & Jenkins 1998)
- *Tourism Ecolabelling* (edited by Font & Buckley 2001)
- *Tourism, Recreation and Climate Change* (edited by Hall & Higham 2005).

Statistical compilations

Tourism statistics are compiled by various government departments and non-governmental organisations. Among the latter, the WTO publishes two very useful and accessible annual compilations of international tourism data:

- *Yearbook of Tourism Statistics* (basic data for the given year for each member country; especially good coverage of regions, such as East Asia and the Pacific, etc.)
- *Compendium of Tourism Statistics* (basic data for countries provided over a five-year timeframe).

Nontourism NGOs that also publish international tourism statistics include the United Nations (included in the *Statistical Yearbook*), the Economist Intelligence Unit (*International Tourism Report* and *Travel & Tourism Analyst*) and the Euromonitor (included in *International (European) Marketing Data and Statistics*).

Within Australia, Tourism Research Australia publishes a number of important compilations, including the *International Visitor Survey* and the *National Visitor Survey* (see section 2.3.5). The Australian Bureau of Statistics (ABS) publishes *Overseas Arrivals and Departures*, which details the origins of inbound tourists and the destinations of outbound Australians. The ABS also publishes the *Survey of Tourist Accommodation (STA)*, which is a quarterly Australia-wide survey of supply and demand for hotels containing at least 15 rooms.

Trade publications

Trade publications include magazines and newsletters published by various industry organisations as well as government. As a source of data, they have the disadvantage of being 'unscientific' and journalistic in orientation. There is no equivalent of a double-blind review process, and the content often mirrors the vested interests and biases of the organisation producing the material. However, they are extremely useful for providing news of events that may have happened within the previous few weeks and indications of industry trends and perspectives. Some of the prominent Australian trade publications relating to the tourism sector are:

- *Tourism on the Move* (DITR)
- *Traveltrade* (Reed Elsevier Group)
- *Travel Week Australia* (Peter Isaacson Publications).

Newspapers and magazines

Newspapers and nonspecialised magazines such as *Time* and *Newsweek* are subject to the same advantages and disadvantages as outlined for trade publications. Students should therefore use these mainly as a source of current news, and also as a basis for content analysis exercises (i.e. a secondary source used to conduct primary analysis).

The Internet

The Internet is now an important source of secondary research information, especially as many of the above-mentioned publications are being made available online as a more accessible alternative to hard copy. While much reliable data can be obtained through the Internet, quality and reputability are major issues that must be considered when using this source. The Internet is an extremely attractive source of information for students and professional academics due to the convenience of being able to access an enormous amount of material on the most obscure topics at a single computer terminal. An Internet search, moreover, requires far less time to undertake than an exploration of conventional research sources. However, there are no standards or controls that regulate material appearing on the Internet, and the result is an enormous oversupply of useless and misleading information that surrounds the reputable material.

Topographical maps and remotely sensed images

Most aspects of tourism possess a spatial dimension, and it is therefore logical that topographical maps and remotely sensed images (e.g. aerial photographs, satellite images) should be widely used as a source of secondary research information. However, this is not the case, except among tourism specialists with a background in geography. This may be due in part to the decline of geography within high school and university curricula in many Western countries, including Australia. Whatever the underlying cause, a change in attitude is warranted. Large-scale topographical maps in particular provide an enormous amount of detailed information about changing landscapes if analysed longitudinally over a series of map editions. As such, they are very valuable for anyone wishing to examine the lifecycle dynamics of a destination for which such maps are available. However, the following limitations of topographical maps should be noted:

- considerable time lag (as much as 20 years) between editions
- need for the researcher to possess technical map-reading skills
- insufficient symbolic differentiation; for example, all wooded areas, no matter how diverse, are often depicted with a uniform light green colour
- need for researcher to have interpretive skills, i.e. how to distinguish tourism-related changes to those associated with other forces.

12.3 *T*HE RESEARCH PROCESS

In order to produce substantive and useful outcomes, research must be carried out in a deliberate and systematic manner. The steps that are required to carry out a research project from its origins to its conclusions comprise the **research process** (figure 12.3). The specific way in which each of these stages and their attendant substages is operationalised will vary from project to project, and the process is seldom one that is strictly sequential. For example, the results that emerge from an analysis of data may prompt a rethinking of the original research questions. Alternatively, the research methods may have to be reconsidered once the researcher has begun to collect the data and discovers that in-depth interviewing would be more effective than a mail-out survey in eliciting information from a particular group. More fundamentally, the methodological biases of the researcher often dictate, in the first instance, the problems that are identified and the questions that are posed.

■ **Figure 12.3**
*The research
process*

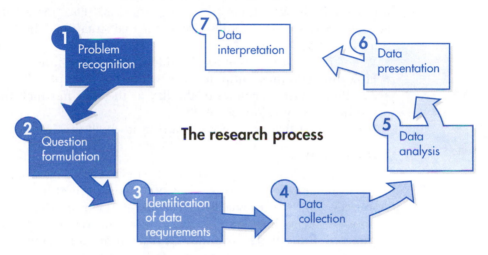

The research process

■ 12.3.1 Problem *recognition*

The first step in any research process is **problem recognition**, or the identification of the broad issues or problems that interest the investigator. For a tourism-based corporation, core issues that require research are reduced patronage and declining market share. From a destination perspective, additional concerns may be harboured about negative community reactions to tourism or declining environmental conditions. Existing theories, such as the Butler sequence or the irridex, may provide a useful framework for clarifying or contextualising the broad problem, which often emerges as a consequence of subjective perceptions, personal experiences or other qualitative input. As suggested above, methodological bias might dictate the problems that are identified. For example, a scientist trained in 'hard' quantitative techniques might not perceive a relatively subjective issue such as cultural commodification (see chapter 9) as being amenable to or worthy of scientific analysis, and hence would not recognise it as a problem that fits into their research agenda.

■ 12.3.2 Question *formulation*

Once these broad problems or issues are identified, the research questions must be focused, at least in applied research, so that time and resources are not wasted on tangential avenues of investigation. As a basis for **question formulation** (which may be expressed as hypotheses or propositions), it is helpful to clarify the level of investigation that is warranted by the problem and the resources of the company or destination that are available. Four levels of investigation (description, explanation, prediction and prescription) are possible, each of which builds on the previous level.

Description

Description is the most basic level of inquiry. Imagine that the managers of a particular destination are concerned that the local people appear to be increasingly hostile towards visiting tourists. The logical first step in addressing this issue is to describe the actual situation. The following questions might be posed:

- What are the attitudes of local residents towards visiting tourists?
- How much do these attitudes vary within the local population?
- Are there particular times of the day or the year in which the antitourist sentiment is more noticeable?
- Are there particular groups of tourists at which this hostility is directed?

Explanation

The decision whether to proceed to the next level of investigation, which is to explain the resultant patterns, is often constrained by the availability of resources. However, the decision should be based on whether one or more serious problems have been revealed after the research process has been completed at the descriptive level. If it is found, for example, that the perceived hostility of residents involves only a few isolated incidents instigated by known troublemakers, then there is probably no compelling reason to proceed any further with the investigation. If, however, the suspicions of emerging hostility within the population at large have been confirmed, then explanation is a necessary stage towards its resolution. In the hypothetical situation described above, the following explanation-based questions may emerge:

- Why does a significant minority of young male adults in the community express negative attitudes towards tourism?
- Why is their hostility directed mainly towards migrant workers employed by hotels?
- Why do most antitourist acts occur in the evening?

The subsequent research process might reveal a high level of unemployment among young males and resentment that 'their' jobs are being taken by outsiders. The evening may be a period of peak alcohol consumption and a time when tourists are visible on the street.

Prediction

Once a plausible explanation for the problems are found, the next level of investigation is to predict the consequences of the problem if no remedial measures are taken. As with any prediction involving humans, this stage of inquiry is speculative and often based on a process of linear extrapolation, but it is possible to engage in intelligent and well-considered speculation that will inform the final stage of prescription. Following on from the above example, the following predictive questions can be posed:

- What will happen to the local tourism industry if no steps are taken to address the hostility of young adults towards tourism?
- What will subsequently happen to the local community in terms of economic and social impacts?

Prescription

Prescription is the culmination of the research process, involving the informed consideration of various solutions to minimise the problem. If the predictive phase reveals that the above situation is highly volatile, and that the community will endure great suffering if nothing is done, then the prescriptive phase will be essential. The following questions may emerge:

- What immediate steps can the community take to ensure that the situation does not escalate out of control?
- What medium- and long-term steps can be taken to defuse the situation and to instil a more positive attitude to tourism among young adult males in the community?

For the first question, the 'research process' may have to be accelerated or abandoned altogether given the immediacy of the crisis (e.g. migrant workers may all be summarily dismissed and replaced by local residents). The second question, however, is more amenable to the rigour that is normally associated with the research process, though it may have to be reformulated depending on the outcome of the immediate measures that are adopted.

The question of intervention, or the actions that should be taken to ensure optimum outcomes for the company or destination, is a core component of the management process, and a very important arena for applied research. However, appropriate solutions or prescriptions will only emerge as a result of the knowledge that is obtained through good preliminary research at the levels of description, explanation and prediction. Furthermore, if the research questions raised at those levels are engaged effectively, it is more likely that problem areas will be intercepted and addressed before they evolve into major crises. Hence, it is difficult to see how good management can be undertaken in the absence of good research.

■ 12.3.3 Identification *of research methodology or methods*

The next stage usually involves the identification of the specific **research methods** that will best allow the questions to be addressed. This is normally informed by a search of secondary literature sources to see how other researchers have approached similar problems. In the descriptive phase of the example used, the investigator may undertake quantitative surveying among residents, tourists and tourism workers. This will provide a statistical basis for determining whether certain groups are more hostile towards tourism than others. Depending on resources and time, observation and community focus groups may augment the surveying process.

Cultural and social context must be considered in selecting an appropriate research methodology. For example, Likert-scaled survey questions (e.g. agreement with a statement on a 1 to 5 scale) are a reasonably effective means of eliciting accurate information from adults in mainstream, 'Western' societies such as those that predominate in Australia. However, there is evidence that east Asians for cultural reasons tend to avoid extreme responses on such instruments (i.e. they avoid 'strongly' agree or 'strongly' disagree), even if this is the way they really feel about the situation. For research issues involving indigenous people, a standard quantitative methodology based on the scientific paradigm is often grossly inappropriate given the importance in those cultures of building trust through face-to-face contact over a long period (Schuler, Aberdeen & Dyer 1999).

At the explanatory level, the researcher, in virtually any cultural context, should consider engaging in qualitative, in-depth interviews (e.g. with a sample of young adults and hotel employees) to identify the reasons for revealed attitudes and behaviour. For prediction, the interviewer has a number of options that can be pursued in conjunction with each other to see whether the different methods yield the same results, or whether the outcomes can be combined to arrive at a probable scenario. These include:

- an interview or survey question that asks the young adults what they are likely to do next if the situation does not change
- a modified Delphi technique to see what experts believe will occur
- a literature review to identify the outcomes of similar situations in other destinations
- extrapolation of past trends (e.g. if the number of hostile encounters has been increasing by 2 per cent a year over the past five years, then it could be assumed that this trend will continue to increase by a similar percentage in subsequent years)
- observation of situations in which the target behaviour is likely to be seen.

To use all of the above techniques in the same research process (whether at the explanatory or some other level of investigation) is to engage in methodological **triangulation**, or the use of several methods to gather information about and gain insight into the research issue (Oppermann 2000; Jennings 2001). If all four methods reveal similar outcomes, then the researcher has a high degree of confidence that the real situation has been identified. Moreover, it is likely that each method will yield its own unique insights into this situation, thereby strengthening the knowledge base that is obtained from the research. Constraints of time, expertise and money, however, often rule out the use of triangulation.

At the prescriptive level, many approaches are also possible, including continued Delphi inquiries as to appropriate solutions, as well as solicitation of the community to see what local residents (and young adult males in particular) are willing to accommodate or suggest. Interviews with tourism managers in other destinations may also provide insight.

12.3.4 **Data** *collection*

Once the most appropriate methods have been identified, the **data collection** phase of the research process can proceed. In most cases, the researcher cannot access the entire population that is being investigated, or observe every event associated with a particular process. It is therefore expedient in such circumstances to select a sample from the target population. Sampling can be carried out on a probability or nonprobability basis. In the former case, a sample is randomly drawn from the population so that each member of that population has an equal or known probability of being selected. This can be done by simply drawing names out of a hat (in a small population), by using random number tables or selecting every nth name from a list or person from a line-up. However attained, it is important to select a large enough sample so that inferences can be made about the entire population. If carried out properly, a sample of 2000 households can accurately reflect all Australian households within a very small margin of error. However, for a small population (e.g. fewer than 1000), it is advisable to sample at least 30 per cent of the population to achieve the same effect (Neuman 1997). Nonprobability or convenience sampling is commonly practised in qualitative research, and involves the deliberate selection of certain cases to build the sample. This type of sampling is not recommended for quantitative research except under certain circumstances.

Once the sample size and selection procedure have been decided, the actual collection of data can begin. Factors that must be considered at this stage include the timing of interviews or observations, consistency in the application of the research method or methods, and the collection of all results in as short a time period as possible. Specific issues may have to be considered depending on the research method and the conditions that are encountered in the 'field'. For example, telephone surveys carried out around suppertime are likely to yield a high response rate (i.e. people are likely to be at home), but a lower participation rate (i.e. because they do not wish to be bothered at that time).

12.3.5 **Data** *analysis*

The **data analysis** stage attempts to answer the relevant research questions by examining and assessing the collected information to identify patterns and meanings. Examination usually involves the filtering and organising of the database to eliminate invalid responses. This is then followed (at least in quantitative research) by the coding and entering of the data into a computer software system such as SPSS (Statistical Package for the Social Sciences), which facilitates further classification and analysis. Once the data are 'cleaned' to eliminate errors in the coding procedure, the actual analysis can be undertaken.

The most basic analysis in quantitative research is the recording of simple descriptive statistics such as frequencies, means and standard deviations (i.e. how much the data clusters around the mean). These are sufficient to answer many types of questions. At a more sophisticated level, tests of significance can be used to see whether the responses of one particular group are significantly different than those of the overall population. The relationships between many different variables and groups can be examined simultaneously using multivariate techniques such as factor analysis, cluster analysis and multidimensional scaling. The level of sophistication that should be adopted depends on the nature of the research questions, the competency of the researcher and the characteristics of the data that are collected.

In qualitative research, analysis can involve the sorting, comparing, classifying and synthesis of the collected information, usually with a much higher level of subjective or personal judgement than occurs in quantitative analysis. Because of this subjectivity, qualitative researchers are more likely to practise triangulation.

12.3.6 Data *presentation*

In the **data presentation** stage, the results of the analysis should be communicated in a way that can be easily interpreted by the target audience. Tables and graphs are the most common devices for presenting data, but great care should always be taken to avoid complexity and clutter particularly if the intended audience is not academic. Confusion often results when researchers wrongly assume that the audience is familiar with specific techniques and jargon. In general, the reader should be able to read a table or figure on its own, without having to resort to the text for an explanation.

Maps are underused not only as a source of secondary data, but also as a means of data presentation. Yet, for the same reasons, maps are an extremely efficient means of presenting spatial information if constructed properly. Imagine, for example, that the researcher wishes to present research results on the regional distribution of inbound tourists in Spain and the means by which they arrive in the regional destination. Figure 12.4 illustrates how this information can be depicted in a way that simplifies the identification of relevant spatial and transportation patterns. The graded circles indicate a concentration of tourists along the Mediterranean coastline (i.e. the Spanish Riviera) and in the offshore islands. At the same time, the division of the circles into wedges clearly reveals the dominance of road and air transport on the mainland and offshore, respectively. The clarity of this thematic map is assisted by the elimination of almost all contextual information except regional and international boundaries.

12.3.7 Data *interpretation*

The final stage, and in many ways the most difficult, is the extraction of meaning from the research results through **data interpretation**. This is where the significance and implications of the results are considered from a theoretical or practical perspective or both. The researcher may consider higher levels of investigation at this stage (e.g. move from description to explanation), or may revisit previous stages. As with earlier stages in the research process, interpretation will be influenced by the methodological and other biases of the researcher. In quantitative research, the acceptance or rejection of a hypothesis at the previous stage is a more objective form of interpretation, since this is determined by the outcome of a particular statistical technique. In such instances, the term 'significance' has a very specific meaning — that is, the result of the technique tells us, for example, whether the difference between two populations is statistically significant within some specified margin of error. Interpretation may or may not in this case lead to broader and more subjective speculations about less tangible matters, such as the implications of these results for the community or company.

While it is possible for two researchers to produce almost identical results up to the point of hypothesis acceptance or rejection, it is likely that their interpretations of the results will differ greatly at this broader level. Interpretation, in essence, can be as much art as science, and the effective interpreter is an individual who is well versed and experienced in the broader topic area and knowledgeable about the external environments that affect tourism. The importance of effective interpretation at the specific or broad level cannot be overstated, since this leads to the translation of research results into policy decisions and other outcomes that are important to the target audience.

■ **Figure 12.4**
Effective cartography: regional distribution of tourism in Spain, by mode of transport, July–December 1993

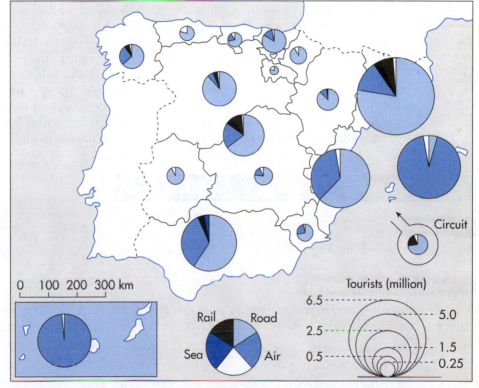

Source: *Pearce & Priestley (1998)*

CHAPTER REVIEW

The essential role of research is to provide a sound knowledge base that allows the managers of destinations and businesses to make the best possible management decisions. Research can be categorised into several contrasting pairs. Basic research uses an inductive or deductive approach to broaden our understanding of tourism, while applied research is directed towards addressing a particular problem or issue. Cross-sectional research is undertaken during a single time period, while longitudinal research considers trends over two or more time periods. Qualitative research tends to examine a small number of cases in great detail, while quantitative research usually considers a large number of cases in less depth. Finally, primary research occurs when the investigator gathers their own data, while secondary research involves the use of data that has already been gathered by other researchers.

The process through which research is undertaken comprises seven stages, although there is usually considerable flexibility in the sequence of steps that are actually followed in a research project. The process begins with problem recognition, then proceeds to the formulation of questions or hypotheses that provide a specific focus for investigation. At this point, the researcher also needs to consider the level of investigation that is of interest — description, explanation, prediction or prescription. Subsequently, a methodology (if not predetermined) and methods must be selected that address the research questions, and data collected that can then be analysed using those techniques. Once the data have been presented, the research process culminates in the interpretation of the results, which allows these to be translated into usable outcomes by the target audience.

SUMMARY OF KEY TERMS

Research

A systematic search for knowledge

Research methodology

A set of procedures and methods that are used to carry out a search for knowledge within a particular type of research

- **Basic research:** research that is broadly focused on the revelation of new knowledge, and is not directed towards specific outcomes or problems
- **Applied research:** research that addresses some particular problem or attempts to achieve a particular set of outcomes; it is usually constrained by set time schedules
- **Induction:** an approach in basic research whereby the observation and analysis of data leads to the formulation of theories or models that link these observations in a meaningful way

- **Deduction:** an approach in basic research that begins with a basic theory that is applied to a set of data to see whether the theory is applicable or not
- **Hypotheses:** tentative informed statements about the nature of reality that can be subsequently verified or rejected through systematic deductive research
- **Cross-sectional research:** a 'snapshot' approach to research that considers one or more sites at one particular point in time
- **Longitudinal research:** a trends-oriented approach to research, which examines one or more sites at two or more points in time or, more rarely, on a continuous basis
- **Qualitative research:** research that does not place its emphasis on the collection and analysis of statistical data, and usually tends to obtain in-depth insight into a relatively small number of respondents or observations
- **Quantitative research:** research that is based mainly on the collection and analysis of statistical data, and hence tends to obtain a limited amount of information on a large number of respondents or observations; these results are then extrapolated to the wider population of the subject matter
- **Primary research:** research that involves the collection of original data by the researcher
- **Secondary research:** researcher in which the investigator uses previously collected data

Research process

The sequence of stages that are followed to carry out a research project from its origins to its conclusions

- **Problem recognition:** the first stage of the research process, which is the identification of a broad problem arena that requires investigation
- **Question formulation:** the posing of specific questions or hypotheses that serve to focus the research agenda arising from problem recognition; these questions can be descriptive, explanatory, predictive or prescriptive in nature
- **Research methods:** the techniques that will be used to answer the questions or prove or disprove the hypotheses
- **Triangulation:** the use of multiple methods, data sources, investigators or theories in a research process
- **Data collection:** the gathering of relevant information by way of the techniques identified in the research methodology stage
- **Data analysis:** the process by which the collected information is examined and assessed to identify patterns that address the research questions
- **Data presentation:** the stage during which the results of the analysis are communicated to the target audience
- **Data interpretation:** the stage during which meaning is extracted from the data

QUESTIONS

1 Why is basic research associated more with universities than the corporate world?

2 (a) What is the difference between induction and deduction?
(b) How do the two approaches work together in long-term research projects?

3 What are the main advantages and disadvantages of
(a) cross-sectional research and
(b) longitudinal research?

4 (a) What are the relative strengths and weaknesses of
(i) qualitative research and
(ii) quantitative research?
(b) In what ways can qualitative and quantitative research display a complementary relationship?

5 Why should the researcher be cautious when considering observation, and webcams in particular, as a means of gathering tourism-related data?

6 (a) Why has the Internet become so popular as a source of information for tourism researchers?
(b) Why should caution be exercised when using the Internet to obtain material for research purposes?

7 (a) How do the four levels of investigation (i.e. description, explanation, etc.) complement each other towards the fulfilment of a complete research agenda?
(b) How do each of these contribute towards the more effective management of businesses or destinations?

8 What are the strengths and weaknesses of methodological triangulation?

9 (a) Why is it usually important for researchers to obtain a representative sample of a particular population for research purposes?
(b) When is it appropriate not to take a representative sample?
(c) What factors must be considered when defining a representative sample for a particular study?

10 (a) Why can interpretation be considered an art as much as a science?
(b) How important is interpretation to the research process?

EXERCISES

1 Obtain a recent copy of one of the trade journals listed on page 393, and prepare a 1000-word report that comments on the strengths and weaknesses of this issue as a source of secondary tourism information for an academic research project.

2 (a) Using any recent article from *Annals of Tourism Research, Tourism Management* or the *Journal of Travel Research,* identify the type of research that is represented and the type of primary and/or secondary research methods and sources that are employed (see section 12.2).

  (b) Describe how these types of research and methods are related to the problem recognition, question formulation and identification of data requirements (i.e. first three stages of the research process in section 12.3) used in the article.

FURTHER READING

Alreck, P. L. & Settle, R. B. 1995. *The Survey Research Handbook.* **Second Edition. London: Irwin.** The *Research Handbook* provides a comprehensible and readable guide to the design and administration of surveys.

Garrod, B. 2003. 'Defining Marine Ecotourism: A Delphi Study'. In Garrod, B. & Wilson, J. (Eds) *Marine Ecotourism: Issues and Experiences.* **Clevedon, UK: Channel View Publications, pp. 17–36.** Garrod's exploration of the definition of 'ecotourism' provides a thorough demonstration of the utility of the Delphi technique in tourism research.

Goodson, L. & Phillimore, J. (Eds) 2004. *Qualitative Research in Tourism: Ontologies, Epistemologies and Methodologies.* **London: Routledge.** This book provides a comprehensive exposure to and analysis of qualitative research methods as they pertain to the tourism sector.

Jennings, G. 2001. *Tourism Research.* **Brisbane: John Wiley & Sons.** Jennings discusses all essential aspects of research from a tourism studies perspective, including data sources, ethical considerations, qualitative and quantative methods, and the preparation of research proposals.

Kemp, S. & Dwyer, L. 2003. 'Mission Statements of International Airlines: A Content Analysis'. *Tourism Management* **24: 635–53.** A good step-by-step application of content analysis is provided by the authors.

Oppermann, M. 2000. 'Triangulation — A Methodological Discussion'. *International Journal of Tourism Research* **2: 141–6.** Oppermann provides a useful critique of triangulation as a research approach in the field of tourism studies.

Raybould, M., Mules, T., Fredline, E. & Tomljenovic, R. 2000. 'Counting the Herd. Using Aerial Photography to Estimate Attendance at Open Events'. *Event Management* 6: 25–32. This intriguing article demonstrates the challenges and creative thinking involved in researching unusual situations, such as crowd size at nonsecured events. The 1998 Wintersun Festival, on the Gold Coast, is the case study.

Sarantakos, S. 2004. *Social Research*. Third Edition. Melbourne: Palgrave Macmillan. This is an excellent introduction to a wide range of methods and issues associated with research in the social sciences and related fields, such as tourism.

Schuler, S., Aberdeen, L. & Dyer, P. 1999. 'Sensitivity to Cultural Difference in Tourism Research: Contingency in Research Design'. *Tourism Management* 20: 59–70. A detailed discussion is provided on issues that should be considered for those wishing to undertake ethical research among indigenous people.

Timothy, D. & Groves, D. 2001. 'Research Note: Webcam Images as Potential Data Sources for Tourism Research'. *Tourism Geographies* 3: 394–404. The possibilities for using webcams as a source of tourism-related data are discussed by the authors.

Backpackers, brochures and photographs

The visual images of iconic attractions and landscapes depicted in films, brochures and other media appear to perpetuate a 'circle of representation', in which tourists deliberately seek and photograph (i.e. 'recapture') these same images — usually with themselves included in the picture, and subsequently share them with friends and relatives as evidence of their personal contact with the iconic site. This process reinforces the power of these images in the public mind and encourages the media to display them even more prominently for marketing purposes (Jenkins 2003). The tendency to be influenced by and to perpetuate iconic imagery through the circle of representation might be expected among psychocentric mass tourists preferring contact with the familiar but should not in theory be encountered among allocentric tourists seeking unusual and offbeat experiences. To investigate the latter proposition, Jenkins conducted a study of backpackers who had visited or were currently visiting Australia.

The first stage of this research involved a content analysis of the photography in 17 brochures on Australia collected in 1998 from retail travel agencies in Vancouver, Canada. This descriptive inventory revealed a dominance of physical features such as beaches (109 occurrences), the Great Barrier Reef and Red Rocks other than Uluru or the Olgas (79 each) and Uluru (45). The dominant cultural feature was the Sydney Opera House, with 45 occurrences. Interestingly, the brochures averaged five images of young adult females wearing swimwear, often a 'rear view' of the individual facing the ocean. The brochures were then divided between those directed towards mainstream tourists and those pitched to backpackers, based on wording and company affiliation. The backpacker brochures were far more likely to depict adventurous outdoor activities such as bungee jumping, sky diving and scuba diving, while the mainstream brochures emphasised passive activities such as eating, walking and petting iconic animals such as koalas. The former were also more likely to depict groups of young people while the latter focused on couples. A semiotic analysis of these images suggests that the mainstream brochures convey a sense of relaxation designed to reinvigorate a sexual relationship, while the backpacker images suggest fun, adventure and social opportunities (including meeting potential sexual partners). This content and semiotic analysis indicated that stereotypical natural images dominated all the brochures but that the depictions of activities and social dynamics were distinctive.

In the next phase of the research, 30 backpackers in Australia (all of whom possessed cameras) were asked in interactive semistructured interviews about the kinds of photographs they were taking on their trip. The responses, which indicated the popularity of natural attractions, informed the development of a photography-content structured face-to-face survey that was administered to 90 Canadian backpackers in Vancouver. In neither case does the author reveal how the backpackers were selected. Seventy-seven per cent of the Canadians reported that they 'always', 'very often' or 'often' take pictures of famous sites, while just 3 per cent claimed that they 'never' did so. One in-depth qualitative interview with a young female backpacker from the Netherlands revealed a rear view beach shot that almost exactly mirrored the stereotypical brochure image of this type.

To gain further insight, five disposable cameras were given to each of then selected backpackers, who were asked to take the pictures at five destinations (i.e. Sydney, Byron Bay, Fraser Island, the Cairns region and central Australia). Presumably, the sample was selected because they were going to all five locations but the author does not indicate this in her article (ibid.). Only three of these subjects returned all five cameras with all pictures taken but the images that were returned yielded an enormous amount of information. Using a bulletin board, the photos were clustered by location and theme and compared with the images conveyed in the backpacker brochures. The researcher found much evidence to refute the proposition that backpackers prefer to photograph unusual or offbeat sites and attractions. Images of the opera house, or opera house and harbour bridge juxtaposed, were featured in the Sydney photographs, as were the Byron Bay lighthouse and the Atherton Tablelands curtain fig tree. 'Strong similarities' between the backpacker photos and the brochure photos are reported by Jenkins (ibid., p. 323). The article, however, does not report any other details about the photographs, for example, whether they tended to imitate the 'action' group shots that are prominently featured in the backpacker brochures.

The author concludes that backpackers, despite their association with alternative tourism, are essentially as susceptible to the myths and stereotypes of mass marketing as other tourists in terms of what constitutes the 'real' Australia. This supports the idea of a circle of representation in which clichéd images are tracked down and 'recaptured', thus reinforcing their iconic value and power. A broader implication is the possibility that this reflects a larger pattern of conformity that ties backpackers even more closely to mainstream modes of tourist behaviour, despite the self-conscious 'antitourist' image that they usually wish to project. If so, then it may be that the backpacker experience, like the Grand Tour experience, reflects a 'normal' pseudorebellious stage of life that precedes and presages a more conformist pattern of tourist activity once the backpacker marries or secures a permanent job. The allocentric, by this logic, is really a 'pseudoallocentric' who eventually becomes a midcentric or even psychocentric in a later life phase. For marketers, these research findings may suggest the receptiveness of backpackers to other trappings of the mainstream tourist experience, including the use of credit cards and indulgence expenditures.

Questions

1 Prepare a 1000-word critique of this research project that includes
   (a) the type or types of research it represents, that is basic or applied, induction or deduction, cross-sectional or latitudinal, qualitative or quantitative, primary or secondary
   (b) the methods that are used
   (c) how far the seven-stage research process (figure 12.3) is followed
   (d) how much the four types of question formulation are pursued and
   (e) the strengths and weakness of the study and recommendations for improvement or clarification.

2 Locate a photo album of a trip taken by yourself or a member of your family during the past five years. Perform a simple content analysis of these photos to determine whether they lend support to the circle of representation theory.

Selected international and Australian tourism organisations

TOURISM ORGANISATION	ORIGINAL DATE ESTABLISHED	PURPOSE	HEAD-QUARTERS
Australian Bureau of Statistics (ABS) www.abs.gov.au/	1976	Australia's official statistical organisation	Belconnen, ACT
Tourism Australia www.tourism.australia.com/ (predecessor Australian Tourist Commission)	1967	The Australian Government statutory authority established to promote Australia as an international tourist destination	Canberra, ACT
Tourism Research Australia (predecessor Bureau of Tourism Research) www.tra.australia.com	1987	A branch of Tourism Australia that collects, analyses and disseminates information regarding the Australian tourism industry to government, industry and the general public	Canberra, ACT
Sustainable Tourism CRC www.crctourism.com.au/	1996	An Australian partnership (cooperative research centre) between universities, government and industry to promote sustainable tourism through the timely delivery of strategic innovation	Gold Coast, QLD
Ecotourism Australia www.ecotourism.org.au/ (predecessor Ecotourism Association of Australia)	1991	Promotes an understanding of ecotourism and environmental issues in Australia, and aims to develop ethics and standards for the industry, and facilitate interaction between ecotourism stakeholders	Brisbane, QLD
Green Globe 21 www.greenglobe.org	1992	A private intercorporate company that promotes certified environmental sustainability among its member tourism companies	Turner, ACT

TOURISM ORGANISATION	DATE ESTABLISHED	PURPOSE	HEAD-QUARTERS
Pacific Asia Travel Association (PATA) www.pata.org/	1951	A nonprofit travel industry association that promotes travel and tourism destinations in the Asia–Pacific region through networking, marketing, promotion and sales, destination promotion and trade shows; consists of approximately 2100 organisations, including governments, travel organisations and companies	San Francisco, United States (administrative headquarters)
Industry, Tourism and Resources www.isr.gov.au	1996	The main federal agency responsible for developing and implementing government tourism policy, managing Australia's participation in international expositions and delivering funding through the government's regional tourism program	Canberra, ACT
The World Tourism Organization (WTO) (predecessor IUOTO – International Union of Official Travel Organisations) www.world-tourism.org/	1975	An international nongovernmental organisation that provides a forum to discuss global tourism policy and issues, and has a mission to promote and develop tourism as a way of encouraging world peace, and as an agent of economic development; includes 133 countries and territories, and more than 300 affiliate members	Madrid, Spain
World Tourism and Travel Council (WTTC) www.wttc.org/	n/a	The main forum for global tourism chief executive officers, including accommodation, catering, cruises, entertainment, recreation, transportation and travel-related services; central goal is to work with governments to fulfil the full economic potential of tourism	London, United Kingdom

Refereed English language tourism journals (2005)

JOURNAL TITLE	DATE OF FIRST ISSUE	COUNTRY OF EDITOR(S)
Journal of Travel Research (formerly *Travel Research Bulletin*) www.sagepub.co.uk/frame.html? www.sagepub.co.uk/journalhome.aspx	1962	United States
Annals of Tourism Research www.sciencedirect.com/science/journal/01607383	1973	United States
Tourism Recreation Research www.TRRworld.com/	1976	India
Tourism Management www.elsevier.com/inca/publications/store/3/0/4/7/2/	1980	New Zealand
Anatolia www.anatoliajournal.com/	1990	Turkey
Journal of Tourism Studies www.jcu.edu.au/fac1/public/business/jts/ Has ceased publication as of 2005.	1990	Australia
Journal of Travel & Tourism Marketing www.haworthpress.com/store/product.asp?sku=J073	1992	Hong Kong SAR (China)
Event Management (formerly *Festival and Event Management*) www.cognizantcommunication.com/	1993	Canada
Journal of Hospitality and Tourism Management (formerly *Australian Journal of Hospitality Management*) www.australianacademicpress.com.au/Publications/Journals/ JHTM/jhtm_absframe.htm	1993	Australia
Journal of Sustainable Tourism www.channelviewpublications.net/jost/default.htm	1993	United Kingdom
Journal of Vacation Marketing www.henrystewart.com/journals/hspindex.htm	1994	Australia
International Journal of Tourism Research (formerly *Progress in Tourism and Hospitality Research*) interscience.wiley.com/jpages/1099-2340/	1995	United Kingdom
Tourism Economics www.ippublishing.com/general_tourism.asp	1995	United Kingdom

JOURNAL TITLE	DATE OF FIRST ISSUE	COUNTRY OF EDITOR(S)
Asia Pacific Journal of Tourism Research www.hotel-online.com/Neo/Trends/AsiaPacificJournal/ www.tandf.co.uk/journals/titles/10941665.asp	1996	Hong Kong SAR (China)
Journal of Sport Tourism www.tandf.co.uk/journals/titles/14775085.asp	1996	Canada
Tourism (formerly Turizam) www.iztzg.hr/turizam/tourism.htm	1996	Croatia
Tourism Analysis www.cognizantcommunication.com/	1996	United States
International Journal of Hospitality and Tourism Administration (formerly Journal of International Hospitality, Leisure and Tourism Management) www.haworthpress.com/web/IJHTA/	1997	United States
Journal of Hospitality & Tourism Research www.sagepub.com/journal.aspx?pid=102	1997	Hong Kong SAR (China)
Tourism Review International (formerly Pacific Tourism Review) www.cognizantcommunication.com/	1997	Australia
Current Issues in Tourism http://angelina.catchword.com/vl=32880129/cl=25/nw=1/ rpsv/cw/mm/13683500/contp1.htm	1998	New Zealand
Information Technology and Tourism www.cognizantcommunication.com/	1998	Austria
Journal of Convention & Event Tourism (formerly Journal of Convention & Exhibition Management) www.haworthpress.com/store/product.asp?sku=J452	1998	United States
Tourism Culture and Communication www.cognizantcommunication.com/	1998	Australia
Tourism Geographies www.geog.nau.edu/tg/	1999	United States
Tourism & Hospitality Research www.henrystewart.com/tourism_and_hospitality/	1999	United Kingdom
Journal of Quality Assurance in Hospitality & Tourism www.haworthpressinc.com/store/product.asp?sku=J162	2000	South Korea/ United States
Journal of Teaching in Travel & Tourism www.haworthpress.com/web/JTTT/	2001	Hong Kong SAR (China)
Scandinavian Journal of Hospitality and Tourism www.tandf.co.uk/journals/titles/15022250.asp	2001	Norway

JOURNAL TITLE	DATE OF FIRST ISSUE	COUNTRY OF EDITOR(S)
Tourist Studies http://tou.sagepub.com/	2001	Australia/ United Kingdom
Journal of Ecotourism www.channelviewpublications.net/jet/default.htm	2002	Canada
eReview of Tourism Research (ejournal) http://ertr.tamu.edu/	2003	United States/ Canada
Journal of Tourism and Cultural Change www.channelviewpublications.com/multi/journals/journals- jtcc.asp?TAG=BH82VX5X9849165X2D104V&CID=	2003	United Kingdom
Tourism and Hospitality Planning & Development www.tandf.co.uk/journals/titles/1479053X.asp	2004	United Kingdom
Tourism in Marine Environments http://cognizantcommunication.com/	2004	New Zealand
Journal of Heritage Tourism jht.asp?TAG=BH82VX5X984916SX2D104V&CID=	2006	United States

Inbound and outbound tourism data

ENTITY	REGION	POPULATION (000s) 2002	GNP PER CAPITA (2002) (US$)	OUTBOUND (000s) 2002	INBOUND (000s) 1990	INBOUND (000s) 2002	INT. TOURISM RECEIPTS 2002 (US$MIL)	TOURISM AS % OF GNP (2002)
Afghanistan	SAsia	27 756	n/a	n/a	n/a	n/a	n/a	n/a
Albania	SEur	3 545	1 420	n/a	30	n/a	446[1]	8.9
Algeria	NAfr	32 278	1 720	1 257	1 137	998	133	0.2
American Samoa	AusSP	69	n/a	44[1]	26	n/a	n/a	n/a
Andorra	SEur	60	n/a	n/a	n/a	3 388	n/a	n/a
Angola	MAfr	10 593	680	n/a	67	91	22[1]	0.3
Anguilla	Car	12	n/a	n/a	31	44	58[3]	74.4
Antigua & Barbuda	Car	67	8 770	n/a	206	n/a	272[1]	46.2
Argentina	SA	37 813	4 220	3 008	1 930	2 820	2 547[1]	1.6
Armenia	CEEur	3 330	810	131	n/a	n/a	123[1]	4.6
Aruba	Car	70	n/a	n/a	433	643	715[3]	41.3
Australia	AusSP	19 547	19 530	3 461	2 215	4 841	8 087	2.1
Austria	WEur	8 170	23 860	3 907	19 011	18 611	11 237	5.8
Azerbaijan	CEEur	7 798	720	1 141	n/a	834	43[1]	0.8
Bahamas	Car	300	15 110	n/a	1 562	n/a	1 636[1]	36.1
Bahrain	ME	656	11 260	n/a	1 376	3 167	366[3]	7.5
Bangladesh	SAsia	133 377	380	1 158	115	207	48[1]	0.1
Barbados	Car	277	8 790	n/a	432	498	687[1]	28.2
Belarus	CEEur	10 335	1 380	1 386[1]	n/a	n/a	82[1]	0.6
Belgium	WEur	10 275	22 940	6 773	n/a	6 724	6 892	2.9
Belize	CA	263	3 190	n/a	197	200	133	15.9
Benin	WAfr	6 788	380	n/a	110	72	60	2.3

ENTITY	REGION	POPULATION (000s) 2002	GNP PER CAPITA (2002) (US$)	OUTBOUND (000s) 2002	INBOUND (000s) 1990	INBOUND (000s) 2002	INT. TOURISM RECEIPTS 2002 (US$MIL)	TOURISM AS % OF GNP (2002)
Bermuda	Car	64	n/a	n/a	435	284	351[1]	n/a
Bhutan	SAsia	2 094	600	n/a	2	6	10[2]	0.8
Bolivia	SA	8 445	910	636	254	n/a	156[1]	2.0
Bonaire	Car	12	n/a	n/a	37	52	75[1]	n/a
Bosnia & Herzegovina	SEur	3 964	1 310	n/a	n/a	160	73[1]	1.4
Botswana	SAfr	1 591	2 990	n/a	543	1 037	309	6.5
Brazil	SA	176 030	2 860	2 364	1 091	3 783	3 120	0.6
British Virgin Is.	Car	21	n/a	n/a	160	285	230[3]	37.3
Brunei	SEAsia	351	n/a	n/a	377	n/a	n/a	n/a
Bulgaria	CEEur	7 621	1 790	3 188	n/a	3 433	1 344	9.9
Burkina Faso	WAfr	12 603	250	n/a	74	149	34[1]	1.1
Burundi	EAfr	6 373	100	35[1]	109	n/a	1[1]	0.2
Cambodia	SEAsia	12 775	290	49[4]	17	787	379	10.2
Cameroon	MAfr	16 185	570	n/a	89	n/a	39[2]	0.4
Canada	NA	31 902	22 390	17 705	15 209	20 057	9 700	1.3
Cape Verde	WAfr	409	1 280	n/a	24	126	20[3]	4.6
Cayman Islands	Car	36	n/a	n/a	253	303	450[3]	60.4
Central African Rep.	MAfr	3 643	250	n/a	n/a	n/a	n/a	n/a
Chad	MAfr	8 997	220	39[1]	9	n/a	n/a	n/a
Chile	SA	15 499	4 350	1 938	943	1 412	733	1.1
China	NEAsia	1 284 304	960	16 602	n/a	36 803	20 385	1.7
Colombia	SA	41 008	1 810	1 277	813	541	962	1.3
Comoros	EAfr	614	380	n/a	8	n/a	16[3]	8.2
Congo	MAfr	2 958	610	n/a	33	n/a	n/a	n/a

ENTITY	REGION	POPULATION (000s) 2002	GNP PER CAPITA (2002) (US$)	OUTBOUND (000s) 2002	INBOUND (000s) 1990	INBOUND (000s) 2002	INT. TOURISM RECEIPTS 2002 (US$MIL)	TOURISM AS % OF GNP (2002)
Congo (Dem.)	MAfr	55 225	90	50[4]	55	n/a	n/a	n/a
Cook Islands	AusSP	21	n/a	9	34	73	34[3]	45.9
Costa Rica	CA	3 835	4 070	364	435	1 113	1 078	6.9
Croatia	SEur	4 391	4 620	n/a	7 049	6 944	3 811	18.8
Cuba	Car	11 224	n/a	111	327	1 656	1 571[3]	8.8
Curacao	Car	n/a	n/a	n/a	219	218	273	n/a
Cyprus	EMed	767	n/a	645	1 561	2 418	1 671[3]	18.7
Czech Republic	CEEur	10 257	5 490	34 303	n/a	4 579	2 941	5.2
Denmark	NEur	5 369	30 260	4 935	n/a	2 010	5 785	3.6
Dominica	Car	70	3 190	n/a	45	67	36	16.1
Dominican Rep.	Car	8 722	2 310	332	1 305	2 811	2 736	13.6
Ecuador	SA	13 447	1 490	627	362	654	447	2.2
Egypt	ME	70 712	1 470	3 330	2 411	4 906	3 764	3.6
El Salvador	CA	6 354	2 080	1 001	194	951	342	2.6
Eritrea	EAfr	4 466	190	n/a	n/a	101	73	8.6
Estonia	CEEur	1 416	4 190	1 849	n/a	1 360	555	9.4
Ethiopia	EAfr	67 673	100	n/a	79	156	75[1]	1.1
Fiji	AusSP	856	2 080	99	279	398	267	15.0
Finland	NEur	5 184	23 890	5 857	n/a	2 875	1 573	1.3
France	WEur	59 766	22 240	17 404	52 497	77 012	32 329	2.4
French Polynesia	AusSP	258	n/a	n/a	132	189	354[3]	n/a
Gabon	MAfr	1 233	3 060	219	109	212	7[1]	0.2
Gambia	WAfr	1 456	310	n/a	100	n/a	n/a	n/a
Georgia	CEEur	4 961	720	317	n/a	298	472	13.2

ENTITY	REGION	POPULATION (000s) 2002	GNP PER CAPITA (2002) (US$)	OUTBOUND (000s) 2002	INBOUND (000s) 1990	INBOUND (000s) 2002	INT. TOURISM RECEIPTS 2002 (US$MIL)	TOURISM AS % OF GNP (2002)
Germany	WEur	83 252	22 740	73 300	17 045	17 969	19 158	1.0
Ghana	WAfr	20 244	280	n/a	146	483	520	9.2
Gibraltar	SEur	28	n/a	n/a	n/a	n/a	n/a	n/a
Greece	SEur	10 645	11 660	n/a	8 873	14 180	9 741	7.8
Grenada	Car	89	3 480	n/a	76	132	84	27.1
Guadeloupe	Car	436	n/a	n/a	331	n/a	418[2]	n/a
Guam	AusSP	161	n/a	n/a	780	1 059	n/a	n/a
Guatemala	CA	13 314	1 750	629	509	881	695	3.0
Guinea	WAfr	7 775	410	n/a	n/a	43	31	1.0
Guyana	SA	698	860	n/a	64	104	52[3]	7.9
Haiti	Car	7 064	430	n/a	144	140	54[1]	1.8
Honduras	CA	6 561	920	285	290	550	342	5.7
Hong Kong SAR	NEAsia	7 303	24 500	4 709	6 581	16 566	10 117	5.7
Hungary	CEEur	10 075	5 240	12 966	20 510	15 870	3 273	6.2
Iceland	NEur	279	27 960	283[2]	142	278	250	3.2
India	SAsia	1 045 845	470	4 940	1 707	2 370	2 923	0.6
Indonesia	SEAsia	231 328	710	n/a	2 178	5 033	5 411[1]	3.3
Iran	SAsia	66 623	1 790	2 921	154	n/a	477[3]	0.4
Iraq	ME	24 002	n/a	n/a	748	n/a	n/a	n/a
Ireland	NEur	3 883	23 030	4 634	3 666	6 476	3 089	3.5
Israel	EMed	6 030	16 020	3 273	1 063	862	1 197	1.2
Italy	SEur	57 716	19 080	25 126	26 679	39 799	26 915	2.4
Ivory Coast	WAfr	16 805	620	n/a	196	n/a	48[1]	0.5
Jamaica	Car	2 680	2 700	n/a	989	1 266	1 209	16.7
Japan	NEAsia	126 975	34 010	16 523	3 236	5 239	3 499	0.08
Jordan	ME	5 307	1 760	1 726	572	1 622	786	8.4
Kenya	EAfr	31 139	360	n/a	814	838	297	2.6

ENTITY	REGION	POPULATION (000s) 2002	GNP PER CAPITA (2002) (US$)	OUTBOUND (000s) 2002	INBOUND (000s) 1990	INBOUND (000s) 2002	INT. TOURISM RECEIPTS 2002 (US$MIL)	TOURISM AS % OF GNP (2002)
Kiribati	AusSP	96	890	n/a	3	5	3[1]	3.5
Korea North	NEAsia	22 224	n/a	n/a	115	n/a	n/a	n/a
Korea South	NEAsia	48 324	11 280	7 123	2 959	5 347	5 277	1.0
Kuwait	ME	2 112	16 340	n/a	15	n/a	118	0.3
Kyrgyzstan	CEEur	4 822	290	45	n/a	n/a	24[1]	1.7
Laos	SEAsia	5 777	310	n/a	14	215	113	6.3
Latvia	CEEur	2 367	3 490	2 306	n/a	848	161	1.9
Lebanon	ME	3 678	3 900	n/a	n/a	956	956	6.7
Lesotho	SAfr	2 208	470	n/a	171	n/a	23[1]	2.2
Libya	ME	5 369	n/a	n/a	96	n/a	n/a	n/a
Liechtenstein	WEur	33	n/a	n/a	78	49	n/a	n/a
Lithuania	CEEur	3 601	3 730	3 584	n/a	1 433	513	3.8
Luxembourg	WEur	449	39 470	261[1]	820	876	2 186	12.4
Macau (China)	NEAsia	462	n/a	200	2 513	6 565	2 622[3]	38.4
Macedonia	SEur	2 055	1 710	n/a	562	123	39	1.1
Madagascar	EAfr	16 473	230	n/a	53	n/a	115[1]	3.0
Malawi	EAfr	10 702	160	n/a	130	285	125	7.3
Malaysia	SEAsia	22 662	3 550	29 866	7 446	13 292	6 785	8.4
Maldives	SAsia	320	2 140	43	195	485	318	46.4
Mali	WAfr	11 340	240	n/a	44	96	71[2]	2.6
Malta	SEur	397	9 260	157	872	1 134	568	15.4
Marshall Islands	AusSP	74	2 380	n/a	5	6	4	2.3
Martinique	Car	422	n/a	306[1]	282	448	245[1]	n/a
Mauritius	EAfr	1 200	3 860	162	292	682	612	13.2
Mexico	NA	103 400	5 940	11 948	17 176	19 667	8 858	1.4

ENTITY	REGION	POPULATION (000s) 2002	GNP PER CAPITA (2002) (US$)	OUTBOUND (000s) 2002	INBOUND (000s) 1990	INBOUND (000s) 2002	INT. TOURISM RECEIPTS 2002 (US$MIL)	TOURISM AS % OF GNP (2002)
Micronesia	AusSP	136	1 970	n/a	n/a	19	13[1]	4.9
Moldova	CEEur	4 435	470	52	n/a	18	55	2.6
Monaco	WEur	32	n/a	n/a	245	263	n/a	n/a
Mongolia	NEAsia	2 694	430	n/a	147	198	39[1]	3.4
Montserrat	Car	8	n/a	n/a	13	10	8[3]	25.0
Morocco	NAfr	31 168	1 170	1 614	4 024	4 193	2 152	5.9
Myanmar	SEAsia	42 238	n/a	n/a	21	217	45[1]	n/a
Namibia	SAfr	1 821	1 830	n/a	n/a	n/a	404[1]	12.1
Nepal	SAsia	25 874	230	238	255	n/a	140[1]	2.4
Netherlands	WEur	16 068	23 390	16 758	5 795	9 595	7 706	2.1
New Caledonia	AusSP	208	n/a	72	87	104	93[1]	n/a
New Zealand	AusSP	3 908	13 250	1 293	n/a	2 045	2 918	5.6
Nicaragua	CA	5 024	720	532	106	472	106	2.9
Niger	WAfr	10 640	180	n/a	21	n/a	18[3]	0.9
Nigeria	WAfr	129 935	280	n/a	190	n/a	156[1]	0.4
Niue	AusSP	2	n/a	n/a	1	2	n/a	n/a
Northern Marianas	AusSP	77	n/a	n/a	426	466	n/a	n/a
Norway	NEur	4 525	38 730	2 629	1 955	3 107	2 738	1.5
Oman	ME	2 713	7 830	2 060	149	602	116	0.5
Pakistan	SAsia	147 663	420	n/a	424	498	105	0.2
Palau	AusSP	19	7 090	n/a	33	59	59	44.0
Panama	CA	2 882	4 020	200	214	534	679	5.9
Papua New Guinea	AusSP	5 172	520	92	41	54	101[1]	3.8
Paraguay	SA	5 884	1 180	141	280	250	62	0.9
Peru	SA	27 949	2 020	859	317	846	841	1.5

ENTITY	REGION	POPULATION (000s) 2002	GNP PER CAPITA (2002) (US$)	OUTBOUND (000s) 2002	INBOUND (000s) 1990	INBOUND (000s) 2002	INT. TOURISM RECEIPTS 2002 (US$MIL)	TOURISM AS % OF GNP (2002)
Philippines	SEAsia	84 526	1 030	1 968	1 025	1 933	1 741	2.0
Poland	CEEur	38 625	4 670	45 043	n/a	13 980	4 500	2.5
Portugal	SEur	10 084	10 720	n/a	8 020	11 666	5 919	5.5
Puerto Rico	Car	3 958	n/a	1 227	2 560	3 087	2 233[3]	6.4
Qatar	ME	793	n/a	n/a	136	n/a	n/a	n/a
Réunion	EAfr	744	n/a	319	200	426	284	n/a
Romania	CEEur	22 318	1 920	5 757	3 099	3 204	612	1.4
Russia	CEEur	144 979	2 130	20 343	n/a	7 943	4 188	1.4
Rwanda	EAfr	7 398	230	n/a	n/a	n/a	9[1]	0.5
Saba	Car	n/a	n/a	n/a	n/a	11	n/a	n/a
St Eustatius	Car	n/a	n/a	n/a	n/a	10	n/a	n/a
St Kitts & Nevis	Car	39	6 440	n/a	73	68	57	22.7
St Lucia	Car	160	3 890	n/a	141	253	256	41.2
St Marten	Car	n/a	n/a	n/a	545	381	493[1]	n/a
St Vincent	Car	116	3 080	n/a	54	78	81	22.7
Samoa	AusSP	179	1 420	n/a	48	89	45	17.7
San Marino	SEur	28	n/a	n/a	45	45	n/a	n/a
São Tome e Principe	MAfr	170	300	n/a	3	n/a	8[1]	15.7
Saudi Arabia	ME	23 513	8 530	7 896	2 209	7 511	3 420[1]	1.7
Senegal	WAfr	10 590	460	n/a	246	427	178[3]	3.7
Serbia & Montenegro	SEur	10 657	1 400	n/a	1 186	448	77	0.5
Seychelles	EAfr	80	6 910	53	104	132	130	23.5
Sierra Leone	WAfr	5 615	140	27	98	28	n/a	n/a
Singapore	SEAsia	4 453	21 180	4 399	4 842	6 996	4 932	5.2

ENTITY	REGION	POPULATION (000s) 2002	GNP PER CAPITA (2002) (US$)	OUTBOUND (000s) 2002	INBOUND (000s) 1990	INBOUND (000s) 2002	INT. TOURISM RECEIPTS 2002 (US$MIL)	TOURISM AS % OF GNP (2002)
Slovakia	CEEur	5 422	4 050	437	822	1 399	724	3.3
Slovenia	SEur	1 933	10 200	2 127	n/a	1 302	1 083	5.5
Solomon Islands	AusSP	495	560	n/a	9	n/a	13[3]	4.2
South Africa	SAfr	43 648	2 630	3 794	1 029	6 550	2 719	2.4
Spain	SEur	40 077	14 580	3 871	34 085	51 748	33 609	5.8
Sri Lanka	SAsia	19 577	850	533	298	393	253	1.5
Sudan	NAfr	37 090	400	n/a	33	52	56[1]	0.4
Suriname	SA	436	1 990	n/a	46	n/a	14[1]	1.6
Swaziland	SAfr	1 124	1 240	n/a	263	332	28	2.0
Sweden	NEur	8 877	25 970	12 927	n/a	7 459	4 496	1.9
Switzerland	WEur	7 302	36 170	11 427	13 200	10 000	7 628	2.9
Syria	ME	17 156	1 090	3 299	562	2 809	1 366	17.5
Taiwan	NEAsia	22 548	n/a	7 319	n/a	2 726	3 372[3]	0.9
Tanzania	EAfr	37 188	280	n/a	n/a	550	730	7.0
Thailand	SEAsia	62 354	2 000	2 250	5 299	10 873	7 902	6.3
Togo	WAfr	5 286	270	n/a	103	n/a	11[1]	0.8
Tonga	AusSP	106	1 400	n/a	21	37	9	6.1
Trinidad & Tobago	Car	1 164	6 600	n/a	195	379	224	2.9
Tunisia	NAfr	9 816	1 990	1 939	3 204	5 064	1 422	7.3
Turkey	EMed	67 309	2 510	5 131	4 799	12 782	9 010	5.3
Turkmenistan	CEEur	4 689	870	n/a	n/a	n/a	n/a	n/a
Turks & Caicos Is.	Car	19	n/a	n/a	49	155	292	n/a
Tuvalu	AusSP	11	n/a	n/a	1	1	n/a	n/a
Uganda	EAfr	24 699	240	387	69	254	185	3.1
Ukraine	CEEur	48 396	780	14 729	n/a	6 326	2 992	7.9

ENTITY	REGION	POPULATION (000s) 2002	GNP PER CAPITA (2002) (US$)	OUTBOUND (000s) 2002	INBOUND (000s) 1990	INBOUND (000s) 2002	INT. TOURISM RECEIPTS 2002 (US$MIL)	TOURISM AS % OF GNP (2002)
United Arab Emirates	ME	2 446	n/a	n/a	973	5 445	1 328	n/a
United Kingdom	NEur	59 778	25 490	59 377	18 013	24 180	17 591	1.2
United States	NA	280 562	35 400	58 050	39 362	41 892	66 547	0.6
US Virgin Islands	Car	123	n/a	n/a	463	553	1240	n/a
Uruguay	SA	3 387	4 350	530	n/a	1 258	318	2.2
Uzbekistan	CEEur	25 563	460	264	n/a	332	68	0.6
Vanuatu	AusSP	196	1 080	12	35	49	46[1]	21.7
Venezuela	SA	24 288	4 090	881	525	432	468	0.5
Vietnam	SEAsia	81 098	430	n/a	250	n/a	n/a	n/a
Yemen	ME	18 701	490	n/a	52	89	38[1]	0.4
Zambia	EAfr	9 959	340	n/a	141	565	117[1]	3.5
Zimbabwe	EAfr	11 377	n/a	331[4]	605	n/a	76	n/a

[1] 2001
[2] 2000
[3] 1998
[4] 1999

Sources: *Finfacts 2004 WTO 2005a WTO 2005b*

REFERENCES

ABS 1997. *Australian Demographic Trends.* ABS Catalogue No. 3201.0. Canberra: Australian Bureau of Statistics.

ABS 1998a. *1998 Year Book Australia.* ABS Catalogue No. 1301.0. Canberra: Australian Bureau of Statistics.

ABS 1998b. *Overseas Arrivals and Departures.* ABS Catalogue No. 3204.0. Canberra: Australian Bureau of Statistics.

ABS 1998c. *Disability, Ageing and Carers: Summary of Findings.* Catalogue No. 4430.0. Canberra: Australian Bureau of Statistics.

ABS 1999. *1999 Yearbook Australia.* ABS Catalogue No. 1301.1. Canberra: Australian Bureau of Statistics.

ABS 2000. 'Tourism Feature Article: Australian Tourism Satellite Account'. *Australian Economic Indicators.* ABS Catalogue No. 1350.0. Canberra: Australian Bureau of Statistics.

ABS 2001. *2001 Year Book Australia.* Canberra: Australian Bureau of Statistics.

ABS 2003a. *Family Characteristics, Australia.* Catalogue No. 4442.0. www.abs.gov.au/Ausstats/abs@.nsf/Lookup/ E6A9286119FA0A85CA25699000255C89 (visited 2 June 2005).

ABS 2003b. *Indirect Economic Contribution of Tourism to Australia, 1997–98 to 2000–01.* Catalogue No. 8634.0. www.abs.gov.au/Ausstats/abs@.nsf/0/ 6e527edc730e9331ca2568a900139401?OpenDocument Canberra: Australian Bureau of Statistics. (visited 5 May 2005).

ABS 2004a. *Australian Historical Population Statistics.* Catalogue No. 3105.0.65.001. www.abs.gov.au/Ausstats/abs@.nsf/0/8439f9fcfc1b 9314ca256a17007b390d?OpenDocument. Canberra: Australian Bureau of Statistics. (visited 15 August 2005).

ABS 2004b. *Population by Age and Sex, Australian States and Territories.* Catalogue No. 3201.0. www.abs.gov.au/Ausstats/abs@.nsf/0/b52c3903 d894336dca2568a9001393c1?OpenDocument. Canberra: Australian Bureau of Statistics. (visited 15 August 2005).

ABS 2005. *Overseas Arrivals and Departures.* Catalogue No. 3401.0. www.abs.gov.au/ausstats/abs@.nsf/0/ be16fd1a189be384ca256cf4000101ee?OpenDocument. Canberra: Australian Bureau of Statistics. (visited 15 August 2005).

Adler, M. & Ziglio, E. 1996. *Gazing into the Oracle: The Delphi Method and its Application to Social Policy and Public Health.* Bristol, PA, USA: Jessica Kingsley Publishers.

Agarwal, S. 1994. 'The Resort Cycle Revisited: Implications for Resorts'. In Cooper, C. and Lockwood, A. (Eds.). *Progress in Tourism, Recreation and Hospitality Management. Volume 5.* Chichester, UK: Wiley, pp. 194–208.

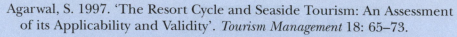

Agarwal, S. 1997. 'The Resort Cycle and Seaside Tourism: An Assessment of its Applicability and Validity'. *Tourism Management* 18: 65–73.

Aglionby, J. 2001. 'On the Philippine Frontier'. *Guardian Unlimited*. www.guardian.co.uk/elsewhere/journalist/story/ 0,7792,503185,00.html (visited 9 June 2001).

Ahmed, Z. 1992. 'Islamic Pilgrimage (Hajj) to Ka'aba in Makkah (Saudi Arabia): An Important International Tourism Activity'. *Journal of Tourism Studies* 3 (1): 35–43.

Airey, D. & Johnson, S. 1999. 'The Content of Tourism Degree Courses in the UK'. *Tourism Management* 20: 229–35.

Akama, J. 1996. 'Western Environmental Values and Nature-based Tourism in Kenya'. *Tourism Management* 17: 567–74.

Alderman, L. 1997. 'How I Found Shangri-la'. *Money* 26 (9): B15–20.

Alford, P. 1999. 'Database Marketing in Travel and Tourism'. *Travel & Tourism Analyst* 1: 87–104.

Alreck, P. L. & Settle, R. B. 1995. *The Survey Research Handbook*. Second Edition. London: Irwin.

Altman, J. & Finlayson, J. 2003. 'Aborigines, Tourism and Sustainable Development'. *Journal of Tourism Studies* 14: 78–91.

Anderson, B., Provis, C. & Chappel, S. 2003. 'The Selection and Training of Workers in the Tourism and Hospitality Industries for the Performance of Emotional Labour'. *Journal of Hospitality and Tourism Management* 10: 1–12.

Ankomah, P. & Crompton, J. L. 1990. 'Unrealized Tourism Potential: The Case of Sub-Saharan Africa'. *Tourism Management* 11: 11–28.

Antigua & Barbuda. 1982. *The State of Antigua and Barbuda: Information Memorandum*. St John's, Antigua.

Ashworth, G. J. & Tunbridge, J. E. 1990. *The Tourist-Historic City*. London: Belhaven Press.

Ashworth, G. J. & Tunbridge, J. 2004. 'Whose Tourist-Historic City? Localizing the Global and Globalizing the Local'. In Lew, A., Hall, C. & Williams, A. (Eds.). *A Companion to Tourism*. Oxford: Blackwell, pp. 210–22.

ATC 1997. *Australia 96/7: Annual Report*. Canberra: Australian Tourist Commission.

ATC 2000. *Financial Reports*. Canberra: Australian Tourist Commission.

ATEC (Australian Tourism Export Council) 2005. 'ATEC Slams Productivity Commission Report'. www.atec.net.au/ MediaRelease_ATEC_slams_Productivity_Commission_report.htm (visited 18 April 2005).

August, M. 1996. 'Exotic Treks Can Lead to Trouble'. *Globe and Mail* (Canada), 14 February, p. A18.

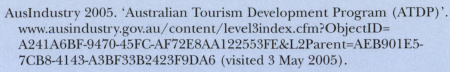

AusIndustry 2005. 'Australian Tourism Development Program (ATDP)'. www.ausindustry.gov.au/content/level3index.cfm?ObjectID= A241A6BF-9470-45FC-AF72E8AA122553FE&L2Parent=AEB901E5-7CB8-4143-A3BF33B2423F9DA6 (visited 3 May 2005).

Ayala, H. 1993. 'Mexican Resorts: A Blueprint with an Expiration Date'. *Cornell Hotel and Restaurant Administration Quarterly* 34 (3): 34–42.

Backman, S. J. & Crompton, J. L. 1991. 'Differentiating Between High, Spurious, Latent, and Low Loyalty Participants in Two Leisure Activities'. *Journal of Park and Recreation Administration* 9 (2): 1–17.

Bailey, M. 1995. *China. International Tourism Reports.* Number 1. London: Economist Intelligence Unit, pp. 19–37.

Bair, A. 1995. 'Pacific Yurts'. In Hawkins, D., Epler Wood, M. & Bittman, S. (Eds) *The Ecolodge Sourcebook for Planners and Developers.* North Bennington, VT, USA: Ecotourism Society.

Balogh, S. 1998. 'Pink Dollars Slam Dunk Sporting Quid'. *The Australian,* 3 August, p. 3.

Baloglu, S. & Brinberg, D. 1997. 'Affective Images of Tourism Destinations'. *Journal of Travel Research* 35 (4): 11–15.

Barke, M. & O'Hare, G. 1991. *The Third World: Diversity, Change and Interdependence.* Second Edition. Harlow, UK: Oliver & Boyd.

Bauer, J. & Herr, A. 2004. 'Hunting and Fishing Tourism'. In Higginbottom, K. (Ed.) *Wildlife Tourism: Impacts, Management and Planning.* Altona, Vic.: Common Ground Publishing, pp. 57–77.

Bauer, T. & McKercher, B. (Eds.). 2003. *Sex and Tourism: Journeys of Romance, Love and Lust.* Binghampton, USA: Haworth Hospitality Press.

Baum, T. 1998. 'Tourism Marketing and the Small Island Environment: Cases from the Periphery'. In Laws, E., Faulkner, B. & Moscardo, G. (Eds) *Embracing and Managing Change in Tourism: International Case Studies.* London: Routledge, pp. 116–37.

Becker, W. 1994. 'Can Las Vegas Go Family Friendly?' *Visions in Leisure and Business* 13 (1): 17–20.

Beech, J., Rigby, A., Talbot, I. & Thandi, S. 2005. 'Sport Tourism as a Means of Reconciliation? The Case of India–Pakistan Cricket'. *Tourism Recreation Research* 30: 83–91.

Beedie, P. & Hudson, S. 2003. 'Emergence of Mountain-based Adventure Tourism'. *Annals of Tourism Research* 30: 625–43.

Beeton, S. & Benfield, R. 2002. 'Demand Control: The Case for Demarketing as a Visitor and Environmental Management Tool'. *Journal of Sustainable Tourism* 10: 497–513.

Bendell, J. & Font, X. 2004. 'Which Tourism Rules? Green Standards and GATS'. *Annals of Tourism Research* 31: 139–56.

Bennett, M., King, B. & Milner, L. 2004. 'The Health Resort Sector in Australia: a Positioning Study'. *Journal of Vacation Marketing* 10: 122–37.

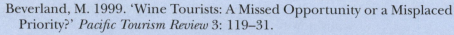

Beverland, M. 1999. 'Wine Tourists: A Missed Opportunity or a Misplaced Priority?' *Pacific Tourism Review* 3: 119–31.

Blamey, R. K. 1997. 'Ecotourism: The Search for an Operational Definition'. *Journal of Sustainable Tourism* 5: 109–30.

Blamey, R. K. 2001. 'Principles of Ecotourism'. In Weaver, D. (Ed.) *The Encyclopedia of Ecotourism.* Wallingford, IK: CABI Publishing, pp. 5–22.

Blamey, R. K. & Hatch, D. 1998. *Profiles and Motivations of Nature-based Tourists Visiting Australia.* Occasional Paper No. 25. Canberra: Bureau of Tourism Research.

Blattberg, R. C. & Deighton, J. 1991. 'Interactive Marketing: Exploiting the Age of Addressability'. *Sloan Management Review* 33 (Fall): 5–14.

Bloor, M. 2001. *Focal Groups in Social Research.* London: Sage.

Boehm, E. 1993. *Twentieth Century Economic Development in Australia.* Third Edition. Melbourne: Longman Cheshire.

Bond, M. 1997. 'Women Travellers: A New Growth Market?' *PATA Occasional Papers Series, Paper No. 20.* Singapore: Pacific Asia Travel Association.

Boniface, B. & Cooper, C. 2005. *Worldwide Destinations: The Geography of Travel and Tourism.* Fourth Edition. Sydney: Elsevier.

Boo, E. 1990. *Ecotourism: The Potentials and Pitfalls.* Volume 1. Washington, DC: World Wildlife Fund.

Bosselman, F., Peterson, C. & McCarthy, C. 1999. *Managing Tourism Growth: Issues and Applications.* Washington, DC: Island Press.

Bowen, D. 2001. 'Antecedents of Consumer Satisfaction and Dissatisfaction (CS/D) on Long-haul Inclusive Tours — A Reality Check on Theoretical Considerations'. *Tourism Management* 22: 49–61.

Bowen, D. 2002. 'Research through Participant Observation in Tourism: A Creative Solution to the Measurement of Consumer Satisfaction/Dissatisfaction (CS/D) among Tourists'. *Journal of Travel Research* 41: 4–14.

Boyle, A. 2004. 'Zero-gravity Flights Go Mainstream: U.S. Company Offers Public the Chance to Experience Weightlessness'. MSNBC News www.msnbc.msn.com/id/5992077/ (visited 18 February 2005).

Bradbury, D. & Mourdant, R. 1996. *The Battle for Byron.* Wilsons Creek, NSW: Frontline Films. [video]

Brady, S. 1998. 'China's Outwardly Mobile'. http://web.lexisnexis.com/univers...5=fe9a4e6dfc78ee0203728c42cbff67 (visited 18 December 1998).

Brewer, K., Poffley, J. & Pederson, E. 1995. 'Travel Interests Among Seniors: Continuing Care Retirement Community Residents'. *Journal of Travel and Tourism Marketing* 4 (2): 93–8.

Bridgewater, P. 1996. 'Opening Address'. In Colgan, K., Prasser, S. & Jeffery, A. (Eds) *Encounters with Whales. 1995 Proceedings.* Canberra: Australian Nature Conservation Agency, pp. 3–4.

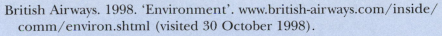

British Airways. 1998. 'Environment'. www.british-airways.com/inside/comm/environ.shtml (visited 30 October 1998).

Brown, D. O. 1998. 'Debt-funded Environmental Swaps in Africa: Vehicles for Tourism Development?' *Journal of Sustainable Tourism* 6 (1): 69–79.

Brown, D. O. 2001. 'Political Risk and Other Barriers to Tourism Promotion in Africa: Perceptions of US-based Travel Intermediaries'. *Journal of Vacation Marketing* 6: 197–210.

Brown, G. & Giles, R. 1994. 'Coping with Tourism: An Examination of Resident Responses to the Social Impact of Tourism'. In Seaton, A. et al. (Eds) *Tourism: The State of the Art*. Chichester, UK: John Wiley, pp. 755–64.

Brown, H. 1999. 'Sex Crimes and Tourism in Nepal'. *International Journal of Contemporary Hospitality Management* 11 (2/3): 107–10.

Brunet, S., Bauer, J., de Lacy, T. & Tshering, K. 2001. 'Tourism Development in Bhutan: Tensions Between Tradition and Modernity'. *Journal of Sustainable Tourism* 9: 243–63.

Brunt, P., Mawby, R. & Hambly, Z. 2000. 'Tourist Victimisation and the Fear of Crime on Holiday'. *Tourism Management* 21: 417–24.

BTR 1987–2004. *Domestic Tourism Monitor*. Canberra: Bureau of Tourism Research. Various years.

BTR 1996. *International Visitor Survey 1995*. Canberra: Bureau of Tourism Research.

BTR 1997. *International Visitor Survey 1996*. Canberra: Bureau of Tourism Research.

BTR 1998. *Domestic Tourism Monitor 1996–97*. Canberra: Bureau of Tourism Research.

BTR 2002. *International Visitor Survey 2002*. Canberra: Bureau of Tourism Research.

BTR 2003. 'Tourism Snapshot – International'. www.tra.australia.com/ (visited 8 February 2005).

Buchanan, I. & Rosetto, A. 1997. *With My Swag Upon My Shoulder: A Comprehensive Study of International Backpackers to Australia*. Occasional Paper No. 24. Canberra: Bureau of Tourism Research.

Buckley, R. 2002. 'Tourism Ecocertification in the International Year of Ecotourism'. *Journal of Ecotourism* 1: 197–203.

Buckley, R. (Ed.) 2004. *Environmental Impacts of Tourism*. Wallingford, UK: CABI Publishing.

Buckley, R., King, N. & Zubrinich, T. 2004. 'The Role of Tourism in Spreading Dieback Disease in Australian Vegetation'. In Buckley, R. (Ed.) *Environmental Impacts of Tourism*. Wallingford, UK: CABI Publishing, pp. 317–24.

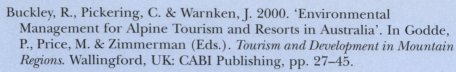

Buckley, R., Pickering, C. & Warnken, J. 2000. 'Environmental Management for Alpine Tourism and Resorts in Australia'. In Godde, P., Price, M. & Zimmerman (Eds.). *Tourism and Development in Mountain Regions.* Wallingford, UK: CABI Publishing, pp. 27–45.

Buhalis, D. 2000. 'Marketing the Competitive Destination of the Future'. *Tourism Management* 21: 97–116.

Bull, A. 1995. *The Economics of Travel and Tourism.* Second Edition. Melbourne: Longman Cheshire.

Burkart, A. J. & Medlik, S. (Eds) 1981. *Tourism: Past, Present and Future.* Second Edition. Oxford: Heinemann.

Burns, D. & Murphy, L. 1998. 'An Analysis of the Promotion of Marine Tourism in Far North Queensland, Australia'. In Laws, E., Faulkner, B. and Moscardo, G. (Eds) *Embracing and Managing Change in Tourism: International Case Studies.* London: Routledge, pp. 415–30.

Burton, R. 1995. *Travel Geography.* Second Edition. London: Pitman.

Bushell, R., Faulkner, B. & Jafari, J. (Eds) 1996. *Tourism Research in Australia: A Strategy for Mobilising National Research Capabilities.* Position paper emerging from the Collaborative ARC Tourism Research Strategic Planning Workshop, University of Western Sydney, Hawkesbury, 24–25 November.

Butler, R. (Ed.) 2005a. *The Tourism Area Life Cycle: Theoretical and Conceptual Implications.* Clevedon, UK: Channel View.

Butler, R. (Ed.) 2005b. *The Tourism Area Life Cycle: Applications and Modifications.* Clevedon, UK: Channel View.

Butler, R. W. 1980. 'The Concept of a Tourist Area Cycle of Evolution: Implications for Management of Resources'. *Canadian Geographer* 24: 5–12.

Butler, R. W. 1992. 'Alternative Tourism: The Thin Edge of the Wedge'. In Smith, V. L. & Eadington, W. R. (Eds) *Tourism Alternatives: Potentials and Problems in the Development of Tourism.* Philadelphia: University of Pennsylvania Press, pp. 31–46.

Butler, R. W. & Boyd, S. (Eds) 2000. *Tourism and National Parks: Issues and Implications.* Chichester, UK: John Wiley.

Butler, R. W., Hall, C. M. & Jenkins, J. (Eds) 1998. *Tourism and Recreation in Rural Areas.* Chichester, UK: John Wiley.

Bywater, M. 1995. 'Switzerland'. *International Tourism Reports*, No. 3, pp. 48–65.

Calvià 1998. 'Calvià 21 Local Agenda'. www.bitel.es/dir~calvia/kindice.htm (visited 22 December 1998).

Campbell, M. 1998. *The Witness and the Other World: Exotic Travel Writing, 400–1600.* London: Cornell University Press.

Carmichael, B., Peppard, D. Jr & Boudreau, F. 1996. 'Megaresort on My Doorstep: Local Resident Attitudes toward Foxwoods Casino and

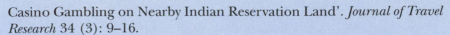

Casino Gambling on Nearby Indian Reservation Land'. *Journal of Travel Research* 34 (3): 9–16.

Carter, B. 1996. 'Private Sector Involvement in Recreation and Nature Conservation in Australia'. In Charters, T., Gabriel, M. & Prasser, S. (Eds) *National Parks: Private Sector's Role.* Toowoomba, QLD: SQU Press.

Casado, M. 1997. 'Mexico's 1989–94 Tourism Plan: Implications of Internal Political and Economic Instability'. *Journal of Travel Research* 36 (1): 44–51.

Casson, L. 1974. *Travel in the Ancient World.* London: Allen and Unwin.

CDT 1994. *National Ecotourism Strategy.* Canberra: Commonwealth Department of Tourism.

CDT 1995a. *National Backpacker Tourism Strategy.* Canberra: Commonwealth Department of Tourism.

CDT 1995b. *Building for Backpackers: Guidelines for Backpacker Accommodation.* Canberra: Commonwealth Department of Tourism.

Ceballos-Lascurén, H. 1996. *Tourism, Ecotourism and Protected Areas.* Gland, Switzerland: IUCN (The World Conservation Union).

Chadwick, R. 1994. 'Concepts, Definitions, and Measures Used in Travel and Tourism Research'. In Ritchie, J. R. B. & Goeldner, C. R. (Eds) *Travel, Tourism, and Hospitality Research: A Handbook for Managers and Researchers.* Second Edition. Chichester, UK: John Wiley, pp. 65–80.

Cherry, J. 1993. *Cassell Business Briefings: Republic of Korea.* London: Cassell.

Chien, G. & Law, R. 2003. 'The Impact of the Severe Acute Respiratory Syndrome on Hotels: a Case Study of Hong Kong'. *International Journal of Hospitality Management* 22: 327–32.

China 1998. *The Outline of China Tourism Statistics.* Beijing: National Tourism Administration of the People's Republic of China.

Chon, K., Inagaki, T. & Ohashi, T. (Eds) 2000. *Japanese Tourists: Socio-economic, Marketing and Psychological Analysis.* New York: Haworth Hospitality Press.

Christaller, W. 1963. 'Some Considerations of Tourism Location in Europe'. *Papers and Proceedings of the Regional Science Association* 12: 95–105.

Clacher, I. 1998. 'Boost for Pink Tourism'. *Queensland Pride.* No. 89 (October), pp. 1 and 3.

Cleaver Sellick, M. 2004. 'Discovery, Connection, Nostalgia: Key Travel Motives Within the Senior Market'. Journal *of Travel & Tourism Marketing* 17: 55–71.

Clifford, H. 2002. *Downhill Slide: Why the Corporate Ski Industry is Bad for Skiing, Ski Towns and the Environment.* San Francisco: Sierra Club Books.

Clift, S. & Carter, S. (Eds) 2000. *Tourism and Sex: Culture, Commerce and Coercion.* London: Pinter.

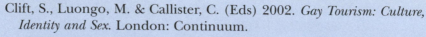

Clift, S., Luongo, M. & Callister, C. (Eds) 2002. *Gay Tourism: Culture, Identity and Sex.* London: Continuum.

CNTA 2003. *China Statistical Yearbook 2003.* Beijing: China National Tourism Administration.

CNTA n.d. 'International Tourists by Locality 2000'. www.cnta.com/lyen/2fact/6–2.htm (visited 9 March 2005).

Cohen, E. 1972. 'Toward a Sociology of International Tourism'. *Social Research* 39: 164–82.

Collins, C. 1979. 'Site and Situation Strategy in Tourism Planning: A Mexican Case Study'. *Annals of Tourism Research* 6: 351–66.

Collins, J. & Wallace J. 1995. 'The Use of Census Data for Target Marketing — The Way Forward for the Tourism Industry'. *Journal of Vacation Marketing* 1: 273–80.

Cooper, C., Fletcher, J., Gilbert, D. & Wanhill, S. 1993. *Tourism Principles and Practice.* Harlow, UK: Longman Cheshire.

Cooper, C., Fletcher, J., Wanhill, S., Gilbert, D. & Fyall, A. 2004. *Tourism Principles and Practice.* Third Edition. London: Prentice Hall.

Cowan, G. 1977. 'Cultural Impact of Tourism with Particular Reference to the Cook Islands'. In Finney, B & Watson, K. (Eds) *A New Kind of Sugar: Tourism in the Pacific.* Honolulu: East–West Center, pp. 79–85.

Cox News Service. 1999. 'What's Ahead for Travel? Let's Trek into the Future'. www.globeandmail.ca/gam/Travel/19990814/TR14FUTU.html (visited 15 August 1999).

Craig-Smith, S., Davidson, M. & French, C. N. 1995. 'Hospitality and Tourism Education in Australia: Challenges and Opportunities'. In Faulkner, B., et al. (Eds) *Tourism Research and Education in Australia.* Proceedings of the Australian National Tourism Research and Education Conferences, 1994. Canberra: Bureau of Tourism Research, pp. 311–20.

Crime Prevention Division 2002. Byron Bay Crime Prevention Plan (part 1). www.lawlink.nsw.gov.au/cpd.nsf/pages/cpplans_byronbay1 (visited 12 June 2005).

Critchley, C. 1998. 'Puffing Billy's Back on Track'. *Courier-Mail* (Brisbane), 17 October, p. 24.

Crompton, J. 1992. 'Structure of Vacation Destination Choice Sets'. *Annals of Tourism Research* 19: 420–34.

Crompton, J. L. 1979. 'An Assessment of the Image of Mexico as a Vacation Destination and the Influence of Geographical Location on that Image'. *Journal of Travel Research* 17 (1): 18–23.

Crystal, E. 1989. 'Tourism in Toraja (Sulawesi, Indonesia)'. In Smith, V. L. (Ed.) *Hosts and Guests: The Anthropology of Tourism.* Second Edition. Philadelphia: University of Pennsylvania Press, pp. 139–68.

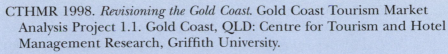

CTHMR 1998. *Revisioning the Gold Coast.* Gold Coast Tourism Market Analysis Project 1.1. Gold Coast, QLD: Centre for Tourism and Hotel Management Research, Griffith University.

D'Amore, L. & Jafari, J. (Eds) 1988. *Tourism — A Vital Force for Peace.* Montreal: First Global Conference.

D'Amore, L. 1988. 'Tourism: The World's Peace Industry'. *Journal of Travel Research* 27 (1): 1–8.

Dahles, H. (Ed.) 2001. *Tourism, Heritage and National Culture in Java: Dilemmas of a Local Community.* Richmond, UK: Curzon Press.

Davidson, T. 2005. 'What Are Travel and Tourism: Are They Really an Industry?' In Theobald, W. (Ed.) *Global Tourism.* Third Edition. Sydney: Elsevier, pp. 25–31.

DCITA (Department of Communications, Information Technology and the Arts) 2003. 'Attendance at Selected Cultural Venues 2002'. www.dcita.gov.au/swg/publications/ Australia%27s%20Culture%20No%2013_8%20June.pdf (visited 15 March 2005).

de Burlo, C. 1996. 'Cultural Resistance and Ethnic Tourism on South Pentecost, Vanuatu'. In Butler, R. and Hinch, T. (Eds) *Tourism and Indigenous Peoples.* London, International Thomson Business Press, pp. 255–76.

DEFRA (Department for Environment, Food and Rural Affairs) 2005. 'How to Bring your Pet Dog or Cat into or Back into the UK under the Pet Travel Scheme (PETS)'. www.defra.gov.uk/animalh/quarantine/ pets/procedures/owners.htm (visited 4 April 2005).

DEH (Department of the Environment and Heritage) 2005. Kakadu National Park. www.deh.gov.au/parks/kakadu/index.html (visited 12 March 2005).

Dernoi, L. A. 1981. 'Alternative Tourism: Towards a New Style in North–South Relations'. *International Journal of Tourism Management* 2: 253–64.

Dick, T. 2005. 'Entry Toll Plan for Byron Bay Visitors'. *Sydney Morning Herald.* www.smh.com.au/news/National/Entry–toll–plan–for–Byron–Bay–visitors/2005/01/21/1106110947569.html?from=more Stories&oneclick=true (visited 6 March 2005).

Dickey, C. 1998. 'A New Breed of Killers'. *Newsweek* 130 (22): 44.

Dieke, P. (Ed.) 2000. *The Political Economy of Tourism Development in Africa.* Elmsford, US: Cognizant Communication.

Digance, J. 2003. 'Pilgrimage at Contested Sites'. *Annals of Tourism Research* 30: 143–59.

DIST 1995. *Best Practice Ecotourism: A Guide to Waste and Energy Minimisation.* Canberra: Department of Industry, Science & Tourism.

DIST 1996. *Ecotourism Education Directory.* Canberra: Department of Industry, Science & Tourism.

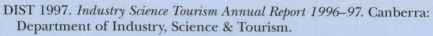

DIST 1997. *Industry Science Tourism Annual Report 1996–97.* Canberra: Department of Industry, Science & Tourism.

DITR (Department of Industry, Tourism and Resources) 2004. 'Economic Impact of the Rugby World Cup 2003 on the Australian Economy – Post Analysis'. www.industry.gov.au/assets/documents/ itrinternet/FinalEconomicImpactOfRWC2003_20040604150504.pdf? CFID=8115941&CFTOKEN=88567173 (visited 1 February 2005).

DITR (Department of Industry, Tourism and Resources) 2005a. 'Regional Australia'. www.industry.gov.au/content/itrinternet/cms content.cfm?objectID=F28D8A57–F4AF–0D91–1798C9751496C2C7 (visited 4 May 2005).

DITR (Department of Industry, Tourism and Resources) 2005b. 'Tourism White Paper Initiatives'. www.industry.gov.au/content/itrinternet/ cmscontent.cfm?objectID=4E01EE73-65BF-4956-B057EC96612BDDCB (visited 4 May 2005).

Dore, C. 1999. 'Crisis-Hit Asians Stay Home in Droves'. *The Australian*, 24 February, p. 5.

Douglas, N. 1997. 'Applying the Life Cycle Model to Melanesia'. *Annals of Tourism Research* 24: 1–22.

Douglass, W. & Raento, P. 2004. 'The Tradition of Invention — Conceiving Las Vegas'. *Annals of Tourism Research* 31: 7–23.

Doxey, G. 1976. 'When Enough's Enough: The Natives are Restless in Old Niagara'. *Heritage Canada* 2 (2): 26–27.

Dunbar-Hall, P. 2001. 'Culture, Tourism and Cultural Tourism: Boundaries and Frontiers in Performances of Balinese Music and Dance'. *Journal of Intercultural Studies* 22: 173–87.

Dwyer, L. 1989. 'Tourism–agricultural linkages in Western Samoa and Tonga'. *World Review* 28 (2): 32–52.

Ecotourism Society. 1998. *Ecotourism Statistical Fact Sheet.* North Bennington, VT, USA: Ecotourism Society.

Elliott, J., O'Brien, D., Leder, K., Kitchener, S., Schwartz, E., Weld, L., Brown, G., Kain, K. & Torresi, J. 2004. 'Imported *Plasmodium Vivax* Malaria: Demographic and Clinical Features in Nonimmune Travelers'. *Journal of Travel Medicine* 11: 213–19.

English, E. P. 1986. *The Great Escape? An Examination of North–South Tourism.* Ottawa, Canada: North–South Institute.

Erisman, H. 1983. 'Tourism and Cultural Dependency in the West Indies'. *Annals of Tourism Research* 10: 337–61.

Essex, S. & Brown, G. 1997. 'The Emergence of Post-Suburban Landscapes on the North Coast of New South Wales: A Case Study of Contested Space'. *International Journal of Urban and Regional Research* 21: 259–85.

Europa Publications 1998. *Europa World Year Book 1998.* Volume 1. London: Europa Publications.

EventPlan 2003. 'Gettysburg Re-enactment 1998' www.eventplan.co.uk/
photopages/Gettysburg%201988.htm (visited 17 March 2005).

Eyefortravel 2002. 'A New State of the Art Tourism Information Service
May Soon Be Available'. www.eyefortravel.com/print.asp?news=31876
(visited 1 June 2005).

Faulkner, B. 1998. 'Some Parameters for Exploring Progress in Tourism
and Hospitality Research'. In Faulkner, B., Tideswell, C. and Weaver, D.
B. (Eds) *Progress in Tourism and Hospitality Research*. Proceedings of the
Eighth Australian Tourism and Hospitality Research Conference.
Canberra: Bureau of Tourism Research, pp. 4–8.

Faulkner, B. & Russell, R. 1997. 'Chaos and Complexity in Tourism: In
Search of a New Perspective'. *Pacific Tourism Review* 1: 93–102.

Faulkner, B. & Tideswell, C. 1997. 'A Framework for Monitoring
Community Impacts of Tourism'. *Journal of Sustainable Tourism* 5: 3–28.

Faulkner, B. & Vikulov, L. 2001. 'Katherine, Washed Out One Day, Back
on Track the Next: A Post-mortem of a Tourism Disaster'. *Tourism
Management* 22: 331–44.

Faulkner, B. & Walmsley, D. J. 1998. 'Globalisation and the Pattern of
Inbound Tourism in Australia'. *Australian Geographer* 29 (1): 91–106.

Feng, R. & Morrison, A. 2002. 'GIS Applications in Tourism and
Hospitality Marketing: a Case in Brown County, Indiana'. *Anatolia* 13:
127–43.

Fennell, D. & Dowling, R. (Eds) 2003. *Ecotourism Policy and Planning*.
Wallingford, UK: CABI Publishing.

Fifer, V. 1988. *American Progress: The Growth of the Transport, Tourist, and
Information Industries in the Nineteenth-Century West*. Chester, Conn, USA:
Globe Pequot Press.

Finfacts 2004. 'Global/World Income Per Capita/Head 2004'.
www.finfacts.com/biz10/globalworldincomepercapita.htm (visited 9
May 2005).

Finney, B. & Watson, K. (Eds) 1975. *A New Kind of Sugar: Tourism in the
Pacific*. Honolulu: East–West Center.

Fisher, D. 2004. 'The Demonstration Effect Revisited'. *Annals of Tourism
Research* 31: 428–46.

Fletcher, K., Wheeler, C. & Wright, J. 1994. 'Strategic Implementation of
Database Marketing: Problems and Pitfalls'. *Long Range Planning* 27:
133–41.

Foley, M. & McPherson, G. 2000. 'Museums as Leisure'. *International
Journal of Heritage Studies* 6: 161–74.

Font, X. 2001. 'Regulating the Green Message: The Players in
Ecolabelling'. In Font, X. & Buckley, R. (Eds.). *Tourism Ecolabelling:
Certification and Promotion of Sustainable Management*. CABI Publishing,
pp. 1–17.

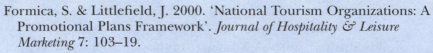

Formica, S. & Littlefield, J. 2000. 'National Tourism Organizations: A Promotional Plans Framework'. *Journal of Hospitality & Leisure Marketing* 7: 103–19.

Fredline, E. & Faulkner, B. 2000. 'Host Community Reactions: A Cluster Analysis'. *Annals of Tourism Research* 27: 763–84.

Freitag, T. G. 1994. 'Enclave Tourism Development: For Whom the Benefit Rolls?' *Annals of Tourism Research* 21: 538–54.

French, P. 1997. *Coastal and Estuarine Management*. London: Routledge.

Frew, E. & Shaw, R. 1999. 'The Relationship between Personality, Gender and Tourism Behavior'. *Tourism Management* 20: 193–202.

Frommer, A. 1991. *New World of Travel*. Fourth Edition. New York: Prentice Hall.

Frost, W. 2004. 'A Hidden Giant: Second Homes and Coastal Tourism in South–Eastern Australia.' In Hall, C.M. & Müller, D. (Eds.). *Tourism, Mobility and Second Homes: Between Elite Landscape and Common Ground*. Clevedon, UK: Channel View, pp. 162–73.

Fyall, A. & Garrod, B. 2005. 'From Competition to Collaboration in the Tourism Industry' In Theobald, W. (Ed.) *Global Tourism*. Third Edition. Sydney: Elsevier, pp. 52–73.

Gammon, S. 2004. 'Secular Pilgrimage and Sport Tourism'. In Ritchie, B. and Adair, D. (Eds) *Sport Tourism: Interrelationships, Impacts and Issues*. Clevedon, UK: Channel View, pp. 30–45.

Garrod, B. 2003. 'Defining Marine Ecotourism: A Delphi Study'. In Garrod, B. & Wilson, J. (Eds.). *Marine Ecotourism: Issues and Experiences*. Clevedon, UK: Channel View Publications, pp. 17–36.

Gartner, W. C. 1993. 'Image Formation Process'. *Journal of Travel and Tourism Marketing* 2 (2/3): 191–216.

GCCC (Gold Coast City Council) 2004. 'Gold Coast City Innovation Stories'. First Edition. www.goldcoast.qld.gov.au/attachment/edmp/Innovation_stories.pdf (visited 5 May 2005).

GCCC (Gold Coast City Council) 2005. 'Gold Coast City Innovation Stories'. Second Edition. www.goldcoast.qld.gov.au/attachment/publications/pb364_innovation_stories_2.pdf (visited 6 May 2005).

Gee, C., Makens, J. & Choy, D. 1989. *The Travel Industry*. Sixth Edition. Melbourne: Van Nostrand Reinhold.

Getz, D. 1992. 'Tourism Planning and Destination Life Cycle'. *Annals of Tourism Research* 19: 752–70.

Getz, D. 1997. *Event Management and Event Tourism*. New York: Cognizant Communications.

Getz, D. 2000. *Explore Wine Tourism: Management, Development & Destinations*. Elmsford, USA: Cognizant Communication.

Giannecchini, J. 1993. 'Ecotourism: New Partners, New Relationships'. *Conservation Biology* 7: 429–32.

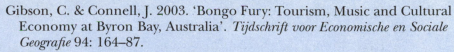

Gibson, C. & Connell, J. 2003. 'Bongo Fury: Tourism, Music and Cultural Economy at Byron Bay, Australia'. *Tijdschrift voor Economische en Sociale Geografie* 94: 164–87.

Gilbert, E. W. 1949. 'The Growth of Brighton'. *Geographical Journal*, 114 (1): 30–52.

Gilbert, N. 1993. 'Research, Theory and Method'. In Gilbert, N. (Ed.) *Researching Social Life*. London: Sage, pp. 18-31.

Glaesser, D. 2003. *Crisis Management in the Tourism Industry*. Sydney: Butterworth–Heinemann.

Gningue, A. 1992. 'Integrated Rural Tourism: Lower Casamance, Senegal'. In Eber, S. (Ed.) *Beyond the Green Horizon: Principles for Sustaining Tourism*. Discussion paper commissioned by Tourism Concern and the WWF, pp. 40–2.

Goeldner, C. & Ritchie, J. 2003. *Tourism: Principles, Practices, Philosophies*. Ninth Edition. Chichester, UK: John Wiley.

Goodall, B. 1991. 'Understanding Holiday Choice'. In Cooper, C. (Ed.) *Progress in Tourism, Recreation and Hospitality Management. Volume 3*. London: Belhaven, pp. 58–77.

Goodson, L. & Phillimore, J. (Eds) 2004. *Qualitative Research in Tourism: Ontologies, Epistemologies and Methodologies*. London: Routledge.

Gordon, J. 2001. 'Jobless Yardstick Wrong: Statistician'. www.theage.com.au/news/2001/01/22FFXWDPDL71C.html (visited 5 June 2001).

Gössling, S. 2003. 'The Political Ecology of Tourism in Zanzibar'. In Gössling, S. (Ed.) *Tourism and Development in Tropical Islands: Political Ecology Perspectives*. Cheltenham, UK: Edward Elgar, pp. 178–202.

Graburn, N. 1989. 'Tourism: The Sacred Journey'. In Smith, V. (Ed.) *Hosts and Guests: The Anthropology of Tourism*. Second Edition. Philadelphia: University of Pennsylvania Press, pp. 21–36.

Graham, P. 1998. 'Weak Canadian Dollar Likely to Affect Snowbird Economy'. *The Record* (Canada), 8 August, p. F3.

Green Globe. 1998a. 'Green Globe Certification'. www.wttc.org/WTTC GATE.NSF/06c4976954bcc5a6a90025654f004e5826?OpenDocument (*v*isited 2 April 1998).

Green Globe. 1998b. 'Green Globe Destinations'. www.wttc.org/WTTC GATE.NSF/06c49762ff648fc213c10025654f0050b9e4?OpenDocument (visited 7 October 1998).

Greenwood, D. 1989. 'Culture by the Pound: An Anthropological Perspective on Tourism as Cultural Commoditization'. In Smith, V. L. (Ed.) *Hosts and Guests: The Anthropology of Tourism*. Second Edition. Philadelphia: University of Pennsylvania Press, pp. 171–85.

Gunn, C. 1994a. 'A Perspective on the Purpose and Nature of Tourism Research Methods'. In Ritchie, J. R. Brent & Goeldner, C. R. (Eds) *Travel, Tourism, and Hospitality Research: A Handbook for Managersand Researchers*. Second Edition. Chichester, UK: John Wiley, pp. 3–11.

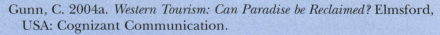

Gunn, C. 2004a. *Western Tourism: Can Paradise be Reclaimed?* Elmsford, USA: Cognizant Communication.

Gunn, C. 2004b. *Tourism Planning: Basics, Concepts, Cases.* Third Edition. London: Taylor & Francis.

Hall, C. M. 1994. 'Gender and Economic Interests in Tourism Prostitution: The Nature, Development and Implications of Sex Tourism in South-east Asia'. In Kinnaird, V. & Hall, D. (Eds) *Tourism: A Gender Analysis.* Chichester, UK: John Wiley, pp. 142–63.

Hall, C.M. 1998. 'Historical Antecedents of Sustainable Development and Ecotourism: New Labels on Old Bottles?' In Hall, C.M. & Lew, A. (Eds) *Sustainable Tourism: A Geographical Perspective.* Harlow, Essex, UK: Longman, pp. 13–24.

Hall, C.M. 2002. 'ANZAC Day and Secular Pilgrimage'. *Tourism Recreation Research* 27: 83–87.

Hall, C.M. & Higham, J. (Eds) 2005. *Tourism, Recreation and Climate Change.* Clevedon, UK: Channel View Publications.

Hall, C. M., Jenkins, J. & Kearsley, G. 1997. 'Tourism Planning and Policy in Urban Areas: Introductory Comments'. In Hall, C. M., Jenkins, J. & Kearsley, G. (Eds) *Tourism Planning and Policy in Australia and New Zealand: Cases, Issues and Practice.* Sydney: McGraw-Hill/Irwin, pp. 198–208.

Hall, C. M. & Macionis, N. 1998. 'Wine Tourism in Australia and New Zealand'. In Butler, R. W., Hall, C. M. & Jenkins, J. (Eds) *Tourism and Recreation in Rural Areas.* Chichester, UK: John Wiley, pp. 197–224.

Hall, C. M. & Page, S. (Eds) 1996. *Tourism in South and Southeast Asia: Issues and Cases.* Oxford: Butterworth–Heinemann.

Hall, C.M., Sharples, L., Mitchell, R., Macionis, N. & Cambourne, B. (Eds) 2003. *Food Tourism Around the World: Development, Management and Markets.* Sydney: Butterworth–Heinemann.

Hamilton, C. & Attwater, R. 1997. 'Measuring the Environment: The Availability and Use of Environmental Statistics in Australia'. *Australian Journal of Environmental Management* 4 (2): 72–87.

Harrell-Bond, B. 1978. A Window on the Outside World, Tourism and Development in the Gambia. American Universities Field Staff Report No. 19. Hanover, New Hampshire.

Harriott, V., Davis, D. & Banks, S. 1997. 'Recreational Diving and Its Impacts in Marine Protected Areas in Eastern Australia'. *Ambio* 26: 173–9.

Harris, R. 2002. 'The Tale of the Little Penguins and the Tourists — Making Tourism Sustainable at Phillip Island Nature Park'. In Harris, R., Griffin, T. & Williams, P. (Eds.). *Sustainable Tourism: A Global Perspective.* Sydney: Butterworth–Heinemann, pp. 238–51.

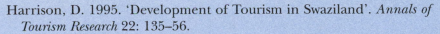

Harrison, D. 1995. 'Development of Tourism in Swaziland'. *Annals of Tourism Research* 22: 135–56.

Harrison, D. 1997. 'Globalization and Tourism: Some Themes from Fiji'. In Oppermann, Martin (Ed.) *Pacific Rim Tourism.* Wallingford, UK: CAB International, pp. 167–83.

Harrison-Hill, T. 2000. 'Investigating Cognitive Distance and Long-haul Destinations'. *Tourism Analysis* 5: 83–90.

Healey, J. 2000. 'USA Today Auto Track: Automakers Prepare Onslaught of New SUVs'. www.usatoday.com/money/consumer/autos/mauto668.htm (visited 27 June 2001).

Hein, K. 1998. 'Egypt's Curse'. *Incentive* 172 (1): 9.

Henderson, J. 2003. 'Terrorism and Tourism: Managing the Consequences of the Bali Bombings'. *Journal of Travel & Tourism Marketing* 15: 41–58.

Henderson, J. 2004. 'Food as a Tourism Resource: A View from Singapore'. *Tourism Recreation Research* 29 (3): 69–74.

Herold, E., Garcia, R. & DeMoya, T. 2001. 'Female Tourists and Beach Boys: Romance or Sex Tourism?' *Annals of Tourism Research* 28: 978–97.

Heung, V. & Cheng, E. 2000. 'Assessing Tourists' Satisfaction with Shopping in the Hong Kong Special Administrative Region of China'. *Journal of Travel Research* 38: 396–404.

Higgins, B. 1996. 'The Global Structure of the Nature Tourism Industry: Ecotourists, Tour Operators, and Local Businesses'. *Journal of Travel Research* 35 (2): 11–18.

Higgins-Desbiolles, F. 2003. 'Reconciliation Tourism: Tourism Healing Divided Societies!' *Tourism Recreation Review* 28: 35–44.

Higham, J. (Ed.) 2005. *Sport Tourism Destinations: Issues, Opportunities and Analysis.* Sydney: Elsevier.

Hinch, T. 1996. 'Urban Tourism: Perspectives on Sustainability'. *Journal of Sustainable Tourism* 4 (2): 95-110.

Hitchcock, M. 1999. 'A Special Island'. *The Guardian* (United Kingdom), 16 October, p. 14.

Holden, P. (Ed.) 1984. *Alternative Tourism With a Focus on Asia.* Bangkok: Ecumenical Council on Third World Tourism.

Horneman, L., Beeton, R. & Huie, J. 1997. 'Environmental Quality Assurance: Are Consumers of Hospitality and Tourism Services Willing to Pay?' *Australian Journal of Hospitality Management* 4: 42–6.

Hovinen, G. 2002. 'Revisiting the Destination Lifecycle Model'. *Annals of Tourism Research* 29: 209–30.

HPCCV Publications 1998. 'The CAVE: A Virtual Reality Theater'. www.evl.uic.edu/pape/CAVE/oldCAVE/CAVE.html (visited 16 June 1998).

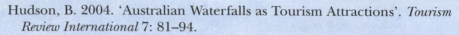

Hudson, B. 2004. 'Australian Waterfalls as Tourism Attractions'. *Tourism Review International* 7: 81–94.

Hudson, S. 2000. *Snow Business: A Study of the International Ski Industry*. London: Cassell.

Hunter, C. 1997. 'Sustainable Tourism as an Adaptive Paradigm'. *Annals of Tourism Research* 24: 850–67.

Hydropolis 2004. 'Hydropolis Underwater Resort Hotel'. www.hydropolis.com/homepage.html (visited 1 June 2005).

ICCL (International Council of Cruise Lines). 2004. 'The Cruise Industry: 2003 Economic Summary'. www.iccl.org/resources/2003_econstudy–analysis.pdf (visited 14 February 2005).

IDABC (Interoperable Delivery of European eGovernment Services to Public Administrations, Business and Citizens) 2004. 'Biometric Border Control System Launched in US Airports and Seaports'. http://europa.eu.int/idabc/en/document/1958/348 (visited 2 March 2005).

ILO (International Labour Organization) 2005. 'After the Tsunami: In Thailand, the Tourist Industry Fights Back'. www.ilo.org/public/english/bureau/inf/features/05/tsunami_thai.htm (visited 7 June 2005).

Inskeep, E. 1991. *Tourism Planning: An Integrated and Sustainable Development Approach*. New York: Van Nostrand Reinhold.

Israeli, A. & Reichel, A. 2003. 'Hospitality Crisis Management Practices: the Israeli Case'. *International Journal of Hospitality Management* 22: 353–72.

Jackson, R. & Davis, J. 1997. 'Religion and Tourism in Western China'. *Tourism Recreation Research* 22 (1): 3–10.

Jacob, T. 2005. 'Dreamscape: Who Says That Waiting for Your Flight Has To Be Boring?' *Travel Savvy* Jan/Feb., pp. 96–9.

Jafari, J. 2001. 'The Scientification of Tourism'. In Smith, V. L. and Brent, M. (Eds) *Hosts and Guests Revisited: Tourism Issues of the 21st Century*. New York: Cognizant, 28–41.

Jang, S., Yu, L., & Pearson, T. 2003. 'Chinese Travellers to the United States: A Comparison of Business Travel and Visiting Friends and Relatives'. *Tourism Geographies* 5: 87–108.

Jansen-Verbeke, M. 1999. 'Industrial Heritage: A Nexus for Sustainable Tourism Development'. *Tourism Geographies* 1: 70–85.

Jenkins, J. 1992. 'Fossickers and Rockhounds in Northern New South Wales'. In Weiler B. and Hall, C. M. (Eds) *Special Interest Tourism*. London: Belhaven Press, pp. 129–40.

Jenkins, O. 2003. 'Photography and Travel Brochures: The Circle of Representation'. *Tourism Geographies* 5: 305–28.

Jennings, G. 2001. *Tourism Research*. Brisbane: John Wiley.

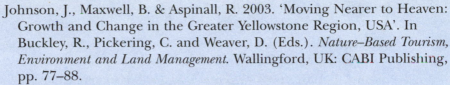

Johnson, J., Maxwell, B. & Aspinall, R. 2003. 'Moving Nearer to Heaven: Growth and Change in the Greater Yellowstone Region, USA'. In Buckley, R., Pickering, C. and Weaver, D. (Eds.). *Nature–Based Tourism, Environment and Land Management.* Wallingford, UK: CABI Publishing, pp. 77–88.

Jones, C. 2003. ' "What Happens Here Stays Here" Strikes Sour Note for Some at Conference'. www.reviewjournal.com/lvrj_home/2003/Dec-18-Thu-2003/news/22822287.html (visited 31 May 2005).

Jones, D. R. 1986. 'Prostitution and Tourism'. In Marsh, J. (Ed.) *Canadian Studies of Parks, Recreation and Tourism in Foreign Lands.* Peterborough, Canada: Trent University, pp. 241–8.

Jones, P. & Phillips, D. 2003. 'What Use Is Research Anyway? Industry and Academe's Differing Views'. *International Journal of Contemporary Hospitality Management* 15: 290–3.

Jutla, R. 2000. 'Visual Image of the City: Tourists' Versus Residents' Perception of Simla, a Hill Station in Northern India'. *Tourism Geographies* 2: 404–20.

Keay, J. 1996. 'Waterworld Set for Foreign Spending Spree'. *Corporate Location* May/June, pp. 68–75.

Keesing's Record of World Events. Volume 43, Numbers 11 and 12.

Kemp, S. & Dwyer, L. 2003. 'Mission Statements of International Airlines: A Content Analysis'. *Tourism Management* 24: 635–53.

Kim, Y.-K. & Crompton, J. 1990. 'Role of Tourism in Unifying the Two Koreas'. *Annals of Tourism Research* 17: 353–66.

King, D. A. & Stewart, W. P. 1996. 'Ecotourism and Commodification: Protecting People and Places'. *Biodiversity and Conservation* 5: 293–305.

Kinnaird, V. & Hall, D. (Eds) 1994. *Tourism: A Gender Analysis.* Chichester, UK: John Wiley.

Kinninment, M. 2005a. 'Ragers, We Don't'. *The Lismore Northern Star.* www.northernstar.com.au/byronbay/index.cfm?part=2 (visited 12 June 2005).

Kinninment, M. 2005b. 'Byron — It's Time the Party Ended'. *The Lismore Northern Star.* www.northernstar.com.au/byronbay/index.cfm?part=1 (visited 12 June 2005).

Knight, D., Mitchell, B. & Wall, G. 1997. 'Bali: Sustainable Development, Tourism and Coastal Management'. *Ambio* 26 (2): 90–6.

Knill, G. 1991. 'Towards the Green Paradigm'. *South African Geographical Journal* 73: 52–9.

Knobloch, J. 2004. 'Long-term Malaria Prophylaxis for Travelers'. *Journal of Travel Medicine* 11: 374–8.

Kotler, P., Bowen, J. & Makens, J. 2003. *Marketing for Hospitality and Tourism.* Third Edition. Upper Saddle River, NJ, USA: Prentice Hall.

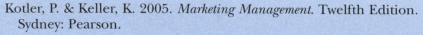

Kotler, P. & Keller, K. 2005. *Marketing Management.* Twelfth Edition. Sydney: Pearson.

Krueger, R. & Casey, M. A. 2000. *Focus Groups: A Practical Guide for Applied Research.* Third Edition. London: Sage.

Kuhn, T. 1962. *The Structure of Scientific Revolutions.* Chicago: University of Chicago Press.

Kurtzman, J. & Zauhar, J. 2003. 'Virtual Sport Tourism'. In Hudson, S. (Ed.) *Sport and Adventure Tourism.* Binghamton, USA: Haworth Hospitality Press, pp. 293–309.

Lang, C-T. & O'Leary, J. T. 1997. 'Motivation, Participation, and Preference: A Multi-Segmentation Approach to the Australian Nature Travel Market'. *Journal of Travel & Tourism Marketing* 6 (3/4): 159–80.

Laws, E. & Scott, N. 2003. 'Developing New Tourism Services: Dinosaurs, a New Drive Tourism Resource for Remote Regions?' *Journal of Vacation Marketing* 9: 368–80.

Lawson, R. 1991. 'Patterns of Tourist Expenditure and Types of Vacation Across the Family Life Cycle'. *Journal of Travel Research* 30 (2): 12–18.

Lawton, L. J. 2000. 'A Profile of Older Adult Ecotourists in Australia'. *Journal of Hospitality & Leisure Marketing* 9 (1/2): 113–32.

Lawton, L. J., Weaver, David B. & Faulkner, Bill. 1998. 'Customer Satisfaction in the Australian Timeshare Industry'. *Journal of Travel Research* 37 (1): 30–8.

Leinwand, D. 2005. 'Please Come to Thailand, at Locals' Request'. *USA Today,* 14 January, p. 7D.

Leiper, N. 1995. *Tourism Management.* Melbourne: RMIT Press.

Leiper, N. 1997a. 'Those Who Oppose University Courses On Tourism and Hospitality'. In Bushell, R. (Ed.) *Tourism Research: Building a Better Industry.* Proceedings from the Australian Tourism and Hospitality Research Conference, 1997. Canberra: Bureau of Tourism Research, pp. 75–9.

Leiper, N. 1997b. 'Big Success, Big Mistake, at Big Banana: Marketing Strategies in Road-Side Attractions and Theme Parks'. *Journal of Travel & Tourism Marketing* 6: 103–21.

Leiper, N. 1999. 'A Conceptual Analysis of Tourism-supported Employment which Reduces the Incidence of Exaggerated, Misleading Statistics About Jobs'. *Tourism Management* 20: 605–13.

Leiper, N. 2000. 'An Emerging Discipline'. *Annals of Tourism Research* 27: 805–9.

Leiper, N. 2004. *Tourism Management.* Third Edition. Sydney: Pearson Education Australia.

Leiper, N. & Hunt, S. 1998. 'Why Australia's Tourist Commissions Should be Promoting Universities and Why Academics Should be on the Commissions' Boards'. *Pacific Tourism Review* 2 (3/4): 191–7.

Lennon, J. & Foley, M. 1999. 'Interpretation of the Unimaginable: The U.S. Holocaust Memorial Museum, Washington, D.C., and "Dark Tourism" '. *Journal of Travel Research* 38 (1): 46–50.

Lennon, J. & Foley, M. 2000. *Dark Tourism: The Attraction of Death and Disaster.* London: Continuum.

Leung, P. & Lam, T. 2004. 'Crisis Management during the SARS Threat: a Case Study of the Metropole Hotel in Hong Kong'. *Journal of Human Resources in Hospitality and Tourism* 3: 47–57.

Lim, C. & McAleer, M. 2001. 'Monthly Seasonal Variations: Asian Tourism to Australia'. *Annals of Tourism Research* 28: 68–82.

Litchfield, C. 2001. 'Responsible Tourism with Great Apes in Uganda'. In McCool, S. and Moisey, R. (Eds) *Tourism, Recreation and Sustainability: Linking Culture and the Environment.* Wallingford, UK: CABI Publishing, pp. 105–32.

Littlefair, C. 2004. 'Reducing Impacts Through Interpretation, Lamington National Park'. In Buckley, R. (Ed.) *Environmental Impacts of Tourism.* Wallingford, UK: CABI Publishing, pp. 297–307.

Litvin, S. 2004. 'A Look Back at SARS and SIP'. *e–Review of Tourism Research* 2 (1). http://ertr.tamu.edu.

Lockwood, A. & Medlik, S. 2001. *Tourism and Hospitality in the 21st Century.* Oxford: Butterworth–Heinemann.

Loker-Murphy, L. & Pearce, P. L. 1995. 'Young Budget Travelers: Backpackers in Australia'. *Annals of Tourism Research* 22: 819–43.

Lovgren, S. 2005. 'Airbus Unveils A380 "Superjumbo" Jet'. *National Geographic News.* http://news.nationalgeographi.com/news/2005/01/0118_050118_airbus.html (visited 18 January 2005).

Lumsdon, L. M. & Swift, J. S. 1994. 'Latin American Tourism: The Dilemmas of the 21st Century'. In Seaton, A. V. et al. (Eds) *Tourism: The State of the Art.* Chichester, UK: John Wiley, pp. 359–65.

Lundgren, J. 1984. 'Geographic Concepts and the Development of Tourism Research in Canada'. *GeoJournal* 9: 17–25.

MacCannell, D. 1976. *The Tourist: A New Theory of the Leisure Class.* New York: Schocken Books.

Macy, R. 1998. 'New Vegas is Tops for Family Fun'. *Weekend Bulletin* (Gold Coast), 24–25 October, pp. 22–3.

Magazine Publishers of Australia 2005. 'Key Circulation Facts'. www.magazines.org.au/driver.asp?page=circulation+%26+readership/key+circulation+facts (visited 7 June 2005).

Mansfeld, Y. 1994. 'The Middle East Conflict and Tourism to Israel, 1967–90'. *Middle Eastern Studies* 30 (3): 646–67.

Marion, J. & Farrell, T. 1998. 'Managing Ecotourism Visitation in Protected Areas'. In Lindberg, K., Epler Wood, M. & Engeldrum, D. (Eds.). *Ecotourism: A Guide for Planners and Managers. Volume 2.* North Bennington, VT, USA: The Ecotourism Society, pp. 155–81.

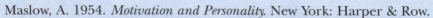

Maslow, A. 1954. *Motivation and Personality.* New York: Harper & Row.

Mason, P., Grabowski, P. & Du, W. 2005. 'Severe Acute Respiratory Syndrome, Tourism and the Media'. *International Journal of Tourism Research* 7: 11–21.

Mather, S. 1998. *Philippines.* International Tourism Reports Number 3, pp. 67–92.

Mathieson, A. & Wall, G. 1982. *Tourism: Economic, Physical and Social Impacts.* London: Longman Cheshire.

Mazur, N. 2001. *After the Ark? Environmental Policy-making and the Zoo.* Carlton South, Victoria: Melbourne University Press.

Mbaiwa, J. 2005. 'Enclave Tourism and its Socio-economic Impacts in the Okavango Delta, Botswana'. *Tourism Management* 26: 157–72.

McElroy, J. & de Albuquerque, K. 1999. 'Measuring Tourism Penetration in Small Islands'. *Pacific Tourism Review* 3: 161–9.

McKean, P. F. 1989. 'Towards a Theoretical Analysis of Tourism: Economic Dualism and Cultural Involution in Bali'. In Smith, V. L. (Ed.) *Hosts and Guests: The Anthropology of Tourism.* Second Edition. Philadelphia: University of Pennsylvania Press, pp. 119–38.

McKercher, B. 1993. 'The Unrecognised Threat to Tourism: Can Tourism Survive "Sustainability"?' *Tourism Management* 14: 131–6.

McKercher, B. 1998. *The Business of Nature Tourism.* Melbourne: Hospitality Press Pty Ltd.

McKercher, B. 1999. 'A Chaos Approach to Tourism'. *Tourism Management* 20: 425–34.

McKercher, B. 2001. 'The Business of Ecotourism'. In Weaver, D. B. (Ed.) *The Encyclopedia of Ecotourism.* Wallingford, UK: CABI Publishing, pp. 565–77.

McKercher, B. 2003. 'SIP (SARS Induced Panic): A Greater Threat to Tourism Than SARS (Severe Acute Respiratory Syndrome)'. *e–Review of Tourism Research* 1 (1). http://ertr.tamu.edu.

McKercher, B. & Lew, A. 2003. 'Distance Decay and the Impact of Effective Tourism Exclusion Zones on International Travel Flows'. *Journal of Travel Research* 42: 159–65.

Meade, K. 'Packing One Day, Bountiful the Next'. The *Weekend Australian,* 11–12 July, p. 46.

Meyer, C. 1997. 'Public-Nonprofit Partnerships and North-South Green Finance'. *Journal of Environment and Development* 6 (2): 123–46.

Meyer-Arendt, K. & Hartmann, R. (Eds.). 1998. *Casino Gambling in America: Origins, Trends, and Impacts.* Elmsford, NY: Cognizant Communications.

Meyer-Arendt, K. & Justice, C. 2002. 'Tourism as the Subject of North American Doctoral Dissertations, 1987 – 2000'. *Annals of Tourism Research* 29: 1171–4.

Michaud, J. 1991. 'A Social Anthropology of Tourism in Ladakh, India'. *Annals of Tourism Research* 18: 605–21.

Millar, R. 2005. 'Rate Slug Plan for Seaside Owners'. *The Age.* January 15. www.theage.com.au/news/National/Rate-slug-plan-for-seaside-owners/ 2005/01/14/1105582718055.html?oneclick=true (visited 6 March 2005).

Miller, M. L. & Kaae, B. 1993. 'Coastal and Marine Ecotourism: A Formula for Sustainable Development?' *Trends* 30 (2): 35–41.

Minca, C. 2000. '"The Bali Syndrome": the Explosion and Implosion of "Exotic" Tourism Spaces'. *Tourism Geographies* 2: 389–403.

Mings, R. & McHugh, K. E. 1995. 'Wintering in the American Sunbelt: Linking Place and Behaviour'. *Journal of Tourism Studies* 6 (2): 56–62.

Mings, R. 1969. 'Tourism's Potential for Contributing to Economic Development in the Caribbean'. *Journal of Geography* 68: 173–7.

Mings, R. 1997. 'Tracking "Snowbirds" in Australia: Winter Sun Seekers in Far North Queensland'. *Australian Geographical Studies* 35: 168–82.

Mistilis, N. & Dwyer, L. 1997. 'Capital Cities and Regions: Economic Impacts and Challenges for Development of the Mice Industry in Australia'. In Bushell, R. (Ed.) *Tourism Research: Building a Better Industry.* Proceedings from the Australian Tourism and Hospitality Research Conference, 1997. Canberra: Bureau of Tourism Research, pp. 390–408.

Moeller, G. & Shafer, E. 1994. 'The Delphi Technique: A Tool for Long-Range Travel and Tourism Planning'. In Ritchie, J. R. Brent & Goeldner, C. R. (Eds) *Travel, Tourism, and Hospitality Research: A Handbook for Managers and Researchers.* Second Edition. Chichester, UK: John Wiley, pp. 473–80.

Morgan, N. & Pritchard, A. 2000. *Advertising in Tourism and Leisure.* Oxford: Butterworth–Heinemann.

Morgan, N., Pritchard, A. & Piggott, R. 2002. 'New Zealand, 100% Pure. The Creation of a Powerful Niche Destination Brand'. *Brand Management* 4: 335–54.

Morgan, N., Pritchard, A. & Pride, R. (Eds) 2004. *Destination Branding: Creating the Unique Destination Proposition.* Second Edition. Sydney: Elsevier.

Morrison, A. 2002. Hospitality and Travel Marketing. Third Edition. Albany, New York, US: Delmar Thomson Learning.

Mowforth, M. & Munt, I. 1998. *Tourism and Sustainability: New Tourism in the Third World.* London: Routledge.

MSNBC 2004. 'Libya Sees Thriving Tourism Industry Ahead'. www.msnbc.msn.com/id/5210117 (visited 1 June 2005).

Murphy, P. E. 1985. *Tourism: A Community Approach.* New York: Methuen.

Needham, P. 1997. 'War is Over. Peace Gives Tourism a Chance'. *Travelweek* No. 897 (16 July), pp. 10–11.

Neuman, W. L. 1997. *Social Research Methods: Qualitative and Quantitative Approaches*. Third Edition. London: Allyn and Bacon.

Newsome, D., Moore, S. & Dowling, R. 2002. *Natural Area Tourism: Ecology, Impacts and Management*. Clevedon, UK: Channel View Publications.

Nicholson, M. H. 1959. *Mountain Gloom and Mountain Glory*. Ithaca, NY, USA: Cornell University Press.

Nielsen, C. 2001. *Tourism and the Media*. Melbourne: Hospitality Press.

North Beach Byron 2005. 'Division Over North Beach Byron'. www.northbeachbyron.com.au/byron/news/releases/ byron_division.asp (visited 13 June 2005).

Nullis, C. 1995. 'Tourism Takes a Plunge in Switzerland'. *Globe and Mail* (Canada), 22 July, p. A13.

OECD 1980. *The Impact of Tourism on Development*. Paris: Organisation for Economic Cooperation and Development.

Oliver, B. 1998. 'Titanic Raises Super Interest'. The *Weekend Australian*, 12–13 September, p. 45.

Oneworld 1998. 'What Oneworld Will Offer'. www.oneworldalliance.com/pressroom/index.htm (visited 6 January 1999).

ONT 1998. *A Monthly Facts Sheet on the Economic Impact of Tourism & The Latest Visitor Arrival Trends*. Canberra: Office of National Tourism. August.

Oppermann, M. 1994. 'Regional Aspects of Tourism in New Zealand'. *Regional Studies* 28: 155–67.

Oppermann, M. 1995. 'Models of Tourist Flow Destinations'. *Journal of Travel Research* 33 (4): 57–61.

Oppermann, M. 1997. *Pacific Rim Tourism*. Wallingford, UK: CAB International.

Oppermann, M. 1998a. 'Service Attributes of Travel Agencies: A Comparative Perspective of Users and Providers'. *Journal of Vacation Marketing* 4: 265–81.

Oppermann, M. (Ed.) 1998b. *Sex Tourism and Prostitution: Aspects of Leisure, Recreation and Work*. Elmsford, NY, USA: Cognizant Communications.

Oppermann, M. 2000. 'Triangulation – A Methodological Discussion'. *International Journal of Tourism Research* 2: 141–6.

Oppermann, M., Din, K. H. & Amri, S. Z. 1996. 'Urban Hotel Location and Evolution in a Developing Country: The Case of Kuala Lumpur, Malaysia'. *Tourism Recreation Research* 21 (1): 55–63.

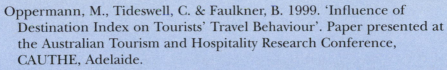

Oppermann, M., Tideswell, C. & Faulkner, B. 1999. 'Influence of Destination Index on Tourists' Travel Behaviour'. Paper presented at the Australian Tourism and Hospitality Research Conference, CAUTHE, Adelaide.

Orchid Hotel 2005. 'Environconstruction'. www.orchidhotel.com/mumbai_hotels/enviroconstruction.htm (visited 23 May 2005).

Parsons, C. 1996. 'Tourism, Whale Watching and the Federal Government'. In Colgan, K., Prasser, S. & Jeffery, A. (Eds) *Encounters with Whales. 1995 Proceedings.* Canberra: Australian Nature Conservation Agency, pp. 87–92.

PATA n.d. *Code for Environmentally Responsible Tourism.* San Francisco: PATA.

Pearce, D. 1983. 'The Development and Impact of Large-scale Tourism Projects: Languedoc-Roussillon (France) and Cancun (Mexico) Compared'. In *Papers of the Seventh Annual Australian/NZ Regional Science Association.* Canberra, pp. 59–71.

Pearce, D. & Priestley, G. 1998. 'Tourism in Spain: A Spatial Analysis and Synthesis'. *Tourism Analysis* 2: 185–205.

Peckham, V. 2003. *BEST Community Profile: The Shaw Heritage Tours.* The Conference Board and WTTC.

Peterson, R. 1998. 'The Depiction of Seniors in International Tourism Magazine Advertisements: A Content Analysis'. *Journal of International Hospitality, Leisure & Tourism Management* 1 (4): 3–17.

Phillips, M. 2001. 'Working Longer, Working Harder? You're Not Alone'. *Weekend Bulletin* (Gold Coast), 17–18 February, p. 30.

PIAS (Petcare Information and Advisory Services Australia). 2005. 'Petnet'. www.petnet.com/au/petcare.html (visited 4 April 2005).

Pickering, C. & Hill, W. 2003. 'Ecological Change as a Result of Winter Tourism: Snow Manipulation in the Australian Alps'. In Buckley, R., Pickering, C. & Weaver, D. (Eds.). *Nature-based Tourism, Environment and Land Management.* Wallingford, UK: CABI Publishing, pp. 137–49.

Pickering, C., Johnston, S., Green, K. & Enders, G. 2003. 'Impacts of Nature Tourism on the Mount Kosciuszko Alpine Area, Australia'. In Buckley, R., Pickering, C. & Weaver, D. (Eds) *Nature–based Tourism, Environment and Land Management.* Wallingford, UK: CABI Publishing, pp. 123–35.

Piggott, R., Morgan, N. & Pritchard, A. 2004. 'New Zealand and *The Lord of the Rings*: Leveraging Public and Media Relations'. In Morgan, N., Pritchard, A. & Pride, R. (Eds) *Destination Branding: Creating the Unique Destination Proposition.* Second Edition. Sydney: Elsevier, pp. 207–25.

Pine, R. & McKercher, B. 2004. 'The Impact of SARS on Hong Kong's Tourism Industry'. *International Journal of Contemporary Hospitality Management* 16: 139–43.

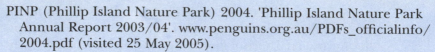

PINP (Phillip Island Nature Park) 2004. 'Phillip Island Nature Park Annual Report 2003/04'. www.penguins.org.au/PDFs_officialinfo/2004.pdf (visited 25 May 2005).

Plog, S. 1991. *Leisure Travel: Making it a Growth Market — Again!* Chichester, UK: John Wiley.

Plog, S. 1994. 'Developing and Using Psychographics in Tourism Research'. In Ritchie, J. R. B. & Goeldner, C. R. (Eds) *Travel, Tourism, and Hospitality Research: A Handbook for Managers and Researchers.* Second Edition. Chichester, UK: John Wiley, pp. 209–18.

Plog, S. 1998. 'Why Destination Preservation Makes Economic Sense'. In Theobold, W. (Ed.) *Global Tourism.* Second Edition. Oxford: Butterworth–Heinemann, pp. 251–66.

Plog, S. 2004. *Leisure Travel: A Marketing Handbook.* Upper Saddle River, NJ, USA: Pearson Prentice Hall, p. 51.

Plog, S. 2005. 'Targeting Segments: More Important than Ever in the Travel Industry'. In Theobald, W. (Ed.) *Global Tourism.* Third Edition. Sydney: Elsevier, pp. 271–93.

Poh, W. P. 1997. 'Singapore: Tourism Development of an Island City–State'. In Lockhart, D. G. & Drakakis-Smith, D. (Eds) *Island Tourism: Trends and Prospects.* London: Pinter, pp. 249–67.

Poirer, R. 2000. 'Tourism in the African Economic Milieu: A Future of Mixed Blessings'. In Dieke, P. (Ed.) *The Political Economy of Tourism Development in Africa.* New York: Cognizant Communications, pp. 29–36.

Poon, A. 1993. *Tourism, Technology and Competitive Strategies.* Wallingford, UK: CAB International.

Prideaux, B. 1996. 'The Tourism Crime Cycle: A Beach Destination Case Study'. In Pizam, A. & Mansfeld, Y. (Eds) *Tourism, Crime and International Security Issues.* Chichester, UK: John Wiley, pp. 59–75.

Productivity Commission 2005. 'Assistance to Tourism: Exploratory Estimates'. www.pc.gov.au/research/crp/tourism/tourism.pdf (visited 18 April 2005).

Prosser, G. 1995. 'Tourist Destination Life Cycles: Progress, Problems and Prospects'. In Shaw, R. N. (Ed.) *Proceedings of the National Tourism and Hospitality Conference 1995.* Melbourne: Council for Australian University Tourism and Hospitality Education, pp. 318–28.

QTTC 1997. *The Queensland Tourist and Travel Corporation Annual Report.* Brisbane: Queensland Tourist and Travel Corporation.

Queensland 1997. *Ecotourism: Queensland Ecotourism Plan.* Brisbane: Department of Tourism, Small Business and Industry.

Ragin, C. 1994. *Constructing Social Research.* Thousand Oaks, CA, USA: Pine Forge Press.

Rajewski, B. (Ed.) 1998. *Countries of the World and Their Leaders Yearbook 1998. Volume One.* Cleveland, USA: Eastword Publications.

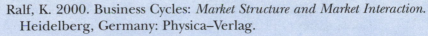

Ralf, K. 2000. Business Cycles: *Market Structure and Market Interaction.* Heidelberg, Germany: Physica–Verlag.

Ranck, S. 1987. 'An Attempt at Autonomous Development: The Case of the Tufi Guest Houses, Papua New Guinea'. In Britton, S. & Clarke, W. (Eds) *Ambiguous Alternative: Tourism in Small Developing Countries.* Suva, Fiji: University of the South Pacific, pp. 154–66.

Raybould, M., Mules, T., Fredline, E. & Tomljenovic, R. 2000. 'Counting the Herd. Using Aerial Photography to Estimate Attendance at Open Events'. *Event Management* 6: 25–32.

Rayno, G. 2003. 'Benson Accepts Old Man Recommendations'. www.theunionleader.com/articles_show.html?article=28910 (visited 1 June 2005).

Richard L. Ragatz Associates. 1993. *An Annual Report of the Worldwide Resort Timesharing Industry — 1992.* Eugene, OR, USA: Richard L. Ragatz Associates.

Richards, G. & Wilson, J. (Eds) 2004. *The Global Nomad: Backpacker Travel in Theory and Practice.* Clevedon, UK: Channel View.

Richins, M. L. 1991. 'Social Comparison and the Idealized Images of Advertising'. *Journal of Consumer Research* 18: 71–83.

Richter, L. 1989. *The Politics of Tourism in Asia.* Honolulu: University of Hawaii Press.

Richter, L. 1993. 'Tourism Policy-Making in South-East Asia'. In Hitchcock, M., King, V. T. & Parnwell, M. J. (Eds) *Tourism in South-East Asia.* London: Routledge, pp. 179–99.

Richter, L. & Waugh, W. L. 1986. 'Terrorism and Tourism as Logical Companions'. *Tourism Management* 7 (4): 230–8.

Rigby, M. 2001. 'Graceland: A Sacred Place in a Secular World?' In Cusack, C. and Oldmeadow, P. (Eds) *The End of Religions? Religion in an Age of Globalization.* Sydney: University of Sydney, pp. 155–68.

Ritter, W. & Schafer, C. 1998. 'Cruise-Tourism: A Chance of Sustainability'. *Tourism Recreation Review* 23: 65–71.

Roberts, J. 1996. 'Green Consumers in the 1990s: Profile and Implications for Advertising'. *Journal of Business Research* 36: 217–31.

Rogers, T. F. 1998. 'The Prospects for Space Tourism'. *Journal of Social, Political, and Economic Studies* 23 (1): 33–7.

Rogerson, C. 2004. 'Urban Tourism and Small Tourism Enterprise Development in Johannesburg: the Case of Township Tourism'. *GeoJournal* 60: 249–57.

Rojek, C. 1993. *Ways of Escape: Modern Transformations in Leisure and Travel.* Basingstoke, UK: Macmillan.

Rowe, M. 1998. 'Going Green Makes Sense'. *Lodging Hospitality,* March, pp. 26–30.

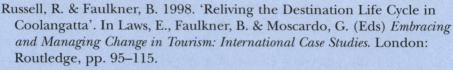

Russell, R. & Faulkner, B. 1998. 'Reliving the Destination Life Cycle in Coolangatta'. In Laws, E., Faulkner, B. & Moscardo, G. (Eds) *Embracing and Managing Change in Tourism: International Case Studies*. London: Routledge, pp. 95–115.

Russell, R. & Faulkner, B. 2004. 'Entrepreneurship, Chaos and the Tourism Area Lifecycle'. *Annals of Tourism Research* 31: 556–79.

Russell, R. 1995. *Tourism Development in Coolangatta: An Historical Perspective*. Bachelor of Business (Honours) thesis, Faculty of Business and Hotel Management, Griffith University, Gold Coast, Australia.

Ryan, C. 1995. *Researching Tourist Satisfaction*. London: Routledge.

Ryan, C. 2002a. 'Tourism and Cultural Proximity: Examples from New Zealand'. *Annals of Tourism Research* 29: 952–71.

Ryan, C. 2002b. 'Equity, Management, Power Sharing and Sustainability — Issues of the "New Tourism"'. *Tourism Management* 23: 17–26.

Santana, G. 2001. 'Tourism in the Southern Common Market: MERCOSUR'. In Harrison, D. (Ed). *Tourism and the Less Developed World: Issues and Case Studies*. Wallingford, UK: CABI Publishing, pp. 77–90.

Sarantakos, S. 1998. *Social Research*. Second Edition. Melbourne: Macmillan Education.

Saunders, P. 2001. 'Household Income and Its Distribution'. In ABS (Australian Bureau of Statistics) *2001 Year Book Australia*. Canberra: Australian Bureau of Statistics, pp. 280–95.

Schwartz, R. D. 1991. 'Travelers Under Fire: Tourists in the Tibetan Uprising'. *Annals of Tourism Research* 18: 588–604.

Seaton, A. 1996. 'Guided by the Dark: From Thanatopsis to Thanatourism'. *International Journal of Heritage Studies* 2: 234–44.

Seideman, D. 1998. 'Final Frontiers'. *Audubon* 100 (5): 18.

Selwood, J. & Tonts, M. 2004. 'Recreational Second Homes in the South West of Western Australia.' In Hall, C.M. & Müller, D. (Eds) *Tourism, Mobility and Second Homes: Between Elite Landscape and Common Ground*. Clevedon, UK: Channel View, pp. 149–61.

Seward, S. & Spinrad, B. 1982. *Tourism in the Caribbean: The Economic Impact*. Ottawa, Canada: International Development Research Centre.

Shackley, M. (Ed.) 2000. *Visitor Management: Case Studies from World Heritage Sites*. Oxford: Butterworth–Heinemann.

Shafer, E. & Moeller, G. 1974. 'Through the Looking Glass in Environmental Management'. *Parks and Recreation* 9 (2): 20–3, 48–9.

Shellito, B., Dixon, J., Inge, C. & O'Neal, J. 2004. 'CIS and 3D Modeling for Tourism Visual Viewscape Issues'. *Tourism Analysis* 9: 167–78.

Shelton, E. & Tucker, H. 2005. 'Tourism and Disability: Issues Beyond Access'. *Tourism Review International* 8: 211–19.

Shire of Augusta–Margaret River. 2004. 'Ordinary Meeting of Council Agenda March 31, 2004: Sea Change Summit — Invitation for Council Representation'.

Shoebridge, N. 1996. 'Village, the Bluechip Blockbuster'. *Business Review Weekly*, 1 July, pp. 32–7.

Silverstein, J. 1992. 'Seeing Dollar Signs: Tourism Investment Goes for the Gold but Offers Something for Everyone'. *Business Mexico* 2 (6): 4–7.

Singapore Infomap 1998. 'Aviation Gateway'. www.sg/flavour/profile/pro-transport1.html (visited 21 December 1998).

Singh, S. 2004. 'Religion, Heritage and Travel: Case References From the Indian Himalayas'. *Current Issues in Tourism* 7: 44–65.

Singh, S., Timothy, D. & Dowling, R. (Eds) 2003. *Tourism in Destination Communities*. Wallingford, UK: CABI Publishing.

Singh, T. V. & Kaur, J. 1986. 'The Paradox of Mountain Tourism: Case References from the Himalaya'. *UNEP Industry and Development* 9: 21–6.

Sisman, R. 1994. 'Tourism: Environmental Relevance'. In Cater, E. & Lowman, G. (Eds) *Ecotourism: A Sustainable Option?* Chichester, UK: John Wiley, pp. 57–67.

Sletto, B. 1996. 'Antigua's Old Mills Turn with New Winds'. *Americas* 48 (6): 6–13.

Smith, C. & Jenner, P. 1997. 'The Seniors' Travel Market'. *Travel & Tourism Analyst* No. 5, pp. 43–62.

Smith, C. & Jenner, P. 2000. 'Health Tourism in Europe'. *Travel & Tourism Analyst*, No. 1, pp. 41–59.

Smith, M. 2004. 'Seeing a New Side to Seasides: Culturally Regenerating the English Seaside Town'. *International Journal of Tourism Research* 6: 17–28.

Smith, R. 1994. 'Scotland's Newest Visitor Attractions'. In Seaton, A. V. (Ed.) *Tourism: The State of the Art*. New York: John Wiley, pp. 510–16.

Smith, S. H. 1988. 'Cruise Ships: A Serious Threat to Coral Reefs and Associated Organisms'. *Ocean and Shoreline Management* 11: 231–48.

Smith, V. 2004. 'Tourism and Terrorism: The "New War"'. In Aramberri, J. and Butler, R. (Eds) *Tourism Development: Issues for a Vulnerable Industry*. Clevedon, UK: Channel View, pp. 275–90.

Smith, V. L. 1989. *Hosts and Guests: The Anthropology of Tourism*. Second Edition. Philadelphia: University of Pennsylvania Press.

Smith, V. L. 1996. 'War and its Tourist Attractions'. In Pizam, A. & Mansfeld, Y. (Eds) *Tourism, Crime and International Security Issues*. Chichester, UK: John Wiley, pp. 247–64.

Sofield, T., & Getz, D. 1997. 'Rural Tourism in Australia: The Undara Experience'. In Page, S. J. & Getz, D. (Eds) *The Business of Rural Tourism: International Perspectives*. London: International Thomson Business Press, pp. 143–61.

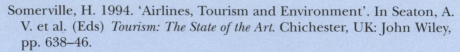

Somerville, H. 1994. 'Airlines, Tourism and Environment'. In Seaton, A. V. et al. (Eds) *Tourism: The State of the Art.* Chichester, UK: John Wiley, pp. 638–46.

Standeven, J. & De Knop, P. 1999. *Sport Tourism.* Champaign, IL, USA: Human Kinetics.

Stansfield, C. 1978. 'Atlantic City and the Resort Cycle: Background to the Legalization of Gambling'. *Annals of Tourism Research* 5 (2): 238–51.

STCRC (Sustainable Tourism CRC) 2005a. 'About STCRC'. www.crctourism.com.au/CRCServer/page.aspx?page_id=42 (visited 17 May 2005).

STCRC (Sustainable Tourism CRC) 2005b. *The Visitor Information Centre Kit – VICkit.* Gold Coast, Australia: Sustainable Tourism CRC.

Steffen, R. 1997. 'The Epidemiology of Travel-related Health Problems'. In Clift, S. & Grabowski, P. (Eds). *Tourism and Health: Risks, Research and Responses.* London: Pinter, pp. 27–37.

Steinecke, A. 1993. 'The Historical Development of Tourism in Europe'. In Pompl, W. and Lavery, P. (Eds) *Tourism in Europe: Structures and Developments.* Wallingford, UK: CAB International, pp. 3–12.

Stolz, G. 1999. 'Chinese are Coming: Group's Arrival a 'Major Milestone' for Tourism'. *Gold Coast Bulletin*, 18 August, p. 4.

Stonehouse, B. & Crosbie, K. 1995. 'Tourist Impacts and Management in the Antarctic Peninsula Area'. In Hall, C. M. and Johnston, M. (Eds) *Polar Tourism: Tourism in the Arctic and Antarctic Regions.* Chichester, UK: John Wiley, pp. 217–33.

Stubbs, D. & MacGregor, L. 1996. 'Towards a Pan-European Environmental Management Programme for Golf in Europe'. *UNEP Industry and Environment* March, pp. 47–9.

Studienkreis fuer Tourismus. 1973–1993. *Urlaubsreisen.* Starnberg, Germany.

Stumbo, N. & Pegg, S. 2005. 'Travelers and Tourists With Disabilities: A Matter of Priorities and Loyalties'. *Tourism Review International* 8: 195–209.

Svenson, S. 2004. 'The Cottage and the City: An Interpretation of the Canadian Second Home Experience'. In Hall, C.M. and Müller, D. (Eds). *Tourism, Mobility and Second Homes: Between Elite Landscape and Common Ground.* Clevedon, UK: Channel View, pp. 55–74.

Symes, C. 1995. 'Taking People for a Ride: Dreamworld, Sea World and Movieworld as Excursive Practice'. *Journal of Australian Studies* 44: 1–12 (March).

Tahana, N. & Oppermann, M. 1998. 'Maori Cultural Performances and Tourism'. *Tourism Recreation Research* 23 (1): 23–30.

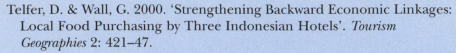

Telfer, D. & Wall, G. 2000. 'Strengthening Backward Economic Linkages: Local Food Purchasing by Three Indonesian Hotels'. *Tourism Geographies* 2: 421–47.

Templeton, R. 2001. 'Nimbin One Day, Noosa the Next?'. *Weekend Bulletin* (Gold Coast), 21–22 April, pp. 56–57.

Teo, P. 1994. 'Assessing Socio-Cultural Impacts: The Case of Singapore.' *Tourism Management* 15 (2): 126–36.

Teye, V. 1986. 'Liberation Wars and Tourism Development in Africa: The Case of Zambia'. *Annals of Tourism Research* 13: 589–608.

Thompson, E. P. 1967. 'Time, Work Discipline and Industrial Capitalism'. *Past and Present* 38: 56–97.

Timothy, D. 1999. 'Cross-border Shopping: Tourism in the Canada–United States Borderlands'. *Visions in Leisure and Business* 17 (4): 4–18.

Timothy, D. & Groves, D. 2001. 'Research Note: Webcam Images as Potential Data Sources for Tourism Research'. *Tourism Geographies* 3: 394–404.

Timothy, D. & Tosun, C. 2003. 'Tourists' Perceptions of the Canada–USA Border as a Barrier to Tourism at the International Peace Garden'. *Tourism Management* 24: 411–21.

Timothy, D. & Wall, G. 1997. 'Selling to Tourists: Indonesian Street Vendors'. *Annals of Tourism Research* 24: 322–40.

Toh, R., Khan, H. & Erawan, S. 2004. 'Bomb Blasts in Bali: Impact on Tourism'. *Tourism Analysis* 9: 219–24.

Toh, R., Khan, H. & Koh, A. 2001. 'A Travel Balance Approach for Examining Tourism Area Life Cycles: The Case of Singapore'. *Journal of Travel Research* 29: 426–32.

Tomljenovic, R. & Faulkner, B. 2000. 'Tourism and World Peace: A Conundrum for the Twenty–first Century.' In Faulkner, B., Moscardo, G. & Laws, E. (Eds.). *Tourism in the 21st Century: Lessons from Experience.* London: Continuum, pp. 18–33.

Torres, R. 2003. 'Linkages Between Tourism and Agriculture in Mexico'. *Annals of Tourism Research* 30: 546–66.

Tourism Australia 2004. 'Top Ten: Activities (Market Insights Tourism Facts)'. www.tourism.australia.com/content/Research/Factsheets/activities_fact_sheet_dec2003.pdf (visited 15 March 2005).

Tourism Australia 2005a. 'Know Your Markets'. www.tourism.australia.com/Markets.asp?lang=EN&sub=0334 (visited 24 March 2005).

Tourism Australia 2005b. 'About Tourism Australia'. www.tourism.australia.com/AboutUs.asp?sub=0281 (visited 20 April 2005).

Tourism Australia 2005c. 'Funding'. www.tourism.australia.com/AboutUs.asp?lang=EN&sub=0311 (visited 4 May 2005).

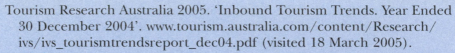

Tourism Research Australia 2005. 'Inbound Tourism Trends. Year Ended 30 December 2004'. www.tourism.australia.com/content/Research/ivs/ivs_tourismtrendsreport_dec04.pdf (visited 18 March 2005).

Tourism New Zealand 2005. 'International Visitor Arrivals November 2004'. www.tourismnewzealand.com/tourism_info/market–research/visitor–arrivals/visitor–arrivals_home.cfm (visited 27 April 2005).

Tourism Queensland 2005. 'Financial Report for the Year Ended 30 June 2004'. www.tq.com.au/tq_com/dms/16A5BB86FF83DF2AEEEC5A5622DC7782.pdf (visited 4 May 2005).

Towner, J. 1996. *An Historical Geography of Recreation and Tourism in the Western World 1540–1940.* Chichester, UK: John Wiley.

Trager, L. 1987. 'A Re-examination of the Urban Informal Sector in West Africa'. *Canadian Journal of African Studies* 21: 238–55.

Trampuz, A., Jereb, M., Muzlovic, I. & Prabhu, R. 2003. 'Clinical Review: Severe Malaria'. *Clinical Care* 7: 315–23.

Tratalos, J. & Austin, T. 2001. 'Impacts of recreational SCUBA diving on coral communities of the Caribbean island of Grand Cayman'. *Biological Conservation* 102: 67–75.

Travelbiz.com 2005. 'Inbound Education Tourism Numbers Jump'. www.travelbiz.com.au/74/0c02e374.asp (visited 24 March 2005).

TravelVideo.TV 2004. 'Libya Opens Door to Tourism'. http://travel video.tv/news/more.php?id=3672_0_1_0_M82 (visited 1 June 2005).

TRCNZ (Tourism Research Council of New Zealand) 2005. 'International Visitor Arrivals February 2005'. www.trcnz.govt.nz/NR/rdonlyres/C9EC04CB-5847-4AEE-80B0-F6754506B742/12450/IVACommentary.pdf (visited 27 April 2005).

Tremblay, P. 2001. 'Wildlife Tourism Consumption: Consumptive or Non-consumptive?'. *International Journal of Tourism Research* 3: 81–6.

Tribe, A. 2004. 'Zoo Tourism'. In Higginbottom, K. (Ed.) *Wildlife Tourism: Impacts, Management and Planning.* Altona, Vic.: Common Ground Publishing, pp. 35–56.

Tse, A. 2003. 'Disintermediation of Travel Agents in the Hotel Industry'. *International Journal of Hospitality Management* 22: 453–60.

Turco, D. 1999. 'Ya' 'At 'Eeh: A Profile of Tourists to Navajo Nation'. *Journal of Tourism Studies* 10(2): 57–68.

Turner, L. & Ash, J. 1975. *The Golden Hordes: International Tourism and the Pleasure Periphery.* London: Constable.

Turpie, J. & Joubert, A. 2004. 'The Value of Flower Tourism on the Bokkeveld Plateau — a Botanical Hotspot'. *Development Southern Africa* 21: 645–62.

Um, S. & Crompton, J. 1990. 'Attitude Determinants in Tourism Destination Choice'. *Annals of Tourism Research* 24: 432–48.

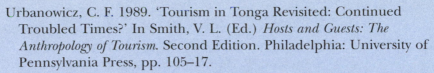

Urbanowicz, C. F. 1989. 'Tourism in Tonga Revisited: Continued Troubled Times?' In Smith, V. L. (Ed.) *Hosts and Guests: The Anthropology of Tourism.* Second Edition. Philadelphia: University of Pennsylvania Press, pp. 105–17.

US Bureau of the Census. 1999. *World Population Profile: 1998.* WP/98. Washington, DC: US Government Printing Office.

Valentine, P. & Birtles, A. 2004. 'Wildlife Watching'. In Higginbottom, K. (Ed.) *Wildlife Tourism: Impacts, Management and Planning.* Altona, Vic.: Common Ground Publishing, pp. 15–34.

Van Doren, C., Koh, Y. K. & McCahill, A. 1994. 'Tourism Research: A State-Of-The-Art Citation Analysis (1971–1990)'. In Seaton, A. V. et al. (Eds) *Tourism: The State of the Art.* New York: John Wiley, pp. 308–15.

Veal, A. & Lynch, R. 2001. *Australian Leisure.* Second Edition. Sydney: Pearson Education Australia.

Viles, H. & Spencer, T. 1995. *Coastal Problems: Geomorphology, Ecology and Society at the Coast.* London: Edward Arnold.

Visser, G. 2003. 'Gay Men, Tourism and Urban Space: Reflections on Africa's "Gay Capital"'. *Tourism Geographies* 5: 168–89.

Vlahakis, V., Ioannidis, N., Karigiannis, J., Tsotros, M., Gounaris, M., Stricker, D., Gleue, T., Dähne, P. & Almeida, L. 2002. 'Archeoguide: An Augmented Reality Guide for Archaeological Sites'. *IEEE Computer Graphics and Applications* 22 (5): 52–60.

Waitt, G. 1996. 'Resorting to Korean Tourism in Australia'. *Tijdschrift voor Economische en Sociale Geografie* 87 (1): 3–18.

Waitt, G. 2004. 'A Critical Examination of Sydney's 2000 Olympic Games'. In Yeoman, I., Robertson, M., Ali-Knight, J., Drummond, S. & McMahon-Beattie, U. (Eds). *Festival and Events Management: an International Arts and Culture Perspective.* Sydney: Elsevier, pp. 391–408.

Waitt, G. & McGuirk, P. 1996. 'Marking Time: Tourism and Heritage Representation at Millers Point, Sydney'. *Australian Geographer* 27: 11–29.

Walker, T. 1985. 'Terrorism Pushes Egypt's Tourism into Steep Decline'. *Globe and Mail* (Canada), 30 December, p. B15.

Walmsley, D. J. & Jenkins, J. M. 1993. 'Appraisive Images of Tourist Areas: Application of Personal Constructs'. *Australian Geographer* 24 (2): 1–13.

Walsh, J., Jamrozy, U. & Burr, S. 2001. 'Sense of Place as a Component of Sustainable Tourism Marketing'. In McCool, S. & Moisey, R. (Eds) *Tourism, Recreation and Sustainability.* Wallingford, UK: CABI Publishing, pp. 195–216.

Wang, K.-C., Hsieh, A.-T., Yeh, Y.-C. & Tsai, C.-W. 2004. 'Who is the Decision-Maker: the Parents or the Child in Group Package Tours?' *Tourism Management* 25: 183–94.

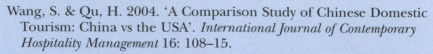

Wang, S. & Qu, H. 2004. 'A Comparison Study of Chinese Domestic Tourism: China vs the USA'. *International Journal of Contemporary Hospitality Management* 16: 108–15.

Wang, Y. & Sheldon, P. 1995. 'The Sleeping Dragon Awakes: The Outbound Chinese Travel Market'. *Journal of Travel & Tourism Marketing* 4 (4): 41–54.

Wanhill, S. 2005. 'Role of Government Incentives' In Theobald, W. (Ed.) *Global Tourism*. Third Edition. Sydney: Elsevier, pp. 367–90.

Wason, G. 1998. 'Taxation & Tourism'. *Travel & Tourism Analyst* No. 2, pp. 77–95.

Waters, S. R. 1997. *Travel Industry World Yearbook: The Big Picture 1996–97. Volume 40.* Rye, New York: Child and Waters.

Watkins, E. 1998. 'Where Do We Go from Here?' *Lodging Hospitality* 54: 66–8 (August).

WCED (World Commission on Environment and Development). 1987. *Our Common Future.* Oxford: Oxford University Press.

Wearing, S. 2001. *Volunteer Tourism: Experiences that Make a Difference.* Wallingford, UK: CABI Publishing.

Weaver, D. 2001. 'Mass Tourism and Alternative Tourism in the Caribbean'. In Harrison, D. (Ed). *Tourism and the Less Developed World: Issues and Case Studies.* Wallingford, UK: CABI Publishing, pp. 161–74.

Weaver, D. 2004. 'The Contribution of International Students to Tourism Beyond the Core Educational Experience: Evidence from Australia'. *Tourism Review International* 7: 95–105.

Weaver, D. 2005. Mass and Urban Ecotourism: New Manifestations of an Old Concept. *Tourism Recreation Research* 30: 19–26.

Weaver, D. 2006. *Sustainable Tourism: Theory and Practice.* London: Elsevier.

Weaver, D. B. 1988. 'The Evolution of a "Plantation" Tourism Landscape on the Caribbean Island of Antigua'. *Tijdschrift voor Economische en Sociale Geografie* 70: 319–31.

Weaver, D. B. 1990. 'Grand Cayman Island and the Resort Cycle Concept'. *Journal of Travel Research* 29 (2): 9–15.

Weaver, D. B. 1991. 'Alternative to Mass Tourism in Dominica'. *Annals of Tourism Research* 18: 414–32.

Weaver, D. B. 1993. 'Ecotourism in the Small Island Caribbean'. *GeoJournal* 31: 457–65.

Weaver, D. B. 1995. 'Alternative Tourism in Montserrat'. *Tourism Management* 16: 593–604.

Weaver, D. B. 1998. *Ecotourism in the Less Developed World.* Wallingford, UK: CAB International.

Weaver, D. B. 2000a. 'The Exploratory War-distorted Destination Life Cycle'. *International Journal of Tourism Research* 2: 151–61.

Weaver, D. B. 2000b. 'A Broad Context Model of Destination Development Scenarios'. *Tourism Management* 21: 217–24.

Weaver, D. B. 2001a. *Ecotourism*. Brisbane: John Wiley.

Weaver, D. B. (Ed.) 2001b. *The Encyclopedia of Ecotourism*. Wallingford, UK: CABI Publishing.

Weaver, D. B. & Elliott, K. 1996. 'Spatial Patterns and Problems in Contemporary Namibian Tourism'. *Geographical Journal* 161: 205–17.

Weaver, D. B. & Fennell, D. A. 1997. 'The Vacation Farm Sector in Saskatchewan: A Profile of Operators'. *Tourism Management* 18: 357–65.

Weaver, D. B. & Lawton, L. J. 1998. 'A Profile of Timesharing on the Gold Coast of Australia'. *Journal of Hospitality and Tourism Research* 22: 225–38.

Weaver, D. B. & Lawton, L. J. 1999a. 'Older Adults as a Distinct Timeshare Market in Australia'. *Australian Journal of Hospitality Management* 6(2): 1–11.

Weaver, D. B. & Lawton, L. J. 1999b. *Sustainable Tourism: A Critical Analysis*. Research Report 1. Gold Coast, Australia: CRC for Sustainable Tourism.

Weaver, D. B. & Lawton, L. J. 2001. 'Resident Perceptions in the Urban-Rural Fringe'. *Annals of Tourism Research* 28: 439–58.

Weaver, D. B. & Lawton, L. J. 2002. 'Overnight Ecotourist Market Segmentation in the Gold Coast Hinterland of Australia'. *Journal of Travel Research* 40: 270–80.

Weaver, D. B. & Oppermann, M. 2000. *Tourism Management*. Brisbane: John Wiley.

Webber, A. 2001. 'Exchange Rate Volatility and Cointegration in Tourism Demand', *Journal of Travel Research* 39: 398–405.

Weber, K. & Ladkin, A. 2003. 'The Convention Industry in Australia and the United Kingdom: Key Issues and Competitive Forces'. *Journal of Travel Research* 42: 125–32.

Webster, K. 2000. *Environmental Management in the Hospitality Industry: A Guide for Students and Managers*. London: Cassell.

Wells, L. 1982. *Sunny Memories: Australians at the Seaside*. Richmond: Greenhouse Publications.

Wells, S. & Price, A. 1992. *Coral Reefs — Valuable but Vulnerable*. Gland, Switzerland: World Wide Fund for Nature.

Wen, J. & Tisdell, C. 1996. 'Spatial Distribution of Tourism in China: Economic and Other Influences'. *Tourism Economics* 2 (3): 235–50.

Wen, Z. 1997. 'China's Domestic Tourism: Impetus, Development and Trends'. *Tourism Management* 18 (8): 565–71.

Western, D. 1982. 'Amboseli National Park: Enlisting Landowners to Conserve Migratory Wildlife'. *Ambio* 11: 302–8.

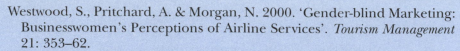

Westwood, S., Pritchard, A. & Morgan, N. 2000. 'Gender-blind Marketing: Businesswomen's Perceptions of Airline Services'. *Tourism Management* 21: 353–62.

Wheeler, D. 1994. 'Content Analysis'. In Witt, S. and Moutinho. L. (Eds) *Tourism Marketing and Management Handbook*. New York: Prentice Hall, pp. 580–84.

Wheeller, B. 1994. 'Ecotourism: A Ruse By Any Other Name'. In Cooper, C. & Lockwood, A. (Eds) *Progress in Tourism, Recreation and Hospitality Management. Volume 6*. Chichester, UK: John Wiley, pp. 3–11.

Whelan, T. (Ed.) 1991. *Nature Tourism: Managing for the Environment*. Washington, DC: Island Press.

Whetton, P., Haylock, M. & Galloway, R. 1996. 'Climate Change and Snow–cover Duration in the Australian Alps'. *Climate Change* 32: 447–79.

Wilks, J., Pendergast, D. & Wood, M. 2003. 'Accidental Deaths of Overseas Visitors in Australia 1997 – 2000'. *Journal of Hospitality and Tourism Management* 10: 79–89.

Williams, A. P. & Hobson, J. S. P. 1994. 'Tourism — The Next Generation: Virtual Reality and Surrogate Travel, is it the Future of the Tourism Industry?' In Seaton, A. V. et al. (Eds) *Tourism: The State of the Art*. Chichester, UK: John Wiley, pp. 283–90.

Wilson, D. 1994. 'Probably as Close as You Can Get to Paradise: Tourism and the Changing Image of Seychelles'. In Seaton, A. V. et al. (Eds) *Tourism: The State of the Art*. Chichester, UK: John Wiley, pp. 765–74.

Withey, L. 1997. *Grand Tours and Cook's Tours: A History of Leisure Travel 1750 to 1915*. London: Autum Press.

Wood, R. 2004. 'Global Currents: Cruise Ships in the Caribbean Sea'. In Duval, T. (Ed.) *Tourism in the Caribbean: Trends, Development, Prospects*. London: Routledge, pp. 152–71.

WTO 1996a. *Compendium of Tourism Statistics*. Seventeenth Edition. Madrid: World Tourism Organization.

WTO 1996b. *What Tourism Managers Need to Know: A Practical Guide to the Development and Use of Indicators of Sustainable Tourism*. Madrid: World Tourism Organization.

WTO 1997. *Yearbook of Tourism Statistics. Volume One*. Forty-ninth Edition. Madrid: World Tourism Organization.

WTO 1998a. *Yearbook of Tourism Statistics. Volume One*. Fiftieth Edition. Madrid: World Tourism Organization.

WTO 1998b. 'WTO News July/Aug 1998: Hot Tourism Trends for the 21st Century'. www.world-tourism.org/index2.htm (visited 12 December 1998).

WTO 1998c. *Compendium of Tourism Statistics 1992–1996*. Eighteenth Edition. Madrid: World Tourism Organization.

WTO 1998d. *Yearbook of Tourism Statistics. Volume Two.* Fiftieth Edition. Madrid: World Tourism Organization.

WTO 2005. 'Inbound Tourism — International Tourist Arrivals & Tourism Receipts by Country'. www.world–tourism.org/facts/tint.html (visited 10 May 2005).

WTTC 1996. *Australia Travel & Tourism: Millennium Vision.* London: World Travel and Tourism Council.

www.amrsc.wa.gov.au/minutes/pdfs2004/040331lateseachange.pdf (visited 6 March 2005).

Yau, K., McKercher, B., & Packer, T. 2004. 'Traveling with a Disability — More Than an Access Issue'. *Annals of Tourism Research* 31: 946–60.

Zakai, D. & Chadwick-Furman, N. 2002. 'Impacts of Intensive Recreational Diving on Reef Corals at Eilat, Northern Red Sea'. *Biological Conservation* 105: 179–87.

Zhang, G., Pine, R. & Zhang, H. 2000. 'China's International Tourism Development: Present and Future'. *International Journal of Contemporary Hospitality Management* 12: 282–90.

Zhang, Y. & Lew, A. 1997. 'The People's Republic of China: Two Decades of Tourism'. *Pacific Tourism Review* 1: 161–72.

Zhou, Z. 1998. 'Destination Marketing: Targeting Different Brochure Users'. *Journal of Segmentation in Marketing* 2: 131–41.

GLOSSARY

3S tourism: a tourism product based on the provision of sea, sand and sun; that is, focusing on beach resorts p. 94

8P model: a product-focused marketing mix model that incorporates place, product, people, price, packaging, programming, promotion and partnerships p. 219

Academic discipline: a systematic field of study that is informed by a particular set of theories and methodologies in its attempt to reveal and expand knowledge about some particular theme; e.g. psychology examines individual behaviour, while geography examines spatial patterns and relationships p. 7

Accommodation: within the context of the tourism industry, commercial facilities primarily intended to host stayover tourists for overnight stays p. 155

Accreditation: the process by which the ecolabel is determined by an overarching organisation to meet specified standards of quality and credibility p. 353

Adaptancy platform: a follow-up on the cautionary platform that advocates alternative forms of tourism deemed to be more appropriate than the mass tourism fostered by the advocacy platform p. 13

Advocacy platform: the view that tourism is an inherent benefit to communities that should be developed under free market principles p. 12

Alternative tourism: the major contribution of the adaptancy platform, alternative tourism as an ideal type is characterised by its contrast with mass tourism p. 354

Amenity migration: migration induced by the quality-of-life characteristics of a place, including comfortable weather and beautiful scenery. Amenity migrants are usually first exposed to such places through their own tourist experiences p. 295

Applied research: research that addresses some particular problem or attempts to achieve a particular set of outcomes; it is usually constrained by set time schedules p. 378

Attraction attributes: characteristics of an attraction that are relevant to the management of an area as a tourist destination and thus should be periodically measured and monitored; includes ownership, orientation, spatial configuration, authenticity, scarcity, status, carrying capacity, accessibility, market and image p. 146

Attraction inventory: a systematic list of the tourist attractions found in a particular destination p. 129

Avalanche effect: the process whereby a small incremental change in a system triggers a disproportionate and usually unexpected response p. 345

Baby boomers: people born during the post–World War II period of high TFRs (roughly 1946 to 1964), who constitute a noticeable bulge within the population pyramid of Australia and other Phase Four countries p. 79

Backstage: the opposite of frontstage; areas of the destination where personal or intragroup activities occur, such as noncommercialised cultural performances. A particular space may be designated as either frontstage or backstage depending on the time of day or year p. 277

Backward linkages: sectors of an economy that provide goods and services for the tourism sector; includes agriculture, fisheries and construction p. 247

Basic research: research that is broadly focused on the revelation of new knowledge, and is not directed towards specific outcomes or problems p. 378

Basic whole tourism system: an application of a systems approach to tourism, wherein tourism is seen as consisting of three geographical components (origin, transit and destination regions), tourists and a tourism industry, embedded within a modifying external environment that includes parallel political, social, physical and other systems p. 24

Behavioural segmentation: the identification of tourist markets on the basis of activities and actions undertaken during the actual tourism experience p. 189

Benchmark: an indicator value, often based on some past desirable state, against which subsequent change in that indicator can be gauged p. 345

Black servility theory: the belief that tourism, in regions such as the Caribbean or South Pacific, is an activity that perpetuates the subjugation of formerly colonised or enslaved peoples through the maintenance of the servant (black) and served (white) relationship p. 279

Broad context model of destination development scenarios: a framework for modelling the evolution of tourist destinations, which takes into account scale and sustainability-related regulations; various transformations are possible among four ideal tourism types CAT, DAT, UMT (unsustainable mass tourism) and SMT (sustainable mass tourism) p. 359–60

Butler sequence: the most widely cited and applied destination lifecycle model, which proposes five stages of evolution that are described by an S-shaped curve; these might then be followed by three other possible scenarios p. 307

Carrying capacity: the amount of tourism activity (e.g. number of visitors, amount of development) that can be accommodated without incurring serious harm to a destination; distinctions can be made between social, cultural and environmental carrying capacity p. 283

Cautionary platform: a reaction to the advocacy platform that stresses the negative impacts of tourism and the consequent need for strict regulation p. 13

Certification: the outcome of a process in which an independent third party verifies that a product or company meets specified standards, allowing it to be certified by the ecolabel p. 353

Circumstantial alternative tourism (CAT): alternative tourism that results from the fact that the destination is currently situated within the early, low-intensity stages of the resort cycle p. 356

Codes of practice: commonly developed and espoused by tourism corp-orations and industry associations, these are intended to provide general guidelines for achieving sustainability-related outcomes p. 350

Commodification: in tourism, the process whereby a destination's culture is gradually converted into a saleable commodity or product in response to the perceived or actual demands of the tourist market p. 276

Condensed development sequence: the process whereby societies undergo the transition to a Phase Four state within an increasingly reduced period of time p. 83

Contagious diffusion: spread occurs as a function of spatial proximity; the closer a site is to the place of the innovation's origin, the sooner it is likely to be exposed to that phenomenon p. 327

Cross-sectional research: a 'snapshot' approach to research that considers one or more sites at one particular point in time p. 382

Crusades: a series of campaigns to 'liberate' Jerusalem and the Holy Land from Muslim control. While not a form of tourism as such, the Crusades helped to re-open Europe to the outside world and spawn an incipient travel industry p. 61

Cultural events: attractions that occur over a fixed period of time in one or more locations, and are more constructed than natural; these include historical commemorations and re-creations, world fairs, sporting events and festivals p. 144

Cultural sites: geographically fixed attractions that are more constructed than natural; these can be classified into prehistorical, historical, contemporary, economic, specialised recreational and retail subcategories p. 137

Dark Ages: the period from about AD 500 to 1100, characterised by a serious deterioration in social, economic and political conditions within Europe p. 60

Dark tourism: tourism involving sites or events associated with death or suffering, including battlefields and sites of mass killings or assassinations p. 138

Data analysis: the process by which the collected information is examined and assessed to identify patterns that address the research questions p. 399

Data collection: the gathering of relevant information by way of the techniques identified in the research methodology stage p. 399

Data interpretation: the stage during which meaning is extracted from the data p. 400

Data presentation: the stage during which the results of the analysis are communicated to the target audience p. 400

Database marketing: a comprehensive marketing strategy that is based on a memory of prior business transactions with customers; the use of accumulated customer data to inform marketing decisions p. 221

Deduction: an approach in basic research that begins with a basic theory that is applied to a set of data to see whether the theory is applicable or not p. 380

Deliberate alternative tourism (DAT): alternative tourism that is deliberately maintained as such through the implementation of an appropriate regulatory environment p. 356

Demarketing: the process of discouraging all or certain tourists from visiting a particular destination temporarily or permanently p. 212

Demographic transition model (DTM): an idealised depiction of the process whereby societies evolve from a high fertility/high mortality structure to a low fertility/low mortality structure. This evolution usually parallels the development of a society from a Phase One to a Phase Four profile, as occurred during the Industrial Revolution. A fifth stage may now be emerging, characterised by extremely low birth rates and resultant net population loss p. 76

Dependables: 'self-centred' tourists who prefer familiar and risk-averse experiences; also known as 'psychocentrics' p. 186

Destination community: the residents of the destination region p. 45

Destination government: the government of the destination region p. 45

Destination lifecycle: the theory that tourism-oriented places experience a sequential process of birth, growth, maturation, and then possibly something similar to death, in their evolution as destinations p. 306

Destination region: the places to which the tourist is travelling p. 43

Direct (or primary) impact: expenditure or direct revenue obtained from tourists p. 245

Direct financial costs: direct expenses that are necessarily incurred to sustain the tourism sector; within the public sector, typical areas of outlay include administration and bureaucracy, marketing, research and direct incentives p. 252

Direct revenue: money that is obtained directly from tourists through advance or immediate expenditures in the destination and associated taxes p. 239

Discretionary income: the amount of income that remains after household necessities such as food, housing, clothing, education and transportation have been purchased p. 57

Discretionary time: normally defined as time not spent at work, or in normal rest and bodily maintenance p. 57

Disintermediation: the removal of intermediaries such as travel agents from the product/consumer connection p. 151

Distance–decay: in tourism, the tendency of inbound flows to decline as origin regions become more distant from the destination p. 97

Domestic excursionists: tourists who stay within their own country for less than one night p. 35

Domestic stayovers: tourists who stay within their own country for at least one night p. 35

Domestic tourist: a tourist whose itinerary is confined to their usual country of residence p. 26

Dominant Western environmental paradigm: the scientific paradigm as applied to environmental and related issues, holding the anthropocentric view that humankind is at the centre of all things, and constitutes the primary focus of reference in all relationships with the natural environment; humans are seen as being superior to nature, which exists only for their benefit p. 339

Double-blind peer review: a procedure that attempts to maintain objectivity in the manuscript refereeing process by ensuring that the author does not know the identity of the reviewers, while the reviewers do not know the identity of the author p. 11

Early modern tourism: the transitional era between premodern tourism (about AD 1500) and modern mass tourism (since 1950) p. 61

Earned time: a time management option in which an individual is no longer obligated to work once a particular quota is attained over a defined period of time (often monthly or annual) p. 73

Ecolabels: mechanisms that certify products or companies that meet specified standards of practice p. 350

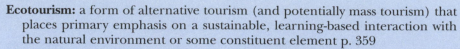

Ecotourism: a form of alternative tourism (and potentially mass tourism) that places primary emphasis on a sustainable, learning-based interaction with the natural environment or some constituent element p. 359

Emotional labour: the expression of the willingness to be of service to customers, as through responsiveness and empathy p. 205

Environmental impact sequence: a four-stage model formulated by the OECD to account for the impacts of tourism on the natural environment: p. 289

Environmental responses: the way that the environment reacts to the stresses, both in the short and long term, and both directly and indirectly p. 289

Environmental stresses: the deliberate changes in the environment that are entailed in the stressor activities p. 289

Ephemeral attraction: an attraction, such as a wildflower display or rarely filled lakebed, that occurs over a brief period of time or on rare occasions only p. 137

e-postcards: virtual postcards that are selected through the Internet and sent to recipients by email p. 227

European Union (EU): an organisation of 25 European countries working towards increased economic integration and efficiency through the elimination of border restrictions (p. 27)

Excursionist: a tourist who spends less than one night in a destination region p. 29

External-intentional actions: deliberate actions that originate from outside the destination p. 324

External-unintentional actions: actions that affect the destination, but originate from outside that destination, and are not intentional; the worst case scenario from a destination perspective p. 324

Family lifecycle (FLC): a sequence of stages through which the traditional nuclear family passes from early adulthood to the death of a spouse; each stage is associated with distinct patterns of tourism-related behaviour associated with changing family and financial circumstances p. 180

Fixed costs: costs that the operation has little flexibility to change over the short term, such as interest costs on borrowed funds and basic facility maintenance costs p. 207

Flexitime: a time management option in which workers have some flexibility in distributing a required number of working hours (usually weekly) in a manner that suits the lifestyle and productivity of the individual worker p. 73

Food tourism: tourism that involves the consumption of usually locally produced food and drink p. 139

Formal sector: the portion of a society's economy that is subject to official systems of regulation and remuneration; formal sector businesses provide regular wage or salaried employment, and are subject to taxation by various levels of government; the formal sector dominates Phase Four societies p. 250

Four major types of tourist: an inclusive group of tourist categories that combines the spatial and temporal components, and assumes adherence to the qualifying purposes of travel p. 34

Freedoms of the air: eight privileges, put in place through bilateral agreements, that govern the global airline industry p. 152

Frontstage: explicitly or tacitly recognised spaces within the destination that are mobilised for tourism purposes such as commodified cultural performances p. 277

Functional adaptation: the use of a structure for a purpose other than its original intent, represented in tourism by canals used by pleasure boaters and old homes converted into bed and breakfasts p. 141

Gender segmentation: the grouping of individuals into male and female categories, or according to sexual orientation p. 177

General demarketing: demarketing that is directed towards all tourists, usually temporarily p. 212

Geographic segmentation: market segmentation carried out on the basis of the market's origin region; can be carried out at various scales, including region (e.g. Asia), country (Germany), subnational unit (California, Queensland), or urban/rural p. 176

GIS (geographic information systems): sophisticated computer software programs that facilitate the assembly, storage, manipulation, analysis and display of spatially referenced information p. 176

Global inequality in tourism: a fundamental distinction pertaining to the relative spatial distribution of tourism at a global level p. 92

Globalisation: The process whereby the operation of businesses and the movement of capital is increasingly less impeded by national boundaries, and is reflected in a general trend towards industry consolidation, deregulation and privatisation p. 161

Golfscapes: cultural landscapes that are dominated by golf courses and affiliated developments p. 142

Grand Tour: a form of early modern tourism that involved a lengthy trip to the major cities of France and Italy by young adults of the leisure class, for purposes of education and culture p. 61

Green consumerism: the proclivity to purchase goods and services that are deemed to be environmentally and socially sustainable; situates along a spectrum from 'true' green to 'veneer' green attitudes and behaviour p. 346

Green paradigm: an emerging ecocentric worldview that is challenging the basic assumptions of the dominant Western environmental paradigm and accounting for its related anomalies and contradictions p. 341

Greenwashing: the process of conveying an impression of environmental responsibility that is not actually deserved; often associated with the misuse of terms such as 'sustainable tourism' and 'ecotourism' p. 343

Growth pole strategy: a strategy that uses tourism to stimulate economic development in a suitably located area (or growth pole), so that this growth will eventually become self-sustaining p. 249

Hard ecotourism: a form of ecotourism that stresses an intensive, specialised and prolonged interaction with nature in a relatively undisturbed natural environment with few available amenities; a form of alternative tourism p. 359

Hierarchical diffusion: spread occurs through an urban or other hierarchy, usually from the largest to the smallest centres, independent of where these centres are located p. 326

Horizontal integration: occurs when firms attain a higher level of consolidation or control within their own sector p. 160

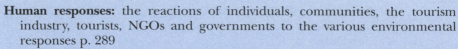

Human responses: the reactions of individuals, communities, the tourism industry, tourists, NGOs and governments to the various environmental responses p. 289

Hyperdestinations: destinations where the annual intake of visitors dramatically outnumbers the permanent resident population; often characteristic of tourist shopping villages p. 118

Hypotheses: tentative informed statements about the nature of reality that can be subsequently verified or rejected through systematic deductive research p. 380

Iconic attraction: an attraction that is well-known and closely associated with a particular destination, such as Mt Fuji (Japan) or the Statue of Liberty (United States) p. 132

Ideal type: an idealised model of some phenomenon or process against which real-life situations can be measured and compared p. 322

Image: in tourism, the sum of the beliefs, attitudes and impressions that individuals or groups hold towards tourist destinations or aspects of destinations. Destination image is a critical factor in attracting or repelling visitors p. 105

Inbound tourist: an international tourist arriving from another country p. 27

Incremental access: a policy, practised most notably in China, whereby new destinations within a country are gradually opened up to international (and possibly domestic) tourists p. 112

Indicators: a variable or parameter that provides information about some phenomenon in order to facilitate its management in a desirable way p. 343

Indigenous theories: theories that arise out of a particular field of study or discipline p. 7

Indirect financial costs: costs that do not entail a direct outlay of funds, but indicate lost revenue p. 253

Indirect impacts: revenues that are used by tourism businesses and their suppliers to purchase goods and services p. 245

Indirect revenues: revenue obtained through the circulation of direct tourist expenditures within a destination p. 245

Induced impacts: revenue circulation that results from the use of wages in tourism businesses and their suppliers to purchase goods and services p. 245

Induction: an approach in basic research whereby the observation and analysis of data leads to the formulation of theories or models that link these observations in a meaningful way p. 380

Industrial Revolution: a process that occurred in England from the mid-1700s to the mid-1900s (and spread outwards to other countries), in which society was transformed from an agrarian to an industrial basis, thereby spawning conditions that were conducive to the growth of tourism-related activity p. 62

Informal sector: the portion of a society's economy that is external to the official systems of regulation and remuneration; dominant in many parts of the less developed world, informal sector businesses are characterised by small size, the absence of regular working hours or wage payments, family ownership and a lack of any regulating quality control p. 250

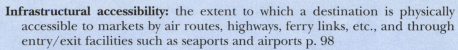

Infrastructural accessibility: the extent to which a destination is physically accessible to markets by air routes, highways, ferry links, etc., and through entry/exit facilities such as seaports and airports p. 98

Inseparability: production and consumption of tourist services both occur at the same time and place and are thus inseparable p. 205

Intangibility: the actual tourism service cannot be seen, touched or tried before its purchase and consumption p. 204

Interdisciplinary approach: involves the input of a variety of disciplines, with fusion and synthesis occurring among these different perspectives p. 8

Internal-intentional actions: deliberate actions that originate from within the destination itself; the best case scenario for destinations in terms of control and management p. 324

Internal-unintentional actions: actions that originate from within the destination, but are not deliberate p. 324

International excursionists: tourists who stay less than one night in another country p. 35

International stayovers: tourists who stay at least one night in another country p. 35

International tourism receipts: all consumption expenditure, or payments for goods and services, made by international tourists (stayovers and excursionists) to use themselves or to give away p. 239

International tourist: a tourist who travels beyond their usual country of residence p. 26

Intervening opportunities: places, often within transit regions, that develop as tourist destinations in their own right and subsequently have the potential to divert tourists from previously patronised destinations p. 41

Irridex: a theoretical model proposing that resident attitudes evolve from euphoria to apathy, then irritation (or annoyance), antagonism and finally resignation, as the intensity of tourism development increases within a destination p. 287

Knowledge-based platform: the most recent dominant perspective in tourism studies, emphasising ideological neutrality and the application of rigorous scientific methodologies to obtain knowledge so that communities can decide whether large- or small-scale tourism is most appropriate p. 14

Leisure class: in premodern tourism, that small portion of the population that had sufficient discretionary time and income to engage in leisure pursuits such as tourism p. 57

Less developed countries (LDCs): countries characterised by a relatively low level of economic development. Until recently, the less developed world has not been very important as a recipient or generator of global tourist flows p. 92

Long-haul trips: trips variably defined as occurring outside of the world region where the traveller resides, or beyond a given number of flying time hours p. 28

Longitudinal research: a trends-oriented approach to research, which examines one or more sites at two or more points in time or, more rarely, on a continuous basis p. 382

Loyalty: the extent to which a product, such as a destination, is perceived in a positive way and repeatedly purchased by the consumer p. 192

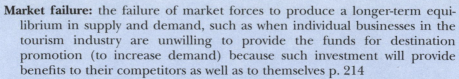

Market failure: the failure of market forces to produce a longer-term equilibrium in supply and demand, such as when individual businesses in the tourism industry are unwilling to provide the funds for destination promotion (to increase demand) because such investment will provide benefits to their competitors as well as to themselves p. 214

Market segmentation: the division of the tourist market into more or less homogenous subgroups, or tourist market segments, based on certain common characteristics and/or behavioural patterns p. 171

Market segments: portions of the tourist market that are more or less distinct in their characteristics and/or behaviour p. 171

Marketing: the interactions and interrelationships that occur among consumers and producers of goods and services, through which ideas, products, services and values are created and exchanged for the mutual benefit of both groups p. 203

Marketing mix: the critical components that determine the demand for a business or destination product p. 219

Markets of one: an extreme form of market segmentation, in which individual consumers are recognised as distinct market segments p. 173

Matrix model of lifecycle trigger factors: an eight-cell model that classifies the various actions that induce change in the evolution of tourism in a destination. Each of the following categories can be further divided into tourism stimulants and depressants p. 323

Merchandise: goods purchased as part of the anticipated or actual tourism experience; includes tour guidebooks and luggage in the origin region, and souvenirs and duty-free goods in the destination region p. 158

Mesopotamia: the region approximately occupied by present-day Iraq, where the earliest impulses of civilisation first emerged, presumably along with the first tourism activity p. 56

MICE: an acronym combining meetings, incentives, conventions and exhibitions; a form of tourism largely associated with business purposes p. 31

Midcentrics: 'average' tourists whose personality type is a compromise between venturer and dependable traits; also known as 'centrics' p. 186

Middle Ages: the period from about AD 1100 to the Renaissance (about AD 1500), characterised by an improvement in the social, economic and political situation, in comparison with the Dark Ages p. 60

Modern mass tourism (Contemporary tourism): the period from 1950 to the present day, characterised by the rapid expansion of international and domestic tourism p. 67

More developed countries (MDCs): countries characterised by a relatively high level of economic development. Collectively, the more developed world remains dominant as a recipient and generator of global tourist flows p. 92

Motivation: the intrinsic reasons why the individual is embarking on a particular trip p. 188

Multidisciplinary approach: involves the input of a variety of disciplines, bu without any significant interaction or synthesis of these different perspectives p. 8

Multilevel segmentation: a refinement of market segmentation that further differentiates basic level segments p. 172

Multiplier effect: a measure of the subsequent income generated in a destination's economy by direct tourist expenditure p. 245

Multipurpose travel: travel undertaken for more than a single purpose p. 33

National tourism authority (NTA): the government agency responsible for broad tourism policy and planning within a destination country p. 216

National tourism organisations (NTOs): publicly funded government agencies that undertake promotion and other forms of marketing at the country-destination scale, usually directed towards inbound tourists; these are distinct from the government departments or bodies, or national tourism authorities, that dictate tourism-related policy p. 214

Natural events: attractions that occur over a fixed period of time in one or more locations, and are more natural than constructed p. 136

Natural sites: geographically fixed attractions that are more natural than constructed; these can be subdivided into topography (physical features), climate, hydrology (water resources), wildlife, vegetation and location p. 130

New traveller: an emerging market niche that is highly discerning and critical in ensuring that its travel behaviour does not negatively affect destinations; similar to Plog's allocentric tourist p. 347

Niche markets: highly specialised market segments p. 173

North–south flow: a common term used to describe the dominant pattern of international tourist traffic from the MDCs (located mainly in the northern latitudes, except for Australia and New Zealand) to the LDCs (located mainly to the south of the MDCs) p. 95

Olympic Games: the most important of the ancient Greek art and athletics festivals, held every four years at Olympia. The ancient Olympic Games are one of the most important examples of premodern tourism p. 57

Opportunity cost: the idea that the use of a resource for some activity (e.g. tourism) precludes its use for some other activity that may yield a better financial return (e.g. agriculture) p. 261

Origin community: the residents of the origin region p. 38

Origin government: the government of the origin region p. 39

Origin region: the region (e.g. country, state, city) from which the tourist originates, also referred to as the market or generating region p. 38

Outbound tourist: an international tourist departing from their usual country of residence p. 27

Package tour: a pre-paid travel package that usually includes transportation, accommodation, food and other services p. 66

Paradigm: the entire constellation of beliefs, assumptions and values that underlie the way that a society interprets the nature of reality p. 338

Paradigm shift: the replacement of one paradigm with another when the formerly dominant paradigm can no longer adequately account for various contradictions and anomalies p. 338

Paradox of resentment: the idea that problems of resentment and tension can result whether tourists are integrated with, or isolated from, the local community p. 284

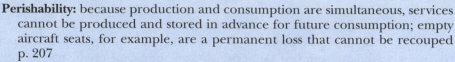

Perishability: because production and consumption are simultaneous, services cannot be produced and stored in advance for future consumption; empty aircraft seats, for example, are a permanent loss that cannot be recouped p. 207

Pilgrimage: generic term for travel undertaken for some religious purpose. Pilgrimages have declined in importance during the modern era compared with recreational, business and social tourism p. 60

Pink dollar: the purchasing power of gay and lesbian consumers, recognised to be much higher than the average purchasing power p. 178

Play in order to work philosophy: an industrial-era ethic, which holds that leisure time and activities are necessary in order to make workers more productive, thereby reinforcing the work-focused nature of society p. 72

Pleasure periphery: those less economically developed regions of the globe that are being increasingly mobilised to provide 3S and alpine tourism products p. 94

Political accessibility: the extent to which visitors are allowed entry into a destination by a governing authority p. 98

Post-Cook period: the time from about 1880 to 1950, characterised by the rapid growth of domestic tourism within the wealthier countries, but less rapid expansion in international tourism p. 66

Postindustrial era: a later Phase Four stage in which hi-tech services and information replace manufacturing and lower-order services as the mainstay of an economy p. 73

Premodern tourism: describes the era of tourism activity from the beginning of civilisation to the end of the Middle Ages p. 56

Primary research: research that involves the collection of original data by the researcher p. 385

Problem recognition: the first stage of the research process, which is the identification of a broad problem arena that requires investigation p. 395

Propulsive activity: an economic activity that is suited to a particular area and thus facilitates the growth pole strategy; in the case of Cancún and other subtropical or tropical coastal regions 3S tourism is an effective propulsive activity p. 249

Psychographic segmentation: the differentiation of the tourist market on the basis of psychological and motivational characteristics such as personality, motivations and needs p. 185

Pull factors: forces that help to stimulate a tourism product by 'pulling' consumers towards particular destinations p. 97

Push factors: economic, social, demographic, technological and political forces that stimulate a demand for tourism activity by 'pushing' consumers away from their usual place of residence p. 69

Qualitative research: research that does not place its emphasis on the collection and analysis of statistical data, and usually tends to obtain in-depth insight into a relatively small number of respondents or observations p. 383

Quality control mechanisms: mechanisms that provide some degree of assurance to consumers, government or others that a particular operation, product or destination follows standards associated with sustainable tourism p. 350

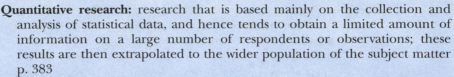

Quantitative research: research that is based mainly on the collection and analysis of statistical data, and hence tends to obtain a limited amount of information on a large number of respondents or observations; these results are then extrapolated to the wider population of the subject matter p. 383

Question formulation: the posing of specific questions or hypotheses that serve to focus the research agenda arising from problem recognition; these questions can be descriptive, explanatory, predictive or prescriptive in nature p. 395

Refereed academic journals: publications that are considered to showcase a discipline by merit of the fact that they are subject to a rigorous process of double-blind peer review p. 11

Renaissance: the 'rebirth' of Europe following the Dark Ages, commenced in Italy during the mid-1400s and spread to Germany and the 'low countries' by the early 1600s p. 61

Research: a systematic search for knowledge p. 378

Research methodology: a set of procedures and methods that are used to carry out a search for knowledge within a particular type of research p. 378

Research methods: the techniques that will be used to answer the questions or prove or disprove the hypotheses p. 397

Research process: the sequence of stages that are followed to carry out a research project from its origins to its conclusions p. 394

Resorts: facilities or urban areas that are specialised in the provision of recreational tourism opportunities p. 57

Revenue leakages: a major category of indirect financial costs, entailing erosion in the multiplier effect due to the importation of goods and services that are required by tourists or the tourist industry, through factor payments abroad such as repatriated profits, and through imports required for government expenditure on tourism-related infrastructure such as airports, road and port equipment p. 253

Rifle marketing: a mode of promotional advertising that is aimed just at the target market p. 225

Scientific paradigm: the currently dominant paradigm, which holds that reality is reducible and deterministic and can be understood through the application of the 'scientific method' p. 339

Seaside resort: a type of resort located on coastlines to take advantage of sea bathing for health and, later, recreational purposes; many of these were established during the Industrial Revolution for both the leisure and working classes p. 63

Secondary (or 'flow-on') impacts: the indirect and induced stages of money circulation in the multiplier effect that follows the actual tourist expenditure p. 246

Secondary research: researcher in which the investigator uses previously collected data p. 385

Secular pilgrimage: travel for spiritual purposes that are not linked to conventional religions p. 32

Selective demarketing: demarketing that is directed towards a particular tourist segment, usually intended as a permanent measure against groups deemed to be undesirable p. 212

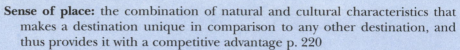

Sense of place: the combination of natural and cultural characteristics that makes a destination unique in comparison to any other destination, and thus provides it with a competitive advantage p. 220

Services marketing: the marketing of services such as those associated with the tourism industry, as opposed to the marketing of the goods industry. The following characteristics distinguish service marketing from goods marketing: p. 204

Short-haul trips: trips variably defined as occurring within the world region where the traveller resides, or within a given number of flying time hours p. 28

Shotgun marketing: a mode of promotional advertising where the message is disseminated to a broad audience on the assumption that this saturation will reach target markets and perhaps attract new recruits p. 225

Simple market segmentation: the most basic form of market segmentation, involving the identification of a minimal number of market segments p. 171

SISODs (small island states or dependencies): geopolitical entities with a population of less than three million permanent residents and a land mass of less than 28 000 km^2. SISODs are overrepresented as tourist destinations because of their ample 3S tourism resources p. 95

Site hardening: increasing the visitor carrying capacity of a site through structural and other changes that allow more visitors to be accommodated p. 150

Sociodemographic segmentation: market segmentation based on social and demographic variables such as gender, age, family lifecycle, education, occupation and income p. 177

Soft ecotourism: a form of ecotourism that emphasises a short-term interaction with nature as part of a multipurpose trip with ample provision for services and facilities; can exist as a form of mass tourism p. 359

Spas: a type of resort centred on the use of geothermal waters for health purposes p. 62

Spatial diffusion: the process whereby some innovation or idea spreads from a point of origin to other locations; this model is more appropriate than the destination lifecycle to describe the development of tourism at the country level p. 326

Standard Industrial Classification (SIC): a system that uses standard alphanumeric codes to classify all types of economic activity. Tourism-related activities are distributed among at least 15 codes p. 6

Stayover: a tourist who spends at least one night in a destination region p. 29

Stopovers: travellers who stop in a location in transit to another destination; they normally do not clear customs and are not considered tourists from the transit location's perspective p. 36

Strategic marketing: marketing that takes into consideration an extensive analysis of external and internal environmental factors in identifying strategies that attain specific goals p. 217

Stressor activities: activities that initiate the environmental impact sequence; these can be divided into permanent environmental restructuring, the generation of waste residuals, tourist activities and indirect and induced activities p. 289

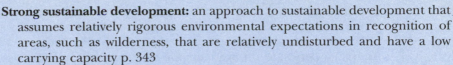

Strong sustainable development: an approach to sustainable development that assumes relatively rigorous environmental expectations in recognition of areas, such as wilderness, that are relatively undisturbed and have a low carrying capacity p. 343

Subnational inequality: the tendency of tourism within countries, states and individual cities to be spatially concentrated p. 117

Sunbelt: the name frequently applied to the 3S-oriented American portion of the pleasure periphery. Well-known destinations within the sunbelt include Hawaii, southern California, Las Vegas (Nevada), Arizona, Texas and Florida p. 94

Sustainable development: in principle, development that meets the needs of present generations while ensuring that future generations are able to meet their own needs p. 342

Sustainable tourism: tourism that is developed in such a way so as to meet the needs of the present without compromising the ability of future generations to meet their own needs p. 343

SWOT analysis: an analysis of a company or destination's strengths, weaknesses, opportunities and threats that emerges from an examination of its internal and external environment p. 217

System: a group of interrelated, interdependent and interacting elements that together form a single functional structure p. 23

Theory: a model or statement that explains or represents some phenomenon p. 7

Thomas Cook: the entrepreneur who applied the principles of the Industrial Revolution to the tourism sector through such innovations as the package tour p. 65

Threshold: a critical value of indicator sustainability; when the threshold is exceeded, this indicates an unsustainable situation p. 345

Timesharing: an accomodation option in which a user purchases one or more intervals (or weeks) per year in a resort, usually over a long peiod of time p. 155

Tour operators: businesses providing a package of tourism-related services for the consumer, including some combination of accommodation, transportation, restaurants and attraction visits p. 157

Tourism: the sum of the processes, activities and outcomes arising from the interactions among tourists, tourism suppliers, host governments, host communities, origin governments, universities, community colleges and nongovernmental organisations, in the process of attracting, transporting, hosting and managing tourists and other visitors pp. 2, 129

Tourism industry: the sum of the industrial and commercial activities that produce goods and services wholly or mainly for tourist consumption p. 46

Tourism participation sequence: according to Burton, the tendency for a society to participate in tourism increases through a set of four phases that relate to the concurrent process of increased economic development p. 69

Tourism platforms: perspectives that have dominated the emerging field of tourism studies at various stages of its evolution p. 12

Tourism product: consists of tourist attractions and the tourism industry p. 129

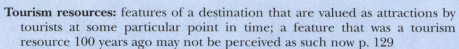

Tourism resources: features of a destination that are valued as attractions by tourists at some particular point in time; a feature that was a tourism resource 100 years ago may not be perceived as such now p. 129

Tourist: a person who travels temporarily outside of his or her usual environment (usually defined by some distance threshold) for certain qualifying purposes p. 2

Tourist attractions: specific and generic features of a destination that attract tourists; some, but not all, attractions are part of the tourism industry p. 129

Tourist market: the overall group of consumers that engages in some form of tourism-related travel p. 171

Tourist shopping villages: small towns where the downtown is dominated by tourism-related businesses such as boutiques, antique shops and cafés p. 118

Tourist–historic city: an urban place where the preservation of historical districts helps to sustain and is at least in part sustained by a significant level of tourist activity p. 275

Transit region: the places and regions that tourists pass through as they travel from origin to destination region p. 40

Transportation: businesses involved with the transportation of tourists by air, road, rail or water p. 152

Travel agencies: businesses providing retail travel services to customers for commission on behalf of other tourism industry sectors p. 151

Travel purpose: the reason why people travel; in tourism, these involve recreation and leisure, visits to friends and relatives (VFR), business, and less dominant purposes such as study, sport, religion and health p. 29

Triangulation: the use of multiple methods, data sources, investigators or theories in a research process p. 398

Urban–rural fringe (or exurbs): a transitional zone surrounding larger urban areas that combines urban and rural characteristics and benefits from proximity to each p. 118

Variability: service encounters, even if they involve a similar kind of experience, are highly variable due to the differences and rapid changes in mood, expectation and other human element factors that affect the participants p. 206

Variable costs: costs that can be readily reduced in the short term, such as salaries of casual staff p. 208

Venturers: according to Plog's typology, 'other-centred' tourists who enjoy exposing themselves to other cultures and new experiences, and are willing to take risks in this process; also known as 'allocentrics' p. 186

Vertical integration: occurs when a corporation obtains greater control over elements of the product chain outside its own sector p. 160

Virtual reality (VR): the wide-field presentation of computer-generated, multi-sensory information that allows the user to experience a virtual world p. 80

War dividend: the long-term benefits for tourism that derive from large conflicts, including war-related attractions, image creation, and the emergence of new travel markets p. 67

Weak sustainable development: an approach to sustainable development that assumes relatively relaxed environmental expectations in recognition of areas, such as intensively developed beach resorts, that are already extensively modified and have high carrying capacities p. 343

Webcasting: the delivery of interactive multimedia to customers through the Internet on either an 'on demand' or 'real-time' basis p. 226

Winescapes: a cultural landscape significantly influenced by the presence of vineyards, wineries and other features associated with viticulture and wine production; an essential element of wine-focused food tourism p. 140

Work in order to play philosophy: a postindustrial ethic derived from ancient Greek philosophy that holds that leisure and leisure-time activities such as tourism are important in their own right and that we work to be able to afford to engage in leisure pursuits p. 74

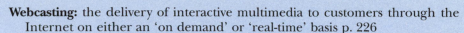

INDEX

external-unintentional actions, 323, 324, 331
face-to-face surveys, 386, 387–8
factory tours, 141
family lifecycle, 180–2, 196
family size, 75–6, 78, 173
farm holidays/tours, 131, 141, 248, 356
fashion, 259–60, 314, 319
feedback, 203–4
feminist travel, 356
festivals and performances, 131, 140, 146, 184, 200, 389
Fiji, 95, 112, 213, 246, 418
Finland, 418
fishing and hunting, 135
'fishing expedition', 379
fixed costs, 297–8, 209, 211, 222, 231, 314
flexitime, 73, 86
Flinders University, 10
flow-on impacts, 246, 264
fluctuations in intake, 256–60
focus groups, 387–8, 397
food and beverages, 47, 102, 240, 241, 316
food tourism, 139–40, 163, 248
forecasting, 215, 388
foreign exchange, 242
formal sector, 250–1, 264
four major types of tourist, 34–5, 49
France, 40, 62, 94, 100, 109, 148, 157, 240, 243, 418
free and independent travellers, 154
free market, 285
freedoms of the air, 152, 153, 161, 164
French Polynesia, 418
French Riviera, 314, 315
frontstage, 277–8, 284, 285, 286–7, 296, 299, 311, 320
functional adaptation, 141, 163

Gabon, 418
Gambia, 418
gambling, 283, 316–17, 325
    see also casinos
garbage, 292, 389
gateway facilities, 98
gay tourism, 178, 182
gender and gender orientation
    segmentation, 173, 174, 177–8, 196
general demarketing, 212, 231
geographic diffusion see spatial diffusion
geographic information systems, 176, 196, 292
geographic scale, 320–1
geographic segmentation, 176–7, 196, 228
geographic strategies, 318, 324, 328
geographical proximity to markets, 97–8
geographical theory, 7–8, 12, 16
Georgia, 418
geothermal waters, 134
Germany, 46, 62, 80, 109, 116, 134, 138, 157, 215, 240, 419
Ghana, 419
Gibraltar, 246, 419
global destination patterns, 92–6
global GDP, 4
global inequality in tourism, 92, 122
global tourism, 39, 71, 251
global tourism economy, 4
globalisation, 4, 161, 164, 285

GNP, 69, 75, 243–4, 416–24
Gold Coast (Qld), 101, 105, 106, 134, 142, 147, 180, 210, 248, 258, 259, 281, 285, 288, 295, 312–13, 314, 315, 318, 321, 328, 363, 367
golf courses, 131, 141–2, 290, 313
golfscapes, 142, 163
government tourism organisations, 214–16, 411
government warnings, 126
governments
    border security &, 99–100
    destination sustainability &, 364
    taxation &, 242–3
    tourism policy &, 3, 4, 13, 106–7, 112, 125, 126
    tourism program sponsorship by, 248–9, 250, 252
    tourism receipts &, 242–3, 244
    see also destination governments; origin governments
Grand Tour, 61–2, 85
Greater Yellowstone area (US), 295–6
Greece, 57–8, 109, 137, 240, 419
'green' code of practice, 351–3
green consumerism, 346–7, 354, 360, 370
Green Globe 21, 353–4, 364, 411
green paradigm, 341–3, 369, 385
Greenland, 310
greenwashing, 343, 369
Grenada, 260, 419
Griffith University, 9
growth, 5, 13, 93, 109
    see also economic growth; tourism growth
growth pole strategy, 249, 250, 264, 366
GST, 242
Guadeloupe, 419
Guam, 112, 419
Guatemala, 273, 419
guidebooks, 62, 158–9, 200
Guinea, 419
Guyana, 419

Haiti, 111, 419
hard and soft ecotourism, 359–61, 362, 363, 371
Hard Rock Café, 224–5
Hawaii, 97, 133, 139, 314, 315
health purpose tourism, 32, 173, 174
heritage districts and landscapes, 138–9, 248
Hervey Bay (Qld), 191–2
hierarchical diffusion, 326, 327, 328, 329, 331
historical development, 56–90
historical re-enactments and commemorations, 144
historical sites, 58, 71, 100, 114, 130, 131, 137–9, 275
history, 16
hi-tech industries, 258, 259
holiday see leisure and recreation
homestays, 356
Honduras, 419
honeymoon market, 190
Hong Kong SAR, 24, 27, 34, 89, 92, 93, 109, 111, 116, 143, 240, 246, 322, 419
Honolulu, 36
horizontal integration, 160, 164, 349
host communities, 3, 4, 5, 25, 44, 45, 46, 106
    see also destination communities

host governments *see* destination governments
hotels and apartments, 6, 155–7, 164, 208, 209, 210, 211, 213, 222, 314, 315, 321, 347, 348, 349, 389
human element factors, 206–7
human responses, 289, 290, 300
Hungary, 109, 419
hunting and fishing, 135
hydrology, 130
Hydropolis (Dubai), 156
hyperdestinations, 118, 123, 285, 287–8, 334
hypotheses, 339, 380–1, 384, 385, 396, 400, 401, 403

Iceland, 134, 246, 419
iconic attractions, 132, 148, 149, 163, 216, 253, 323, 407, 408
ideal type, 322, 331, 354
image, 105–6, 108, 122, 125, 147, 204, 224, 316, 407
   see also market image
imagery, 278–9
immigration, 77
impacts, 4, 13, 24, 39, 44, 245, 246, 264, 271–304, 317, 334, 356, 357, 359
   see also economic impacts
imported goods and services, 253, 260
inbound tour operators, 157, 164
inbound tourists, 27–8, 29, 33, 37–8, 46, 49, 93–6, 97, 112, 120, 130, 131, 190, 199–201, 243, 244, 256, 327, 328, 400, 401, 416–24 *see also* international stayovers; international tourists
incentive tourists, 31
income *see* discretionary income; wages
incremental access, 112, 122
India, 32, 34, 69, 70, 77, 83, 103, 113, 132, 273, 350, 356, 419
Indian Ocean basin, 94
indicators, 343–5, 370
indigenous people/ communities, 248, 249, 277–8, 341, 398
   see also Aboriginal communities/culture
indigenous theories, 7, 14, 15, 19
indigenous tourism, 356
indirect financial costs, 253–5, 265
indirect impacts, 245, 246, 294–5
indirect incentives, 254
indirect resources, 288
indirect revenues, 245–6, 247, 264
Indonesia, 34, 77, 102, 112, 116, 117, 125–6, 249, 251, 277, 324, 366, 419
induced impacts, 245–6, 264, 294–5
induction, 380–1, 385, 402
Indus Valley, 57
Industrial Revolution, 62–5, 66, 69, 85, 93, 132, 141, 260, 312, 340
industrialisation, 62–5, 66, 69, 70, 72, 73, 83
industry research, 379, 381
Industry Tourism Resources, 412
infant mortality, 75
informal sector, 250–1, 265
information for tourists, 216
information technologies, 80
infrastructural accessibility, 98, 107, 122, 125
infrastructure, 41, 59, 112, 113, 214, 250, 253, 256, 296, 304, 320, 322, 324, 334

inseparability, 205, 230, 250
intangibility, 204–5, 230
integrated global tourism network, 4, 5, 13
integration, 160–1
intellectual property, 382
interdependence, 23, 24
interdisciplinary approach, 8, 12, 19
interest rates, 254
'internal customers', 204
internal destination patterns, 117–20
internal environment, 216, 217, 218, 219
internal forces, 311
internal-intentional actions, 323, 324, 331
internal spatial patterns, 326
internal-unintentional actions, 323, 324, 331
International College of Tourism and Hotel Management, 11
international excursions, 65
international excursionists, 35, 36, 49
international marketing, 252
international stayovers, 35, 37, 49, 93, 95, 107, 108, 109, 112, 239, 268
international students, 32–3, 34, 244
international tourism, 65, 67, 68, 327
international tourism receipts, 239, 240, 264, 416–24
international tourist destination patterns, 107–17
international tourists
   data problems &, 37
   definition of, 26–7, 48
   outbound and inbound, 27–8, 31–2
   travel purpose &, 30, 31–4
Internet, 151–2, 159, 172, 226–8, 390, 394
intervening opportunities, 41, 49
involvement stage, 307, 309, 310–13, 318, 319, 323, 328, 331, 355, 356
Iran, 113, 419
Iraq, 103, 105, 110, 114, 419
Ireland, 419
   see also Northern Ireland
irridex, 287–8, 299, 307, 309, 310, 379, 391, 395
Islam, 32, 101, 113, 327
Israel, 101, 103, 115, 294, 419
Italy, 61, 101, 109, 137, 212, 240, 419
   see also Rome
Ivory Coast, 419

Jamaica, 41, 246, 278–9, 356, 419
James Cook University, 9
Japan, 34, 70, 83, 94, 116, 132, 192, 199–201, 243, 419
Jordan, 113, 419
journals *see* refereed academic journals

Kakadu National Park (NT), 136, 167–9, 363
Katherine (NT), 322
Kenya, 95, 190, 279, 293, 361–2, 367, 419
Kiribata, 420
knowledge-based platform, 14, 19, 23, 44
Korea, North, 39, 46, 98, 420
Korea, South, 70, 83, 93, 116, 117, 175, 228, 240, 420
Kuwait, 92, 420
Kyrgystan, 420

museums, 7, 131, 139, 146, 200
music and theatre productions, 7
Myanmar, 126, 421

Namibia, 105, 421
national parks, 129, 130, 131, 135, 136,
    147, 150, 167–9, 212, 248, 304, 310, 362,
    363, 367
National Sea Change Task Force, 365
national stereotypes, 105–6
national tourism authority, 216, 231
national tourism development, 326–9
national tourism organisations, 214–15, 216–
    17, 223, 231, 236, 411, 412
National Voluntary Tourism Accreditation
    System, 252
natural events, 129, 130, 136–7, 163
natural sites/environment, 129, 130–6, 163,
    248, 288, 289, 323, 359, 362
negative impacts, 4, 13, 24, 39
Nepal, 113, 421
Netherlands, 109, 240, 421
New Age movement, 32, 341
New Caledonia, 112, 421
New Guinea see Papua New Guinea
New South Wales
    destination development &, 313, 321, 334–6
    destination patterns in, 119, 120
    ecotourism in, 363
    inbound visitors to, 199, 200
    tourist attractions of, 101, 130, 138, 140
    university sector of, 9, 10, 11
    see also Byron Bay
new traveller, 347, 356, 370
New Zealand, 32, 89, 92, 116, 362
    advertising campaigns of, 215, 235–7
    destination development &, 325
    Maori tourism product, 274, 277
    SIC &, 6, 7
    tourism data &, 6, 180–2, 421
    tourist attractions of, 131, 134, 135, 137, 362
    tourist receipts of, 244, 421
newspaper advertising, 226
newspapers and magazines, 393–4
Niagara Falls, 318, 323
Nicaragua, 421
niche markets/products, 172, 173, 196, 221,
    235, 248, 252
Niger, 421
Nigeria, 421
Niue, 421
non-governmental organisations, 3, 25, 393
nonprobability sampling, 399
North America
    destination development &, 315, 316–17, 318,
        323
    inbound and outbound tourism data
        on, 417, 420, 424
    tourist attractions of, 133, 135, 141
    see also Canada; Mexico; United States
North American Industry Classification
    System, 6
North American regional destination
    patterns, 108, 110–11
North Korea, 39, 46, 98, 420
north-south flow, 95, 122

North-East Asia, 108, 111–12, 417, 419, 420,
    421, 423
Northern Ireland, 246
Northern Marianas, 421
Northern Territory, 120, 136, 167–9, 275,
    322, 363
Norway, 421

'100% Pure New Zealand' campaign, 215,
    235–7
objectives, 217, 218, 219
observation, 381, 384, 389–90, 397
occupancy rates, 208, 209, 222, 258
Oceania, 97, 112, 116
    see also under country eg New Zealand
oil prices, 115
Old Man of the Mountain (US), 149
older adults, 178–80
    see also ageing population
Olympic Games, 31, 57, 85, 116, 145
Oman, 421
'100% Pure New Zealand' campaign, 215,
    235–7
opportunity cost, 261, 265
Orchid Hotel, Mumbai, 350
Organisation for Economic Cooperation and
    Development, 289–90
orientation of attractions, 147
origin community, 38–9, 49
origin governments, 3, 25, 39–40, 49
origin regions, 38–40, 49, 220
outbound tour operators, 157, 164
outbound tourists, 27–8, 36, 39, 48, 66,
    70–1, 81, 82, 89–90, 95–6, 416–24
overnight stays, 4, 29, 36, 38, 81, 118
    see also stayovers
ownership, 147, 309, 355
    see also private ownership; public ownership
ozone depletion, 340, 350

Pacific Asia Travel Association, 412
Pacific islands, 92, 94, 108, 112, 416, 418, 419,
    420, 421, 422, 423, 424
package tours, 66, 86, 158, 223, 240, 241,
    268–9, 314, 355
packaging (8P model), 223
Pakistan, 103, 113, 273, 421
Palau, 246, 421
Panama, 421
Papua New Guinea, 112, 358, 421
parabolic flights, 44–5
paradigm, 338, 369
paradigm shifts, 338–43, 346, 369, 381
paradox of resentment, 284, 299
Paraguay, 421
partnerships (8P model), 223, 228–9
passports, 46, 99
peace, stability and safety, 103–5, 108, 112,
    113, 125
    see also political uncertainty; terrorist attacks
people (8P model), 220–1
perishability, 207, 231
personal awareness travel, 358
personal safety, 104–5, 113, 125
personal selling, 224
personality, 173, 174, 185–8, 205, 206, 207,
    284